MANAGING ACROSS CULTURES

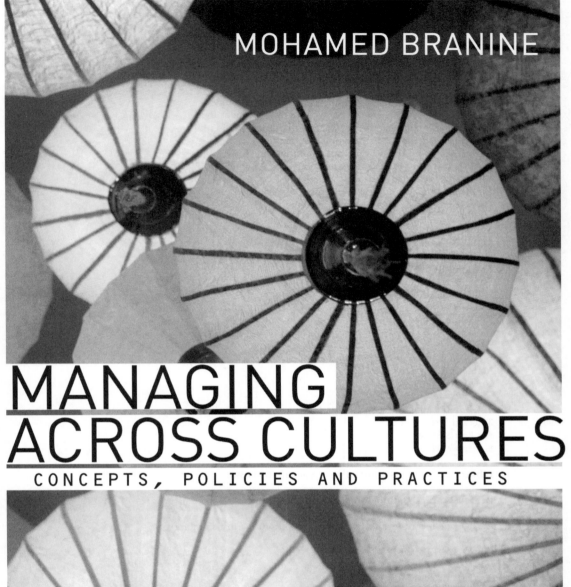

MOHAMED BRANINE

MANAGING
ACROSS CULTURES
CONCEPTS, POLICIES AND PRACTICES

SAGE

Los Angeles | London | New Delhi
Singapore | Washington DC

SAGE Publications Ltd
I Oliver's Yard
55 City Road
London ECIY ISP

SAGE Publications Inc.
2455 Teller Road
Thousand Oaks, California 91320

SAGE Publications India Pvt Ltd
B III I Mohan Cooperative Industrial Area
Mathura Road
New Delhi 110 044

SAGE Publications Asia-Pacific Pte Ltd
33 Pekin Street #02-01
Far East Square
Singapore 048763

Library of Congress Control Number: 2010931692

British Library Cataloguing in Publication data

A catalogue record for this book is available from the British Library

ISBN   978-1-84920-728-7
ISBN   978-1-84920-729-4 (pbk)

Typeset by C&M Digitals (P) Ltd, Chennai, India
Printed in Great Britain by CPI Antony Rowe, Chippenham, Wiltshire
Printed on paper from sustainable resources

Summary of Contents

Contents

List of Tables and Figures

List of
Mini Case Studies

Author Biography

Professor Mohamed Branine is Director of Postgraduate Research Degrees and Postgraduate Admissions, and MBA Programme Director at Dundee Business School (DBS), University of Abertay Dundee. He graduated in economics and management from Algiers University, Algeria and received a PgDipBA, an MPhil and a PhD from Lancaster University in England. In 1991 he became a United Nations human resource management specialist teaching in its UNDP (United Nations Development Program) projects. He has taught at several universities including Lancaster, Manchester, Bradford and Stirling in the UK, the University of British Columbia in Vancouver (Canada), and the University of International Business and Economics in Beijing (People's Republic of China). Before joining the University of Abertay Dundee in 2002 he was a senior lecturer and MBA Programme Director at Stirling University. He is a well-known scholar in many African, Middle and Far Eastern countries for his comparative work which is published in several academic papers, research monographs and professional articles. His research interests are in international and comparative human resource management with particular focus on:

- The determinants of different approaches to management and organization in different countries;
- The practical challenges of managing across cultures for international managers in a competitive business environment;
- The effects of international strategic alliances on national and international human resource development;
- Graduate recruitment, job creation and labour market trends in Europe;
- Culture and environmental awareness in the workplace; and
- Perceptions of age and gender in work and employment in different cultures.

Dr Branine is an active supervisor of doctoral students and masters' degree dissertations as well as teaching Human Resource Management, International Business and Business Research Methods to undergraduate and postgraduate students.

Acknowledgements

This book has drawn on many sources and it would have not been completed without the support of many people. I am indebted to all my colleagues, students, friends and family members for their support, encouragement and patience. I am indebted to all the authors whose work is reviewed, developed or just cited in this book. My particular thanks are to the reviewers and the editors of the first draft of the manuscript for their constructive comments and professional suggestions for improvements. My sincere thanks are to the team at Sage for their professional assistance and patience, in particular Natalie Aguilera, Clare Wells, Ruth Stitt, Rachel Eley and Ben Griffin-Sherwood. I would also like to take this opportunity to thank my mentors and former colleagues at Lancaster University, in particular Professor David H. Brown, Professor Frank Blackler and Dr Colin Brown for setting me on the right path to an academic career and for inspiring the ideas for this book; all my former colleagues at Stirling University, in particular Professor Chris Baldry and Dr Ian Glover for reviewing and supporting the proposal for this book; and all my current and former colleagues at Abertay University for their friendship and continuous support. My thanks are also to Professor Farhad Analoui and Professor Frank McDonald at Bradford University; Professor Kamel Mellahi at Warwick University; Professor Pawan Budhwar at Aston University; Professor Alex Scott and Iain Lauder at Herriot Watt University; Dr Aminu Mamman, Dr Chris Rees, Derek Edridge and Dr Farhad Hussein at Manchester University; Professor Peter Rosa at Edinburgh University, Martin Dowling at St Andrews University; Professor Robert Chia at Strathclyde University; Dr David Pollard at Leeds Metropolitan University; Professor Mike Hughes and Professor Jeff Hyman at Aberdeen University and Dr Azhdar Karami at Bangor Business School for their support over the years and their direct or indirect contribution to the completion of this project. Last but not least, I would like to thank and dedicate this book to my wife Nadia and our children Salim, Sarah and Nassim for their enduring patience and endless support over the years in which I have given more time to the completion of this book. Although every effort has been made to seek permission of the owners of copyright material and to fully acknowledge the authors whose work has been used, there may still be instances where this has been mistakenly overlooked in the process of undertaking this extensive project and I am very sorry in advance for any unwitting infringements.

Guided Tour

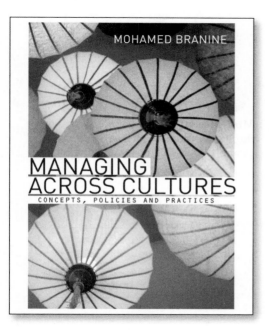

Learning outcomes: A clear set of key learning objectives are provided for each chapter.

Introduction: The introduction outlines the main topics and issues to be covered in each chapter.

6 Many companies are merging or forming strategic alliances with companies from other countries, involving negotiations and partnerships, and then having to work with managers and workers from different cultures and backgrounds.

7 Managing across cultures is not confined to what multinational companies (MNCs) or profitable organizations do. It affects every organization that operates internationally, regardless of its size, nature or location. Therefore the need to study the subject of managing across cultures is not just for those who want to work for multinational companies but for everyone who may become involved in managing resources in different countries and societies.

ACTIVITY 1

1 List what you consider to be the three best reasons for you to study this subject.
2 How might an understanding of this subject either (a) contribute to your career development or (b) enhance the performance of the organization (if any) you work for?

This book: rationale, aims and structure

Rationale

This book provides a detailed and comprehensive treatment of the concepts, policies and practices of managing resources – especially human resources – in various socio-economic, political and cultural contexts. It provides the reader with an understanding of the theory and practice of different national approaches to management, moving from conceptual analysis to the discussion of policies and practices. The book seeks to develop a broad understanding of the determining characteristics of national management approaches and to enable the reader to distinguish between different approaches to management and to learn from examples of 'good and bad' practice of management in different national cultural settings. While recognizing the importance of cultural influences on management theories and practices and at the same time accepting the argument that many societies are becoming similar rather than different in their management objectives, this book defines the process of managing across cultures simply as the management of local employees globally and international employees locally. In doing so it helps to establish the ways by which national cultural differences influence employment policies and practices of different countries and the ways by which national and international organizations have responded to them in a world that is determined by a globalizing power of business on the one hand and a localizing power of culture and politics on the other.

Activity: In-class activities encourage discussion and provoke thought.

MINI CASE STUDY 1

The Western Expatriate in West Africa

When asked about the working and living conditions of expatriates, Mrs Celia Ugboko, the managing director of a major petroleum company in West Africa, replied, 'Western expatriates are highly valued, highly paid, well respected and admired for their knowledge and expertise, commitment to their work, dedication, careful attention to detail, respect for time, and tolerance and sensitivity to other cultures. Our respectful treatment of foreigners has led to increasing numbers of Western and non-Western (third country) expatriates and has facilitated forward diffusion of Western management practices and policies to my country.'

Questions

1 Speculate on (a) the context in which this comment was made and (b) what might be the positive and the negative connotations of Mrs Ugboko's statement.
2 Judging from the manager's comment, what types of knowledge and skills do you think the local employees may learn from forward diffusion?

Managing global employees locally

Just as local employees have to be managed globally through the building of global corporate culture and the forward diffusion of knowledge and skills, global employees, mainly expatriates, have to be managed locally in order to achieve their assignment objectives successfully. Global employees, as home country expatriates or third country expatriates, have to understand the local working environment, the local employees, the local institutions and the local norms and values in order to work with or to manage the local workforces globally. In other words, global employees have to respond to the localizing power of culture and, very often, politics as well.

National differences in norms, values, traditions and beliefs, in levels of economic growth and development, and in institutional settings are the main sources for divergence in management policies and practices between societies. Though it is possible to assimilate organizational structures, to rationalize processes and to standardize products and services between countries, it is not, as Adler (2002) pointed out, easy to assimilate people's behaviour because of their culturally, economically and politically based differences. Therefore managing across cultures requires managers to be aware of the effects that these differences may have on their management policies and practices. They should be aware of the main national norms and values, of the national economic trends and organizational characteristics, and of the national institutions and the legal system.

Mini case study: The mini case studies throughout each chapter provide 'real life' examples that enhance understanding.

activities is to share learning and generate new knowledge from the local operations. Encouraging reverse diffusion of management theories and practices can lead to better understanding of the local working environment and to the development of appropriate approaches to managing across cultures.

Summary

1 The subject of managing across cultures has emerged in recent years as a significant field of academic research and study as a result of a number of triggers and drivers. Among the triggers are: the failure of expatriates to complete their assignments abroad; the economic recession of the 1980s; the rise and successes of South-east Asian countries; the openness of China and later India to the west; and the end of the Cold War and the 'Westernization' of Eastern Europe. The main drivers have been: the growth and spread of multinational companies; international competition; regional economic integration; technical changes and information mobility of information; open trading and availability of financial services; political and cultural influences; internationalization of Western management education with the use of English as the international language of business; and the liberalization and democratization of developing countries.

2 Most of the definitions of managing across cultures focus on the concept of culture and the effects of cultural differences on management in different countries. This book acknowledges the importance of culture and its effects on management and goes beyond the need to understand the similarities and differences between societies to see the process of managing across cultures as the management of local employees globally and third country employees locally, including expatriates, host and third country employees, national and international employee regulations, and national and international employee and employer organizations.

3 The management of local employees globally requires, at least, the building of a global corporate culture that local employees can understand and identify with, and having a strategy of forward diffusion of knowledge and skills from the home to the host countries.

4 Just as local employees have to be managed globally, global employees, mainly expatriates, have to be managed locally in order to achieve their assignments successfully. Global employees have to understand the local working environment, employees, institutions, and norms and values in order to manage the local workforce globally.

5 The process of managing across cultures sits between the globalizing power of business and the localizing power of culture and politics. The problem in implementing such a process effectively lies in knowing the unknown. The more familiar the international manager (expatriate) is with the local working environment and local employees, and the more the local employees know about the corporate culture and its operations, the greater and better the global integration and local responsiveness. The factors that may facilitate the process of knowing the unknown are the ability to assess and avoid risks, and the encouragement of 'reverse diffusion' of management good practice from the host to the home country.

Summary: The main points of each chapter are pulled together, making revision easy.

Revision questions

1 Discuss with the use of examples the main factors and events that have led to the emergence of cross-cultural management as a significant field of academic research and study.
2 What does 'managing across cultures' mean? Elaborate your answer by referring to at least two contrasting definitions.
3 What do you think are the main things that international organizations can do to be successful in (a) managing global employees locally and (b) managing their local employees globally?

References

Adler, N. (2002) International Dimensions of Organizational Behaviour, 4th edn. Cincinnati, OH: South-Western College Publishing/Thomson Learning.
Ball, D.A. and McCulloch, W.H. (1993) International Business: Introduction and Essentials, London: Irwin.
Bamber, G.J. and Lansbury, R.D. (eds) (2004) International and Comparative Employment Relations, 4th edn, London: Sage.
Bartlett, C.A. and Ghoshal, S. (1998) Managing Across Borders: The Transnational Solution, 2nd edn, London: Century Business.
Branine, M. (1997), 'Change and continuity in Chinese employment relationships', New Zealand Journal of Industrial Relations, 22(1): 77-94.
Brewster, C. and Harris, H. (1999), International HRM: Contemporary Issues in Europe, London: Routledge.
Brewster, C. and Tyson, S. (eds) (1991) International Comparisons in Human Resource Management, London: Pitman.
Briscoe, D.R. and Schuler, R.S. (2004), International Human Resource Management, 2nd edn, London: Routledge.
Browaeys, M.J. and Price, R. (2008) Understanding Cross-cultural Management, Harlow: Prentice-Hall/Financial Times.
Budhwar, P. and Debrah, Y.A. (eds) (2001) Human Resource Management in Developing Countries, London: Routledge.
Budhwar, P. and Mellahi, K. (eds) (2006) Managing Human Resources in the Middle East, London: Routledge.
Budhwar, P. and Sparrow, P. (2002a), 'An integrative framework for determining cross-national human resource management practices', Human Resource Management Review, 12(3): 377–403.
Budhwar, P. and Sparrow, P. (2002b) 'Strategic HRM through the cultural looking glass: mapping cognitions of British and Indian HRM managers', Organization Studies, 23(4): 599–638.
Chen, M. (2004) Asian Management Systems, 2nd edn, London: Thomson Learning.
Child, J. (1994) Management in China in the Era of Reform, Cambridge: Cambridge University Press.

Revision questions: Questions at the end of each chapter help you to check your understanding of the key issues in each chapter.

Part I

Introduction

Part 1: Introduction
Map 1: The World with its borders (2010)

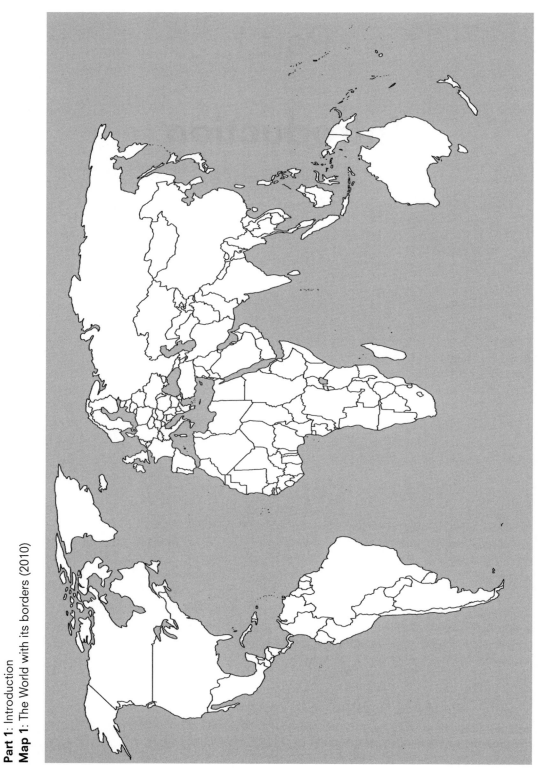

Activity: Write the names of as many countries as you know on the map above.

1

Why Study Managing Across Cultures?

══════════ **LEARNING OUTCOMES** ══════════

This chapter is designed to help the reader to:

1   Recognize the need to study the subject of managing across cultures;
2   Understand the aims and objectives of this book;
3   Understand how the book is structured;
4   Use the book effectively.

Why study the subject of managing across cultures?

Managing across cultures is not a new phenomenon, but it is more important now than ever before. For centuries, travellers, traders, explorers, conquerors, colonizers, knowledge seekers (students and scholars), job seekers and asylum seekers, and employees and/or managers of international organizations have travelled across borders and have had to come to terms with the demands of living in different societies and experiencing new cultures. They had to manage themselves and manage others, when necessary, in tougher and more hostile living environments than those of today. Many empires were built in part on their efficient management of resources across cultures. One of the main reasons for their demise was conflict resulting from misunderstanding or not respecting cross-cultural differences.

However, until the later part of the second half of the twentieth century there were few studies, textbooks or courses on the subject of managing across cultures, and it was given very little attention by economists, political analysts and international business scholars. It was not until the 1980s that cross-cultural management became a common subject of academic research and study – and then most of the literature was on the management of expatriates and the problems of staffing US multinational companies in foreign countries (Evans et al., 1989; Bartlett and Ghoshal, 1989; Adler, 2002; Dowling, Schuler and Welch, 1994; Dowling, Festing and Engle, 2008).

Now, however, managing across cultures is a well-established subject that is taught in universities and practised by managers. It has become one of the main challenges in understanding contemporary management practices and organization theories. The reason why such challenges are important is that management in general and human resource management in particular have become more complex and more problematic than in any time before. A number of textbooks (for example, Dowling, Welch and Schuler, 1999; Brewster and Harris, 1999; Deresky, 2001; Briscoe and Schuler, 2004; Harzing and Van Ruysseveldt, 2004; Moran et al., 2007) have documented with the use of examples the reasons for the need to learn how to manage across cultures by practitioners and decision-makers involved in cross-cultural management.

They include the following:

1   There has been strong evidence to suggest that understanding the behaviours, attitudes, values, beliefs, arts and artefacts of the host country nationals is a key success factor for organizations operating in different countries. Managers working in different cultures have to explore and identify what is hidden in the behaviours and actions of people from different cultural backgrounds and value-orientations. This is summarized by an HR manager of British Petroleum (BP) in Azerbaijan when he said: 'to understand each other better we need to be more aware of the peculiarities and the hidden aspects of the national culture because the key to our success is that understanding'.

2   The composition of international organizations' workforce is becoming more diverse than ever not just in terms of their employees but management as well. For example, Ford has more than half of its employees outside the USA and Philips has more than three-quarters of its employees outside the Netherlands.

3   More and more companies are dependent on managers from different cultures and nationalities operating in different countries and holding high managerial positions that would previously have been held by home country nationals.

4   The free movement of labour between countries, such as within the European Union (EU), and the international movement of people with skills from mainly less developed to more developed countries have made it possible to access a wider pool of labour but at a cost. The cost may be high or low depending on the way people are employed and the extent to which international managers are aware of and able to implement the different national policies, rules and regulations in relation to emigrant workers, skilled workers, and expatriate workers.

5   The recruitment and retention of a highly qualified and competent workforce has become crucial for both indigenous and international companies. The main factor for achieving competitive advantage in the global market economy is to see people as equal and valuable assets that can be utilized effectively at the national and international levels.

6 Many companies are merging or forming strategic alliances with companies from other countries, involving negotiations and partnerships, and then having to work with managers and workers from different cultures and backgrounds.

7 Managing across cultures is not confined to what multinational companies (MNCs) or profitable organizations do. It affects every organization that operates internationally, regardless of its size, nature or location. Therefore the need to study the subject of managing across cultures is not just for those who want to work for multinational companies but for everyone who may become involved in managing resources in different countries and societies.

ACTIVITY 1

1 List what you consider to be the three best reasons for you to study this subject.
2 How might an understanding of this subject either (a) contribute to your career development or (b) enhance the performance of the organization (if any) you work for?

This book: rationale, aims and structure

Rationale

This book provides a detailed and comprehensive treatment of the concepts, policies and practices of managing resources – especially human resources – in various socio-economic, political and cultural contexts. It provides the reader with an understanding of the theory and practice of different national approaches to management, moving from conceptual analysis to the discussion of policies and practices. The book seeks to develop a broad understanding of the determining characteristics of national management approaches and to enable the reader to distinguish between different approaches to management and to learn from examples of 'good and bad' practice of management in different national cultural settings. While recognizing the importance of cultural influences on management theories and practices and at the same time accepting the argument that many societies are becoming similar rather than different in their management objectives, this book defines the process of managing across cultures simply as the management of local employees globally and international employees locally. In doing so it helps to establish the ways by which national cultural differences influence employment policies and practices of different countries and the ways by which national and international organizations have responded to them in a world that is determined by a globalizing power of business on the one hand and a localizing power of culture and politics on the other.

The rationale for its content and structure has been influenced by the growing interest in comparative research. The understanding of how management is practised in particular contexts can provide the opportunity to establish differences and similarities between particular countries and societies, and to assess the reasons for their occurrences. In order to understand the insights of managing across cultures it is important to have the knowledge and skills of managing in different national contexts in which the behaviour of organizations and people is determined to a great extent by cultural and economic factors. This is the main reason for this book's policy of bringing together in clusters countries that are similar in terms of historical heritage, cultural background, economic development, and political and legislative system. This textbook allows the reader to gain knowledge of different national contexts, make comparisons between them, and learn the knowledge and skills of managing in different national contexts.

Aims

The aims of this book are as follows.

1 To present a conceptual and theoretical analysis of managing across cultures by explaining the various definitions of key concepts and providing a critical review of relevant theories and models of culture and management.
2 To discuss the different national cultural values and norms, and their implications for management, in order to develop a theoretical framework for understanding the subject.
3 To provide description, analysis and discussion of employment policies and human resource management practices in different national and cultural contexts. In this respect, a country-by-country or cluster of countries study is provided for comparative purposes and to improve our understanding of the factors that influence labour market trends, and organization and employment policies and practices in different countries.

Structure

To meet the aims above, this book is divided into six parts comprising nineteen chapters. Part I provides a conceptual and theoretical analysis of the subject of managing across cultures. Parts II to V provide a description and analysis of management practices and policies in clusters of countries, covering most of the globe, organized according to their socio-economic, historical, cultural and political similarities. Each part consists of three to five chapters each providing discussion and critical analysis of the main aspects of cross-cultural management in general and the policies and practices of human resource management in particular. The structure of these chapters is designed to facilitate comparison between countries. Each chapter covers the socio-economic and political context of the countries studied, their labour market trends, their management and organization characteristics, and their human resource management policies and practices, focusing on recruitment and selection, training and development, rewards and remuneration, and employee relations. Part VI concludes the book with a discussion of the main emerging issues and future directions in the subject of managing across cultures.

Each of the Chapters in Parts II–V (i.e. the geographically based chapters) is based on a common structure. Each of these chapters (namely Chapters 4–18) contains:

1   An introduction.
2   An overview of economic, political and cultural contexts.
3   A survey of labour market trends. The particular themes covered vary between territories. Typical themes include: employment and unemployment rates; the supply of labour (including such topics as female participation, age structure and migration); the nature of employment (including, for example, flexible working practices); and types of employer.
4   An outline of management policies and practices and organizational structures and behaviour.
5   A description of human resource management. Typical themes include:

   a   Recruitment and selection.
   b   Training and development.
   c   Rewards and remuneration.
   d   Employee relations.

6   A summary of the chapter.
7   A list of references.

Chapters also contain activities and mini case studies, as well as revision questions at the end.

Each chapter is designed as an essay in its own right and so may be read independently of other chapters. However, the common structure facilitates comparison between chapters. Some of the activities are designed to support comparative study.

How to use the book

This book is designed both for class use and individual study. The book as a whole can be used on a 12-week semester/term of 24 hours of lectures and six hours of tutorials. There are 6 parts and each part can be taught over two weeks of four hours of lectures and one hour of tutorials. The case study at the end of each part (Parts I–V) can be used for tutorial discussion, allowing for a revision session at the end of Part VI. It will be possible to use it also over a 10-week semester/term by reducing parts I and VI to one week each (with two hours of lectures and one hour of tutorials). More information about how to use the activities, mini-case studies and the end-of-part case studies is given in the accompanying tutor's manual or can be found on the book's website.

Learning outcomes

To help you focus your learning, each chapter begins with a specification of desired learning outcomes. In Parts I and VI, learning outcomes are unique to each chapter. In Parts II–V (i.e. Chapters 4-18) the learning outcomes are common to each chapter. These are shown in Box 1.1.

BOX 1.1

Learning outcomes for Chapters 4–18

The chapter is designed to help you understand, for the nation or region in question:

1   the (a) economic, (b) political and (c) cultural contexts in which managers work;
2   the main trends in the labour market;
3   the typical features of (a) management policies and practices and (b) organizational structure and behaviour;
4   the main policies and practices of human resource management with regard to: (a) recruitment and selection; (b) training and development; (c) rewards and remuneration; and (d) employee relations.

Chapter review

Each chapter finishes with some revision questions, which are unique to each chapter. In addition, for Parts II–V (i.e. Chapters 4–18), Box 1.2 provides a common task to bear in mind with each chapter. The task is designed to help you (a) review the chapter in question and (b) make connections and comparisons between chapters in order to deepen your learning from them.

BOX 1.2

Review task for Chapters 4–18

Imagine you are the HR director of an MNC from one of the following countries: (a) America; (b) China; (c) Germany; (d) Japan; or (e) a country of your choice. Please select and specify one of these (Obviously, the country you select should not be the one covered in the chapter in question.).

Your company is considering investing in the country or region covered in this chapter. Write a concise report to your company's board, explaining your views on the following questions:

a Which are the most significant features of the prospective host country or region?
b How similar is the prospective host country or region to the one from which your company originates?
c How welcoming and conducive do you think the prospective host country or region would be to investment from your company?
d If your company were to proceed in investing in the host country or region, which aspects of that country or region would expatriates from your company require briefing on most?

In your report, aim to cover the following topics:

e The context (economic, political, and/or cultural).
f Labour market trends.
g Management policy and practice and organizational types and behaviour.
h HR management.

References

Adler, N. (2002) *International Dimensions of Organizational Behaviour*, 4th edn, Cincinnati, OH: South-Western College Publishing/Thomson Learning.

Bartlett, C.A. and Ghoshal, S. (1998) *Managing Across Borders: The Transnational Solution*, 2nd edn, London: Century Business.

Brewster, C. and Harris, H. (1999) *International HRM: Contemporary Issues in Europe*, London: Routledge.

Briscoe, D.R. and Schuler, R.S. (2004) *International Human Resource Management*, 2nd edn, London: Routledge.

Deresky, H. (2003) *International Management: Managing Across Borders and Cultures*, London: Prentice Hall.

Dowling, P.J., Festing, M. and Engle, A.D., Sr (2008) *International Human Resource Management*, 5th edn, London: Thomson Learning.

Dowling, P.J., Schuler, R.S. and Welch, D.E. (1994) *International Dimensions of Human Resource Management*, 2nd edn, Belmont, CA: International Thomson Publishing and Wadsworth Publishing Company.

Dowling, P.J., Welch, D.E. and Schuler, R.S. (1999) *International Human Resource Management: Managing People in a Multinational Context*, 3rd edn, Cincinnati, OH: South-Western College Publishing.

Evans, P., Doz, Y. and Laurent, A. (1989) *Human Resource Management in International Firms*, London: Macmillan.

Harzing, A.W. and Van Ruysseveldt, J. (eds) (2004) *International Human Resource Management*, 2nd edn, London: Sage.

Kanter, R.M. (1995) *World Class: Thinking Locally in the Global Economy*, New York: Simon & Schuster.

Moran, R.T., Harris, P.R. and Moran, S.V. (2007) *Managing Cultural Differences: Global Leadership Strategies for the 21st Century*, 7th edn, Oxford: Butterworth-Heinemann.

Ohmae, K. (1990) *The Borderless World*, New York: McKinsey & Co Inc.

Peters, T. and Waterman, R. (1982) *In Search of Excellence*, New York: Harper & Row.

Pfeffer, J. (1994) *Competitive Advantage Through People: Unleashing the Power of the Workforce*, Boston, MA: Harvard Business School Press.

Rosenzweig, P.M. and Nohria, N. (1994) 'Influences on human resource management practices in multinational corporations', *Journal of International Business Studies*, 25: 229–51.

Schneider, S.C. and Barsoux, J.L. (2003) *Managing Across Cultures*, 2nd edn, Harlow: Prentice-Hall/Financial Times.

Schuler, R.S., Dowling, P.J. and De Cieri, H. (1993) 'An integrative framework of strategic international human resource management', *International Journal of Human Resource Management*, 4(6): 717–64.

Schuler, R.S., Jackson, S.E. and Luo, Y. (2004) *Managing Human Resources in Cross-Border Alliances*, London: Routledge.

2

The Meaning and Importance of Managing Across Cultures

━━━━━━━━━━ **LEARNING OUTCOMES** ━━━━━━━━━━

This chapter is designed to help the reader to:

1　Explain the triggers and drivers that have led to the emergence of managing across cultures;

2　Critically analyse interpretations of the concept of 'managing across cultures';

3　Outline the theoretical framework for the analysis of managing across cultures in diverse cultural settings.

Emergence of managing across cultures

Since the 1980s managing across cultures has emerged as a significant field of academic research and study. Its emergence is the result of a number of 'triggers' and 'drivers'. The triggers are those factors and events that raised the alarm about the importance of understanding cultural differences when operating in different countries; the drivers are those factors that resulted from, or contributed, to the triggers as shown in Table 2.1 below.

The triggers

First, we consider the triggers.

Table 2.1 The triggers and drivers of managing across cultures

Triggers	Drivers
Expatriates' failure to complete assignments abroad	Multinational companies
Recession in the 1980s	International competition
Economic development of Japan and South-east Asia	Regional economic integration
Economic development of China and India	Technical changes and flow of information
'Westernization' of Central and Eastern Europe	Trade and financial services
	Political and cultural influences
	Western management education and the use of English in business
	Reforms in developing countries

Expatriates' failure to complete assignments abroad

In international business, the first people to feel the crunch of working and living in different cultural settings are expatriates. Multinational companies (MNCs) depend on the knowledge and expertise of their expatriates to sustain the growth of their foreign investments (Bartlett and Ghoshal, 1989; Adler, 2002; Deresky, 2001). The role of an expatriate is to transfer the know-how, to control operations and to develop expertise in working in different countries. However, many expatriates have found it difficult to complete their assignments and this has created financial and operational problems for many MNCs. A number of studies reported that in the early 1980s as many as 70 per cent of US companies' expatriates did not complete their assignments abroad (Bartlett and Ghoshal, 1989; Evans et al., 1989; Adler, 2002; Deresky, 2001; Moran et al., 2007). Multinational companies started to feel the high cost failure of such. It became apparent that such failures originated in the expatriates' inability to understand the complexities of cultural differences and their consequent inability to successfully manage across cultures. Therefore many organizations have had to reconsider their recruitment, training and expatriation policies (Harris and Moran, 1991; Dowling, Welch and Schuler, 1999). Cultural awareness training has become a core subject in expatriates' pre-expatriation training.

Recession in the 1980s

The economic recession of the 1980s resulted in plant closures, mass redundancies and a sharp decline in international investments in the USA and Western Europe. Many US and European companies started to expand by shifting investments from home to a number of host countries, taking advantage of increased economies of scale and scope, and producing for different markets overseas in order to increase their profit margins. They benefited by shifting production from the west to the east and from the economically developed to the developing countries. They soon realized that they had to operate differently in the host countries. They had to introduce employment policies and practices that were more appropriate to the new socio-economic, political and cultural contexts. In order to gain competitive advantage, they have had to introduce international approaches to the employment, training, appraisal and reward of their increasingly culturally and nationally diverse workforce.

Economic development of Japan and South-east Asia

The emergence of Japan as a major industrialized nation in the 1970s, followed by South-east Asian countries, generated attempts to explain the causes of such success (Whitley, 1992; Chen, 2004; Tang and Ward, 2003). The success of Japanese companies was attributed to the management of their human resources and the implementation of manufacturing systems such as quality circles, just-in-time management and total quality management, as well as to the commitment and loyalty of their employees. Therefore, many large employers in the USA and Western Europe attempted to adopt Japanese production practices and employee relations policies with the aim of regaining competitive advantage they had lost in the world markets.

Moreover, the smaller economies – Hong Kong, South Korea, Taiwan, Singapore, Thailand and Malaysia – that followed in Japan's footsteps were known as 'tigers' because of their fast-growing and aggressive economic growth in the 1980s. While many Western countries experienced economic growth of less than 2 per cent, many South-east Asian countries grew at over 10 per cent. Therefore, many western companies became attracted to investing in South-east Asia. The move required not only the recruitment and development of employees who were inspired by and able to cope with the work ethics of Asian people but also an understanding of the socio-economic and political context in which people are employed.

Economic development of China and India

In late 1970s the government of the People's Republic of China (PRC) announced an open-door policy and began economic reforms aimed at moving the country from a centrally planned to a free market economy. Consequently the PRC became an increasingly important destination for foreign investment (Child, 1994; Nolan, 2001; Yan and Child, 2002). Companies investing in China have had to consider how to manage their resources in a country in transition between central planning and market economics. One of the major challenges for employers investing (most investments being joint ventures) in China is understanding Chinese culture and its impact on work and managerial behaviour (Tung, 1986, 2002; Easterby-Smith, Malina and Lu, 1995; Branine, 1997; Warner, 2003).

India has since the early 1990s embarked upon major economic reforms that have made it one of the largest stable and successful economies in the world. Foreign firms have been attracted by the formally educated and skilled workforce that is available throughout India. The recent move of some multinational companies' call centres from the US and Europe to India is an example of benefiting from an international labour market, though that has necessitated the introduction of cross-cultural training.

'Westernization' of Central and Eastern Europe

The end of the Cold War following the collapse of the communist bloc, the unification of Germany, and the dismantling of the Soviet Union has led to a gradual 'Westernization' of Eastern European countries. These developments have brought opportunities for multinational companies to expand their investments in central and Eastern Europe and in the former Soviet Union states. Many enterprises in the former communist countries have faced the need to implement economic reforms and to use Western ideas of free enterprise management. Polish, Hungarian and Czech companies, for example, no longer operate within the framework of national economic plans. The 'Westernization' process has required the transfer of market-related skills and management knowledge as well as investments from the US, Canada, Japan and Western European countries. However, for international investors to be successful in former communist countries they needed to understand local operations and to introduce locally responsive employment practices.

The drivers

Next, let us consider the drivers.

Multinational companies

Though multinational companies (MNCs) or transnational companies (TNCs) are not new, the rate by which they have developed since the 1970s has been extraordinary. Rapid increases in international activity have involved high levels of mergers and acquisitions, takeovers and joint ventures. While operating in different countries, MNCs have had to develop appropriate human resource strategies for attracting, recruiting and retaining local and international employees who are able to produce high-quality products and to provide high standards of services to meet the needs of customers in a competitive global market. There is no country in the world that has not been 'invaded' by multinational companies. Whether you are in the middle of the Sahara Desert or Siberia you can always find Coca Cola. As the number of MNCs increases the need for internationally minded managerial, professional and technical staff becomes greater and more attention has to be given to the way in which employees are employed, rewarded, trained and motivated to work effectively in different countries.

International competition

Many organizations have become similar in their distribution channels, technical standards and marketing approaches, products and production methods, giving customers similar choices worldwide. Increasingly, consumers from different countries are demanding products and services that are labelled world class. Customers are very much aware of the choices that are available to them at competitive prices. Therefore, local as well as international companies are being forced to compete on world-class standards to increase their chances of survival in uncertain business environments.

There is no one pattern of international competition because the forces that drive internationalization differ by industry, business, sector and location. However, the evidence from different international investors has shown that competitive successes or failures in the global market are strongly influenced by the quality of organizations' workforces (Peters and Waterman, 1982; Pfeffer, 1994; Ulrich and Black, 1999; Schuler, Jackson and Luo, 2004). Well-trained, skilled, and innovative employees can provide a competitive edge in markets where similar material and financial means of production are available. It is possible for almost any multinational company to acquire the necessary technology and capital, at a cost, but in many cases 'it is rather difficult to acquire a ready pool of highly qualified and highly motivated employees' (Sparrow, Schuler and Jackson, 1994: 269). The processes of obtaining and retaining the needed pool of skilled, motivated and highly qualified employees in different cultural settings require efficient management of resources across cultures.

Regional economic integration

The process of regional economic integration has driven the emergence and development of cross-cultural management. Trade relations between many countries have been improved by the establishment of bilateral and multilateral agreements, the creation of regional economic treaties such as the European Union (EU), the North American Free Trade Area (NAFTA) and the Association of South-east Asian Nations (ASEAN), and the involvement of international agencies such as the World Bank and the World Trade Organization (WTO). Economic integration and the commonality of regulations, as well as the equalization of taxes on a regional basis, have led to the development of common approaches to business and employment practices.

Technical changes and flow of information

Technical changes have led to the introduction of more productive and flexible working arrangements. The use of electronic control systems has made production and distribution processes more efficient, sophisticated and economic than before. For example, the advent of the internet has facilitated growth of international trade, international communications and easy access to information worldwide. Electronic mailing and information systems as well as the computerization of flight and shipping services are examples of current developments in information technologies. Customers can learn more about the goods they consume and many manufacturers are better informed about the needs of their customers. The international mobility of information has been enhanced by the integration of data processing and telecommunications networks on a global scale. Information can flow easily across borders, making geographical barriers less relevant and reducing the cost of travelling. Moreover, as information can be transferred quickly, rapid innovations can be effected in different countries, reducing lead times and product life cycles and increasing competition and cooperation between geographically dispersed organizations.

The speed and accuracy of information transmission are changing the nature of the international manager's job. Technology allows managers to access information and share it instantly. The internet is used increasingly by national and international companies for crucial HRM functions such as advertising job vacancies, contacting potential employees and online learning. The use of information technologies has led to an increasing demand for a workforce that is not just IT skilled but for also talented people with creative and innovative ideas as well as competency in languages.

Trade and financial services

Open trading between countries and instant availability of financial services has greatly facilitated global economic integration of capital markets. With the deregulation of financial services for international trade, it has become easier, faster and safer for companies to operate on the global scale. Many companies are no longer limited to capital sources within closed national boundaries. The global integration of national capital markets has led to freer flows of funds and easier investment between countries than at any time before.

As explained above, information technologies have facilitated international capital flows and provision of financial services to individual customers, suppliers and producers. Credit and debit card payments have led to virtual customers and virtual suppliers of worldwide products and services. The introduction of internet banking and the establishment of online businesses have opened up more opportunities for national and international, public and private companies to reach their customers, clients and employees in different locations.

Such developments have also created new challenges for MNCs as many small and medium size enterprises (SMEs) are trading internationally without requiring subsidiaries overseas. Consequently, managing diverse human resources across cultures has become important to all type and kind of organizations not just MNCs. There are examples of internationally successful companies that started with one person and his or her personal computer from the study in their own homes.

Political and cultural influences

Economic and political dependence of many developing countries on the west has led to the transfer of Anglo-Saxon and European education, political systems, technology, products, art works, and management theories to many countries of the world. Western cultural influences are evident globally and are embedded in people's daily encounters, from what we see and hear to what we consume in and outside our homes. People in developing countries have sometimes become more familiar with Western products, pop stars, film stars, football players, television presenters and politicians than with those in their own countries. Because of perceptions of Western progress, modernization, superiority and high standards, Western brands are sometimes preferred even when they are of poorer quality than those produced domestically. Here the role of the international media in advertising and promoting Western values is strong. This has strengthened a culture of capitalist consumerism and dependence on Western technology and investments.

Western culture is spreading around the world and penetrating people's lives everywhere. For example, in the Middle East the increasing presence of multinational companies is not only bringing requisite technology and management knowledge and skills from the west but also a culture of consumerism through their mass media advertising. Almost all major multinational companies of the world can now be found in the Middle East. Symbols of capitalism and Americanization such as McDonalds, Pizza Hut and KFC can be seen just metres away from the courtyard of the Holy Mosque in Mecca, Saudi Arabia. It is evident that the sustainability of increasing investments in different countries requires the employment and management of people with different cultural backgrounds and therefore the need to understand and implement cross-cultural management at both local and international levels.

Western management education and the use of English in business

Look at the composition of an MBA class in any American or British university and you get the picture of an ever-increasing internationalization of Western management education. More and more non-westerners are exposed to Western management education by attending courses at colleges and universities.

Moreover, the rapid dissemination of knowledge through international conferences, exchange programmes, publications, licensing, internet access and expatriation are narrowing the gap in the management 'know-how' between countries. Education has become one of the main drivers towards global integration as people are exposed to similar or the same knowledge and skills, and aspire to similar academic qualifications.

One way or another, management education is becoming universal. The management theories taught in MBA programmes, for example, in Chinese universities are likely to be the same as those that are being taught in MBA programmes in French, South African, Egyptian, Brazilian, Canadian or Indian universities. American and British management textbooks, which rarely make references to non-Western management experiences and practices, are adopted in universities, colleges and business schools throughout the world. What has made it even easier to disseminate such knowledge is the use of English as the international language of business. As more people are exposed to Western management knowledge and use English as their medium of instruction and as a means for business transactions, it becomes easier for companies to invest in different countries and therefore the drive to manage across cultures.

Reforms in developing countries

Many of the developing countries in Africa, South America and Asia have embarked on economic and political reforms that are aimed at liberalizing their economies and democratizing their political systems. Their socio-economic reforms have attracted increasing amounts of multinational investment. Economic reforms have led to large-scale privatizations of state-owned companies and to providing more opportunities for foreign direct investment. Many multinational companies have gained easy access to foreign assets and to overseas markets through direct ownership of foreign assets or forming joint ventures. The growth and expansion of international investments has driven the need for more knowledge and skills in managing across cultures.

ACTIVITY 1

What barriers or problems may be encountered by international managers seeking to manage across cultures?

The meaning of managing across cultures

So far we have seen the main reasons for studying the subject of managing across cultures and the major triggers and drivers for the emergence of the current widespread knowledge on cross-cultural management. We need now to consider of what 'managing across cultures' really consists. The subject is of course still evolving. Most of the available literature to date on managing across cultures or cross-cultural management (for example, Handy et al., 1988; Brewster and Tyson, 1991; Redding, 1994; Jackson, 1995; Hickson and Pugh, 1995; Gatley et al., 1996; Warner and Joynt, 2002; Budhwar and Sparrow, 2002a,b; Schneider and Barsoux, 2003; French, 2007; Browaeys and Price, 2008) has focused on the concept of culture and on the influence of cultural differences on doing business in different countries, rather than specifically on the process of *managing* across cultures. Though culture does indeed matter greatly in this context, the concept of culture is too complicated to be used in the kind of definition we require. The concept of culture and the different models of cultural differences will be discussed in the next chapter, where the context of managing across cultures is explained and critically analysed.

According to Adler (2002: 11), 'cross-cultural management explains the behaviour of people in organizations around the world and shows people how to work in organizations with employees and client populations from many different cultures'. Adler (2002: 11) adds that the aim of the study of cross-cultural management is to describe and compare organizational behaviour within countries and cultures, and to seek 'to understand and improve the interaction of co-workers, managers, executives, clients, suppliers, and alliance partners from countries and cultures around the world'. This description, however, concerns the study of cross-cultural management, rather than the process of managing across cultures.

Similarly, in the conventional literature on comparative management studies, the subject of managing across cultures has been assimilated to comparative management (see Negandhi, 1974; Ouchi, 1981), which in turn has been defined as a process of describing, analysing and discussing the policy and practice of management in two or more countries that makes it possible to see the main similarities and the main differences between them (Redding, 1994; Bamber and Lansbury, 2004).

It should be pointed out that the word 'across' in 'managing across cultures' implies, theoretically, having to go in between and within countries and cultures, and hence being able to observe, describe and analyse their similarities and differences. In practice, however, the process of managing across cultures is broader than comparative management because it implies (a) a broader understanding of the determining characteristics of national management systems and (b) the ability to distinguish between different systems and to learn from models of good (or bad) practice. This view of managing across cultures is supported by a number of recent studies. Some of these have focused on the ways in which national trends and characteristics, including socio-economic and political reforms, have influenced employment policies and practices in different countries (Brewster and Tyson, 1991; Budhwar and Debrah, 2001; Kamoche et al., 2004; Budhwar and Mellhi, 2006), while others have looked at aspects of management within and between countries by focusing on the impact of culture on business activities (Warner and Joynt, 2002; Schneider and Barsoux, 2003; Chen, 2004; French, 2007; Moran et al., 2007; Browaeys and Price, 2008). For instance, French (2007: 5) states that 'cross-cultural encounters might, for example, occur when companies decide to outsource work to new countries, or when organizations enter into new forms of networked relationships with overseas partners, or as a result of increased migration of labour'.

However, the study of managing across cultures should go beyond examination of the cultural encounters of multinational companies or of the similarities and differences between countries so as to determine the ways by which national differences have influenced employment policies and practices of different countries and the ways by which international companies have responded to them as shown in Figure 2.1 below. In this respect, Budhwar and Sparrow (2002b: 600) make the point that managers have become 'eager to know how human resources (HRs) are managed in different regions of the world' and added that 'in order to maximize cross-national management capabilities, we need to understand *how* people in different national settings respond to similar concepts within their particular functions' (p. 600).

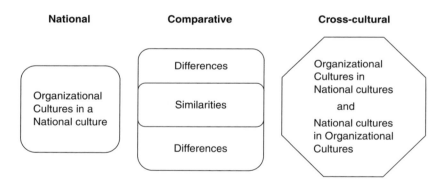

Figure 2.1 National, comparative and cross-cultural management

Managing across cultures is thus a two-way process that involves national and international employees and employers of different organizations in different countries and cultural settings. In this book, managing across cultures is defined simply as the process of *managing local employees globally and global employees locally*. This process involves a strategic approach whereby every employee is expected to act locally and think globally (see Figure 2.2 below). Understanding this process leads, not only to gaining knowledge of different national contexts and to comparing them, but also to international organizations learning the knowledge and skills of managing resources internationally in different national contexts.

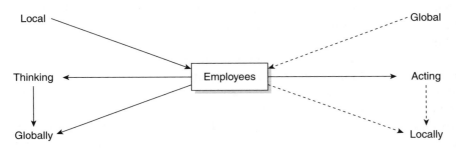

Figure 2.2 The process of managing across cultures

Managing local employees globally

It can be concluded from the drivers outlined above that the globalizing power of business has created common economic, technical and managerial imperatives, despite social, ideological and legal differences. Multinational companies have been the creators of cross-cultural management policy and practice, and have been the main drivers for international convergence rather than divergence. Multinational companies are the main contributors to the globalizing power of business as they have a significant presence in world business in terms of production, trade and employment.

However, one of the main challenges for international organizations in general and multinational companies in particular is to manage local employees globally, strategically and successfully in response to an ever increasing internationalization or globalization of business. The management of local employees globally requires, at least, the building of a global corporate culture that local employees can understand and identify with, and having a forward diffusion employment strategy.

Building a global corporate culture

Global corporate culture is the glue that can keep a global network of activities together (Rhinesmith, 1993). Corporate culture consists of shared visions, systems, mechanisms and processes. These four factors are created by the people on whom the organization depends, from the visions of the founding members or managing directors of the organization to the processes being carried out by employees at the shop-floor level. The building of a sustainable global corporate culture requires an international human resource development strategy that forms an integral part of corporate culture and that helps to create a global mindset in its key employees regardless of their place of work (Hendry, 1991; Srinivas, 1995). In other words, all employees become aware of the main features of that corporate culture and contribute effectively to the achievement of its objectives.

One of the main aspects of a globalising corporate culture is standardization of policies and practices throughout the organization (Bartlett and Ghoshal, 1998; Dickmann et al., 2009). Standardization throughout the organization enhances efficiency through the streamlining of production processes, employment policies, product development, and other activities. As more organizations engage actively in global operations, their activities are likely to lead to social as well as economic changes in societies around the world. For example, all employees working for McDonalds in London, Manhattan, Beijing or Moscow are expected to behave the same way and to serve the same products. The uniform, the grading stars, the service with a smile, the up-selling, the french fries, etc. are all standardized throughout the company in different parts of the world. However, standardization of operations, behaviours and products requires efficient training of local employees to carry out their tasks in the organization's way and the development of local and international managers to make sure that their organization operates in such a way. This process requires a forward diffusion of knowledge and skills and an HR strategy at the core of the organization's corporate strategy.

Forward diffusion of knowledge and skills

To ensure that local employees are successfully managed globally it is crucial to develop a global employment strategy that enables local employees to learn the knowledge and skills that make them globally employable. This process is very often referred to in the international management literature as 'forward diffusion' of knowledge and skills from the home to the host country (Edwards and Ferner, 2004; Edwards et al., 2005).

The forward diffusion of management theory and practice affects not only the local employees of a particular multinational organization but also employees of other indigenous and international organizations. For example, the Japanization of local industries through the increasing presence of Japanese MNCs has led to the adoption of employment policies and practices such as quality circles, total quality management, just-in-time management, pendulum arbitration, and single union representation by many non-Japanese companies in different countries.

================= MINI CASE STUDY 1 =================

The Western Expatriate in West Africa

When asked about the working and living conditions of expatriates, Mrs Celia Ugboko, the managing director of a major petroleum company in West Africa, replied, 'Western expatriates are highly valued, highly paid, well respected and admired for their knowledge and expertise, commitment to their work, dedication, careful attention to detail, respect for time, and tolerance and sensitivity to other cultures. Our respectful treatment of foreigners has led to increasing numbers of Western and non-Western (third country) expatriates and has facilitated forward diffusion of Western management practices and policies to my country.'

Questions

1 Speculate on (a) the context in which the comment was made and (b) what might be the positive and the negative connotations of Mrs Ugboko's statement.
2 Judging from the manager's comment, what types of knowledge and skills do you think the local employees may learn from forward diffusion?

Managing global employees locally

Just as local employees have to be managed globally through the building of global corporate culture and the forward diffusion of knowledge and skills, global employees, mainly expatriates, have to be managed locally in order to achieve their assignment objectives successfully. Global employees, as home country expatriates or third country employees, have to understand the local working environment, the local employees, the local institutions and the local norms and values in order to work with or to manage the local workforces globally. In other words, global employees have to respond to the localizing power of culture and, very often, politics as well.

National differences in norms, values, traditions and beliefs, in levels of economic growth and development, and in institutional settings are the main sources for divergence in management policies and practices between societies. Though it is possible to assimilate organizational structures, to rationalize processes and to standardize products and services between countries, it is not, as Adler (2002) pointed out, easy to assimilate people's behaviour because of their culturally, economically and politically based differences. Therefore managing across cultures requires managers to be aware of the effects that these differences may have on their management policies and practices. They should be aware of the main national norms and values, of the national economic trends and organizational characteristics, and of the national institutions and the legal system.

National norms and values

National norms and values shape the ways in which organizations are designed and run in different countries because the degree to which people regard their work as a central life interest or as an onerous task is affected by their national values, norms and beliefs. The types of social relations and the power structure in family and society, the different norms and expectations related to leadership, social interaction and relationships, and perceptions of emotions differ significantly between countries (Hofstede, 1980a, 1991; Adler, 2002; Deal and Kennedy, 1982; Laurent, 1986; Whitley, 1992; Tayeb, 2003; 2005). As will be explained in more detail in Chapter 3, culture seriously matters in managing across cultures: cultural misunderstandings can easily cause business relationships to be broken, resources and time to be wasted, employees to be offended and international managers ashamed. Selmer (2001: 17) rightly states that 'not being able to interact with the host country nationals in daily life outside work makes expatriates ignorant about local thinking and mentality, which influences their ability to assess work situations and makes them develop erroneous assumptions about the people they are managing'. Therefore it is important for expatriates to interact frequently with the locals and to learn from the local values and norms. This process of national acculturation makes expatriates 'less surprised and frustrated by differences in non-work circumstances of the host country' (Selmer, 2001: 17).

When managing across cultures, international managers become more aware of social differences within individual countries and have to understand the impact of regional, tribal and other in-group and within-group alliances and differences in the way organizations are managed. Therefore, understanding the different norms, values and ways of life in the host country helps not only with the introduction of appropriate employment policies, but also the production of the right products and the provision of needed services. For example, Procter and Gamble faced problems of national preferences and differences when it developed the Visor washing power. It found that Germans generally preferred front-loading washing machines and they thought that the only way to clean white clothes was to use boiling hot water, while French consumers preferred the top-loading machines and did not think it was necessary to use boiling hot water to wash whites. However, the newly introduced Visor washing power was developed to clean whites best in cool water and in front-loading washers. It satisfied neither the Germans nor the French. According to Ulrich and Black (1999: 43), 'as the firm discovered, it is not easy to change people's deeply held beliefs on laundering their whites. Neither is it easy to get a nation to change from front-loading washing machines to top-loading ones'.

When managing across cultures it becomes apparent that what is moral or not, whether religious or just customary, is defined clearly in the relationships of people and is culturally specific. For example, respecting and protecting older people, hospitality, decency and pity, not wasting food and water, and even showing shyness and humility are common cultural values in many countries in the world, but some societies express them more openly than others. In Eastern cultures, it is very unlikely that a younger person would oppose the opinion of an older one. This does not mean, however, that talented and skilled young employees are denied respect and promotion. Therefore, international managers should be aware of such cultural values and take into account how their employees in a particular social context expect them to react and behave.

While emphasizing the importance of cultural awareness, we should also stress that international managers do not need to learn all the languages, convert to the religions of the host countries, or behave exactly like the local people (Torrington, 1994). This happens rarely. The process of managing global employees locally implies that international managers need a good understanding of the local norms, values, customs, history, geography and laws because these are among the main determinants of local identity and national pride. For example, until recently the expatriates who criticize or even refuse to attend a bull-fighting match in Spain may lose the support of local employees who see such a game as part of their national culture.

Host country values and practices have a significant influence on management practices and employment policies at all levels. Therefore, international managers will have to adapt to different working conditions and sometimes operate differently from the way they did in their home countries. For example, when working in African or Middle Eastern countries they may have to accept the hiring of friends and relatives, giving more consideration to trustworthiness and loyalty, and using red tape and cumbersome bureaucratic procedures, because such practices are customary in the host country and respected by the local managers and employees. Such differences should be seen as an opportunity to doing good business rather than a threat.

National economic trends and organizational characteristics

It has very often been argued that societies differ in their management systems according to their levels of economic growth and organizational characteristics (Lammers and Hickson, 1979; Hickson and McMillan, 1981; Ouchi, 1981; Hickson and Pugh, 2001). Countries with similar levels of economic growth and development may develop, and should at least be able to share, some managerial practices. A number of studies have concluded that the difficulties encountered by international managers in developing countries, when trying to implement Western management theories, occur mainly because such theories reflect the level of economic development of their inventors (Hofstede, 1980b, 1993; Srinivas, 1995). Hence, in managing across cultures, understanding the economic environment of the foreign operating country can help international managers to operate effectively when dealing with suppliers and customers, for example, and to predict trends and events that might affect their organizations' future performance.

Moreover, it is also important in managing across cultures to understand the main characteristics of organizations in the host country because the way organizations are managed differs from one society to another; depending on their structure, culture and process (Hickson et al., 1974; Ouchi, 1981; Hickson and McMillan, 1981). For example, in many African, Middle Eastern and South-east Asian countries, organizations are centralized and bureaucratic, and the delegation of authority is often made to relatives and trusted close friends. Misunderstanding of different organizational structures and management practices in the host countries can result in international managers making inappropriate business decisions, as seen from Mini Case Study 2 below.

National institutions and legal systems

A number of studies have found that patterns of national distinctiveness such as the country's history, its national and regional institutions, its political system and its legislative procedures have strong influence on management and employee relations (Whitley, 1992; Child, 1994; Chen, 2004). In managing across cultures, one of the most important institutions that international managers have to be aware of is the host country's education system. The types of education and training programmes delivered in a country are very likely to influence the structure and development of organizations, and to shape the nature and quality of its workforce. By understanding the education system and the types and levels of education in the host country it will be easier for international managers to decide how local employees could be trained and how easily technology can be transferred and implemented effectively. Also, it is important for international managers to understand how local employees learn in order to design appropriate training programmes for them.

The other important institutional factor in managing across cultures is the legal system of the host country. Being aware of international laws as well as host country legal systems and employment legislation is mandatory in cross-cultural management. Ball and McCulloch (1993: 370) argued that 'international business is affected by many thousands of laws and regulations on hundreds of subjects that have been issued by states, nations, and international organizations'. These laws can be divided into international and national laws, and they affect factors such as taxation, employment, trade relations, health and safety, imports and exports (including tariff controls), financial reporting, product liability, intellectual property, contracts, and currency control within and between countries.

Assessing and avoiding risks

The process of managing across cultures sits between the globalizing power of business and the localizing power of culture and politics. The problem in implementing such a process effectively lies in knowing the unknown. In this respect, it can be argued that the more is known by the international manager (expatriate) about the local working environment and the local employees, and the more the local employees know about the corporate culture and its operations, the greater and the better global integration and local responsiveness there will be and hence greater effectiveness in managing across cultures. The factors that facilitate the process of knowing the unknown are: the ability to assess and avoid risks by both local and international employees; and the encouragement of 'reverse diffusion' of management good practice from the host to the home country.

Although many countries have opened their doors to foreign investment, there are still problems of local acceptance that should not be underestimated in managing across cultures. When investing in a foreign country, MNCs should assess the risks involved in employing expatriates and local employees. It should be stressed that though the governments of many countries welcome foreign direct investment, they also have responsibility for protecting their own industries and citizens. Protectionism takes different forms, from trade barriers and quotas to employment restrictions, which MNCs have to be prepared for and deal with effectively. Moreover, the outcomes of inter-governmental conflicts, pacts and bilateral relations can have significant effects on managing across cultures.

Although many developing countries offer large market potential and exhibit strong economic growth, investing in them can be riskier than investing in industrialized countries. Most of the developing countries in Asia, Africa and South America have experienced complex and unstable political systems in their attempts to develop suitable frameworks and ideologies for their socio-economic development. There may also be financial and economic risks because of environmental (climate) changes, terrorism, international labour migration, fluctuations in demand for certain products, shortages in the supply of raw materials, international financial crisis, and so on, that international managers should be able to assess and avoid their impact whenever possible. Such risks have serious implication for the international operations of a firm and for the process of managing across cultures.

Local employees and governments should also be able to assess the risks of increasing presence of international corporate cultures and of forward diffusion of knowledge and skills from other countries. Local industries and business could be seriously affected by the direct international competition created by MNCs. The privatization of public utilities, mergers and takeovers could result in the restructuring of newly created companies and the downsizing of operations, resulting in mass redundancies in countries where unemployment, especially among the young people, is already very high. Another risk is the cultural influence of MNCs in countries that are already very receptive to Western capitalist norms and values. It will be seen from the relevant chapters of this book that the culture of consumerism, greed and competition is spreading throughout Eastern societies with increasing rapidity, partly, if not mainly, because of the spread of foreign investment in that part of the world.

MINI CASE STUDY 2

General Electric in Hungary

In the late 1980s the USA's General Electric Company (GE) moved into Hungary, which was then a communist state. It bought 51 per cent of the Tungsram Company, a producer of lighting products. It believed that it was making a good investment decision to take advantage of Hungary's move towards democracy and a free market economy.

What the company did not expect were the organizational problems that it encountered. Under years of communism there was a strong tradition of waste and inefficiency. There was no motive for individual employees to produce good-quality products. The concepts of customer care and customer satisfaction were alien to many Hungarian employees. The American managers thought that the Hungarian workers were too 'laid back' and the Hungarian employees thought that their American managers were 'too aggressive'.

It took eight years, $440 million and a 50 per cent cut in the workforce before the company began to make profits (Ulrich and Black, 1999).

Question

1   What are the main lessons for managing across cultures to be drawn from this case study?

Reverse diffusion of knowledge and skills

It is argued above that 'forward' diffusion is important for managing local employees globally and for global business integration. Equally, 'reverse' diffusion of management policies and practices from the host to the home country should be encouraged for managers to learn more about local management systems (Edwards, 1998; Edwards et al., 2005).

Reverse diffusion is part of the national identification process as international managers are informed of the national characteristics of organizations and managements in different countries. Ulrich and Black (1999) argued that one of the managerial competencies that may enable international companies to integrate and concentrate global activities while attempting to separate and adapt to local activities is to share learning and generate new knowledge from the local operations. Encouraging reverse diffusion of management theories and practices can lead to better understanding of the local working environment and to the development of appropriate approaches to managing across cultures.

Summary

1   The subject of managing across cultures has emerged in recent years as a significant field of academic research and study as a result of a number of triggers and drivers. Among the triggers are: the failure of expatriates to complete their assignments abroad; the economic recession of the 1980s; the rise and successes of South-east Asian countries; the openness of China and later India to the west; and the end of the Cold War and the 'Westernization' of Eastern Europe. The main drivers have been: the growth and spread of multinational companies; international competition; regional economic integration; technical changes and international mobility of information; open trading and availability of financial services; political and cultural influences; internationalization of Western management education with the use of English as the international language of business; and the liberalization and democratization of developing countries.

2   Most of the definitions of managing across cultures focus on the concept of culture and the effects of cultural differences on management in different countries. This book acknowledges the importance of culture and its effects on management and goes beyond the need to understand the similarities and differences between societies to see the process of managing across cultures as the management of local employees globally and global employees locally, including expatriates, host and third country employees, national and international employee regulations, and national and international employee and employer organizations.

3   The management of local employees globally requires, at least, the building of a global corporate culture that local employees can understand and identify with, and having a strategy of forward diffusion of knowledge and skills from the home to the host countries.

4   Just as local employees have to be managed globally, global employees, mainly expatriates, have to be managed locally in order to achieve their assignments successfully. Global employees have to understand the local working environment, employees, institutions, and norms and values in order to manage the local workforce globally.

5   The process of managing across cultures sits between the globalizing power of business and the localizing power of culture and politics. The problem in implementing such a process effectively lies in knowing the unknown. The more familiar the international manager (expatriate) is with the local working environment and local employees, and the more the local employees know about the corporate culture and its operations, the greater and better the global integration and local responsiveness. The factors that may facilitate the process of knowing the unknown are the ability to assess and avoid risks, and the encouragement of 'reverse diffusion' of management good practice from the host to the home country.

Revision questions

1 Discuss with the use of examples the main factors and events that have led to the emergence of cross-cultural management as a significant field of academic research and study.
2 What does 'managing across cultures' mean? Elaborate your answer by referring to at least two contrasting definitions.
3 What do you think are the main things that international organizations can do to be successful in (a) managing global employees locally and (b) managing their local employees globally?

References

Adler, N. (2002) *International Dimensions of Organizational Behaviour*, 4th edn, Cincinnati, OH: South-Western College Publishing/Thomson Learning.
Ball, D.A. and McCulloch, W.H. (1993) *International Business: Introduction and Essentials*, London: Irwin.
Bamber, G.J. and Lansbury, R.D. (eds) (2004) *International and Comparative Employment Relations*, 4th edn, London: Sage.
Bartlett, C.A. and Ghoshal, S. (1998) *Managing Across Borders: The Transnational Solution*, 2nd edn, London: Century Business.
Branine, M. (1997), 'Change and continuity in Chinese employment relationships', *New Zealand Journal of Industrial Relations*, 22(1): 77–94.
Brewster, C. and Harris, H. (1999), *International HRM: Contemporary Issues in Europe*, London: Routledge.
Brewster, C. and Tyson, S. (eds) (1991) *International Comparisons in Human Resource Management*, London: Pitman.
Briscoe, D.R. and Schuler, R.S. (2004), *International Human Resource Management*, 2nd edn, London: Routledge.
Browaeys, M.J. and Price, R. (2008) *Understanding Cross-cultural Management*, Harlow: Prentice-Hall/Financial Times.
Budhwar, P. and Debrah, Y.A. (eds) (2001) *Human Resource Management in Developing Countries*, London: Routledge.
Budhwar, P. and Mellahi, K. (eds) (2006) *Managing Human Resources in the Middle East*, London: Routledge.
Budhwar, P. and Sparrow, P. (2002a), 'An integrative framework for determining cross-national human resource management practices', *Human Resource Management Review*, 12(3): 377–403.
Budhwar, P. and Sparrow, P. (2002b) 'Strategic HRM through the cultural looking glass: mapping cognitions of British and Indian HRM managers', *Organization Studies*, 23(4): 599–638.
Chen, M. (2004) *Asian Management Systems*, 2nd edn, London: Thomson Learning.
Child, J. (1994) *Management in China in the Era of Reform*, Cambridge: Cambridge University Press.

Deal, T.E. and Kennedy, A.A. (1982) *Corporate Cultures: The Rites and Rituals of Corporate Life*, Reading, MA: Addison-Wesley.

Deresky, H. (2001) *International Management: Managing Across Borders and Cultures*, London: Prentice-Hall.

Dickmann, M., Müller-Camen, M. and Kelliher, C. (2009) 'Exploring standardisation and knowledge networking processes in transnational human resource management', *Personnel Review*, 38(1): 5–25.

Dowling, P.J., Festing, M. and Engle, A.D., Sr (2008) *International Human Resource Management*, 5th edn, London: Thomson Learning.

Dowling, P.J., Schuler, R.S. and Welch, D.E. (1994) *International Dimensions of Human Resource Management*, 2nd edn, Belmont, CA: Thomson International and Wadsworth.

Dowling, P.J., Welch, D.E. and Schuler, R.S. (1999) *International Human Resource Management: Managing People in a Multinational Context*, 3rd edn, Cincinnati, OH: South-Western College Publishing.

Easterby-Smith, M., Malina, D. and Lu, Y. (1995) 'How culture sensitive is HRM?: A comparative analysis of practice in Chinese and UK companies', *The International Journal of Human Resources Management*, 6(1): 31–59.

Edwards, T. (1998) 'Multinationals and the process of reserve diffusion', *International Journal of Human Resource Management*, 9(4): 696–709.

Edwards, T. and Ferner, A. (2004) 'Multinationals, national business systems and reverse diffusion', *Management International Review*, 24(1): 51–81.

Edwards, T., Almond, P., Clark, I., Colling, T. and Ferner, A. (2005) 'Reverse diffusion in US multinationals: barriers from the American business system', *Journal of Management Studies*, 42(6): 1261–86.

Evans, P., Doz, Y. and Laurent, A. (1989) *Human Resource Management in International Firms*, London: Macmillan.

French, R. (2007) *Cross-Cultural Management in Work Organisations*, London: CIPD.

Gatley, S., Lessem, R. and Altman, Y.(1996), *Comparative Management: A Transcultural Odyssey*, London: McGraw-Hill.

Handy, C., Gordon, C., Gow, I. and Randlesome, C. (1988) *Making Managers*, London: Pitman.

Harris, P.R. and Moran, R.T. (1991) *Managing Cultural Differences: High-performance Strategies for a New World of Business*, Texas: Gulf Publishing.

Harzing, A.W. and Ruysseveldt, J.V. (2004) (eds.), *International Human Resource Management: An Integrated Approach*, 2nd edn, London: Sage.

Hendry, C. (1991) 'International comparisons of human resource management: putting the firm in the frame', *The International Journal of Human Resource Management*, 2(3): 415–40.

Hickson, D.J., Hinings, C.R., McMillan, C.J. and Schwitter, J.P. (1974) 'The culture-free context of organization structure: a tri-national comparison', *Sociology*, 8: 59–80.

Hickson, D.J. and McMillan, C.J. (eds) (1981) *Organization and Nation: The Aston Programme IV*, Aldershot: Gower.

Hickson, D.J. and Pugh, D.S. (1995) *Management Worldwide: The Impact of Societal Culture on Organizations Around the Globe*, London: Penguin.

Hickson, D.J. and Pugh, D.S. (2001) *Management Worldwide*, 2nd edn, Harmondsworth: Penguin.

Hofstede, G. (1980a) *Culture's Consequences: International Differences in Work Related Values*, London: Sage.

Hofstede, G. (1980b) 'Motivation, leadership and organization: do American theories apply abroad?', *Organizational Dynamics*, Summer, 1980.

Hofstede, G. (1991) *Culture and Organizations: Software of the Mind*, London: McGraw-Hill.

Hofstede, G. (1993) 'Cultural constraints in management theories', *Academy of Management Executive*, 7(1): 81–94.

Jackson, K. and Tomioka, M. (2004) *The Changing Face of Japanese Management*, Routledge: London.

Jackson, T. (1995) *Cross-Cultural Management*, Oxford: Butterworth-Heinemann.

Kamoche, K.N., Debrah, Y., Horwitz, F. and Muuka, G.N. (eds) (2004) *Managing Human Resources in Africa*, London: Routledge.

Kanter, R.M. (1995) *World Class: Thriving Locally in the Global Economy*, New York: Simon & Schuler.

Lammers, C.J. and Hickson, D.J. (1979) *Organizations Alike and Unlike: International and Inter-institutional Studies in the Sociology of Organizations*, London: Routledge & Kegan Paul.

Laurent, A. (1986) 'The cross-cultural puzzle of international HRM', *Human Resource Management*, 25: 91–102.

Moran, R.T., Harris, P.R. and Moran, S.V. (2007) *Managing Cultural Differences: Global Leadership Strategies for the 21st Century*, 7th edn, Oxford: Butterworth-Heinemann.

Negandhi, A.R. (1974) 'Cross-cultural management studies: too many conclusions, not enough conceptualizations', *Management International Review*, 14: 59–72.

Nolan, P. (2001) *China and the Global Business Revolution*, London: Palgrave, New York: St.Martin's Press.

Ohmae, K. (1990) *The End of the Nation State*, New York: Free Press.

Ouchi, W.G. (1981) *Theory Z: How American Management Can Meet the Japanese Challenge*, Reading, MA: Addison-Wesley.

Peters, T. and Waterman, R. (1982) *In Search of Excellence*, New York: Harper & Row.

Pfeffer, J. (1994) *Competitive Advantage Through People: Unleashing the Power of the Workforce*, Boston: Harvard Business School Press.

Redding, G.S. (1994) 'Comparative management theory: jungle, zoo or fossil bed?', *Organisation Studies*, 15(3): 323–59.

Rhinesmith, S.H. (1993) *A Manager's Guide to Globalization: Six Keys to Success in a Changing World*, Chicago: Richard D. Irwin.

Rosenzweig, P. M., Nohria, N. (1994) 'Influences on human resource management practices in multinational corporations' *Journal of International Business Studies*, 25(2): 229–251.

Schneider, S.C. and Barsoux, J.L. (2003) *Managing Across Cultures*, 2nd edn, Harlow: Prentice-Hall/Financial Times.

Schuler, R.S., Dowling, P.J. and De Cieri, H. (1993) 'An integrative framework of strategic international human resource management', *International Journal of Human Resource Management*, 4(6): 717–64.

Schuler, R.S., Jackson, S.E. and Luo, Y. (2004) *Managing Human Resources in Cross-Border Alliances*, London, Routledge.

Selmer, J. (2001) 'Adjustment of Western European vs. North American expatriate managers in China', *Personnel Review*, 30(1): 6–21.

Sparrow, P., Schuler, R.S. and Jackson S.E. (1994) 'Convergence or divergence: human resource practices and policies for competitive advantage world-wide', *The International Journal of Human Resource Management*, 5(2): 267–99.

Srinivas, K.M. (1995) 'Globalization of business and the third world: challenges of expanding the mindsets', *Journal of Management Development*, 14(3): 26.

Tang, J. and Ward, A. (2003) *The Changing Face of Chinese Management*, Working in Asia Series, London: Routledge.

Tayeb, M.H. (2003) *International Management: A Cross-cultural Approach*, Harlow: Prentice-Hall/Financial Times.

Tayeb, M.H. (2005) *International Human Resource Management: A Multinational Company Perspective*, Oxford: Oxford University Press.

Torrington, D. (1994) *International Human Resource Management: Think Globally, Act Locally*, Hemel Hempstead: Prentice-Hall.

Tung, R.L., (1986) 'Corporate executives and their families in China: the need for cross-cultural understanding in business', *The Columbia Journal of World Business*, 21(1): 21–6.

Tung, R.L. (2002) 'Managing in Asia: cross-cultural dimensions', in Warner, M. and Joynt, P. (eds), *Managing Across Cultures: Issues and Perspectives*, 2nd edn, London: Thomson Learning, 137–42.

Ulrich, D. and Black, S. (1999) 'Worldly wise', *People Management*, 5(21): 42–6.

Warner, M. (1995) *The Management of Human Resources in Chinese Industry*, Basingstoke: Macmillan and New York: St. Martins Press.

Warner, M. (ed.) (2003) *Culture and Management in Asia*, London: Routledge Curzon.

Warner, M. and Joynt, P. (2002) *Managing Across Cultures: Issues and Perspectives*, 2nd edn, London: Thomson Learning.

White, M. and Trevor, M. (1983) *Under Japanese Management*, London; Heinmann.

Whitley, R.D. (1992) *Business Systems in East Asia: Firms, Markets and Societies*, London: Sage.

Yan, Y. and Child, J. (2002) 'An analysis of strategic determinants, learning and decision-making in Sino–British joint ventures', *British Journal of Management*, (13): 109–22.

3

Contexts and the Cultural Dilemma of Managing Across Cultures

================ LEARNING OUTCOMES ================

This chapter is designed to help the reader to:

1 Recognize the impact of globalization and its implications for operational strategies of managing across cultures;

2 Identify the main economic, political, legal and technological challenges faced by international managers when operating in different countries;

3 Recall the main arguments for (a) convergence and (b) divergence of management policies and practices between countries;

4 Analyse critically the main theoretical models of culture and management;

5 Determine the effects of cultural differences on management theory and practice in different countries.

Introduction

The process of managing across cultures is described in the previous chapter as a strategic approach whereby (a) local employees are managed globally and (b) global employees are managed locally, while (c) every employee is expected to act locally and think globally. This chapter aims to develop this conception further by explaining the contexts in which the process of managing across cultures takes place. It also seeks to place the subject within a theoretical framework of analysis. The development of this framework begins with the question: 'Is management a universal phenomenon?' Consideration of this question leads to a discussion of convergence and divergence theories. Convergence theorists argue that management is culture free while the divergence theorists argue that management is culture specific. The debate over the transfer of management theories and practices from one country to another leads us to the analysis of the culture dilemma in managing across cultures. Finally the chapter considers the concept of culture and provides a review of relevant literature on culture, society and management.

The contexts of managing across cultures

The process of managing across cultures takes place in global, local and organizational contexts (see Figure 3.1). The global context is the sphere in which international managers operate and is measured by the number of countries and subsidiaries that have to be managed across cultures. It is influenced by international laws and regulations, international political alliances and conflicts, international labour movements, international monetary systems, the conditions of the international economy, and the level of international transfer of knowledge and technology.

Figure 3.1 The contexts of managing across cultures

The local context of managing across cultures is made up of home, host and third country nationals, organizations and systems. National and regional cultures, political and economic systems, historical events, labour market trends, laws and regulations, level of economic growth and industrialization, and the country's infrastructure, are the factors that influence how international managers operate in different countries.

The organizational context is formed by the international organization or the multinational company for which the international manager works. This context is influenced by the organization's approach to staffing its subsidiaries, which is in turn dependent of the organization's culture, structure and operations.

The global–international context

Cross-cultural management takes place in a global context and is both a cause and effect of a globalizing power of business. 'Globalisation' is often seen as a cause of international political conflicts, economic recession, financial crisis, information revolution, consumerism, and so on. However, perceptions and interpretations of globalization vary, not least because of the multi-disciplinary nature of the phenomenon: from the globalization of trade to the globalization of arts, language and types of food, there are almost as many conceptualizations of globalization as there are disciplines. Even within the globalization of business and management we find the globalization of marketing, finance, entrepreneurship, information, and human resource management.

Generally speaking, globalization concerns activities that take place in a 'borderless world' (Ohmae, 1990). In society, Giddens (1990: 4) sees globalization as 'the intensification of world-wide social relations which links distant localities in such a way that local happenings are shaped by events occurring many miles away and vice versa'. Most of the literature on management and globalization concerns the *effects* of globalization, rather than the question of what globalization *is*. The effects of globalization in the electronics, computer, telecommunications and automobile industries, as well as in the increasing number of services from banking to fast food restaurants, are well documented. It has been argued that as a result of the globalization of certain products and services, many organizations of different sizes have been forced to reassess their strategic approaches to international operations by revising their organizational structures and corporate cultures (Bartlett and Ghoshal, 1989; Deresky 2003; House et al., 2004; Lewis, 2004). The changes brought by globalization are far-reaching. Reich (1991: 77) has argued that because of globalization 'there will be no national products or technologies, no national corporations, no national industries ... industries are ceasing to exist in any form that can meaningfully be distinguished from the rest of the global economy'.

Organizations have become, through the rise in foreign trade, foreign direct investment, strategic alliances and joint ventures, inextricably related to each other through complex international business networks. The main elements of the global context for managing across cultures include international business, international labour movement and migration, international laws and regulations, international political alliances or clashes, the international monetary system and international transfers of knowledge and technology. Such elements create a number of challenges for managing resources in different cultural settings. These challenges can be classified as economic, political, legal and technological.

Economic challenges

Multinational companies face all the economic challenges of international business from international competition, negotiating strategic alliances, establishing joint ventures and dealing with changes in international monetary and financial systems. An international organization adapts itself to different economic stages and cycles, namely boom or recession. In conditions of economic boom, national income and profits increase as well as wages and investments. Organizations grasp the good economic conditions to increase sales, expand their market shares and reinvest to enlarge their operations at home and abroad. The opposite happens in conditions of economic recession. Organizations seize the opportunity to acquire foreign assets and gain access to markets through acquisitions, takeovers, strategic alliances and joint ventures. Therefore, those managing across cultures have to adjust to the different changes in international economic trends.

Political challenges

Multinational companies prefer to invest in countries that are politically stable and have low rates of inflation, a high real growth rate, favourable employment laws, skilled labour, plenty of natural resources, and easy access to the technologies needed. The main political challenges for international investors are taking political risks seriously and dealing with political instabilities wisely. A political risk can be defined as 'any governmental action or politically motivated event that could adversely affect the long-run profitability or value of a firm' (Deresky, 2003: 12). All organizations are exposed to levels of political risks, but for multinational companies the risk is greater (Tayeb, 2003, 2005) because they have to deal with home country politics, host country politics, and international political constraints and conditions.

Political instability disrupts the operations of the local and international markets and threatens international investments. The world is prone to many political conflicts, religious tensions, and wars. Some countries are occupied under different pretexts, leading to national resistance and military struggle for independence, while others go to war or find themselves driven to it as a result of conflicts over borders, water and other resources. Intergovernmental conflicts, pacts and bilateral relations all affect the process of managing across cultures.

However, it should be noted that MNCs can benefit from political conflicts by seizing opportunities to increase their sales and lobbying to win contracts for rebuilding the war destroyed countries. For example, many American and European companies benefited from the Gulf War by investing heavily in the rebuilding of Kuwait. It has been argued that the occupation of Iraq was driven by the desire of American companies to control the wealth of the oil rich country. Moreover, political conflicts and wars lead to the migration of skilled and non-skilled people from wartorn countries to safer and more stable ones. This movement of labour creates more 'third country' employees for MNCs and hence more opportunities to access a wider pool of resources, but the process of managing different employees becomes more complex and challenging.

Legal challenges

Managing across cultures requires adherence to various international and regional laws and regulations. For example, there are many international as well as regional and national employment laws to which international employers have to adhere. The International Labour Organization (ILO) issues codes of practice on employment practices and produces annual reports on employment trends and labour statistics in different countries. In developing countries employment legislation is usually less protective of employees than in more developed countries. There are international laws concerning the employment of young people, the employment of emigrant workers, overtime work, equal opportunities, and so on. In all cases, international employers have to understand the different laws and implement them accordingly.

Technological challenges

One of the main challenges for international companies is to achieve sustainable growth based on continuous development and use of new technologies by innovative, creative and well-trained employees. Technological superiority is the aim of many organizations, but it is especially important to international firms because it enables them to stay competitive in the world markets. It gives them a better chance for survival when entering a foreign market, especially where other companies are already established.

There are many technological factors that affect the process of managing across cultures. According to Deresky (2003: 31), such factors include: 1) the level of technology required by different operations in different countries; 2) the availability of local technical skills and expertise; 3) the technical requirements of the host country; 4) the level of knowledge and technology transfer required in each country involved; 5) the type of infrastructure needed in each country to support the use of the technology required; and 6) the environmental protection that is imposed by international, regional or local laws. The risk of piracy and technology espionage has been a real problem for many multinational companies operating across cultures because some governments have very limited control over intellectual property rights and the reproduction of other companies' products.

ACTIVITY 1

Consider the above global challenges in relation to a multinational company with which you are familiar. Draw up a table indicating (a) each challenge and (b) how to deal with it.

The local–national country context

The main elements of the local or national context for managing across cultures are the national culture, the political and legislative systems, the historical background, the labour market, employment laws, and the levels of economic growth and industrialization of the host and the home country. Though the major challenge for international managers is to understand and to cope with the host country's national culture, most of the challenges of managing across cultures are related to the demands of the national political, legal and economic environments in which they operate.

The political environment

Managing across cultures involves dealing with governments of different countries and responding to the local political environment. Often a change in government is followed by new economic and social measures, which can affect the way business is carried out and people are employed. In some countries the state intervenes through the expropriation of multinational businesses and the imposition of operational restrictions. Governments may also impose restrictions relating to currency inconvertibility, employment of foreign and local workers, local ownership, product requirements, wages, labour unions, and so on. They may set tariff barriers and other regulations to protect domestic firms, and foreign firms may be affected. Many government actions are aimed at protecting domestic industries, as well as the social structure and political system. Many governments protect their domestic industries on the grounds that these industries are new and need protection from foreign competitors. Political risks arise not only from change in government but also from factors such as civil war, mass arrests, social unrest and terrorism. Problems of ethnicity, identity and nationalism are behind most of the political instabilities in many countries.

The legal environment

The legal environment of a country consists of the country's laws and regulations. Legal systems vary from country to country in terms of complexity, interpretation and application. The international manager should be aware of the type of laws and regulations, especially employment laws, which are enacted in the host country. Such laws may be divided into common, civil and Islamic. Common law is based on custom and practice and is practised in countries such as the UK, where there is no written constitution and the courts base their decisions on previous relevant cases. Civil law is based on a comprehensive set of regulations organized in the form of statutes and codes of practice. Civil law is practised in most countries of the world. Islamic law is based on the interpretation of the Koran (words of God) and the *Hadith* (teachings of the Prophet Mohammed) in what is known as *Sharia* law. Many Muslim countries use a combination of Islamic and civil laws. Therefore international managers should be familiar with the type of laws that are implemented in the countries they find themselves in.

The economic environment

The economic environment of a country determines the level and type of foreign investment in it. Normally a healthy and stable economic environment enjoys a high level of foreign investment. The more industrialized the country, the less the risk of economic instability and the more likely a favourable environment for the international firm to operate. Understanding the economic environment of the host country can help the international firm to predict trends and events that might affect its future performance there.

The strength of an economy is also indicated by its balance of payments. This affects exchange rates, the level of employment, interest rates, and prices of goods and services. A high deficit can create obstacles to international firms, as they will find it hard to import goods, causing a shortage of products in the marketplace. Countries with balance of payments surpluses can see their currencies appreciating against others and this can affect international firms engaged in exports, as demand for their products will decrease due to the appreciation of currencies.

Often international managers find themselves dealing with the effects of different national financial and banking systems, and the fluctuation of currencies, inflation rates, and interest rates. International firms revenues can be severely affected by the constant fluctuation or the devaluation of a national currency. Moreover, international investments are dependent on good infrastructure for business planning, product distribution, logistics and market entrance. Companies operating in an economic environment with poor infrastructure may find it difficult to deliver their goods on time, meet deadlines, get raw materials and reach suppliers and customers according to plans. Poor transport and communication facilities can be a major obstacle for international companies wanting to invest in some developing countries.

The organizational context

The organizational context of managing across cultures is the international organization or the multinational company in which managers and employees both operate locally and think globally in different cultural settings. Of course, national companies and institutions are also involved in cross-cultural management, though only when they aspire to become international or when they are directly related to a multinational company such as in joint ventures. Multinational companies can be described as organizations that have operating facilities in several different countries around the world (Dowling et al., 1994; 1999). In this book the term 'multinationals' is interchangeable with multinational companies (MNCs), multinational enterprises (MNEs), and international, transnational or global companies. A multinational's headquarters, which coordinates all operations in different countries, is normally based in the home country. Multinationals operate in different countries with the aim of achieving global organizational objectives by utilizing the resources available to them at a profitable cost. For example, Acer's computer project 'Aspire' designed the main computer system in its Taiwanese headquarters, the monitor and keyboard were produced in Malaysia, and the development of the prototype and software and assemblage of the completed product happened in the United States.

Multinationals can source staff in three ways: by assigning parent country nationals (PCNs), appointing host country nationals (HCNs) or recruiting third country nationals (TCNs). The PCNs are expatriates who are employed by the company as managers, supervisors, experts and trainers; the HCNs are the locals or the citizens of the host country, often employed by the company as supervisors, administrators, and manual workers; and the TCNs may be expatriates sent by the company from a third country or emigrants living in the host country and therefore considered locals.

The staffing of multinational companies for international operations is of critical importance for their competitive advantage and sustainable growth. The process involves dealing with different cultures, regulations and working environment. Normally, as in any organization, the recruitment and selection process starts with human resource planning and the production of job descriptions and job specifications after conducting a job analysis. A well-defined job description and person specification can help to plan the company workforce and identify the necessary behaviours and qualities necessary for managing across cultures. However, the staffing policy of a multinational company's subsidiary determines also its international management orientation and its human resource management strategy. MNCs' staffing approaches have been classified as ethnocentric, polycentric, geocentric and regiocentric. Let us consider each type in turn.

The ethnocentric approach

The companies that adopt this approach prefer to have their managers from the home rather than the host country. One often finds that key managerial positions in the subsidiaries are held by parent country nationals (PCNs) or citizens of the country where the headquarters is situated. It is often believed that PCNs are better trained and informed about company policies, procedures and practices. This approach is also used when the parent company management believes that the HCNs lack the knowledge and skills required from managers in the top positions in the subsidiary. In most cases PCNs are preferred when a high level of technical expertise is needed (Dowling, Schuler and Welch, 2004). Hence, the HCNs are used only in lower-level, unskilled and supporting jobs. In such cases the strategic decisions on the management and operation of subsidiaries are made at the headquarters, giving very little autonomy to the subsidiaries. Many examples of ethnocentric companies are found among Japanese and South Korean companies, but also some US and German multinationals.

The ethnocentric approach is also used where a company observes the inadequacy of local managerial skills and decides to maintain close communication and coordination with headquarters. The headquarters determines the decision-making process so that the parent country's national, business and organizational cultures have great influence over all aspects of management in the subsidiaries.

The advantage of an ethnocentric staffing policy is that PCNs are usually more familiar with the company's policies, objectives, products and procedures. This approach is more suitable for companies setting up new subsidiaries or in countries where there is a shortage of local managers. The main disadvantage of this approach is the lack of promotion and advancement opportunities for the HCNs, which may result in employee resentment, reduced commitment, poor performance and increased staff turnover of HCNs (Dowling, Schuler and Welch, 1994; Dowling, Festing and Engle, 2008). Other disadvantages are the possibility of not understanding the host country culture leading to expatriates making mistakes. The main challenge for the successful management of resources across cultures by ethnocentric companies is the effective management of global employees locally.

The polycentric approach

The opposite of ethnocentric is polycentric, where the host country management is preferred over the use of expatriates. Subsidiaries are treated as distinct national entities with some decision-making autonomy. They are managed with minimum intervention from the headquarters personnel. With a polycentric staffing approach, local managers are hired to occupy key positions in their own country. The belief here will be that HCNs are naturally familiar with the local culture, language and ways of doing business, and they may already have contacts with local businesses and government bodies and institutions. In addition, local managers are more likely to be accepted by people both inside and outside the subsidiary, and they may provide role models for the other members of staff. This approach to staffing is more likely to be successful when the company pursues a multi-domestic investment strategy. Examples of such companies are found amongst British, French, Swiss and some US multinationals.

The main advantage of this approach is the reduction of language barriers and avoidance of adjustment problems of expatriate managers and their families. The need to employ and train expensive expatriates is eliminated. It also increases the opportunities for HCNs to develop their careers with the company, which in turn can increase local commitment and attachment to the organization (Dowling, Schuler and Welch, 1994; Scullion and Collings, 2006).

The major disadvantage of a polycentric approach to staffing is the likely problem of coordinating policies and activities between the HCN subsidiary managers and the headquarters. Cultural differences, conflicting national loyalties and language barriers may segregate the HCNs from the headquarters. Another problem is that companies adopting this approach provide limited opportunities to the PCNs to gain the foreign experience necessary for the development of international managers. The main challenge for companies following a polycentric approach is to manage the local employees globally.

The geocentric approach

Geocentric organizations are those that depend on international teams of managers regardless of their country of origin or nationality. In this approach, the best managers are recruited from inside and outside the company. Selected employees are sent on a number of short overseas assignments to introduce them to different ways of doing things. Companies that adopt a geocentric approach simply appoint the best-qualified employees to manage their subsidiaries. This type of company is more likely to have managers with international mindsets than do organizations with an ethnocentric or polycentric approach (Scullion and Collings, 2006). Examples of such companies include IBM, Shell, NCR, Unilever and Nestlé.

The main advantage of this approach is that the company will have a wider pool of international managers and experts to draw from for its international operations. The knowledge, skills and experience that managers transfer throughout the company provide a pool of shared learning and best practices and knowledge that spread across the company as employees bring these practices when they move from one country to another. One of the main disadvantages of this approach is cost: the approach can be expensive to implement, especially when families have to move from one country to another.

The regiocentric approach

Companies that adopt a regiocentric approach employ managers on a regional basis: employees may move outside their home country but stay within a particular geographic region. This type of organization depends on the use of regionally selected managers and professionals. Examples of such companies include Chinese multinationals that use managers from Hong Kong, Singapore and other countries in the region. This approach can produce a mix of parent country, host country and third country nationals, according to the needs of the company or the product strategy within the region. Regional managers have a relatively large degree of regional autonomy in decision-making (Scullion and Collings, 2006). However, they are not always brought into jobs at headquarters (Deresky, 2003).

The main advantage of the regiocentric approach is that it uses the managerial talent that is available in the region and that such managers are familiar with the culture and the working conditions of the region. A major disadvantage is that it may hinder the organization to develop a truly global expertise, as management knowledge is usually limited to a regional level.

Each of the above approaches has its advantages and disadvantages (see also Dowling, Festing and Engle, 2008). In practice most multinational companies have some degree of each one of them. The company that pursues an international strategy will most likely implement an ethnocentric staffing policy; the company that pursues a multi-domestic strategy will most likely implement a polycentric staffing policy; and the company that pursues both global and transnational strategies will more likely implement a geocentric staffing policy. Managing across cultures depends on the extent to which the company's organizational culture is strong or weak in relation to the national culture of the host country.

ACTIVITY 2

Produce a table listing the advantages and the disadvantages of each of the above types of multinational companies for the host and for the home country economy.

Organizational culture

The culture of an organization affects the way in which corporate strategy is decided, how objectives are set, and how they are achieved (Schein, 1999, 2004). In managing across cultures, the type of organizational culture concerned is 'corporate culture' which is characteristic of multinational companies whereby the culture of headquarters influences that of the subsidiaries and vice versa. In other words, corporate culture is determined by internal as well as external factors: it both adapts to and responds to the demands of national and regional cultures. The internal factors are the shared values of all employees working together, rules and procedures, policies and strategies, images and symbols, and the management vision that makes the organization. The external factors are similar in their kind to the internal ones but found in different countries where subsidiaries are located.

The determinant factor in international corporate culture is the international manager who is seen as the manager with the ability, knowledge and skills to manage in different countries and different cultural settings. An international manager has to deal with people from different countries and with different cultural values and norms. According to Torrington (1994: 17), international managers are 'people who are not only familiar with different countries and regions, but who also operate internationally with other managers occupying similar roles in other companies'. Such managers are not merely internationally mobile: they also 'in their minds, travel across boundaries by understanding the international implications of their work' (Barham and Antal, 1994).

Among other personal, organizational and professional attributes, adaptability, spirit of inquiry, and flexibility are some of the main criteria for identifying, selecting and developing managers who would be able to understand cultural influences on their managerial tasks.

1 Adaptability is the readiness to change and to compromise, to adopt and adapt to what is new or different, to have a more generalized expertise across all areas of management (this is developed through job rotation, continuous training and regular foreign assignments).
2 Spirit of inquiry involves logical reasoning and systematic methods of observation and deduction, and the review of one's value orientations, otherwise the manager may learn new skills but fail to be motivated to use them, instead of seeing cultural differences as an opportunity for development rather than a threat. Cross-cultural management should be seen as a challenge, as should learning local languages in order to communicate cross-culturally and win the trust of local people.
3 Flexibility is the ability to monitor the organization's internal and external environment, to implement change effectively and innovate swiftly, and to possess a variety of skills to adapt to diverse situations.

International managers should possess the above competencies in order to operate successfully in new and different environments. These are the qualities that determine whether a manager can work in an overseas assignment or not. A manager's ability to work cross-culturally is a critical success factor for MNCs in competing effectively in the global market.

Is management a universal phenomenon?

If we assume that managerial activities take place in a borderless world and that international managers are able to deal with the economic, political, legal and technological challenges they face in different societies, does this mean that the practice of management is a universal phenomenon? In other words, using our definition (from Chapter 2) of managing across cultures, would it be possible to use the *same* policies and practices when (a) managing the local employees globally and (b) managing the global employees locally?

Though there have been many attempts to answer this question, there is no consensus. Scholars have been split between those who argue for and those who argue against. The debate has developed since the early 1960s, initially amongst modernization theorists in economics and sociology (Rostow, 1960; Kerr et al., 1960; Parsons, 1964, 1971; Frank, 1971), and then amongst scholars of organizational behaviour and analysis (Hofstede, 1980a, 1991, 2001; Laurent, 1983; Negandhi, 1974, 1983; Lammers and Hickson, 1979; Hickson and McMillan, 1981; Whitley, 1992; Tayeb, 1988, Trompenaars and Hampden-Turner, 1997), and writers on human resource management and industrial relations (Laurent, 1986; Locke et al., 1995; Sparrow and Hiltrop, 1994; Harris, Brewster and Sparrow, 2003). The debate continues whenever transfer of management comes to question. The debate has been described as 'culture-free' versus 'culture-specific' (see Lammers and Hickson, 1979; Braun and Warner, 2002), as low context versus high context perspectives (see Child, 2002), and as convergence versus divergence theories.

Convergence theory

Convergence theory argues that management, in theory and practice, is becoming increasingly similar across the world, regardless of location or culture because a number of forces are making for convergence. They include trends in technology, economic policy, management education, and managerial functions. According to Kerr et al. (1960), technological developments make industrial organizations around the world increasingly similar to each other. It is argued that the transfer of knowledge and technology between countries will accelerate the convergence process. Management structures and practices become similar across the world through the spread of multinational companies' work processes and organizational design (Hickson and Pugh, 2002). Mueller and Purcell (1992) support convergence theory, arguing that global markets and multinational company operations lead to similar structures and practices across the world. According to this argument, a factory is a factory, a school is a school, a hospital is a hospital, no matter where they are in the world: each type of organization requires certain types of employees – engineers for factories, teachers for schools and doctors for hospitals, and so on. Moreover, it is argued that the huge growth in global media communications (Hickson and Pugh, 2002) via satellite television and the internet, providing immediate access to information, goods and services, has accelerated convergence. Broadly speaking, we receive the same news (from the BBC, CNN, Aljazeera) and the same banking and financial services (provided by the top ten major banks and insurance companies in the world), consume the same food (Indian curries, Chinese noodles, American burgers, etc.), watch the same films (mainly American, British, French and Indian), and drive the same cars (mostly American, German, French and Japanese). Another factor is the convergence of economic systems as a result of regional integration, lateral and bilateral economic relations, the decline of communism and the domination of free market economics, and strategic economic and political alliances. For example, the European Union provides an example of converging economic systems where economic integration accompanied by changes in political and educational systems have led to the gradual development of similar management policies and practices (Sparrow and Hiltrop, 1994; Brewster, 2007) being adopted throughout the member states.

Convergence theorists argue that, as a result of convergence, management in general and the management of human resources in particular becomes just a function or a technique that can be learnt by anyone and implemented anywhere in the world. They see the practice of management as culture-free because, they argue, managers perform the same functions – such as staffing, planning, training, rewarding, budgeting and leading – throughout the world. They argue that the nature of management problems is similar in organizations anywhere, regardless of their geographical location, and hence the solutions to such problems require the application of similar methods and techniques. In other words, managers subscribe to similar aims and objectives in their management and they become 'driven to carry out their functions in ways which have been found to be the most effective in comparable situations elsewhere across the world' (Pugh and Hickson, 2002: 8).

It can be seen that the convergence theory bases its arguments on macro-level variables, such as the technologies used, the level of economic development, and organizational size and structure (Child, 1981). In comparative management a number of studies of the relationship between management systems and the size and technology of organizations (Child and Kieser, 1979; Child, 1981) concluded that there was a social effect that influenced management in different countries, making convergence theory less convincing.

Divergence theory

In contrast to convergence theory, divergence theory holds that the practice of management is culture-specific and differs from one society to another. It is argued that situational factors, such as a country's industrial relations, employment policies, economic and legislative circumstances, cultural norms and values, national institutions and historical trends, all shape management policies and practices in different countries. According to this theory, any kind of management transfer involves not only the technical dimension of management, but also human behaviour – and the latter is culturally bound and influenced by local economic and political factors.

Divergence theory bases its arguments on micro-level variables (such as the behaviour of employees within the organization), starting from the premise that culture has strong effects on individual employees and hence on organizational behaviour (see Child, 1981; Adler, 1983; Hofstede, 1980b, 1983, 1991, 1993).

The following arguments have been put forward against the universality of management theories and practices:

1. Management, in general, not only influences the cultural values of people it deals with, but is also influenced by such values. For example, Kamoche (1992) tested the four goals of the HRM model of Guest (1987) – integration, commitment, flexibility and quality – in Kenyan organizations and concluded that such goals were difficult to achieve because of several contextual factors such as cultural values.

2. Management theory reflects the levels of economic development of the country in which it is carried out. For example, Hofstede (1985) and Zeffane and Rugimbana (1995) argue that motivation theories like the ones of Maslow, Herberg, Vroom and McGregor cannot be applied to developing countries (LDCs), such as those in Africa, because such theories apply only to individualistic behaviour and are all based on self-interest and self-actualization. They explain: 'many management principles emanate from proponents of individualistic cultures, which emphasize individual interest and individual achievements as a means of defining and distinguishing themselves. By contrast, an understanding of management in LDCs requires greater comprehension of group-oriented societies where people define themselves as members of clans or communities and consider the group welfare most important' (1995: 28).

3. Management is affected by national legislative frameworks, especially in countries where the rewards system and employee relations are heavily legislated

(Schuler and Rogovsky, 1998; Sparrow, 2000). For example, from a study of 6,600 employees in 11 countries, Schuler and Rogovsky (1998) concluded that there was a strong link between cultural values and reward systems. They found that in highly individualistic countries such as the US, Canada, Australia and the UK, employees showed a preference for individual performance-related pay schemes.

It can be concluded that there is evidence for both the convergent and divergent sides of the argument (see Child, 2002). There are management methods and techniques that can be put into practice universally but the management approach can differ from one country to another and even from one organization to another within the same sector in one country. Some practices are culture-specific and contingent upon the situation in which they are implemented. The process of convergence depends upon forces of economic integration arising from a globalizing power of business, which necessitates the management of the local employees globally. In the current 'globalization revolution', the process of convergence 'is seen to arise from ubiquitous economic and technological forces that are in turn motivated by universal human needs and drives' (Child, 2002: 28). In contrast, the process of divergence implies the existence of localizing power of culture and politics which necessitate the management of a global workforce locally in order to be responsive to the needs of the local operations.

A closer look into the arguments of both theories reveals that managerial decisions and solutions given to universal or specific management problems will naturally involve actions and interactions of people, which are forms of human behaviour and are culturally bound. Management reflects the ideological and political interest, the level of economic and technological requirements, and the objectives and power relations of the various actors involved. Understanding cultural differences is important in management because they suggest ways of reasoning, communicating, explaining, perceiving and thinking in different cultural settings. Thus culture is a dilemma that cannot be avoided in the process of managing across cultures – a point we will now examine in detail.

The cultural dilemma of managing across cultures

Culture exists at a number of levels. There are not only national cultures (such as French culture or Chinese culture), but also corporate or organizational cultures (for example, McDonald's culture or Toyota's culture) and industrial or sectoral cultures (for example, football culture or health service culture).

In this book the main focus is national cultures. Before analysing the models and dimensions of national cultures, we will examine the concept of culture itself.

The word culture comes from the Latin word *cultura*, which is connected to the concept of *cultus* or *cult*, meaning worship or action according to a set of beliefs. The modern concept is much wider and broader than this. According to the *Oxford Modern Dictionary* (1992: 253), culture consists of 'the arts and other manifestations of human intellectual achievement regarded collectively'. In general, culture is perceived as the physical and metaphysical aspects of human behaviour that are readily distinguished from each other. After analysing 164 different definitions of culture, Kroeber and Kluckhohn (1952: 86) concluded that

> Culture consists of patterned ways of thinking, feeling and reacting, acquired and transmitted mainly by symbols, constituting the distinctive achievements of human groups, including their embodiments in artefacts; the essential core of culture consists of traditional (i.e. historically derived and selected) ideas and especially their attached values

This classic definition of culture is still relevant and widely cited (Sparrow and Hiltrop, 1994: 61). However, it is very broad and not directly related to the concept of managing organizations. Hall (1959) took Kroeber and Kluckhohn's definition a step further by stating that culture is the pattern of assumptions underlying how a group of people should think, act, and feel as they deal with their daily affairs. However, this definition is still very broad. Like many other definitions of culture before the 1980s, it was associated with anthropological studies that saw culture as something holistic, historically determined and characteristic of a tribal life in remote areas far away from the developed world. The norms, values, beliefs, traditions and other ways of surviving that make a culture of a society are the determinants of how that society perceives, and is perceived by, others. However, as Child (1981) and Redding (1994) observed, most such definitions did not offer an explicit explanation of culture and treated it as a 'trash-can' residual variable.

It was not until Hofstede (1980a) and, to some extent, Ouchi (1981), Laurent (1983), Hampden-Turner and Trompenaars (1993) published their research findings that the concept of culture became explicitly defined or explained in relation to management and organizational behaviour. Hofstede (1991: 260) defines culture as the 'collective programming of the mind which distinguishes members of one group or category of people from another'. In one of the recent major studies of cultural differences and leadership, the Global Leadership and Organizational Behaviour Effectiveness (GLOBE) project, culture is defined as 'shared motives, values, beliefs, identities, and interpretations of meanings of significant events that result from common experiences of members of collectives that are transmitted across generations' (House et al., 2004: 15). From a recent analysis of 93 empirical studies of culture published in 16 world leading management journals, Tsui, Nifadkar and Ou (2007: 430) found that the definitions of culture 'suggest that common experiences and shared meaning are important delimiters of a cultural group'. They added that 'even though scholars generally agree that variations between groups can exist on multiple dimensions (cognitions, behaviours, and values), cross-cultural research has focused on shared cultural values as the major source of differentiation among national groups'.

In the contemporary literature on culture and management, the concept of culture is generally seen as something that is: (a) shared by most of the members of a particular social group and that can be inherited (passed from generation to generation); (b) learnt (from childhood to adulthood in the family, education institutions and society); (c) adopted (from other cultures and societies); or (d) imposed (by laws or by force).

The fact that it is something shared implies that it is group-based and can only exist in a collective entity (Hofstede, 1980a, 1991; Adler, 1983). Moreover, culture is neither visible nor sensed until it manifests itself in group behaviours and common artefacts. Usually the visible manifestations of culture are the symbols, heroes, and rituals of a social group (Schneider and Barsoux, 2003). Normally, the symbols, heroes, and rituals are the outer layers or the elements that can be seen by outsiders, but their cultural meanings are the hidden behaviours or values, which are the core elements of culture (Hofstede, 2001).

In managing across cultures, managers move from the observable artefacts and behaviours to the hidden beliefs and values, and then to the treasures of culture that make the cultural assumptions in management (Schneider and Barsoux, 2003). For more discussion of cultural assumptions in management refer to Schein (2004).

The different studies of culture, from anthropology to management and organizational behaviour, have attempted to classify cultural differences in terms of value orientations and dimensions for comparative and analytical purposes. The purpose of the next section is to review some of the main classifications that have influenced our understanding of culture and management in different countries.

Dimensions of culture

An increasing number of empirical studies, using quantitative research, have attempted to explain cultural differences between different societies. They have identified sets of cultural dimensions and developed models and theoretical frameworks for the analysis of culturally oriented work and social behaviour. Such frameworks have proliferated over the years and have contributed to the development of cross-cultural management literature. The following are among the most popular and the most influential frameworks.

Kluckhohn and Strodtbeck (1961): cultural value orientations

Two American anthropologists whose work influenced Geert Hofstede and other scholars of culture and management were Florence Kluckhohn and Fred Strodtbeck. They carried out fieldwork research and analysed other previous studies of culture in general, and then identified the core elements of culture that distinguish societies from each other as cultural value orientations. They studied five cultural groups in the South-west of the USA. Among the groups they studied were the Mexican-Americans, members of the Church of Jesus Christ of Latter-day Saints (Mormons) and the Native American Navajo Indians. They found six value orientations common to all groups. These were: relations to nature; relationships between people; views of human nature; attitudes to time; focus of activity; and use of space. (The last of these was not included in their original findings but added later.)

Here we consider each value orientation in turn.

- Relations to nature: concerns the extent to which the members of a social group control or are controlled by the environment. Some cultures control nature (mastery) while others submit to it (subjugation), and others have a harmonious relationship with it (harmony).
- Relationships between people: this concerns the level of concern and responsibility people have for each other. Some cultures have concern for themselves and their close families only (individualistic) while others have concerns for others (collectivist) and others see their relationships with others arranged in a lineal order (hierarchical).
- Views of human nature: this concerns how people see themselves in society. In some cultures, human nature is seen as inherently good while in others it is bad, and in others in between (neutral).
- Focus of activity: this concerns people's perception of work in their lives. In some cultures people 'work to live' (being) while in others they 'live to work' (doing) and in others they avoid extremes and are rational in balancing work with living (being-in-becoming).
- Attitudes to time: this concerns how people make decisions. In some cultures people make decisions based on traditions and historical events (past orientation) while in other cultures they base on current events (present orientation) and in others they base on events in the future (future orientation).
- Use of space: this concerns what people think about the physical space they use. In some cultures people prefer to keep their space private while in others they are open (public) and in others they are in between private and public.

The pioneering work of Kluckhohn and Strodtbeck (1961) formed the bedrock of many studies to come in the area of cross-cultural management (Fink et al., 2005). Among these is the famous work of Geert Hofstede.

Geert Hofstede: cultural dimensions of societies

Possibly the most popular and widely disseminated research on culture in relation to management and organizational behaviour is that of the Dutch scholar

Geert Hofstede. In the 1970s, after analysing survey data collected from 116,000 employees of the multinational company IBM in 48 different countries between 1968 and 1973, Hofstede identified four key dimensions of cultural differences among countries that affect people's perceptions of their work and employee relations (Hofstede, 1991, 2001). He argued that since IBM had a very strong corporate culture, differences between countries would be the result of national cultures. The results of his study concern differences between countries rather than individuals and are expressed in relative, rather than absolute, terms (see Table 3.1).

Table 3.1 Summary of Hofstede's cultural dimensions

Countries	Individualism		Power Distance		Uncertainty Avoidance		Masculinity		Long Term Orientation	
	Rank	Index	Rank	Index	Rank	Index	Rank	Index	Rank	Index
Argentina (ARG)	28–29	46	18–19	49	36–41	86	30–31	56		
Australia (AUL)	49	90	13	36	17	51	35	61		31
Austria (AUT)	33	55	1	11	26–27	70	49	79		
Belgium (BEL)	43	75	33	65	45–46	94	29	54		
Brazil (BRA)	25	38	39	69	29–30	76	25	49		65
Canada (CAN)	46–47	80	15	39	12–13	48	28	52		23
Chile (CHL)	15	23	29–30	63	36–41	86	8	28		
Columbia (COL)	5	13	36	67	31	80	39–40	64		
Costa Rica (COS)	8	15	10–12	35	36–41	86	5–6	21		
Denmark (DEN)	42	74	3	18	3	23	4	16		
Ecuador (ECA)	2	8	43–44	78	24	67	37–38	63		
Finland (FIN)	34	63	8	33	20–21	59	7	26		
France (FRA)	40–41	71	37–38	68	36–41	86	17–18	43		
Germany (FRG)	36	67	10–12	35	23	65	41–42	66		31
Great Britain (GBR)	48	89	10–12	35	6–7	35	41–42	66		25
Greece (GRE)	22	35	26–27	60	50	112	32–33	57		
Guatemala (GUA)	1	6	48–49	95	48	101	11	37		
Hong Kong (HOK)	16	25	37–38	68	4–5	29	32–33	57		96
India (IND)	30	48	42	77	9	40	30–31	56		61

Table 3.1 (Continued)

Countries	Individualism		Power Distance		Uncertainty Avoidance		Masculinity		Long Term Orientation	
	Rank	Index	Rank	Index	Rank	Index	Rank	Index	Rank	Index
Indonesia (IDO)	6–7	14	43–44	78	12–13	48	22	46		
Iran (IRA)	27	41	24–25	58	20–21	59	17–18	43		
Ireland (IRE)	39	70	5	28	6–7	35	43–44	68		
Israel (ISR)	32	54	2	13	32	81	23	47		
Italy (ITA)	44	76	20	50	28	75	46–47	70		
Jamaica (JAM)	26	39	17	45	2	13	43–44	68		
Japan (JPN)	28–29	46	21	54	44	92	50	95		80
South Korea (KOR)	11	18	26–27	60	34–35	85	13	39		75
Malaysia (MAL)	17	26	50	104	8	36	26–27	50		
Mexico (MEX)	20	30	45–46	81	33	82	45	69		
Netherlands (NET)	46–47	80	14	38	18	53	3	14		44
New Zealand (NZI)	45	79	4	22	14–15	49	34	58		30
Norway (NOR)	38	69	6–7	31	16	50	2	8		
Pakistan (PAK)	6–7	14	22	55	26–27	70	26–27	50		
Panama (PAN)	3	11	48–49	95	36–41	86	19	44		
Peru (PER)	9	16	31–32	64	42	87	15–16	42		
Philippines (PHI)	21	32	47	94	10	44	39–40	64		19
Portugal (POR)	18–19	27	29–30	63	49	104	9	31		
Salvador (SAL)	12	19	34–35	66	45–46	94	14	40		
Singapore (SIN)	13–14	20	40	74	1	8	24	48		48
South Africa (SAF)	35	65	18–19	49	14–15	49	37–38	63		
Spain (SPA)	31	51	23	57	36–41	86	15–16	42		
Sweden (SWE)	40–41	71	6–7	31	4–5	29	1	5		33
Switzerland (SWI)	37	68	9	34	19	58	46–47	70		
Taiwan (TAI)	10	17	24–25	58	25	69	20–21	45		87
Thailand (THA)	13–14	20	31–32	64	22	64	10	34		56
Turkey (TUR)	24	37	34–35	66	34–35	85	20–21	45		
United States (USA)	50	91	16	40	11	46	36	62		29

(Continued)

Table 3.1 (Continued)

Countries	Individualism		Power Distance		Uncertainty Avoidance		Masculinity		Long Term Orientation	
	Rank	Index	Rank	Index	Rank	Index	Rank	Index	Rank	Index
Uruguay (URU)	23	36	28	61	47	100	12	38		
Venezuela (VEN)	4	12	45–46	81	29–30	76	48	73		
Regions:										
Arab World (ARA) (1)	21–25	38	44–45	80	24–25	68	28–29	52		
Eastern Africa (EAF) (2)	18–19	27	31–32	64	17–18	52	14–15	41		25
West Africa (WAF) (3)	13–14	20	40–42	77	18–19	54	20–22	46		16

(1) Arab World (selected countries: Egypt, Iraq, Kuwait, Lebanon, Libya, Saudi Arabia and United Arab Emirates)
(2) Eastern Africa (selected countries: Ethiopia, Kenya, Tanzania and Zambia)
(3) Western Africa (selected countries: Ghana, Nigeria and Sierra Leone)

Source: Hofstede, G. (2001) *Culture's Consequences: International differences in work-related values* (2nd edn), Newberry Park, CA: Sage Publications (Reproduced with permission).

Hofstede (1991, 2001) argued that culture can be influenced by different factors and under different situations it can change and develop to involve different aspects of an identity, group or society. However it does not change as fast as technological, economic or other components of a society. He explained that a society does not have only one culture: there are various subcultures, which are normally influenced by religion, gender, generation, region and class. He concluded that national cultures were determined by five cultural dimensions: (i) power distance, (ii) uncertainty avoidance, (iii) individualism versus collectivism, (iv) masculinity versus femininity, and (v) time orientation. Below we consider each dimension of Hofstede's model in turn.

Individualism versus collectivism

This dimension refers to the extent to which a person sees himself or herself in relation to others in a society, and the extent to which personal freedom and privacy are valued in a society. In individualist cultures, people tend to be self-centred and concerned mainly with their own interests and those of their immediate families. Individual interests take priority over group interests. Individuals prefer to depend on themselves and have control over their own lives. They prefer not to be a burden on anyone and, in turn, not to be bothered by others.

In individualist societies' organizations, motives of self-interest dominate relationships at work. Behaviours of individual motivation are reflected in overt rivalries and competition between the members of a group. Such behaviours are interpreted in terms of the individual asserting independence from his/her group or organization, and as an explanation for the emergence of calculative motivations in organizations. According to Hofstede's classification of countries, most Anglo-Saxon and European societies are found to reflect aspects of individualistic cultures.

In a collectivist culture, people respect and adhere to the norms of the group to which they belong. The group's interests take precedence over those of the individual. In collectivist societies, people expect help and support from their relatives, friends and work colleagues. People act and react in relation to the main objectives of the groups, clans, clubs, tribes, families and societies they belong to. According to Hofstede's results, most people from developing countries in Africa, Asia and Latin America belong to collectivist cultures.

Large versus small power distance

Hofstede (2001) argued that societies differ from one another in the extent to which power and authority are exercised among people. Inequality is more tolerated in some cultures than in others. The level of power differentiations (or distance) is influenced by national norms and values concerning status, wealth, gender, age, religion, race and education.

In large power distance societies, the people who have more power are the wealthy, religious, educated, old men from the indigenous race or tribal background (or some combination of these factors). The level of power differentiations depends also on the type of relationships people have with others. For example, a person may have power in the home as a parent but may be powerless in the workplace.

Such differences in power distance are reflected in the way organizations are structured and managed in different societies. In large power distance cultures, managers and leaders have higher status and are entitled to certain privileges that their subordinates do not have. Inequality is accepted and appreciated by both the more and the less powerful. In a small power distance culture, in contrast, power and status are not as important as competency and achievement because subordinates can bypass their leaders in order to get their work done.

High versus low uncertainty avoidance

Uncertainty avoidance concerns the extent to which people in a culture feel nervous or threatened by uncertainty and ambiguity, and create institutions and rules to try to avoid it. This cultural dimension concerns the anxiety levels in a society or 'tolerance of the unpredictable' (Hofstede, 1991: 110).

The level of people's uncertainty avoidance depends on many factors, especially those that have affected their background and previous experiences of success or failure. Most cultures have been affected by unfortunate events such as wars, natural disasters, and political instability. Such events have conditioned their level of risk taking when making decisions. People from cultures with strong or high uncertainty avoidance tend to experience more stress, and have more written and unwritten laws. They try to resist change because the result is unpredictable and they do not want to take any risks. They avoid uncertainty and reduce anxiety by working in groups and sharing responsibilities for planning and decision-making or by not delegating responsibilities to others. It takes a long time and a lot of patience to reach agreements when negotiating a deal with people from high uncertainty avoidance cultures.

In weak or low uncertainty avoidance cultures, people accept uncertainty as a fact of life, take risks, and introduce changes whenever they think they are necessary. In these societies, few rules and regulations are used to guide people's actions, as people are encouraged to test their ideas and take risks. Hofstede (2001) states that the Germans, for example, tend to exhibit low uncertainty avoidance because of their tolerance for ambiguity and taking risks, while people from Asian countries tend not to tolerate ambiguities and exhibit higher uncertainty avoidance.

Masculinity versus femininity

In a masculine culture, the dominant values are advancement, ambition, assertiveness, performance, the acquisition of money and material objects, and caring less for others. In a feminine culture, values of love and care, such as maintaining personal relationships, care for others, and care for the environment, are emphasized.

Hofstede (2001) argued that one of the social components of cultural differences between societies is the perception of gender and the role of women in society, business and management. However, the masculinity versus femininity dimension is broader than the perceptions of gender differences. For example, 'masculine' patterns of behaviour are related to the desire to strive for material success through tough deals and competition, while the 'feminine' patterns of behaviour tend to show modesty and concern for others by striving for a better quality of life.

Long- versus short-term orientations

This dimension was not identified in Hofstede's original study of IBM in mainly Western or Western-influenced countries. It was added later after the study was replicated by Michael Bond (1988) including China and other Asian countries. Initially Bond and associates developed the Chinese Values Survey (CVS) to measure Chinese value orientations, among which was Confucian dynamism. (The principles of Confucianism will be discussed later in Chapter 8, on managing in China and Hong Kong). On the basis of Bond's studies, Hofstede (1991, 2001) developed the fifth dimension, namely long-term versus short-term orientations.

A long-term orientation can be found in cultures that are geared towards the future, and exhibit values of perseverance and thrift, order relationships by status and observe order, and have a sense of shame. A short-term orientation can be found in cultures that promote values related to the past and present, and assume that there is an absolute truth. Short-term orientation cultures involve personal steadiness and stability, protecting one's face, exchanging greetings, favours and gifts, and showing respect for traditions. Although these time orientation values are not unique to the countries in East Asia, they are mostly found in the Confucian traditions that characterize Asian cultures.

ACTIVITY 3

There are four people on a boat: a baby, mother and father, and a grandparent. The boat is going to sink unless one of them is thrown in the water. None of them can swim. Either one of them or all of them will end up in the water.

Who do you think should be thrown in the water for the rest to survive? Why? After you have decided who should go and why, see where you fit in each of Hofstede's dimensions. For example, if you think the grandparent should go in order to protect the nuclear family, you belong to an individualistic culture.

Although Hofstede's work has received much criticism (see McSweeney, 2002), it has helped to put the concept of culture at the heart of understanding organizational and work behaviour. As a strong divergence theorist, Hofstede often questioned the relevance of Western-derived theories of management to non-Western societies (1983, 1991). He argued that such theories were related to behaviour found predominantly in the USA and reflected American cultural patterns because, for example, those who share the view of motivation through self-interest will fail to understand collectivist behaviour among people in developing countries, where the individual is more likely to be motivated by group interest. Furthermore, Hofstede argued that self-actualization is not the supreme need for collectivist countries, where the actualization of the in-group, which may even call for self-effacement, is important.

In support of Hofstede's arguments, Mendonca and Kanungo (1996) used the first four dimensions to analyse performance management in developing countries. They found enough evidence to support some of Hofstede's work and added a further dimension, which they called abstractive versus associative thinking. They related associative thinking to developing countries, where people use associations between events that may not have much logical basis, and abstractive thinking to Western societies. They found that job autonomy, for example, is a highly valued non-economic reward in North America but is not necessarily so in developing countries, where rewards that satisfy the social and security needs are more valued. Another example is feedback during performance appraisal review: the confrontational mode is not appropriate to employees who regard face-saving as more important than the benefits of an appraisal. They concluded that the characteristics of the socio-cultural environment in developing countries seem to be incompatible with effective performance management practices of Western countries, and therefore it would be ethically and morally wrong and ineffective to apply policies and practices which would coerce the employees into giving up their deeply held cultural values and beliefs.

One of the main criticisms of Hofstede's work concerns his research methodology. The validity of his questionnaire was questioned, as was his choice of IBM as the only multinational company to study. He replied to such criticisms in his subsequent publications (Hofstede, 1991, 2001). Despite such criticisms, his work provided the impetus for the development of other significant and popular studies such as those of Fons Trompenaars and Charles Hampden-Turner.

Fons Trompenaars' (1993) Cultural Framework

Trompenaars is a business consultant and management scholar who was also influenced by Kluckhohn and Strodtbeck and Hofstede. In part collaboration with Charles Hampden-Turner he carried out research over more than 15 years involving more than 50,000 participants from over 50 countries. Analysis of their extensive quantitative data led them to identify seven cultural dimensions which they claim have practical implications for doing business. The seven dimensions are summarized below.

Universalism versus particularism

This dimension concerns the extent to which behaviours and rules are applied universally or specifically to particular situations. In universalistic cultures people believe that truth and goodness can be defined and applied universally, whereas in particularistic cultures such behaviours are determined by unique circumstances. For example, China scores more highly on particularism than the USA, which is classified as universalistic.

Individualism versus communitarianism (collectivism)

This dimension is very similar to the one suggested by Hofstede (2001). It deals with the extent to which individuals behave independently or as members of a group to which they feel loyal and committed.

Affective versus neutral relationships

In affective cultures it is natural to express emotions and to show one's feelings, whereas in neutral cultures individuals tend to 'mask' their emotions and not express them openly. In the latter, there is a great emphasis on self-control and not, for example, showing distress at work. However, Trompenaars' findings in relation to this dimension were not precise and in some countries the scores seem to differ from one group of the population to the other. As a result, this dimension was further revised to include a question that separated emotions from reasoning. By doing so they were able to get a clearer understanding of the reasons for expressing affective or neutral relationships. For example, 'Americans tend to exhibit emotion yet separate it from "objective" and "rational" decisions' (Trompenaars and Hampden-Turner, 1997: 73).

Specificity versus diffuseness

This dimension is about the extent to which individuals allow access to their inner selves to others. In specific cultures, individuals tend to be straightforward in their relationships with others, whereas in diffused cultures (such as the Chinese, for example) individuals will seek not to be confrontational in order not to lose face. In the former, individuals distinguish between work and non-work relationships, while in the latter they cannot easily separate them.

Achievement versus ascription

In achievement cultures, status and power are determined by what individuals do, whereas in ascription cultures, status and power are determined by who individuals are. Interestingly, in relation to this dimension, Trompenaars (1993) found that religious beliefs are influential. For example, he stressed that the Catholic, Buddhist and Hindu faiths influenced the development of ascriptive cultures, while Protestantism led to achievement cultures.

Sequential versus synchronic

This dimension is similar to 'attitudes to time' in Kluckhohn and Strodtbeck's model (1961). However, instead of past, present and future orientations, Trompenaars (1993) divided time into linear versus holistic views of time (sequentiality), and future orientation versus past orientation (synchronicity). In sequential cultures, people are punctual, they use their time rationally and effectively, and they tend to relate to the past and use the present to plan for the future. In synchronic cultures, people perceive time as circular and made of repetitive events.

Outer versus inner control

This dimension concerns people's relations to the environment. It is similar to Kluckhohn and Strodtbeck's (1961) relations to nature. In their recent work,

Trompenaars and Hampden-Turner (2004) called it 'internal versus external' control. The outer control cultures tend to believe that forces outside their own making control their actions, whereas the inner control societies tend to believe that they control their own destiny.

The above cultural dimensions have been tested by many other studies. They have also been used in practice by managers worldwide, partly because of the hundreds of international training programmes that Trompenaars and colleagues conducted over the years. However, like any other study of cultural differences, the work of Trompenaars and Hampden-Turner is not immune from criticisms. It is not surprising that one of the main critics is Hofstede (1997), who argues that the seven dimensions identified by Trompenaars and Hampden-Turner are specific to US culture and have limited international applicability. He also asks whether each dimension stands alone or is related to other dimensions: in his own studies he develops country profiles made of a combination of the five dimensions, while Trompenaars and Hampden-Turner focus on advising international managers on how to deal with each single dimension in different countries. The debate continues and many studies have been carried out since the pioneering work of these scholars was published. One of the recent major projects is GLOBE, which we will now consider.

The Project GLOBE cultural framework (House et al., 2004)

The GLOBE (Global Leadership and Organizational Behaviour Effectiveness), project is a worldwide study of the relationship between national culture, organizational culture and leadership within organizations. The project sought to identify the dimensions of societal and organizational culture, and analyse the intracultural similarities and intercultural differences. Its aim was to develop an empirically based theoretical framework for the understanding and predicting the impact of specific cultural variables on leadership and organizational processes (House et al., 2001, 2004). It was 'a multi-phase, multi-method project examining the interrelationships between societal culture, organizational culture, leadership, and societal achievements' (Javidan and Dastmalchian, 2009: 44).

The survey started with an extensive review of relevant literature and then collected quantitative data through the use of a questionnaire targeted at 17,000 managers in 950 organizations from 62 different countries. Analysis of the data led the researchers to propose nine cultural dimensions, which they refer to as 'culture construct definitions'. Six of the nine dimensions are similar to ones suggested by Hofstede (1980a), discussed above, while the other three are based on the work of Kluckhohn and Strodtbeck (1961). A brief description of each of the nine dimensions of culture, according to GLOBE project, is given in Table 3.2.

The GLOBE project reinforces the findings of previous research. It has tested the validity of some of the previous studies, responded to criticism of previous research, and provided an opportunity for further research to test

Table 3.2 The GLOBE project cultural dimensions

Cultural dimension	Description
Collectivism I. Institutional collectivism	The degree to which work organization and national institutions practise, encourage and reward collective distribution of resources and collective action.
Collectivism II. In-group collectivism	The degree to which individuals show pride, loyalty and commitment in their work organizations or families.
Power distance	The degree to which members of a social group expect power to be distributed in their work organizations or their society.
Uncertainty avoidance	The degree to which members of a society or work group rely on social norms, rules and procedures to alleviate unpredictable and uncertain events.
Gender egalitarianism	The degree to which men and women are treated equally in a society or work group organization, and gender-based role differences are important for such social groups.
Assertiveness	The degree to which individuals are assertive, confrontational or aggressive in their relationships with others within a particular cultural setting.
Humane orientation	The degree to which members of a society or work organization elicit, encourage and reward individuals for their kindness, fairness, altruism and generosity to others.
Performance orientation	The degree to which members of a society or work organization encourage and reward individuals for high performance.
Future orientation	The degree to which individuals plan and calculate the future implications of their actions.

Source: Developed with permission from House et al., 2004.

and revise its findings with the aim of establishing a generally acceptable framework. A further contribution of the GLOBE project is the identification of dimensions of leader behaviour or leadership styles that exist in different cultures (see House et al., 2004; Javidan and Dastmalchian, 2009).

The GLOBE project identified, in line with the previous studies, clusters of countries that share similar cultural dimensions. The clustering of countries is not new in comparative management studies, but with the studies of culture and management it became a useful way of showing how cultural differences affect management preferences. For example, Hofstede (1991, 2001) suggested the following typology of countries:

- *Village market* (Anglo-Nordic countries), where low power distance is combined with low uncertainty avoidance;
- *Family* (Asian societies), where high power distance is combined with high uncertainty avoidance;
- *Well-oiled machine* (Germanic cluster), where low power distance is combined with low uncertainty avoidance;
- *Pyramid of people* (Latin countries), where high power distance is combined with high uncertainty avoidance.

The GLOBE project identified ten clusters of countries as shown on Table 3.3. If we accept that the GLOBE project is the most comprehensive study of

Table 3.3 The GLOBE project country clusters

Cluster name	Cluster countries
Anglo	England, Australia, Canada, Ireland, New Zealand, USA, South African (White sample)
Latin Europe	France, Italy, Portugal, Spain, Switzerland (French/Italian), Israel
Nordic Europe	Finland, Sweden, Denmark
Germanic Europe	Austria, Switzerland (Germanic), Netherlands, Germany
Eastern Europe	Albania, Hungary, Russia, Poland, Slovenia, Georgia, Greece, Kazakhstan
Latin America	Argentina, Brazil, Bolivia, Costa Rica, Colombia, Guatemala, Ecuador, El Salvador, Mexico, Venezuela
Sub-saharan Africa	Nigeria, Zambia, Namibia, Zimbabwe, South Africa (Black sample)
Arab countries	Egypt, Kuwait, Morocco, Qatar, Turkey
Southern Asia	India, Indonesia, Malaysia, Iran, Thailand, Philippines
Confucian Asia	China, Hong Kong, Japan, South Korea, Taiwan, Singapore

Source: Hofstede, G. (2001) *Culture's Consequences: Comparing Values, Behaviors, Institutions and Organizations Across Nations*, (2nd edn). Thousand Oaks, California: Sage Publications.

cultural differences and that it is a recent study, it is reasonable to adopt the above classification for the time being. However, one has some doubts about including Iran alongside Thailand and the Philippines, and Israel alongside Latin Europe. These countries can be clusters on their own (see Sparrow et al., 1994).

It may be argued that culture does not provide a sufficient criterion for clustering. Economic, political and historical factors should also be taken into consideration when attempting to group countries for comparative analysis. As explained in Chapter 1, the logic for the design of this book is to use a combination of cultural, economic, political and historical factors when categorizing countries. Table 3.4 shows this book's classification of countries into perspectives and management approaches for comparative purposes, after taking into consideration more than just cultural similarities.

Table 3.4 The present study's classification of global approaches to management

Perspectives	Approaches	Countries
Anglo-Saxon	North American	USA and Canada
	Anglo-European	UK and Ireland
	Australasian	Australia and New Zealand
South-east Asian	Japanese	Japan and South Korea
	Asian-Islamic	Malaysia and Indonesia
	Chinese	China and Hong Kong
European	Francophone	France and Belgium
	Germanic	Germany and Holland
	Scandinavian	Denmark, Norway and Sweden
	Southern European 'Olive'	Spain, Italy and Greece
Developing countries	African	Subsaharan Africa
	Arabic-Islamic	North Africa and the Middle East
	Latin American	South America
	Post-Soviet transitional	Eastern Europe and Russia
	Emerging economies	India and others

Summary

1   The process of managing across cultures takes place in global, local and organizational contexts.
2   The main elements of the global context are international business, international labour movement and migration, international laws and regulations, international political alliances or clashes, the international monetary system, and international transfer of technology and knowledge.
3   The main elements of the local or national context for managing across cultures are the national culture, the political and legislative system, the historical background, the labour market, employment laws; and the level of economic growth and industrialization of the host and the home country. The organizational context of managing across cultures is the international organization in which managers and employees operate locally and think globally in different cultural settings. MNCs have been described, according to their HR policies and staffing approaches, as ethnocentric, polycentric, geocentric and regiocentric.
4   There is a continuing debate between convergence and divergence theories. Convergence theory advocates see management as a function or technique that can be learnt and implemented in different contexts. Divergence theory holds the view that management theories can be affected by each country's individual situation.
5   Culture is generally seen as something that is shared by most of the members of a particular social group and that can be inherited (passed from generation to generation); learnt (from childhood to adulthood in the family, and in educational institutions and society); adopted (from other cultures and societies); or imposed (by laws or by force).
6   Different studies of culture, from anthropology to management and organizational behaviour, have attempted to classify cultural differences in terms of value orientations and dimensions for comparative and analytical purposes.

Revision questions

1   What arguments are there for and against the transfer of management knowledge from developed to developing countries? Use examples to support your arguments.
2   Critically analyse Hofstede's framework of cultural differences.
3   Use the GLOBE project cultural dimensions to produce a cultural profile of a country of your own choice.

References

Adler, N. (1983) 'Cross-cultural Management Research: The Ostrich and the Trend', *Academy of Management Review*, 8(2): 226–32.

Barham, K. and Antal, A. (1994) 'Competencies for the pan-European manager', in Mabey, C., Salaman, G. and Storey, J. (eds), *Human Resource Management: A Strategic Introduction*, Oxford: Blackwell.

Bartlett, C.A. and Ghoshal, S. (1989) *Managing Across Borders: The Transnational Solution*, Boston: Harvard Business School Press.

Bond, M.H. (1988) 'Finding dimensions of individual variation in multicultural studies of values: the Rokeach and Chinese value surveys', *Journal of Personality and Social Psychology*, 55(6): 1009–115.

Braun, W. and Warner, M. (2002) 'The "culture-free" versus "culture-specific" management debate', in Warner, M. and Joynt, P. (eds), *Managing Across Cultures: Issues and Perspectives*, 2nd edn, London: Thomson Learning, 13–25.

Brewster, C. (2007) 'A European Perspective on HRM', *European Journal of International Management*, 1(3): 239–59.

Child, J. (1981) 'Culture, contingency, and capitalism in the cross-national study of organizations', *Research in Organizational Behaviour*, 3: 303–56.

Child, J. (2002) 'Theorizing about organization cross-nationality: part 1, an introduction', in Warner, M. and Joynt, P. (eds), *Managing Across Cultures: Issues and Perspectives*, 2nd edn, London: Thomson Learning, 26–39.

Child, J. and Kieser, A. (1979) 'Organizational and managerial roles in British and West German Companies: an examination of the culture-free thesis', in Lammers, C. and Hickson, D.J. (eds), *Organizations Alike and Unlike: International and Inter-institutional Studies in the Sociology of Organizations*, London: Routledge & Kegan Paul.

Deresky, H. (2003) *International Management: Managing Across Borders and Cultures*, London: Prentice-Hall.

Dowling, P.J., Festing, M. and Engle, A.D. (2008) *International Human Resource Management*, 5th edn, London: Thomson Learning.

Dowling, P.J., Schuler, R.S. and Welch, D.E. (1994) *International Dimensions of Human Resource Management*, 2nd edn, Belmont, CA: International Thomson Publishing and Wadsworth Publishing Company.

Dowling, P.J., Welch, D.E. and Schuler, R.S. (1999) *International Human Resource Management: Managing People in a Multinational Context*, 3rd edn, Cincinnati: South-Western College Publishing.

Fink, G., Kolling, M. and Neyer, A.K. (2005) 'The cultural standard method', *EI Working Paper* no. 62, Vienna: University of Vienna.

Frank, A.G. (1971) *Sociology of Development and the Underdevelopment of Sociology*, London: Luto Press.

French, R. (2007) *Cross-Cultural Management in Work Organisations*, London: CIPD.

Giddens, A. (1990) *The Consequences of Modernity*, Cambridge: Polity Press.

Guest, D. (1987) 'Human Resource Management and Industrial Relations', *Journal of Management Studies*, 24(5): 503–521.

Hall, E.T. (1959) *The Silent Language*, New York: Doubleday.

Hampden-Turner, C. and Trompenaars, F. (1993) *The Seven Cultures of Capitalism: Value Systems for Creating Wealth in the United States, Britain, Japan, Germany, France, Sweden and the Netherlands*, New York: Doubleday.

Harris, H., Brewster, C. and Sparrow, P. (2003) *International Human Resource Management*, London: CIPD.

Hickson, D.J. and McMillan, C.J. (eds) (1981) *Organization and Nation: The Aston Programme*, Farnborough, Hants: Gower Press.

Hickson, D.J. and Pugh, D.S. (2002) *Management Worldwide: Distinctive Styles among Globalization*, 2nd edn, Harmondsworth: Penguin.

Hofstede, G. (1980a) *Culture's Consequences: International Differences in Work Related Values*, London: Sage.

Hofstede, G. (1980b) 'Motivation, leadership and organization: do American theories apply abroad?', *Organizational Dynamics*, Summer, 1980.

Hofstede, G. (1983) *Culture and Management Development*, Discussion Paper, Management Development Branch, Training Department, Geneva: ILO.

Hofstede, G. (1991) *Culture and Organizations: Software of the Mind*, London: McGraw-Hill.

Hofstede, G. (1993) 'Cultural constraints in management theories', *Academy of Management Executive*, 7(1): 81–94.

Hofstede, G. (1997) *Cultures and Organizations: Software of the mind*, London: McGraw-Hill.

Hofstede, G. (1998) 'Think locally, act globally: cultural constraints in personnel management', *Management International Review*, Special Issue, 98(2): 7–26.

Hofstede, G. (2001) *Culture's Consequences: International Differences in Work Related Values*, 2nd edn, London: Sage.

House, R.J., Hanges, P.J., Javidan, M., Dorfman, P. and Gupta, V. (2004) *Culture, Leadership and Organization: The GLOBE Study of 62 Societies*, Thousand Oaks, CA: Sage.

House, R.J., Javidan, M. and Dorfman, P. (2001) 'The Globe Project', *Applied Psychology: An International Review*, 50(4): 489–505.

Javidan, M. and Dastmalchian, A. (2009) 'Managerial implications of the GLOBE project: a study of 62 societies', *Asia Pacific Journal of Human Resources*, 47(1): 41–58.

Kamoche, K. (1992) 'Human resource management: an assessment of the Kenyan case', *The International Journal of Human Resource Management*, 3(3): 497–521.

Kerr, C., Harbison, F.H., Dunlop, J.T. and Myers, C.A. (1960) *Industrialism and Industrial Man*, Cambridge, MA: Harvard University Press.

Kluckhohn, F. and Strodtbeck, F. (1961) *Variations in Value Orientations*, Evanston, IL: Row, Peterson.

Kroeber, A. and Kluckhohn, C. (1952) 'Culture: a critical review of concepts and definitions', *Cambridge Papers of the Peabody Museum of Archaeology and Ethnology*, 47(1), Cambridge, MA: Harvard University Press.

Lammers, C.J. and Hickson, D.J. (1979) *Organizations Alike and Unlike: International and Inter-institutional Studies in the Sociology of Organizations*, London: Routledge & Kegan Paul.

Laurent, A. (1983) 'The cultural diversity of western conceptions of management', *International Studies of Management and Organization*, 13(1–2): 75–96.

Laurent, A. (1986) 'The cross-cultural puzzle of international HRM', *Human Resource Management*, 25: 91–102.

Lewis, R. (2004) *When Cultures Collide: Leading, teamworking and managing across the globe*, London: Nicholas Brealey.

Locke, R., Kochan, T. and Piore, M. (1995) 'Reconceptualizing comparative industrial relations: Lessons from international research', *International Labour Review*, 134(2): 139–61.

McSweeney, B. (2002) 'Hofstede's model of national cultural differences and their consequences: a triumph of faith – a failure of analysis', *Human Relations*, 55(1): 89–118.

Mendonca, M. and Kanungo, R.N. (1996) 'Impact of culture on performance management in developing countries', *International Journal of Manpower*, 17(4/5): 65–75.

Mueller, F. and Purcell, J. (1992) 'The Europeanization of Manufacturing and the Decentralization of Bargaining', *International Journal of Human Resource Management*, 3(1): 15–31.

Negandhi, A.R. (1974) 'Cross-cultural management studies: too many conclusions, not enough conceptualizations', *Management International Review*, 16: 59–72.

Negandhi, A.R. (1983) 'Cross-Cultural Management Research: Trends and Culture Directions', *Journal of International Business Studies*, 14(2): 17–28.

Ohmae, K. (1990) *The Borderless World: Power and Strategy in the Interlinked Economy*, New York: McKinsey & Co.

Ouchi, W.G. (1981) *Theory Z: How American Management Can Meet the Japanese Challenge*, Reading, MA: Addison-Wesley.

Oxford Modern Dictionary (1992) Oxford: Oxford University Press.

Parsons, T. (1964) 'Evolutionary Universals in Society', *American Sociological Review*, 29(3): 339–57.

Parsons, T. (1971) *The System of Modern Societies*, Englewood Cliffs, NJ: Prentice-Hall.

Pugh, D. and Hickson, D.J. (2002) 'On organizational convergence', in Warner, M. and Joynt, P. (eds.) *Managing Across Cultures: Issues and Perspectives*, 2nd edn, London: Thomson Learning.

Redding, S.G. (1994) 'Comparative management theory: jungle, zoo or fossil bed?', *Organization Studies*, 15: 323–59.

Reich, R.B. (1991) *The Work of Nations: Preparing Ourselves for 21st-Century Capitalism*, New York: Vintage Books.

Rostow, W.W. (1960) *Stages of Economic Growth: a Non-Communist Manifesto*, Cambridge: Cambridge University Press.

Schein, E.H. (1985) *Organizational Culture and Leadership*, San Francisco, CA: Jossey-Bass.

Schein, E.H. (1999) *The Corporate Culture Survival Guide*, San Francisco: Jossey-Bass.

Schein, E.H. (2004) *Organizational Culture and Leadership*, 3rd edn, San Francisco: Jossey-Bass.

Schneider, S.C. and Barsoux, J.L. (2003) *Managing Across Cultures*, 2nd edn, Harlow: Prentice-Hall/Financial Times.

Schuler, R.S. and Rogovsky, N. (1998) 'Understanding compensation practice variations across firms: the impact of national culture', *Journal of International Business Studies*, 29(1): 159–78.

Scullion, H. and Collings, D. (2006) *Global Staffing*, London: Routledge.

Sparrow, P. (2000) 'International Reward Management', in White, G. and Drucker, J. (eds), *Reward Management: A Critical Text*, London: Routledge, 196–214.

Sparrow, P. and Hiltrop, J.M. (1994) *European Human Resource Management in Transition*, Harlow: Prentice-Hall.

Sparrow, P., Randel, S., Schuler, R.S. and Jackson, S.E. (1994) 'Convergence or divergence: human resource practices and policies for competitive advantage worldwide', *The International Journal of Human Resource Management*, 5(2): 267–99.

Tayeb, M.H. (1988) *Organizations and National Culture: A Comparative Analysis*, London: Sage.

Tayeb, M.H. (2003) *International Management: A Cross-cultural Approach*, Harlow: Prentice-Hall/Financial Times.

Tayeb, M.H. (2005) *International Human Resource Management: A Multinational Company Perspective*, Oxford: Oxford University Press.

Torrington, D. (1994) *International Human Resource Management: Think Globally, Act Locally*, Hemel Hempstead: Prentice-Hall.

Trompenaars, F. (1993) *Riding the Waves of Culture: Understanding Cultural Diversity in Business*, London: Economist Books.

Trompenaars, F. and Hampden-Turner, C. (1997) *Riding the Waves of Culture: Understanding Cultural Diversity in Business*, 2nd edn, London: Nicholas Brealey.

Trompenaars, F. and Hampden-Turner, C. (2004) *Managing People Across Cultures*, Oxford: Capstone.

Tsui, A.S., Nifadkar, S.S. and Ou, A.Y. (2007) 'Cross-national, cross-cultural organizational behaviour research: advances, gaps, and recommendations', *Journal of Management*, 33(3): 426–78.

Whitley, R.D. (1992) *Business Systems in East Asia*, London: Sage.

Zeffane, R. and Rugimbana, R. (1995) 'Management in the less-developed countries: a review of pertinent issues, challenges and responses', *Leadership and Organization Development Journal*, 16(8): 26–36.

Part I

Case Study: Bob Over the Globe – Chevron and Saudi Aramco

Introduction

Chevron, the giant American petroleum company, and Saudi Aramco, the largest state-owned oil company of Saudi Arabia, provide examples of what happens when the globalizing power of business is met by the localizing power of culture and politics.

Chevron's original company, Standard Oil of California, was the first to explore for oil in Saudi Arabia in 1933 and has since established a stronghold in the Gulf States. Its major concern has always been the management of people across different cultures. Its management is very much aware of the important role of culture in exploring for and producing oil in different parts of the world. It has subsidiaries in many countries in Africa, Asia, Europe and South America. It operates in about 118 countries around the world and has experienced some difficulties in terms of culture or politics in a number of countries. For example, it was the first to find oil in the south of Sudan and then it had to withdraw because of the civil war. Its main challenge is to be seen in the host countries as a national, rather than foreign, company.

In contrast, Saudi Aramco is a state-owned national company that has very limited difficulties in understanding or dealing with the local or regional cultures and political systems: its main challenge is to have an international presence and to operate at an international level as a major explorer, producer and exporter of oil.

The birth and growth of Saudi Aramco

Aramco is an acronym for 'Arabian American Oil Company'. It ranks among the top ten hydrocarbon companies in the world. It controls the largest off-shore and onshore oil fields and the largest and most modern fleet of super-tankers in the world. It employs more than 54,000 people of over 50 different nationalities, uses leading-edge technology for exploring, producing, refining and marketing the hydrocarbon, and has many strategic alliances and joint ventures with companies throughout the world. It currently produces and exports about 8 million barrels of oil per day and oversees proven oil reserves of 259 billion barrels (about a quarter of the world's total oil reserves). It is also a major producer of natural liquefied gas.

Chevron's original company, Standard Oil of California (Socal), was formed from the break-up of Standard Oil in 1911. When Socal discovered large fields of oil in Saudi Arabia, it created a new company called California-Arabian Standard Oil Company in 1938 to evolve into what could be seen as a national oil company of the Arabian Gulf countries. In 1944 the latter was renamed the Arabian American Oil Company (Aramco). By 1980 it was com-pletely owned by the Saudi government and then renamed as Saudi Aramco in 1988. Thus, Saudi Aramco was born from Standard Oil but nurtured and adopted by the Saudis. However in 1984, before Saudi Aramco was estab-lished, Socal merged with another company, Kuwait Gulf Oil Company, to form the largest oil company in the region, which became Chevron Corporation. After a number of other mergers, Chevron Corporation merged with Texaco in 2001 to form a petroleum giant, ChevronTexaco. In 2005 they decided to drop the word 'Texaco' from the name: the company has since been called just Chevron or Chevron International Exploration and Production Oil Corporation.

Chevron–Saudi Aramco interface

It seems that it is in the best interest of the two companies, Chevron and Saudi Aramco, to work together, rather than compete against each other. Chevron cannot compete directly, at least in the Gulf region, against Saudi Aramco, which is heavily subsidized and protected by the Saudi government, and Aramco cannot compete with Chevron, which is an international company with a long history, expertise and knowledge of the petroleum industry. They tend to work together at the official level, especially in the use and develop-ment of technology, in product development and in international marketing.

However, since both of them require skilled and experienced labour they have pursued different and rather competitive approaches to the management of their human resources. Chevron has had regularly to reconsider its recruitment, training and expatriation policies in Saudi Arabia. The cost and benefits of recruiting local, rather than using international managers, have become a strategic employment matter for Chevron and Aramco in Saudi Arabia.

Saudi Arabian Chevron is a subsidiary of Chevron International Exploration and Production. Its mission is: 'To deliver to the Kingdom of Saudi Arabia, Chevron, employees and stakeholders the greatest possible value in a safe and environmentally responsible manner, by efficiently exploring, producing and marketing the energy resources entrusted to us' (Chevron website, 2007). To achieve its mission, Chevron works closely with Saudi Aramco in order to develop its petroleum reserves, capitalize on the value chain for derived petroleum products, and realize the potential of its human resources. In order to do so, a steady flow of talented earth scientists, petroleum and reservoir engineers, surface facilities engineers and operations personnel, as well as other business support staff, is required.

It is estimated that more than 80 per cent of Saudi Arabia Chevron employees are Saudi and Kuwaiti nationals. Chevron offers a variety of direct recruitment of opportunities to applicants from all nationalities, but it has comprehensive early career development initiatives open to Saudi and Kuwaiti nationals. This approach is also adopted by Saudi Aramco which attracts more and better educated nationals. Moreover, Chevron offers a very competitive salary package and a variety of incentive awards to all its employees, but Saudi Aramco offers similar or higher salaries and better job security to its nationals, who prefer jobs for life. It is estimated that about 87 per cent of Saudi Aramco employees are Saudi nationals.

The globalizing power of business versus the localizing power of culture in managing people internationally

Saudi Arabia Chevron's corporate citizenship is seen everywhere throughout the Kingdom of Saudi Arabia to the extent that some citizens do not understand the difference between Saudi Aramco and Saudi Chevron. The latter supports a wide range of educational and environmental programmes in the region. It has sponsored a number of social, cultural and economic projects to make its presence felt everywhere and to sustain stronger public relations. For example, it supported the ongoing beautification and greening projects in the city of Khafji and makes regular financial contributions to King Fahad University of Petroleum and Mineral Resources, the King Abdul Aziz Foundation for the Gifted, the King Fahad National Center for Children's Cancer Research, and many other charitable projects.

In its attempt to become more local, Chevron has been committed to the achievement of three nationally strategic objectives. These are: the 'Saudization' of jobs; the transfer of advanced technology; and the improvement of productivity and quality product and services. The Saudization objective has been met by employing as many Saudis as possible. However, since not all Saudis are sufficiently trained, Chevron has had to bring in expertise and highly skilled labour (comprising about 17 per cent of its employees in Saudi Arabia) from the US and other Western countries to help implement the state-of-the-art advanced petroleum technologies and to deliver a variety of employee development programmes aimed at building job performance competencies and quality enhancement initiatives. Chevron's diversity principles are summarized in the following statement: 'We learn from and respect the cultures in which we work. We value and demonstrate respect for the uniqueness of individuals and the varied perspectives and talents they provide. We have an inclusive work environment and actively embrace a diversity of people, ideas, talents and experiences. Our principles endorse a spirit of inclusion and foster an environment where everyone can reach his or her full potential. We are committed to being recognized as a global leader that backs its words with accountable actions and quantifiable results' (Chevron website, 2007).

Chevron is proud to be the recipient of numerous international awards and recognition for promoting diversity in the workplace. Its experience and international reputation have enabled it to integrate its global activities while attempting to adapt to local differences through its diverse workforce and act locally while thinking globally. However, despite its experience in managing human resources, Saudi Arabia is still a major challenge for Chevron. The box below considers the example of Peter Martin, one of Chevron's international team of managers who were sent to Saudi Arabia in 1998.

Although Peter Martin was trained in cross-cultural management, he was not well informed about the living conditions in a country that is recognized as strict in its cultural norms, values and religion. Before going to Saudi Arabia, Peter Martin read parts from a book entitled *The Arabian Nights* which was full of stories of love and magic, and watched the film, 'Lawrence of Arabia'. When he was a child he read at school that the Saudis live in tents made of goat's hair and their best pets were ugly camels. He also learnt that every Saudi man had to grow a black beard that had to be at least 10 centimetres long. He was told by a friend that all Saudis prayed for hours, five times a day, and nobody dared to disturb them when they perform their prayers, and that they listened all the time to the reciting of the Koran (holy book) rather than to music. He was also told that drinking alcohol was forbidden and anyone caught with alcohol could be beheaded. Thus Peter, and perhaps all his colleagues, had a very scary picture of the people he would be working with.

When Peter arrived in Saudi, he found none of what he read or thought of about the new workplace and its people. The Saudi managers and officials, men and women, he had to work with were highly educated, well behaved and spoke quite good English. Most of them did not have beards and only prayed when the prayer is called for, that is only twice during the working time, and lasted for about five minutes each.

One day when leaving his four-bedroom villa (modest in comparison with the luxurious houses of his Saudi colleagues), he came across the young computer programmer, Faysal Al-Garni, in a tracksuit jogging with headphones plugged into an iPod. He was taken by what he saw and started walking faster to catch up with him. When he arrived at the company's gates he found Faysal resting on a wooden chair, legs apart and moving his head from side to side with the headphones still on his ears. Peter said hello but Faysal did not reply because he did not hear him. Peter was very curious to know what Faysal was listening to. He wondered: 'listening to the Koran while jogging? Isn't it forbidden in Islam to listen to music?' To his surprise, he found that Faysal was listening to music by Bob Marley. He heard Faysal singing along with the song, 'let's get together and feel alright'. Peter asked with amusement: 'Are you listening to Western music?' Faysal replied in Arabic '*Bob feel globe*'. Peter said, 'That's globalization for you', and went to his office.

Actually, Peter had misunderstood what Faysal told him: he thought he had heard Faysal saying, 'Bob (meaning Bob Marley) is known over the globe', whereas what the young man said is 'pop' (the Arab pronounced the p as b), meaning 'pop music touches people's hearts'.

In this instance, it was not very important whether Peter understood what Faysal said. What is significant is that Peter became aware that most young Saudi employees were like any other young people elsewhere. He would not then have been surprised if he had known that this young Saudi man graduated in 1994 with a BSc (Hons) degree in computing from a British university and spent six months in the US on a short course in petroleum management before starting work in Saudi Chevron. Also, Faysal wanted to work for Saudi Aramco, but he failed the entry examination test. Saudi Aramco is very selective and offers jobs only to those who pursue its company-specific programmes and pass them successfully. Applicants with qualifications from outside its approved programmes have to take rigorous entry tests and examinations. Faysal was not very strong academically and could not pass the entry examination test. He got a job at Chevron thanks to the intervention and recommendation of his uncle, who was a manager at Jubail Chevron Phillips (JCP). He was accepted as part of Chevron's Saudization policy commitment.

The largest proportion of the Saudi Aramco workforce is made of geophysicists and geologists who are highly educated and most of them trained abroad.

There is no problem concerning culture or managing diversity because most of the workforce is Saudi, while the managers and the experts are hired from different countries to do their work the Saudi way. The main problem is to make the performance of its workforce meet international standards. In each of its operations (drilling and workover, refining and distribution, and shipping) it has had to compete with other national and international oil producers for the recruitment of thousands of highly skilled engineers. It has invested heavily in the training and development of a national workforce in order to keep abreast of international developments. In other words it has had to manage its local (national) workforce globally. In contrast, Chevron's challenge has been to manage its international workforce locally.

Questions

1   Describe the position of Chevron in Saudi Arabia in relation to Saudi Aramco.
2   Discuss how Saudi Aramco should manage its local employees globally.
3   Discuss how Chevron should manage its global employees locally. What does the story of Peter Martin's experience suggest is wrong in Chevron's diversity management strategy?
4   How should Peter Martin have been prepared for his new assignment in Saudi Arabia?
5   What lessons can we learn from the Peter and Faysal encounter?

References

http://www.saudiaramcoworld.com/issue/200706/ accessed November 2007.
http://saudinf.com/main/d19.htm, accessed October 2007.
http://www.chevron.com/ accessed October 2007.

Part II

Managing in Anglo-Saxon Countries

Part 2: Managing in Anglo-Saxon Countries
Map 2

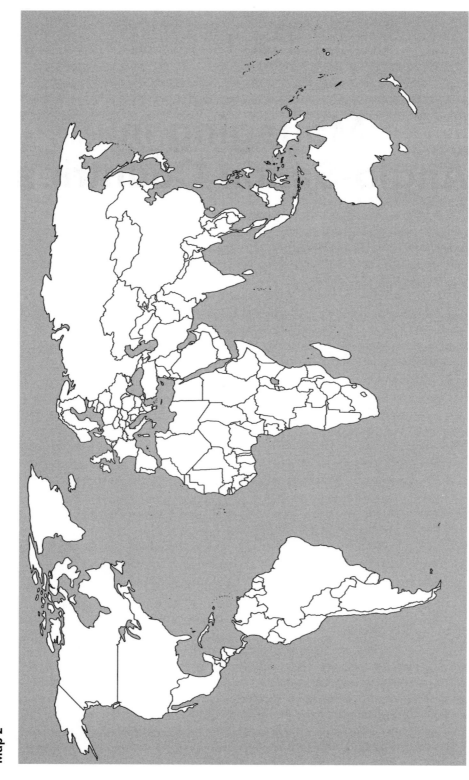

Activity: Put the number allocated for each of these countries on the map above: Ireland (1), UK (3), Canada (6), US(4), Australia (5) and New Zealand (2).

4

The US and Canada

Introduction

The United States (US) and Canada are economically intertwined because of their close geographical location, strong trade relations, common socio-economic and historical backgrounds, and similar organizational characteristics. As the founding members of the North American Trade Agreement (NAFTA), which includes Mexico, they have harmonized their business operations through the free movement of employees and goods between each other. The high level of investment by US corporations in Canada has had an impact on the employment decisions and management policies and practices of Canadian employers.

Though the two countries have much in common, there are also some distinct differences in the details of employee relations and the practice of some HRM functions. Management theory and practice in both countries has gone through numerous transformations as a result of industrial development, technological changes and increasing trade and business competition at home and

Table 4.1 Basic statistical indicators, the US and Canada

Country	Area (sq km)	Population (July 2010 est.)	Population growth (2010 est.) %	GDP – real growth rate (2009) %	Inflation rate (2009 est.) %	Workforce (2009 est.) Million	Unemployment rate (2009) %
Canada	9 984 670	33 487 208	0.817	−2.5	0.3	18.39	8.3
USA	9 826 675	307 212 123	0.977	−2.6	−0.3	154.2	9.3

Source: CIA *World Factbook*, 2010.

from abroad (see Werner, 2007). Each of the two countries has had to follow employment approaches that best meet its economic and employee relations needs. (See Table 4.1 for comparative statistical indicators.)

Contexts: economics, politics and culture

Economics

The US economy is the largest in the world. It represents between 25 to 35 per cent of the world market. It is a leading industrial power with highly diversified and technologically advanced production systems. It produces and exports commodities, such as agricultural products, and capital goods such as aircrafts, weapons, military equipments, motor vehicle parts, machinery, chemicals, computers, and many consumer goods.

Like the US, Canada is a competitive free market economy. It is heavily dependent on international trade and international investments, which are related mainly to the US. More than 77 per cent of Canadian exports in 2008 were to the US (CIA World Factbook, 2010). Canada dominated the world market in the exports of grain and lumber for most of the twentieth century and still enjoys a comparative advantage in the production and export of raw materials and semi-processed products. Oil and gas have now become Canada's main exports. Canada is the US's largest foreign supplier of energy, including oil, gas, uranium and electricity. The country remains an important exporter of coal, iron and industrial goods to Europe, China, Mexico and Japan and a major exporter of agricultural products to many developing countries. Canada meets about 10 per cent of the world's demand for grain (CIA World Factbook, 2010).

Both Canada and the US have been magnets to foreign investments from all parts of the world. Unlike many other countries (except the members of

European Union), they do not require foreign investors to take national companies as joint venture partners and they have very limited restrictions on foreign investment. They are seen as safe havens for foreign investors because of the comparatively stable and safe business environment. As a result, many US companies have to compete aggressively against foreign investors who have been allowed to acquire established businesses or to build new ones in the US. On the other hand, many US companies are multinational companies and have investments in many other countries – notably Canada, where about a third of the assets of all industrial investments are owned by foreign firms, mainly by the US multinational corporations (www.canadianeconomy.gc.ca). Both countries' management practices provide good examples of managing across cultures.

Politics

Both the US and Canada enjoy stable political systems. Both are federal democracies: each state (USA) or province (Canada) has substantial powers in running its own economic and social affairs, including the introduction of employment and civil laws. However, the two countries differ in their approach to government and in their political agendas. Canada has a constitutional monarchy and a parliamentary democracy, where the head of state is formally the British monarch represented by a Governor General and the head of government is an elected prime minister. In contrast, the US has a constitution-based federal system led by an elected president who is both the chief of state and head of government. Politics in the US has been dominated by two major political strands, the Republicans and the Democrats. Though in theory they are opposed, in practice they agree on many aspects of economic and foreign affairs. The main difference is that the Democrats have adopted some policies that are more liberal and more supportive of the welfare system and the working classes.

Canadian federal politics has been dominated for most of the last seven decades by the Liberal party, though there have been occasional minority and Conservative governments. In the 1990s the New Democratic party (NDP) emerged with strong support from the unions, but was unable to get enough support from the working classes to get to power. In general, the Liberal and the Conservative policies of the Canadian governments stand somewhere between the US and Europe in terms of employment laws and regulations.

Culture

The US and Canada are multicultural societies with ethnically diverse populations. Since most of the population is originally foreign there is a level of tolerance and acceptance of other cultures. According to Gesteland (1996) American culture is deal-focused, informal, monochromic, and moderately expressive. Americans tend to do business immediately and like to express their business concerns explicitly. According to Hofstede's (2001) dimensions of cultural differences, both the US and Canada have a small power distance, low uncertainty avoidance, individualism, masculinism, and have short-term orientation cultures. However, they differ in some ways: the US is lower in uncertainty avoidance and more masculine than Canada (Hofstede, 2001). The drive for industrialization, achievement and better economic development in the US and Canada is also influenced by Protestant work ethics, according to which people believe in the efficacy of their individual efforts to achieve self-actualization and success, and also by the commitment and dedication of skilled, educated, business-minded and hard-working immigrants.

Labour market trends

The labour markets of both Canada and the US are flexible, diverse, relatively stable and increasingly knowledge-based. The demand side of their labour markets has been driven by a knowledge-based economy associated with international competition and technological developments. The supply side has been characterized by a rise in the highly educated workforce, a relative increase in older employees, and a significant participation of women and ethnic minorities (immigrant labour). It can be seen from Table 4.2 that the majority of the population is at the working age (15–64). Employees most affected by cyclical changes in the economy are those under the age of 26 or over 55.

Table 4.2 Age structure (%) 2010, the US and Canada

Country	0–14 years %	15–64 years %	Over 65 years %	Median age (years)	Life expectancy at birth (men & women)
Canada	16.1	68.7	15.2	40.7	81.23
USA	20.2	67	12.8	36.8	78.11

Source: CIA *World Factbook*, 2010.

The current labour markets of both countries are generally characterized by: a growing services sector; increasing unemployment rates; flexible working practices; job insecurity and high turnover; a shortage of skilled workers; a diverse workforce; an older working population; and competitiveness.

The services sector

The sectors that grew in the 1990s, such as automobile, computer, and electronics production, contracted over the 2000s. Those that struggled in the 1980s such as construction, mining and oil and gas, saw a high growth between 2001 and 2007. Employment in the manufacturing sector has declined in both countries over the last five years. (See Table 4.3.)

Table 4.3 Workforce distribution by occupation in 2007 (%), the US and Canada

Country	Agriculture	Industry	Services	Construction	Other
Canada	2	13	76	13	3
USA	0.6	22.6	76.8	–	0.6

Source: CIA World Factbook, 2009.

In both countries, white-collar employment grew in the 1990s and has continued to grow over the last few years because of a growth in public sector investments, especially in education and health. Although there has been an increase in public sector employment, the main employers in both the US and Canada are the large private multinational companies in the mining, oil and gas, construction, farming, and transport sectors where managerial, professional, technical, skilled and administrative employment fluctuates with the economy.

Unemployment

The rate of unemployment in both countries was relatively stable from the year 2000, until the 'credit crunch' recession saw a sharp increase in the number of people out of work. The recent recession forced many US companies to close down or to downsize their operations, creating mass redundancies and hence leading to a high level of unemployment. The rate of unemployment in Canada has been better than that of the US. For example, in the US it increased from 5.1 percent to 7.2 percent between 2005 and 2008, while in Canada it improved slightly as it moved from 6.8 percent to 6.2 percent over the same period.

Flexible working practices

Increasingly, companies in the US and Canada have been forced by internal and global competition to attract and retain skilled employees. They have introduced flexible working practices in order to retain core employees who are unable to work full time because of other commitments. The use of flexible working patterns such as part-time work, home-based working, temporary working, and job sharing is becoming increasingly popular in both the US and Canada (Jain and Verma, 1996; Perrewé, 2007). Part-time employment as a proportion of total employment has tended to rise in Canada but decline in the US (see Table 4.4). The main reason for the decline in part-time work in the US is the decline in female employment since the late 1990s.

Table 4.4 Part-time employment as a percentage of total employment, the US and Canada

Country\year	1980	1985	1990	1995	2000	2005	2007
Canada	14.3	17.1	17	18.8	18.1	18.3	18.2
US	14.4	14.7	14.1	14	12.6	12.8	12.6

Source: OECD *Factbook*, 2009.

Job insecurity and high turnover

In highly competitive and free market economies such as those of the US and Canada, no employers can promise jobs for life to their employees. Job insecurity has become a symptom of today's labour markets. Since they do not expect long-term commitment from their employers, many employees tend to change jobs whenever they get an opportunity. Turnover has become a reality to many active members of the population. Many employees have become attracted to learning new skills, earning high income in the short term, and being free from any legal obligations that make them stay in their current jobs. According to Greco (1998), the attitude of American employees, especially the skilled and the knowledgeable, has tended to change from being loyal to the organizations they work for to being loyal to themselves. Since no job is guaranteed, the only way to guarantee a job is to learn new skills that enhance employability potential. The Mini Case Study below encapsulates this point.

MINI CASE STUDY 3

No Job is Good Enough for Me Yet! (The US)

David Wilson of the International Association of Graduate Business Schools in the US is reported as saying: 'My father was born in 1907 and he retired in 1973 from the same company that he began with 44 years earlier. Since I entered the workforce in 1965, I've lived in about a dozen different places, and I've had three different careers. My son will probably have eight or nine careers. The old employer – employee contract implicitly promised employment-for-life. Now, we're at employment-for-now. Once employees started feeling that corporate entities had violated their contracts, they lost much of their sense of loyalty. Today, people prepare for their own futures' (cited in Greco, 1998: 44).

Questions

1 What do you think are the motives that might make employees stay with one employer?
2 What do you think causes some employees to change their jobs regularly?

Diversity

Though the race and gender composition of the US labour market has not changed significantly over the last twenty years, there has been a moderate rise in Hispanics and Asians. The number of Hispanics increased from 9 to 15 per cent of the population and that of the Asians from 4 to 5 per cent between 1996 and 2008. Similarly, the Canadian labour market has changed very little despite an influx of immigrants from Asia, mainly from Hong Kong, India and mainland China, over the last 20 years.

There has been a steady increase in the participation of women in the labour market in Canada (81.6 per cent of women aged 25–54 were at work in 2005), but a slight decline in the US since 1997 (65.8 per cent of US women aged 25–54 were at work in 2005). The number of women (14–64 years) in employment has increased by nearly 18 per cent in Canada and about 10.5 per cent in the US between 1980 and 2007 (see Table 4.5). The slight decline in the participation of women in the US labour market since 2000 has been attributed partly to the increase by 23 per cent in child bearing by women aged 30 to 44 (Cross, 2005a).

Table 4.5 Share of women of working age (14–64 years) in employment (%), the US and Canada

Country\year	1980	1990	1995	2000	2005	2007
Canada	52.6	62.8	61.6	65.6	68.3	70.1
USA	55.4	64	65.8	67.8	65.6	65.9

Source: OECD *Factbook*, 2009.

Ageing working population

The population of both countries is becoming older and healthier. Older people account for a growing proportion of the workforce. A study by Schellenberg et al. (2002) found that about 25 per cent of the Canadians who retired between 1992 and 2002 returned to work, though nearly half of them returned to work on a part-time basis. Cross (2005a: 3.8) commented that 'the increase in both the number of people aged 55 and over and their participation rate meant that they contributed over one-third of the 2.35 million increase in Canada's labour force since 1996'.

ACTIVITY 1

Imagine you are a labour market consultant. Write a short report to the ILO (International Labour Organization) summarizing the strengths and weaknesses of the Canadian and US labour markets.

Management and organization

Most of the principles of modern management were developed in the US and Western Europe. It is often argued that contemporary management and organizational behaviour theories were derived from US companies', best management practice and they have their roots in the development of management thinking since the start of the twentieth century – especially the development of 'scientific management' by Frederick Taylor (1856–1915). Taylorism is based on the view that managers develop the best methods for their workers to carry out their tasks. Managers select the workers who have appropriate abilities, train them when necessary to do the job in the most efficient and cost effective way, and use pay incentives to increase output (Gatley et al., 1996). Individual employees have equal obligations and opportunities to meet not only their organizations' objectives but their individual ambitions too. In highly specialized and formalized organizations, operations are standardized and clearly described and written as rules and standard operating manuals, so both management and production processes are expected to be effective. The McDonald's operations manual, for example, contains in minute details the steps that should be followed in cooking burgers, serving customers, or cleaning the ice cream machine. In a critical evaluation of HRM in the USA, Guest (1990: 379) states that HRM in America is 'optimistic, apparently humanistic and also superficially simple. In short it has rediscovered elements of the American Dream'.

The systems of employee relations and management in both the US and Canada have gone through many changes over the years as a result of industrial developments and socio-economic and political changes. Such changes have culminated in the development of management and organization systems that are generally characterized by strategic awareness, trade union avoidance, legally binding employee–employer agreements, and management of diversity.

Strategic awareness

Historically, management in the US is associated with forms of strategic awareness based on employment policies linked to corporate objectives (Fombrum et al., 1984; Beer et al., 1984, 1985), the integration of employee goals with those of the organization (Kochan et al., 1986), the belief that high levels of organization performance depend on high levels of employee commitment (Beer et al., 1984, 1985; Walton, 1985), and the need for an organizational culture that values the commitment of human resources (Beer et al., 1984, 1985).

Downsizing, labour process re-engineering, quality management, and the use of information technologies have dominated the practice of management in the USA (Konrad and Deckop, 2001). Over the 1980s and the 1990s, a number of large companies had to introduce downsizing (or rightsizing, as the employers prefer to call it) programmes in order to reduce costs and maintain their profitability by introducing voluntary and compulsory redundancies at all levels of their organizational hierarchy, despite the fact that they made record corporate profits (Wheeler and McClendon, 1998). Eastern Kodak and Digital Equipment are examples of such companies (Kochan and Dyer, 1995). As in the US, Canadian employers have also been under pressure since the 1980s to reduce costs because of increased international and national competition and the deregulation of public industries (Belout et al., 2001). According to Thompson (1998: 101), 'many responses by employers to these changes were traditional: Layoffs dramatically reduced employment in many industries, and the use of part-time and casual workers rose substantially'.

Avoidance of trade unions

US employers avoid trade unions and collective bargaining by all means. Historically, trade unions have had a bad name among managers, economic thinkers and political decision-makers. The Cold War era had many serious repercussions on trade unions, as they were believed to be associated with communism. Caute (1979) states that:

> at least 1.5 million employees in private industry were subjected to security programmes ... Bell Telephone accounted for 780,000 and General Electric for 280,000 of such company-instituted security checks ... in Michigan the large automobile companies of Ford, General Motors and Chrysler all made extensive

use of local police departments to spy on and police their employees. Ford went further by employing the former head of the FBI's Detroit Bureau, John Bugas, to spy on company employees. Other companies, including GE, Honeywell, Stewart-Warner, Motorola, Lockheed Aircraft Corp., US Steel, and the Emerson Electric Company, employed the American Security Council (ASC), prominently staffed by ex-FBI agents, to list, monitor and exercise surveillance over suspected radicals among their employees. (Caute, 1979: 370–2)

Students of business and management, managers and politicians have often been taught that trade unions are bad for the American economy and social structure. Many American management textbooks are written in a way that does not give credit to trade unions in organizations. When industrial conflict and strikes are mentioned, they are described negatively in terms of days lost and a cost to the economy, or even as anti-American activities that should have never happened (Mills and Hatfield, 1999). Many management consultants advise managers on how to avoid trade unions and collective bargaining.

The emergence of HRM thinking over the 1980s came to consolidate the view that it is not necessary to have trade unions to protect the interests of the workers. It argued that there is no need for trade union representatives in organizations where management considers every employee as a 'valued' asset and communicates with him or her directly, meets employees' individual needs, and rewards all employees fairly and adequately according to their performance. Many commentators have criticized the American logic of employee relations and trade union avoidance. For example, David Guest (1990: 515) argues that the emergence of HRM was a reinvention of the 'American dream' that people aspired to in the land of industrialization, supposedly with endless opportunities and prosperity for every citizen, but as far as industrial relations are concerned it was 'a smokescreen behind which management can introduce non-unionism or obtain significant concessions from trade unions'. He adds that the alleged organizational successes of some American companies as a result of introducing HRM policies are myths: the reality was the introduction of downsizing and redundancy programmes. He argued that,'like the myths of the cowboy and the Wild West which served to obscure the reality of the massacre of the Indians, so HRM can serve to obscure the assault on the union movement in the USA' (Guest, 1990: 519).

The non-recognition of trade unionism and collective bargaining by many US employers has strengthened the development of a management-driven approach to employee relations. Managers prefer to approach their employees informally and individually rather than through a representative body. This approach is aimed at generating individual employee commitment to the goals of the organization where employees compete individually for better rewards, higher positions and security of employment. Describing employee relations in the US, Wheeler and McClendon (1998: 72) state that 'the conditions under which employment takes place are essentially employer-determined, although limited by labour market forces'. The main reason for avoiding trade unions is cultural: managers believe that their managerial activities and decisions should not be shared with or challenged by their subordinates. In line with Taylor's principles of scientific management, many US managers believe that there should be a clear distinction between those who manage and those who are managed.

In Canada, in contrast, avoidance of trade unions is very limited and less openly expressed than in the US. Many Canadian companies have recognized trade unions. Employers, mainly in manufacturing, transport and the public sector, have historically accepted the unions and have managed to work with them quite successfully (Belout et al., 2001; Thompson, 1998). According to Thompson (1998: 101), 'militant anti-unionism is not a popular public position among Canadian employers, although many managers privately express hostility to labour organizations'. He adds that 'legal restrictions on employer tactics make de-unionization very difficult, and protections for union organization are effective' (1998: 101). Most of the non-unionized companies attempt to match their wages and working conditions to those that are unionized. However, the presence of an increasing number of US companies in Canada is changing the attitude of some managers towards trade unions. Many employers have opted for direct forms of employee involvement and participation rather than collective bargaining through trade unions.

In both Canada and the US, a number of employers have introduced forms of employee direct participation such as problem-solving teams, quality circles, joint employee–management groups, team briefing, and self-managing teams. These measures aim to empower individual employees in the work they do. It has been argued that such forms of employee direct involvement 'have the potential to undermine the union within the workplace, and it may be that in some instances these schemes have been introduced as part of a union-avoidance strategy' (Hollinshead and Leat, 1995: 289). This is certainly true for the US companies, but in Canada many companies have introduced forms of direct employee participation not to avoid trade unions but to empower their employees and to benefit from their views (Belout et al., 2001).

Employee–employer agreements

In Canada and the US, all aspects of employee–employer relations are legally governed. Many laws have been introduced in the areas of pay, health and safety at work, pensions, discrimination, termination of employment, and leave entitlements (Elkins, 2007). There is no area that is not covered by the law. There are even laws that deal with ethical and controversial issues such as alcoholism, drug abuse, and theft, which cost US companies tens of billions of dollars each year. Collective agreements in the US typically contain 'force *majeure'* clauses that protect the authority and supremacy of management's decisions over the workers in cases of crises, as described in the case study at the end of Part II.

Managing diversity

One of the main themes of management and organization in the US and Canada is diversity. In the 1980s the issue of managing diversity was adopted by employers as a means of responding positively and effectively to demographic changes affecting the labour market (see Jain and Verma, 1996). In the US, managing diversity was seen as a response to affirmative action, which had been practised for many years but created more problems of discrimination than it eliminated. In Canada, managing diversity has been seen as a response to inequality in employment or specifically to the failure to implement the Employment Equity Act (1986, amended 1995).

In the US, affirmative action focuses not on the fair and equal recruitment and retention of people from ethnic minorities, women, older people and other so-called insecure groups but rather on the numerical representation of one or more of these groups. According to Agócs and Burr (1996: 32) 'affirmative action in employment might be called "hiring by the number" because of its focus on increasing the representation of the designated groups through targeted hiring, and to a lesser extent, training and promotion'. In contrast, managing diversity is about having employment policies and practices in place that give everyone equal rights and opportunities. It is to ensure that employees from different groups – ethnic, age, gender, ability, and so forth – are considered as 'equal participants in the workplace, enjoying equitable career development opportunities and rewards for their contributions' (Agócs and Burr, 1996: 32). In Canada, where there is no affirmative action, managing diversity is aimed at eliminating inequality in the workplace, especially since the labour market is becoming increasingly diverse (Jain and Verma, 1996).

ACTIVITY 2

Please answer the following questions in the light of the above discussion of management and organization in the two countries:

1 Why do US employers often seek to avoid trade unions?
2 Why do US employers use affirmative action? How strategic is the issue of managing diversity in US and Canada?

Managing human resources

In this section we focus on the conduct of the main functions of human resource management in more detail.

Recruitment and Selection

As well as the use of conventional methods of recruitment (such as newspapers, magazines, journals, radio and TV advertising, recruitment agencies and direct graduate recruitment contacts), employers in the US and Canada use more aggressive approaches to recruitment such as poaching and headhunting employees from competitors and other successful organizations, and taking affirmative action in recruiting women, the old and the disabled (Konrad and Deckop, 2001; Belout et al., 2001; Tarique and Schuler, 2007). Most companies use the internet to advertise their vacancies and to solicit individuals to apply or to request application information. There are also agencies that specialize in headhunting employees with particular qualities, qualifications and skills. The process of recruitment is commonly characterized by:

- recruitment of employees, especially managers, from the private sector to work in the public sector and vice versa;
- a preference to hire already trained employees rather than the ones that companies will have to train themselves;
- targeting the overseas labour market in the search for a talented and skilled workforce. Here companies benefit from the use of information technologies by advertising throughout the world or in specific countries, and conduct interviews through phone or video-conferencing;
- not showing the salary and other benefits and rewards when advertising jobs in order to attract as many applicants as possible. Such rewards are normally negotiated and agreed only when the job is being offered.

Equal opportunities

In both the US and Canada, employers are very cautious about discrimination in the process of recruitment and selection because of many legally binding employment laws and regulations. Recruiters are expected to be fair and objective in their recruitment and selection of new employees. In the US, the Civil Rights Act of 1964 prohibits discrimination in employment on the basis of gender, race, colour, religion or nationality. The act was amended further by the Age Discrimination Act of 1967, which made it illegal to discriminate in employment against people above the age of 40 on the grounds of age, and in

1978 by the Pregnancy Discrimination Act, which prohibited discrimination against pregnant women in employment and at work. The Disabilities Act 1990 made it illegal to discriminate in employment against people with physical or mental disabilities. The Equal Opportunities Employment Commission (EOEC) strictly monitors all recruitment and selection procedures to make sure that the right procedures were followed, but in practice discrimination still exists. In Canada there are similar laws to those in the US, though discrimination is less of a problem.

Graduate recruitment

The labour markets of both the US and Canada are knowledge-based and the supply side is characterized by an increasing number of highly educated workers. Many job seekers are college and university graduates, often with higher degrees. Many companies have introduced graduate recruitment programmes and some even have graduate recruitment departments. Increasingly, graduate recruitment is driven by international competition and is becoming part of the international resourcing strategy of multinational companies (Tarique and Schuler, 2007).

The process of graduate recruitment in the US and Canada, as in most of the industrialized countries, has been standardized in terms of what organizations look for in graduates and the methods they use to recruit and select them. For most professional jobs, employers look for drive, transferable skills, ability to learn, vision, and academic achievements. For most managerial positions, employers look for leadership skills, social skills, vision, ability to learn, the right attitude, cultural awareness, and academic achievements. They require that the applicant holds a good degree in business and management at undergraduate level. Holders of an MBA or a graduate qualification in management are very often preferred. There has been a high demand by US companies for specialized MBA graduates and for MBA internships. With the increase in the number of MBAs on offer, many employers scrutinize where the MBA was taught and when it was awarded. They prefer graduates with MBAs from well-known and reputable business or management schools, colleges and institutes.

However, having an MBA or a degree in management does not always guarantee a job in management in either the US or in Canada. Many graduates find themselves unemployable either because they graduated from unknown or non-reputable business schools, or lack the requisite skills. The process of graduate recruitment has become a stressful experience for many graduates who have to go through at least two interviews and attend an assessment centre. Therefore many graduates have resorted to applying for manual school leavers' jobs in order to gain the experience that enables them to develop their future career.

MINI CASE STUDY 4

The Assembly Line is Better than the Office: US Recruitment

When asked to comment about the status of graduate recruitment in the US, the managing director of a fast-growing recruitment agency in New York, Louisa Baker, replied:

> Higher educated graduates are finding the assembly line more appealing than management careers. US employers have become tougher in their recruitment in order to employ the best educated and the highly trained to do operational tasks that were twenty years ago given to school leavers. The car manufacturing companies, for example, have realized that to compete with the Japanese they have to hire not just the qualified to do the jobs but the well experienced as well. American graduates have found assembly line work less physically demanding, more rewarding, less stressful and more intellectually challenging than their counterparts did two decades ago. With the increase in highly qualified employees there has been less demand for line managers because employees have become self-directed and the work more technical. What is needed is not supervisors telling workers what to do but workers who are able to read and understand instruction manuals and to discuss and solve quality related problems.

Question

1 Why do some graduates do jobs that school leavers did twenty years ago? Does it mean that the graduates of today are less educated than those of twenty years ago? Discuss.

Selection

Selection processes in the USA and Canada are formalized, structured and rigorous. Employers use a variety of tests and selection methods, depending on the type and level of the jobs being offered. For example, when hiring their assembly line workers the car manufacturing companies test the ability of their candidates to read, write and reason, as well as testing their mathematical, manual dexterity, computer and interpersonal skills. Employers in the US and Canada use all means to get the employees they need.

To avoid claims of discrimination in the selection process, employers in both countries use objective and properly validated methods of selection, such as structured interviews and quantitatively measured tests. They use a number of ability, personality and psychometric tests. Most large companies use assessment centres for the selection of applicants for managerial and professional jobs.

Education, training and development

In a knowledge-based economy, having an educated, knowledgeable and skilled workforce is essential. Continuous improvement through lifelong learning creates opportunities for better rewards, upward mobility and wider choice of career paths. In both countries most citizens have at least a school education. An emphasis on education throughout one's life and the desire for more learning and for better self-development are part of the American national culture. According to Handy (1989: 54),

> education plays a big part in American life. Teachers and professors are respected. Degrees and qualifications are desired and sought after. It is a natural and normal instinct in America to want to go back to school throughout life. Faced with new problems or new opportunities Americans often turn first to the universities and colleges for help through research, teaching or consultancy.

Literacy is widespread and often there is very little difference between the blue- and white-collar workers in terms of educational background. For example, by 1994, more than 20 per cent of assembly plant workers at Chrysler's Windsor plant in Ontario were college graduates, and about 5 per cent of blue-collar workers at Ford Motor Company were university graduates (Griffith, 1994). However, an educated workforce is not necessarily well trained to meet the demands of the country's knowledge-based economy. In both the US and Canada, not enough is being done at the organizational and federal levels: there are still shortages of skilled employees.

Organizational training

Many people express amusement when they hear of McDonald's Hamburger University, Popcorn University or Holiday Inn University. These are real corporate universities that offer certificates, diplomas and degrees. They have hundreds of professors and teach thousands of students not just in the US but also throughout the world, where their companies have subsidiaries. Many US multinational companies have their own training centres, corporate colleges and even universities. They spend billions of dollars every year on the education, training and development of their employees. As well as providing training in-house, they also send their employees to attend generic or specialized university or college courses, consultants' courses, seminars and workshops, and national and international conferences.

Corporate universities and colleges such as Apple University, McDonald's Hamburger University, the Xerox Learning Centre, and the Western Electric Corporate Education Centre, offer university-standard courses and award certificates and degrees. The courses they offer do not differ very much from those offered by specialized departments within universities, except that they are related to one particular industry and one organization. Such organizational training provides the opportunity for many employees to enhance their careers by studying formally and qualifying with an award. A school leaver who starts a job at McDonald's as a crewmember could become a store manager within five years if he/she qualifies to study at McDonald's Hamburger University and graduates with a degree in hamburgerlogy. However, although large companies spend huge sums of money ($30–40 billion per annum) on training their employees, they have been able to meet only some of their corporate needs and not the needs of the economy as a whole. They have not matched the level of training provided by their main competitors in Japan and Europe (Kochan and Dyer, 1995). Therefore, it can be argued that since organizational training is not sufficient to meet the demands of the economy, it is the responsibility of individuals to get trained and of the federal governments in both countries to provide the training needed. Federally funded job training in the US has been available under the Workforce Investment Act since 2000, but 'accounts for less than one-tenth of the total annual job training investment' (O'Leary et al., 2005: 1). It is only aimed at enabling the disadvantaged members of the population to get employment.

Business and management education

The first business schools and the first formal and specialized courses in business and management began in the US in the first quarter of the twentieth century. As explained earlier, a university degree followed by a graduate degree in business administration is a prerequisite for a career in management. The most popular undergraduate degree is a business major and the most popular graduate (or postgraduate) degree is the Master of Business Administration (MBA). Management training is seen as the natural way into management through programmes such as MBAs with special emphasis on strategy, finance and HRM. The training includes modules designed to enhance managerial skills such as effective negotiating techniques, risk management, stress management and cross-cultural awareness.

Business education in the US and, to a lesser extent, in Canada is seen as a means of getting to know the 'one best way' of managing effectively: management is considered science that can be learnt in North America and implemented anywhere in the world. The focus is on universal education standards because managers are taught to manage in any environment (Tarique and Schuler, 2007). Critics have argued that this system produces international managers who 'talk more than they listen' and who manage by 'remote control' (Hampden-Turner and Trompenaars, 1993: 28).

Vocational education

In both countries the use of vocational education is limited. In the US, a vocational qualification normally can be achieved through two years of further education in a junior college. Further education is generally self-funded, though help is sometimes provided in the form of federal loans or scholarships (full or partial) that are offered by state departments, local authorities and for-profit and non-profit organizations to selected individuals. In the US, apprenticeships are not widespread and are held in very low esteem: the practice is not seen as part of the American education tradition. Vocational education is more available in Canada than in the US but is still limited in comparison with other industrialized nations.

It can be argued, however, that organizational training, mentioned above, is a form of vocational education. In practice the two are not the same: organizational training is a post-occupational training that is offered to employees already at work, while vocational education is normally a pre-occupational training that is mainly provided to young people (school leavers) to help them get into full-time employment. Most of the jobs in the services and retail sectors that would normally require vocational education and training in the UK, for example, are designed in the US in a way that does not require much of training. Employees in the US are trained to do the basics by following operation manuals and without having to think very much, and then motivated to be highly effective in doing routine and simple tasks.

Rewards and remuneration

In both countries, rewards are related to performance, though they differ greatly from one organization to another. Most organizations use job evaluation and performance appraisal to determine the wages and salaries of their employees, after taking into consideration the rate of the current minimum wage where applicable.

Performance appraisal

Performance appraisal is used by most organizations in both countries both developmentally (i.e. for establishing the training and development needs of employees) and judgementally (i.e. for establishing individual employees' achievement and rewarding them accordingly). However, there is scepticism over appraisal: one report showed that only 49 per cent of American employees thought that their managers had taken performance reviews seriously; about 44 per cent said they had received constructive feedback; 24 per cent believed that the reviews were not given regularly; and about 18 per cent felt that their long-term career objectives had not been discussed (HRM Guide. com., US, 6 March 2006). Although performance appraisal is widespread, the level of pay and other rewards in both countries often depends on whether the organization is unionized or non-unionized.

Performance-related pay and negotiated pay

In the private sector and non-unionized organizations, it is the employer who determines the level of pay, types of reward, and the working conditions. In both the US and Canada, performance appraisal is widely used in order to determine the appropriate reward for each employee. For example, companies such as Gillette, Hewlett Packard and IBM have adopted individualistic payment policies where individual employees are paid according to their performance. They use job evaluation to determine the value of the job to the firm and performance appraisal to relate performance to pay and other rewards as well as training needs. They pay a number of competitive allowances and fringe benefits such as health insurance, pension schemes, and leave entitlements.

Salary differentials between managers and workers are very high. Top managers or 'executives' are sometimes paid as much as 85 times the average worker's salary. This high financial incentive is partly a result of the widespread headhunting recruitment style used to attract management executives from competitors and successful organizations. It should be noted that promotions are based on drive and achievement rather than long-term service and seniority. All rewards are made 'with an eye to the external labour market, with total compensation having to be adequate to attract and keep needed workers' (Wheeler and McClendon, 1998: 81). In this respect, the main difference between US and Canadian non-unionized firms is that in Canada the non-unionized firms tend to follow the lead of unionized firms when it comes to pay rises.

In the public sector and unionized companies, pay and working conditions are normally influenced by collective bargaining agreements between trade unions and management, but not very often determined by them because all rewards are primarily based on individual performance. In Canada pay rises are still collective in most organizations. Many companies provide profit-sharing payments to their employees. It can be concluded that since the level of unionized firms in Canada is higher than that in the US, rewards in the US are more employer-driven and performance-related than in Canada, where many rewards are still employee-driven and negotiated.

Minimum wage

In the US, the Fair Labour Standards Act 1938 (FLSA) regulates the pay and hours of employees. It specifies the federal minimum wage, the rate of overtime pay and the training wage minimum. The FLSA was amended by the Equal Pay Act of 1963, which made it illegal to discriminate between men and women in payment for equal work. The minimum wage varies between states but it has changed very little over the last 20 years. The federal minimum wage rate was $7.25 per hour in 2009, but there are states (such as Alabama and Louisiana) that have no minimum wage, states that have a lower rate than the federal minimum wage (such as Georgia ($5.15) and Arkansas ($6.25)), and states that have a higher rate than the federal minimum wage (such as California ($8.00) and Illinois ($8.25)) (US Department of Labour, 2009). The minimum wage rate in Canada also differs from one province to another, though all provinces apply a minimum wage policy. The difference between the provinces is not wide: they range from the lowest in NWT at $8.25 per hour to the highest in Nunavut at $10.00 per hour (Human Resources and Social Development Canada, 2009).

Employee relations

As stated earlier, US employers prefer not to deal with trade unions and avoid them as much as they can. In Canada, there has always been a tradition of union recognition and collective bargaining. The Canadian system has been the most stable among those of the Anglo-Saxon countries. Describing employee relations in Canada, Thompson (1998: 107) writes that the main reasons for this stability are: 'the lack of a crisis sufficiently important to provoke change; the decentralized structure of employment relations and political systems; and the entrenched nature of employment relations institutions'. Though the two countries seem to be fundamentally different in their approach to employee relations, there have been signs of convergence as a result of the increasing presence of US multinational companies in Canada.

Trade unions

The first trade unions in the US were the craft unions formed around the 1880s. It was not until the 1930s that trade unionism became relatively active: unions took the opportunity amidst increasingly deteriorating working conditions in the Great Depression to organize a wave of effective strikes. Such events led to the introduction of the Wagner Act in 1935 during the administration of Franklin Roosevelt. The act gave the workers for the first time the right to organize and join trade unions and to go on strike. For example, Section 7 of the act states that employees have the right to 'form, join or assist labour organizations, to bargain collectively through representatives of their own choosing and to engage in concerted activities for the purpose of collective bargaining'. Consequently, many trade unions were formed, especially in the industrial sector and in particular in the car manufacturing industry, mining, and steel production. The trend of organized labour continued after the Second World War, with a significant growth in both industry and services (government) unions. In 1947, the Taft–Hartley (Labour–Management Relations) Act amended the Wagner Act in relation to trade union financial and bargaining practices. For example, it required the unions to prepare and provide annual financial statements, to give 60 days' notice of strike action, to denounce any act of violent revolution, and to express their opposition to communism (Wheeler and McClendon, 1998). The president was given the right to intervene and stop any strike action that was seen by the government as harmful to the country's economy. In 1959, the Wagner Act was further amended by the Landrum–Griffin Act (Labour–Management Reporting and Disclosure Act) which incorporated a Bill of Rights of Union Members granting legal rights to union members to inspect their unions' accounts and records, to nominate and to elect their representatives and to participate in union meetings. Since then unions have been legally recognized and employees have been allowed to form and to join trade unions, but there has been no obligation on the employers to recognize the unions. In general, trade unions in the US have been weaker and less organized than their counterparts in the other Anglo-Saxon countries.

In Canada, the first trade unions were formed by craftsmen around the 1870s, but it was not until the 1930s that most of the manufacturing industries were unionized. Many Canadian workers also joined US international trade unions in the manufacturing sector and in particular the automobile industry. It was the car workers' strike at General Motors, Oshawa, Ontario, in 1937 that established industrial trade unionism in Canada (Thompson, 1998). Until the late 1960s, labour relations in Canada were very similar to those in the US, as most of the US trade unions had a significant membership in Canada. According to Thompson (1998: 97), the Canadian 'labour relations legislation combines many features of the US National Labour Relations Act (Wagner Act) and older Canadian pattern of reliance on conciliation of labour disputes', though there are differences in the details of implementing such legislation. The rise of public sector trade unionism and the change of labour policies in Canada led to a significant decline in Canadian workers' membership in the US trade unions. For example, they declined from more than 70 per cent in 1966 to less than 30 per cent in 1996 (Thompson, 1998: 94). The labour movement in Canada has become more organized and grown further apart from its US counterparts over the last 20 years. The Liberal government, which dominated Canada's politics in this period, developed a comprehensive labour law system by which many codes and regulations were issued to protect employees from unfair treatment. Trade unions in general and those in the public sector in particular became more protected, more accepted, better organized, and stronger in Canada than in the US.

A number of factors have changed the role of trade unions in both countries. For example:

- Trade union membership has declined significantly, leading to the reduction in the financial conditions, organizational integration and bargaining power of trade unions. In the US, trade unions' membership density reached its highest levels in the 1950s. The main decline has been in the manufacturing sector, while the government and services sectors have maintained a reasonable membership. In Canada union density has declined more gradually (Gunderson et al., 2005; Cross, 2005b).
- Many trade unions had to merge in order to reorganize their membership and strengthen themselves. Some small unions were taken over by large ones in order to consolidate their power in the face of increasing employer oppression.
- In both countries, the major growth in trade unionism since the 1960s has been among while-collar workers, mainly in the public sector (civil service, education and health). The rate of growth has been higher in Canada than in the US.
- Japanese employee relations' practices such as single-status, single-union, strike-free agreements, and pendulum arbitration, have been adopted by a number of companies in both countries. Single-company unions and single-workplace agreements are now common in the manufacturing sector in both the US and Canada.

In both countries, trade unions are normally affiliated to a congress, federation or confederation. The Canadian Labour Congress (CLC) represents more than 80 trade unions or about 60 per cent of Canada's trade union members, but most of the negotiations between the unions and management take place at the local level. There is also the Confederation of National Trade Unions (CNTU), which represents about 6 per cent of trade union members (mainly from Quebec). In contrast to the CLC, the CNTU has been politically active, supporting the independence of Quebec, and has a centralized structure with considerable power in representing its members. In the US, the American Federation of Labour–Congress of Industrial Organizations (AFL-CIO), does not get involved in collective bargaining. It has a public relations and a civic representational role on behalf of its affiliates.

Collective bargaining

In both countries, although most collective bargaining takes place between a single union and a single employer at the local (organizational) level, there are also multi-employer and multi-union agreements at industry and national levels. Regardless of the level or place of bargaining, the process is always formal and has to be with a certified trade union only. In the US, the National Labour Relations Board (NLRB) has overall responsibility for making sure that labour–management negotiations are conducted according the existing employment laws and that both parties use fair labour practices and bargain with the aim of reaching an agreement. The mandatory issues that the parties bargain over are pay, wages, hours of work, and the terms and conditions of employment. The refusal to bargain over these issues by either of the parties constitutes an unfair labour practice. Both parties are required by law to meet at an appropriate time and place, and to produce a contract that is legally binding; the unions must make a reasonable demand and the management must make a realistic offer. When one of the parties complains that the other party has used unfair labour practices, the NLRB intervenes by making an order which is enforced by law. Strikes during the period of collective bargaining can be seen as unfair practice because in most cases the contract of agreement contains a no-strike clause.

In Canada, the process of collective bargaining is decentralized and takes place at the unit level as management–single union negotiation followed by multi–management–single union negotiation. This does not mean, however, that there are no company-wide, regional and federal bargaining processes. They exist in large provinces and in big companies in the transport, telecommunications, steel, paper, construction and automobile industries. There are also a number of joint management–worker committees, such as the health and safety committee, the public relations committee, and the research and development committee – depending on the type and size of the organization – which use their regular meetings as collective bargaining venues.

In countries where collective bargaining agreements are legally binding, such as in the US and Canada, the unions tend to adopt a cooperative rather than an adversarial approach to dealing with management, and they prefer to negotiate treaties such as giving up the right to strike in return for long-term job security and better quality of working life. A number of trade unions in the US, such as the United Steelworkers Union, have opted for a cooperative or 'concession bargaining' approach to meet their demands. They do so not just because collective agreements are legally binding but also because they have become too weak to fight.

Industrial action

The level of industrial action in the US and Canada is very low and has dropped significantly over the last twenty years. For example, the average annual amount of time lost in the 1990s due to industrial action in Canada was only half of that lost in the 1980s (Akyeampong, 2001). In both countries, strike action or an action short of a strike is legal only after a majority vote by the members in a secret ballot. In the US, the NLRB regulates the secret ballot elections to ensure that all eligible workers have a free choice in deciding for or against strike action. When there is a majority vote for industrial action 'the NLRB issues a certification that requires the employer to bargain in good faith with the union' (Wheeler and McClendon, 1998: 79).

Settlement of industrial disputes

When the two bargaining parties fail to reach an agreement they resort to third party intervention, which can be in a form of conciliation, mediation or arbitration. The most popular form of settling disputes in both the US and Canada is mediation. In the US, the Federal Mediation and Conciliation Service (FMCS) is authorized by the Labour Relations Act 1947 (revised in 1978) to provide mediation to the parties in dispute when they fail to reach an agreement. The FMCS mediates all collective bargaining disputes except those in the railway and the airline industries because their disputes are normally referred to the National Mediation Board (NMB). In Canada, the settlement of industrial disputes is through mediation except in some public sector organizations or essential services, where arbitration is compulsory.

The number of mediation cases in both countries has declined steadily over the last two decades. This decline is attributed to the overall decline in industrial action, the decline in trade union power, the rise in an interest-based approach to negotiations, the long-term agreements between the unions and management, and the rise in the use of preventive mediation. Many companies use preventive mediation (PM) to prevent the risk of strike action. In the US, one of main roles of the FMCS is to help the unions and management to understand each other and to prevent industrial disputes. The help is normally in the form of workshops in labour–management partnership building, cultural diversity in the workplace, interest-based bargaining, and even violence prevention in the workplace.

Summary

1 The US and Canada are economically intertwined because of their close geographical location, strong trade relations, common socio-economic and historical backgrounds, and similar organizational characteristics.

2 Although they have much in common, they also have some distinct differences in the details of approach to employee relations and in the practice of some HRM functions.

3 The management theory and practice in both countries has gone through numerous transformations over the years as a result of industrial development, technological changes and increasing trade and business competition at home and from abroad. The labour markets of both countries can be described as flexible, diverse, relatively stable, and increasingly knowledge-based. The demand side of the labour markets of both countries has been driven by a knowledge-based economy associated with international competition and technological developments. The supply side has been characterized by a rise in the highly educated workforce, a relative increase in older employees, and significant participation by women and ethnic minorities (immigrant labour).

4   Contemporary management and organisational behaviour in the US have their roots in the development of management thinking since the start of the twentieth century and in particular since the advent of 'scientific management', which was based on the view that managers develop the best methods for their workers to carry out their tasks. However, such changes over the last five decades have culminated in the development of a management approach that has been characterized by strategic awareness, trade union avoidance, legally binding employee–employer agreements, and managing diversity.

5   As well as the use of conventional methods of recruitment, employers in the US and Canada use more aggressive methods such as poaching and headhunting employees from competitors and other successful organizations, and taking affirmative action in recruiting women, the old and disabled people.

6   The process of selection in both the US and Canada is formalized, structured and rigorous. To avoid claims of discrimination in recruitment and selection, they use more objective and properly validated methods of selection such as structured interviews and quantitatively measured tests. They make use of a number of ability, personality and psychometric tests.

7   In both the US and Canada, nearly everyone is literate and educated, though this does not mean that the workforce is well trained to meet the demands of the country's knowledge-based economy. In both countries, there are still shortages of skilled employees.

8   US and Canadian organizations have been unable to match the level of training provided by their main competitors in Japan and Europe. Vocational education is more available in Canada than in the US but still limited in comparison with other industrialized nations.

9   In both countries, rewards are related to performance but they differ greatly from one organization to another and between the unionized and non-unionized organizations. Most organizations uses job evaluation and performance appraisal to determine the wages and salaries of their employees, after taking into consideration the rate of the current minimum wage.

10 In the public sector and unionized companies, pay and working conditions are normally influenced by collective bargaining agreements between trade unions and management. In Canada pay rises are still collective in most organizations and many companies provide profit-sharing payments to their employees. Since the level of unionized firms in Canada is higher than that of the US, rewards in the US are more employer driven and performance related than in Canada, where many rewards are still employee driven and negotiated.

11 Trade unions in general and those in the public sector in particular are more protected, more accepted, better organized and stronger in Canada than in the US.

12 In countries where collective bargaining agreements are legally binding, such as the US and Canada, the unions tend to adopt a cooperative rather than an adversarial approach to management.

13 US employers prefer not to deal with trade unions and they avoid them as much as they can. In Canada, there has always been a tradition of union recognition and collective bargaining. Though the two countries seem to be fundamentally different in their approach there have been signs of convergence as a result of the increasing presence of US multinational companies in Canada.

Revision questions

Chapter 1 provides a review task designed to consolidate your learning from this chapter. Please see Box 1.2.

In addition, the following questions are designed to help you revise this chapter:

1 What are the main management issues that characterize the North American approach to management?
2 As an HR manager of a French company in Canada, write a report to the company's board of directors in Paris describing the main similarities and the main differences in HRM functions (recruitment and selection, training and development, rewards system, and employee relations) between the US and Canada.
3 How far is managing diversity in the US and Canada a new strategic HRM policy of equal employment and how far is it a substitute for employment equity?

References

Agócs, C. and Burr, C. (1996) 'Employment equity, affirmative action and managing diversity: assessing the differences', *International Journal of Manpower*, 17(4/5): 30–45.

Akyeampong, E. (2001) 'Time Lost due to Industrial Disputes', *Canadian Economic Observer*, Sep. 2001, Statistics Canada, Catalogue no. 11-010-XPB.

Beer M., Spector B., Lawrence P.R., Quinn Mills D. and Walton, R.E. (1984) *Managing Human Assets*, New York: Free Press.

Beer, M., Spector, B., Lawrence, P.R., Quinn Mills, D., and Walton, R.E. (1985) *Human Resource Management: A General Manager's Perspective – Text and Cases*, New York: Free Press.

Belout, A., Dolan, S.L. and Saba, T. (2001) 'Trends and emerging practices in human resource management: the Canadian scene', *International Journal of Manpower*, 22(3): 207–15.

Caute, D. (1979) *The Great Fear: The Anti-Communist Purge under Truman and Eisenhower*, New York: Touchstone.

CIA World Factbook (2010) accessed online at: www.cia.gov/library/publications/the-world-factbook/geos/ca.html_and www.cia.gov/library/publications/the-world-factbook/geos/us.html, on 07 September 2010.

Cross, P. (2005a) 'Recent changes in the labour market', *Canadian Economic Observer*, March 2005, Statistics Canada, Catalogue no. 11-010.

Cross, P. (2005b) 'Canada's economic growth in review', *Canadian Economic Observer*, April 2005, Statistics Canada, Catalogue no. 11-010.

Elkins, T.J. (2007) 'New HR challenges in the dynamic environment of legal compliance', in Werner, S. (ed.), *Managing Human Resources in North America*, London: Routledge, 44–58.

Fombrum, C.J., Tichy. N.M. and Devanna, M.A (1984) *Strategic Human Resource Management*, New York: John Wiley.

Gatley, S., Lessem, R. and Altman, Y. (1996) *Comparative Management: A Transcultural Odyssey*, London: McGraw-Hill.

Gesteland, R. (1996) *Cross-Cultural Business Behaviour*, Copenhagen: Copenhagen Business School.

Greco, J. (1998) 'America's changing workforce', *Journal of Business Strategy*, 19(2):.43–7.

Griffith, V. (1994) 'Blue-collar team, white-collar wise', *Financial Times*, 11 May 1994.

Guest, D. (1990) 'Human resource management and the American dream', *Journal of Management Studies*, 27: 503–23.

Gunderson, M., Ponak, A. and Taras, D.G. (2005) (eds.) *Union-Management Relations in Canada*, 5th edition, Toronto: Pearson Addison Wesley.

Hampden-Turner, C. and Trompenaars, F. (1993) *The Seven Cultures of Capitalism: Value Systems for Creating Wealth in the United States, Britain, Japan, Germany, France, Sweden and the Netherlands*, New York: Doubleday.

Handy, C. (1989) 'The United States', in Handy, C., Gordon, C., Gow, I. and Randlesome, C. (eds), *Making Managers*, London: Pitman, 51–81.

Hofstede, G. (1980) *Culture's Consequences: International Differences in Work Related Values*, London: Sage.

Hofstede, G. (2001) *Culture's Consequences: International differences in work related values*, 2nd edn, London: Sage.

Hollinshead, G. and Leat, M. (1995) *Human Resource Management: An International and Comparative Perspective*, London: Pitman.

Jain, H.C. and Verma, A. (1996) 'Managing workforce diversity for competitiveness: the Canadian experience', *International Journal of Manpower*, 17(4/5): 14–29.

Kochan, T. and Dyer, L. (1995) 'HRM: an American view', in Storey, J. (ed.), *Human Resource Management: A Critical Text*, London: Thomson International Business, 332–51.

Kochan, T.A., Katz, H.C. and McKersie, R.B. (1986) *The Transformation of American Industrial Relations*, New York: Basic Books.

Konrad, A.M. and Deckop, J. (2001) 'Human resource management trends in the USA: challenges in the midst of prosperity', *International Journal of Manpower*, 22(3): 269–78.

Mills, A.J. and Helms Hatfield, J.C. (1999) 'From Imperialism to Globalization: Internationalization and the Management Text' in Clegg, S.R., Ibarra-Colado, E. and Bueno-Rodriquez, L. (eds.), *Global Management: Universal Theories and Local Realities*, London: Sage, 37–67.

O'Leary, C.J., Straits, R.A. and Wandner, S.A. (2005) 'Reconsidering job training and the workforce investment Act', *Employment Research*, 12(2): 1–4.

Perrewé, P.L. (2007) 'The changing family and HRM', in Werner, S. (ed.), *Managing Human Resources in North America*, London: Routledge, 60–71.

Schellenberg, G., Turcotte, M. and Ran, B. (2002) 'Post-retirement employment', in *Perspectives on Labour and Income*, 6(9), Statistics Canada, Catalogue no. 75-001-XIE.

Tarique, I. and Schuler, R.S. (2007), 'Staffing and developing the multinational workforce', in Werner, S. (ed.), *Managing Human Resources in North America*, London: Routledge, 11–25.

Thompson, M. (1998) 'Employment relations in Canada', in Bamber, G.J. and Lansbury, R.D. (eds), *International and Comparative Employment Relations*, 3rd edn, London: Sage, 89–109.

Walton, R. (1985) 'From control to commitment in the workplace', *Harvard Business Review*, 63 (March-April): 76–84.

Werner, S. (ed.) (2007) *Managing Human Resources in North America*, London: Routledge.

Wheeler, H.N. and McClendon, J.A. (1998) 'Employment relations in the United States', in Bamber, G.J. and Lansbury, R.D. (eds), *International and Comparative Employment Relations*, 3rd edn, London: Sage, 63–88.

5

The UK and Ireland

LEARNING OUTCOMES

The chapter is designed to help you understand, for the UK and Ireland:

1. The (a) economic, (b) political, and (c) cultural contexts in which managers work;
2. The main trends in the labour market;
3. The typical features of (a) management policies and practices and (b) organizational structure and behaviour;
4. The main policies and practices of human resource management with regard to: (a) recruitment and selection; (b) training and development; (c) rewards and remuneration; and (d) employee relations.

Introction

Introduction

The United Kingdom (UK) and the Republic of Ireland (Ireland) are closely related geographically and historically. Ireland was part of the UK from 1801 until 1921 and inherited much of the UK's management and employee relations system. Until the 1970s they had similar economic and labour market policies, there was a flow of labour from Ireland to the UK, and most of Irish trade was with the UK. A number of British trade unions operate in Ireland, and in both countries the practice of HRM is formally accredited by the UK-based Charted Institute of Personnel and Development (CIPD, formerly IPD and IPM).

In recent years, both countries' systems of management and organization have diverged as a result of economic, political and legal reforms. They have diverged in, for instance, their international trade policies, their relations with other members of the European Union (EU) and with the US, and in their internal policies, especially education and training, and employee relations.

Table 5.1 Basic statistical indicators, the UK and Ireland

Country	Area (sq km)	Population (July 2010 est.)	Population growth (2010) %	GDP – real growth rate (2009) %	Inflation rate (July 2010 est.) %	Work-force (2009 est.) Million	Unemployment rate (2009) %
UK	243610	61113205	0.279	−4.9	2.2	31.37	7.6
Ireland	70280	4203200	1.12	−7.6	−4.5	2.187	11.8

Source: CIA World Factbook, 2010 and World Bank, 2009

Ireland joined the EU in 1973 and has had a positive approach to European integration. It was one of the first states to sign the Social Charter and to adopt the Euro as its national currency. The UK joined the EU in 1974 and has adopted a sceptical approach to many European policies. It has not joined the Euro zone. Ireland did not introduce the kind of radical and anti-union employee relations reforms that the UK's Conservative government introduced in the 1980s and 1990s. (See Table 5.1 for basic statistical indicators.)

Socio-economic and political context

Economics

Both countries are members of the OECD and are among the most industrialized nations in the world. When the UK was the cradle of the Industrial Revolution and the pioneer of modern industrialization, migrant workers from Ireland contributed significantly the UK's manual workforce. The UK developed a larger and more technologically advanced manufacturing system than Ireland, which remained dependent on agriculture and had very limited industrial activity.

Both countries have been transformed over the years. Ireland has seen an exceptional socio-economic development since the 1990s and has become a modern industrialized country with one of the highest economic growth rates in the European Union (Heraty and Morley, 2000, 2003). In the late 1980s the Irish government introduced the 'Tallaght Strategy' aimed at tackling economic and social problems by cutting taxes, reducing borrowing, and freeing the economy to foreign direct investment and internal competition. Such reforms sparked the economic miracle that made Ireland a 'Celtic Tiger' akin to the 'Asian Tigers' of Singapore, Hong Kong, South Korea and Taiwan (Dundon et al., 2007). These economic reforms have been strengthened by the adoption of a 'social partnership' approach to employee relations since the 1990s. Foreign investors flocked to Ireland because of a low corporate tax rate (10 per cent), low inflation, the availability of a young and skilled workforce, and its stable political system. The US and the EU member states invested heavily in Ireland, which suddenly became one of the world exporters of machinery and high-tech equipment. Ireland also became one of the world's call centre capitals, with a share of about 30 per cent of Europe's operations (Cooke, 1999: 4). Therefore the increase in foreign direct investment led to a fall in the level of unemployment and a substantial rise in consumer spending, making the country one of the thriving members of European Union. Although the economy is heavily dependent on exports, there has been a significant growth in construction, retailing and services. However, the country has been very hard hit by the 'credit crunch' recession. The real growth rate (GDP) declined from 5.6 per cent in 2007 to −3.5 per cent in 2008 and to −7.6 per cent in 2009 (OECD Factbook, 2010).

The British economy is the fifth largest in the world and the second largest in Europe. It has grown over the years from being driven by industry and manufacturing, and the export of machinery, cars, coal and finished products, to a services- and knowledge-based economy, and from an economy dominated by public entities to a free market economy driven by the private sector. Over the 1980s and 1990s most publicly owned companies such as telecommunications, airlines, railways, coal and steel, and many utilities such as gas, electricity and water, were privatized as a result of government policies aimed at promoting enterprise culture, flexibility in the labour market, and small business development (Kessler and Bayliss, 1995; Goodman et al., 1997; de Menezes and Wood, 2006). The biggest transformation has been in the decline of the manufacturing sector and the rise of the service sector, the financial sector in particular. The manufacturing industry, which was the backbone of the British economy, declined gradually over the years to account currently for about 16 per cent of the national output, employing less than 13 per cent of the total workforce, though it remains an important producer of foreign exports. The current knowledge-based economy is based on the service sector, which accounts for more than 46 per cent of the GDP.

Politics

Both countries have a parliamentary democracy with a prime minister as the head of government. The UK is a monarchy, while Ireland is a republic with an elected president. In the UK there has been a partial devolution of power to Scotland, Wales and Northern Ireland. Scotland has its own parliament and Wales and Northern Ireland have assemblies. The legal system is based on custom and practice, and there is no written national constitution. The two parties that have dominated British politics for more than 60 years are Labour and Conservative.

By contrast, in the Republic of Ireland, there has not been a single-party government since the late 1980s. There is a written constitution of 1937 which prescribes the functions of the country's bicameral parliament (*Oireachtas*) which consists of a senate or upper house (*Seanad Éireann*) and a lower house (*Dáil Éireann*). The constitution prescribes also the judiciary system and defines the basic rights of Irish citizens. Administratively, Ireland is divided into 26 counties and each county is made up of constituencies depending on its size. The local government is administered according to the Local Government Act of 1991 in a two-tier structure. Local governments are funded by the central government and have responsibility for the planning and provision of local services.

Culture

Ethnically, both countries have become increasingly diverse. Historically, the UK comprises a mixture of English, Scottish, Welsh and Irish cultures that are still distinctive. By contrast, Ireland was, until recently, a homogenous nation dominated by one ethnic group, namely the Celts. The country had virtually no minorities until the last quarter of the twentieth century: emigration had been mainly out of, rather than into, Ireland. In the UK, the post-Second World War economic boom required a supply of foreign labour. This was drawn mainly from people in the former colonies of the British empire, in particular Afro-Caribbeans, Indians, Pakistanis and Bangladeshis. Over the years new cultural norms and values, though sometimes alien and alienating, have complemented and added value to the richness of the diverse British culture. Both the UK and Ireland are now multicultural societies. In terms of work-related values, Hofstede (2001) attributed the same cultural dimensions to the UK and Ireland: they scored low on power distance and uncertainty avoidance but high on individualism and relatively high on masculinity. They also scored low on long term orientation.

================ **ACTIVITY 1** ================

List seven artefacts and symbols that can be associated with British culture (for example, the red double decker bus) and with Irish culture (for example, Guinness).

Labour market trends

Equal opportunities legislation is a critical feature of both British and Irish labour markets. In both countries it is illegal to discriminate between employees on the grounds of gender, race, nationality, colour, sexual orientation, disability and religion. The British labour market is one of the least regulated in the developed world and is characterized by a trend towards self-employment, short-term employment and flexible working. The total workforce stands at about 30 million (CIPD, 2006). Most of the working population is in the services and the government sectors (52.4 per cent and 28 per cent respectively) while the manufacturing and construction sectors share 18.2 per cent of the workforce, and agriculture accounts for only about 1 per cent (see Table 5.2). There has been a significant shift from the large plant with many thousands of long-term and full-time employees to small plants with less than 500 employees, most of them on temporary or part-time employment. Heavy, large-scale production manufacturing plants have given way to light, hi-tech industries and services. The largest increases in employment have been in professional, managerial, administrative, clerical, and personal and protection services jobs.

Table 5.2 Workforce distribution by occupation in 2006 (%), UK and Ireland

Country	Agriculture %	Industry %	Services %
UK	1.4	18.2	80.4
Ireland	6	27	67

Source: CIA *World Factbook*, 2010

The Irish labour market has been less deregulated than that of the UK. About two-thirds of the workforce are employed in the services. The Irish workforce has grown since the late 1980s. It increased by more than 35 per cent over the 1990s. Until the recent 'credit crunch' recession, there was strong growth in financial and retailing sectors. There was also a significant growth in the number of people employed in the catering and the social and personal services sector. The construction sector increased sharply as a result of the boom in the property market and then dropped suddenly because of the recession.

All indicators show that the labour markets of both countries are often characterized by shortages in skilled labour, increasing female employment, increasing migrant labour, an increasingly older workforce, and by the use of flexible working practices.

Shortages of skilled labour

The skills shortage is a continuous global problem. It has become more and more acute in the UK and Ireland over recent years, especially in the IT and knowledge-based professions on which their current economies depend. According to a CIPD quarterly report (2004), about 28 per cent of British employers had problems recruiting employees with technical and professional skills. Also about 19 per cent had difficulties in recruiting people with management skills. Similarly, Ireland, which used to export skilled labour to other countries, has come to experience significant shortages of skilled and professional labour. For example, at the turn of this century Ireland needed between 8,000 to 10,000 skilled construction workers from outside the country each year (Cooke, 1999: 4). Some of these skills have been met by accepting emmigrants from Eastern Europe.

Employment of women

The long-term growth in the number of female employees in both countries has been attributed to changes in labour market needs, as many jobs that are available seem to be more attractive, or are seen as more suitable for, women. In the UK, the participation rate of women in the labour market has increased sharply over the last three decades, while that of men has dropped slightly. The major employers of women in the UK and Ireland are the retail and hospitality sectors, followed by the health service sector, but most of the women who work in this sector are in lower-paid jobs (Harris et al., 2007).

Hakim (2000) argues that women exercise work–life preferences according to their social conditions. Their preferences divide them into three groups; work-centred, adaptive, and non-career-oriented. The work-centred women, who make up about 20 per cent of female workforce, are likely to have no children and are committed to their jobs and work on a full-time basis. The non-career-oriented or the 'home-centred' women, who also make up about 20 per cent of the female workforce, are likely to have children and to stay at home, and prefer not to work. The adaptive women, who make up the remaining 60 per cent, are the most responsive to employment, as they prefer to work, but most of them work on a part-time basis because of family and other commitments that prevent them from having a continuous working career. From a study of sales assistants in 31 outlets of three major retailers, Harris et al. (2007: 497) state that 'whilst working part-time enabled women to manage their family and domestic commitments, it was widely perceived ... that part-time staff were disadvantaged in terms of career opportunities compared to full-time staff'.

MINI CASE STUDY 5

Ladies First (the UK)

In the preparations for the 2010 general elections the British Conservative party leader David Cameron said he would impose all-women shortlists in order to increase the number of female MP candidates. At a conference on equality at Westminster Cameron said that almost 30 per cent of Conservative candidates would be women because, he argued, the shortage of women MPs had been a real problem for parliament and even greater problem for his party.

Questions

1 To what extent was David Cameron's decision driven by changes in the labour market rather than by political motives?
2 Discuss the advantages and the disadvantages (if any) of targeting women for political and senior management positions.

The older workforce

In contrast to the UK, Ireland has the youngest population in Western Europe with a median age of 34.5 (compared to 39.8 for the UK) years, while only 12 per cent (16.2 per cent for the UK) of the population are above the age of 65 (see Table 5.3). While the number of people in employment between the ages of 15 and 24 has declined, the number of those above the age of 55 has increased in both countries.

Table 5.3 Age structure (%) (2010), the UK and Ireland

Country	0–14 years %	15–64 years %	Over 65 %	Median age (years)	Life expectancy at birth (for men and women)
UK	16.7	67.1	16.2	39.8	79
Ireland	20.9	67.1	12	34.5	78.24

Source: CIA *World Factbook*, 2010

In the UK, after years of age discrimination, especially in the 1980s and 1990s when many people above the age of 50 were considered unemployable (see Glover and Branine, 2001), there has been a slight increase in the employment of older people. According to a CIPD survey, the over-50 employees were ranked by their employers as performing better than the rest of the workforce, and they were seen to be more productive, more loyal and less likely to be absent from work than other employees (CIPD, 2005).

Employment of migrant workers

The UK has traditionally been dependent on the flow of immigrant labour from all over the world. Ireland has, after many years of being described as the 'exporter' of hard-working manual labour to the Anglo-Saxon countries, become one of the highest 'importers' of migrant workers in Europe. With increasing international competition and the high demand for special knowledge-based professional and technical skills, many employers in the UK and Ireland have had to recruit from overseas to find talented and skilled labour. In 2007 it was estimated that 'in comparative terms, Ireland's current rate of immigration per capita is double that of the US' (Dundon et al., 2007: 502). Immigrant labour made up about 8 per cent of the total Irish labour force of about 2,180,300 in May 2006 (CSO, 2007). In the UK, according to a CIPD survey, almost one in three employers thought that they would employ immigrant workers because they found them committed, loyal and hard working (CIPD, 2004). Sectors like agriculture, retailing, construction and transport have benefited most from migrant labour from Eastern and Central Europe (Dench et al., 2006; Morgan and Finniear, 2009). In 2006, about 50 per cent of foreign labour was from Poland (Dundon et al., 2007).

Flexible working practices

The labour market of both countries has seen an increase in the use of flexible working practices such as part-time work, job sharing and home-based working. A CIPD survey (2005) found that 4 in 10 employers planned to recruit employees on temporary or fixed-term contracts. Successive CIPD quarterly reports have shown that the recruitment of part-time, temporary and fixed-term staff has been on the increase. The most common practice was part-time work, which was used by some 81 per cent of the employers surveyed. It was reported that although other forms of flexible working practice had been less common, many employers intended to introduce them in the future. Many employers have used part-time work because it provides them with the flexibility to meet the fluctuations in demand for their goods and services, and to respond to the needs of individual employees who prefer to combine work with family commitments (Penn, 1995; Hakim, 1997; Branine, 1999; Dick and Hyde, 2006). Goodman et al. (1997: 56) pointed out that 'many of the new jobs for women or men are based on atypical contracts – such as part-time, short-term, fixed contracts, contracts subsidised by government training programs – or other forms of less-skilled, less-secure and poorly paid employment'. Most of those who work part time are women, particularly working mothers (DTI, 2003), although many studies have found that in the UK women, whose children are above the school age, like to work on a full-time rather than part-time basis (EOC, 2006; Harris et al., 2007).

The unemployment rate

The rate of unemployment in both countries was relatively low over the 1990s and the 2000s until the recent economic downturn created by the credit crunch. In the UK, unemployment had grown significantly over the 1980s to reach about 12 per cent. It then fell to around 6 per cent by the late 1990s and to around 4 per cent in 2003. Most of the unemployment in the 1980s and early 1990s was created by the decline in manufacturing industries and the privatization of public companies. For example, over 2 million jobs were lost in the manufacturing sector between 1979 and 1987. The number of people looking for work before the credit crunch (2008) was at about 1.42 million or about 4.7 per cent of the workforce. In Ireland, the level of unemployment dropped from about 18 per cent in 1986 to around 4 per cent of the active population in 2007, and then started to rise from just above 6 per cent in 2008 to nearly 12 per cent by the end of 2009 (OECD, 2009).

MINI CASE STUDY 6

Work As You Like and Do What We Ask You to (the UK)

The HR manager of a large British supermarket in Edinburgh was quoted as saying:

> in our superstore we have full-time and part-time workers working together in all shifts. You cannot tell the difference between them. Some of our cashiers job share while others work flexitime. It is good for them and for us. When we offer jobs to our applicants we tell them to work as they like but they have to do what we ask them. It sound confusing but it is true. Perhaps it is too good to be true.

Questions

1 Why is it good for a supermarket to employ full-time and part-time workers?
2 List the main advantages and disadvantages of working flexibly for women with school age children, for people above the age of 65, and for students in full-time education.

Management and organization

The type of management that is practised in the UK and Ireland stands between the US and European management perspectives, or, in other words, between unitarist and pluralist traditions. While the British system seems to be becoming more American unitarist, the Irish system is more European pluralist. In the UK, there have been many changes in employment relations since the 1980s. Many changes were introduced by the Conservative government between 1979 and 1997 in order to curb the power of trade unions and to promote 'the decentralisation and individualisation of the employment relationship' (Goodman et al., 1997: 34). The process of individualization has been pursued through the introduction of a variety of techniques such as performance-related pay, employee direct involvement, outsourcing, and flexible working policies.

A number of studies have reported that the management of employee relations and organizational behaviour in the UK (see for example Guest, 1987; Handy et al., 1988; Storey, 1995; Legge, 1995; Cully et al., 1999; Budhwar, 2000; Poole et al., 2005; Watson et al., 2007) and in Ireland (Gunnigle et al., 1995; Gunnigle et al., 2001; D'Art and Turner, 2002; Wallace et al., 2004) are generally characterized by strategic integration, the devolution of HR activities to line managers, the outsourcing of management functions, the use of collective bargaining with or without the unions, pragmatism, flexibility and cost reduction, commitment to quality improvement, and an international orientation. We shall look at each of these factors in turn.

Strategic integration

In both countries management functions are integrated with corporate strategy. For example, from a study of HRM practices in 93 British organizations, Budhwar (2000) found that about 35 per cent had the HR department involved in the formation of corporate strategy from the outset and 42 per cent had actively involved HRM in the implementation stage of their organizational strategies. He concluded that there was a growing strategic and proactive role for HRM managers in the process of decision-making. Similarly, Gunnigle et al. (1995) analysed the Cranet Survey data related to the practice of human resource management in the Republic of Ireland and reported that the majority of Irish companies had a formal HR strategy, that nearly 50 per cent of HR managers were involved in the company's strategy formulation, and that many of them were members of the board of directors.

However, it has been observed that since the 1980s HRM activities have been devolved to line managers. The move of HRM activities from HR specialists to line managers occurred not just because of the decline in personnel and the rise of human resource management, but also because of the realization that people management is too important for organizational performance and competitive advantage to be left to HR specialists alone (Watson et al., 2007). The line managers become fully or partly responsible, for example, for the recruitment and selection, training and development, reward and remuneration, and health and safety of employees. While line managers take control of HR practices, HR managers concentrate on strategic organizational issues.

Outsourcing

British and Irish employers have often relied on management consultants for the delivery of some of their management practices. Some companies find it more cost effective and more professional to have some of their managerial activities carried out by external experts rather than internal managers (Ward et al., 2001; Houseman et al., 2003; Forde et al., 2008). For example, many small and medium size enterprises that have no HR specialists or HR departments rely on external agencies for the delivery of HR functions such as recruitment and selection, training, performance appraisal and the production of payroll (TUC, 2007; Forde and Slater, 2006; Forde et al., 2008). According to the 2004 UK Workplace Employment Relations Survey (WERS) (Kersley et al., 2006), 86 per cent of all organizations that employed 10 people or more had arrangements in place for outsourcing some of their activities, including building maintenance and cleaning, computer services, security, payroll, transport and training, temporary employment, printing, catering and recruitment. From a study of outsourcing human resource management, Woodall et al. (2007: 249) conclude that 'outsourcing represents a step change beyond simple sub-contracting, and is now extensively used in respect of a range of low skilled work throughout UK workplaces'. They add: 'the outsourcing of core management functions such as HRM is a growing area that has only just begun to receive attention'.

Collective bargaining

Until recently most British and Irish employers recognized trade unions and tended not to avoid them as the US employers do. There were some cases of de-recognition but they were not widespread (Kessler and Bayliss, 1995). In fact most of the companies that did not recognize the unions were either small in size or historically known for their non-recognition of trade unions. For example, Marks and Spencer has never recognized trade unions. Some US companies in the UK and Ireland such as IBM and Hewlett Packard, and fast food companies such as McDonald's, Burger King, KFC and Pizza Hut, also do not recognize trade unions. In the UK, the number of organizations with no union membership increased from 27 per cent in 1984 to 36 per cent in 1990 and 47 per cent in 1998 (Cully et al., 1999). However, according to Goodman et al. (1997: 42) the decline of trade union power did not lead to a significant shift in employers' attitude to collective bargaining arrangements. Many of them retained their contacts with the unions while 'initiating improved direct employee communications arrangements, total quality management (TQM), team working and other techniques associated with human resource management' with the aim of seeking 'more flexibility and employee commitment'. Collective bargaining is the preferred way of employer–employee relations with or without the recognition of trade unions.

Since the 1990s the adversarial relationship between the management and trade unions has been replaced by a more cooperative approach, called partnership (Ackers and Payne, 1998; Ackers et al., 2005), as will be explained below under the section on employee relations. From a longitudinal study of British managers' attitudes and behaviour in industrial relations over 20 years, Poole et al. (2005) found that as the unions have become weaker, managers have become less hostile to them, and there has been a 'lack of any real evidence of the replacement of representative, trade-union-based modes of employee participation by individual or group forms' (131).

Pragmatism

Managers in the UK and to a lesser extent in Ireland take a pragmatic approach to management, especially in their relationships with each other. They tend not to show their emotions strongly to their colleagues or their subordinates. A common attitude is that what is good can be better and what is bad can be worse: when asked 'How are you?' the reply will often be, 'not too bad'. This type of pragmatism is described thus by Torrington and Holden (1992: 22): 'open conflict is avoided at all costs and the British manager seeks to convince everyone that he is pleasant, sociable and wishing to please everybody'. Although there may be a lot of interaction and exchange of information within the organization, it is not easy to get access to company secrets and to decisions made behind closed doors. Managers are secretive and very discreet in their dealings with outsiders.

Flexibility and cost reductions

The flexible firm model (see Atkinson, 1984; Atkinson and Meager, 1986) was developed in the UK as a management strategy adopted by British employers in response to fluctuations in demand for their products in difficult times. Numerical and functional flexibility are being used as strategic decisions in order to reduce fixed costs and improve productivity. By dividing employees into core and periphery, the theory of the flexible firm seems to have characterized much of the change in employment policy. There has been a shift from the standard eight hours a day and five days a week to more fragmented and individually-tailored arrangements that are deemed to be in the interests of both employees and employers. Such employment policies have led to an increase in flexible working, subcontracting, home-based working and out-sourcing, which characterize both the British and the Irish labour markets, as explained earlier.

Moreover, the main reason for introducing redundancies is the need to improve organizational competitiveness through labour cost reductions. British and Irish managers are highly cost conscious and tend to reduce costs through reducing the head count (making redundancies). It is often argued that because of financial constraints many employers in the UK and Ireland resort to the use of vulnerable employees who produce more for less and who are easier to hire and fire (Hakim, 1997). However it is also argued that the main reason for cost reduction policies is the intensification of competition at home and from abroad, which has increased the need for labour flexibility and for reduced labour costs.

Commitment to quality improvement

Commitment and quality are the two ultimate goals of human resource management (Guest, 1987). According to Legge (1995: 44) 'in the theory of HRM these concepts are seen as symbiotic. Employees, through careful selection and intensive socialization, become committed to the values that drive business strategy'. British and Irish employers are committed to improving the quality of their products and services in order to compete in a highly competitive international market. Many employers have introduced quality improvement techniques such as 'quality circles', 'Just-in-time operations', 'total quality management', 'lean production', and so forth. For example, a study by de Menezes and Wood (2006), using data from Britain's Workplace Employee Relations Survey of 1998, examining whether a managerial orientation underlies high-performance work systems and any association that may exist between them and total quality management (TQM), concluded that:

> First, the core of HR management is the flexible work practices associated with it and the implied orientation towards employee involvement for continuous improvement. Second, flexible work practices are being used in conjunction with quality practices associated and seen to be part of TQM. Third, motivational practices such as variable pay and job security guarantees, whilst to some extent more likely to be used in flexible workplaces, are not distinctive to them. (2006: 135)

International management orientation

Many multinational companies have invested in the UK and Ireland and in doing so have brought with them their employment and management practices. Japanese management practices such as single status, quality circles, and pendulum arbitration are examples of practices that have been introduced to the British management and employee relations systems. The increasing presence of US companies in the UK has also brought some changes in the way British managers perceive employee relations, such as strategic awareness and the decentralization of collective bargaining.

The influence of multinational companies on Irish management and employee relations has also become apparent, especially in recent years. It is estimated that more than two-thirds of the manufacturing industry in Ireland is dominated by foreign-owned companies, in particular the US multinationals (Gunnigle et al., 2007; McDonnell, 2008). The role of multinational companies in the diffusion of American-style management is becoming increasingly prominent. Such diffusion is gradually changing the traditional modes of Irish employee relations.

Managing human resources

Following on from the above discussion of the main characteristics of management in both countries, this section will focus on the conduct of the main functions of human resource management in more detail.

Recruitment and selection

The process of employee recruitment and selection in both the UK and Ireland is not dissimilar from those found in other major Anglo-Saxon and European countries. As the competition for skilled and professional employees intensifies, the process of recruitment and selection has become the most strategic and complex management function. Many employers have had to adopt new ways of attracting (recruitment) and choosing (selection) their potential employees (Herriot, 1990; Herriot and Anderson, 1997). Both British and Irish employers use a combination of methods ranging from the conventional methods of advertising, interviewing and seeking references to more sophisticated methods requiring the use of agencies and expert consultancies. According to a CIPD quarterly survey report (2004) more than two-thirds of British employers adopted new approaches to attracting potential applicants such as offering new learning and development opportunities, introducing family-friendly employment policies and flexible working practices, and changing their approach to communication with employees.

Recruitment

In both the UK and Ireland, once an employer has decided that a vacancy has to be filled, a number of methods are used to recruit the needed employee. These include the use of advertisements, employment agencies, recruitment consultants, executive search consultants, career conventions, job centres, open days, recruitment fairs, websites, and other less common forms of recruitment such as word of mouth, recommendations and headhunting (CIPD, 2007a,b,c). In short, they use all means to get the workforce they need. The difference in such methods is in the extent to which they are used. While some methods are used more often then others there are also methods that are used for some particular jobs only. For example,

- Job centres are very often used by small employers to get first time job seekers and unemployed people looking for manual and temporary jobs. It is unusual for managerial and professional jobs to be advertised in the local job centres. Such jobs are normally advertised in national and international newspapers, special journals and magazines, on websites, and with recruitment agencies. Agencies and consultants are increasingly used to recruit employees for professional and managerial jobs.
- Large organizations tend to recruit their managers through external recruitment and they very often use the services of international agencies. However, they also sometimes use recruitment agencies for the recruitment of skilled manual workers. There are many recruitment agencies in the UK and Ireland. They are used by many national and multinational companies for attracting and obtaining employees that may not be easily acquired.

Graduate recruitment

Graduate recruitment in the UK and Ireland has become one of the tough challenges for an increasing number of employers who have realized that the future of their organizations depends on the recruitment of the best among an increasing number of graduates in different disciplines from a widening range of higher education institutions (Keenan, 1995; Pollitt, 2005; Branine, 2008). Graduate recruitment is a process of searching for and obtaining potential job applicants from graduates in sufficient numbers and of sufficient quality so that employers can select the most suitable candidates to fill their job vacancies. In practice there is no commonly agreed procedure on how to recruit and select graduates because different employers have different recruitment methods, depending on their operations, size and needs (Ryan, 1996; Nabi and Bagley, 1999; Ryan et al., 2006). They have had to introduce a variety of more effective recruitment methods to ensure that appropriate graduates apply and are recruited (Raybould and Sheedy, 2005). More and more employers have had to cope with high volumes of applicants in order to fill in very limited vacancies. Normally, most graduate employers in the UK and Ireland begin recruiting in November for those graduating in June of the following year to start work in September or October. Some employers only recruit graduates when they need them and do not have a set timescale for graduate recruitment. In the process, university careers advisory services play an important role in not only assisting graduates with their searches for employment but also assisting employers in attracting and targeting students. By the late 1990s, the trend in graduate recruitment was changing in both the UK and Ireland because of developments in information technology and the growth of graduate student numbers (Stewart and Knowles, 1999). For example, the internet started to dominate the process of graduate recruitment as more and more employers use it to advertise their vacancies, provide an online application process, and even conduct online testing (Lievens, van Dam and Anderson, 2002; Sackett and Lievens, 2008; Parry and Tyson, 2008). There has been also greater use of agencies and work placements and lesser use of standardized application forms (Sackett and Lievens, 2008).

However, despite the increasing use of the internet for advertising job vacancies, most companies still use print media to reach potential applicants. A recent CIPD (2007b) report showed that more than 75 per cent of UK companies still advertise in local and national newspapers, magazines and journals. Many graduate employers still use graduate recruitment literature (such as the Prospects and GET directories) that are directly targeted to graduates. They also use organizational recruitment brochures that are distributed at graduate recruitment fairs or given on request (CIPD, 2007a). A study of 326 graduate employers in the UK (Branine, 2008) found that the most popular method of graduate recruitment was the internet, which was used by 91 per cent of the respondents and by all employers with more than 500 employees. The second most popular method was the use of careers literature such as the Prospects Directory, the GET Directory and Prospects Today. These were used by 89 per cent of the respondents, and significantly by 78 per cent of employers with less than 500 employees and 95 per cent of larger employers. The 'milk round', which was used by 45 per cent of the respondents, appeared to be less popular than methods such as graduate recruitment fairs (55 per cent), which employers preferred because of the elements of direct contact and availability to answer prospective applicants' questions. The least popular method of graduate recruitment was the use of recruitment agencies. They were used by only 15 per cent of the respondents. About 45 per cent of the respondents reported that they targeted students at particular universities by contacting those universities' careers advisory services, directors of programmes and heads of department. About 14 per cent of the 326 graduate employers studied indicated that they had targeted only universities that offered particular degree courses with good reputations. Only 9 per cent of the respondents indicated that they preferred the old universities. More than a third (37 per cent) preferred universities where graduates undertook work placements as part of their studies.

Selection

In terms of selection, both British and Irish companies do not usually use too many sophisticated selection techniques such as psychometric testing or assessment centres. Interviews and reference checks are still the most commonly used selection methods. The reason for this may be related to the nature of the labour market and the type of industries that dominate the economies of the two countries. However, while the use of interviews is still the most popular method of selection, there has been a growing interest in the use of attitude and psychometric tests and of assessment centres by large companies (CIPD, 2007d; Sackett and Lievens, 2008). A pre-selection process is very often used. For example, Keenan (1995: 307) reported that 94 per cent of the 536 organizations he surveyed carried out an initial pre-selection on application forms. Keenan (1995:309) also found that all employers surveyed used interviews in their selection process, while 44 per cent used assessment centres. Gabb (1997) found interviews to be the main part of the selection process and that there was awareness of the danger of subjectivity in the conduct of interviews. To avoid such dangers, Gabb (1997: 64) found that 'companies often prefer an interview panel of two or sequential interviews with different people'.

While the trio of application form, interview and references is still popular in both countries, there have been further developments in incorporating these methods with the use of assessment centres which are reportedly on the increase. Assessment centres have become popular venues for the selection of candidates, identification of their potentials, and assessment of their training and development needs (CIPD, 2007d; Sackett and Lievens, 2008; Branine, 2008). However, although it is illegal in both the UK and Ireland to discriminate in the process of recruitment and selection on the grounds of gender, race, colour, nationality, religion and sexual orientation, a number of studies have found that employers are able to discriminate in the process against some applicants. For example, a survey by the CIPD (2005) found that 6 in 10 employers deliberately discriminated against people with a criminal record, a history of drug or alcohol problems, or a history of long-term sickness. Also about a quarter of employers surveyed did not consider homeless people for jobs.

Training and development

In both the UK and Ireland education is compulsory for all children until the age of 16, and most of the population is literate. They are nations of educated people. The education sector is one of the major public sector employers in both countries. However, they are fundamentally different in their systems of education, and as there are differences even within the UK. The Scottish education system, for example, is different from the English and the Welsh. The Irish government has invested more on education than the British, where most education institutions, especially universities, have suffered serious cuts in state funding in recent years. In terms of training, neither country has done enough to meet the demands of their economies, although the Irish government has invested more heavily and effectively on training at all levels.

Apprenticeship training

Apprenticeship training was very common in both countries for most of the last century and many skills were learnt through on-the-job training. Prior to the early 1960s, employers had to rely on the use of apprenticeship to maintain the levels of skilled workforce they required. The number of apprenticeships has been in continual decline since the 1980s because of a number of changes in employment and the nature of work as well as in employee relations. Changes in production systems and in the provision of many services because of the use of technology have resulted in many unskilled jobs that required very little training and no need for formal apprenticeship programmes. Moreover, the subcontracting and outsourcing of many skilled and professional operations have also contributed to the apparent decline in the use of apprenticeship training.

It should be emphasized that such a decline has been more apparent in the UK than in Ireland, where many companies are still dependent on apprenticeship schemes that are supported and funded by the state. In the UK, the apprenticeship system has been substituted to some extent by the introduction of National Vocational Qualifications system that was expected to be competency-based and provide broader, rather than specific, transferable skills. As a result, training became employer-led and the Industrial Training Boards (ITBS) were replaced with Training and Enterprise Councils (TECs) at the local level.

Employee training and development

Employee training and development in the UK and Ireland is still limited in comparison with that of other industrialized countries such as Japan, the USA and Germany (Handy et al., 1988; CIPD, 2007; Heraty and Collings, 2006). In the UK, employee training is seen as the responsibility of employers not that of the state and, as a result, the government has done very little to improve the knowledge and skills of the working population. At the same time many employers invested very little in the training of their employees (Tregaskis and Brewster, 1998; Meager, 2008, McDowall and Saunders, 2010).

According to Tregaskis and Brewster (1998: 182), 'the state appears to be taking on the role of facilitator, building a qualifications infrastructure and means and mechanisms for both employers and individuals to engage in training and learning'.

In Ireland the state has funded a number of employee training programmes which have proven insufficient, while many employers have invested very little in the training and development of their employees (Heraty and Morley, 2000, 2003). Until recently many employers in both countries were reluctant to spend on employee training because training was very often considered a cost rather than an investment in the future of the organization. A significant difference between the two countries in this respect is that training in the UK is more concerned with the creation of empowerment and self-development, as training is very often requested by employees rather than initiated by employers, while in Ireland training is more concerned with the development of a mobile European workforce and is usually supported by the state. In Ireland, the government has invested in training and retraining initiatives aimed at youth and the unemployed workforce. Such initiatives have eventually paid off as Ireland has built up a supply of skilled employees.

Management education, training and development

In the late 1980s, Charles Handy (1988: 168) wrote that 'in Britain management education and training is *too little, too late, for too few*' (original emphasis). He added, commenting on the lack of management education and training, that 'the British have rationed something which should be universally available and turned a potential common good into a special reserve. What should be a prerequisite of all managers has become a perk for the minority.' This statement is probably still true today, because not much has changed for the better despite the availability of many business and management courses and the co-existence of three approaches to management education and training that Handy (1988) described as the corporate, the academic and the professional.

The corporate approach is one in which managers are provided with the necessary training and experience needed to do their managerial work and develop their career in management. In most cases this learning experience is related to a specific management function such as marketing, sales and operations. This approach is common in the UK, Ireland and many EU countries. Most of the large companies in the UK and Ireland recruit their managers among university graduates and employ them as trainee managers. Unlike the type of organizational training found in the US, as explained in Chapter 3, this corporate approach to training is also found in Japanese companies. With this approach, management education and training are strongly linked to each other because managers are expected to grow and develop through experience, education and training, on and off the job.

The academic approach is based on the belief that management can be learnt in colleges and business schools, and then implemented in the workplace. Normally, a manager is expected to have an undergraduate or postgraduate degree in business and management before starting a career in management. This is gaining momentum in the UK and other European countries (Meager, 2008). Many universities in the UK are offering a variety of management courses leading to the awarding of degrees, certificates and diplomas that are increasingly demanded by employers as prerequisites for management positions. Having completed an MBA degree, for example, is considered a step into a managerial career in the USA, Canada and Australia, but in the UK and Ireland a good first degree or a master's degree (MSc or MA) in marketing, finance or HRM is as important as an MBA degree for a career in management.

The professional approach is based on the principle that those who practise a profession in an area of expertise have to be recognized by the professional body that accredits that expertise. For managers to qualify as professionals in certain managerial functions they have to complete a course that is accredited by a professional body. This is a common practice in the UK and Ireland, where all traditional professions from accounting to law and from human resource management to psychology require professionally accredited qualifications. There are many professional bodies in the UK and Ireland that are related to management education and development. The most popular of such professional bodies are: the Chartered Institute of Management Accountants (CIMA); the Chartered Institute for Personnel and Development (CIPD); and the Chartered Institute of Management (CIM).

ACTIVITY 2

Discuss the strengths and weaknesses of each one of the above approaches to management education, training and development in the UK.

Some British employers, especially small and medium size organizations, prefer to poach or buy-in trained and skilled managers rather than investing in the training of their current managers (CIPD, 2007e; McDowall and Saunders, 2010). This US approach is gaining momentum in the UK and Ireland, especially among employers who fear the loss of their managers after investing in their training and development. It is also influenced by the presence of an increasing number of US multinational companies in both countries.

Vocational training

As explained above, the traditional practice of craft apprenticeship in the UK was replaced in the 1980s by award-bearing courses related to commerce and industry. The successful completion of the courses leads to the award of National Vocational Qualifications (NVQs). NVQs were made available to the young people (16 to 19 year olds) and to adults who wanted to learn specific skills. However, it seems that such initiatives on vocational training have been unable to maintain a coherent national institutional framework for vocational training. In the pursuit of NVQs what has become important to many trainees is passing the courses, rather than learning the skills. In a country where there is a low volume of training activity and a high concern for identifying training needs and monitoring the outcomes of training programmes, vocational training has become a mere opportunity to have a qualification. NVQs have become more academic and theoretically based than practical and vocationally oriented qualifications, leading very often to further and higher education than to finding employment opportunities.

Vocational training in Ireland is provided from the senior level of secondary education by combining class education with workplace apprenticeship. The national body responsible for vocational training is the FÁS in coordination with the Department of Education, and they provide training to young people in sectors such as construction, electrical and mechanical engineering, printing and artworking. The trainees work as employees and attend school or college for two to three days per week. They complete their studies and training by taking trade examinations leading to the award of a national craft certificate. Most trainees spend about four years working and studying before qualifying to do the jobs they train for. Despite the existence of such state funded and widely available vocational training programmes, there is still a shortage of skilled workforce to meet the demands of a fast-growing economy.

Lifelong learning

The British government paper on *Lifetime Learning, A Policy Framework* (DfEE, 1996) encouraged employers and individual employees to invest in continuous training and development. The paper set targets for communication, numeracy and information technology skills. It states that learning is for life and is significant throughout one's career.

However, the evidence has shown that not much progress has been made. One of the reasons for non-attainment of targets is the lack of government investment in employee training, as explained earlier.

Investors in People (IP)

The Investors in People (IP) scheme in the UK is a national benchmark for good practice in achieving business objectives through people. It was introduced in 1990 in order to provide a framework of good practice for effective investment in training and development of employees in the different sectors of the economy. The initiative is based on the principles of developing human resources by focusing employees on business objectives, training them to achieve those objectives, and then evaluating the results of the training (Emberson and Winters, 2000). By 1997, one-third of UK employers were IP accredited (Cully et al., 1999). The main benefits of the scheme are to improve employees' skills, motivate employees, increase employees' career prospects, improve the relations between business objectives and training and development programmes, and enhance the reputation of the employer as an investor in people.

Rewards and Remuneration

As explained earlier, the British and Irish labour markets are the most deregulated among the industrialized countries and there are no specific statutory regulations of pay determination at any level, except for a statutory minimum wage and equal pay legislation. The terms and conditions of employment were traditionally set through collective agreements between management and the unions at the national level, and to a lesser extent at the organization or unit level. When the UK Conservative government came to power in 1979, monetarist policies and fiscal restraints were adopted to control price inflation and rising unemployment. It was argued that the contribution of individual employees could be differentiated by objective performance measures. Rewards and compensation became more driven by an individualistic model of performance appraisal as opposed to a collectivist approach based on collective bargaining agreements.

In the 1990s, the Conservative government abandoned the Fair Wages Resolution and abolished the Wages Councils in an attempt to further deregulate the labour market and take away the wage agreements from the long-established collective bargaining system, therefore reducing the power of trade unions in negotiating wage settlements. That led to the introduction of compulsory competitive tendering and the removal of all constraints on pay (Goodman et al., 1997: 46). Most of the private sector companies opted for company-wide or even unit-level negotiation rather than national collective bargaining agreements, and by the late 1990s the company and division or unit-level wage agreement for all grades of employees became acceptable. Despite the promotion of partnership under Labour governments since 1997 (Ackers and Payne, 1998; DTI, 1998) the reward systems have become increasingly decentralized and individualized (see Marginson et al., 2008; Johnstone et al., 2009), although the use of collective bargaining is still dominant. Drawing evidence from retail banking and machinery and equipment companies, Marginson et al. (2008: 345) conclude that 'the introduction of variable pay has not undermined collective bargaining in the sense of its core focus on delivering inflation-based increases to basic pay'.

In Ireland, the changes in the rewards system have been less radical and comparatively different from those introduced in the UK in this respect. Unlike the UK where rewards have become more and more decentralized, the Irish system has since the late 1980s been based on social partnership agreements between the Irish Congress of Trade Unions, the Irish Business and Employers Confederation, and the government. Rewards for employees at all levels are largely determined through centralized collective bargaining agreements. However, as a result of increasing multinational investment, mainly from the US, there has been more emphasis on the individual rather than the group, moving away from collective bargaining agreements to individually based rewards (Gunnigle et al., 1995, 2001). In general, the main features of the reward and remuneration systems in both the UK and Ireland, considering their differences, are: the use of performance appraisal for developmental and judgemental purposes; the use of performance-related pay; the implementation of a statutory minimum wage; and the apparent wage inequalities.

Performance appraisal

The use of performance appraisal has been a common HRM practice in both the UK and Ireland. It has been used for developmental and judgemental purposes. In other words, the purpose of performance appraisal is to identify areas in which the employee needs improvements to meet agreed performance objectives. This may involve the identification of training needs and the design of training programmes for the employee's improvement and career development. It has also been used to assess the contribution of individuals to the organization and to reward them accordingly. Performance appraisal has been carried out regularly, every six months or annually, depending on the type and level of jobs undertaken. Although such practice is still not too widespread in Ireland it is common in the UK. Currently it is rare to find an organization in the UK that does not have a form of performance appraisal in place.

Performance-related pay

As we noted above, in the UK there has been a move away from collective to individual rewards as many employers aim to reward their employees for individual rather than group achievements. In doing so, they have introduced a variety of payments related to performance such as merit pay, individual bonuses, team bonuses, share option schemes, and so on. Such rewards are expected to make pay reflect an individual's contribution to the organisation they work for. By the mid-1990s more than two-thirds of British companies used performance-related pay to reward their managerial, professional and skilled employees. Similarly, in Ireland, despite the use of collective agreements in determining national pay levels, many employers use performance-related pay to reward individual employees for their effort and achievements (Gunnigle et al., 2001; Wallace et al., 2004). Performance-related pay, skill-based pay and personalized contracts were introduced in most foreign-owned companies and started spreading into national ones.

Statutory minimum wage

Both the UK and Ireland were among the last countries to introduce a statutory minimum wage in Western Europe. The main reason for the delay in introducing the minimum wage was the fear that a minimum wage would not be good for the economy and in particular for the growth and sustainability of the small businesses on which the national economy depends. Although no national minimum wage rate existed until recently, there was always a mechanism by which minimum wages for particular industries and sectors were determined. A UK national minimum wage rate was introduced for the first time by the Labour government in April 1999 at £3.60 per hour for those aged 22 and over. The minimum wage rate was recommended by the Low Pay Commission (LPC), which is an independent body appointed by the government in July 1997 to advise on the rate of the minimum wage. The LPC is made up of three trade unionists, three employers and three labour market relations experts. The current (as from the 1 October 2009) minimum wage rate is £5.80 per hour for those aged 22 and over, £4.83 per hour for those 18 to 21, and £3.57 per hour for those aged 16 and 17. There has been no strong evidence of a decline in small businesses as a result of introducing the minimum wage, and there have been very limited cases of employers not paying the minimum wage.

The republic of Ireland introduced a statutory minimum wage in 2000, but unlike the UK it distinguishes between the experienced adult worker, and those over 18, and those under 18, as follows: From 1 July 2007, €8.65 per hour for experienced adult workers aged 18 or over; €6.92 for the first year from date of first employment of those aged over 18; €7.79 for the second year from date of first employment of those aged over 18; and €6.06 for those under 18 and over 16. There are also exceptions to the rule, as some people may still get paid less than the minimum wage if they are provided, for example, with food and accommodation as benefits for the job. However, most employers have paid above the minimum wage in order to attract the employees they need, especially when unemployment was low and there was a shortage of skilled labour. For example, in 2004 only 3.1 per cent of employees received the minimum wage. Following the recent financial crisis there have been calls by employers' associations and some economists for the reduction of the minimum wage.

Wage inequalities

Wage inequalities still exist in the UK and Ireland despite the introduction of legislation forbidding all kinds of discrimination between employees (Hills, 1996, 1999; Barrett et al., 1999, 2000; Nolan and Russell, 2001; Bell and Van Reenen, 2010). In the UK, men's wages are still slightly higher than those of women and there have been significant inequalities in pay between managerial and non-managerial jobs. Similarly, Ireland has also had the highest wage inequality among the OECD countries (D'Art and Turner, 2002; Wallace et al., 2004).

ACTIVITY 3

Argue for and against the introduction of a minimum wage in a country like the UK, and then in a developing country of your choice.

Employee relations

The UK was the first country to industrialize in the Western world and the Republic of Ireland played a significant role in that revolutionary industrialization process. The development of the factory system and mass production industrialization led to a mass exploitation of labour from the last quarter of the nineteenth century. However, in response to poor conditions of work, low wages and unfair treatment at work, the workers had to organize themselves by forming trade unions in order to demand better working conditions, higher wages and fair treatment at work. In the UK, associations of skilled workers and craftsmen were formed in the nineteenth century and the Trades Union Congress (TUC) was established in 1868. It was the trade unions that created the Labour party in 1906 (initially formed in 1883 as the Independent Labour Party), and since then most of the major trade unions have been supporting it politically and financially.

Most of the trade unions that were formed in the UK also had branches and membership in Ireland. Until around the mid-1960s, there were only small differences between the British and Irish industrial relations systems, and in both countries the government had little involvement in employee–employer relations except in their capacities as employers and owners of public sector utilities.

The 1960s brought much new legislation in the area of employment relations. However, the UK Conservative government from 1979 to 1997 reduced the direct involvement of the state in employee relations and in the management of the economy by privatizing public sector companies and passing laws that deregulated the labour market further, strengthened enterprise culture, and curbed the power of trade unions. The Labour government's policies over the 1990s and 2000s, despite some legal changes, did not reverse any of the anti-union laws introduced by the Conservatives (see Poole et al., 2005; Parker, 2008; Johnstone et al., 2009). In contrast to the Labour party leadership of the 1960s and 1970s, the leadership of the 1990s and 2000s gradually distanced itself from the unions, giving them less scope for involvement in political decision-making. It also distanced itself from the working classes. The current British employee relations system is based on three principal features of voluntarism:

1 Collective agreements are not legally binding;
2 Employers are not obliged to recognize trade unions; and
3 Industrial disputes and their settlements are independent from any form of state intervention.

The Irish industrial relations system was very similar to that found in the UK post-1979, until the late 1980s. In 1987 the Irish government introduced the Programme for National Recovery (PNR) which limited annual wage increases to 2.5 per cent for three years from 1988. The government agreed to compensate wage limits by cutting income tax and improving the welfare system. The programme was heralded as a success because it led to a decline in industrial conflicts and an increase in economic growth. The PNR was followed by a number of other programmes such as the Economic and Social Progress programme (1991–4), the Competitiveness and Work programme (1994–7), the Partnership programme (1997–2000), and the Prosperity and Fairness programme (2000–3). These programmes have contributed to the transformation of the Irish workplace and employee relations, and hence the management of the economy in general. The Partnership programme changed the collective bargaining process from that of union–management negotiation to a process where a third party (government) is also involved. Overall, the current system of employee relations in Ireland is characterized by the following principles (see Gunnigle et al., 1995; D'Art and Turner, 2002; Wallace et al., 2004):

1 Centralized collective bargaining based on 'social partnership' involving representatives from the unions, the government and employers.
2 High exposure to international employee relations systems because of the increasing presence of multinational companies in Ireland.
3 Government support for the right to form and to join trade unions.
4 Limited anti-union feelings and no trade union avoidance by Irish employers.

Although the Irish system of employee relations originated within the British system, it has not evolved in the same direction since the late 1980s.

Trade unions

The coming to power of the Conservatives in 1979 had a major impact on the direction and tradition of employee relations in the UK and mainly on the role of trade unions: a series of employee relations legislation was introduced with the aim to curb the power of trade unions. For example, it was made illegal for the unions to take industrial action without the use of a secret ballot, and the process of secondary industrial action was outlawed. The practice of picketing was limited to a small number of employees and only at the gates of the their own workplace. The Employment Act 1988 gave more rights to individual employees by making it illegal for the trade unions to take any action against members who refuse to take part in industrial action, and mandated the selection of trade union officials through a secret ballot. Further, the Employment Act 1989 limited the rights of trade union officials to time off for trade union activities, and the Employment Act 1990 outlawed closed shops and made it illegal to refuse employment on the grounds of union membership. Moreover, in 1993 the secret ballot for industrial action was made fully postal and union membership dues were made payable directly from the employee's wage, to be reaffirmed by the member every three years. The weakening of trade unions coincided with the economic recession of the mid-1980s and the early 1990s, as well as changes in labour market composition, as outlined above, and led to a new era in the British employee relations system (see Poole et al. 2005; Johnstone et al., 2009).

Trade unionism in Ireland has not been affected by any direct anti-union legislation. On the contrary, trade unions have been protected and supported by all political parties, and there has been since the late 1980s a gradual shift from the traditional adversary nature of union–management collective bargaining and conflict settlements (the British type) to cooperative tripartite bargaining agreements involving the state, unions and employers. Tripartite agreements have given trade unions some kind of participative role in economic and social matters and have made them important partners rather than the enemies of employers. Gunnigle et al. (2001) point out that a significant characteristic of the employee relations system in Ireland is the absence of a strong anti-union ideology among any of the main political parties. The difficulties that Irish trade unions have had are not with national employers but with the increasing number of international employers, especially US multinational companies, which do not recognize trade unions or have anti-union policies (see Linehan et al., 2002; Wallace et al., 2004).

As far as trade union membership and density are concerned, they have declined in both countries, but relatively faster in the UK than in Ireland. In the UK trade union membership was 13.26 million members in 1979, representing a density of 57.2 per cent of the overall working population. Then between 1979 and 1985 it dropped by about 10 per cent and continued to drop sharply, especially in the industrial sector, over the 1980s, to reach about 29 per cent by the middle of the 1990s. There are many interrelated factors that led to the sharp decline in trade union membership from the 1980s (see Hollinshead and Leat, 1995; Goodman et al., 1997; Kelly, 1997; Machin, 2000; Poole et al., 2005; Johnstone et al., 2009). The most significant factors include:

1 The closure of large manufacturing plants led to significant decreases in blue-collar workers and therefore in trade union density.
2 The decline in employment in large public sector organizations such as the National Health Service, the public services and the local authorities as a result of government cost saving measures.
3 The bad name given by the government to trade union militancy and to collective bargaining. Trade union leaders were portrayed in the 1980s as corrupt, undemocratic and aggressive. The unions were heavily criticized publicly through the media, especially at the time of the miners' strike.
4 The rise of uncompromising macho management. Many employers replaced their older by younger managers who pretended publicly to be working with the unions while they did all they could to implement laws restricting the powers of trade unions.
5 Employer introduction of non-union communication channels with individual employees. Therefore many employees saw no need for trade unions to represent them since they were able to 'negotiate' their terms and conditions of employment individually with their managers.
6 The increasing presence of international employers, mainly from the US, that did not recognize trade unions.
7 The failure of some trade unions to organize and recruit new members because of legal restrictions and lack of resources.
8 The rise in part-time, temporary and self-employment. Many employees who worked flexibly did not join trade unions.
9 Splits and conflicts between some unions, creating more uncertainty and bad feelings among the members.
10 The merger of some trade unions that resulted in the dissatisfaction of members whose loyalty to their unions was affected.

ACTIVITY 4

Why do people join trade unions? Argue for and against employees joining trade unions in the UK and Ireland. Are there countries where it is better or worse for workers to join trade unions?

Collective bargaining

In both the UK and Ireland, the terms and conditions of employment as well as pay were traditionally settled through collective bargaining, which took place at the national, organizational and unit levels. Although collective bargaining is still prominent, there has been a shift since the 1980s towards more decentralized and individualized forms of employee representation in the UK (Poole et al., 2005; Marginson et al., 2008) and more cooperative forms of negotiations in Ireland (Wallace et al., 2004). In the UK, there has been a gradual shift from national to local and from centralized to decentralized collective bargaining. The significant development has been the move from company-wide to workplace bargaining. Although there has been an overall decline in the use of collective bargaining it is still high in the public sector, which is generally highly unionized, and low in the private sector, which has become less and less unionized (Poole et al., 2005). There has been a shift away from multi-employer and multi-union negotiations to single employer and single union negotiations in most private sector organizations. The multi-employer negotiations that had traditionally been conducted in, for example, the engineering and national newspapers industries, were ended by the late 1980s. The shift from national to unit- and company-level bargaining led to an increase in single table bargaining (Gall, 2004). Moreover, with the emergence of HRM policies, collective bargaining became little more than 'an empty shell' or a 'form without substance' (see Storey, 1995) because in many cases union representatives have found themselves with one option, which is to accept the offer or leave it (Goodman et al., 1997; Gall, 2004).

In Ireland, there has been a move towards a more corporatist model of employee relations where the state becomes directly involved in negotiations, creating a tripartite agreement based on a more centralized bargaining system that is gradually influenced by legislation from within and from outside (i.e. from the EU). Currently, centrally negotiated agreements cover pay, welfare provision, job creation, and tax reform.

Strikes and industrial action

Strikes and other industrial action short of a strike, such as short stoppages and work to rule, were common practice in the UK and to some extent in Ireland (Beardsmore, 2006; Bird, 2007; Hale, 2010). The highest volume of strikes was in the 1970s and early 1980s. Since the late 1980s the number of strikes has declined significantly for many reasons, namely the decline of trade unions power and changes in labour market trends. The decline in the rate of industrial action in Ireland has been even sharper than that in the UK, partly because of the non-adversarial approach that Irish unions have taken in relation to their employers. For example, the number of industrial disputes resulting in strike action dropped form 192 in 1984 to just 12 in 2008 (Central Statistics Office, Ireland, 2009).

Settlement of industrial disputes

As explained earlier, collective agreements are normally reached through collective bargaining, but in some cases the negotiating parties fail to reach an agreement and they need third party assistance. Third party intervention can be in the form of conciliation, mediation and/or arbitration, which is provided in the UK by the Advisory, Conciliation and Arbitration Service (ACAS), which is an independent body. When the parties in dispute require conciliation, mediation or arbitration, ACAS makes use of its appointed pool of industrial relations experts, although it has no powers to secure the acceptance of its assistance or to impose any solution for an issue in dispute. In the UK, arbitration is voluntary and not compulsory, as in Australia, and is not legally binding, as in the US. Moreover, as a way of preventing industrial disputes, ACAS assists in preventing and resolving problems at work by providing advisory mediation (AM). AM extends to collective bargaining arrangements, industrial employment rights, pay and reward systems, communication consultation and employee involvement, and organization effectiveness and handling change. A similar mechanism for the settling of industrial disputes exists in Ireland, where the Labour Relations Commission (LRC) is responsible for providing advisory, conciliation and arbitration services to the parties in industrial dispute. Most of the cases are resolved through conciliation which is voluntary and is the most effective process in Ireland's industrial relations system. When the parties fail to reach an agreement through conciliation or, less often, arbitration, the dispute is referred to the labour court.

Employee involvement and participation

Forms of employee involvement such as joint consultation committees, problem-solving groups, quality circles, suggestion schemes, team working, profit sharing, employee share ownership and many other kinds of individual direct involvement, depending on the type, size and specilization of the organization, have been introduced, but none of them seem to have replaced the practice of collective bargaining. Goodman et al. (1997) report that the most common form of direct involvement in the UK was the joint consultative committee, which was present in about 25 per cent of all organizations that had more than 25 employees. Recent surveys (Poole et al., 2005; Marginson et al., 2008; Johnstone et al., 2009) have concluded that such employee involvement initiatives have not changed the traditional forms of employee representation in the

UK, despite the apparent decline in trade union power. Similarly, direct employee involvement in Ireland is very limited. Collective bargaining through tripartite representation is still the predominant form of employee involvement in all sectors of the Irish economy.

Summary

1 The United Kingdom (UK) and the Republic of Ireland (Ireland) are very similar in many aspects because of their geographic location and shared historical and industrial backgrounds.

2 The labour markets of both the UK and Ireland are characterized by shortages in skilled labour, increasing female employment, increasing migrant labour, employment of older workers, and flexible working practices.

3 Management and organization strategy in the UK and, to some extent, in Ireland is characterized by integration of management in corporate strategy, devolution of HR activities to line managers, outsourcing of management functions, decentralization of collective bargaining, pragmatism, flexibility and an emphasis on cost reduction, and an international orientation.

4 Both British and Irish employers use a combination of recruitment methods ranging from the conventional methods of advertising, interviewing and seeking references to more sophisticated methods using the services of agencies and expert consultancies. In terms of selection, they do not usually use psychometric testing or assessment centres.

5 In terms of training, both countries have not done enough to meet the demands of their economies, although the Irish government has invested heavily and effectively on training at all levels.

6 Unlike the UK decentralized rewards system, the Irish system has since the late 1980s been based on social partnership agreements between the Irish Congress of Trade Unions, the Irish Business and Employers Confederation, and the government. Employee rewards in Ireland are still determined through centralized collective bargaining agreements.

7 The current British employee relations system is based on three principal features of voluntarism, namely that: (a) collective agreements are not legally binding; (b) employers are not obliged to recognize trade unions; and (c) industrial disputes and their settlements are independent from state intervention.

8 The Irish industrial relations system originated from the British system but has changed significantly. The current system of employee relations in Ireland is characterized by: (a) centralized collective bargaining based on 'social partnership' between unions, the government and employers; (b) high exposure to international employee relations systems through multinational investments in Ireland; (c) government support for the right to form and to join trade unions; and (d) limited anti-union feelings – and no trade union avoidance by Irish employers.

Revision questions

Chapter 1 provides a review task designed to consolidate your learning from this chapter. Please see Box 1.2.

In addition, the following questions are designed to help you revise this chapter.

1 Discuss critically the main characteristics of the Anglo-European approach to management. Analyse the similarities and differences between this approach and the North American one.
2 As a Japanese expatriate in Ireland, write a letter to the head office of your company describing the socio-economic context and the conditions of the labour market in the host country. What advice would you give to potential expatriates?
3 As an HR manager of a French company in the UK, write a report to the company's board of directors in Paris describing the similarities and differences in HRM functions (recruitment and selection, training and development, rewards system, and employee relations) between France and the UK.
4 Discuss the concept of 'social partnership' in the Irish industrial relations system and the pros and cons of its application in the UK.

References

Ackers, P. and Payne, J. (1998) 'British trade unions and partnership: rhetoric, reality and strategy', *The International Journal of Human Resource Management*, 9(3): 529–49.

Ackers, P., Marchington, M., Wilkinson, A. and Dundon, T. (2005) 'Partnership and voice, with or without trade unions: changing UK management approaches to organisational participation', in Stuart, M. and Martinez-Lucio, M. (eds), *Partnership and Modernisation in Employment Relations*, London: Routledge, 23–45.

Atkinson, J. (1984) *Flexibility, Uncertainty and Manpower Management*, IMS Report No.89, Brighton: Institute of Manpower Studies.

Atkinson, J. and Meager, N. (1986) *Changing Working Patterns: How companies achieve flexibility to meet new needs?*, Institute of Manpower Studies, National Economic Development Office: London.

Barrett, A., Callan, T. and Nolan, B. (1999) 'Rising Wage Inequality, Returns to Education and Labour Market Institutions: Evidence from Ireland', *British Journal of Industrial Relations*, 37(1): 77–100.

Barrett, A., Callan, T., Doris, A., O'Neill, D., Russell, H., Sweetman, O. and McBride, J. (2000) *How Unequal? Men and women in the Irish Labour Market*, Dublin: Oak Tree Press.

Beardsmore, R. (2006) *International comparisons of labour disputes in 2004*, Special Feature, Office for National Statistics, Labour Market Trends, available on line at:

http://www.statistics.gov.uk/articles/labour_market_trends/Int_labourdisputes.pd, accessed on 12 July 2010.

Bell, B. and Van Reenen, J. (2010) 'Bankers' pay and extreme wage inequalities in the UK', Centre for Economic Performance, London School of Economics, available on line at: http://cep.lse.ac.uk/pubs/download/special/cepsp21.pdf, accessed 17 September 2010.

Bird, D. (2007) 'Indicators to measure trade union membership, strikes and lockouts in the UK', *Economic & Labour Market Review*, 1(9): 40–7.

Branine, M. (1999) 'Part-time work in the public health service of Denmark, France and the UK', *The International Journal of Human Resource Management*, 10(3): 411–28.

Branine, M. (2008) 'Graduate recruitment and selection in the UK: a study of the recent changes in methods and expectations', *Career Development International*, 13(6): 497–513.

Budhwar, P.S. (2000) 'A reappraisal of HRM models in Britain', *Journal of General Management*, 26(2): 72–91.

CIPD (Chartered Institute of Personnel and Development) (2004) *Quarterly HR trends and Indicators*, Survey Report, Autumn, London: CIPD.

CIPD (Chartered Institute of Personnel and Development) (2005) *Labour Market Outlook*, Quarterly Survey Report, Summer/Autumn, London: CIPD.

CIPD (Chartered Institute of Personnel and Development) (2006) *Labour Market Outlook*, Quarterly Survey Report, Spring, London: CIPD.

CIPD (Charted Institute of Personnel and Development) (2007a) *Annual Survey Report 2007: Recruitment, Retention and Turnover*. Available online from: www.cipd.co.uk/NR/rdonlyres/746F1183-3941-4E6A-9EF6-135C29AE22C9/0/recruitmentsurv07.pdf. [Accessed 12 May 2008.]

CIPD (Charted Institute of Personnel and Development) (2007b) *E-Recruitment*. Available online from: www.cipd.co.uk/subjects/recruitmen/onlnrcruit/onlrec. htm?IsSrchRes = 1. [Accessed 12 May 2008.]

CIPD (Charted Institute of Personnel and Development) (2007c) *Psychological Testing*. Available online from: www.cipd.co.uk/subjects/recruitmen/tests/psytest. htm. [Accessed 12 May 2008.]

CIPD (Charted Institute of Personnel and Development) (2007d) *Assessment Centres for Recruitment and Selection*. Available online from: www.cipd.co.uk/ subjects/recruitmen/assmntcent/asscentre.htm?IsSrchRes = 1. [Accessed 12 May 2008.]

CIPD (Charted Institute of Personnel and Development) (2007e), *Latest trends in learning, training and development: reflections on the 2007 learning and development survey*, London: CIPD, available on line at: www.cipd.co.uk/onlineinfodocuments/atozresources.htm, visited on 16 may 2010.

Cooke, K. (1999) 'Skilled workers are in short supply: Ireland', *Financial Times*, 4 Oct. p. 4.

CSO (Central Statistics Office) (2007) *Census 2006*, CSO: Republic of Ireland.

CSO (Central Statistics Office, Ireland) (2009) *Industrial disputes involving stoppages of work*, Cork: CSO.

Cully, M., Woodland, S., O'Reilly, A. and Dix, G. (1999) *Britain at Work: As Depicted by the 1998 Workplace Employee Relations Survey*, London: Routledge.

D'Art, D. and Turner, T. (eds) (2002) *Irish Employment Relations in the New Economy*, Dublin: Blackhall.

De Menezes, L.M. and Wood, S. (2006) 'The reality of flexible work systems in Britain', *International Journal of Human Resource Management*, 17(1): 106–38.

Dench, S., Hurstfield, J., Hill, D. and Akroyd, K. (2006) *Employers' Use of Migrant Labour*, UK Home Office Reports 03/06 and 04/06.

DfEE (Department of Education and Employment) (1996) *Lifetime Learning: a policy framework*, London: DfEE.

Dick, P. and Hyde, R. (2006) 'Line manager involvement in work–life balance and career development: can't manage, won't manage?', *British Journal of Guidance & Counselling*, 34(3): 345–64.

DTI (UK Department of Trade and Industry) (1998) *Fairness at Work*, Cmnd 3968, London: DTI.

DTI (UK Department of Trade and Industry) (2003) *Balancing Work and Family Life: Enhancing Choice and Support for Parents*, London: HM Treasury.

Dundon, T., González-Pérez, M.-A. and McDonough, T. (2007) 'Bitten by the Celtic Tiger: immigrant workers and industrial relations in the new "glocalized" Ireland', *Economic and Industrial Democracy*, 28(4): 501–22.

Emberson, M. and Winters, J. (2000) 'Investors in People: How a Large Public Sector Organization in the UK Dealt with a New National Training Initiative?', *International Journal of Training and Development*, 4(4): 259–71.

EOC (Equal Opportunities Commission) (2006) *Equal Opportunities Commission Annual Report and Accounts 2005–2006*, accessed online at: www.official-documents. gov.uk/document/hc0506/hc14/1423/1423.pdf on 24 April 2009.

Forde, C. and Slater, G. (2006) 'The nature and experience of agency working in Britain: what are the challenges for human resource management?', *Personnel Review*, 35(2): 141–57.

Forde, C., MacKenzie, R. and Robinson, A. (2008) 'Help wanted? Employers' use of temporary agencies in the UK construction industry', *Employee Relations*, 30(6): 679–98.

Gabb, A. (1997) 'University challenge', *Management Today*, Dec.: 62.

Gall, G. (2004) 'Trade union recognition in Britain 1995–2002: turning a corner?', *Industrial Relations Journal*, 35(3): 249–70.

Glover, I. and Branine, M. (eds) (2001) *Ageism in Work and Employment*, Aldershot: Ashgate.

Goodman, J., Marchington, M., Berridge, J., Snape, E. and Bamber, G.J. (1997) 'Employment relations in Britain', in Bamber, G.J. and Lansbury, R.D. (eds), *International and Comparative Employment Relations*, 3rd edn. London: Sage, 34–62.

Guest, D. (1987) 'Human Resource Management and Industrial Relations', *Journal of Management Studies*, 24(5): 503–21.

Gunnigle, P., Lavelle, J., McDonnell, A. and Morley, M. (2007) *Managing HR in Multinational Companies in Ireland: Autonomy, Coordination and Control*, Report to the Labour Relations Commission (LRC), November 2007, Employment Relations Unit, Department of Personnel and Employment Relations, University of Limerick, Ireland.

Gunnigle, P., MacCurtain, S. and Morley, M. (2001) 'Dismantling pluralism, indus-trial relations in Irish Greenfield sites', *Personnel Review*, 30(3): 263–79.

Gunnigle, P., McMahon, G. and Fitzgerald, G. (1995) *Industrial Relations in Ireland: Theory and Practice*, Dublin: Gill & Macmillan.

Hakim, C. (1997) 'A sociological perspective on part-time work', in Blossfield, H.P. and Hakim, C. (eds), *Between Equalization and Marginalization: Women Part-time Workers in Europe and the USA*, Oxford: Oxford University Press.

Hakim, C. (2000) *Work–Lifestyle Choices in the 21st Century: Preference Theory*, Oxford: Oxford University Press.

Hale, D. (2010) 'Labour disputes in 2009', *Economic & Labour Market Review*, 4(6): 47–59.

Handy, C. (1988) 'Britain' in Handy, C., Gordon, C., Gow, I. and Randlesome, C. (eds), *Making Managers*, London: Pitman.

Handy, C., Gordon, C., Gow, I. and Randlesome, C. (1988) (eds), *Making Managers*, London: Pitman.

Harris, L., Foster, C. and Whysall, P. (2007) 'Maximising women's potential in the UK's retail sector', *Employee Relations*, 29(5): 492–505.

Heraty, N. and Collings, D.G. (2006) 'Training and development in the Republic of Ireland', *International Journal of Training and Development*, 10(2): 164–74.

Heraty, N. and Morley, M. (2000) 'Human resource development in Ireland: organizational level evidence', *Journal of European Industrial Training*, 24(1).

Heraty, N. and Morley, M. (2003) 'Management development in Ireland: the new organizational wealth', *Journal of Management Development*, 22(1).

Herriot, P. (1990) *Recruitment in the 1990s*, London: Institute of Personnel Management.

Herriot, P. and Anderson, N. (1997) 'Selecting for change: how will personnel and selection psychology survive?', in Anderson, N. and Herriot, P. (eds), *International Handbook of Selection and Assessment*, Chichester: Wiley, 1–34.

Hills, J. (1996) (ed.) *Inequalities: The Changing Distribution of Income and Wealth in the United Kingdom*, Cambridge: Cambridge University Press.

Hills, J. (1999) *Income and Wealth: the Latest Evidence*, York: Joseph Rowntree Foundation.

Hofstede, G. (2001) *Culture's Consequences: International differences in work related values*, 2nd edn, London: Sage.

Houseman, S., Kalleberg, A. and Erickcek, G. (2003) 'The role of temporary agency employment in tight labor markets', *Industrial and Labor Relations Review*, 57(1): 105–27.

Johnstone, S., Ackers, P. and Wilkinson, A. (2009) 'The British partnership phenomenon: a ten year review', *Human Resource Management Journal*, 19(3): 260–79.

Keenan, T. (1995) 'Graduate recruitment in Britain: a survey of selection methods used by organization', *Journal of Organizational Behaviour*, 16(2): 303–17.

Kelly, J. (1997) 'Industrial relations: looking to the future', *British Journal of Industrial Relations*, 35: 393–8.

Kelly, J. (2004) 'Social partnership agreements in Britain: labour, co-operation and compliance', *Industrial Relations*, 43: 267–92.

Kersley, B., Alpin, C., Forth, J., Bryson, A., Bewley, H., Dix, G. and Oxenbridge, S. (2006) *Inside the Workplace: Findings from the 2004 Workplace Employment Relations Survey*, London & New York: Routledge.

Kessler, S. and Bayliss, F. (1995) *Contemporary British Industrial Relations*, 2nd edn, Basingstoke: Macmillan.

Legge, K. (1995) *Human Resource Management: Rhetoric and Realities*, London: Macmillan Business.

Lievens, F., van Dam, K. and Anderson, N. (2002) 'Recent trends and challenges in personnel selection', *Personnel Review*, 31(5): 580–601.

Linehan, M., Morley, M. and Walsh, J. (eds) (2002) *International Human Resource Management and Expatriate Transfers: Irish Experiences*, Dublin: Blackhall.

McDonnell, A. (2008) 'Outward foreign direct investment and human capital development: A small country perspective', *Journal of European Industrial Training*, 32(6): 452–71.

McDowall, A. and Saunders, M.N.K (2010) 'UK managers' conceptions of employee training and development', *Journal of European Industrial Training*, 34(7): 609–30.

Machin, S. (2000) 'Union decline in Britain', *British Journal of Industrial Relations*, 38(4): 631–45.

Marginson, P., Arrowsmith, J. and Gray, M. (2008) 'Undermining or reframing collective bargaining? Variable pay in two sectors compared', *Human Resource Management Journal*, 18(4): 327–46.

Meager, N. (2008) *The Role of Training and Skills Development in Active Labour Market Policies*, Institute for Employment Studies Working Paper: WP15 available online at: www.employment-studies.co.uk/pdflibrary/wp15.pdf, accessed on 16 May 2010.

Morgan, A. and Finniear, J. (2009) 'Migrant workers and the changing psychological contract', *Journal of European Industrial Training*, 33(4): 305–22.

Nabi, G.R. and Bagley, D. (1999) 'Graduates' perceptions of transferable personal skills and future career preparation in the UK', *Education and Training*, 41(4): 184–93.

Nolan, B. and Russell, H. (2001) *Pay Inequality and Economic Performance in Ireland: A Review of the Applied Literature*, The Economic and Research Institute, Dublin, available on line at: cep.lse.ac.uk/piep/papers/Ireland.pd, accessed on 17 May 2010.

OECD (Organization for Economic Cooperation and Development) (2009) *Harmonized Unemployment Rates, October 2009*. Available online at: http:// stats. oecd.org/Index.aspx?QueryName = 251&QueryType = View&Lang = en. [Visited Oct. 2009.]

Parker, J. (2008) 'The Trades Union Congress and civil alliance building: towards social movement unionism?', *Employee Relations*, 30(5): 562–83.

Parry, E. and Tyson, S. (2008) 'An analysis of the use and success of online recruitment methods in the UK', *Human Resource Management Journal*, 18(3): 257–74.

Penn, R. (1995) 'Flexibility, skill and technical change in UK retailing', *The Service Industries Journal*, 15(3): 229–4.

Pollitt, P. (2005) 'Testing graduates at Lloyds TSB: how banks select the people who will lead it into the future', *Human Resource Management International Digest*, 13(1): 12–14.

Poole, M., Mansfield, R., Gould-Williams, J. and Mendes, P. (2005) 'British managers' attitudes and behaviour in industrial relations: a twenty-year study', *British Journal of Industrial Relations*, 43(1): 117–34.

Raybould, J. and Sheedy, V. (2005) 'Are graduates equipped with the right skills in the employability stakes?', *Industrial and Commercial Training*, 37(5): 259–63.

Ryan, L. (1996) *An Overview of the Demand for Graduates*, Policy Studies Institute for Employment Research, March, London: HMSO.

Ryan, P., Gospel, H. and Lewis, P.A. (2006) *Large Employers and Apprentice Training in the UK*, London: CIPD.

Sackett, P.R. and Lievens, F. (2008) 'Personnel selection', *Annual Review of Psychology*, 59: 419–50. Available online at: http:// psych.annualreviews.org. [Accessed on 2 June 2008.]

Stewart, J. and Knowles, V. (1999) 'The changing nature of graduate careers', *Career Development International*, 4(2): 370–83.

Storey, J. (ed.) (1995) *Human Resource Management: A Critical Text*, London: Thomson International Business Press.

Torrington, D. and Holden, N. (1992) 'Human Resource Management and the International Challenge of Change', *Personnel Review*, 21(2): 19–30.

Tregaskis, O. and Brewster, C. (1998) 'Training and development in the UK context: an emerging polarisation?', *Journal of European Industrial Training*, 22(4/5): 180–9.

TUC (UK Trades Union Congress) (2007) *Agency Workers: Counting the Cost of Flexibility*, London: TUC Equality and Employment Right Units.

Wallace, J., Gunnigle, P. and McMahon, G. (2004) *Industrial Relations in Ireland*, 3rd edn, Dublin: Gill & Macmillan.

Ward, K., Crimshaw, D., Rubery, J. and Bevnon, H. (2001) 'Dilemmas in the management of temporary work agency staff', *Human Resource Management Journal*, 11(4): 3–21.

Watson, S., Maxwell, G.A. and Farquharson, L. (2007) 'Line managers' views on adopting human resource roles: the case of Hilton (UK) hotels', *Employee Relations*, 29(1): 30–49.

Woodall, J., Scott-Jackson, W., Newham, T. and Gurney, M. (2007) 'Making the decision to outsource human resources', *Personnel Review*, 38(3): 236–52.

6

Australia and New Zealand

═══════════════ **LEARNING OUTCOMES** ═══════════════

The chapter is designed to help you understand, for Australia and New Zealand:

1   The (a) economic, (b) political, and (c) cultural contexts in which managers work;
2   The main trends in the labour market;
3   The typical features of (a) management policies and practices and (b) organizational structure and behaviour;
4   The main policies and practices of human resource management with regard to: (a) recruitment and selection; (b) training and development; (c) rewards and remuneration; and (d) employee relations.

Introduction

Geographically, Australia and New Zealand form a continent of their own. Australia is larger and more industrialized than New Zealand. Both are former British colonies. They had similar employment policies and employee relations systems until the 1980s, when the New Zealand government began a strategy of 'market liberalism'. Over the long term, both countries have transformed themselves from agrarian countries dependent on limited exports into internationally competitive and industrialized market economies with world leading technological capabilities. (See Table 6.1 for basic statistical indicators).

Table 6.1 Basic statistical indicators, Australia and New Zealand

Country	Area (sq km)	Population (July 2010 est.)	Population growth (2010) %	GDP – real growth rate (2009) %	Inflation rate (Jan. 2009 est.) %	Work-force (2009 est.) Million	Unemployment rate (2009) %
Australia	7741220	21262641	1.19	1.3	1.8	11.45	5.6
New Zealand	267710	4213418	0.93	−1.6	2.1	2.3	6.2

Source: Australian Labour Statistics (ABS, 2009); CIA *World Factbook* (2010).

Contexts: economics, politics and culture

Economics

Australia's economy has shifted from reliance on exports of iron ore, coal, wool, wood, meat and other natural resources to become a leading provider of industrial expertise, entertainment products, international education, and information and communications services, and a world resort for tourism, sports and leisure activities. By the turn of the century Australia was ranked among the top 15 industrialized countries in the world (*The Economist*, 26 Feb. 2000). The Australian economy grew at an average rate of 4 per cent between 1987 and 2007, as investments grew at record levels and unemployment was at its lowest. Reforms such as floating the Australian dollar and liberalizing trade and capital flows have resulted in a strong economy.

New Zealand has moved from a state-subsidized agrarian economy, known for its kiwis, to a free market economy competing worldwide through technology-based mass production of commodities. Its exports include meat, dairy products, fish, wood and wood products, fruit and vegetables, paper, textiles, processed foods, and agricultural machinery. Reforms in employee relations, information and communications technology, transport, civil service, education, health, leisure and tourism, contributed to fast growth until the 'credit crunch' recession.

The spread of multinational companies and with them the increasing use of information and communications technologies, the growth in international tourism and a high level of international trade have all contributed to the transformation of the Australian and New Zealand economies. A significant element in this transformation is their focus on the Asia-Pacific region after many years on being economically related to the British and the US economies. They have strengthened their trade and economic ties with Asian countries, notably China, Singapore and Thailand. Both Australia and New Zealand are partners with the Association of South–east Asian Nations (ASEAN), members of the East Asia Summit, and participants in the Asia-Pacific Economic Cooperation (APEC) group.

Politics

Both Australia and New Zealand are parliamentary democracies with the British monarch as sovereign. Both have a federal state system: New Zealand comprises 16 regions and one territory; Australia comprises six states and two territories.

Australian politics has oscillated between Labour and Liberal–National governments. The Liberal–National party coalition government of 1996–2007 favoured a deregulated employment system. It introduced the Workplace Relations and Other Legislative Amendments Act 1996. This provided for non-union bargaining through workplace agreements with individual employees rather than unions. The Act also emphasized freedom of association and the right of employees to join or not to join trade unions. By contrast, Labour governments (1983–96 and 2007–10) have been characterized by strong ties with the trade unions. They have encouraged the adoption of a cooperative approach between the government and the unions as well as employer and trade union partnerships. They have also supported decentralized collective bargaining (this will be discussed in more detail later in the chapter). The recent parliamentary elections in June 2010 brought back the Liberal–National party to power with a very narrow majority.

New Zealand politics has oscillated between the conservative National party and the left-wing Labour party. The National party government of 1990–99 introduced many radical and anti-union laws. The most radical was the Employment Contracts Act 1991, explained in more detail later in this chapter. The Labour party government of 1999–2008 replaced the Employment Contract Act 1991 with the Employment Relations Act 2000, aimed at restoring the power of trade unions and the role of collective bargaining – though in fact not much progress was made in this respect. The National party returned to power in November 2008 with a promise to review the system of employee relations and to strengthen the free market economy.

Culture

Australia and New Zealand share a British cultural heritage. The Australian population is diverse and composed of a mixture of natives (Aborigine) and immigrants. It is estimated that more than 40 per cent of Australians are migrants or children of migrants from mainly the UK, Ireland and North America. In recent years there has been an increase of immigrants from Asia. Native Australians represent only about 2 per cent of the total population. They have very limited participation in economic activities of the country and tend to be less skilled and less qualified than other groups (ABS, 2000; Patrickson and Hartmann, 2001).

Similarly, New Zealand is also made of a mixture of indigenous people (Maori), British and other European settlers, and recent immigrants from Asia. The Maori make about 8 per cent of the New Zealand population and they are relatively educated and politically active. New Zealanders have been described as generally 'hands on' and practical people who tend not to give much attention to intellectual and theoretical issues and who often undervalue their own achievements and abilities. In relation to Hofstede's cultural dimensions (described in Chapter 3) Australia and New Zealand occupy a similar position. Both are categorized as having small power distance, being high on individualism, weak on uncertainty avoidance, and relatively masculine.

Labour market trends

Australia and New Zealand are sparsely populated, have plentiful natural resources and a high capacity for growth and development. Australia has a workforce of 11.45 million, mostly located in Adelaide, Brisbane, Melbourne, Perth and Sydney. New Zealand has a workforce of about 2.3 million (World Factbook, 2010). Both countries are nations of small and medium enterprises despite the recent influx of multinational companies.

As shown in Table 6.2, most of the workforce of both countries is in the services sector. The hosting of the 2004 Olympics and Commonwealth games in 2006 boosted employment in the services industry and the tourism sector. In New Zealand, the high level of employment in services has been attributed to the public sector and to the increasing number of multinational companies in finance and tourism.

Table 6.2 Workforce distribution by occupation in 2005 (%), Australia and New Zealand

Country	Agriculture	Industry	Services
Australia	3.6	21.4	75
New Zealand	7	19	74

Source: CIA *World Factbook,* 2010.

Currently, the most significant factors in the composition of the labour market of both countries are the rising participation of women in the labour market, the use of flexible working practices, the employment of older people, the employment of immigrant workers, and a low unemployment rate.

Employment of women

In both countries the law prohibits discrimination against women in employment. In some cases the law encourages employers to take affirmative action in recruiting women. For example, in Australia, the Federal Affirmative Action (Equal Employment Opportunity for Women) Act 1986 required all private sector employers with 100 employees or more to take eight specific steps to avoid any kind of discrimination against women in employment. The Industrial Relations Act 1988 endorsed the Federal Affirmative Action (Equal Employment Opportunity for Women) Act 1986, giving equal opportunities to men and women in pay and all other benefits.

In Australia, the number of women in employment increased from about 25 per cent of the total workforce in 1961 to 44.6 per cent in 2004 and to 58 per cent in 2009 (Davis and Harris, 1996; Davis and Lansbury, 1998; ABS, 2005). According to Lansbury and Baird (2004: 151), 'major demographic, educational and social shifts have resulted in significant increases in female participation rates and decreases in male participation rates, meaning that the traditional separation between home and work can no longer be sustained'. In New Zealand the rate of female participation in the labour market increased from 32.01 per cent of the workforce in 1976 to 45.43 per cent in 1996 (www.stats.govt.nz, accessed July 2006). The employment of women reached its peak at 68.7 per cent of the workforce in 2008 and then dropped to 67.4 per cent in 2009 (OECD, 2010).

However, most female employment has been confined to low paid jobs in the retailing, health, education, and clerical sectors. Fewer than 1 per cent of women employees in Australia are in senior management positions at company director level. By 2001, about 73 per cent of all part-time workers were women. More than 60 per cent of women with children under the age of 15 worked part time (ABS, 2005, 2010). In New Zealand, 71 per cent of those who work part time are women (EEOT, 2005; OECD, 2010).

Flexible working practices

A study by De Cieri et al. (2005) found that in Australia the most popular flexible working practices were, in order of popularity, part-time work, study leave, flexitime, home-based working and job sharing. Part-time work in Australia has more than doubled between 1978 and 2004 (ABS, 2005) and then stabilized at around 24 per cent of the workforce between 2005 and 2009

(OECD, 2010). More than a third of employees in the retail and wholesale industries, public services and recreation and personal services are in part-time employment (ABS, 2005; Bardoel et al., 2008). In New Zealand, the number of part-time increased from 18 per cent of the workforce in 1991 to 23 per cent in 2001 and then started to decline slightly to 22.5 per cent in 2009 (EEOT, 2005; OECD, 2010). Most jobs created over the past decade are casual and part time, making Australia one of the countries with 'the highest proportion of "atypical" or non-full-time employees in its labour force in the industrialised world' (Lansbury and Baird, 2004: 149).

There has been a marked growth in teleworking and home-based working. In 2005 the Australian government set up an advisory committee on teleworking called ATAC (the Australian Telework Advisory Committee), in order to monitor the practice of teleworking throughout the country. A survey by Sensis found that a third of Australians had experienced teleworking and that more than a third of small and medium enterprises used it. In New Zealand, the use of teleworking has also increased. For example, a partnership between Telecom New Zealand and iPass, a connectivity specialist company, resulted in the introduction of Telecom Office Anywhere (TOA) allowing employees to access their organizations' network systems from a PC or laptop almost anywhere in the country and worldwide.

Employment of older people

People in Australia and New Zealand are living longer and getting healthier. (See Table 6.3.) Many employees prefer to continue working after the official age of retirement. In Australia the number of older people (55–64 years) in employment increased from 44.3 per cent of the workforce in 1999 to 59 per cent in 2009 (OECD, 2010). Similarly, in New Zealand the proportion of older people in employment increased from 56.5 per cent to 72.1 per cent over the same period (OECD, 2010). The reason for the high number of older people in employment in New Zealand is the change in the age of eligibility for pensions from 60 to 65, making many employees remain in employment longer than before.

Table 6.3 Age structure (%) (2009), Australia and New Zealand

Country	0–14 years %	15–64 years %	Over 65 %	Median age (years)	Life expectancy at birth (for men and women)
Australia	18.6	67.9	13.5	37.3	81.6
New Zealand	20.7	66.5	12.8	36.6	80.3

Source: CIA *World Factbook*, 2010.

Employment of ethnic minorities

The concept of ethnic minorities in Australia and New Zealand is different from that of most other countries. The native peoples are part of the ethnic minority while the ethnic majority is mainly made up of British, Irish and American settlers. Aboriginal peoples make up only 2 per cent of the Australian population while the native Maori people make about 7 per cent of the population of New Zealand. In New Zealand, the group with the highest participation rate in the labour market is the European (Pakeha) ethnic group (62.7 per cent), followed by the Maori ethnic group (54 per cent). Many large companies, mainly the MNCs, recruit foreign labour, especially from Asia.

MINI CASE STUDY 7

I Wish I Were an Old Foreign Woman (Australia)

Jim Logan is a graduate from Queensland University with a first-class degree in sociology and social work. Although he has a strong CV and good communication skills, he has not been able to find employment for the last 10 months. He thinks that employers have been discriminating against him because he is a young Australian male. One day he woke up and said, 'I wish I were an old foreign woman'.

Questions

1 Discuss why Jim Logan said 'I wish I were an old foreign woman'.
2 In the light of the above description of current labour market trends, discuss the positive and the negative aspects of affirmative action in Australia and New Zealand.

Unemployment

The level of unemployment has fluctuated over the years depending on the state of the economy in the two countries. For example, in the 1970s and up to the late 1980s the level of unemployment was relatively low. In the early 1990s the level of unemployment increased significantly because of a decline in the manufacturing sector, cuts in public sector employment, and pressure on many private sector employers to reduce labour costs. Also, more capital-intensive methods of production were introduced. By 1994 the rate of unemployment in Australia was 10.2 per cent, but as the state of the economy improved the rate gradually declined to 4.2 per cent in 2008, before going back to 5.8 in 2009 (OECD, 2009). New Zealand experienced a trend similar to that in Australia in the 1970s and 1980s. In June 2006, the rate of unemployment in New Zealand was about 3.8 per cent before it started to increase steadily to reach about 4.8 per cent in 2009 (OECD, 2009).

Management and organization

Until the mid-1980s, the practice of management and organization in Australia and New Zealand was similar to that in the UK in the 1970s. However, economic and political changes and the increasing level of US and Japanese investment in Australia and New Zealand led to the development of new approaches to management, including human resource management (Boxall, 1996; Haynes and Fryer, 1999; Allan et al., 1999; Lansbury and Baird, 2004). Allan et al. (1999) have shown that managers in Australia and New Zealand have adopted a number of strategic management practices. These include: becoming aware of the necessity of linking HRM strategies to corporate strategy; using legal expertise in dealing with management problems; and focusing more on performance indicators at the organizational, group and individual levels.

HR and corporate strategy

What triggered Australian managers to think strategically was a Commonwealth Government Task Force report (Karpin, 1995), which concluded that the standard of Australian managers was much behind that of their counterparts in the industrialized world. It argued that they had to break away from the personnel management practices they had practised previously and embrace a strategic approach to the management of people. Moreover, the high exposure of many managers to international management practices from the increasing presence of MNCs in both Australia and New Zealand has led to the transfer of management practices that were seen as good practice by international standards.

Consequently, more companies in both countries have had to concentrate on value-added products and services that require a more strategic approach to management (Boxall, 1996; Kane et al., 1999; Fisher and Dowling, 1999; Lansbury and Baird, 2004). Australian and New Zealander employers have had to adopt strategies aimed at improving their domestic operations, introducing new technologies, redesigning jobs, developing employee skills, gaining employee commitment, downsizing the workforce, allowing greater flexibility in working practices, improving quality products, and cutting costs in order to remain competitive.

Allan et al. (1999) found that both countries had experience with the three strategies of productivity enhancement, cost minimization and work intensification, though New Zealand employers were much more likely than Australians to implement cost reduction and productivity enhancement measures. In terms of work intensification, they found that New Zealand employers introduced new payment systems and made their employees work harder, while the Australians resorted to other measures such as not replacing the workers who left their jobs. They also found that in implementing the productivity improvement strategy the responsibility for HR practices had been shifted from human resource managers to line managers.

Reliance on legal experts

With the continuous decline in trade union membership in both countries, employers have had to use more individualistic approaches in dealing with their employees. There has been a move towards more decentralized bargaining arrangements at the enterprise level, where every employee is considered individually (Bamber, 1992). Employers are allowed to negotiate with individual employees over hours of work and the terms and conditions of employment. There has been an increasing need to refer to legal experts for advice to protect individual employees' interests and those of the organization. Also, to avoid claims of discriminations and unfair treatment, managers have had to rely very often on the services of legal experts.

ACTIVITY 1

Refer to Chapter 4 (on the US and Canada). What do you think are the main similarities and differences between the profiles of US and Australian managers?

Managing human resources

The management of human resources in Australia and New Zealand is similar to that of the UK and also has much in common with that of the US (Pennington and Lafferty, 2002; Lansbury and Baird, 2004; De Ceiri, 2007). In this section, the main policies and practices of HRM in both countries are discussed.

Recruitment and selection

The process of recruitment and selection is particularly important in Australia and New Zealand because the labour market is very diverse and there is a shortage of skilled workforce. As in many other countries, employers in Australia and New Zealand use job analysis and human resource planning, and apply the conventional methods of recruitment and selection, from advertising the job to making the offer of employment (Taylor, 1998; Breaugh and Starke, 2000; Taylor et al., 2002; Daly et al., 2005). The use of human resource planning is more common in New Zealand than in Australia. Job analysis is traditionally used in both countries, though more so in Australia than in New Zealand (CCH Survey, 1999: 4; Taylor et al., 2002). The process of recruitment and selection in both countries has been influenced by the growth of international recruitment by large international companies using global recruiting agencies. Below we discuss three themes: recruitment in general; graduate recruitment; and selection.

Recruitment

Employers in both countries use a variety of recruitment methods ranging from advertising vacancies on notice boards internally, in newspapers and on the internet, to contacting job centres and agencies, to targeting and poaching individuals. The common features of recruitment in both countries are:

- The use of word of month, which is very common among employees in manual and low-skilled jobs.
- Unsolicited job seekers who just walk in into a farm or turn up at the gate of a plant to ask for employment.
- Extensive use of the internet. Note that internet recruitment has had major effects on the proliferation of agency recruitment at an international scale. It enabled employers to reach a wider pool of potential employees beyond the boundaries of Australasia.

Graduate recruitment

Both Australia and New Zealand have a growing population of students graduating each year. The graduate labour market has become increasingly competitive as many companies are recruiting skilled employees from overseas as well as from home. Australian and New Zealander graduates have had to compete internationally for jobs in their own country. For more information on graduate recruitment in Australia please refer to Carless (2007).

Selection

The use of interviews is traditional and still very popular in both countries. Until recently, the use of tests in Australia and New Zealand was very limited. Hicks (1991) stated that the use of tests in Australian companies was similar to that found in the UK. Moreover, a survey of management selection practices in the state of Victoria by Vaughan and McLean (1989) found very little evidence of the use of tests in their managerial selection practices. Similarly a study of selection practices in New Zealand by Dakin and Armstrong (1989) concluded that the use of tests was very limited.

However, a number of recent studies have reported an increase in the use of testing, not just to recruit new staff but also for promotion, training and redundancies (Hicks, 1991; Dakin et al., 1994; Taylor, 1998; Taylor et al., 2002; Daly et al., 2005). The main reasons for the rise in the use of tests are: the increasing availability of tests through commercial consultancies; changes in the laws requiring equal opportunities in recruitment and selection; and the growing belief by users in the benefits of testing for their organizations. Dakin et al. (1994: 5) points out that such tests were 'marketed in a much more active fashion by commercial test producers'.

Another feature in the selection process is the decline in the use of written references. Many employers rely on written references less frequently than they used to. For example, in Australia, the use of references declined from 37 per cent in 1994 to 16 per cent in 1999 (CCH Survey, 1999).

MINI CASE STUDY 8

The Wan Tan Slaughter House in the Asia-Pacific

Wan Tan International is a Malaysian company specializing in the production and export of Hallal corned beef in Australia and New Zealand. Most of its 2,000 employees are immigrants from Indonesia, Egypt and Iraq. When the general manager, Rudwan Abdul Rahman, was asked, 'Why don't you employ the local people?' he replied, 'We employ those who can do the job better not those who look smarter.'

Questions

1 Explain Wan Tan's employment policy in the light of the information provided in this chapter.
2 To what extent is Wan Tan's recruitment policy discriminating against local employees? Discuss the arguments for and against such policy.

Training and development

Both Australia and New Zealand employers use on-the-job training, off-the-job training, and organizational training at different levels. However, they vary in their approaches and their level of spending on training. For example, until the 1990s, spending on vocational education and industrial training in Australia was limited and had less effect than those of other countries in the region.

This was so despite a number of initiatives aimed at improving the knowledge and skills of its workforce – for example, the establishment of a National Training Authority (ANTA) and the National Training Board (NTB) in order to set national training standards, competency and accreditation guidelines (Anderson, 1994; Noe and Winkler, 2009). In both countries, the federal government expects public and private sector organizations to invest in the training and development of their employees. For example, they have been actively promoting back-to-education initiatives and implementing training policies that may help the unemployed to become employable. Private sector employers have been urged to keep up with technological changes by training their employees. Moreover, employers in both countries make use of the services of training and accrediting bodies such as the Human Resources Institute of New Zealand (HRINZ) and the Australian Human Resources Institute (AHRI). The HRINZ and the AHRI are professional accrediting bodies similar in their roles to the UK Chartered Institute for Personnel and Development (CIPD).

On-the-job training and apprenticeships

In Australia, by the start of the 1990s more than 23 per cent of all those employed who were 15–19 years old had apprenticeship training (Baker, 1994). In New Zealand, the government has been promoting the use of apprenticeship training by allocating a federal budget, which amounted to NZ$41 million in 2002, for the purpose of providing on-the-job training to young people. The reason for implementing this traditionally British inherited training method (apprenticeship) can be related to the type of dominant businesses in both countries. Their economies have been based on small and medium enterprises where a small number of employees are normally recruited and trained on the job. The recent growth in the level of foreign direct investment has led to large investors (multinational companies) having to introduce a variety of training methods. This development has led to a decline in the use of apprenticeship, but not in the level of training in general because many employees benefit from off-the-job training to improve their knowledge and skills (Selvarajah et al., 2000; Lansbury and Baird, 2004; Noe and Winkler, 2009).

Off-the-job training and education

The standard of education in both countries is amongst the best in the world. More than 99 per cent of the population is literate (OECD, 2009). They have some world-class, internationally recognized universities, and there are excellent opportunities for vocational and technical education in specialized colleges, centres and institutes. More than 1.7 million Australians enrol in publicly funded vocational and technical training and education each year. Australian universities have become international centres of excellence in higher education and research, and they have attracted thousands of students from throughout the world, significantly from South-east Asian countries, to study in them. Moreover, many Australians are going back to college/university to sharpen their skills and enhance their employment prospects.

However, it has been argued that although the education system is good, the workforce is not well trained and many graduates lack the basic transferable skills that employers require. In this respect, Lansbury and Baird (2004: 153) state: 'While Australia has been fortunate to achieve economic stability in recent times, it has not paid sufficient attention to the development of human capital and a skilled, educated nation'. The type of training, in the form of short-term traineeship, which has replaced the traditional apprenticeship system is not adequate: it produces 'qualifications which are "tickets to nowhere" ... Australia is simply not keeping up with the level and quality of training provided by most other advanced industrialised economies for their citizens' (Lansbury and Baird, 2004: 152).

Organizational training

As in the US, many large companies in Australia and New Zealand have their own training facilities but they tend also to use the services of specialist and international consultancies (Avery et al., 1999; Noe and Winkler, 2009). Major international training providers such as DDI, Forum, Siebel and Achieve Global have established strong networks of training outlets delivering training in different areas of expertise. Moreover, many large companies have made online courses easily available to their employees.

ACTIVITY 3

Refer to the passage on Training and Development in Chapter 4 (US and Canada). Compare and contrast North American and the Australasian management approaches to training.

Rewards and remuneration

The level of rewards and remuneration in Australia and New Zealand was until the late 1980s decided through a centralized wage determination process of collective agreements between the government, the unions and the employers.

Over the last twenty years the trend has been towards a decentralized rewards system (with rewards set by individual arrangements). 'In practice, under the arbitral system, wages and conditions were set by industrial tribunals through conciliation and arbitration' (Holland et al., 2009: 69). The arbitral system 'operated on the recognition of organizations, meaning union representation was entrenched as the primary mode of employee voice' (Holland et al., 2009: 69). The current reward and remuneration system is more complex and varied, as discussed below.

Centralized rewards system (rewards set by collective agreement)

Until recently, Australian federal wage policy had been determined by the government, the Australian Council of Trade Unions (ACTU), and the employers. Each party made a submission to the Federal Arbitration Commission, which arbitrated and made the appropriate wage decision that very often was applied throughout the country. The involvement of the federal commission in the settlement of wages through arbitration made the reward system in Australia relatively centralized (Davis and Lansbury, 1998). For example, in 1975 the commission issued new wage-fixing guidelines that made it illegal to grant wage increases without the permission of the commission. A similar mechanism existed in New Zealand until the introduction of the Employment Contracts Act 1991. Although the federal wage system is still in operation, many employers have moved towards a more decentralized system of rewards and remuneration.

Decentralized rewards system (rewards set by individual arrangements)

Deregulation of industrial relations and employment policies in both countries since the 1990s has encouraged many employers to introduce flexible systems of rewards related to individual performance. Many employers started to use employee performance appraisal for performance-related pay. In New Zealand, the introduction of the Employment Contracts Act 1991 and the Workplace Relations Act of 1996 (WRA) changed the role of trade unions and the ways in which employees are rewarded (Hanley and Nguyen, 2005). In both countries, performance appraisal was used regularly but for developmental rather than judgemental (pay) reasons. Recently it appears that there has been a move away from the regular form filling and interviewing performance appraisal system to a more empowering and discussion-based system of performance management linked to performance-related pay (Hanley and Nguyen, 2005). Many employers have used performance management indicators when deciding on the rewards of their employees.

=== **MINI CASE STUDY 9** ===

The 2002 New Zealand Cricket Pay Dispute

The New Zealand cricket season (2002/3) was postponed for six weeks because of a pay dispute between the Cricket Players' Association and New Zealand Cricket. The association claimed that the New Zealand cricket team did not bargain in good faith as provisioned in the Employment Relations Act 2000.

Question

1 Discuss the advantages and disadvantages of setting rewards by collective agreements.

The minimum wage

Both countries operate a statutory minimum wage. In Australia, a minimum wage system has been operated since 1907 when the Commonwealth Court of Conciliation and Arbitration set a basic minimum wage that was aimed at meeting the normal needs of an average unskilled worker with a family unit of five. Since then a number of changes have been introduced to the national minimum wage: rather than a basic wage that is just enough for an average unskilled worker's family, it eventually became a total award for a standard work week and was set relative to increases in the consumer price index (i.e. a full wage indexation policy). Wage indexation had to be abandoned in 1981 as result of changes in the economy and political system. The Labour government from 1983 to 1996 was in favour of direct negotiations and collective bargaining at the enterprise level, giving more power to the Federal Commission on wage determination (Davis and Lansbury, 1998). The commission reintroduced the indexation wage system, which the unions had to accept and agree not to make any extra claims. This led to stability in wages because unions became unable to press for wages higher than the agreed national wage rates. However, by 1987 the wage indexation system had to be replaced because of a decline in trade and poor balance of payments, forcing the government to review its income policy. In 1987 and 1988, the Australian Industrial Relations Commission (AIRC) introduced new wage guidelines aimed at improving 'efficiency, productivity and functional flexibility at the workplace' (Allan et al., 1999: 830). The Federal minimum wage in Australia is currently at AU$15.00 per hour or AU$569.90 per week (ABS, 2010).

In 1894 the government of New Zealand enacted the first minimum wage law in the world. From then until the 1990s the minimum wage was determined by collective agreements between the state, trade unions and employers. Currently, the statutory minimum wage is decided in relation to the customer price index. It was NZ$12 per hour in 2008 for adults over the age of 18 and NZ$9 per hour for 16-17 years old. A proposal was made in the Minimum Wage (Abolition of Wage Discrimination) Amendment Bill introduced in parliament on 7 December 2005 to end age discrimination in employment by requiring employers to pay employees aged 16 and 17 years old the same minimum wage as adult employees. A number of companies, mainly MNCs, have abolished the youth minimum wage rate and offer the adult minimum rate to all their employees.

MINI CASE STUDY 10

The KiwiSaver Bill, New Zealand

The New Zealand labour government introduced the KiwiSaver Bill into parliament on 28 February 2006. The bill proposes a work-based savings scheme that encourages employees to save for retirement. A deduction of 4 to 8 per cent is made by the employer from a participating employee's gross pay and forwarded to the Inland Revenue Department along with the employee's PAYE. The scheme is voluntary and allows those in financial hardship or emigrating permanently to opt out within the first six weeks. Employees aged 18 to 65 are automatically considered for the scheme when taking up a new job but employees may choose their own KiwiSaver scheme if they prefer not to take the one chosen by their employers. The government has introduced incentives to encourage participation in the scheme, including a NZ$1,000 saving kickstart and a contribution of up to NZ$5,000 towards a first home.

Questions

1 What do you think were the real motives for introducing the scheme?
2 Discuss the advantages and disadvantages of such voluntary schemes to the employee, the employer and the government.

Employee relations

The practice of employee relations in Australia and New Zealand has historically been similar to that in the UK. The development of trade unionism started in the nineteenth century and by the 1920s more than half of the Australian workforce had joined trade unions. The first confederation of all trade unions was formed in 1927 as the Australian Council of Trade Unions (ACTU), which is still an important party to the federal employee relations agreements. Trade union activity concentrated, traditionally, on the betterment of the terms and conditions of their members' employment and on the improvement of their wages and salaries (Davis and Lansbury, 1998; De Cieri, 2007; Holland et al.,

2009). However, there have been significant changes since the 1990s. Radical changes started first in New Zealand with the introduction of the Employment Contracts Act 1991 by the conservative National party government, and then in Australia with the introduction of the Workplace Relations Act 1996 by the conservative Liberal–National coalition government.

In New Zealand, the Employment Contracts Act 1991 disbanded the arbitration system and replaced it with a system of enterprise-based bargaining and voluntary conciliation and arbitration. The act also abolished collective awards and replaced them with a system of collective and individual contracts whereby it is possible for individual employees to represent themselves or to nominate a bargaining agent other than a trade union. Although employers had to recognize employees' bargaining options, they were no longer obliged to bargain in good faith (Allan et al., 1999: 831). However, when the Labour party returned to power in 1999 they repealed the Employment Contracts Act 1991 and replaced it with the Employment Relations Act (ERA) 2000, which was amended in 2005, and strengthened the position of trade unions by supporting union membership, collective bargaining, and good faith in employment relationships.

In Australia, the decentralization of employment relations in the 1990s was extended to include enterprise flexibility agreements and made the negotiation of workplace agreements possible in non-unionized enterprises. The Workplace Relations Act 1996 started the 'radical deregulation of industrial relations although it still provided parties with a choice between remaining in the award system or opting for a workplace agreement' (Davis and Lansbury, 1998: 138). Unlike the Employment Contracts Act 1991 in New Zealand, the WRA 1996 of Australia did not abolish the arbitration system, but it moved the Australian employee relations system 'away from a collectivist approach, in which there was a strong role for unions and tribunals, to a more fragmented system of individual bargaining between employees and employers' (Davis and Lansbury, 1998: 138).

The changes introduced at the federal level were followed to varying degrees at the state level. Conservative governments at the state level, in Victoria and Western Australia, introduced more radical changes than those in New Zealand. For example, Victoria 'abolished the award system in 1992 and replaced it with a system of industrial and collective contracts' (Allan et al., 1999: 830). The Workplace Relations Amendment (Work Choices) Bill 2005 was intended to further undermine the role of trade unions and collective bargaining, and to give more power to employers. Among its many radical proposals are the replacement of the separate state and federal systems with a single national employee relations system, the replacement of the National Wage Cases at the Australian Industrial Relations Commission (AIRC) by a new body called the Australian Fair Pay Commission, a reduction in allowable award matters, the exemption of businesses with fewer than 101 employees from unfair dismissal laws, the increase of restrictions on allowable industrial action, and the discouraging of pattern bargaining and industry-wide industrial action.

In summary, there have been significant changes in the systems of employee relations of both countries since the early 1990s because of changes in government, as well as technological changes and international competitive pressures, mainly due to the influence of multinational companies and the liberalization of international trade. Such 'changes have had a significant effect on the focus and structure of employment relations and the variety of employee voice regimes in Australia. A major effect has been the shift of decision-making power on employment relations to the workplace, with direct communications between employers and employees becoming the norm' (Holland et al., 2009: 68).

Trade union organization, membership and density

As in the UK, the types of unions have moved from craft to general and industrial unions, and from blue- to white-collar unions. Trade unionism grew faster from the early 1920s to the 1950s because of governments using legislation that was favourable to trade unions (Haynes et al., 2005, 2008). Trade union membership increased rapidly to reach its highest levels by the middle of the 1970s, and then started to decline over the 1980s and 1990s. One feature of current employee relations is the existence of an increasing number of free riders. Haynes et al. (2008: 8) found that 'large and increasing numbers of Australian workers take a "free ride" on union membership, gaining the benefits of union coverage without contributing to the costs of provision'. They estimated that about 39.2 per cent of those in unionized workplaces who had the opportunity to be members of their union did not join (Haynes et al., 2008: 25).

In general, trade unions in both countries are still well organized and still considered by some employers as good bargaining partners. Despite the conservative governments' laws – such as the Employment Contracts Act 1991 in New Zealand, aimed at weakening the power of trade unions and encouraging employees to sign individual contracts with their employers rather than be represented by the unions – trade union membership is still significant in some sectors of the economy. In New Zealand, trade union membership has stabilized at around 22 per cent of the working population since 2004 (OECD, 2009).

In Australia, the number and membership of trade unions have declined significantly since the 1980s, though the decline has been in the private rather than the public sector. The public sector saw a rise in trade union membership especially among white-collar employees. There has been also a decline in the number of trade unions, in part because of the merger of small and medium sized unions to form amalgamated unions in order to establish, as Davis and Lansbury (1998: 117) point out, 'larger, better-resourced unions, which would be better able to serve their members and assist them in workplace bargaining'.

=========== MINI CASE STUDY 11 ===========

Minimum Union Membership in Australia

Before the Industrial Relations Act 1988, trade unions in Australia could be formed with a minimum of 100 members, but the Act required federal unions to register with the arbitration authorities in order to be given full legal status and to have access to an industrial tribunal. Two years later, in 1990, the amended act required the federal unions to have a minimum of 10,000 members, but this proposal was criticized by many employers and was opposed by the Confederation of Australian Industry (CAI). The CAI complained to the International Labour Organization (ILO) on the grounds of freedom of association. As a result, the Industrial Relations Reform Bill 1993 reverted to the required minimum of 100. Three years later, the Workplace Relations Act 1996 reduced the required minimum to just 50.

Questions

1 What were the reasons for the amended Act of 1990 requiring a minimum of 10,000 members, and why was it legislated at a time when trade union membership was in decline?
2 Why did the CAI oppose the proposed minimum membership of 10,000 members? (Please note that it was the CAI not the ACTU.)
3 Taking into consideration the current economic and social conditions in Australia, discuss the benefits of trade unions to Australian employers.

The low trade union density in both countries is attributed to a decline in manufacturing industry, a rise in part-time work (part timers do not join the unions), and to an increase in job insecurity (employees do not stay in employment long enough to join the unions).

Collective bargaining

As indicated earlier, collective agreements in both Australia and New Zealand before the mid-1990s were only achieved through collective bargaining between registered trade unions and registered employers. Collective agreements could be reached through single-party or multi-party bargaining, according to a set of procedures. As a result of economic and political changes, radical reforms were made to the collective agreements tradition, first in New Zealand and then in Australia. In New Zealand, the Employment Contracts Act 1991 allowed individual employees to bargain individual contracts with their employers without the need for trade union representation. The act was aimed at systematically undermining the use of collective bargaining and strengthening the position of employers *vis-a-vis* trade unions. However, the next Labour government in 1999 abandoned the Employment Contracts Act 1991 and replaced it with the Employment Relations Act (ERA) 2000: this reverted to the previous practice of collective bargaining, mediation and arbitration processes, and bargaining in good faith. The ERA 2000 (subsequently amended in 2004 and in 2005) encouraged collective bargaining in good faith between the trade unions and employers. The act set out basic requirements for good-faith bargaining. It required, for example, that the employers and the unions involved in collective bargaining:

- do their best to agree on an effective bargaining procedure;
- consider each other's proposal, meet and respond to each other;
- carry on bargaining until they reach an agreement on matters they have not agreed yet, even if they have come to a deadlock on another matter;
- respect the role of the other's representative by not seeking to bargain directly with those being represented;
- not undermine the bargaining process or the status of the other party;
- not pass on collectively bargained terms and conditions to employees not covered by collective bargaining or agreements; and
- conclude a collective agreement, unless there is a genuine reason based on reasonable grounds not to. (www.ers.dol.govt.nz/bargaining/good_faith.html, accessed 23 July 2006)

In Australia, the introduction of the Workplace Relations Act 1996 (amended in 2006) further provided for the decentralization of collective bargaining, defined the rights and duties of employees, determined the acceptable employment practices, regulated occupational health and safety, prohibited all forms of discrimination in employment, and promoted positive action and equal opportunity policies. As far as collective bargaining is concerned, the act initiated radical changes by institutionalizing 'individual and workplace collective bargaining as the preferred system of bargaining. The role of unions and the Industrial Commission was curtailed although the award system was retained, albeit in a much reduced form' (Allan et al., 1999: 831). The Workplace Relations Act 1996 was based on the principle that individual and collective agreements were equal. Thus it encouraged employers to opt for individual workplace agreements known as Australian Workplace Agreements (AWAs).

The AWAs gave employers the power to enter into agreement with non-unionized groups of employees or individuals. Employers are required only to have agreement contracts registered at the office of the Employee Advocate to ensure that the agreement meets the no-disadvantage test, or to refer to the Commission as a final arbiter. The introduction of the AWAs reduced pluralism in employee relations and increased management's prerogative at the enterprise level (Waring, 1999; Thornwaite and Sheldon, 2000; Hanley and Nguyen, 2005). One of the claims made by the ACTU against the AWAs is that they led to the exploitation of individual employees, especially those who wish to balance work with family commitments. A report by the Department of Employment and Workplace Relations confirmed the ACTU claim by stating that of all individual contracts less than 1 in 12 (8 per cent) provided paid maternity leave and only 1 in 20 (5 per cent) provided paid paternity leave (HRM Guide Network, 17 March 2006). Also, a study by the Employment Advocate reported that about 1 in 3 (32 per cent) employees on individual contracts were working more hours than they did two years earlier (ibid.). Also, the introduction of AWAs led to a significant decline in trade union membership and a reduction in strike action.

Industrial conflicts and strikes

Until 1930, all strike activity in both Australia and New Zealand was illegal and subject to penalties under the Commonwealth Conciliation and Arbitration Act. Despite the restrictions, there were strikes in both public and private sectors. As in most industrialized nations, strike activity coincided with the increasing exploitation of employees and became widespread in the 1960s and the 1970s, before starting to decline over the 1980s and 1990s for reasons to do mainly with changes in labour market composition and the introduction of new legislation restricting industrial action.

Currently, employment law provides for the right to strike during a designated bargaining period, but gives more power to the Arbitration Commission to make use of traditional compulsory arbitration and to intervene when parties are not acting in good faith. For example, in New Zealand, the total number of stoppages (complete strikes, partial strikes and lockouts) dropped from 72 in 1996 to their lowest (21) in 2000 and started to go up to 53 stoppages in 2005 (Statistics New Zealand, 2005, Quarterly Employment Survey). In Australia there have been a number of industrial action activities other than strikes, such as work-to-rule and bans. A ban is an action short of a strike and is the refusal by workers to carry out certain tasks, use certain equipment or cooperate with others in their workplace. This type of industrial action, which is referred to by Davis and Lansbury (1998) as a 'silent strike', is becoming the most popular action in Australia, especially after the introduction of legislation limiting strike action.

Settlement of industrial disputes

The settlement of industrial disputes in both countries has been through compulsory conciliation and arbitration that was introduced in New Zealand by the Industrial Conciliation and Arbitration Act 1894, and in Australia by the Conciliation and Arbitration Act of 1904. According to Allan et al. (1999: 829), the process of 'arbitration provided unions with compulsory employer recognition and allowed unions to exert considerable influence in the setting of legally enforceable minimum labour standards'. The main difference here between the two is that in Australia, the legislation designed to protect arbitration and conciliation tends to differ slightly from one state or territory to another, while in New Zealand the legislation covers the entire country and affects all employees. In Australia, the Industrial Relations Act 1988 required all federal unions to register with the arbitration authorities in order to be given full legal corporate status and to have access to an industrial tribunal. The use of industrial tribunals is common in both Australia and New Zealand, especially for dealing with individual cases of unfair treatment or unfair dismissal.

Employee involvement and participation

When workers' participation and industrial democracy schemes were in fashion throughout the world in the 1970s, Australia was no exception (Bowes, 1975; Lansbury, 1978). The Labour governments of that time sought to extend the power of workers beyond the common practice of collective bargaining (Holland et al., 2009; Markey and Patmore, 2009). However, direct employee involvement never materialized because of the change of government in 1975 from Labour to a Liberal–National coalition (Davis and Lansbury, 1998; Markey and Patmore, 2009). When the Labour party returned to government in 1983 it attempted to introduce direct workers' participation, giving employees the right to information and involvement in issues of technological change under the Accord Mark I. The federal government paper on Industrial Democracy and Employee Participation stated that 'employee participation is now a major government priority and the government sees it as essential to a successful response to the significant challenges of the present time' (Department of Employment and Industrial Relations, 1986). Over the 1980s a number of National Wage Case Decisions were made in order to enhance the practice of workers' participation, but this did not last for a long (Markey and Patmore, 2009). The trend seems to have reversed gradually since the 1990s as the attention of government turned to the use of employee consultation (Davis and Lansbury, 1998; Holland et al., 2009). The move towards employee consultation, rather than workers' direct participation, has been related to the increasing emphasis on enterprise bargaining. However, there has been little evidence of any real workers' consultation or significant employee involvement in the process of decision-making (Moorehead et al., 1997; Benson, 2000; Markey and Patmore, 2009). A number of studies (see Holland et al., 2009; Markey and Patmore, 2009) have concluded that while respecting the practice of collective bargaining, many Australian and New Zealander managers are resistant to employee direct involvement in the process of decision-making because management is seen as the exclusive domain of managers who make decisions and are responsible for organizational performance. Trade unions are also sceptical of direct employee involvement practices, which they see as a means of undermining their representative role.

Summary

1   Both Australia and New Zealand are former British colonies and inherited similar employment policies and employee relations systems until the 1980s when they started to pursue different political and economic reforms.
2   The most significant factors in the composition of the labour markets of both countries are the rising participation of women, the use of flexible working practices, the employment of older people, the employment of immigrant workers, and low unemployment rate.
3   Managers in Australia and New Zealand have adopted a number of strategic management practices such as becoming aware of the necessity to link HRM strategies to corporate strategy, becoming reliant on legal expertise in dealing with management problems, and focusing more on performance indicators at the organizational, group and individual levels.
4   The process of recruitment and selection is crucial in countries such as Australia and New Zealand where the labour market is very diverse and short of skilled workforce. Employers in both countries use job analysis and human resource planning, and apply conventional methods of recruitment and selection from advertising the job to making the offer of employment. The use of human resource planning is more common in New Zealand than in Australia. Job analysis is traditionally used in both countries but more so in Australia than in New Zealand.
5   Australia and New Zealand have much in common in terms of training and development. They both use on-the-job training (apprenticeship), off-the-job training (formal education and vocational training), and organizational training at different levels, but they vary in their approaches and availability of resources.
6   The level of rewards and remuneration in both Australia and New Zealand was until the late 1980s decided through a centralized wage determination process of collective agreements between the government, the unions and the employers. There has been a significant move towards a decentralized rewards system over the last twenty years.
7   There have been significant changes in the systems of employee relations of both countries since the early 1990s. Such changes have had their effects on trade union organization, membership and density, collective bargaining, industrial conflict and the settlement of industrial disputes.

Revision questions

Chapter 1 provides a review task designed to consolidate your learning from this chapter. Please see Box 1.2.

In addition, the following questions are designed to help you revise this chapter.

1   Show in a table the main similarities and differences between the labour markets of Australia and New Zealand on the one hand and the US and Canada on the other.
2   Critically analyse the main issues concerning the Australasian approach to management.

3   As an HR manager of a British company in Australia, write a report to the company's board of directors describing the main similarities and the main differences in HRM functions (recruitment and selection, training and development, rewards system, and employee relations) between Australia and the UK.

References

ABS (Australian Bureau of Statistics) (2000) *Educating and Training Australia's Workers*, Special article, Canberra: AGPS.

ABS (Australian Bureau of Statistics) (2005) *February 2005 Employment Figures*, Canberra: AGPS.

ABS (Australian Bureau of Statistics) (2010) September 2010, *Australian Economic Indicators*, Canberra: AGPS.

Allan, C., Brosnan, P. and Walsh, P. (1999) 'Human resource strategies: workplace reform and industrial restructuring in Australia and New Zealand', *International Journal of Human Resource Management*, 10(5): 828–41.

Anderson, A.A. (1994) 'Vocational education and industry training in Australia', *Education and Training*, 36(2): 31–5.

Avery, G., Everett, A., Finkelde, A. and Wallace, K. (1999) 'Emerging trends in Australian and New Zealand management development practices in the twenty-first century', *Journal of Management Development*, 18(1): 94–108.

Bamber, G.J. (1992) 'Industrial relations and organizational change: is human resource management strategic in Australia?', in Towers, B. (ed.), *The Handbook of Human Resource Management*, Oxford: Blackwell.

Bardoel, E.A., De Cieri, H. and Santos, C. (2008) 'A review of work–life research in Australia and New Zealand', *Asia Pacific Journal of Human Resources*, 46(3): 316–33.

Benson, J. (2000) 'Employee voice in union and non-union Australian workplaces', *British Journal of Industrial Relations*, 38(3): 453–9.

Bowes, L.B. (1975) 'Worker Participation in Management: The South Australian Developments', *Journal of Industrial Relations*, 17(June): 119–34.

Boxall, P. (1996) 'The strategic HRM debate and the resource-based view of the firm', *Human Resource Management Journal*, 6(3): 59–75.

Breaugh, J.A. and Starke, M. (2000) 'Research on employee recruitment: So many studies, so many remaining questions', *Journal of Management*, 26(2): 405–34.

Carless, S.A. (2007) 'Graduate Recruitment and Selection in Australia', *International Journal of Selection and Assessment*, 15(2): 153–66.

CCH Survey (1999) *Survey of Recruitment, Selection and Induction Practices in Australian and New Zealand Organizations: 1999*, CCH Australia Ltd and the Australian Graduate School of Management, pp. 1–18.

Dakin, S.R. and Armstrong, J.S. (1989) 'Predicting job performance: a comparison of expert opinion and research findings', *International Journal of Forecasting*, 5(2): 187–94.

Dakin, S., Nilakant, V. and Jensen, R. (1994) 'The role of personality testing in managerial selection', *Journal of Managerial Psychology*, 9(5): 3–11.

Daly, A., Barker, M. and McCarthy, P. (2005) 'Preferences in recruitment and selection in a sample of Australian organizations', *International Journal of Organizational Behaviour*, 9(1): 581–93.

Davis, E.M. and Harris, C. (eds.) (1996) *Making the Link: Affirmative Action and Industrial Relations*, vol. 7, Canberra: Australian Government Publishing Service, pp. 61–3.

Davis, E.M. and Lansbury, R.D. (1998) 'Employment relations in Australia', in Bamber, G.J. and Lansbury, R.D. (eds), *International and Comparative Employment Relations*, 3rd edn, London: Sage, 110–43.

De Cieri, H. (2007) *Human resource management in Australia: Strategy, people, performance*, Canberra: McGraw-Hill Australia.

De Cieri, H., Holmes, B., Abbott, J. and Pettit, T. (2005) 'Achievements and challenges for work/life balance strategies in Australian organizations', *The International Journal of Human Resource Management*, 16(1): 90–103.

Department of Employment and Industrial Relations (1986) *Industrial Democracy and Employee Participation*, Canberra: Australian Government Publishing Service.

The Economist (2000), February 26th 2000.

EEOT (Equal Employment Opportunities Trust) (2005) *Parents and work – online survey analysis*, available online at: www.eeotrust.org.nz, accessed on 22 November 2009.

Fisher, C. and Dowling, P.J. (1999) 'Support for an HR approach in Australia: the perspective of senior HR managers', *Asia Pacific Journal of Human Resources*, 37(1): 1–19.

Hanley, G. and Nguyen, L. (2005) 'Right on the money: what do Australian unions think of performance-related pay?', *Employee Relations*, 27(2): 141–59.

Haynes, P. and Fryer, G. (1999) 'Changing patterns of HRM and employment relations in New Zealand: the large hotel industry', *Asia Pacific Journal of Human Resources*, 37(2): 33–43.

Haynes, P., Boxall, P. and Macky, K. (2005) 'Non-union voice and the effectiveness of joint consultation in New Zealand', *Economic and Industrial Democracy*, 26(2): 229–56.

Haynes, P., Holland, P., Pyman, A. and Teicher, J. (2008) 'Free-riding in Australia', *Economic and Industrial Democracy*, 29(1): 7–34.

Hicks, R.E. (1991) 'Psychological testing in Australia in the 1990s', *Asia-Pacific Human Resource Management*, 29(1): 94–101.

Holland, P., Pyman, A., Cooper, B.K. and Teicher, J. (2009) 'The development of alternative voice mechanisms in Australia: the case of joint consultation', *Economic and Industrial Democracy*, 30(1): 67–92.

Kane, B. (1996) 'HRM: changing concepts in a changing environment', *International Journal of Employment Studies*, 4(2): 115–77.

Kane, B., Crawford, J. and Grant, D. (1999) 'Barriers to effective HRM', *International Journal of Manpower*, 20(8): 494–515.

Karpin, D. (1995) *Enterprising Nation: Renewing Australia's Managers to Meet the Challenges of the Asia-Pacific Century* (Report of the Industry Task Force on Leadership and Management Skills), Canberra: AGPS.

Lansbury, R.D. (1978) 'Industrial democracy through participation in management: the Australian experience', *Industrial Relations Journal*, 9(2): 71–9.

Lansbury, R.D. and Baird, M. (2004) 'Broadening the horizons of HRM: lessons for Australia from the US experience', *Asia Pacific Journal of Human Resources*, 42(2): 147–55.

Markey, R. and Patmore, G. (2009) 'The role of the state in the diffusion of industrial democracy: South Australia, 1972–9', *Economic and Industrial Democracy*, 30(1): 37–66.

Moorehead, A., Steel, M., Alexander, M., Stephen, K. and Duffin, L. (1997) *Changes at Work: the 1995 Australian Workplace Industrial Relations Survey*, Melbourne: Longman.

Noe, R.A. and Winkler, C. (2009) *Employee training and development: for Australia and New Zealand*, Canberra: McGraw-Hill Australia.

OECD (Organization for Economic Cooperation and Development) (2009) *OECD Harmonised Unemployment Rates*, Paris, 12 Oct., pp. 1–4.

OECD (Organization for Economic Cooperation and Development) (2010) *OECD Employment Outlook: How does your country compare -Australia, -New Zealand*, Paris, 6 July 2010.

Patrickson, M. and Hartmann, L. (2001) '*Human Resource Management in Australia-Prospects for the twenty-first century*', *International Journal of Manpower*, 22(3): 198–206.

Pennington, A. and Lafferty, G. (2002) *Human Resource Management in Australia: An Introduction*, Oxford: Oxford University Press.

Selvarajah, C., Sung-Wai Lau, T. and Taormina, R.J. (2000) 'Management training and development: a New Zealand study', *Journal of Management and Organization*, 6(1): 28–41.

Taylor, P. (1998) 'Seven staff selection myths', *New Zealand Management*, 45(1): 61–5.

Taylor, P., Keelty, Y. and McDonnell, B. (2002) 'Evolving personnel selection practices in New Zealand organizations and recruitment firms', *New Zealand Journal of Psychology*, 31(1): 8–18.

Thornwaite, L. and Sheldon, P. (2000) 'Employer matters in 1999', *Journal of Industrial Relations*, 42(1): 83–108.

Vaughan, E. and McLean, J. (1989) 'A Survey and Critique of Management Selection Practices in Australian Business Firms', *Asia-Pacific Human Resource Management*, 27(1): 20–33.

Waring, P. (1999) 'The rise of the individualism in Australian industrial relations', *New Zealand Journal of Industrial Relations*, 24(3): 291–318.

Part II

Case Study: 9/11 – The Effects and Organizational Response

Introduction

On the morning of 11 September 2001, the twin towers of the World Trade Center in New York City were completely destroyed by hijacked US commercial airliners crashing into them. A third hijacked airplane hit the Pentagon and a fourth crashed in Pennsylvania before reaching its intended destination – the White House in Washington DC. These horrifying terrorist attacks had considerable effects on the politics and economics of the US and many other countries in the world. The sectors of the economy most immediately affected after the attacks were travel and tourism. This case study examines such effects on and the organizational response of the organizations that were most affected.

The impact of 9/11 on travelling and tourism

The World Travel and Tourism Council (WTTC) expected a decline in the industry of around 10 per cent, resulting in a loss of 8.8 million jobs worldwide, including 190,000 jobs in the UK, 1.2 million jobs in the EU, and 1.1 million jobs in the US. The WTTC called upon governments to provide financial support and to introduce policies to help private sector employers, especially hotel and restaurant owners, to cope with and survive the short-term effects of the crisis. In a letter to the members of congress, the chairman and CEO of Loews Hotels stated that the attacks had crippled the travel and tourism industry as the public's confidence in the safety of travel had been severely reduced. He wrote: 'Hard data as well as anecdotal experience suggest that meetings are being postponed, all but critical corporate travel is being delayed, and individuals are cancelling or postponing personal travel plans within the US and abroad' (www.tbr.org. accessed 23 Nov. 2007).

Immediately after 9/11 many airline flights were cancelled for security reasons and because many travellers cancelled their flights within and outside the US. Air travel continued to decline in the following months and into 2002. All airline companies suffered loss of revenue, but while some of them have recovered, others have struggled to stay in business. Major airlines had to 'cut their flights by an average of 20% and laid off an average of 16% of their workforces in the weeks following the attacks' (Gittell et al., 2003: 301). Airline companies such as Delta, US Airways, United, Continental and Northwest were badly affected, despite the rescue package of US$5 billion that the US government introduced to help the airline industry to recovery. Others, such as JetBlue and Southwest Airlines, were the less affected by the crisis. It seems that even within the same industry the effects and the survival strategies were different.

Dealing with and responding to the crisis

Most US airline companies are multinationals. They should, by virtue of the size of their operations and type of global management strategy, be able to deal with and respond effectively to instances of short-term economic crisis. They can normally adapt to different economic cycles because, as explained in Chapter 4, management in US companies is associated with forms of strategic awareness that tend to link employment policies to corporate objectives. In other words, the management of American organizations is strategic, flexible and dynamic, and can respond effectively to sudden changes in the market and fluctuations in the supply and demand for labour, goods and services. Managers are not always restricted by collective agreements (although all agreements are legally binding when and where they are concluded).

It should also be remembered that HRM strategies in the US have their roots in the development of management thinking since the start of the twentieth century, and in particular since the advent of 'scientific management' based on the view that managers exist to develop the best methods for their workers to carry out tasks. Managers select those workers who have appropriate abilities and train them, when necessary, to do the job in the most efficient and cost-effective way. Individual employees have equal obligations and opportunities to meet not only their organizations' objectives but their individual ambitions too. By applying these basic management principles, most

US companies were able to cope with the effects of the attacks and to recover in a very short time.

It is important to see what lessons can be learnt from their responses to the crisis and the different human resource management strategies they used in this respect. The Society for Human Resource Management (SHRM) in the US conducted a survey of 120,000 of its members to discover the effects of and the responses to the attacks a week after the 9/11. The analysis of more than 5,600 responses found that the majority of employers felt that their employees were coping with the situation as expected, about 66 per cent of employers expected their employees to be more caring toward one another, 62 per cent of employers allowed their employees to take time off if needed, 56 per cent introduced tighter security controls and became more concerned with crisis management plans, and 45 per cent cancelled meetings and events (SHRM, 2001; also reported in Kondrasuk, 2004: 30). Other surveys found that the immediate responses were: making redundancies to save costs; recruiting and retaining key employees; training for possible attacks; improving communication procedures; and implementing crisis management plans.

Redundancies – the common response to a crisis

The immediate response to the crisis by most organizations in the US and other countries affected by the 9/11 terrorist attacks was to make some of their employees redundant in order to reduce labour costs. It should be noted that the major running costs of many organizations consist of the wages and salaries they pay their employees. However, in most cases the decision to lay off employees leads to negative reactions, resistance to change, lack of trust, deception, low morale, increased conflict, feelings of victimization, less team work, the spread of rumours, low commitment, and overall employee dissatisfaction. All these reactions have to be managed effectively – otherwise the solution to a problem becomes another problem.

For example, the US Airways response to the crisis – reducing its workforce by 24 per cent resulted in the deterioration of employee–employer relations, low employee morale, and poor organizational performance. However, the case of US Airways is interesting because it is not clear whether it was the effects of the 9/11 attacks or the US Airways leadership bungling restructuring that led to making nearly a quarter of the company's workforce redundant. The president of US Airways, Rakesh Gangwal, was known for his anti-union and cost-cutting management strategy. According to Barakat (2001), Gangwal said: 'the September 11 attacks have allowed the airline to restructure and downsize in ways that would have been impossible otherwise. Specifically, the attacks allow the airline to invoke "force majeure" clauses in union contracts and eliminate unprofitable routes.' The expression *force majeure* in the US employee relations system is a legal term allowing the employer to evade contractual obligations under exceptional circumstances. Moreover, Gangwal was also reported as saying: 'I don't want to take advantage of the situation but we have to do what is right for the company ... And the events of September 11th have opened certain doors for the company that were pretty much closed before' (cited in Gittell et al., 2003: 317). The approach taken by the US Airways leadership resulted in grievances and in damage to the relationship between management and employees. The US Airways president was replaced in early 2002, perhaps because of his response to the crisis. However, the company continued to cut costs by reducing the number of flights and making more employees redundant. For example, in addition to the 286 pilots who were laid off just after 9/11, another 471 pilots were asked to leave in 2002, while another 915 flight attendants were added to the 2,760 that were made redundant after 11 September (Gittell et al., 2003). The US Airways response to the crisis was explained by the fact that the company had been hit not only by the 9/11 attacks but also by the debt it had accumulated of almost $8 billion over the years before 2001. It was under pressure from the lenders to pay back the debt, at a time when it was losing money because of declining confidence in air travel.

Recruiting and retaining key employees

Some companies responded to the crisis by recruiting and retaining a core of well-trained and highly skilled employees. Many US employers have always thought strategically about the recruitment, training and development of their employees but now they have had to think politically. For example, some employers became very selective in their recruitment process and sometimes they had to discriminate by favouring nationals over the foreigners, especially foreigners of certain faiths and nationalities. American employers have been urged by the government to be extra vigilant and to carry out close checks of job applicants before they hire them, as well as checking profiles of current employees from different ethnic backgrounds. There has been more employee screening and reference checking than at any time before. Some employers used the opportunity to get rid of employees they did not like and to hire new ones from among nationals or from friendly countries. For example, when they introduced redundancies, the first employees who were asked to leave were those from ethnic backgrounds. Therefore there was 'a significant increase in the number of charges alleging discrimination based on religion and/or national origin. These charges most commonly allege harassment and discharge' (www. eeoc.gov/facts/backlash-employer.html, accessed on 23 Nov. 2007).

Unlike US Airlines, Southwest Airlines did not have to lay off any of its employees, even though it was equally affected by declining numbers of passengers. Instead of creating redundancies, Southwest Airlines announced in February 2002 that it would 'hire about 4,000 new employees, drawing in part from the employees laid off from other airlines' (Gittell et al., 2003: 323). Southwest Airlines' management always argued that their approach is to have a better understanding of the needs of their employees, to motivate them to work hard and to stay in the company, and to support them in times of crisis, rather than 'adding salt to injury' by making them redundant. Hence, Southwest Airlines' management insisted on recruiting, training, retraining and retaining the best pilots and cabin crew they could find in the country. Their catchphrase is: 'if you care about your employees they will care about your customers'. However, the company introduced a very stringent recruitment process that guaranteed the selection and employment of the best pilots and cabin crew from among the US applicants. A very small number of foreign nationals were considered and not many of them were recruited.

Training for possible attacks

Normally training is offered to employees in order to improve their job-related knowledge and skills, but after 9/11 some employers gave priority to training their employees on what to do when there is a terrorist attack. More employers started to train their employees in skills that help them recognize, prevent and respond to threats of terrorism. For example, according to the SHRM (2001) survey, about 35 per cent of employers had plans for the introduction of training programmes in crisis management and disaster recovery (Kondrasuk, 2004: 32). Moreover, the attacks led many employers to focus on in-house and on-the-job training in order to reduce travel by planes and to make more use of the intranet, internet and video-conferencing.

Communication and crisis management plans

All organizations need a communication system to enable them to operate effectively. In the US, many employers pride themselves of having clear communication channels that enable them to communicate directly with their employees, rather than having to go through the medium of trade unions or employee representatives. However, most of them realized after the 9/11 attacks that it was not easy to reach all their employees individually at short notice, despite the availability and accessibility of advanced information and communication technologies. Many employers did not have up-to-date records on their employees and did not have contact details for all employees who were outside the workplace. Therefore, employers have had to improve their communication methods and to use a variety of communication channels. Many have now developed company disaster recovery plans and trained their employees in crisis management and on how to contact others and get help in case of an attack. For example, 'Deloitte & Touche used its voicemail system to leave information for employees across the country, asking everyone to contact a toll-free number to account for their whereabouts' (Hurley-Hanson, 2006: 3). Moreover, in times of crisis and uncertainty rumours tend to spread very quickly, and they can cause stress and anxiety, resulting in the loss of trust among workers and between management and employees, poor productivity and low morale (DiFonzo and Bordia, 2000). Many organizations have had to improve their formal communication channels in order 'to help prevent or neutralize the detrimental effects of rumors' (Dicke and Ott, 2003: 110).

Conclusion

The initial effects of the 9/11 terrorist att0acks were catastrophic in human and material terms. Some organizations were more affected than others and the impact on the travel and tourism industry as well as the insurance and financial sectors was great, at least in the short to medium terms. Some of the risks were more serious than others and organizations within the same sector used different HRM strategies in dealing with the crisis. In such circumstances the role of state intervention cannot be overestimated. While the different airline companies responded differently to the crisis in order to stay in business, the US and many other countries' governments responded by using tighter security and control measures at airports and on the people who travel to and from their territories. Whatever the responses, travelling by air is now a frustrating experience for travellers and holiday-makers. As a result of increased security procedures, travelling has become slower and the movement of goods and people has become more difficult and very often much more expensive than before, despite the introduction of better and more competitively priced commercial flights. Incidents of company executives missing important meetings, travellers missing their connection flights, luggage going missing, and so on, have been experienced by many people throughout the world. As a result, the tourism industry has been severely affected. Moreover, it is not easy to restore public confidence in travelling by air while the threat of terrorism is still imminent.

Questions

1   How did different US organizations respond to the crisis? Discuss the main reasons for the difference between the US Airlines and Southwest Airlines responses.
2   To what extent were organizational responses influenced by political or economic motives? Discuss how HRM functions such as recruitment and selection have changed as a result of the 9/11 attacks.
3   How prepared are American organizations to respond to future terrorist attacks? Explain how and with the use of examples if possible.
4   To what extent do you think the lack of effective communication channels may lead to poor employee relations in cases of crisis?

References

Barakat, M. (2001) 'US Airways loses $766 million in third quarter, worse than analysts expected', *Arlington Journal*, October 31, 2001 available online at: http://www.co.arlington.va.us/NewsDigest/Scripts/ViewDetail.asp?Index = 593, accessed 24 November 2008.

Dicke, L.A. and Ott, J.S. (2003) 'Post-September 11 human resource management in non-profit organizations', *Review of Public Personnel Administration*, 23(2): 97–113.

DiFonzo, N. and Bordia, P. (2000) 'How top PR professionals handle hearsay: corporate rumors, their effects, and strategies to manage them', *Public Relations Review*, 26(1): 173–90.

Gittell, J.H., Cameron, K., Lim, S. and Rivas, V. (2003) 'Relationships, layoffs, and organizational resilience – airline industry responses to September 11', *The Journal of Applied Behavioural Science*, 42(3): 300–29.

Hurley-Hanson, A.E. (2006) 'Organizational responses and adaptations after 9–11', *Management Research News*, 29(8): 480–94.

Kondrasuk, J.N. (2004) 'The effects of 9/11 and terrorism on human resource management: recovery, reconsideration, and renewal', *Employee Responsibilities and Rights Journal*, 16(1): 25–35.

SHRM (Society for Human Resource Management) (2001) 'More caring, security predicted following attacks, poll shows', *HR News*, 20(11): 14 & 17.

Part III

Managing in South-East Asian Countries

REGENTS COLLEGE
LONDON

Inner Circle, Regent's Park, London, NW1 4NS
T: +44 (0)20 7487 7505 F: +44 (0)207 487 7425

Part 3: Managing in South East Asian Countries
Map 3

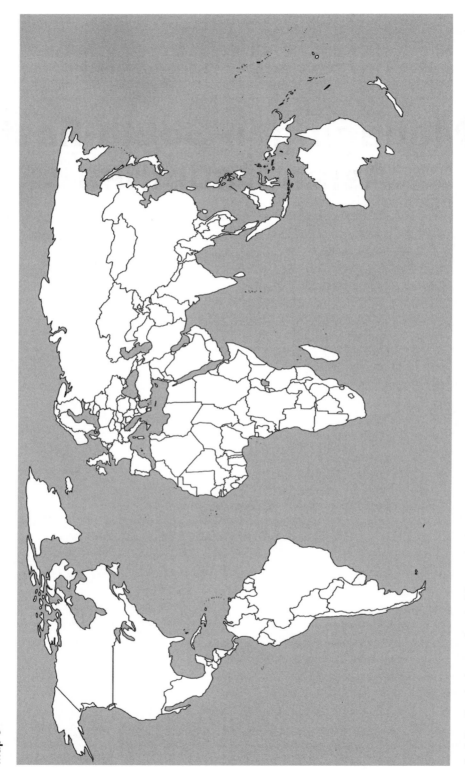

Activity: Put the letter allocated for each of these countries on the map above: Mainland China (C), Hong Kong (H), Japan (J), South Korea (S), Indonesia (I) and Malaysia (M)

7

Japan and South Korea

LEARNING OUTCOMES

The chapter is designed to help you understand, for Japan and South Korea:

1 The (a) economic, (b) political and (c) cultural contexts in which managers work;

2 The main trends in the labour market;

3 The typical features of (a) management policies and practices and (b) organizational structure and behaviour;

4 The main policies and practices of human resource management with regard to: (a) recruitment and selection; (b) training and development; (c) rewards and remuneration; and (d) employee relations.

Introction

The theory and practice of management in South Korea has been developed largely in line with the Japanese approach. The two countries are geographically and culturally related. Korea was controlled directly by Japan from 1910 until the end of the Second World War. From about 1948, both countries embarked upon similar socio-economic reforms and challenges. Although they have very limited natural resources and are very reliant on the importation of raw materials and hydrocarbons, they have enjoyed extraordinary economic success. It is often argued that their success lies with the quality of their human resources and the credibility of their management systems (see, for example, Nonaka and Takeuchi, 1996; Lincoln and Nakata, 1997; Bae and Rowley, 2001, 2003; Kim and Kim, 2003; Kim and Bae, 2004). Both countries are known for distinctive production practices and employment policies which have led to a reputation for manufacturing excellence and efficiency (Amsden, 1989; Jackson and Tomioka, 2004; Rowley et al., 2004). In both countries national

Table 7.1 Basic statistical indicators, Japan and South Korea

Country	Area (sq km)	Population (July 2010 est.)	Population growth (2010) %	GDP – real growth rate (2009) %	Inflation rate (Jan. 2009 est.) %	Workforce (2009) Million	Unemployment rate (2009) %
Japan	377915	127078679	–0.19	–5.3	–1.4	65.93	5.1
South Korea	99720	48508972	0.26	0.2	2.8	24.40	3.7

Source: Compiled from Japan Statistics Bureau, MIC, 2009 and CIA *World Factbook*, 2010.

businesses are protected by the state from external competition and their labour markets are highly regulated. However, the countries differ in their levels of economic growth and maturity, and in their labour movements and labour organization.

Contexts: economics, politics and culture

Economics

Japan and South Korea are among the world's largest and most technologically advanced producers and exporters of automobiles, electronic goods, semiconductors, wireless telecommunications equipment, computers, machine tools, chemicals and processed foods. They have small subsidized agricultural sectors but large fishing fleets. Despite their limited natural resources, they developed a strong manufacturing base after the Second World War. Japan achieved admirable levels of economic growth over the 1960s and 1970s, though more recently economic growth has stalled. Over the past two decades, the Japanese economy has been shifting from manufacturing to the services industry. There has been a strong emphasis on placing production overseas, slimming down supplier networks, and rationalizing distribution.

South Korea has been transformed from being a destitute, wartorn agricultural country, to a modern, industrialized nation (Amsden, 1989; Gross, 1996; Kong, 2000) with full membership of the World Trade Organization (WTO) since 1995 and the Organization of Economic Cooperation and Development (OECD) since 1996. The rapid economic growth has enabled it to enter the world trade community as a leading trade partner and the largest manufacturer of memory chips, a major maker of automobiles and electronics, and the world's second largest shipbuilder. The major investors in South Korea are the US, with about 50 per cent of all foreign investments, and then Japan with about 20 per cent. American investors have concentrated on the services sector while the Japanese have dominated the manufacturing sector.

The Asian financial crisis of 1997 affected both countries, though 'the Korean economy did seemingly recover quickly, at least in terms of growth, incomes, debt, reserves and also employment' (Rowley and Bae, 2002: 529). A number of measures were taken by the governments of both countries to bring about economic recovery. They included the control of interest rates to keep them very low or even at a nil rate, the deregulation of the financial sector to make financial transactions more transparent, the enforcement of stronger anti-monopoly policies, the reduction of restrictions on foreign direct investment, the deregulation of land use and construction projects, and the encouragement of organizational restructuring including initiatives for downsizing. Both countries recovered and turned their economies around faster than any of the other countries in the region (*Financial Times*, 1 Dec. 2004), though both economies have been affected by the 'credit crunch' recession.

Politics

Japan is a constitutional monarchy with a parliamentary government. The head of state is the emperor, who has a symbolic role. The head of government is the prime minister. Legislative authority rests with the national diet of Japan (*Kokkai*), which gathers the House of Representatives (parliament) and the House of Councillors (upper house). The members of both houses are elected democratically by direct vote every four years. Japan's politics has been dominated by the Liberal Democratic party (LDP) which has been in power for most of the period since 1955. The LDP, which is known for its conservative policies, lost in September 2009 to the Democratic party of Japan (DPJ), which is known for its more liberal and social policies.

South Korea is a democratic republican state where the head of state and commander-in-chief of the armed forces is an elected president and the unicameral legislature is an elected national assembly. The president is elected by popular vote for a single five-year term and has substantial political power. The members of the national assembly or *Kukhoe* (parliament) are elected by popular vote. The president appoints the leader of the majority party as the prime minister, confirms the members of cabinet (the state council) after they are recommended by the prime minister, establishes the chief justice of the law courts, and directs the National Intelligence Service and the Audit and Inspection Board. The extensive power held by the president is a remnant of a country in transition from the years when leaders assumed office under non-democratic circumstances, especially in the 1960s and 1970s when a succession of military leaders seized power. It was only after violent civilian protests in the 1980s that the military leaders were forced to hold free and democratic elections in 1987. The government still plays a central role in employee relations and has a significant impact on the policy and practice of management at all levels of the economy.

Culture

Both countries are influenced by Confucianism, which stresses the values of harmony, conformity, avoiding conflict and maintaining long-term relationships. In Confucianism all human relationships are vertically organized in a hierarchy of duties and responsibilities from the government down to the simple individual in society (Hofstede and Bond, 1988; Bond, 1992; McNamara, 2002). Such social vertical relations are observed in all aspects of life and are very important in social interactions and ways of addressing each other. In both Japanese and Korean languages, which are very much similar, there is a range of verbs for distinguishing ways of addressing people according to their rank, class, age, gender, qualifications, status and so on. Paying attention to class, status, education level, age and seniority is very important because these factors determine the level of respect an individual should get. Not responding in the right way to the right people may damage personal relationships and destroy opportunities for business deals (Gross, 1996; Kim and Park, 2003; Lee and Trim, 2008).

In both countries, there is a stronger emphasis on the role of the group than that of the individual. Normally an individual cannot progress and achieve a successful career without the support of the community or without being part of the harmonious group, and any individual who breaks the harmony by trying to do it alone is seen as an outcast or misfit. It is the extent of the contribution of an individual to the group interest that is valued (Song and Meek, 1998). This is why when an individual expresses an opinion, he or she always says 'we' rather than 'I', and in referring to one's company, school, home or country they say 'our company', 'our school', etc. This group-oriented and collectivist behaviour has a powerful impact on employee relations, business operations and management practices, as explained in the rest of this volume.

ACTIVITY 1

After reading the above section, answer the following questions:

1 Discuss the main cultural norms and values that might have contributed to the Japanese and South Korean economic success.
2 Identify the main differences and similarities between the political systems of Japan and South Korea.
3 What advice would you give to an international manager going to work in South Korea?

Labour market trends

Both Japan and South Korea have very limited natural resources, but they have a highly skilled and committed workforce (Kim and Kim, 2003; Duignan and

Yoshida, 2007). Japan's workforce has been relatively stable. It has grown by less than 1 per cent over the last three decades. The number of those in employment has been between 62 to 65 per cent of the working-age population. The level of employment in agriculture, forestry and fishing declined from about 17 per cent in the 1970s to less than 5 per cent in the 2000s. There has been also a slight decline in employment in the industrial sector and a rise in the services sector.

Similarly, in South Korea only about 7 per cent of the working population are in agriculture, 26.4 per cent in industry and 67.2 per cent in the services sector. Both countries are known for their MNCs' investments around the world rather than for attracting foreign companies' investments.

In summary, both countries have a low level of unemployment; the domination of conglomerates (*chaebol* and *zaibatsu*) with corresponding employment practices; a hard-working, committed and loyal workforce; limited employment opportunities for women; and a relatively older workforce characterize the labour markets of both countries. (see Table 7.2.)

Table 7.2 Employment by sector in Japan and South Korea (%)

Sector	Japan (2009)	South Korea (2007)
Agriculture	4	7.2
Industry	28	25.1
Services	68	67.7

Source: Compiled from CIA *World Factbook*, 2010.

Low unemployment rates

The level of unemployment in both Japan and South Korea has been low in comparison with other industrialized nations: it has been between 1 and 4 per cent since the 1960s. The practice of lifetime employment has practically prevented the rise of unemployment. Also, from the mid-1950s until the late the 1990s, large-scale redundancies were very limited because the law made it harder for employers to dismiss their employees. However, across many sectors of the Japanese economy job insecurity is rising among the middle-aged population. Unemployment is high amongst men aged 45 and 54. There has also been a general move away from lifetime employment to 'employment adjustment' (Rowley and Bae, 2002: 538) and this kept the level of unemployment at a steady average of about 4 per cent between 2000 and 2007. Unemployment in Japan is currently at around 5 per cent.

Similarly, in South Korea, unemployment fell from around 8 per cent in the early 1960s to just above 4 per cent by 1970, and then continued to decline to stand at around 2 to 3 per cent over the last three decades, except for the two years following the 1997 financial crisis when company closures resulted in

Table 7.3 Unemployment rates 1990–2009 (%), Japan and South Korea

Country\year	1990	1995	2000	2005	2006	2007	2008	2009
Japan	2.1	3.2	4.7	4.4	4.1	3.9	4.0	5.2
South Korea	2.4	2.1	4.4	3.7	3.5	3.2	3.2	3.7

Source: Statistics Bureau, MIC, Cabinet Office, Japan and South Korea, 2007; OECD, 2010.

mass redundancies. It should be noted that although the rate of unemployment is low, it has especially affected young people in their twenties and those among the highly educated (graduates). The economic recovery and rapid economic growth led to a significant rise in industrialization and therefore job creation, and reduced the level of unemployment to around 3.2 per cent between 2006 and 2008, before it began to rise to about 3.7 in 2009, as shown in Table 7.3. A recent rise in unemployment in both countries has been triggered by the sudden economic downturn following the international financial crisis starting 2008.

Chaebol and *zaibatsu*

Both Japan and South Korea are known for their large business conglomerates established by founding families and kept together by cross-share holdings, cross-subsidies and loan guarantees. In Japan, they are called *kobal* or *zaibatsu* and in South Korea they are known as *chaebol*. Examples of such internationally famous South Korean *chaebols* are Samsung, Daewoo, Hyundai and Lucky-Goldstar. *Chaebol* translates as 'financial clique'. In practice they are family controlled and owned conglomerates, structured into a number of companies in various sectors (Leggett, 1996; Miles, 2008). Unlike the *chaebol*, the Japanese *zaibatsu* have their own financial resources and are more competitive and less dependent on state funds. In both cases the founder is basically the supreme controller of the whole conglomerate (*chaebol* or *zaibatsu*) and the family members become controllers of the subsidiaries. Usually the eldest son succeeds the father as owner, once the latter retires or dies. About 60 per cent of the top 30 *chaebol* families in South Korea are associated with high-level politicians or public servants (Leggett, 1996). Often the wife of the owner's son is the daughter of a politician and the husband of the owner's daughter is the son of another *chaebol*'s owner or a politician. Many of the families that own conglomerates are linked to each other and with the power elite by marriage. This link is used by politicians to strengthen their political power and by the owners of conglomerates to connect themselves to the ruling elite and to influence economic policy decisions.

A hard-working, committed and loyal workforce

It has often been said that the main reason for Japanese and South Korean economic success is their hard-working, committed and loyal workforce (Gross, 1996; Song, 1997; Bae and Rowley, 2001; Rowley and Bae, 2004; Cho, 2009). Japanese and Korean employees tend to work longer hours, do not take all their holidays, are seldom absent from work, and work for the same employer for as long as they are needed. In Japan they work on average 46 hours per week, 6 days a week. In South Korea a 5-day, 40-hour work week was introduced by law in 2002, but many Koreans still work more than 40 hours per week. However, the issue of employee loyalty and commitment is debatable and has generated a lot of controversy. Some studies have found that Korean workers are not loyal to the company but rather to the management or the owner of the company. For example, Song (1997) found that loyalty was mainly to individuals, regardless of whether that individual was the owner or the manager of the company; there was little loyalty to the organization. The opposite can be found in Japan, where employees are loyal and committed to the organization rather than to its owners or managers (Rowley and Bae, 2004). A study by Usugami and Park (2006: 284) found that Korean employees preferred to have their own business and had little loyalty to their companies. It has also been argued that the outward appearance of harmony and commitment to the organization does not mean that all the workers are content and satisfied in their workplaces (Briggs, 1991). In Asian cultures, personal desire must not interfere with company loyalty, and therefore, despite the low satisfaction of employees, perhaps little dissent is openly expressed.

Female employment

In both Japan and South Korea, the male and female roles are quite culturally and socially defined, as men are seen as the breadwinners and women as the home and family caretakers. For many years there existed a two-tier employment status system. One represents the regular workers, who are mostly male, make up the core workforce, and enjoy privileges such as job security, good rewards and high career prospects. The other represents the non-regular or peripheral workers who are primarily women and immigrants workers (Nagase, 1997). Despite the introduction since the 1980s of legislation on equal pay for equal work and equal promotion opportunities for women and men, little progress has been made in this regard. Normally women have no problem in finding jobs, especially graduates who have equal opportunities to men in their early working careers, but problems often arise when the women marry and have children. Most women feel obliged to leave employment at a certain time between the ages of 25 and 35 to marry and have children. Even

Table 7.4 Share of women of working age in employment (%) (selected industrialized countries)

Country\year	1980	1990	2000	2005	2007
Australia	47.9	57.4	61.4	64.7	66.1
Canada	52.6	62.8	65.6	68.3	70.1
China	–	–	68.8	66.6	68
Japan	51.4	55.8	56.7	58.1	59.5
South Korea	44.6	49	50	52.5	53.2
UK	56.7	62.8	65.6	66.7	66.3
USA	55.4	64	67.8	65.6	65.9

Source: OECD *Factbook* 2009: Economic, Environmental and Social Statistics.

if they decide to work they find it difficult to cope with the demands of full-time employment and many of them eventually quit their jobs.

Overall, the main reasons for the limited opportunities for female employment are:

1 Many employers prefer not to hire temporary employees to cover for maternity leave and are inclined to replace the employee by a new one with the expectation that the woman on maternity will not return.

2 Since employees are expected to be committed and to stay with the same company for years until reaching the mandatory retirement age, many employers do not see the employment of women, who may marry and quit after a few years, as a good investment.

3 Women who stay on in employment are very often labelled as 'old maids' or 'old aunts' and are considered of lower status because they have chosen a career over a family life.

4 There is a belief in Japanese and Korean societies that the cause of juvenile delinquency is improper maternal care. This belief has been exploited very often in the media and has discouraged many mothers from seeking employment.

5 There are limited opportunities for part-time work, job sharing and home-based working for female employees in professional and managerial positions. Full-time work is the norm. Very often 'the official eight hours of the working day extend to 10 or 12 at many companies and a woman can be made to feel she is letting down the team if she leaves at 5pm, even if she has been more productive than her colleagues during the day' (Hutton, 2000: 22).

6 Corporate nurseries are rare, private nurseries are oversubscribed and very expensive. Nannies are unheard of in many parts of the country. Even when it is possible to find and to afford a nursery place, the timing may not be convenient because many nurseries close at 6 p.m. when the women employee is still at work.

Older working population

As in most industrialized nations, the proportion of older people in Japan and in South Korea has been increasing rapidly. By the mid-1980s about 17.6 per cent

Table 7.5 Age structure (%) (2009), Japan and South Korea

Country	0–14 years %	15–64 years %	Over 65 %	Median age (years)	Life expectancy at birth (for men and women)
Japan	13.5	64.3	22.2	44.2	82.12
South Korea	16.8	72.3	10.8	37.3	78.72

Source: CIA *World Factbook*, 2010.

of the Japanese working population were aged 55 years or over, and by 2000 this proportion had jumped to more than 23 per cent (*Financial Times*, 12, Oct. 2004: 5). It is estimated that more than a fifth (22.2 per cent) of the Japanese population is over the age of 65 and this is expected to reach a quarter (25 per cent) by 2014, while the birth rate is the lowest in the developed world. In South Korea, the age structure is also moving upwards as birth rates keep falling and life expectancies are rising. It is estimated that only about 16.8 per cent of the population is less than 14 years of age and that about 11 per cent of the population are over the age of 65 (see Table 7.5).

From full-time employment to flexible employment

Although full-time employment is still the norm in most of the large companies in both Japan and South Korea, there has been, since the 1997 financial crisis, an increasing reliance by many small and medium sized enterprises on temporary and part-time employees (Dalton and Benson, 2002; Rowley et al., 2004). Many Japanese employers 'are now changing their hiring practices. They are increasingly resorting to cost-cutting measures that involve expanding their pool of non-regular workers and in some cases recruiting cheaper non-regular workers to undertake regular work assignments' (Salmon, 2004: 66). It can be seen from Table 7.6 that the number of people in part-time employment has been increasing despite the dominant culture of full-time employment.

Table 7.6 Part-time employment as a percentage of total employment (selected industrialized countries)

Country\year	2000	2001	2002	2003	2004	2005	2006	2007
Australia	–	24.2	24.3	24.7	23.8	24.5	24.4	24.1
Japan	–	–	17.7	18.2	18.1	18.3	18	18.9
South Korea	7	7.3	7.6	7.7	8.4	9	8.8	8.9
UK	23	22.7	23.3	23.7	24	23.5	23.4	23.3
Netherlands	32.1	33	33.9	34.6	35	35.7	35.5	36.1

Source: OECD *Factbook* 2009: Economic, Environmental and Social Statistics.

Management and organization

Although many factors have contributed to the success of the Japanese and Korean economies, it has often been argued that their distinctive approach to management and organization is the most significant success factor (Whitehill, 1991; Kim and Bae, 2004; Jackson and Tomioka, 2004; Duignan and Yoshida, 2007; Cho, 2009). The Japanese management approach, which is similar to the management and organization in South Korea, is characterized by: (i) a high emphasis on quality; (ii) having clear mechanisms for consultation, communication and decision-making (the *ringi* system); (iii) exercising a kind of paternalistic leadership style, emphasizing single status between the leaders and the subordinates; and (iv) relative job security.

Quality improvement

In both countries, with Japan taking the lead, there has been an emphasis on quality in work organization systems that are based on functional flexibility, team-working and quality circles, and on manufacturing systems based on total quality management and just-in-time operations (Kawakita, 1997). A study by White and Trevor (1983) of Japanese manufacturing companies found there was an emphasis on production, valuing the details of work, stressing quality not quantity, and demanding high levels of task-related discipline.

The competitiveness of Japanese industries is largely due to continuous minor improvements and modifications to existing processes and products rather than to major technological breakthroughs in research and development. Many of the small modifications start at the workplace unit and are initiated by a group of individual employees. Although such modifications may be minor, the cumulative effect on costs can be very significant. New ideas and suggestions not only provide inputs and benefits for producing good-quality products, but also motivate workers to work harder and stay committed to their organisations.

Moreover, computer-assisted manufacturing systems have become well established in most Japanese and South Korean companies. Through the use of integrated technologies and networked information and communication systems all work teams, consisting of managers and subordinates, contribute their ideas to improving quality and building it into the product. Within Japanese organizations group identity and consequent effective team-working are considered essential elements of their success. The group as a whole takes responsibility for its own actions and no individual can be separated from it. The group works as a community where the spirit of consensus is regarded as important for driving quality initiatives.

The main strengths of the manufacturing systems in Japan and South Korea are the development of new products in highly competitive and technically superior sectors of the economy, such as electronics and automobile industries, through the use of quality control circles (QCC), total quality management (TQM), just-in-time (JT) operations, 'six sigma' and other innovation and quality initiatives (see, for example, Nonaka and Takeuchi, 1996; Keeley, 2001; Kim and Bae, 2004; Cho and McLean, 2009).

Consultation, communication and decision-making: the *ringi* system

Both Japan and South Korea are known for having clear mechanisms for consultation, communication and decision-making. An important aspect of the Japanese approach to management is the existence of the so-called *ringi* system, or consensual decision-making process, where subordinates are allowed to question the decisions of their managers and suggest solutions to work-related problems. Normally, the subordinate prepares a document outlining the problem and a suggested solution. This process is called *ringisho*. The *ringisho*, once prepared, is passed on to management to be circulated to relevant work units for discussion and improvement, before it is approved, moderated or rejected by senior management.

Since consensus is important, rejection of a suggestion could be a serious setback for the employee who initiated it. Usually, to avoid such setbacks, the subordinate makes an informal suggestion before a proposal is made formally to the superior. This process is called *nemawashi*. According to Fukuda (1983: 22), 'the abrupt submission of a proposal without *nemawashi* is seen as a lack of sensitivity contrary to the Japanese spirit, which reveres the preservation of a harmonious atmosphere within an organization'.

Management encourages an upward flow of communication from the lowest to the highest levels of the organization, and the role of managers in the process is to facilitate decision-making, guide discussions and create an atmosphere in which subordinates feel motivated to find solutions to problems and to initiate new work-related proposals. Although the final decisions have to be made at the appropriate level of authority, subordinates know that they have had the opportunity to have their views heard. The process is slow but when action is taken any potential difficulties have already been overcome and collective commitment has been given (Oliver and Wilkinson, 1992: 52). Very often the consensual decision-making process is reinforced and complemented by the emphasis on personal contacts between management and employees throughout their working lives. Face-to-face communication is very important, and it is manifested at the organizational level where employees communicate directly with their leaders and their work colleagues.

Paternalistic leadership

In most Japanese and South Korean companies senior managers tend to regard their subordinates as junior colleagues in an enterprise community with shared objectives rather than as wage earners with conflicting interests (Fukuda, 1983; Oliver and Wilkinson, 1992). In general, they exercise certain godfatherly characteristics over their management teams, which in turn look after the welfare of their subordinates. In response, most employees get a sense of belonging to the organization and feel responsible for achieving organizational objectives (Gross, 1996; Duignan and Yoshida, 2007; Miles, 2008). Line managers are therefore expected to be more than administrators and supervisors but also caretakers and personal advisors. They listen to their subordinates' suggestions and complaints, and endeavour to solve their problems. In some cases managers' concern for their subordinates' welfare goes beyond the workplace, as they may act as matchmakers or even perform wedding ceremonies for their employees (Gross, 1996). Also, when an employee is, for example, unwell or has personal problems, the manager often calls or visits to ask about their health, and to offer support and assistance if needed. At work, single status is very often emphasized as all employees, regardless of their status, use the same canteen, wear similar uniforms, and share the same carpark spaces.

Job security: from lifetime employment to employment adjustment

Until recently, most Japanese and South Korean employees had jobs for life. Lifetime employment was guaranteed as far as possible, or as long as the company was still in business. Most employees stayed with one employer until the age of retirement. Such an employment practice helped to build a stable working environment for many employees, who in turn showed great commitment and loyalty to their only employer. Even when lifetime employment could no longer be guaranteed, many employers have tried to relocate or transfer employees from one work unit to another within the organization rather than making them redundant.

There has been a general move away from lifetime employment to 'employment adjustment' (Rowley and Bae, 2002: 538). The employer's commitment to lifetime employment through employment adjustment has required the continuous implementation of training, education and considerable job rotation programmes throughout the organization (Salmon, 2004). Currently, even the most secure conglomerates, such as Toyota, Sony, LG and Samsung, cannot guarantee a safe and secure future for their employees, but in comparison with companies in other countries there is still relative provision of job security in Japan and South Korea.

Managing human resources

As stated in the introduction, both Japan and South Korea have very limited natural resources and their economies are reliant on the import of raw materials and hydrocarbons from other countries. They have been exemplary in their economic success because of the quality of their human resources and the credibility of their management systems, especially their human resource management. In this section the main features of HRM are discussed.

Recruitment and selection

Most of the methods of recruitment and selection that are known in Western countries are used in Japan and South Korea, but with different levels of emphasis. For example, it is reported that Japanese and Korean companies put the same effort into the recruitment of blue-collar workers as US and European companies put into the recruitment of managers (*Financial Times*, 11 May 1994). As in the other chapters of this volume, this section presents the recruitment process in general, graduate recruitment, and the selection process.

Recruitment

The Japanese approach to recruitment in general is characterized by the recruitment of generalists than specialists, the hiring of friends and relatives through word of mouth, and the use of headhunting.

New employees are recruited to take up general positions before they start training on new company-based skills. Most companies tend to employ young and adaptable employees who have no or very little experience and then train them to acquire the knowledge and skills required to do the job. In other words, Japanese employers prefer their new recruits to be 'blank canvases' that can be painted with corporate experience. Young and supposedly hard-working employees are hired and then introduced to the organization's culture, structure and processes before they are retained through a system of job rotation, continuous training and internal transfers. In Japan, the new recruits share a common induction programme in which they are made aware of the history and culture of the organization as well as their duties and obligations, the organization's rules and procedures, the product market and the work environment. Once settled within the company the new recruits are absorbed into the normally highly group-oriented atmosphere that most large/middle sized companies have. In South Korea, the new recruit spends about three to six months (Leggett, 1996) being inducted through collective training to socialize them into the organizational culture and to strengthen their basic knowledge of the organization.

The hiring of friends and relatives is more common in South Korea than in Japan because of the former's strong family control of conglomerates. In keeping with Confucianism, which emphasizes family tradition, the hiring of friends, relatives and family members is very common and acceptable (Rowley and Bae, 2002; Kim and Kim, 2003). As explained above, most of the managers of the large conglomerates are members of one family or they come from the same region. Recruitment through word of mouth and recommendations by friends and relatives is very common among the small and medium size organizations that are also family owned.

The shortage of professional and skilled employees has led many Japanese and South Korean companies to look for recruits in other companies and even in other countries. In a competitive business environment the best way to stay ahead of your competitors is to recruit their best employees. According to Salmon (2004: 65), in Japan 'some 70 per cent of firms who have found themselves in this situation have resorted to hiring experienced mid-career workers from the external labour market'. More and more companies are using recruitment agencies to headhunt highly skilled, talented and professional employees from competitors.

Graduate recruitment

Both Japanese and South Korean employers recruit their future managers and professional employees directly from universities and colleges through open screening tests and examinations offered to groups of students once or twice a year, depending on organizational needs. Large companies (*chaebol* in Korea and *zaibatsu* in Japan) tend to recruit top graduates from the top colleges and universities in the country. Most of the reputable organizations have no problems attracting the best graduates from the most prestigious universities (Kim and Briscoe, 1997; Rowley and Bae, 2004). Normally, the recruitment process starts with announcements being made to universities in the summer indicating the job vacancies available. Applications, personal contacts, interviews and medical checks follow before the candidate is chosen, to ensure that good-quality applicants are selected. In a number of cases, the top executives of the South Korean *chaebol* are from the same region as the founders because it is believed that managers who share the same accent, behaviour, attitudes and personality are likely to have the same work ethics and managerial views.

Selection

The selection process involves a combination of written exams and interviews. While the written exams focus on the candidates' knowledge about the job for which they have applied, interviews are used to evaluate the behavioural qualities of the candidates. The selection process emphasizes attitude and personality, as well as having the right qualifications and experience, but more importance is given to the former for managerial and professional jobs. Since such qualities are not easily detected during an interview, the selectors tend to gather more information about the candidate from university or college records. Teachers' recommendations are very often sought and are taken seriously. Many companies have good relations with the universities from which they regularly recruit their candidates. Job interviews are usually influenced by Confucianism (Cho, 1994; Leggett, 1996; Kim and Park, 2003), which emphasizes qualities of sincerity, loyalty, honesty, diligence and determination when evaluating candidates. Salmon (2004: 65) explains that this selection process 'places considerable value on the social and attitudinal characteristics of candidates'. He adds that 'this reliance upon a closed institutional network for company recruitment has helped to sustain the corporate culture and foster company loyalty, nurturing the "company man"'.

ACTIVITY 2

The Republic of Cousins (South Korea)

In South Korea, most of the large conglomerates are family owned and controlled by the members of one family, their friends and relatives. They are also linked to each other and to those in power (such as politicians) through marriage. Companies control the business and the political system.

Question

Discuss the South Korean business culture in comparison with other countries where management is separated from ownership. What are the arguments for and against the recruitment of family members, friends and relatives to occupy managerial posts?

Training and development

Both Japan and South Korea value education highly and see it as an important aspect of citizenship. The literacy rate is close to 100 per cent in Japan and about 98 per cent in South Korea. The education and training received by the Japanese is one of the best in the world. The Japanese workforce is well educated: more than 80 per cent of shopfloor workers complete compulsory education until the age of 19 and most of the managers of large companies are university graduates (Sano et al., 1997). The Japanese value lifelong learning and continuous training. Certificates and diplomas are common and widely used as evidence of successful completion of training courses and individual achievement.

Similarly, South Korea has a well-organized and properly resourced education system. The Korean government has invested heavily in education and in improving the quality of the Korean workforce through vocational training. For example, the country spent between 3 and 4 per cent of its GDP on education between 1980 and 2000 (Asian Development Bank, 2001). The state-sponsored National Manpower Agency (KOMA) provides training in basic skills and new technology skills to all job seekers to prepare them for employment. By the end of the 1990s, more than 70 per cent of the workforce in South Korea had graduated from high schools (Morden and Bowles, 1998). By the mid-1990s more than 90 per cent of secondary school pupils went to universities or vocational training centres (Gross, 1996; Cho and McLean, 2009). South Korea has some of the best universities in the world and there is also a tradition of sending students to study abroad to gain higher degrees in science and technology, and managers to train in Japan and the US in order to acquire further management knowledge and skills.

In summary, the process of training and development in Japan and South Korea is characterized by the use of induction training, on-the-job training, company-specific training, continuous training, self-development training, and a company-based approach to management training and development. Let us look at these more closely.

Company induction training

Japanese and South Korean employers consider induction training to be the most important step in integrating the employee into his or her organization. Very careful attention is given to the details of organizational culture and basic work behaviours. Since many employees are hired without previous work experience, they are trained to learn the basics and given a broad knowledge of and basic skills for doing the job through on-the-job and occasional off-the-job training. In Japan, new employees are provided with 6 to 12 months of induction training, in the form of on-the job training, in each of the organization's offices, divisions and workstations. The employee is introduced to all aspects of the organization's operations within the first year of his/her employment.

In South Korea new employees are provided with 3 to 6 months of in-house induction training that takes place in their training centres or 'socialization' camps, as they are commonly called. In these camps, new employees 'are inculcated in company history, culture, business philosophy, core values and vision, to develop "all-purpose" general skills through which to enhance team spirit, "can-do" spirit, adaptability and problem-solving' (Rowley and Bae, 2004: 52–3). By the end of the induction period the employees are expected to have mastered the protocols, values and mission of the company. They learn the philosophy that underpins the company's organizational behaviour, which emphasizes the importance of loyalty, team spirit and dedication. The 'socialization camps' are venues for social interaction and learning opportunities because they extend beyond the workplace to include recreational outdoor activities, indoor and outdoor sports events, parties and other activities that make the employee not just part of the team but a member of the company family.

On-the-job training and job rotation

All employees learn job-related skills from their seniors and they experience them through job rotation. It is believed that knowledge and skills can only be gained through observing, listening to, and practising under the supervision of more experienced and older employees. Job rotation is seen as the best way to gain new skills and to contribute to the development of new ones. However, it should be noted that while on-the-job training is the most popular method of training in Japanese companies, it was less common in South Korea until the 1990s (Leggett, 1996; Rowley et al., 2004) because of the prevalence of fragmented and deskilled tasks; one needed very little training to operate the automated production process in most of the heavy, automobile and electronics industries.

In Japan, on-the-job training and job rotation are considered important to all employees, not just to those on the production line. Managers are usually moved around different departments of the organization, or sent to subsidiaries overseas to broaden their managerial experience, to develop more networks, and to gain a greater understanding of how the organization operates as a whole. An important aspect of on-the-job training in Japan is that training is formalized and results in the awarding of qualifications. It helps employees to learn how to do their jobs properly and to enhance their career progression opportunities.

Enterprise-specific skills training

Employees are trained to gain enterprise-specific skills because they are expected to stay with one employer for life, as explained earlier. Most employees learn company-specific rather than transferable skills. In other words, the longer employees stay with one employer the less the chance of them becoming employable somewhere else. One might argue that Japanese employees effectively become qualified to work for only one particular employer, and that the system therefore produces a 'captive workforce' (Briggs, 1991). However, although training is company-specific it is not job-specific, because employees are trained to gain knowledge and skills for working in many functional areas. Learning enterprise-specific skills does not mean that labour mobility is low or limited. On the contrary, Japanese and Korean companies provide training in specific skills in order to make their employees more mobile within the organization and to help them open up future career prospects within the company. To make sure that employees learn the company's specific skills, many large organizations have their own training centres and they emphasize on-the-job training and in-house training (Rowley and Bae, 2004).

Continuous training

For most Japanese and Korean employers, training is seen as a long-term investment rather than a short-term cost (Gow, 1988; Leggett, 1996). The concept of quality in Japanese companies is expressed in relation to 'continuous improvement' (*kaizen*). Training is strongly associated with quality improvement. One of the main reasons for the success of quality control circles and the retention of quality excellence in Japan and, more recently, South Korea is their continuous training of employees. In South Korea, this process has been formalized at the national level by requiring all companies with more than 150 employees to have in-house vocational training facilities and to have plans for the continuous development and training of their employees (Gross, 1996; Kim and Kim, 2003). Organizations that fail to provide training to their employees will have to pay a tax levy which is equal to the cost that would have been spent on continuous training.

Self-development

Self-development through formal education and training is part of the Japanese and, to a lesser extent, the South Korean workforce's way of advancing their career prospects. Many employees enhance their knowledge and skills through attending evening courses or distance learning programmes. According to Usugami and Park (2006: 284) 'Korean people have a strong desire for career development. They take a more positive attitude toward improvement of work and language skills that contribute to their job performance'. The increasing number of Open University and college educated employees, and the high number of employees attending weekend and evening classes are evidence of a desire by employees to develop themselves for better career prospects.

Management training and development

While the South Koreans have long had US-type MBAs and US-designed business schools, the Japanese have always believed in the development of their own style of holistic managers through on-the-job training and job rotation. The Japanese have developed their own distinctive management policies and practices, and these have inspired many Western managers and management educators. In Japan there are only a few business schools that provide specialized courses in business and management. Most Japanese companies provide their own management training and show a strong preference for young people who can be trained in the company way. This type of management training is 'focused more on moulding managers to the company's core values and philosophy than developing their job-related abilities and knowledge. Programs placed more emphasis on building character and developing positive attitudes than on professional competence' (Rowley and Bae, 2004: 53). However, as the demand for more internationalized management techniques increased because of the intensification of international competition, many Japanese have had to adopt and then adapt management and business techniques from the US and Western Europe (Harney, 2000: 22). Also, many Japanese companies send their managers to study in the US and Europe in order to learn specific management knowledge and skills that are needed for their international operations. However, it has been argued that 'sending students to the US produced a lot of "vacuum cleaners" – students who sucked up a lot of information but participated little in the classroom' (Hutton, 2000: 22). Therefore, some Japanese universities have started to offer their own MBA programmes. Currently, a number of Japanese and South Korean universities run their own MBA programmes with the aim of bringing Western management education to the east and forming a bridge between the old and the new economies, as explained in the Mini Case Study.

MINI CASE STUDY 12

From the US to Japanese MBA

In April 1998, Waseda University in Japan launched an MBA programme to train graduates to do business the Western way in the east. This came following the Asian financial crisis of 1997, but many other Japanese universities already had MBA programmes. For example, Keio University introduced an MBA programme in 1979. Traditionally Japanese companies prefer to train their managers in-house and have never been in favour of the American-style MBA, but they seem to have a change of heart as a result of international competitive pressures. Japanese universities have sought to provide MBAs at home rather than sending managers to be trained abroad. The problem is that most Japanese graduates prefer to study for an MBA in reputable business schools in the US, UK or Australia. Being aware of this desire, Waseda University announced that its MBA was tailor-made for doing business in Asia and would be better for Asian people than studying in Western universities. They also argued that an MBA made in Asia would be useful for European and American graduates who wish to work in Asia because the programme included courses about Asian culture and the Asian style of doing business, taught in Japanese and English by an international team of

(Continued)

(Continued)

professors. In May 2000 this 'Asian-made MBA' was ranked number 16 out of 46 of the best full-time MBA programmes in a survey by *Asia Week* magazine. Many of the graduates are now working for large international companies such as PricewaterhouseCoopers as well as major Japanese companies. (Case developed from *The Financial Times*, 6 Nov. 2000, p. 27.)

Questions

1 Is an MBA really necessary for managers in general and managers in Japan in particular? Why?
2 How beneficial might Western-style or Eastern-made MBAs be for a Japanese manager? Why?

Rewards and remuneration

In Japan all wages are determined at the organizational level as agreed between the management and the company union, whereas in South Korea rewards are determined at the national and organizational levels. At the national level the Ministry of Labour in consultation with the Federation of Korean Trade Unions (FKTU) and the employers' associations determines the levels of pay annually. At the organizational level, especially in the small and medium size and non-unionized enterprises, it is the management that determines the pay. Until the late 1990s, all rewards, regardless of how they were determined in each of the two countries, were generally collective and seniority-based because of the influence of Confucianism, which emphasizes collectivism, status and seniority. There has, however, been a shift from pay based on seniority to pay related to performance.

In South Korea, the partial move away from seniority-based rewards to more performance-related ones has included new rewards such as employee share-holding and profit sharing (Rowley and Bae, 2002; Lee and Kim, 2006; Kwon and Holliday, 2007; Miles, 2008). The current system of rewards and remuneration in both countries is generally characterized by the implementation of a statutory minimum wage, the persistence of some emphasis on seniority and age in pay and promotion, a strong link between organizational size and pay, the offer of generous bonuses, and increasing emphasis on performance-related pay.

Minimum wage

The minimum wage in Japan varies according to industry and region. The Minister of Labour or the Chief of the Prefectural Labour Standards Office reviews the recommendations of the Minimum Wage Council and sets the minimum wage for the different industries in different regions. In South Korea, a statutory minimum wage is national and is revised annually by taking into consideration the price index. Very few South Koreans work for minimum wage because in most manufacturing and low-paid jobs the average hourly rate is higher than the state-defined minimum hourly rate.

Seniority-based rewards

Seniority-based rewards are influenced by the culture of Confucianism that determines the value system of Asian countries. The belief in seniority-based rewards comes from the assumption that the older the employee the greater the experience and the longer the commitment to the organization. Therefore age, seniority, loyalty, punctuality and reliability are used as criteria for pay increases and other rewards such as bonuses and promotion. This belief is also related to the Asian culture of respecting seniority. In the early years of employees' careers they are paid very low wages to test their loyalty and commitment to the organization, and then they start going up gradually. The longer employees stay with an organization the more training they get, the better they perform and the higher they get paid. Despite recent economic changes that have forced many organizations to adopt performance-related rewards (Kim and Kim, 2003; Chang, 2006) it has not been possible to move away completely from culturally anchored seniority-based pay (Miles, 2008).

Rewards and organizational size and sector

In both Japan and South Korea, rewards also vary from one organization to another by size, industry and type of employment. In Japan, wage levels, bonus earnings, overtime pay, working hours and benefits all differ considerably according to the size of the organization. This is because large organizations are wealthier and they can afford to pay higher wages; they adhere to employment regulations in relation to pay and benefits in order to protect their reputation; and they face more wage competition than small employers. Moreover, in both Japan and South Korea wages are higher in sectors such as banking and finance, public services, publishing and high-technology industries than in other sectors.

Bonus systems

In both Japan and South Korea employees are paid generous bonuses. In Japanese companies bonuses can be up to 30 per cent of annual income and they are normally related to increases in productivity in general, individual achievements, good behaviour, loyalty and commitment. Workers receive two large bonuses over their normal wage, one at mid-year and the other at the end of the year. Besides the generous bonuses, workers also receive a number of tangible and intangible fringe benefits such as allowances for the cost of living, for travel, for good behaviour, for good attendance, and for special job conditions. South Korean companies provide good annual bonuses and most of them provide profit sharing bonuses when the company makes a surplus. Also, most employers provide a wide range of welfare provisions, from the normal pension schemes, insurance funds, medical help, and sickness benefit, to grants and loans for housing, buying a car, paying childrens' school fees, and family-related events such as weddings, birthdays and funerals. Usugami and Park (2006: 284) note that 'a fringe benefits programme plays a more important role in HRM in Korea than in Japan'.

Performance-related pay

As explained earlier, there has been a move in both countries from seniority-based to performance-related rewards. Currently more and more organizations in both countries are explicitly favouring ability and performance over tenure and age in salary decisions. In Japan there has been a move away from 'the more predictable fixed annual entitlements and allowances based on seniority towards a far greater emphasis on individual ability and greater use of merit evaluations' (Salmon, 2004: 68–9). In South Korea, Rowley and Bae (2004: 49) observed that some conglomerates such as Samsung and Hyosung introduced a 'zero-sum' approach to rewards, which means that the poor performers have their pay reduced and the good performers have their pay increased by the same amount. They also found that 'companies such as Doosan, Daeang and SK used a 'plus-sum' method, which means increasing salaries of good performers without reducing those of poor performers'.

The basis for performance-related pay is a performance appraisal system. Therefore, most Japanese and Korean companies have introduced a combination of performance appraisal methods (Kim and Briscoe, 1997; Rowley and Bae, 2004). Nevertheless, not many employers have been able to use performance appraisal on all their employees because of problems in relating pay to performance through a procedure (appraisal) that is alien to an Asian culture of harmonious and collective rewards (Miles, 2008). Many managers are not keen on giving negative evaluations of their subordinates because that could undermine the harmonious relations that exist between them. For example, in South Korea, there is the value of *koenchanayo* (that's good enough) which usually 'encourages tolerance and appreciation of people's efforts and not being excessively harsh in assessing sincere efforts' (Rowley and Bae, 2004: 52).

Many managers are very careful not to transgress *koenchanayo* as a result of excessive use of performance appraisal indicators.

Promotion

It seems that in both Japan and South Korea, employee career progression is straightforward because of the existence of a clear career path from induction to continuous training and to seniority-based rewards and promotion. The employment process allows for promotions to be steady and with little differentiation in one's career, but they are linked to extensive training and evaluation of potential. Seniority as well as ability and performance criteria are regularly used for promotion, but because of the seniority requirement it is very often difficult and frustrating for many young and talented employees to progress quickly. It is unusual for a senior manager to be younger than 30 years old unless he/she is a member of the founder–owner family, which means experience is inherited by age rather than through formal employment. The culture of respecting seniority and old age has helped to consolidate the senior/junior or *sempai/kohai* relationship whereby the experience of the senior is given to the junior person in a relatively smooth and progressive manner; thus one is said to learn from the mistakes and successes of the past while dealing with the present and preparing for the future.

MINI CASE STUDY 13

Age Before Beauty (Japan)

If rewards are seniority based the eminent problem has been the promotion of senior employees who cannot be progressed higher than their current level. Many employees reach a certain level in their careers and they get stuck because there are no positions for them to progress to. Senior employees have occupied all the high positions, they do not want to leave their jobs before the retirement age. However, as a result of international competition, an increasing number of Japanese companies, especially those operating abroad, have had to change their promotion policies and promote their employees on the basis of performance and achievement regardless of age and seniority. Interestingly, many young employees have been reluctant to accept promotions before their older colleagues. When a junior manager was asked, 'Why don't you accept promotion?', he replied: 'I believe in age before beauty'.

Question

1 Discuss the advantages and disadvantages of seniority-based promotion in Japan and in another country of your choice.

Employee relations

Japanese employees have a constitutional right to organize trade unions, to bargain with management for better pay and working conditions, and to go on strike when necessary. Article 28 of the Japanese constitution (1947) states that the right to organize is 'unavoidable'. The rights of workers to bargain and to go on strike, if needed, are also enshrined. Despite these constitutional rights, the Japanese employee relations system has been exemplary in promoting industrial peace and employee–employer cooperation. One of the main characteristics of this non-adversarial and cooperative approach to employee relations is the institution of enterprise union (Holzhausen, 2000; Jackson and Tomioka, 2004; Suzuki, 2008). The enterprise or company union is a single union that unites both blue- and white-collar core (full-time) employees. Unlike the Japanese system, employee relations in South Korea have been characterized by state control and violent industrial action. It was not until recently that trade unions were allowed to exist, bargain with management and call for strikes. The Korean system is highly regulated as almost all aspects of employee relations are stated in codes of practice and statutes. The Korean government uses such laws and regulations in order to control labour organization and operations. All collective agreements are legally binding and mandatory. Overall, as will be explained below, the Japanese employee relations system is rather stable while that of South Korea is dynamic and highly volatile.

Trade unions

In Japan, trade unions are organized into enterprise-based unions, industrial federations, and a national centre called RENGO (the Japanese Trade Union Confederation). Industrial federations are made of enterprise-based unions within the same industry. Their affiliated member unions gather and exchange information on the conditions of work in that particular industry, debate the work-related policies and employment problems, and seek solutions to them before presenting them to the management (Lincoln and Nakata, 1997; Suzuki, 2008). RENGO is made up of about 58 affiliated industrial federations and 47 local organizations representing a total of more than 6.5 million workers by 2006. The role of RENGO is to work with the government and employers' organizations to protect the interests of workers on issues that cannot be settled at the industry or local levels. Also, there are 47 local union confederations (called local RENGOs) spread over the Japanese prefectures. More than 70 per cent of enterprise unions are linked to some type of industrial federation of unions such as the Federation of Japanese Automobile Workers and the Japanese Electronic and Information Union. Industrial federations are affiliated mainly to the nationwide Japanese Trade Union Confederation (RENGO).

The federations coordinate the activities of their member unions in political lobbying and guiding them in specific disputes with their employers. Trade union density has declined slightly from about 22.2 per cent in 1999 to about 18.3 per cent in 2007 (OECD Statistics, 2009).

Traditionally, trade unions in South Korea have been more powerful than in Japan (Usugami and Park, 2006). They are militant and well organized, especially in some of the large companies in automobile manufacturing, transportation, shipbuilding and telecommunications. Also, while trade unionism in Japan has been peaceful and stable, trade unions in South Korea have had a history of struggle with the state. Following the declaration of the First Republic of Korea, the General Federation of Korean Trade Unions (GFKTU), which emerged in 1946 after a labour movement struggle, was reorganized and renamed in 1948 as the Federation of Korean Trade Unions, FKTU (*Daehan Nochong*). It has often been at loggerheads with the government. Trade unions were suppressed by the military rulers from 1961 to the mid-1980s, when democracy and freedom of organization were restored and a genuine trade unionism was allowed to emerge again.

In the late 1980s there were massive demonstrations and protests that were followed by a series of national strikes affecting the whole of the South Korean economy. Such industrial action led to fundamental changes in the Korean industrial relations system, which became less regulated by the state and more by the employer and unions in the workplace (Kim, 1993; Leggett, 1996). A number of independent trade unions were set up over the 1990s, but trade union membership dropped back to about 12 per cent again after the 1997 financial crisis when the role of trade unions became weaker because of the government's emphasis on cooperation and 'consultation through legally prescribed Labour Management Councils' (Rowley et al., 2004: 925). Before 2002, when multiple trade unionism was recognized, most trade unions had been company based and each company was legally permitted only one trade union. Trade union density declined slightly from about 11.7 per cent in 1999 to about 10 per cent in 2007 (OECD Statistics, 2009). Korean trade unions are still strong, especially in the shipbuilding and automobile industries and in the transportation and telecommunications sectors.

Enterprise unions

When the workers in a single enterprise form one union that is confined to that individual enterprise rather than being organized across crafts or industries, it is called an enterprise union. The system of a single enterprise union is expected to create an atmosphere where workers equate their livelihood with the prosperity of the company they work for. The enterprise union has a limited adversarial role and has little real influence in decision-making because of the *ringi* system, as explained earlier, and the belief that personal desires should not interfere with company loyalty (Kawanishi, 1992). Employees see their prosperity and that of the company as concurrent. This is indicative of the Japanese word for company, *kaisha*, which literally translates as 'our company'. The enterprise unions' leaders work with managers rather than against them, creating an atmosphere of partnership rather than the 'them and us' attitude that exists in some Western organizations.

However, this does not mean that other forms of employee representation do not exist in Japan. Other forms of union organization are limited but not insignificant. For example, the *Kaiin* (Japan's Seaman's Union) is one of the most powerful industrial unions in Japan. There are also some craft and occupational unions akin to those found in Western industrialized countries. They are organized under standard apprenticeships or occupations recognized by the government.

As in Japan, the majority of trade unions in South Korea are enterprise based. The company unions are affiliated with federations at the industry level which in turn are members of federations at the national level. Another aspect of employee representation in South Korea is the establishment of labour management councils in all organizations with 50 or more employees. The councils are expected to promote harmonious employee relations between employees and their managers; and to discuss work-related issues such as health and safety and job design, and employee concerns, grievances and welfare; but they do not discuss or negotiate industrial conflict issues such as strikes and pay rises. The latter are normally dealt with by the company unions through a more adversarial and aggressive collective bargaining process than that in Japan.

Collective bargaining

In Japan most collective bargaining is conducted at the local or plant levels between the company union and management. Labour–management negotiations are normally held in the spring and very often referred to as 'the Spring Struggle for a Better Life' and 'the Spring Offensive', because it is the time when enterprise unions submit claims for pay increases in coordination with the trade union confederations as well as the industrial union federations. It is also the time when most companies recruit new employees, carry out a review of current employees' salaries, and consider the transfer or promotion of employees. When collective agreements are reached and signed, they become legally binding for a maximum period of three years. However, enterprise unions play a small role in negotiating general wage changes and how they are distributed to individual employees. For example, a company bonus may be negotiated collectively but the individual employee receives a payment that is calculated in proportion to a the basic wage according to a personal performance appraisal review.

In South Korea, collective bargaining is widely practised, especially in large conglomerates (the *chaebol*), which are normally unionized. Collective agreements are legally binding and override the terms and conditions set in the labour contract and employment regulations. The negotiating parties have to report their agreements in writing and register them with the relevant authorities (the Ministry of Labour) within 15 days of concluding the deal. However, because of heavily regulated employee relations, the agreed deal should not violate any of the laws in force. Any deal that contravenes state-imposed laws is void and any deal that is acceptable is valid for a maximum of two years.

Industrial action

The popular stereotypical image of Japanese industrial relations suggests that industrial conflict rarely occurs, but in reality industrial conflict is as common as in many other industrialized nations. In fact, countries like Sweden, Norway, the Netherlands and Ireland have fewer industrial disputes than Japan. According to the Trade Unions Law (art. 1, para. 2, 1949), for an industrial action to be legal it has to be called for by a legally registered trade union and there should be no use of violence. Strikes tend to be short in duration but they are usually accompanied by work-to-rule, go slow, sit ins, slow downs, rallies, picketing, flyers, billboards, headbands and even sometimes physical harassment of managers (Kim, 1990; Kim, 1993). One of the reasons for the short duration of strikes is societal pressure towards consensus that places responsibility on the enterprise union and the management to resolve disputes without resorting to conflict that may damage the performance and/or the reputation of the enterprise. Thus strikes in Japan are very rare not because they are not allowed but because of:

- the strike-free agreements that the unions have with the management of their enterprises;
- the high cost of legal proceedings in settling industrial disputes;
- the long time the courts take to settle a dispute; and
- the cultural value of avoiding conflicts.

In contrast to Japan, industrial actions in the form of strikes are widespread in South Korea and they tend to be violent at times. The government has often responded by using force because such actions seemed to be potentially damaging to the country's economic growth and competitiveness. Until recently, whenever employees went on strike the government intervened to stop them by putting pressure on union leaders. For example, in 2002 the president of the Korean Confederation of Trade Unions (ICFTU) was arrested and sentenced to two years in prison for organizing a general strike (ICFTU, 2003). For industrial disputes to be recognized they have to adhere to the legal procedures defined by the Labour Dispute Adjustment Act 1987. The law states that for a strike to be legitimate it has to be fully justified by a recognized and registered trade union that has to meet the following conditions:

- The strike has to be voted for by the majority of the members through a direct, secret and unsigned ballot;
- The administrative authorities and the Labour Relations Commission have to be informed in advance of the action, and that both the action and the methods to be taken must be justified;
- The action must be intended for the improvement of either working conditions or the workers' welfare and income level; and
- No strike action can involve violence or destruction and occupation of production facilities.

In case of a strike action, the Law (art. 46, para. 1 of the Trade Union and Labour Relations Adjustment Act 1998) encourages employers to introduce lockouts in order to protect industrial facilities as they are not allowed to recruit more non-striking workers or to subcontract the work to outsiders. The government's intervention by law and with force to limit industrial action has had very limited effects on trade unions' militancy. Korean workers believe that industrial action in the form of strikes and noisy and colourful protests is a way of expressing employees' democratic rights and a natural stage in the country's economic and social development. Strikes are still very common and present one of the major problems for foreign investors in South Korea. To encourage foreign investment and reduce the risk of violent industrial actions the Office of Industrial Relations Policy at the Korean Ministry of Labour set up a consultation office where foreign companies can meet when they have problems with the unions. This seems to have worked because the number of foreign companies has increased significantly over the recent years.

MINI CASE STUDY 14

Strikes at Citibank's Seoul Office

After almost a month on strike, the workers of Citibank's Seoul Office returned to work in November 2004. It seems that industrial action had been a problem for Citigroup since it decided to take over the South Korean lender KorAm. In June 2004 KorAm workers went on strike for 18 days. The action resulted in a settlement by which the workers were offered a large bonus and job security. Consequently, the workers at Citibank Seoul walked out, asking for rewards similar to those offered to KorAm workers. In November 2004, the workers agreed to go back to work only after the management of Citibank had promised to meet their demands. The vice-president of the American Chamber of Commerce in South Korea was reported as saying that 'the Korean people must realise that the window of opportunity is closing quickly and images of angry, striking demonstrators do not encourage investment'. (Case developed from *Financial Times*, 1 Dec. 2004, Special Report.)

Question

1   The case shows the difficulties that foreign investors such as Citibank may encounter in South Korea because of labour union militancy. What are the arguments for and against industrial action in companies owned by foreign investors in South Korea?

The settlement of industrial disputes

Labour disputes in Japan are referred first to a joint consultation committee of labour and management representatives at the enterprise level. If the dispute is not resolved it will proceed on to collective bargaining between the enterprise union and the management. And then if they fail to reach an agreement the dispute can be settled by conciliation, mediation or arbitration upon submission to the Labour Relations Commission (LRC) of a case made by either or both of the parties in dispute. The LRC imposes a waiting period of up to 15 days before starting the conciliation and mediation process. In practice, most of the disputes are dealt with through conciliation and rarely through arbitration, because most of the disputes are dealt with at the organization level and solved at an earlier stage. Finally the conciliator and the mediation committee, which are appointed by the LRC, help the parties in dispute to reach an agreement by drafting the settlement, whereas the arbitrator or arbitration committee, which is also appointed by the LRC, meets and listens to the parties in dispute, considers their offers and makes a decision in writing (known as an arbitration award) that has the same effect as a collective agreement (art. 34 of the Labour Relations Adjustment Law, no. 25, 1946). It is very uncommon to bring disputes to the labour courts because disputes are rarely not solved through arbitration. However, all individual labour disputes are settled by filing complaints with the district court as a court of first instance.

In South Korea, the Labour Dispute Adjustment Act (1987) sets the legal framework for settling industrial disputes and provides for conciliation, mediation and arbitration. Normally, the Labour Board (similar to the Japanese Labour Relations Commission), which deals with industrial disputes, is made of 30 members (10 employee representatives, 10 employer representatives and 10 public figures). The board examines cases of labour disputes related to unfair dismissal and unfair labour practices and makes judgements. According to the Trade Unions Labour Relations Adjustment Act (arts 53 and 54, para. 1, 1998) mediation and arbitration are normally used for adjustment procedures. A mediation proposal needs to be accepted by both parties for it to have the same effect as a collective agreement (art. 61, paras 1 and 2). An arbitration committee designated by the Labour Board conducts the arbitration procedure. When the arbitration procedure starts, no industrial action is allowed for 15 days. The Arbitration Committee makes an award which is legally binding and has the same effect as a collective agreement (arts 63 and 70, para. 2, 1998).

Summary

1   Although their economies are reliant on imports of raw materials and hydrocarbons, Japan and South Korea have achieved prosperity through the quality of their human resources and their management.
2   The Japanese and the South Koreans pay particular attention to class, status, education level, age and seniority. Not responding in the right way to the right people may damage personal relationships and destroy opportunities for concluding business deals.
3   The labour markets of both countries are characterized by: a low level of unemployment; the domination of conglomerate (*chaebol* and *zaibatsu*) employment practices; a hard-working, committed and loyal workforce; limited opportunities for female employment; and an increasingly older working population.
4   The Japanese approach to management is characterized by: an emphasis on quality; having clear mechanisms for consultation, communication and decision-making (the *ringi* system); a paternalistic leadership style, emphasizing shared status between the leaders and the subordinates; and relative security in employment.
5   The Japanese employee relations system has been exemplary in promoting industrial peace and employee–employer cooperation, while the South Korean system has been characterized by state control and violent industrial action.

Revision questions

Chapter 1 provides a review task designed to consolidate your learning from this chapter. Please see Box 1.2.

In addition, the following questions are designed to help you revise this chapter:

1   What are the main management issues that characterize the Japanese approach to management? Analyse each one of them in comparison to similar issues in Australia and New Zealand.
2   Discuss critically the main reasons for the move from seniority-based payment to performance-related pay and from lifetime employment to the use of employment adjustment in both Japan and South Korea.
3   Imagine you are the HR manager of an American company in South Korea. Write a report to the company's board of directors in New York summarizing the main similarities and differences in HRM (recruitment and selection, training and development, rewards system, and employee relations) between Japan and South Korea.

References

Amsden, A. (1989) *Asia's Next Giant: South Korea and Late Industrialization*, Oxford: Oxford University Press.

Asian Development Bank (2001) *Annual Report 2001*, available online at: http://www.adb.org/documents/reports/annual_report/2001/kor.asp, accessed 13 November 2009.

Bae, J.S. and Rowley, C. (2001) 'The impact of globalization on HRM: the case of South Korea', *Journal of World Business*, 36(4): 402–28.

Bae, J.S. and Rowley, C. (2003) 'Changes and continuities in South Korean HRM', *Asia Pacific Business Review*, 9(4): 76–105.

Bond, M.H. (1992) *Beyond the Chinese Face – Insights from Psychology*, Oxford: Oxford University Press.

Briggs, P. (1991) 'Organisational commitment: the key to Japanese success', in Brewster, C. and Tyson, S. (eds), *International Comparisons in Human Resource Management*, London: Pitman, 33–43.

Chang, E. (2006) 'Individual pay for performance and commitment HR practices in South Korea', *Journal of World Business*, 41(4): 368–81.

Cho, E. (2009) 'Work values and business ethics in Korea', *Advances in Developing Human Resources*, 11(2): 235–52.

Cho, L.J. (1994) 'Culture, institutions and economic development in East Asia', in Cho, L.J. and Kim, Y.H. (eds), *Korea's Political Economy: An Institutional Perspective*, Boulder, CO: Westview Press.

Cho, Y. and McLean, G.N. (2009) 'Successful IT start-ups' HRD practices: four cases in South Korea', *Journal of European Industrial Training*, 33(2): 125–41.

Dalton, N. and Benson, J. (2002) 'Innovation and change in Japanese human resource management', *Asia Pacific Journal of Human Resources*, 40(3): 345–62.

Duignan, R. and Yoshida, K. (2007) 'Employee perceptions of recent work environment changes in Japan', *Personnel Review*, 36(3): 440–56.

Fukuda, K.J. (1983) 'Transfer of management: Japanese practices for the orientals?', *Management Decision*, 21(4): 17–25.

Gow, I. (1988) 'Japan', in Handy, C., Gordon, C., Gow, I. and Randlesome, C. (eds), *Making Managers*, London: Pitman.

Gross, A. (1996) 'Human resource issues in South Korea', at http://www.pacificbridge.com/publication.asp?id = 15, accessed 23 Aug. 2007.

Harney, A. (2000) 'Turning management education Japanese', *Financial Times*, Oct. 30, p. 22.

Hofstede, G. and Bond, M.H. (1988) 'The Confucian connection: from cultural roots to economic growth', *Organizational Dynamics*, 16(4): 5–21.

Holzhausen, A. (2000) 'Japanese employment practices in transition: promotion policy and compensation systems in the 1990s', *Social Science Japan Journal*, 3(2): 221–37.

Hutton, B. (2000) 'Working mothers with a yen for family life', *Financial Times*, p. 22. Accessed 2 March 2010.

ICFTU (International Confederation of Free Trade Unions) (2003), Korea, Republic of: Annual Survey of Violations of Trade Union Rights (2003), available online at: http://www.icftu.org/displaydocument.asp?Index = 991217715&Language = EN, accesses on 16 November 2009.

Jackson, K. and Tomioka, M. (2004) *The Changing Face of Japanese Management*, London: Routledge.

Kawakita, T. (1997) 'Corporate strategy and human resource management', in Sako, M. and Sato, H. (eds), *Japanese Labour and Management in Transition: Diversity, Flexibility and Participation*, London: Routledge.

Kawanishi, H. (1992) *Enterprise Unionism in Japan*, London: Kegan Paul.

Keeley, D. (2001) *International Human Resource Management in Japanese Firms*, London: Palgrave.

Kim, A.E. and Park, G.S. (2003) 'Nationalism, Confucianism, work ethics and industrialisation in South Korea', *Journal of Contemporary Asia*, 33(1): 37–49.

Kim, D. and Kim, S. (2003) 'Globalisation, financial crisis and industrial relations: the case of South Korea', *Industrial Relations*, 42(3): 341–67.

Kim, D. and Bae, J. (2004) *Employment Relations and HRM in South Korea*, Aldershot: Ashgate.

Kim, H.J. (1993) 'The Korean union movement in transition', in Frenkel, S. (ed.), *Organized Labor in the Asia-Pacific Region: A Comparative Study of Trade Unionism in Nine Countries*, Ithaca, NY: International Labor Relations Press, 133–61.

Kim, K.C. and Kim, S. (1989) 'Kinship group and patrimonial executives in a developing nation: a case study of Korea', *Journal of Development Areas*, 24(1): 27–45.

Kim, S. and Briscoe, D. (1997) 'Globalization and a new human resource policy in Korea: Transformation to a performance-based HRM', *Employee Relations*, 19(4): 298–308.

Kim, T.K. (1990) *Industrial Relations and Collective Bargaining in Korea: Recent Developments*, Seoul: Korea Labor Institute.

Kim, Y.S. (1990) 'Korea's export-managed industrialization and its lessons', *Human Systems Management*, 9(3): 173–85.

Kong, T.Y. (2000) *The Politics of Economic Reform in South Korea: A Fragile Miracle*, New York: Routledge.

Kwon, S.M. and Holliday, I. (2007) 'The Korean welfare state: a paradox of expansion in an era of globalisation and economic crisis', *International Journal of Social Welfare*, 16(3): 242–8.

Lee, E.S. and Kim, S.S. (2006) 'Best practices and performance based HR system in Korea', *Seoul Journal of Business*, 12(1): 3–17.

Lee, Y.-I. and Trim, P.R.J. (2008) 'The link between cultural value systems and strategic marketing: Unlocking the mindset of Japanese and South Korean Managers', *Cross-cultural Management: An International Journal*, 15(1): 62–80.

Leggett, C. (1996) 'Recent developments in Korean industrial relations', paper presented at a Research Seminar, University of Stirling, 22 April.

Lincoln, J. and Nakata, Y. (1997) 'The transformation of the Japanese employment system: nature, depth and origins', *Work and Occupations*, 24(1): 33–55.

McNamara, D. (2002) *Market and Society in Korea: Interest, Institution and the Textile Industry*, London: Routledge.

Miles, L. (2008) 'The significance of cultural norms in the evolution of Korean HRM practices', *International Journal of Law and Management*, 50(1): 33–46.

Morden, T. and Bowles, D. (1998) 'Management in South Korea: a review', *Management Decision*, 36(5): 316–30.

Nagase, N. (1997) 'Wage differentials and labour supply of married women in Japan: part-time and informal sector work opportunities', *The Japanese Economic Review*, 48(1): 29–42.

Nonaka, I. and Takeuchi, H. (1996) *The Knowledge Creating Company: How Japanese Companies Create the Dynamics of Innovation*, Oxford: Oxford University Press.

OECD (Organization for Economic Cooperation and Development) (2009) *OECD Harmonized Unemployment Rates & levels*, available online at http://stats.oecd.org/Index.aspx?QueryName = 251&QueryType = View&Lang = en, accessed on 10 March 2010.

Oliver, N. and Wilkinson, B. (1992) *The Japanization of British Industry*, 2nd edn, Oxford: Blackwell.

Rowley, C. and Bae, J. (2002) 'Globalization and transformation of human resource management in South Korea', *International Journal of Human Resource Management*, 13(3): 522–49.

Rowley, C. and Bae, J. (2004) 'HRM in South Korea', in Budhwar, P.S. (ed.), *Managing Human Resources in Asia-Pacific*, London: Routledge, 35–60.

Rowley, C. and Benson, J. (eds) (2003) *HRM in the Asia Pacific region: Convergence Revisited*, London: Frank Cass.

Rowley, C., Benson, J. and Warner, M. (2004) 'Towards an Asian model of human resource management? A comparative analysis of China, Japan and South Korea', *International Journal of Human Resource Management*, 15(4): 917–33.

Salmon, J. (2004) 'HRM in Japan', in Budhwar, P.S. (ed.), *Managing Human Resources in Asia-Pacific*, London: Routledge, 61–73.

Sano, Y., Morishima, M. and Seike, A. (eds) (1997) *Frontiers of Japanese Human Resource Practice*, Tokyo: Japanese Institute of Labour.

Song, B.N. (1997) *The Rise of the Korea Economy*, Oxford: Oxford University Press.

Song, H.Y. and Meek, C.B. (1998) 'The Impact of culture on the management values and beliefs of Korean firms', *Journal of Comparative International Management*, 1(1): 1–38.

Suzuki, A. (2008) 'Community unions in Japan: similarities and differences of region-based labour movements between Japan and other industrialized countries', *Economic and Industrial Democracy*, 29(4): 492–520.

Usugami, J. and Park, K.-Y. (2006) 'Similarities and differences in employee motivation viewed by Korean and Japanese executives: empirical study on employee motivation management of Japanese-affiliated companies in Korea', *International Journal of Human Resource Management*, 17(2): 280–94.

White, M. and Trevor, M. (1983) *Under Japanese Management*, London: Heinmann.

Whitehill, A.M. (1991) *Japanese Management: Tradition and Transition*, Chippenham: Antony Rowe.

8

China and Hong Kong

LEARNING OUTCOMES

The chapter is designed to help you understand, for China and Hong Kong:

1   The (a) economic, (b) political and (c) cultural contexts in which managers work;

2   The main trends in the labour market;

3   The typical features of (a) management policies and practices and (b) organizational structure and behaviour;

4   The main policies and practices of human resource management with regard to: (a) recruitment and selection, (b) training and development, (c) rewards and remuneration, and (d) employee relations.

Introter

Introduction

The Chinese approach to management is evident, to a great extent, in the management policies and practices of mainland China (the People's Republic of China), Hong Kong, Taiwan, Thailand, Singapore and some other neighbouring countries. However, though they may be similar in terms of work ethic, organizational behaviour, and management systems, there are of course many political and economic differences. This chapter focuses on the mainland China (PRC) and its special administrative region, Hong Kong, which have become known as one country with two different economic systems. The two parts of one country share the same cultural values and are gradually becoming politically and economically similar.

China is an interesting country to study because of its history of major achievements and its ancient civilization, diverse culture, large population, and strategic geographical location. It is a huge country with immense natural resources. Child (1994) describes it as a very complex and often surprising

Table 8.1 Basic statistical indicators, China and Hong Kong

Country	Area (sq km)	Population (July 2010 est.)	Population growth (2010) %	GDP – real growth rate (2009) %	Inflation rate (Jan. 2009 est.) %	Workforce (2009) Million	Unemployment rate (2009) %
Mainland China	9,596961	1,338,612968	0.65	9.1	–0.7	813.5	4.3
Hong Kong	1,104	7,055,071	0.50	–2.8	–0.5	3.695	5.3

Source: CIA World Factbook, 2010.

society that is almost impossible to understand from the outside: it is 'so old, so big, so diverse and so deep'. As economic policy has shifted from central planning towards market economics, the PRC has emerged as an economic superpower. (See Table 8.1 for basic statistics.)

Contexts: economics, politics and culture

Economics

China has been transformed from an agricultural country with basic industrial activity to one of the world's major manufacturers. The transformation started with a policy decision, made in 1978, to make the economy more open to the rest the world. Economic reforms were introduced gradually through the 1980s. By the late 1990s, when Hong Kong (previously a British colony) was returned to China, the Chinese economic growth rate was amongst the highest in the world. The GDP per capita increased by about 4.5 times from 1980 to 2000 (OECD, 2002), and strong growth has continued since and even during the recent international financial crisis.

China is very rich in natural resources such as coal, iron ore, mercury, tin and uranium. It is the largest producer of cement, zinc, antimony, tungsten and natural graphite in the world. There is a large agricultural sector: the country is self-sufficient in the production of many essential commodities such as rice, wheat, corn, tea, cotton, potatoes and apples. China's notable industries include textiles, chemicals, electronics, automobiles, telecommunications equipment, toys and aviation.

The Chinese economic reforms were founded on four modernization initiatives: (a) the decentralization and partial privatization of the agricultural sector; (b) the reduction of industrial central planning (industrial liberalization); (c) the establishment of special economic zones; and (d) the development of education in science and technology. Initially most reforms were in agriculture: more power was given to farmers, enabling them to make decisions about levels of crop production and product diversification. The reforms were extended cautiously onto the industrial sector: special economic zones (SEZs) were established and priorities were shifted from heavy to light industry. In 1984 the Communist Party Central Committee approved a policy document on China's economic reform, making public sector enterprises more accountable for their profit and loss, and giving greater attention to training and management development, rewards, and employment contracts.

The Chinese economy was strengthened further in 1997 when Hong Kong, one of the world's most successful capitalist economies, was returned to China. Hong Kong has a free market economy based heavily on the provision of international financial and trade services (92.6 per cent of GDP in 2008). By the time Hong Kong was returned to China, it was developing a knowledge economy that provided the value-added services which the Chinese economy needed to sustain its high level of economic growth (Chan and Lui, 2004). Hong Kong's economy is founded on privately owned small and medium size companies. Many Hong Kong-based companies have developed extensive trade and investment projects in China's fast-growing economy where manufacturing is much more cost effective.

By the start of this century China had combined two successful economies under one political system. It became a full member of the World Trade Organization (WTO) in December 2001. By joining the WTO the Chinese government committed to cut tariff barriers and to provide greater opportunities to foreign companies. There has been an increasing emphasis on the attraction of foreign direct investment in high-technology and primary industries which are export-oriented, and in services sectors such as tourism, retailing and insurance. China has become the second largest economy in the world after the US. However, in terms of per-capita income it is still classified among the developing countries. Further structural reforms are still needed in order to improve quality standards, competition laws, intellectual property rights, enterprise governance and other frameworks and regulations required for sustaining a high economic growth.

Politics

The People's Republic of China is a communist country with a one-party system. The power to run the country rests in the leadership of the Chinese Communist Party (CCP), which derives its constitution from Marxism-Leninism, Mao Zedong's thought, Deng Xiaoping's theory, Jiang Zemin's views, and the aspirations and ideas of the current leadership. There is a CCP constitution and a state constitution: both have been revised regularly since the late 1980s to incorporate the ideas of emerging leaderships and evolving socio-economic policies. Party members elect the representative bodies of both party and state, and they in turn elect their administrative officers at different levels. Although the highest political institution of the state power is the National Party Congress (NPC), the real political power rests with the CCP Central Committee and Party Political Bureau. The NPC operates as the state's legislative authority. Deputies to the NPC are elected for five years from the provinces, autonomous regions, centrally administered municipalities, special administrative regions, and the armed forces. They meet each year for two to three weeks to debate and approve the country's policies, to examine and agree the national economic and social development plans and the state budget, and to elect the president and vice-president of the state, the head of the army, the president of the court, and the procurator general. The State Council (like a government cabinet) is the Central People's Government and the executive organ of state power, led by a premier (prime minister) nominated by the president and approved by congress. There are also five vice-premiers and five state councillors.

Administratively, China is divided into 22 provinces (Taiwan is considered as its 23rd province), 5 autonomous regions, 4 municipalities, and 2 special administrative regions (Hong Kong and Macau). With the approval of the National People's Congress (NPC), the central government in Beijing appoints the governors of the provinces and autonomous regions and the mayors of the centrally controlled municipalities. Hong Kong has some political autonomy, with its own political parties, a constitution and a legal system that is based on English common law. It has a unicameral Legislative Council (parliament) made of 60 seats (in 2004) with 30 members directly elected by functional constituencies and 30 members elected by popular vote. The head of state of Hong Kong is that of the mainland China, while the head of government (chief executive) is appointed by the NPC in Beijing. The executive council (the cabinet) is made up of members of the majority party in the parliament. Foreign affairs and the national security of Hong Kong come under the control of the central government in Beijing.

Culture

Chinese culture can be described as collectivist and high power distance: its people typically value family ties, have great respect for age, seniority and status, are law abiding, hard working, and committed to establishing formal and informal networks and relationships (Hofstede and Bond, 1988; Bond, 1992; Chan, 1999; Chew and Lim, 1995). Ethnically, more than 90 per cent of the population of China belong to the Han Chinese ethnic group. In terms of religion, the PRC is officially atheist, but there are well-established and growing Christian, Muslim and Buddhist communities. The overriding Chinese cultural norms and values that have persisted down through generations are derived from Confucianism.

Confucianism is a moral philosophy and a system of ethical conduct that promotes harmony, peace and good morals in family life and society in general. It remains influential in business and in social and family relations (Liu and Vince, 1999). Chinese leaders, regardless of their political views and ideologies, are guided by Confucianism, which instructs them to lead with 'benevolence and justice' and suggests that the only way forward in a hierarchical Chinese society was to develop a 'morally-motivated bureaucracy' (Chan, 1999: 297). Confucius observed that the path to happiness for any society lies in the degree to which individuals understand and accept their given roles in the order of things. Symbols and images are an integral part of Chinese culture. Communication in China often means employing symbols (for example, the colour red, the number eight, the dragon), so one must master implied meanings. In general, Confucianism is based on the concept of harmony that can be achieved through collectivism, control of emotions, conflict avoidance and inner peace and harmony (Kirkbride and Tang, 1992). These norms and values provide the ethical and moral foundation for Chinese business and social structure, and influence the way the Chinese think and behave (Chan, 1999; Tang and Ward, 2003).

Labour market trends

It can be seen from Table 8.2 that the Chinese workforce has been increasing by about 10 million employees per annum since 2001. The current working population was estimated at around 813.5 million in 2009 and the participation rate is at around 98 per cent (World Factbook 2010). State-owned enterprises and the government sector are still the main employers. There are an increasing number of joint ventures and foreign-owned firms as a result of the foreign direct investment that the Chinese government has encouraged in high-technology exporting sectors in order to attract the transfer of advanced technologies and develop a skilled Chinese workforce.

Hong Kong's workforce consists of nearly 4 million workers; most of them are skilled and highly educated. The participation rate is around 70 per cent. Most jobs are created by small and medium size enterprises (SMEs) in the manufacturing and service sectors. Statistics on the distribution of the workforce by occupation in 2008 show that most jobs are created by the wholesale

Table 8.2 Labour and employment, China and Hong Kong

Year	Labour force (10,000s)		Labour force participation rate (%)		Unemployment rate (%)	
	PRC	HK	PRC	HK	PRC	HK
2001	74,432	342.7	98.10	61.4	3.6	5.1
2002	75,360	348.7	97.85	61.8	4.0	7.3
2003	76,075	349.6	97.84	61.4	4.3	7.9
2004	76,823	355.1	97.88	60.3	4.2	6.8
2005	77,877	358.6	97.36	60.9	4.2	5.6

Source: compiled from http:www.stats.gov.cn/tjsj/ndsj/2006/html/, accessed 7 Sept. 2007.

and retail trades, and restaurants and hotels (42.9 per cent), followed by finance, insurance and real estate at 19.7 per cent (CIA World Factbook, 2009).

China has a youthful workforce (see Table 8.3). However, as the standard of living has improved, the Chinese are living longer and in better health, which is pushing up the older demographic. As a result of the one-child policy, the number of young people will decline over time. It is estimated that by 2020 about 12 per cent of the population will be over 65 years. Currently, Hong Kong has a slightly older population than the PRC. In China there is a comparatively high level of equal opportunities between men and women in employment and in society. However, the gap between the rich and the poor has been widening significantly.

Table 8.3 Age structure (%) (2009), China and Hong Kong

Age	PRC %	Hong Kong %
0–14 years	19.8	12.2
15–64 years	72.1	74.6
65 years and over	8.1	13.1

Source: CIA *World Factbook*, 2009.

Overall, the current labour market is characterized by a shortage of skilled labour, rural–urban migration, emphasis on attracting joint ventures and foreign-owned companies, and the stratification and exploitation of the labour force.

Skills shortages

There is an acute shortage of skilled and sufficiently qualified workers throughout all sectors of China's economy (*Economist*, 2005). Although there is no shortage of people, there has been a serious lack of qualified managers, certified experts, and accredited professionals to meet the needs of a market economy. Though the Chinese government has made huge efforts to train as many people as possible to overcome the shortage of skilled labour, there is still a 'structural imbalance in the labour market, with a shortage of skilled professionals and over-supply of unskilled labour' (Cunningham and Rowley, 2007: 420).

Rural–urban migration

With increasing industrialization and large construction projects, there has been a high demand for manual labour in the cities. Also, the use of modern agricultural practices and the diminishing agricultural workforce has resulted in rural poverty, forcing people to migrate to large cities in search of employment. Rural–urban migration has created a mass movement of labour from underdeveloped regions (central and Western China) to the developed ones (Eastern and Coastal China). For example, between 1980 and 2000, urbanization went from 20 per cent to 31 per cent. The share of employment in agriculture fell from 69 to 50 per cent, while that of manufacturing industry rose from 18 to 23 per cent and services from 13 to 27 per cent (OECD, 2002).

Migration from rural to urban areas has become a problem because many rural migrants find it difficult to get formal-sector jobs. Also, they are not entitled to any state support if they do not have permission to move from one region to another. Farmers who decide to look for jobs in the cities may risk losing their land-use rights if they stay away from their rural homes for more than 12 months. Technically local authorities issue permits for the movement of skilled labour to places when there is a high demand, but in reality it has not been possible to control the flow of low-skilled and manual labour from one region to another. Consequently 'problems in the labour market may get worse since regional and income disparity encourage a "floating population" of economic migration and widening gaps between skilled professionals and unskilled workers' (Cunningham and Rowley, 2007: 421).

Since the return of Hong Kong to China, many skilled and business-minded (entrepreneurial and managerial) people have been given permission to move from Hong Kong to mainland China, but there have been strict controls on people moving in the opposite direction, from the mainland to Hong Kong.

Joint ventures and foreign-owned companies

The presence of a large number of MNCs in China has had significant implications for the composition of the Chinese labour market. MNCs have acted as a magnet to young, highly educated, very skilled and hard-working Chinese graduates. They prefer to work for foreign-owned companies and joint ventures because of the high salaries and the career opportunities they provide to their employees. A study by Wang and Fang (2001) found that the majority of Chinese workers who worked for MNCs were less than 30 years old and about 95 per cent of them had at least an advanced diploma qualification. The study found also that the main reasons for choosing to work in foreign-owned companies were opportunities to use their acquired skills and knowledge and to realize their own value as well as to get high salaries (cited in Cooke, 2004: 28). The attraction of foreign-owned enterprises has given an opportunity to foreign employers to choose and select the best Chinese workers. Many highly qualified employees who decide to work for MNCs have not found the opportunities they were looking for and have found themselves doing jobs below their level of qualification such as working in foreign-owned hotels and restaurants doing clerical, cleaning and catering work. There have also been reports of long working shifts (16 hours a day, for example), poor health and safety procedures, and bad working conditions in a number of joint ventures and foreign-owned enterprises in the manufacturing and service sectors.

Stratification and exploitation of the labour force

In most Chinese enterprises there is a clear stratification of the labour force represented in three types of employee (permanent, contract and temporary), 'each with its own work conditions, career prospects and opportunities in life' (Ip, 1995: 282). Besides the increasing number of contract workers, there are the many casual and temporary workers who migrate from the rural areas to seek employment in cities and towns, as explained above. Under the household registration system, which approves jobs for locals only, most of the casual and temporary workers find themselves unprotected by either the law or unions. They cannot join the unions because only permanent and contract workers can join. Therefore, casual and temporary workers are among the poor, uneducated and most vulnerable members of society who find themselves at the mercy of the notorious entrepreneurs and managers of manufacturing and construction plants. The increasing number of casual workers moving to already overpopulated cities has also led to problems such as homelessness, prostitution and theft, outcomes that the Chinese government does not tolerate and for which severe penalties are usually imposed.

ACTIVITY 1

Compare and contrast the Chinese labour market with that of the UK. How does culture influence the composition of each country's labour market trends?

Management and organization

From the founding of the PRC in 1949 to the declaration of the open door policy in 1978, Chinese management was influenced to a great extent by the Soviet system because the Chinese saw the Soviet Union as a model of successful communism (Warner, 1995, 1996; Cooke, 2005). It was also, to some extent, influenced by Japanese administration because of the Japanese occupation of China during the Second World War and the economic success of Japan as a neighbouring Asian economic power. With the introduction of free market economic reforms, which required corresponding management skills, the Chinese had to look to the West for examples of best practice in management and organization. However, many commentators argued that, despite the adoption of the 'Look West' policy, there has been no strong evidence of Chinese companies' management in general and HRM in particular being practised along Western lines (Child, 1991; Warner, 1992; 1995; 1997; 2004; Easterby-Smith et al., 1995; Brown and Branine, 1995; and many others).

According to an earlier study by Child (1991: 102) there was 'a wide gap between Chinese and foreign practice in human resource management'. Warner (1992) expressed doubts about the possibility of convergence between Western HRM practices and Chinese personnel management. Also, findings from a comparative study of British and Chinese companies showed that there were few similarities and several distinct differences in management between the two countries (Easterby-Smith et al., 1995). Most of the similarities were found in planning and career development procedures, while there were differences in terms of criteria for promotion, job rotation, recruitment and selection, and the role of trade unions. Similarly, from a study of the impact of economic reforms on managing people in 20 Chinese foreign trade corporations, Brown and Branine (1995) found that despite the reforms having been in progress for some 15 years, there was little evidence of radical change in the way personnel-based policies were carried out. Enterprise directors were, in theory, given the right to recruit, select, promote, train, demote and dismiss their employees 'within the limits of the system'. In practice the phrase 'within the limits of the system' is broad in its interpretation and prevents many decisions having to be made. That was mainly because the aim of the Chinese government was to introduce economic reforms in a way that would not affect the communist ideological orientation of the country, and so that state control over all organizations and institutions could be retained despite the increasing number of joint ventures, the growth of an active private sector, and the success of free-trade zones.

The practice of management in Hong Kong before the late 1990s was in principle similar to that of the British system, though modified to accommodate Chinese work ethics. For example, most of the institutions of the British industrial relations system such as trade union recognition, the practice of collective bargaining, the right to strike, the settlement of industrial disputes, the accreditation of management professions by a professional bodies such as, the Institute of Personnel and Development, and the recognition of the strategic role of personnel or HR managers in organizations, were all in place at the national and organizational levels throughout Hong Kong. Since around 2001 the whole system of employee–employer relations and the management system started to change gradually, not because of the imposition of the Chinese system by the Beijing government, but because of changes in the Hong Kong economy and labour market structure. As a result of economic decline between 2001 and 2003, resulting in company closures and mass redundancies, managers in Hong Kong had to implement new Chinese employment laws in relation to employees' rights and obligations, and adopt more strategic management approaches to overcome the problems of a sudden economic downturn. Since 2003, a number of new employment laws have been introduced in line with China's employment policies, and gradually many managers in Hong Kong have adopted management approaches similar to those practised in mainland China.

State- and party-orientated management

The one-party state controls every aspect of a Chinese citizen's life. Between the 1950s and early 1980s, all resources were allocated to prioritized sectors of the economy such as heavy industry and military development. The economy was weak and the country was isolated from the outside world partly because of some unusual and sometimes bizarre ideas, such as those driving the Cultural Revolution (1966–76) in the name of communism. At the level of each state-owned enterprise the state was in charge of allocating raw materials, managing the production system, and distributing the products. The enterprise was just a unit within the central planning system. Since all business projects and all activities, from the allocation of quotas to the production process and volume and the determination of the price of the products, had to be approved by the state, there was no room for entrepreneurial activities or individual initiatives (Boisot and Child, 1988; Newell, 1999: 286). There was 'no need for marketing, financial controls or human resource management – three of the most striking skill shortages in China today' (Southworth, 1999: 325). Managers of state-owned enterprises were merely civil service administrators and state bureaucrats who implemented state and party orders. It was the enterprise's party committee that selected employees for crucial positions in the different departments and offices, and made sure that its policies were adhered to by anyone in a position of authority (Walder, 1989; Child, 1994; Warner, 1995). As mere administrators, who saw management as no more than a systematic activity, Chinese managers avoided making their own decisions or challenging their leaders' ideas.

Even after the liberalization of the economy and the introduction of legislation making the managers more accountable for the operations of their enterprises and reducing Communist Party control of enterprises, the party remained central and dominant in managerial decision-making processes. The party has strong control of all sensitive decisions in enterprises. It is the party rather than trade unions that challenge the power of managers. While the managers are in charge of the day-to-day operation of their organizations, the party committee is responsible for making enterprise policies (Lu and Child, 1996). The Enterprise Law introduced in May 1988 required consultation between the director of the enterprise, the party committee, and the unions on all strategic decisions, but it did not define the term 'strategic decisions'. It also stated that the role of the party committee is to support the enterprise director, though it did not explain how. This is an example of making legislation as ambiguous as possible in order to give the party plenty of scope in interpretation of the texts. Therefore the ambiguity in defining the specific duties of the party was an attempt to preserve the party's position on strategic decision-making. This is why it was easy for party officials to regain their dominant roles in implementing the austerity programme after the Tiananmen Square demonstrations in June 1989. The influence and involvement of Communist party members in the management of enterprises is still apparent, despite the fact that enterprise managers have been made more accountable and autonomous. 'Although politics should, in principle, be separated from administration and production, political cadres continued to be involved because enterprise managers have been unable to make decisions without the consent of the party of which most of them are members' (HR manager of a state-owned company, personal communication).

Heavily regulated management

The practice of management in both mainland China and Hong Kong is highly regulated, despite the fact that the level of Hong Kong government intervention in employee relations seems to be minimal in comparison with that in Beijing. It is understood that legal reforms were needed for the regulation of the growing economy and the social changes that accompanied it. In the PRC, the first statutory document that tried to define the role of managers, trade unions and party committees was the Enterprise Law introduced in May 1988. It stated that the enterprise manager (director) is the sole legal representative of the enterprise, exercising full responsibility for all business activities. It also provided a breakthrough in the traditional relationship between the party, managers and unions by specifying that the director would replace the party secretary as the chief leader of the enterprise. Consequently, the stream of legislation increased over the 1990s and 2000s to cover every aspect of organizational life. For example, issues such as product labelling, food product contents, property rights and responsibilities, and many other issues requiring legal clarification were covered by the legal reforms of the 1990s. There were also laws that regulated mergers of state-owned enterprises and the restructuring and privatization of underperforming organizations, as well as many other laws covering organizational relationships, the setting up of new companies, the introduction of new products, and so on. Taxation reforms were introduced to cover all the different types of organizations and the varied needs of different sectors. For example, tax incentives have been offered to the growing number of joint ventures in the retailing, cosmetics and luxury goods markets in order to meet the increasing domestic demand for such products.

Culturally determined management

The practice of management in China is also deeply rooted in the society's traditional values, which include an egalitarian society, respect for age, family loyalty, mutual assistance, honesty, friendship, and obedience to law. The Chinese managers' tendency to conform to what their seniors and leaders tell them to do, the treatment of employees like members of one family (paternalism), and the avoidance of industrial conflict are all influenced by Confucianism. Most Chinese managers focus on previous successful experiences and the advice of their superiors in order to avoid failure and loss of face (Chen, 1995; Chew and Lim, 1995; Jaw et al., 2007). They represent a high power distance and high uncertainty avoidance culture (Hofstede and Bond, 1988), where central autocracy combined with local bureaucracy has always been the way to manage in China for centuries. Chinese cultural norms and values have their roots in the country's history and ideology, and have influenced, to a great extent, aspects of work behaviour, but this does not mean the absence of management policies and practices that are similar to those in the UK, Japan or the USA. For example, it was found that in many Chinese foreign trade corporations there had been recognition of individual commitment, despite the domination of a collectivist culture, as a means of enhancing an organization's effectiveness (Brown and Branine, 1995; Jaw et al., 2007; Tong and Mitra, 2009). It has become apparent that as more reforms are introduced, many organizations will have to adopt managerial practices and policies that are more appropriate to their business needs but not in conflict with their cultural values.

Western management

The open door policy was not just about foreign direct investment in China, it also concerned the transfer of technology, the adoption of management knowledge and skills, and the opening of new markets abroad for Chinese products and services (Wang, 1992; Li, 1999). Also, many Chinese managers are eager to learn Western management theories by attending management courses at home and abroad. Very often the managers of MNCs are 'hailed by the media as good models to be followed by domestic firms in China' (Cooke, 2004: 31). The spread of MNCs throughout China has brought with it the implementation of international standards in production and quality management, marketing and financial operations, and HRM practices (Warner, 2004). Fukuda (1989: 49) argues that the attitudes of the Chinese towards external agents has been changing due to economic reforms because foreign investment has come to be seen as a means of increasing the financial strength of the economy and the transfer of technology for further economic growth. He also argues that foreign involvement in resource extraction and foreign trade in China have become a necessity for the success of economic reforms and therefore have to be accepted and encouraged. He concludes that the Chinese have to import, learn and implement management theories from Western organizations.

MINI CASE STUDY 15

Do As You Are Told (China)

When one lives in China it can seem that everything is forbidden unless permitted by law. No couple is allowed to have more than one child and many female employees may not get maternity leave without getting the permission of their enterprise unit manager to get pregnant! Also, many employees are not allowed to move from one region to another or from one organization to another without having a permit. The employees of certain companies are not even allowed to speak to foreigners without the knowledge and approval of their managers. In some cases no private meetings with foreigners are allowed without the presence of the unit manager or the party representative. As one friend put it; 'when you are in China, do as you are told or you get into trouble with the big brother'.

Questions

1 Chinese officials argue that imposing rules is the best way to avoid social and political conflict and to make sure that more than one billion citizens live in a law-abiding and harmonious society. How far do you agree with this argument and why?
2 Discuss the implications of state intervention at all levels on the management of the economy.

Managing human resources

There has been a raft of literature on HRM in China but so far there is no agreement on its type and nature, and there is still a need for more research to clearly analyse and identify the exact format of an evolving Chinese HRM system (see Cooke, 2009). Many studies have reported that until the early 1990s the role of the personnel department in Chinese organizations was to allocate employees to operation units, allocate wages according to the national wages policy, implement disciplinary procedures and investigate cases of corruption and inefficiency (Warner, 1992; Ding et al., 2001; Law et al., 2003; Rowley et al., 2004; Cooke, 2005). Managing human resources was the same as managing any means of production, and all employment policies were state imposed and employee relations state controlled. The practice of HRM equates to neither personnel management nor human resource management, as known in the West, but a Chinese way of managing people. It is very often described as an HRM 'with Chinese characteristics' (Warner, 1992, 1995).

After more than two decades of economic reform, the work unit (*danwei*) or the enterprise and people's living standards have changed significantly, but HRM and employee relations have changed very little. Warner (2004: 619) reported an HR manager saying: 'we are still the policemen of the *danwei*'. That means that the role of HR managers is still confined to 'applying personnel rules and regulations to control employee behaviour' and that 'it is still very far from the initial concept of HRM as understood internationally. The prevalence of the *status quo* in China, however, cannot be ignored' (Warner, 2004: 619). However, the little that has changed is quite significant in relation to HRM functions such as recruitment and selection, training and rewarding of employees. For example, the introduction of a labour contract system, the decentralization of the staffing system, and the liberalization of the reward system, have been significant developments in managing human resources.

Recruitment and selection

In the PRC, the employment system, which guaranteed jobs for life and cradle-to-grave welfare protection, has been changing gradually over the last 20 years. Before the 1990s, the process of recruitment and selection was centralized and job seekers had no or very limited choice in the jobs they wanted to do. Work was assigned to people and was guaranteed for life, but labour mobility was strictly controlled. Jobs were centrally allocated within each region through local employment bureaus (Esterby-Smith et al., 1995; Warner, 1995). However, as the reforms have intensified there has been a change from lifetime employment to labour contract assignments, from a centralized to a decentralized recruitment system, and from non-existent to more formalized recruitment and selection methods.

From lifetime employment to labour contract assignments

The labour contract system was no doubt the most significant aspect of the labour reforms because it revoked the longstanding tradition of lifetime employment in China. It was first implemented in the Shenzheng Special Economic Zone in 1983 and then it was introduced gradually into other parts of the economy. There has been a large increase in the number of contract workers, especially in township industries, joint ventures and privately and/or foreign-owned enterprises. State-owned enterprises, however, have applied the contract system reluctantly and to varying degrees.

In theory, both the employee and the employer agree a contract that specifies the duration of employment, the tasks to be carried out and the standards to be achieved, the responsibilities of each party, the rewards to be received, and the terms and conditions of renewal or cancellation. Every labour contract has to include the provisions made by article 8 of the 1986 Labour Contract Regulations which are: performance targets; the period of employment; working conditions; pay; insurance and welfare benefits; discipline and penalties; and so on (Warner, 1995). The contract, which can be for a period of 2 or 3 years and for up to 20 years, has to be formally approved at the Contract Certification Office of the Local Municipal Labour Bureau which is normally in charge of labour allocation to enterprises in the area. In practice the labour contract system has not affected the continuation of lifetime employment because many contracts are renewed automatically, except in cases of serious infringement of labour discipline.

From centralized to decentralized recruitment

Until recently, all Chinese enterprises recruited their employees through local bureaus according to a centralized manpower planning system. All applications for employment went through a local bureau of recruitment that allocated people to jobs regardless of their preferences. People had no choice of jobs but they had job security. Enterprises were sent employees whom they had to train and retain for life under a quota system, which absorbed the labour market surplus regardless of business needs and demand. Enterprise managers were not involved directly in the recruitment and selection of their employees, and they were not even allowed to 'discuss an employee on the grounds of unsuitability for the job' (Ip, 1995: 271). The system made it very difficult to change jobs or to be transferred from one work unit to another. Jobs were assigned for life and in some cases the employees' children inherited them after retirement. The system was able to eliminate unemployment but created overstaffing because many factories were pressed by their local bureaus 'to recruit more employees than necessary' (Ip, 1995: 271). It was estimated that all large and medium size enterprises throughout China were 10–15 per cent overstaffed, putting more than 20 million people at work with nothing to do.

It was not until the introduction of the enterprise reforms of 1984 that enterprise managers were given the power to hire and fire their employees as needed. Under a system of local rather than central manpower planning, managers can now recruit their own staff according to their annual human resource plans. However the HR plan has to be approved by the ministry in charge of the sector in which the enterprise belongs. At the same time, job seekers are free to choose the jobs they prefer, but they have to get permission from the local bureau in charge of labour allocation in the region because there are still some jobs that have to be allocated centrally. For example, because of the shortage in secondary-school teachers, graduates with teaching qualifications are not allowed to get jobs other than in the schools to which they are allocated. The role of the local bureau has changed from that of the administration and allocation of employment to that of an agency, making recommendations and giving advice to job seekers and enterprises (Zhu, 1995). There also is an increasing number of labour service agencies to which job seekers and those who wish to change employment can refer for advice and support.

The decentralization of staffing has been met with great enthusiasm by many employers, especially the non-state-owned enterprises, and many young employees who were afraid of being allocated to jobs which they did not like, as was the case with the old system. Job seekers are now given the right to choose the jobs they like but they become more responsible for the fate of their own future employment. Such freedom of employment created a challenge for applicants to compete for better jobs with better career prospects, but nothing comes without a price. Job opportunities with better career prospects can now be found in joint ventures and foreign-owned multinational companies, but the work is often highly demanding and employment can be insecure. In most cases, the failure to perform up to expectations during the contractual period may lead to the loss of employment and make it hard to get a job in another enterprise.

From non-existent to more formalized recruitment and selection methods

Before the decentralization of the recruitment process, the recruitment bureau carried out all recruitment and selection according to a quota system that was supposed to meet the needs of all local enterprises, and there were no formal or rational methods of recruitment and selection in use. Since everyone was assigned to a job, the allocation process depended on the candidate's qualifications, conduct, loyalty to the communist party, and relationships. Most employees were recruited through word of mouth and recommendations from friends, party members and government officials. Although many job seekers had no choice of jobs allocated to them, a number of people could choose where to work because they were related to those in high places – in the party and government.

After the enterprise reforms of the 1980s, many companies started to have some kind of recruitment and selection procedure similar to that found in Western countries. As Rowley et al. (2004: 921) state, 'many firms now select and recruit their labour force with a freedom unthinkable in the almost half a century preceding the economic reforms, although some limited personal connections (*guanxi*) persist'. Moreover, although job interviews are widely used in most countries they are not the most favoured selection method in China (Zhu and Dowling, 2002). Similarly, the use of assessment centres and psychometric tests is very limited (Cunningham and Rowley, 2007).

While some employers, mainly state-owned enterprises, are still dependent on the recruitment bureau for initial recruitment and recommendations, many others request their potential applicants to submit an application form, attend an interview, and take tests. However, the use of these formalized methods of recruitment and selection depends on the type and level of jobs on offer. The more specialized and the higher the level the more sophisticated the methods, but in all cases the use of word of mouth and nepotism are still prevalent. Cooke (2004) comments that in an attempt to combat the effects of nepotism in recruitment and selection, the Chinese government recommended the introduction of examinations and tests in all public sector organizations.

The process of recruitment and selection in Hong Kong is comparable to that in the UK in terms of using traditional recruitment and selection methods such as advertising the vacancy, sifting through application forms, seeking references, conducting interviews and tests, and making offers, though these are all carried out in a more competitive and more regulated labour market than in the UK. Word of mouth and personal recommendation are also widely used.

MINI CASE STUDY 16

Got to be Tall, Fit and Good Looking (China)

The China National Packing Import and Export Corporation (CNPIEC) is one of the largest import and export corporations in China. With more than 20 subsidiaries at the provincial level and a wide branch network abroad, it has been transformed from a purely operational organization to an international

(Continued)

(Continued)

corporation with offices throughout the world in 68 countries. Its rapid expansion has required the use of more sophisticated and advanced methods of recruitment and selection. Each of its branches can now obtain its employees by using personnel exchange centres (new labour bureaus), recruiting directly from universities and colleges, advertising in local newspapers and magazines, using the company website, and accepting unsolicited (many of them) applicants.

A typical recruitment procedure would involve an initial meeting with potential applicants, a thorough investigation of the applicants' profile and achievements, interviewing and testing, and then making decisions. Normally a detailed investigation of each applicant is made. 'Information is gathered from their school days up to their recent graduation or their recent job in order to know their moral integrity, national loyalty, diligence and professional ability', said Mr Ling, the HR Manager.

Interestingly, the main requirements for a managerial post are university education and an age less than 35, and height for men should be more than 1.70 metres and for women 1.60 metres. Mr Ling explains: 'a manager is seen to reflect the company's image. This is why our employees should be tall, fit, good looking and pass the physical test.'

Questions

1 CNPIEC uses a combination of recruitment and selection methods: which ones are traditional (i.e. from before the reforms) and which ones are recent (i.e. after the reforms)?
2 Which of the CNPIEC recruitment and selection practices would be seen in the West as discriminatory? Why?

Training and development

The Chinese are learned and well-educated people because education is free and is traditionally held in high esteem. More than 90 per cent of the Chinese population are literate (Population Census 2000). As far as training is concerned, many Chinese were trained for the jobs they had to do under the centralized planned economy, but when the reforms were introduced there were serious shortages of trained employees to meet the needs of a free and fast-growing economy. A lot of efforts have been made to improve the education system and to train as many employees as possible, but shortages persist (Warner, 1985, 1986, 1997; Branine, 1996; Cooke, 2005).

Education and learning process

Education in China is divided into primary, junior secondary, senior secondary and higher levels. Children start school at the age of 6 and spend 9 compulsory years in primary and junior secondary education. Senior secondary education is for 3 years during which pupils decide to follow an art or science discipline in preparation for higher education. There are also opportunities to follow technical or vocational education after junior secondary school for those who wish to learn specialized skills. Admission into a higher education institution (college, institute or university) requires the passing of the National College Entrance Examination (just like the baccalaureate in France). The Ministry of Education is responsible for the provision of education and the awarding of qualifications.

To understand how the Chinese learn it is important to understand the process by which they learn the Chinese language. According to Pun (1992), the process of learning Chinese involves memorizing and repeating the meaning of single characters. Each word is made of a single character and each character has its own meaning, fixed form and sound. The Chinese characters are monosyllabic and are made of different strokes. At school, children are taught to memorize each character and its pronunciation. They develop the ability to visualize and grasp the written text and accept it as knowledge not to be questioned. Chan (1999) argues that what seems to be rote memorizing from a Western perspective is just the Chinese process of learning by repetition. 'In this case, repetition is used to assist students in the accurate recall of information. Unlike rote learning, repetitive learning enabled the learner to attach meaning to the material learned' (Chan, 1999: 300).

It has also been argued that the process of learning by rote and memorizing makes the Chinese learner very dependent on teachers. According to Newell (1999: 291), 'the teacher is the expert and the learner can simply learn by listening and following. Dialogue would be avoided in this situation because dialogue presupposes a process of joint knowledge production, which would undermine the belief in the expert teacher'. This way of learning makes the Chinese learner more passive and less analytical. They become dependent on their teachers, who provide them with information, and they seldom question or criticize what is being provided. Being obedient and respectful to the teacher or the 'master' is seen by the Chinese as being a good learner and is the main principle of the teacher–student relationship in Confucianism. Challenging the authority of the teacher is seen to be a sign of disrespect, deviance and unwillingness to excel in what is being learnt (Chan, 1999; Cunningham and Rowley, 2007).

This passive process of learning does not stop after the school or university levels but carries into the workplace as well. Employees learn instructions from their managers and the managers learn the rules and regulations by learning policy documents produced by their seniors. It is believed that the more Chinese 'characteristics' managers are able to inculcate into their minds, the better informed they become. By this process, managers of Chinese state-owned enterprises had to think the same way and to speak the same language, having no opportunities for self-expression or innovation.

Even after the reforms, there has been little change in the way Chinese managers and employees learn. Mao Zedong's *Red Book* has merely been supplemented, rather than outmoded, by Western management textbooks. A number of recent studies on how Chinese managers learn (Chan, 1999; Newell, 1999; Tang and Ward, 2003; Branine, 2005) observed that the managers who attended management development programmes in Western countries preferred a trainer-centred approach. They appeared to be conditioned to the teacher-led approach they experienced in their early stages of formal education. Many managers were found to be very much interested in acquiring information that was put together for them by their trainers. They liked structured lectures rather than tutorials and group discussions, and they preferred to take notes and to memorize them for examinations (Branine, 2005; Tong and Mitra, 2009).

ACTIVITY 2

An American professor once said: 'group work does not work with the Chinese student'. This statement has been echoed by many academics who taught Chinese students in the West or in China because most Chinese students prefer to be lectured to and not to participate in group discussions. Some commentators say that all Eastern people share this learning behaviour, while others argue that it is only the way the Chinese learn.

Questions

1 To what extent do you agree with the professor's statement? Why?
2 Compare the way the Chinese learn with that of one or two other countries of your choice.

Vocational training and education

In both the PRC and Hong Kong, learning is more academic and theoretical than vocational because of the importance given to formal theoretical education at all levels of learning. Vocational education is perceived to be for manual and less intelligent workers. It is seen as the last resort for those who fail to progress up the ladder of formal education (Kwan and Ng, 1999). It was not until recent years that the Chinese authorities realized that one of the ways to overcome the skills shortages is to provide vocational education and training at the national level to young people (school leavers) and at the organizational level to all employees who need to improve or to acquire new skills to enhance their career prospects (Rowley et al., 2004). They have invested heavily in vocational training over the last two decades, but the supply of skilled employees is still much lower than the demand.

Organizational training

By the mid-1980s all state-owned companies and public sector institutions were requested by the government to upgrade the knowledge and skills of their employees. Every employee had to undertake some kind of formal training in-house or away from the workplace. As a result, training became an end in itself because many employees were rewarded for their loyalty and good behaviour by sending them on training courses abroad or to training centres in luxurious holiday resorts away from the workplace. As Child (1991: 102) observes:

> Chinese employees tend to regard attendance at a training course as a perk rather than as an investment which should take account of the potential of the person in relation to the needs of the organization. This is especially the case when the training is abroad. Chinese candidates for training have therefore often been selected by their compatriot superiors on the basis of seniority rather than of capacity and promise.

Moreover, the successful completion of a training course was also, in most cases, followed by promotion to a higher post and/or a transfer to a different location, even though what had been learnt was never seen to be useful for the new job. Training in many Chinese organizations tends to be for a short period of time and given on the job (Hassard et al., 2004).

Management education, training and development

Economic reforms created a fast-growing economy that led to an unusual, uncertain and uncomfortable working environment for many Chinese managers, who found themselves in the unprecedented position of having to 'think business', to improve the quality of their products and services, to compete for better jobs and/or higher positions, and to face the possibility of losing their employment. This new managerial context is different from what they had been used to before the reforms, when there were very few incentives for improving individual performance because an employee's efficiency and achievement had little effect on his/her personal rewards, as every employee was guaranteed an income under the 'Iron Rice Bowl' policy (Warner, 1995, 1997; Ding et al., 2000). There was no pressure on management or workers to improve the quality of their products or services, and hence there was no need to improve their knowledge and skills (Borgonjon and Vanhonacker, 1994; Branine, 1996). The Chinese became eager to train as many employees as possible, and Western management became 'an acceptable means of introducing elements of a foreign managerial approach into the Chinese situation' (Child, 1991: 104). Therefore their approach to management training aimed to: i) provide management education on a wider scale; ii) train as many managers as possible at home and abroad; and iii) support Chinese managers in learning from joint ventures and foreign-owned companies.

Management education on a wider scale

Soon after the reforms were initiated, the whole of China witnessed an eruption of colleges and universities offering a wide range of management and business courses. By 2004, there were 1,396 universities offering courses in business and management, and over 300 specialized schools and institutions in management. The number of MBA programmes proliferated over the 1980s and 1990s to the extent that nearly every Chinese university had an MBA or a master's in management and related subjects such as marketing and finance. As well as all the colleges and universities that currently teach business and management, a number of courses are offered online through distance learning, the Chinese Open University, and radio and television programmes. Management education is also being transferred from the West by strengthening the relationships between Chinese and foreign institutions of higher education (Fan, 1998).

Training as many managers as possible at home and abroad

Many Chinese managers attended management courses and completed master's and doctoral degrees as well as short-term executive programmes at home and abroad. Many managers have been sent overseas to study business and management subjects such as marketing, entrepreneurship, human resource management, accounting, finance, business strategy, information technology and other specialist disciplines such as computing and engineering.

Supporting Chinese managers in learning from joint ventures and foreign-owned companies

The Chinese have also realized that management development does not take place in the classroom only. It is a continuous learning process that has also been facilitated by the interaction and operation of Chinese managers with their Western partners in joint ventures, the settlement of an increasing number of overseas Chinese in mainland China, and the international competitive pressures on Chinese managers for better-quality products and services. A study of 20 joint ventures by Yan and Child (2002: 119) found that local Chinese managers were 'enthusiastic to learn about partner-specific knowledge and resource inputs through the IJV (International Joint Ventures) partnership'. They concluded that

> the common mechanisms for achieving the Chinese partner's desired 'objectives of learning from the foreign partner' include the appointment of senior managers to IJV management positions, the creation of communication channels with their Chinese parent companies via reporting lines and an increase in the frequency of informal visits to strengthen the relationship between the venture and its parents. (Yan and Child, 2002: 121)

MINI CASE STUDY 17

Western Management for Chinese Managers

One of the major problems that Western educators face when introducing management programmes to Chinese managers is the applicability of Western management concepts to Chinese management practices (see Bu and Mitchell, 1992; Branine, 1996, 2005). Since most of Western management theories have originated from American and European management practices they cannot be easily transferred to China even when the Chinese are willing to adopt them. For example, the use of case studies based on management best practice from Western organizations may be inadequate because such cases tend to neglect the direct role of the state in managing organizations. Teaching material may become less useful or even irrelevant when translated from, say English to Chinese. It should always be borne in mind that the Chinese perception of management is still influenced by their culture and political system. Learning from an expert's experience and following the advice of previous leaders and managers is more important to the Chinese than attempting to develop one's own learning abilities through self-development, critical thinking and action learning, because there is greater risk of failure and more individual responsibility for the outcomes from the latter approach than the former.

Questions

1 What are the difficulties in, and obstacles to, transferring Western management knowledge to China?
2 What should Western management educators do to ensure that Chinese managers benefit from the management courses they provide?

Rewards and remuneration

Before the reforms were introduced, the rewards and remuneration system was uniform and centralized. The communist state provided for everything from the cradle to the grave. The work unit was responsible for the welfare of the employee and was allocated a state budget, which covered the education, housing, transport, subsistence, health care, child care, and elderly care for the employee and his/her dependants. The policy was based on the view that since everything was taken care of there was no need for a weekly or monthly cash reward. Average industrial wages were virtually stable for about 25 years. From 1953 to 1978 they increased by only 0.3 per cent in real terms (Henley and Nyaw, 1986; Jackson and Littler, 1991). Employees in state-owned enterprises were paid in goods, cash and tokens at subsistence levels; savings were not thought to be in the spirit of communism (Takahara, 1992). There was little difference between the monthly cash incomes of manual and non-manual workers or between leaders and subordinates. Age, seniority (length of service) and loyalty to the state system and party rather than effort or performance were the main factors considered when financial or non-financial rewards were allocated. There was no incentive to work hard and to increase organizational performance as everyone was paid more or less the same. The only significant income disparities were between the regions and the sectors of the economy. For example, the average wage in Shanghai was significantly higher than that in other regions because Shanghai was economically more developed and contributed more to the state's budget. Also, since priority was given to heavy industry and the military, employees in such companies or in the army were paid much more than those in other sectors. However, although the gap between the pay of leaders and subordinates seemed to be very narrow, the former benefited from handsome bonuses and status-related privileges.

With the introduction of economic reforms, the 'Iron Rice Bowl' welfare system was changed. Reform of the rewards system started with a series of national pay adjustments between 1979 and 1984 (Leung, 1988). Major reforms such as relating pay to performance criteria, making workers pay a social security contribution, and institutionalizing a minimum wage according to a price index system, were introduced from 1988. Later, the 1994 Labour Law provided for worker contributions to several insurance funds, including pension, medical, accident and disability, maternity and unemployment. Among its significant resolutions, the 1994 Labour Law allowed all enterprises, regardless of type of ownership, to set their wages at or above a guaranteed minimum wage set up by the local authorities according to the local living standards. It also specified a maximum of 44 hours per working week and one hour of overtime per day. Payment for overtime work was set at 150 per cent on normal days, at least 200 per cent on holidays, and at least 300 per cent on public holidays. The law covers health and safety at work, training and development, social insurance and welfare benefits, as well as the protection of female workers and those workers between the age of 16 and 18.

The reforms led to the introduction of a bonus system, a floating payment system and a structural payment system (Jackson and Littler, 1991; Goodall and Warner, 1997). These include the traditional basic or standard pay, functional pay that is related to status and seniority, and floating pay that involves any payment for increased performance (Zhu, 1995). However, as Cooke (2004: 25) points out, 'the basic wage is still based largely on the seniority-based egalitarian wage structure which does not reflect competence, and egalitarianism in the bonus distribution remains a key characteristic in order to maintain stability and harmonization'.

Minimum wage

A national statutory minimum wage was introduced in 2004 to cover all full-time and part-time employees. At the same time the Regulations on Enterprises

Minimum Wage provided for the provinces, autonomous regions and the municipalities to set their own minimum wage below or above the national one according to their labour needs and the standard of living in each province, region or municipality. For example, there were five categories of minimum wage in Guangdong province in September 2008, ranging from the highest at 5.92 yuan (about US$0.88) per hour in Guangzhou to the lowest at 3.79 yuan (about US$0.56) an hour in the rural areas. There has been no statutory minimum wage in Hong Kong where wages have been determined by the level of labour supply and demand, but, as a result of recent renewed demands by trade unions for the introduction of a minimum wage, the Legislative Council of Hong Kong (LegCo) passed, in July 2010, a minimum wage bill which has been approved. To date, there is no agreed minimum wage, but it is expected to be between HK$ 24 (US$ 3) per hour, supported by employers' associations, and HK$ 33 (US$ 4) per hour, demanded by trade unions (*The Economist* ,July 15th 2010).

Performance appraisal and performance-related pay

By the mid-1990s, a number of state-owned enterprises were under pressure to balance their accounts or close down. Therefore, they began to set targets for their units and sub-units so that employees would be clearer about their objectives and their achievements. Performance appraisal criteria were introduced in many companies for the first time, but most of them were very subjective. For example, a study by Easterby-Smith et al. (1995) found that the main performance appraisal criteria were:

- Good moral practice (*de*), which is also linked to political loyalty and harmonious relations with others;
- Adequate competence (*neng*);
- Working hard (*qin*);
- Excellent performance records (*ji*).

Chinese managers have used these performance criteria not to reward their employees but to decide on their suitability to stay or leave after the end of their employment contract. In fact in many state-owned enterprises the system of performance-related pay was never implemented. It is believed that performance-related pay would lead to income differentials and inequalities that could drive the country away from its egalitarian principles. It has also been observed that inadequate implementation of performance related pay has led many talented and highly skilled employees to start looking for jobs in other companies, mainly joint ventures and foreign-owned companies. Therefore, in order to retain talented and skilled employees who are otherwise attracted to work in MNCs, domestic private and state-owned companies have had to introduce individual wages to meet the demands of individual employees

(Cooke, 2004: 28–9). 'Indeed, bonus and performance-related pay schemes are still post-related and a traditional ideology of egalitarian rewards still persists' (Cunningham and Rowley, 2007: 372).

In Hong Kong, the rewards and remuneration system is similar to that of the UK, where pay awards are normally set through collective agreements. However, unlike in mainland China, performance-related pay is widely implemented. The standards of living in Hong Kong are quite high, requiring higher and more competitive wages. In the PRC, economic reforms have brought an end to the equality principle, which emphasized collective rewards and was fundamental in building a socialist state and a classless society. This has been challenged in recent years because of widening income disparities between employees. The gap between the rich and the poor in Chinese society began to appear over the 1990s and is widening rapidly.

ACTIVITY 3

As an HR manager of a Chinese–British joint venture in Beijing, you have been asked to review the current reward policy, which is similar to that in the UK, and to suggest a new policy that is more appropriate to Chinese employees. What reward policy would you suggest and how would you implement it?

Employee relations

At present there are two channels through which Chinese workers are expected to be involved in the management of their enterprises and by which employment relationships are regulated. These are the trade unions and the workers' congresses. Trade unions exist at the national, provincial and enterprise levels, while workers' congresses only exist at the enterprise or unit level.

Trade union composition and membership

All employees regardless of their level or position in an enterprise can join the same union. This is stated in article 1 of the All China Federation of Trade Unions (ACFTU) Constitution (1988), which states that 'membership in trade unions is open to all manual and non-manual workers in enterprises, undertakings and offices, whose wages constitute their principal means of livelihood'. Employees have a constitutional right to form trade unions at the industry and sector levels, but all trade unions come under the umbrella of the state-controlled ACFTU. Trade union membership is voluntary, but since having a membership card means being entitled to many welfare benefits nearly all employees in state-owned enterprises are union members. Temporary employees are not eligible to join trade unions, whereas contract employees are expected to join trade unions and to have the same rights and benefits as permanent workers. Membership increased from 2.4 million in 1949 to more than 100 million in 1988 (*Beijing Review*, 13–26 Feb. 1989: 27–31). By 2009, there were more than 226 million members of about 1.8 million trade unions affiliated to ACFTU, according to Xinhua news at: (http://news.xinhuanet.com/english2010/china/2010-09/26/c_13529940 htm, accessed 26 September 2010).

In Hong Kong, the system of employee relations paralleled that of the UK in terms of having the right to form and join trade unions, and to engage in collective bargaining. In 2001 there were more than 600 trade unions representing employees in different sectors, but generally they have been weak for many reasons. According to Snape and Chan (1999), the main reasons for trade union weakness are the small size of manufacturing and private sector organizations, the attitude of Chinese workers towards joining the unions and challenging the authority of management, and employers' opposition to trade unions (cited in Chan and Lui, 2004). In practice the role of trade unions in Hong Kong has become similar to their role in the PRC, although theoretically they are different. According to Chan and Lui (2004: 84), a number of surveys have shown that 'instead of work-related issues, unions engage mostly in activities outside the workplace, such as organizing recreational and social activities, and providing educational and health services to members'. This is exactly what trade unions in the PRC do, as we will see next.

The role of trade unions

The All China Federation of Trade Unions (ACFTU) was established in 1925. Like most other communist parties, the CCP made full use of the labour movement in gathering support to establish the PRC's government in 1949. The ACFTU mobilized the working class to rally for the creation of a communist state. After the nationalization of all enterprises in 1956 the role of the unions had to change from being adversarial to basically becoming a transmission belt between the state and the workers (Han and Morishima, 1992). During the Cultural Revolution from 1966 to 1976 the unions were suspended. They re-emerged only after the launch of the economic reforms. Until the middle of the 1980s it was notably the state, through its party committees, that was in charge of all employee relations decisions, from employment to training and development, and to promotions and remuneration. There was no industrial action and no real collective bargaining. Littler and Lockett (1983: 38) describe the trade unions in China as 'having the task of promoting production and productivity, with some concern for the welfare of employees by providing housing, education, sports and cultural facilities'. Warner (1995: 32) lists the main functions of Chinese trade unions as follows:

1 Protection of the whole country's interest but at the same time safeguarding the legitimate rights and interests of the workers;
2 Helping their members participate in the management of their own work units;
3 Mobilizing the workforce to raise productivity and the economy's performance; and
4 Educating the workers to be better members of society.

In theory, these functions are carried out at the enterprise, local or provincial, and national levels. In practice, however, the main role of Chinese trade unions is to take care of employees' social welfare and benefits such as supervising the distribution of houses, keeping watch over safety standards, organizing recreational activities and taking care of various other benefits (Warner, 1995; Branine, 1997; Ng and Warner, 1998). This welfare role, which includes the provision of education, housing, transport, sport and health care facilities, has given the unions considerable support from and influence over their members. At the national level the unions transmit the party policies to employees, encourage production in a variety of ways, engage in political and ideological education, and carry out numerous welfare and cultural responsibilities (Helburn and Shearer, 1984; Lee, 1986; Warner, 1992, 1995). At the organizational level Chinese trade unions do not bargain with management over better terms and conditions of employment. Instead they sometimes discipline workers who do not respect the rules or who fail to perform as expected. Their role was and still is centred on 'labour productivity, worker morale and welfare' (Henley and Nyaw, 1986: 648).

It seems that whilst all the policy reform initiatives are in the direction of decentralizing authority and responsibility to enterprise management, there is no evidence that the power of trade unions has increased in any way, and there are no significant proposals for a revised trade union role. The Trade Unions Law introduced in 1992 was expected to revise the Trade Unions Law 1950 in accordance with the new spirit of reform, but it contained no resolutions for the revision of existing practices. Current changes in employee relations, such as the imposition of the contract system, and introduction of redundancies and performance-related pay, will make the role of trade unions more adversarial and cause them to take industrial action when necessary. Many foreign-owned firms, joint ventures and privately-owned small businesses take advantage of current employee relations to exploit their employees by paying them low wages and making them work in poor conditions.

The workers' congress

In 1950, one year after the founding of the People's Republic of China, a law was passed requiring all industrial enterprises that employed more than 200 workers to set up their own workers' congresses. A workers' congress at the level of each work unit or enterprise was regarded as an important means for keeping a check on the performance of state-owned enterprises (Lansbury, Ng and McKern, 1984). The congress or council (as it is sometimes called) consists of representatives from the management, the workers and the unions. Within a typical enterprise, a workers' congress elects its own executive council according to the size of the enterprise. For each 100 employees there are 8 to 10 representatives. The members of the congress are selected to represent the workers in special committees such as the health and safety committee and the discipline committee of the enterprise. The congress meets twice a year while the committees meet regularly as needed. According to the Provisional Regulations of June 1981, establishing the functions of workers' congresses, a workers' congress is expected to:

1   Discuss production targets, workers' concerns and changes in the structure of the enterprise or the methods of work;
2   Examine the management's reports, the plans and budgets of each department, the health and safety procedures, and the implementation of enterprise regulations; and
3   Propose new work arrangements, training programmes, bonuses and welfare benefits, and the list of employees eligible for an award.

In practice, however, it seems that the role of workers in the congress/council is merely symbolic, because they are often dominated by management representatives (Lansbury, Ng and McKern, 1984; Warner, 1992; 1995). The enterprise's general manager has the power to veto decisions made by the congress. Also, the existence of two employee representative bodies, the workers' congress and trade union, at the level of each enterprise proved to be practically problematic. It is not only that a 'workers' congress is functionally not too distinct from the union' but also that 'the workers elected to the workers' congress are usually drawn from the union faithful' (Warner, 1992: 210). The Labour Law 1994, which is considered to be the most comprehensive piece of employment legislation to date (Markel, 1994; Zhu, 1995), does not cover the role of the workers' congresses vis-à-vis that of trade unions and it only clarifies the position of the unions in cases of industrial disputes. It states that a union has the right to express an opinion if it sees that the termination of a worker's employment is inappropriate. Collective bargaining is not a key feature of the Chinese industrial relations system, and both the unions and the workers' congresses have no more than a welfare role in the Chinese employee relations system.

Industrial action

There is no right to strike in any organization on mainland China, while in Hong Kong employees in both public and private sector organizations are allowed to call a strike if it is agreed by the majority of the members in a secret ballot. However, unofficial strikes have occurred now and then on the mainland, while official strikes have been very rare in Hong Kong. The reason is not just cultural (i.e. the Chinese avoid conflict), it is political on mainland China and economic in Hong Kong. In the former, any industrial action is seen by the Beijing government as a kind of social unrest and therefore not allowed, especially in the state-owned enterprises. In the latter, the economy is mostly dominated by small employers who very often do not recognize trade unions and threaten to make all employees redundant in cases of industrial action.

Settlement of industrial disputes

In a system of industrial relations where there are no real negotiations and no collective agreements there is no room for collective or individual disputes. In theory, industrial disputes are dealt with at the enterprise level through 'a degree of arbitration and conciliation' (Rowley et al., 2004: 922), but in practice this does not happen often. Individual employees' grievances are raised with the workers' congress and then they are taken to the local labour arbitration committee. In practice, since many workers expect very little from their workers' congresses, they refer directly to party officials because it is with the latter that the power lies, and then the party official refers the individual's case to the labour arbitration committee only when necessary. According to Tang and Ward (2003: 104), although the majority of employees do not complain, an increasing number of young workers are 'more ready to make use of the Labour Arbitration Committees. Principally this stems from their being more likely to be employed under a fixed-term labour contract.' Similarly, industrial disputes rarely occur in Hong Kong, and when they do they are usually classified as minor employment claims by individual employees and referred to the Minor Employment Adjustment Board. Only a small number of cases are referred to the industrial tribunal as exceptional cases of failure to comply with the Employment Ordinance or a breach of terms of contract of employment.

Summary

1   As the economic reforms have progressed, more laws concerning employment relationships have been introduced.
2   The Chinese approach to management is party-orientated, heavily regulated, culturally determined, and partially adopted from the West.
3   The management of human resources in China is deeply rooted in the country's history, and characterized by tacit socialist norms of solidarity, equality, mutual assistance, and obedience to the law.
4   The Chinese approach to learning and management development is generally passive rather than active.
5   The ideology behind the Chinese rewards policy was to keep the rates of pay as low as possible and to use normative or symbolic rewards as performance incentives. Reforms have led to the introduction of bonuses, floating payments, and structural payments.
6   The main role of Chinese trade unions has been to take care of employees' social welfare and benefits.

Revision questions

Chapter 1 provides a review task designed to consolidate your learning from this chapter. Please see Box 1.2.

In addition, the following questions are designed to help you revise this chapter:

1 Provide, in a table, a comparative analysis of HRM functions of recruitment and selection, training and development, rewards and remuneration, and employee relations before and after the reforms in China.
2 Discuss how the return of Hong Kong to the People's Republic of China has affected the Chinese labour market and the development of a distinctive Chinese approach to management.

References

Boisot, M. and Child, J. (1988) 'From fiefs to clans and network capitalism: explaining China's emerging economic order', *Administrative Science Quarterly*, 41(3): 600–28.

Bond, M.H. (1992) *Beyond the Chinese Face – Insights from Psychology*, Oxford: Oxford University Press.

Borgonjon, J. and Vanhonacker, W.R. (1994) 'Management training and education in the People's Republic of China', *The International Journal of Human Resource Management*, 5(2): 327–56.

Branine, M. (1996) 'Observations on training and management development in the People' Republic of China', *Personnel Review*, 25(1): 25–39.

Branine, M. (1997) 'Change and continuity in Chinese employment relationships', *New Zealand Journal of Industrial Relations*, 22(1): 77–94.

Branine, M. (2005) 'Cross-cultural training of managers: an evaluation of a management development programme for Chinese managers', *Journal of Management Development*, 24(5): 459–72.

Brown, D.H. and Branine, M. (1995) Managing people in China's foreign trade corporations: some evidence of change, *The International Journal of Human Resource Management*, 6(1): 159–73.

Bu, N. and Mitchell, V.F. (1992) 'Developing the PRC's managers: how can Western experts be more helpful?', *Journal of Management Development*, 11(2): 42–53.

Chan, A. and Lui, S. (2004) 'HRM in Hong Kong', in Budhwar, P.S. (ed.), *Managing Human Resources in Asia-Pacific*, London: Routledge, 75–92.

Chan, S. (1999) 'Chinese learner – a question of style' *Education and Training*, 41(6/7): 294–304.

Chen, M. (1995) *Asian Management Systems*, London: Routledge.

Chew, K.H. and Lim, C. (1995) 'A Confucian perspective on conflict resolution', *The International journal of Human Resources Management*, 6(1): 143–57.

Child, J. (1991) 'A foreign perspective on the management of people in China', *The International Journal of Human Resource Management*, 2(1): 93–107.

Child, J. (1994) *Management in China in the Age of Reform*, Cambridge: Cambridge University Press.

Cooke, F.L. (2004) 'HRM in China', in Budhwar, P.S. (ed.), *Managing Human Resources in Asia-Pacific*, London: Routledge, 17–34.

Cooke, F.L. (2005) *HRM, Work and Employment in China*, London: Routledge.

Cooke, F.L. (2009) 'A decade of transformation of HRM in China: a review of literature and suggestions for future studies', *Asia Pacific Journal of Human Resources*, 47(1): 6–40.

Cunningham, L.X. and Rowley, C. (2007) 'Human resource management in Chinese small and medium enterprises: a review and research agenda', *Personnel Review*, 36(3): 415–39.

Ding, D.Z., Ge, G. and Warner, M. (2001) 'A new form of Chinese human resource management? Personnel and labour–management relations in Chinese township and village enterprises: a case study approach', *Industrial Relations Journal*, 32(4): 328–43.

Ding, D.Z., Goodall, K. and Warner, M. (2000) 'The end of the "Iron-Bowl": whither Chinese human resource management?', *International Journal of Human Resource Management*, 11(2): 217–36.

Easterby-Smith, M., Malina, D. and Lu Yuan (1995) 'How culture sensitive is HRM? A comparative analysis of practice in Chinese and UK companies', *The International Journal of Human Resource Management*, 6(1): 31–59.

Economist (2005) 'Human resources: China's people problem', 16 April, pp. 59–60.

Fan, Y. (1998) 'The transfer of western management to China', *Management Learning*, 29(2): 201–21.

Fukuda, J.K. (1989) 'China's Management tradition and reform', *Management Decision*, 27(3): 45–9.

Goodall, K. and Warner, M. (1997) 'Human Resources in Sino-foreign Joint Ventures: Selected Case Studies in Shanghai Compared with Beijing', *International Journal of Human Resource Management*. 8(5): 569–93.

Han, J. and Morishima, M. (1992) 'Labour system reform in China and its unexpected consequences', *Economic and Industrial Democracy*, 13(1): 233–61.

Hassard, J., Morris, J. and Sheehan, J. (2004) 'The "third way": the future of work and organization in a "corporatized" Chinese economy', *The International Journal of Human Resource Management*, 15(2): 314–40.

Helburn, I.B. and Shearer, J.C. (1984) 'Human resources and industrial relations in China: a time of ferment', *Industrial and Labour Relations Review*, 38 (1): 3–15.

Henley, J.S. and Nyaw, M.K. (1986) 'Introducing market forces into managerial decision-making in Chinese enterprises', *Journal of Management Studies*, 23(6): 635–56.

Hofstede, G. and Bond, M.H. (1988) 'The Confucian connection: from cultural roots to economic growth', *Organizational Dynamics*, 16(4): 5–21.

Ip, O.K.M. (1995) 'Changing employment systems in China: some evidence from the Shenzhen Special Economic Zone', *Work, Employment and Society*, 9(2): 269–85.

Jackson, S. and Littler, C. (1991) 'Wage trends and policies in China: dynamics and contradictions', *Industrial Relations Journal*, 22(1): 12.

Jaw, B.-S., Ling, Y.-H., Wang, C.Y.-P. and Chang, W.-C. (2007) 'The impact of culture on Chinese employees' work values', *Personnel Review*, 36(5): 763–80.

Kirkbride, P.A. and Tang, S.F.Y. (1992) 'Management development in the Nanyang Chinese societies of Southeast Asia', *Journal of Management Development*, 11(2): 56–66.

Kwan, P.Y.K. and Ng, P.W.K. (1999) 'Quality indicators in higher education – comparing Hong Kong and China's students', *Managerial Auditing Journal*, 14(1&2): 20–7.

Lansbury, R.D., Ng, S.K. and McKern, B. (1984) 'Management at enterprise level in China', *Industrial Relations Journal*, 15(1): 56–64.

Law, K., Tse, D.K. and Zhou, N. (2003) 'Does human resource management matter in a transitional economy? China as an example', *Journal of International Business Studies*, 34(3): 255–65.

Lee, L.T. (1986) *Trade Unions in China: 1949 to the Present*, Singapore: Singapore University Press.

Leung, W.Y. (1988) *Smashing the Iron Rice Pot: Workers and Unions in China's Market Socialism*, Hong Kong: Asia Labour Monitor Centre.

Li, S.T.K. (1999) 'Management development in international companies in China', *Education + Training*, 41(6/7): 331–5.

Littler, C.R. and Lockett, M. (1983) 'The significance of trade unions in China', *Industrial Relations Journal*, 14(4): 31–42.

Liu, S. and Vince, R. (1999) 'The cultural context of learning in international joint ventures', *The Journal of Management Development*, 8(8): 666–75.

Lu, Y. and Child, J. (1996) 'Decentralization of Decision – Making in China's State Enterprises' in Brown, D.H. and Porter, R. (eds), *Management Issues for China in the 1990s: Domestic Enterprises*, London: Routledge.

Markel, D.C. (1994) 'Finally, a national labour law', *The China Business Review*, Nov.–Dec.: 46–9.

Newell, S. (1999) 'The transfer of management to China: building learning communities rather than translating Western textbooks?', *Education and Training*, 41(6/7): 286–93.

Ng, S.H. and Warner, M. (1998) *China's Trade Unions and Management*, Basingstoke: Macmillan; New York: St. Martin's Press.

OECD (Organization for Economic Cooperation and Development) (2002) *China in the World Economy: The Domestic Policy Challenges–Synthesis Report*, available on line at: http://www.oecd.org/dataoecd/45/57/2075272.pdf, accessed 10 April 2009.

Pun, A. (1992) 'Action learning: encountering Chinese culture' in Jones, M. and Mann, P. (eds) *HRD: International Perspectives on Development and Learning*, New York, NY: Kumarian Press.

Rowley, C., Benson, J. and Warner, M. (2004) 'Towards an Asian model of human resource management? A comparative analysis of China, Japan and South Korea', *International Journal of Human Resource Management*, 15(4): 917–33.

Snape, E. and Chan, A. (1999) 'Hong Kong trade unions: In search of a role', in P. Fosh, A.W. Chan, W.W.S. Chow, E. Snape and R. Westwood (eds.) *Hong Kong management and labour: Change and continuity*, London: Routledge, pp.255–70.

Southworth, D.B. (1999) 'Building a business school in China: the case of the China Europe International Business School (CEIBS)', *Education + Training*, 41(6/7): 325–31.

Takahara, A. (1992) *The Politics of Wage Policy in Post-Revolutionary China*, Basingstoke: Macmillan and New York: St. Martin's Press.

Tang, J. and Ward, A. (2003) *The Changing Face of Chinese Management*, Working in Asia Series, London: Routledge.

Tong, J. and Mitra, A. (2009) 'Chinese cultural influences on knowledge management practice', *Journal of Knowledge Management*, 13(2): 49–62.

Walder, A. (1989) 'Factory and manager in an era of reforms', *Chinese Quarterly*, 118 (June): 241–64.

Wang, G.G. and Fang, W. (2001) 'Cultural adaptation and cooperation: an important aspect that MNCs face in China' *XinhuaWenjai*, 12(1): 19–24.

Wang, Z.M. (1992) 'Managerial psychological strategies for Sino-foreign joint ventures', *Journal of Managerial Psychology*, 7(3): 10–17.

Warner, M. (1985) 'Training China's managers', *Journal of General Management*, 11(2): 12–26.

Warner, M. (1986) 'The long march of Chinese management education', *China Quarterly*, 106: 326–42.

Warner, M. (1992) *How Chinese Managers Learn*, London: Macmillan.

Warner, M. (1995) *The Management of Human Resources in Chinese Industry*, Basingstoke: Macmillan and New York: St. Martin's Press.

Warner, M. (1996) 'Human resources in the People's Republic of China: The 'three systems reforms', *Human Resource Management Journal*, 6(2): 32–43.

Warner, M. (1997) 'China's managerial training revolution', in Warner, M. (ed.), *Management Reforms in China*, London: Frances Pinter Publishers.

Warner, M. (2004) 'Human resource management in China revisited: introduction', *The International Journal of Human Resource Management*, 15(4): 617–34.

Yan, Y. and Child, J. (2002) 'An analysis of strategic determinants, learning and decision-making in Sino–British joint ventures', *British Journal of Management*, 13(1): 109–22.

Zhu, C.J. and Dowling, P.J. (2002) 'Staffing Practices in Transition: Some Empirical Evidence in China', *The International Journal of Human Resource Management*, 13(4): 569–97.

Zhu, Y. (1995) 'Major changes under way in China's industrial relations', *International Labour Review*, 134(1): 37–49.

9

Indonesia and Malaysia

LEARNING OUTCOMES

The chapter is designed to help you understand, for Indonesia and Malaysia:

1 The (a) economic, (b) political and (c) cultural contexts in which managers work;

2 The main trends in the labour market;

3 The typical features of (a) management policies and practices and (b) organizational structure and behaviour;

4 The main policies and practices of human resource management with regard to: (a) recruitment and selection; (b) training and development; (c) rewards and remuneration; and (d) employee relations.

Introduction

Indonesia and Malaysia are the two major Muslim countries in South-east Asia. They have much in common in terms of history, culture, and post-independence political and economic challenges. Although they are different in terms of geographic size, availability of resources and level of industrialization, they share a management approach strongly influenced by Islamic values. More than a third of their populations is of Chinese, Indian and Western European origins, and so the traditions of Confucianism, Buddhism and Christianity have also influenced management practices and social relations. As former colonies of major Western empires (Britain for Malaysia and Holland for Indonesia), they have acquired Western education, technology and industrial infrastructure that have eased the development of advanced manufacturing systems and adoption of aspects of Western management and organizational behaviour. This has resulted in the development of a distinctive mixture of Asian and Western management systems influenced by Islam.

Table 9.1 Basic statistical indicators, Indonesia and Malaysia

Country	Area (sq km)	Population (July 2010 est.)	Population Growth (2009) %	GDP – real growth rate (2009) %	Inflation rate (2009 est.) %	Work-force (2009 est.) Million	Unemployment rate (2009) %
Indonesia	1904569	240271522	1.13	4.5	4.8	113.3	7.7
Malaysia	329847	25715819	1.72	−1.7	0.6	11.38	3.7

Source: Compiled from the CIA *World Factbook,* 2010 and OECD Statistics, 2009.

Contexts: economics, politics and culture

Economics

The Indonesian economy and political system have evolved in three main eras: the Old Order (1945–65), the New Order (1966–97) and the Reform Order (1998–present). At the start of the 'Old Order' in 1945, when Indonesia became independent from the Dutch and the Japanese, the Indonesian economy had been described as a 'basket case' (Hill, 2000). During the era of the 'New Order' (1966–97), Indonesia's economy was transformed through the development of heavy industries centred on steel, aluminium and cement. As a result of economic growth, the economy came to be described by the World Bank (1993) as one of the Newly Industrialized Economies (NIEs). It was characterized by a controlled rate of inflation, a rapid transition from a centrally controlled to a market-based economy, and a successful exchange rate policy, especially during the oil boom period from 1973 to 1982. The economy became less dependent on oil revenues (Nasution, 2001). According to Hill (2000), the most obvious outcomes of the New Order era were strong economic growth, rapid structural and technological reform, and an improved welfare system. The manufacturing sector experienced extraordinary growth and became the dominant sector within Indonesia's economy. It created new job opportunities and helped to reduce poverty (Fujita and James, 1997). The New Order government welcomed foreign investment, which created new jobs and advanced the level of economic growth.

The Reform Order started as a result of the 1997 financial crisis. The economic miracle of Indonesia became an economic meltdown by the mid-1997. Indonesia was the most affected country in the region. The crisis led to a fall in GDP; political instability; long-lasting social and labour market problems such as high unemployment; high inflation; weak infrastructure; a weak financial and banking sector; rampant corruption; and a low level of foreign direct investment. However, Indonesia managed to recover quite quickly. All outstanding IMF debt was paid off ahead of schedule and heavy investment has been made in improving the education and skill levels of the population. This has been possible because Indonesia is rich in mineral and natural resources, and has fertile land for agriculture. Its main exports are oil and gas, electrical appliances, rubber, textiles, rice and plywood. It is a prominent member of the Organization of the Petroleum Exporting Countries (OPEC) and is one of the world's popular tourist destinations.

The Malaysian economy has also gone through three economic policy periods, namely: The Post-independence (PI) era (1957–70), the New Economic Policy (NEP) era (1971–90), and the National Development Plan (NDP) era (1991–present). During the PI era, Malaysia was mainly a producer and exporter of primary commodities such as rubber and tin. The NEP (1971–90) era started with the development of light manufacturing of goods in the 1970s and then moved on to the development of heavy industry and hydrocarbons supported by foreign direct investment. By the beginning of the 1980s, the economy exhibited rapid growth and structural transformation. Moreover, the New Economic Policy (NEP) aimed to eradicate poverty across the different ethnic groups and to reduce inequality in the distribution of wealth among the different groups, thereby sustaining the unity and prosperity of the country. To achieve this national unity objective through economic means the emphasis was placed on export-led manufacturing and the attraction of foreign direct investment. In the 1980s, the 'Look East Policy' (LEP) 'was inspired by the perceived success of Japan and South Korea in their heavy industrialization' (Smith, 2003: 119). A component of the Look East Policy was the introduction in 1983 of the 'Malaysia incorporated policy' which called 'for the public and the private sectors to work closely, support, facilitate and supplement each other for socio-economic development', making the whole country operate like 'a business corporation' (Siddiquee, 2006: 344).

The post-NEP period or the National Development Plan (1991–present) saw the continuation of previous plans and policies, but with strong emphasis on promoting a knowledge-based economy using state-sponsored advanced information communication technology projects (Smith, 2003). The NDP focused on the development of human resources in order to achieve what it termed its 2020 vision. 'Vision 2020' was introduced in 1992 by Prime Minister Mahathir Mohamad: the aim was for Malaysia to attain the status of a 'highly developed nation' – not just economically but also politically and socially. The vision projected a Malaysian society 'imbued with spiritual values and the highest ethical standards, and economically just, society with inter-ethnic economic parity' (Gomez and Jomo, 1999: 169). By 1993, the country was rated by the World Bank as among the eight High Performing Asian Economies (HPAEs) (World Bank Report, 1993).

Like the rest of the region, Malaysia suffered very badly from the 1997 financial crisis, which consequently led the government to take drastic measures to counter the economic and financial effects of the crisis. The economy recovered well, as low inflation, low imports and increasing foreign investment coincided with opportunities to export oil and gas at high prices.

As exporters of hydrocarbons, both Indonesia and Malaysia have benefited from the recent rises in oil and gas prices, but they have also been affected by the world economic downturn created by the 'credit crunch' because both economies are heavily dependent on changes in the world markets and international trade.

Politics

Both countries have experienced a one-party authoritarian political system but they have been institutionally different. Indonesia's current political system is a presidential and parliamentary democracy where the publicly elected president is the head of state and head of government. Theoretically, the two institutions responsible for national policies are the house of representatives or parliament (*Dewan Perwakilan Rakyat*, DPR) and the house of regional representatives (*Dewan Perwakilan Daerah*, DPD) which provides support to the DPR on regional legislative issues. The members of both houses are elected by public vote to serve for a five-year term. The members of both houses make up the People's Consultative Assembly (*Majelis Permusawaratan Rakyat*, MPR), which is the highest authority of the state. In practice, politics in Indonesia is a one-person show: the president is the sole policy-maker, with substantial powers despite recent political changes and the existence of political parties and two houses of representatives.

The current head of state and head of government is the supreme leader and decision-maker. There was very little political freedom or democracy in Indonesia for nearly sixty years (1945–2004). The post-independence politics of the 'Old Order' was dominated by the nationalist leader and founder of the state Republic of Indonesia, Ahmed Sukarno, for 20 years (1945–65). The second era of the 'New Order' was also dominated by the authoritarian regime of Suharto for 33 years (1965–98). The first democratically contested parliamentary elections since the 1950s were held in 1999, resulting in an elected president, Abdurrahman Wahid, who was eventually impeached in July 2001 following a number of serious allegations. He was succeeded by his vice-president, Megawati Sukarnowati, Sukarno's eldest daughter, who was defeated in the September 2004 elections in favour of a retired army general, Susilo Bambang Yudhoyono. There has been little political opposition in the houses of representatives. The party that has dominated the legislative system has been the Golkar party, the party of the former president, Suharto. Thus despite the recent multi-party elections the party that ruled the country for decades remains in power. The Law on Regional Autonomy (Act no. 22 of 1999) provided for the decentralization of power and decision-making to the regions and districts, but little progress has been made in this respect.

Malaysia is a constitutional monarchy with a bicameral parliament consisting of an elected house of representatives (*Dewan Rakyat*) and a non-elected senate (*Dewan Negara*). The members of the house of representatives are elected by popular vote to serve for a five-year term whereas the members of the senate or upper house of representatives are partly appointed by the paramount ruler (the king) and partly appointed by the government. Political power is held by the cabinet, which is appointed by the prime minister from among the members of the house of representatives with consent of the king. Although there are political parties and democratic elections, one ruling coalition of parties has been in power for the last three decades, and that is the National Front or BN (*Barisan Nasional*). The dominant party among the coalition is the United Malays National Organization (UMNO) which has ruled the country since independence. The head of state is the paramount ruler (king) who has a symbolic role in politics and is normally elected for a five-year term by and among the nine hereditary state rulers (sultans). The head of government or prime minister is the leader of the elected party with the majority in the house of representatives. Administratively, Malaysia is made of 13 states and three federal territories (Kuala Lumpur, Labuan and Putrajya). Nine states have hereditary rulers (sultans) and four states (Melaka, Penang, Sabah and Sarawak) have governors appointed by government.

ACTIVITY 1

In the light of the above discussion of the economic and political contexts of both countries, produce a report comparing the stages of economic and political development the two countries have gone through since their independence.

Culture

Both Indonesia and Malaysia are multi-ethnic societies. Both countries have a collectivist culture (Hofstede, 2001) where the integration of the family, social relations, cooperativeness, mutual help, and group pressure are very dominant (Taib and Ismail, 1982; Noordin et al., 2002). Indonesia is more ethnically diverse (with about 350 recognized ethno-linguistic groups) than Malaysia. However, in terms of religion Indonesia is more homogenous with a prominent religious group (more than 88 per cent of the population are Muslim) than Malaysia, which has at least four distinctive religious groups (60.4 per cent Muslim, 19.2 per cent Buddhist, 9.1 per cent Christian and 6.3 per cent Hindu). Indonesia is the most populous Muslim country in the world. It comprises a cluster of thousands of culturally diverse islands with diverse norms, values and social structures. This is why Indonesians always say *'Bhineka Tunggal Ika'*, which means 'unity in diversity'. In Malaysia three different ethnic groups (61.4 per cent Malay and indigenous, 23.7 per cent Chinese and about 14.9 per cent Indians and others) co-exist. For a good description and analysis of the co-existence of the three cultures in Malaysia, see Smith (2003).

In both countries the values that influence people's social interactions, work behaviour and management practices are derived from the Muslim faith and aspects of Confucianism. All in all, Islam emphasizes respect for status, authority, knowledge, age and women, and gives importance to family, cooperation, brotherhood/sisterhood, harmony, kinship, compassion, peace and forgiveness in society. These values are common in Islam and Confucianism and they are taught to children from primary school (Taib and Ismail, 1982; Wolfe and Arnold, 1994). Children are taught, for example, that dedication and commitment to doing good work is a virtue, and, therefore, in striving to achieve that virtue, one has to be forever mindful of the observance of almighty God and to be cooperative, sincere, passionate, efficient, just, truthful, patient, pious, moderate, promise-keeping, accountable, grateful, disciplined and forgiving (Alhabshi and Ghazali, 1994; Darwish, 2000; Mellahi and Wood, 2004).

Another aspect of the cultural values of both countries is the importance of saving face and avoiding loss of face. Indonesians and Malays strongly try to avoid conflict to save face and they use various words to avoid upsetting others. Writing from his experience of working in Indonesia, Mann (1994: 116) says that 'Indonesians, especially Javanese, do not like people to strike aggressive postures or to speak loudly'. Also, 'standing with arms folded or legs apart or crooking the finger should ... be avoided'. Moreover, according to Munandar (2003: 93), Indonesians avoid saying 'no' directly and they always find indirect ways. For example, when invited to attend a meeting which they do not want to go to, they reply by saying *'Inshaa Allah'* ('if God permits or God willing') or 'I will try to come', etc., instead of saying 'sorry, I can't come'.

MINI CASE STUDY 18

No Compulsion in Religion: South-east Asia

In both Indonesia and Malaysia, no one is systematically obliged to follow the religion of the other. The mutual respect that exists between the members of the different religious and ethnic groups is exemplary of successful multi-cultural societies. When living in Malaysia, it is easy to distinguish between the three different groups, by the way they dress, the food they eat, the drinks they consume, and the way they worship. For example, the Malays dress modestly and traditionally, and most of their women cover their heads with a headscarf; they eat rice with lamb or chicken curries. Eating pork and drinking alcohol is strictly forbidden. They perform their daily prayers regularly and fast during the lunar month of Ramadan. Malaysian Chinese wear Western-style and traditional Chinese clothes, eat a lot of pork and like to drink alcohol, especially in social and business events. Most Malaysian Indians wear Western-style clothes, but some men, especially the Sikhs, dress according to their religious code of dress, and most of their women cover themselves in a sari or Punjabi dress. They do not eat beef, they are likely to be vegetarian, and they may not drink alcohol. What is culturally common to these three ethnic groups, according to Smith (2003: 121), 'is the love of socializing informally with friends, neighbours or relatives and chatting while sharing food and drink'.

Questions

As a manager of a multinational company in Malaysia, you want to invite your Malaysian work colleges to your home for a party.

Consider the following scenarios and remember that the loss of face may cause embarrassment that may result in devastating business outcomes. Which one would you choose and why?

1 Invite each religious group separately and provide the appropriate food and drink;
2 Invite them all and provide any food and drink you like; or
3 Invite them all and do not serve any pork, beef or alcohol.

Labour market trends

The labour markets of Indonesia and Malaysia historically have been characterized by the availability of cheap and compliant labour, and by strong state regulation. In Indonesia, the New Order era created a high level of growth in industrial investment and a high demand for skilled and professional labour. However, poverty, low education levels and a high percentage of child labour are still characteristic of Indonesia's labour market. In comparison, the Malaysian labour market is more stable and more regulated. Both countries have young working populations (see Table 9.2).

Table 9.2 Age structure (%) (2009), Indonesia and Malaysia

Country	0–14 years %	15–64 years %	Over 65 years %	Median age (years)	Life expectancy at birth (men & women)
Indonesia	28.1	66	6	27.9	70.76
Malaysia	31.4	63.6	5	26.5	73.29

Source: CIA *World Factbook*, 2010.

In both countries, the labour market has been dominated by large state-controlled companies, especially in the manufacturing of light goods and the petroleum sector, as well as a growing number of small and medium size privately owned companies and an increasing number of foreign-owned multinational companies. In terms of sectors, Malaysia's labour market is concentrated in the industrial sector (36 per cent) and the services sector (51 per cent). Whereas Indonesia is still quite heavily dependent on agriculture, which employed more than 50 per cent of the workforce in the 1990s before declining to 42.1 per cent in 2006, the number of those employed in industry increased from 11.8 per cent to 18.6 per cent over the same period. The number of those employed in the services sector declined from 41.7 per cent in 2000 to 39.3 per cent in 2006 (see Table 9.3).

Table 9.3 Distribution of labour force by sector (%), Indonesia and Malaysia (2006)

	Indonesia	Malaysia
Agriculture	42.1	13 %
Industry	18.6	36 %
Services	39.3	51 %

Source: CIA *World Factbook*, 2010.

Unemployment rate

The rate of unemployment in Indonesia has fluctuated between about 8 and 14 per cent over the last two decades, which is typical of many developing countries. In a populous country like Indonesia, with a workforce of more than 100 million people, an unemployment rate of 10 per cent (on average) means more than 10 million people are out of work at any one time. There are also millions of people in under-employment, doing seasonal and part-time work, and others in 'disguised' unemployment, those still at work and claiming unemployment benefits. In Malaysia unemployment has been much less of a problem. It stands currently at its highest, with less than four per cent.

Employee turnover

In Malaysia where there has been high economic growth, a shortage of skilled labour and low unemployment it is natural to find that employees do not stay with one employer for life. The high level of employee turnover constitutes a real problem for many employers, who struggle to retain a core of well-trained workforce. However, some employers prefer a situation of high employee turnover: it allows them to adjust their staffing levels (Elger and Smith, 2001; Mellahi and Wood, 2004). In other words, the high employee turnover provides a natural functional flexibility and reduces the level of employer spending on training and development, as many new employees are already trained somewhere else. The problem of labour turnover is less significant in Indonesia, where the rate of unemployment is typically higher and many people struggle to find employment.

Demand for skilled and professional labour

The long-term trends in industrialization and economic growth are creating a high demand for skilled labour that cannot be met by the current supply. Colleges, universities and vocational training centres are not producing enough trained employees. The governments of both countries have had to train more people and to introduce initiatives to attract a more skilled workforce. For example, the Malaysian government introduced a number of measures in 2001 aimed at Malaysians living abroad and encouraging them to return to work in Malaysia. Those with special skills and high-level qualifications are given priority in employment. Moreover, the Malaysian government has encouraged businesses to move whenever possible from the use of labour-intensive to capital-intensive production systems in order to reduce the shortage of skilled labour and the dependence on foreign labour. Much impressed by Japanese automation, the Malaysian government has often called for the introduction of robots and new modes of cost-effective and efficient production of high-quality products, as well as for the delivery of excellent services.

Employment of women and ethnic groups

The employment laws of both countries forbid all kinds of exploitation or discrimination in employment. In Malaysia, the law protects ethnic groups and provides for affirmative action in the recruitment and training of native Malays (bumiputra). According to the Indonesian census of 2000, women made up 38.5 per cent of the total working age population, but female participation in employment was only 51.7 per cent while that of men was 84.2 per cent. Considering the large population size, the social structure and culture of the country, and the level of economic growth, however, the rate of female participation in the labour market is greater than that in similar countries around the world. The position of women in the Malaysian labour market is better because of the higher level of government investment in education, training and development of women. For example, many women, especially Malays, benefit from state scholarships to study for higher degrees (master's and doctorate) in top universities in the US, UK and Australia. Both Indonesia and Malaysia, as Muslim countries, have shown that there is nothing in Islam that prevents a woman from contributing fully to the development of her country.

Employment of immigrant workers

The shortage of skilled and professional labour in the home labour markets necessitated the employment of an increasing number of foreign workers. This applies more in Malaysia than Indonesia, where there is a large population and a surplus of manual labour. Indonesia does not suffer too much from the shortage of skilled and professional labour and there has always been a high level of migration from one island to another.

To control the flow of immigrant labour, the Malaysian government produced a list of jobs where labour had to be imported in order to 'ensure that only appropriate foreign workers with required skills were employed and would not hinder the employment of Malaysian workers' (Mellahi and Wood, 2004: 214). By October 1996 there were about half a million legally registered foreign workers in Malaysia, but the unofficial figure including illegal immigrants exceeds one million workers. The 1997 financial crisis led to the deportation of many immigrants back to their home countries, but by 2002, as the economies of both countries started to grow faster, more immigrant workers were needed again. However, the governments of both countries have tightened their borders in order to stop illegal immigrants and admit only the skilled and professional workforce from neighbouring countries.

MINI CASE STUDY 19

A Trapped Workforce (Malaysia)

Some Malaysian employers prefer foreign workers to local ones because foreign workers are found to have better skills and are cheaper to employ than the locals. This leads to hiring as many immigrants as possible regardless of their status of whether they are legal. As a result, there have been cases of such workers being hired by reckless agents to work for non-existent companies or companies other than those mentioned in their travel documents. This type of worker cannot complain of poor working conditions or unpaid wages because they are illegal and unable to seek help from the labour courts, as they have no proper documentation. Such workers may risk being arrested, imprisoned or deported for breaking the immigration laws. The Malaysian Trade Unions Congress (MTUC) argues that the present labour laws do not protect foreign workers and they urge the government to let foreign workers join the unions. Some trade union leaders claim that following the economic downturn in 1997, a number of employers brought down Malaysia's image internationally by the 'shameful behaviour' of exploiting vulnerable immigrants.

Questions

In considering the current socio-economic conditions and the composition of the current labour market in Malaysia, discuss:

1 The extent to which the employers' actions are justified;
2 The extent to which foreign workers are exploited and the reasons for that;
3 What should be done to attract and retain a reasonable number of foreign workers?

Management and organization

The Asian-Islamic approach to management that is practised in Indonesia and Malaysia can only be understood if it is seen in the context of a mixture of Islamic, Confucian and Anglo-Saxon principles of management (Mansor and Ali, 1998). Being a former British colony, Malaysia inherited much of its industrial relations and management system from the UK, but soon after independence a US management education (although still Anglo-Saxon) became more attractive to the Malaysian government and managers. By the 1980s, with the rise of Japanese management, Malaysia adopted the 'Look East' policy, using Japan as a model for economic growth and development (Wolfe and Arnold, 1994). A similar strategy has been also adopted in Indonesia. This led to a process of forward diffusion of management practice from Western countries (mainly the US and the UK) and Japan, as foreign direct investment through MNCs increased and a large number of Indonesian and Malaysian managers were educated in Western universities. While preserving their cultural values and work ethic, they adopted from both West and the East those features that harmonized with their cultural values and met their economic needs. The fusion of Eastern cultural values with Western management thinking has led to the development of a distinctive management system that can be described as heavily regulated, highly paternalistic, closely integrated, quality driven and increasingly adaptive.

Regulated management

In both countries there are few aspects of management that are not regulated. There are laws and regulations governing a great many activities in the workplace and most aspects of relations between employee and employer. This arose because the state was the largest employer, but in recent years, although many state-owned companies have been privatized, government has been still in control of all aspects of employment and employee relations. In Malaysia, the ministry of labour, which was renamed the Ministry of Human Resources (MoHR) in 1990, is responsible for formulating HR policies, helping in the process of human resource planning, and overseeing the training and development of the workforce in different sectors. The MoHR plays a significant role in shaping the policies and practices of management in all sectors of the Malaysian economy (Mellahi and Wood, 2004: 215). The MoHR is also responsible for administering employee relations and overseeing the smooth running of the Malaysian HRM system through various departments, especially the Industrial Relations Department (IRD), the Trade Unions Affairs Department (TUAD) and the Labour Department (LD). It works closely with employers' associations and trade union organizations to ensure the maintenance of an integrated and harmonious system of employee relations that is directly controlled by the state. Similarly, in Indonesia the government intervenes through the use of various laws and regulations that give rights to its institutions, including the military and the secret services, to curb the power of trade unions and to maintain a state-imposed employee relations system.

Paternalistic management

Paternalistic management is prevalent in both Indonesia and Malaysia because of cultural values that emphasize a need for strong harmony, the preservation of face, and the acceptance of status differences. In both countries, relationships take priority over tasks, managers have strong obligations towards their relatives, and employee–employer relations are moral rather than calculated, showing mutual obligations and loyalty (Habir and Larasati, 1999). For example, in recruitment and selection, the managers feel obliged to offer the job to family members and relatives or members of the same ethnic background, and see their roles in the companies they work as extensions of family responsibilities. Managers of state-owned companies are regarded as caretakers who are expected to look after their companies and their employees. This idea of 'caretaking' is derived from the Islamic concept of *khalifa* which means that a person is expected to take care of the resources that are in their trust. God has made mankind *khalifa* on the earth to look after the bounties of his creation (this will be explained in more detail in Chapter 15).

Integrated management

Indonesian and Malaysian managers take a comprehensive and integrated approach to management. For example, in Malaysia every manager is expected to deal with HR issues, and therefore there is no preference for having HR specialists (Othman et al., 2001). All line managers are trained to deal with HRM issues. The HRM function is seen as part of the overall organizational strategy. Therefore HR managers are expected 'to be sensitive to issues beyond their immediate functional responsibilities. This is indicative of a desire to attain consistency between HRM and strategy as well as internal conditions' (Othman et al., 2001: 72). However, the practice of management in Indonesia is less integrated because of the immaturity of local corporate management strategy in comparison with that of Malaysia. For example, in many Indonesian companies the role of HR or personnel managers is still administrative rather than strategic.

Quality-based management

Following in the footsteps of Japan and South Korea, Malaysia and Indonesia have emphasized the need for quality and productivity improvement. In Malaysia a culture of quality improvement has become a way of life at all levels, from very small, privately owned firms to large, state-owned public sector companies. Almost all companies have adopted the practice of quality control circles, introduced strategic planning and implemented quality assurance initiatives (Siddiquee, 2006: 348). According to Othman et al., the ability to introduce quality projects and quality improvement initiatives is one of the ten most important capabilities of managers in Malaysia (2001: 71).

Adopted management

Both countries have adopted aspects of management theory and practice that were developed somewhere else either by copying examples of good practice from Japan and the West or by learning from the presence of an increasing number of multinational companies. In Indonesia, the 'open-door' policy of the New Order government in the 1980s and 1990s attracted foreign investment from all over the world, with a lot of interest from American, Australian, Japanese, Dutch, German and South Korean companies. Malaysia experienced a similar influx of multinational companies after the introduction of the New Economic Policy initiatives of the 1970s and 1980s. Export-oriented economic policies depended on foreign investment and eventually attracted many foreign companies who brought with them technology, expertise and management know-how. The era brought in a variety of international management policies and examples of good practice that local managers have had to adopt in order to improve the performance of their organizations. Thousands of Indonesian and Malaysian students are sent annually to study abroad in order to gain more skill in management and other disciplines, and when they return they adapt what they learnt to their own cultures in their domestic organizations.

Managing human resources

In both countries the concept of human resource management (HRM) is very often associated with human resource development (HRD). The training and development of employees are seen as the main function of an HR department. When the author asked a group of Indonesian managers taking part in an executive training programme to describe the role of a human resource manager, most of them said that it was to make sure that the organization is well staffed with well-trained employees. In Malaysia, the main concern of managers is to improve the quality of products and services and to have well-educated, highly trained and motivated employees. This view of development-focused HRM is very often echoed by senior managers, government officials and politicians through speeches in the national media and at conferences. In Malaysia, the success of Vision 2020 is said to depend on the training and development of the Malaysian workforce. Although both countries share the view that HRM is HRD and they are similar in their recruitment and selection practices, they differ, to some extent, in their rewards and employee relations systems.

Recruitment and selection

As in other Asian countries, the process of recruitment and selection in Indonesia and Malaysia is influenced by the composition of the labour market, the dominant cultural values, the level of state intervention (legislation) and the local and international economic conditions. For example, a labour market of multi-ethnic job seekers has forced the Malaysian government to take affirmative action on the recruitment of Malays because they were under-represented in employment in a number of sectors. Also, the dominant cultural values of harmony and strong family ties have meant that very often friends and family members are given priority in employment and that many employees are recruited through word-of-mouth recommendations. Furthermore, in both countries, as the economy develops and moves from agriculture to industry, from light to heavy industrialization, or from a manufacturing to a knowledge-based economy, and from the use of labour-intensive to capital-intensive methods of production, the demand for labour changes from manual to skilled employees, requiring the use of a variety of more sophisticated methods of recruitment and selection.

Affirmative action

In Malaysia there is affirmative action for the employment of Malays (bumiputra) because, according to the Industrial Coordination Act of 1974, the ethnic distribution of society should be reflected in organizations. The Malaysian government argues that the Malays who make 60 per cent of the population may become under-represented in the labour market if no affirmative action is taken. Affirmative action started in the education system when Malays were given priority in public education and were encouraged to enrol in institutions of higher education to study for science, management and engineering degrees. As a result, many Malay graduates are recruited to fill managerial and professional positions in government offices and public sector organizations. Initially many foreign observers and some non-Malay citizens criticized the affirmative action programme for promoting favouritism and discrimination, but the Malaysian government argued that the main objective of the programme was social cohesion and equality in the distribution of national wealth. The policy is enforced at all levels by the Ministry of Human Resources (MoHR), which intervenes in the process of human resource planning by cooperating with employers on the recruitment and selection of job seekers. In Indonesia, there is also a kind of covert (implicit) affirmative action that gives priority to endogenous groups in public education and in employment in public sector and government organizations.

Word of mouth

Word of mouth is the most common recruitment method for blue-collar workers in both Indonesia and Malaysia. Most employees in Malaysian manufacturing enterprises are recruited through the recommendations of other employees, friends and relatives (Smith, 2003: 124). In a culture of trust, managers feel comfortable with the recruitment of someone who is recommended by those they trust, especially when the person making the recommendation is a hard-working employee, a member of the family or someone in a high position.

Kinship recruitment

Although most companies, especially the large ones, use Western methods of recruitment and selection such as advertising vacancies in newspapers, in magazines and on the internet, using application forms, requesting references and conducting tests and interviews, the process is very much influenced by the traditions, norms and values that exist in each region, state or community. Very often when a vacancy occurs, the persons to be considered first by the manager are members of his/her family. It is normal to find a father and sons or a number of brothers and cousins working for the same company. Kinship recruitment can also be found among the members of ethnic groups. Smith (2003: 123) confirms that in Malaysia it is very likely for 'Malay personnel managers to find jobs for their relatives and the members of their rural village communities of origin'.

Need-based recruitment

With increasing shortages of skilled and highly qualified employees, managers have had to look for suitable employees beyond members of their families, friends and people who share their ethnic background. In these changing conditions, some companies have resorted to the use of recruitment agencies to supply them with the workers they need (Prijadi and Rachmawati, 2002). While the use of word of mouth and kinship recruitment practices is still prevalent in small and medium size enterprises, most large companies are using recruitment and selection methods similar to those used by their multinational company counterparts in order to attract and retain the skilled employees they need.

Training and development

As explained earlier, in both countries there has been a shortage of skilled and professional labour and there has been an urgent need for the education of a skilled and highly qualified workforce as well as the training of those already employed in order to improve and upgrade their skills. In Malaysia the MoHR intervenes in order to make sure that the workforce is trained to the standards required to meet the demands of economic growth. The Labour Department of the MoHR has a pool of trained staff with managerial and organizational skills, and provides in-house training programmes, that are expected to help employers improve the knowledge and skills of their employees.

Education

In Indonesia primary education is compulsory for six years followed by optional three years of junior high school and three years of senior high school.

The Ministry of National Education is responsible for non-religious public schools while the Ministry of Religious Affairs is responsible for religious and private schools. In Malaysia, the national education policy has been geared towards the foundation and sustainability of national unity and rapid economic growth. The Ministry of Education aims to provide educational opportunities to all citizens irrespective of race, religion, locality or state. The Malaysian government's affirmative action programme in education led to an increase in *bumiputra* students at public universities (from 12 per cent in 1969 to around 70 per cent by the mid-1990s (Lucas and Verry, 1996, 1999)). Since the 1990s the government has passed a number of educational laws aimed at reforming the educational system in line with the country's socio-economic objectives to achieve the 2020 Vision. The reforms, which included the corporatization of higher education institutions by making them operate like businesses, were all aimed at improving the quality and standards of higher education. The MoHR envisaged that the education system had to be market-driven and that higher education programmes had to be more relevant to the needs of industry.

Training

In both countries, the concept of training is very much equated with education. Many employers do not give much attention to the training of their employees and many employees stop becoming active learners after graduation from college or university. The responsibility for company-level and vocational training is usually assumed by government rather than employers. The only way to learn new skills for many employees is from their seniors through job rotation and on-the-job learning rather than through formal and management-driven on-the-job training. Vocational training is provided as a substitute for formal education to those who are unable to complete their learning to university level. In Indonesia, for example, the level of vocational training is described as being poor in quality rather than limited in quantity (Prijadi and Rachmawati, 2002). In this respect, the Malaysian government has been more successful than its Indonesian counterpart in making vocational training more accessible, better organized, more relevant to business and industry, and more respected by employers.

Although both countries have been influenced by the Japanese industrial success, it was only the Malaysians who formally attempted to adopt the Japanese approach to training and development as part of their 'Look East Policy'. The Malaysian government called repeatedly upon all employers to follow the Japanese model of HRM, especially in adopting on-the-job training and Japanese trade union approach. The Human Resource Development Act 1992 required all private sector employers with more than 50 workers to contribute one per cent of their monthly payroll to a training fund which would be used to support 'employers to undertake and accelerate systematic training programs to equip the workforce with high skills, knowledge and positive industrial attitudes' (Mellahi and Wood, 2004: 215). However, since these contributions were made to central government, some individual organizations benefited more than others. Many employers relied on the government to help them provide the training rather than doing it themselves. Consequently, the training provided by the government through its MoHR's Training and Development Department has not always been relevant to the needs of all organizations.

MINI CASE STUDY 20

Developing Tourism in Sabah State, Malaysia

Sabah State aims to become a major tourist destination in Malaysia, but the quality of the local workforce needs to be improved to serve the needs of the sector within the context of the tourist strategy and the business plan of the main operators. This will necessitate training a pool of tour guides, tour operators, hoteliers and taxi-drivers, in a courteous manner of handling tourists, as well as increasing their knowledge of the local history, arts and culture. The local people need to be trained in how to operate tourist-oriented businesses such as handicrafts, marinas, resorts and service-related facilities. Unemployment in the state is quite high, affecting around 8 per cent of the total working population. The officials of Sabah State are faced with two options represented by two different points of view: on the one hand, there are those who suggest that the best way to attract tourism and to provide world-class services is to invite MNCs that have experience and expertise in tourism to invest in the state and therefore provide employment and on-the-job and company training to the local workforce. On the other hand, there are those who argue that MNCs would destroy the cultural heritage of the state because they do not understand the local culture and history and their main objective is to make money. They suggest that local authorities should help local businesses to invest in tourism and train local people so as best to project the real image of the state.

Questions

1 If you support the first option, how would you convince those opposed to accept it? What arguments would you use?
2 If you support the second option, how would you convince the Sabah State officials to accept it? What arguments would you use?

Rewards and remuneration

Both countries have a state-controlled income policy that determines the level of wage increases, compensations and benefits in the public sector and state-owned companies. In Malaysia, a royal commission which was appointed in 1971 determines the salaries of employees in all government institutions. The royal commission recommended in 1995 that all employees in the public sector be paid the same salary for doing the same type of work, thereby implementing the concept of equal pay for equal work of equal value. Although rewards in the private sector are supposed to be collectively agreed between the management and the unions, it is the employer, in line with the government's income policy, who very often determines the wages of its employees. However, it should be noted that most employers reward their employees on the basis of seniority and performance. Performance appraisal is widely used for judgemental and developmental purposes.

Minimum wage

In Indonesia, a statutory regional minimum wage was introduced during the era of the New Order when the country experienced a high level of economic growth and a low level of unemployment; but it was not properly implemented, and many employees in manual jobs accepted wages that were less than the minimum wage (Prijadi and Rachmawati, 2002). Employers, especially in small and medium size organizations, violated the minimum wage because of the high demand for employment and employees' ignorance of their rights. Therefore in 1989 new legislation set the minimum wage according to the cost of living and conditions of the labour market in each region, but this meant that the minimum wage had to be increased regularly. Currently, each region or province has its own minimum wage because they have different labour market conditions and different standards of living. But in a country where unemployment among young, uneducated and unskilled people is high, many companies have no problem in finding job seekers who would be pleased to work for much less than the minimum wage.

There is no national statutory minimum wage in Malaysia despite many attempts by the Malaysian Trade Unions Congress (MTUC) to convince the government to introduce it. The government has insisted that a minimum wage would deter foreign investment and reduce the competitiveness of domestic businesses. The MTUC has argued that the introduction of a statutory minimum wage will prove how much the Malaysian economy has developed and that it is time to leave income policy to market forces. The government's position has been strengthened by the private sector employers' argument that a minimum wage would put many small companies out of business, which would result in declining investment in crucial sectors such as manufacturing and services, and in turn would result in increasing the level of unemployment. In response to international labour organizations' criticisms and internal pressure from trade unions and opposition parties, there have been talks about the possible introduction of a minimum wage in specific sectors to protect those on low wages.

Performance appraisal and performance-related pay

With the introduction of the National Development Plan (NDP), the Malaysian government tried to make the public sector the same as the private sector and called for all rewards to be made performance related. Performance-related pay (PRP) was seen to be important in order to create a more efficient, committed, loyal and reliable public sector workforce. The Malaysian Trade Unions Congress (MTUC) supported the New Remuneration Scheme (NRS) introduced in 1992 and the new performance appraisal system introduced in 1993 because PRP was regarded as a way of acknowledging the quality of work in the public sector (Milliman et al, 2002). Circular no. 4 of NRS 1992 describes in detail the new performance appraisal system. At the level of each work unit appraisal work targets (AWTs) have to be set at the beginning of the appraisal year and then reviewed mid-year to evaluate progress and to check for any performance problems. In circumstances where work targets were unrealistic, the AWTs could be rectified. At the end of the appraisal cycle, the appraisee is required to record actual work achievement against the AWTs. If the work targets are not met, the appraisee is required to explain why. Following each annual review, the employee can stay at the same pay point, move horizontally to a higher job scale and receive a pay rise and a promotion, move diagonally to a higher job scale (promotion) but not necessarily with a pay rise, or move vertically within a job scale and receive a pay rise. Regardless of the frequency of moves in the matrix, the pay rise is restricted to 5 per cent per annum. However, as a result of employees' complaints (See Mini Case Study 22) the government finally decided in 2002 to introduce a new scheme called the Malaysian Remuneration System (SSM) as an alternative to the NRS. Employees can opt to be appraised through either of them.

MINI CASE STUDY 21

Appraisal and Favouritism: Malaysia

When the Malaysian government introduced the New Remuneration System (NRS) in 1992 it argued that the NRS was comprehensive and closely linked to corporate governance and strategic planning. However, many public sector employees reported a number of weaknesses and drawbacks in the implementation of the system. They complained of favouritism by heads of department in rating employees' performance, thereby discriminating against employees who really deserved pay rises and promotion. More than 90 per cent of employees were not satisfied with the new performance appraisal system and claimed that the assessors had been incompetent and lacked knowledge of performance appraisal. They asked the government to consider not relating performance appraisal to salary increases and to just use it to determine the strengths and weaknesses of the employee's performance. The government, arguing that the system was working satisfactorily, rejected their proposal and suggested the extension of the system to '360-degree assessment' where, as well as the superior assessing subordinates, subordinates can also evaluate their superiors and each other.

Questions

1 Why did the Malaysian government introduce performance-related pay?
2 Why were employees dissatisfied with the implementation of performance appraisal?
3 Argue for and against the use of performance-related pay in countries like Malaysia.

Employee relations

In the mid-1970s, during the era of the New Order, the Indonesian system of industrial relations known as Pancasila Industrial Relations (HIP) was established. The five basic principles of the Pancasila, as listed by Kelly (2002: 7), are:

1 Belief in the one and only God, i.e. not working only for oneself but as a devotion to God;
2 A just and civilized humanity, including valuing the dignity of workers as human beings and not just as factors of production;
3 The unity of Indonesia, where employers and workers should strive for a common goal;
4 Democracy guided by the inner wisdom of deliberations of representatives, as differences should be resolved through consensus rather than through strikes and lockouts; and
5 Social justice for all the people of Indonesia, with an emphasis on balancing the rights and duties of both parties in an enterprise, and an equal sharing of the results achieved between workers and employers on the basis of partnership.

Kelly (2002: 7) comments that the above principles were used by the authoritarian regime of President Suharto to control the development of trade unionism and to undermine democratic freedoms under the disguise of national unity, national security and economic growth. It was not until the post-1997 financial crisis (during the Reform Order) when the new political leadership was in crisis, that the employees were allowed to organize themselves into independent trade unions, as it will be explained later.

Malaysia inherited the British industrial relations system, with legislation giving employees the right to form and join trade unions and to bargain collectively, but soon after independence in 1957 the government intervened heavily by regulating all aspects of employee relations with the aim of containing industrial conflict and maintaining a high level of managerial prerogatives in the name of, as in Indonesia, national unity, national security and national economic development and prosperity. However, unlike Indonesia, where political reforms led to some freedom in trade unionism, there has been very little change in the Malaysian system of employee relations, which is described by Peetz and Todd (2001: 334) as a system that 'serves as an adjunct to economic policy – to attract investment and provide modestly priced and disciplined labour'.

Trade unions

In Indonesia trade unionism started in the early 1920s with increasing labour unrest over working conditions and pay, but the Dutch colonial authorities banned the organization of unions in 1926. This colonial action resulted in clandestine union organizations. After independence in 1949, the nationalist government tried to keep the unions under state control, but the union confederation (Labour Central Organization for All Indonesia or SOBSI) continued to represent the workers' interests and gather membership that reached 20 per cent of the working population in the early 1960s (Manning, 1993). In 1966 the 'New Order' began. The government dissolved the SOBSI because it was accused of being affiliated to the outlawed Indonesian Communist Party. In 1973 a new, and the only legal, labour organization, FBSI (Labour Federation for All Indonesia), was established and no other union was allowed. In November 1985 the FBSI was renamed the SPSI (All Indonesian Workers' Union). As a centralized trade union federation, the SPSI was under the direct influence of the military and the secret services with one aim, which was to protect the regime rather than the workers. Moreover, to make the public sector workers easier to control, they were all made members of the ruling party, Golkar, and of the corps of government employees, KORPRI. The latter was not a trade union but another state-made social association aimed at preventing the workers from organizing into free and independent trade unions (Gall, 1998). The SPSI was between a rock and a hard place because of its awkward position between growing unorganized and sporadic workers' unrest and a dominating and ruthless government. It had no control over its members or its finances because of direct intervention by the state in all aspects of employee–employer relations, including even the collection of trade union membership fees. It was also reported that about 85 per cent of SPSI trade union stewards had been selected by employers rather than the workers they represented and many local SPSI officials were former military personnel (Abdullah and Etty, 1995). The SPSI was excluded from joining the International Confederation of Free Trade Unions (ICFTU) because it was not really representing the Indonesian workforce (Gall, 1998).

The monopoly power of the state-controlled SPSI was broken in 1999 following the change of government and the start of the 'Reform Era'. The Trade

Unions Act no. 21 of 2000 consolidated the right of employees to join and to form independent trade unions and made a number of provisions that met the international standards of labour organization and operations (Kelly, 2002: 18). The SPSI is still the state-controlled and recognized trade union confederation in Indonesia. There are many independent trade unions but these are less organized and less powerful than the ones affiliated to the SPSI. The newly established independent trade unions 'are not officially controlled by political parties, and they are free to associate as they wish, but most have political connections and tend to be affiliated with one or more political parties' (Kelly, 2002: 25).

In Malaysia, trade unions were established during British colonial rule as early as 1894 to represent the workers in tin production and the rubber plantations. The pan-Malayan General Labour Union (PMGLU) was formed in 1946 and became the leading organization of the Malaysian Communist Party (MCP). The PMGLU was later reconstituted as the Pan-Malayan Federation of Trade Unions (PMFTU). The British government welcomed the development of democracy through a trade union movement modelled on the British type. However, because of continued industrial action and labour unrest, the PMFTU and the MCP were made illegal by the amendment of the Trade Unions Ordinance on 31 May 1948 (Jomo and Todd, 1994). Therefore, until independence in 1957 the Malayan industrial relations system consisted of government-nurtured unionism and independent trade unions with declining left-wing influence. The first government after independence promised to respect a free and democratic trade union organization but it soon introduced legislation that curbed the power of trade unions. New labour laws (Trade Unions Ordinance 1959; Trade Unions Act 1965; Industrial Relations Act 1967) were introduced in order to consolidate the state control of trade union organization and operations. After the introduction of the New Economic Programme (NEP) in 1971, the role of trade unions was to meet the national objectives of unity and economic development through the organization of loyal, hard-working, committed, obedient and non-striking workers. All labour laws were amended with the aim of making trade unions part of the government's apparatus for economic growth and national unity. Trade unions were urged to change their role from representing workers against management and to focus on workers' education programmes and social and cultural projects.

In Malaysia, the government ensured that no trade union activity would deter foreign companies from investing in Malaysia. For example, no trade unions and no strikes were allowed in the electronics industry because it was seen as the most important sector for economic growth and development in the 1980s. Also, the Industrial Relations Act 1967, amended in 1980, made it illegal to take industrial action in essential services such as transport and banking (Arudsothy and Littler, 1993). The ban on industrial action in the electronics sector continued. The government has always tried to make sure that trade

Table 9.4 Number of trade unions and membership by gender, Malaysia, 2001–5

Year	No. of unions	Membership		
		Male	Female	Total
2001	592	472,401	313,040	785,441
2002	595	504,305	303,497	807,802
2003	609	479,607	309,556	789,163
2004	611	474,470	308,638	783,108
2005	621	464,308	296,852	761,160

Source: Department of Trade Union Affairs, Ministry of Human Resources, Malaysia, 2006.

unions are not a threat to its national planning programmes, to attract foreign investment and, in particular, to ensure the smooth running of the private sector as a catalyst for economic growth. Although the number of trade unions registered with the Department of Trade Union Affairs has increased slightly since 2001, their membership has declined (see Table 9.4).

From state unions to company unions

In 1994, the International Labour Organization (ILO) received a formal complaint from the International Confederation of Free Trade Unions (ICFTU) against the Indonesian government for not allowing the workers to set up independent trade unions outside the affiliation of the SPSI, for harassing trade union leaders, and for not adhering to the international standards on the right to organization and to collective bargaining (cited in Kelly, 2002: 8). In response to international pressure the Indonesian government allowed the setting up of company unions (SPTPs) similar to those found in Japan. Currently there is a mixture of industry and sector trade unions at the regional and national levels, and an increasing number of company-based unions.

Impressed by Japanese economic success, the Malaysian government, in pursuit of its 'Look East Policy', called for the setting up of enterprise unions similar to those found in Japanese companies in all Malaysian private and public sector organizations. It argued that in-house unions (company unions) would protect the interests of workers and develop more harmonious employer–employee relations. Initially, the MTUC accepted the idea of enterprise unions because they were expected to bring lifelong employment and a seniority wage system as in Japan, but that never happened. The number of company unions has continued to increase while that of the large national unions has decreased over the last two decades, marking a significant move in trade unionism from state-controlled to the employer-dominated trade unions.

When a Malaysian politician was asked, 'Why do you prefer in-house unions?', he replied: 'we prefer to keep our problems indoors'. After referring to Chapter 7, on Japan and South Korea, write a comparative analysis of trade unions' positions in Japan and Malaysia.

Collective bargaining

In Indonesia since the early 1980s Tripartite Cooperation Boards (LKSs) made up of employee, employer and government representatives have been set up at the national and regional levels, and all across the municipalities and regions, to discuss and reach collective agreements on the terms and conditions of employment. But since the SPSI has been controlled by the government and the state has been the largest employer, the LKSs have been no more than a state apparatus to rubber stamp its decisions. The LKSs existed 'in name and in number' but their role was highly ambiguous because the 'the government was the dominant force in any discussions' (Kelly, 2002: 10). When enterprise unions were permitted, as explained above, enterprise collective agreements outside the remit of the SPSI were also allowed, but they have had very limited effect because enterprise agreements have to be in line with national collective agreements. In companies where there are no trade unions and no collective agreements the government required the employer to have a set of corporate regulations that defines the terms and conditions of employment. The regulations are reviewed every two years and have to be approved by the Ministry of Manpower and Transmigration. However, most small and medium size organizations prefer to have a set of regulations endorsed by the government rather than having to bargain with the unions. In recent years, as a result of some freedom of association and the establishment of multiple and independent unions, many large employers have advocated the use of company unions and corporate regulations because they have found it difficult to bargain with different unions (Kelly, 2002: 38).

Collective bargaining in Malaysia is often a mere formality to discuss the implementation of state-imposed regulations over the terms and conditions of employment: negotiations between the management and unions do not include matters of promotion, transfer, employment, termination of service, dismissal, and assignment or allocation of duties. The company unions are expected to bargain with management for better terms and conditions of employment, but collective agreements are heavily regulated and restricted to items that are outside the managerial prerogatives. That means the unions cannot bargain over the hiring and dismissing of employees, promotion, training or re-allocation of responsibilities. Moreover, the legislation also prevents employees 'in pioneer industries from negotiating working conditions more favourable than the minimum standards embodied in the Employment Act. This minimises the incentive to form unions in companies with pioneer status' (Peetz and Todd, 2001: 335).

Industrial action

In both Indonesia and Malaysia, industrial action is highly restricted. In Indonesia, Labour Department Decree no. 22 (1957) and Decree no. 1108 (1986) allowed workers to go on strike only after a dispute had been subject to collective bargaining and had gone through a process of conciliation, mediation and arbitration organized through the Ministry of Labour and Department of Manpower. There were also cases when the right to strike was undermined by Labour Department Decree no. 4 (1986), which considers workers to have resigned from their jobs if they are absent for more than six days (Gall, 1998). In other words, the law made it extremely difficult for workers to go on strike. However, as the economy grew, the workforce became better organized and more militant. Although there are laws and procedures that make it harder for workers to take industrial action, strikes do occur and some of them tend to be violent. Whenever they happen, the military and police are called in to break them up. The number of strikes increased significantly in the 1990s despite the government's continued efforts to repress trade union activities. Most of the strikes were in the manufacturing of export-based products in and around the big cities and the capital, Jakarta. They involved workers in textiles, footwear, chemicals and metals production (Manning, 1993; Gall, 1998). The government's use of force to stop industrial action has always been justified by referring to its traditional slogan of national security, national unity, national development and the stability of foreign investments.

In Malaysia the level of strike action is insignificant because there have hardly been any strikes since the 1970s. Many industrial disputes are dealt with very quickly before any strike action becomes possible. Strikes have been severely restricted by making them legal only when at least two-thirds of union members vote for the strike in a secret ballot. No strikes are permitted once a dispute is referred to the industrial court for arbitration. The law makes it extremely difficult to organize a legal strike, and those who organize illegal strikes are severely punished. To make it even harder to take industrial action every member of the union executive committee involved in an illegal strike is personally liable to a fine or imprisonment. Because of the low rate of unemployment, when workers are unhappy with their jobs they leave the company to work somewhere else instead of taking the risk of putting pressure on the employer to meet their demands. Although the number of strikes is negligible, the unions have sometimes organized effective nationwide pickets such as those in 2007 in support of the Malaysian

Trade Union Congress campaign for a national minimum wage for workers in private sector organizations.

The settlement of industrial disputes

There are legal procedures for settling industrial disputes in both countries but they are designed to protect the employer rather than the employee. In Indonesia, when there is an industrial dispute, the first step is to start negotiations between the management and the unions. When the two negotiating parties fail to reach an agreement they refer their case to the Regional Committee for the Settlement of Labour Disputes (*Penyelesaian Perselisihan Perburuhan daerah*, PPPD). When the PPPD has not enabled the disputing parties to reach an agreement, the case is referred to the Central Committee for the Settlement of Labour Conflicts (*Peneyelesaian Perselisihan Perburuhan Pusat*, PPPP), which is a government body from the Department of Labour, until an agreement is reached (Munandar, 2003). The final decision is legally binding. This procedure, which is designed, implemented and controlled by the state, has been described by Kelly (2002: 10) as 'fairly ineffective in terms of presenting and resolving industrial disputes' because of the 'union members' belief that the dispute resolution committees tended to side with employers'.

In Malaysia, the preferred method of settling industrial disputes is conciliation, which is provided by the Industrial Relations Department (IRD) of the MoHR. Normally, the disputed parties refer their case in writing to the IRD and then the IRD officers would try to help them reach an agreement. If they fail to reach an agreement, the case would be referred to the minister, who decides on the case or refers it to an industrial relations court. The conciliation method seems to have worked satisfactorily because of the limited number of disputes, the expertise of the IRD officers, the employers' preference for the IRD rather than the courts, and the restrictions imposed by the state on the unions taking industrial action.

Summary

1   Indonesia and Malaysia have developed a distinctive model of economic development and management based on a combination of Western management practices and Eastern cultural values.
2   Their labour markets are highly regulated. There is a shortage of skilled and professional labour, a high level of employee turnover, and a preference for capital-intensive production systems. There are good employment prospects for women.
3   The practice of management can be described as regulated, paternalistic, integrated, quality-based, and adapted.

4   The process of recruitment and selection is characterized by the use of affirmative action in Malaysia, and reliance on word of mouth and the dominance of kinship recruitment in both countries.

5   Both countries have state-controlled income policies that determine the level of wage increases, compensations, and benefits in the public and private sectors.

6   Malaysia inherited the British-style industrial relations system, but soon after independence the government intervened heavily by regulating all aspects of employee relations in the name of national unity, national security and national economic development and growth. The situation is similar in Indonesia.

Revision questions

Chapter 1 provides a review task designed to consolidate your learning from this chapter. Please see Box 1.2.

In addition, the following questions are designed to help you revise this chapter.

1   Compare and contrast the Asian-Islamic approach to management described in this chapter and the Anglo-European approach described in Chapter 5.

2   Imagine you are an expatriate of a German MNC in Malaysia who has been asked to write a memo briefing German colleagues about to move to Malaysia. Write the memo, paying careful attention to which aspects of the Malaysian (a) context and (b) labour market require highlighting, and also (c) what advice you would provide.

3   Imagine you are the HR manager of a British company in Indonesia. Write a brief report to the company's board of directors identifying the differences between HRM functions (namely, recruitment and selection, training and development, a rewards system, and employee relations) in Indonesia and the UK.

References

Abdullah, F. and Etty, T. (1995) 'Would Be and Make Believe in Crisis', in Harris, D.R. (ed.) *Prisoners of Progress: A review of the Current Indonesian Labour Situation*, rNDOC/FTNtV/INHD, Leiden, pp.33–6.

Alhabshi, S.O. and Ghazali, A.H. (1994) *Islamic Values and Management*, Kuala Lumpur: Institute of Islamic Understanding Malaysia.

Arudsothy, P. and Littler, C. (1993) 'State regulation and fragmentation in Malaysia', in Frenkel, S. (ed.), *Organized Labour in the Asia-Pacific Region: A Comparative Study of Trade Unions in Nine Countries*, Ithaca: ILR Press.

Darwish, A.Y. (2000) 'Organizational commitment as a mediator of the relationship between Islamic work ethics and attitudes towards organizational change', *Human Relations*, 45(4): 513–37.

Elger, T. and Smith, C. (2001) 'The global dissemination of production models and the recasting of works and employment relations in developing societies', in Coetzee, J.K., Graaff, J., Hendricks, F. and Wood, G. (eds), *Development: Theory, Policy and Practice*, Cape Town: Oxford University Press.

Fujita, N. and James, W. (1997) 'Employment Creation and Manufactured Exports in Indonesia 1980-90', *Bulletin of Indonesian Economic Studies*, April, 33(1): 103-15.

Gall, G. (1998) 'The development of the Indonesian labour movement', *The International Journal of Human Resource Management*, 9(2): 359-76.

Gomez, E.T. and Jomo, K.S. (1999) *Malaysia's Political Economy: Politics, Patronage and Profits*, Cambridge: Cambridge University Press.

Habir, A.D. and Larasati, A.B. (1999) 'Human resource management as competitive advantage in the new millennium: an Indonesian perspective', *International Journal of Manpower*, 20(8): 548-62.

Hill, H. (2000) *The Indonesian Economy*, 2nd edn, Cambridge: Cambridge University Press.

Hofstede, G. (2001) *Culture's Consequences: International differences in work related values*, 2nd edn, London: Sage.

Jomo, K.S. and Todd, P. (1994) *Trade Unions and the State in Peninsular Malaysia*, Kuala Lumpur: Oxford University Press.

Kelly, P. (2002) *Promoting Democracy and Peace Through Social Dialogue: A Study of the Social Dialogue Institutions and Processes in Indonesia*, Geneva: International Labour Office.

Lucas, E.B. and Verry, D. (1996) 'Growth and income distribution in Malaysia', *International Labour Review*, 135(5): 553-75.

Lucas, E.B. and Verry, D. (1999) *Restructuring the Malaysian Economy: Development and Human Resources*, London: Palgrave-Macmillan.

Mann, R.I. (1994) *The Culture of Business in Indonesia*, Mississauga, Ontario: Gateway Books.

Manning, C. (1993) 'Structural change and industrial relations during the Suharto period: an approaching crisis?', *Bulletin of Indonesian Economic Studies*, 29(2): 59-95.

Mansor, N. and Ali, M. (1998) 'An exploratory study of organizational flexibility in Malaysia: a research note', *International Journal of Human Resource Management*, 9(3): 506-15.

Mellahi, K. and Wood, G.T. (2004) 'HRM in Malaysia', in Budhwar, P. (ed.), *Managing Human Resources in Asia-Pacific*, London: Routledge, 201-20.

Milliman, J., Nason, S., Zhou, C. and De Cieri, H. (2002) 'An exploratory assessment of the purposes of performance appraisals in North and Central America and the Pacific Rim', *Asia Pacific Journal of Human Resources*, 40(1): 105-21.

Munandar, A.S. (2003) 'Culture and management in Indonesia', in Warner, M. (ed.), *Culture and Management in Asia*, London: Routledge Curzon, 82-98.

Nasution, A. (2001) 'Meltdown of the Indonesian economy: causes, impacts, responses, and lessons', in Smith, A.L. (ed.), *Gus Dur and the Indonesian Economy*, Singapore: Institute of Southeast Asian Studies (ISEAS).

Noordin, F., Williams, T. and Zimmer, C. (2002) 'Career commitment in collectivist and individualistic cultures: a comparative study', *International Journal of Human Resource Management*, 13(1): 35-54.

Othman, R., Abdul-Ghani, R. and Arshad, R. (2001) 'Great expectations: CEOs' perception of the performance gap of the HRM function in the Malaysian manufacturing sector', *Personnel Review*, 30(1): 61–80.

Peetz, D. and Todd, P. (2001) '"Otherwise you're on your own": unions and bargaining in Malaysian banking', *International Journal of Manpower*, 22(4): 333–48.

Prijadi, R. and Rachmawati, R. (2002) 'Indonesia' in Zanko, M. (ed.), *The Handbook of Human Resource Management Policies and Practices in Asia-Pacific Economies*, Northampton, MA: Edward Elgar.

Siddiquee, N.A. (2006) 'Public management reform in Malaysia: recent initiatives and experiences', *International Journal of Public Sector Management*, 19(4): 339–58.

Smith, W.A. (2003) 'Culture and management in Malaysia', in Warner, M. (ed.), *Culture and Management in Asia*, London: Routledge Curzon, 115–34.

Taib, A. and Ismail, M.Y. (1982) 'The social structure', in Fisk, E.K. and Osman-Rani, H. (eds), *The Political Economy of Malaysia*, Kuala Lumpur: Oxford University Press.

Wolfe, D. and Arnold, B. (1994) 'Human resource management in Malaysia: American and Japanese approaches', *Journal of Asian Business*, 14(4): 80–103.

World Bank (1993) *The East Asian Miracle: Economic Growth and Public Policy*, *Oxford University Press*: Oxford, September, World Bank ISBN: 0-19-520993-1.

Part III

Case Study: The 1997 Asian Financial Crisis

Introduction

Between the 1970s and the 1990s, most of the South-east Asian countries were transformed into industrialized nations internationally recognized for their high-quality products and efficient services. However, by the end of 1997 that much-admired economic success turned into an economic nightmare for all the Asian countries. Within less than a year, from the end of 1996 to the autumn of 1997, the Thai currency exchange rate dropped by 42.8 per cent against the US dollar, the South Korean dropped by 50.7 per cent, the Malaysian by 33.6 per cent and the Singaporean by 16.3 per cent. Within a few months the Asian financial and banking system collapsed, inflation rates rocketed, consumer spending plummeted, and investors lost confidence in Asian markets. Consequently many businesses went bankrupt, making their employees redundant. This case study highlights the implications of the crisis for management and employee relations policies and practices in the countries affected.

Causes

Some people – mainly foreign investors and advisors to international financial organizations – argued that the crisis was internally created. They saw it as the outcome of years of institutional corruption and inadequate political and economic decisions. They contended that the Asian economic bubble had to burst because the political and financial systems of most Asian countries were too weak to meet the demands of economic growth.

Others, however, – mainly politicians and domestic investors – blamed international financial investors and an external conspiracy against the successful Asian countries. They argued that foreign investors pursuing short-term gains initiated the panic in the domestic financial markets. The Malaysian government, for example, argued that Malaysian political institutions were strong enough to control the fast-growing economy and that the crisis was deliberately created by foreign currency exchange speculators.

Many studies have concluded that the main cause of the crisis was a combination of political, social and economic factors, including: the lack of proper controls and economic safeguards on high economic growth; inappropriate investment projects; inadequate financial practices (for example, making bank loans on the basis of political recommendations rather than on sound economic decisions); inadequate financial laws and regulations that did not respond to the needs of a capitalist economy; excessive foreign direct investment; and high levels of foreign currency transfers (see Chotigeat and Kim, 1998; Chotigeat, 2001; Aggarwal, 1999; Kim, 2001).

It has also been argued, however, that the root cause of the crisis was the lack of attention to the importance of employee relations and human resource management in a fast-growing economy. On this account, weak trade unions and limited opportunities for employee involvement in decision-making processes were significant contributors to the crisis (see Lee, 2000). It has been observed that countries such as Japan and Singapore that had well-established policies and practices for employee–employer relations and for managing employees effectively were not severely affected by the crisis, whereas the countries that had weak trade unions and poor employee relations systems (such as Thailand and Indonesia) were.

It is also argued that inadequate investment in people was a factor leading to the crisis because employees did not have the knowledge and skills required for sustaining fast-growing, highly industrialized and knowledge-based economies. The countries that had invested heavily in the training and development of their workforce, such as Japan, Singapore and Taiwan, were those least affected by the crisis.

The effects

Within a few months interest rates had increased, the level of economic growth slowed down, overall standards of living deteriorated, and labour markets had become saturated. Unemployment increased dramatically. Many national, and most international, companies in the region were affected by the sudden currency exchange fluctuations. Because some currencies were devalued by up to

50 per cent, foreign companies experienced lower earnings and had to reduce their production levels or move to other countries.

China and Taiwan were less affected than Indonesia and Thailand: the economies of the former were stronger and better controlled. Indonesia suffered most because its banking sector collapsed very quickly and many companies became unable to get credit and had to close down. More than 1,500 companies went bankrupt within days, making more than 300,000 people redundant. Within the first six months of the crisis more than 13 million people became unemployed, pushing the total number of unemployed to over 35 million. More than 80 million people (40 per cent of the population) were living under the poverty line. In early 1998, prices increased by as much as 300 per cent for most essential commodities. The government increased the minimum wage by 15 per cent in June 1998, but that put more pressure on small businesses, which continued to go bankrupt and to lay off more employees. Such economic problems sparked popular unrest, mass demonstrations, and riots that led to a political crisis that in turn led to the resignation of President Suharto, who had ruled the country for 33 years.

In other countries too unemployment became a serious problem. In Malaysia, where unemployment had been very low for many years, the number of those out of work jumped from 2.6 per cent in 1997 to 4.9 per cent in 1998 as many companies resorted to rationalizing costs through downsizing. In South Korea the level of unemployment went from 2.6 per cent in 1997 to 6.8 per cent in 1998. In Thailand, unemployment jumped from 0.9 per cent in 1997 to 5.2 per cent in 1999. In these countries, great pressure was put on managers to reduce costs by cutting the number of workers.

Compulsory redundancies had to be introduced, though many companies encouraged voluntary redundancies by, for example, luring older employees with attractive early retirement and other rewards packages. However, those companies that managed to survive the crisis needed the skills and the expertise of their senior employees. Therefore, many companies had to retain their skilled and experienced employees while freezing recruitment and saving on the cost of training. As a result, young and inexperienced people, the less skilled, and the long-term unemployed were the most affected by the crisis because they were unemployable.

Responses and recovery measures

Each of the countries affected by the 1997 financial crisis devised its own way of responding to it and dealing with its outcomes, but all had to develop survival strategies involving more cost-effective use of their available resources.

At the organizational level, a typical recovery programme involved cutting salaries, closing down unprofitable operations, cutting overheads, not renewing expired work contracts, and introducing voluntary redundancies, early retirement packages and flexible working practices – whilst retaining core competencies. Some companies sought strategic alliances, while others had to be merged or taken over by their rivals to avoid bankruptcy.

In countries such as Malaysia, South Korea and Thailand many foreign workers did not have their work permits renewed and were sent back to their home countries in an attempt by governments to preserve jobs for the local workforce. Many of the repatriated workers had come from neighbouring countries that were also badly hit by the crisis, and therefore a partial reduction of unemployment in one country merely led to a significant increase in unemployment in another. Some of the jobs that foreign workers had done could not be done by the local workforce, either because they were considered low status jobs or because the jobs were too skilled and needed expert employees (Lee, 1998). Hence, countries such as Malaysia and Thailand had labour shortages soon after they repatriated foreign workers and then had to re-admit some foreign workers and attract back their citizens living abroad.

Trade unions worked with the government and employers' organizations to try to find the best solutions to the problems. In countries such as Thailand, where trade unions were relatively weak, the unemployed did not receive any benefits or state support, whereas in countries such as South Korea, where trade unions were better organized, and in Taiwan, where the opposition parties were stronger, the government had to provide unemployment benefits and support the unemployed financially. In Indonesia, the trade union federation (SPSI), established a committee to liase with employers to ensure that redundancies would be the last resort. The committee's aim was to help the dismissed employees find jobs and to get training for better job opportunities.

The World Bank, the International Monetary Fund (IMF), the Asian Development Bank (ADB) and a number of donor (governmental and non-governmental) organizations offered to help in rebuilding the confidence in the national financial institutions and in encouraging international reinvestment in the affected countries. However, the help was provided with conditions, such as pressure to establish democratic political and economic institutions, stable employee relations, appropriate labour market standards, and policies to encourage foreign direct investment. The IMF agreed to inject some cash, in terms of a loan, in order to maintain the liquidity of the international financial system. The funds were used to redress the balance-of-payments gap and to restore foreign currency reserves. The main aim of the IMF plan was to restore the economies of the countries affected by encouraging some capital outflows, stimulating consumer spending and rebuilding domestic and foreign investors' confidence in the local financial and economic systems. However, in order to meet the objectives of the plan, the IMF imposed a number of restrictions ranging from reducing government spending, the privatization of weaker public sector organizations, and control of inflation and interest rates.

The Thai government had difficulties meeting the IMF targets and standards, and had to change its spending policy to stimulate the demand for local goods and services (Chotigeat, 2001). Indonesia, on the other hand, despite the effects of successive natural disasters – earthquakes and tsunamis – managed to pay back the IMF loan, to bring inflation under control, and to restore consumer confidence. The new government had to call upon the ILO (International Labour Organization) to help in the reform of its employment laws, to allow the formation of independent trade unions, and to open the country to more foreign investors. It can be argued that Indonesia's recovery and its repayment of IMF's loan in a short period of time were achieved only because of the huge oil revenues generated as a result of high oil prices.

By contrast, the Malaysian government rejected IMF financial support and decided to deal with the crisis on its own, without having any restrictions imposed on it by any international organization. They introduced a series of austerity measures immediately. A special fund was set up to help those Malaysian businesses that were most affected. After a number of unsuccessful recovery measures, the economy was brought under control by managing to sustain a level of consumer spending just sufficient to keep inflation and wages at an acceptable level. In November 1998 they set up a National Economic Action Council (NEAC) that became responsible for introducing financial and economic reforms aimed at accelerating the recovery process. The NEAC produced a proposal with six objectives. They were: i) to stabilize the national currency, the ringgit, without having to resort to devaluation or revaluation measures; ii) to maintain a stable financial market with no need to resort to borrowing or reducing public spending; iii) to restore consumers' and investors' confidence in the local market; iv) to strengthen economic infrastructure, partially by restructuring the banking system; v) to continue with the principles of social and economic equity; and vi) to restore and support the most affected sectors of the economy (National Economic Recovery Plan, 1998).

Conclusion

The strong economic growth in South-east Asia, that was accompanied by low inflation, high interest rates, positive balances of payment, increasing foreign investment, and sound macro-economic indicators, suddenly turned into a drastic financial and economic crisis as the national currencies of most Asian countries dropped in value one after the other at astonishing rates. As national currencies lost value, inflation rates went up, interest rates went up, the level of economic growth slowed down, national companies went bankrupt, international investments were withdrawn, and the overall standard of living deteriorated, putting all countries affected into recession and serious economic, social and political difficulties. The causes were debatable, the effects were similar, but the recovery measures were different.

Questions

1 Describe how the 1997 Asian financial crisis started, which countries were most affected, and why.
2 Provide a critical analysis of the different views about the main causes of the crisis. Which explanation would you support and why?
3 Discuss the effects of the crisis on a selected number of countries that were most affected and explain the implications for their human resource management.
4 Compare and contrast the recovery measures used by at least two of the affected countries.
5 What lessons can be learnt from the crisis for the countries in the region and for other countries around the world? What should be done to avoid a similar crisis happening again?

References

Aggarwal, R. (1999) 'Restoring growth in Asia after the late 1990s economic crisis: need for domestic and international economic reforms', *Multinational Business Review*, Fall 1998: 22–30.

Chotigeat, T. (2001) *Coping with the 1997 Financial Crisis: Policy Issues in Southeast Asia*, College of Business Administration, University of Detroit Mercy, Fall 2001. Paper provided by ProQuest Information and Learning Company.

Chotigeat, T. and Kim, D.J. (1998) 'The east Asian financial malaise: analysis and perspectives', *Journal of Euro-Asian Management*, 4(3): 45–58.

Kim, S.H. (2001) 'The Asian financial crisis of 1997: the case of Korea', *Multinational Business Review*, Spring: 50–8.

Lee, S.J. (1998) 'The Impact of the Asian financial crisis on foreign workers in Taiwan', *Asian and Pacific Migration Journal*, 7(2/3): 145–69.

Lee, S.J. (2000) 'Asia in the 21st century: challenges and opportunities in work and labor', in *Proceedings of the 12th IIRA World Congress*, Raporteur's Report, vol. 5, Tokyo, June 1. http://www.jil.go.jp/jil/bulletin/year/2001/vol40-02/05.htm, accessed 4 Dec. 2007.

National Economic Recovery Plan (Malaysia) (1998), *The Crisis and Policy Response*, Kuala Lumpur: Government of Malaysia.

Part IV

Managing in Western European Countries

Part 4: Managing in West European Countries
Map 4

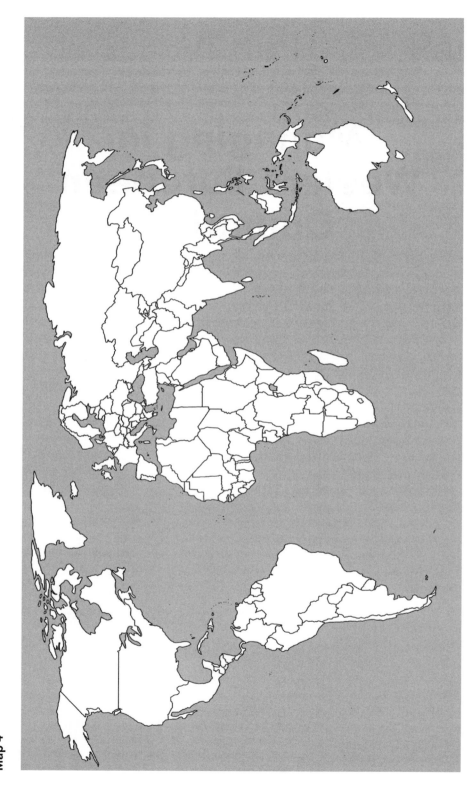

Activity: Put the number allocated for each of these countries on the map above: France (2), Belgium (3), Germany (7), Holland (6), Denmark (8), Sweden (9), Norway (10), Spain (1), Italy (4) and Greece (5)

10

Belgium and France

━━━━━━━━━━ **LEARNING OUTCOMES** ━━━━━━━━━━

The chapter is designed to help you understand, for Belgium and France:

1 The (a) economic, (b) political, and (c) cultural contexts in which managers work;

2 The main trends in the labour market;

3 The typical features of (a) management policies and practices and (b) organizational structure and behaviour;

4 The main policies and practices of human resource management with regard to: (a) recruitment and selection; (b) training and development; (c) rewards and remuneration; and (d) employee relations.

Introduction

The Francophone approach to management encompasses employment policies and management policies and practices found in France, much of Belgium, Luxembourg, and Western Switzerland, as well as in most of the former French colonies and current French overseas departments and territories. This chapter will focus on France and Belgium. They have much in common in terms of history, geography, culture, economic and institutional infrastructure, and political orientation within the European Union (EU). Their systems of administration, organization, and human resource management exhibit many similarities.

French is the second most spoken language in Belgium, after Flemish. It is widely used for business purposes within and outside the country (with other countries). Analysing the practice of management in Belgium and France, Buyens et al. (2004) noticed a significant shift in managing employees in Belgium towards the French approach and away from the Flemish or Dutch approach. (See Table 10.1 for basic statistics.)

Table 10.1 Basic statistical indicators, Belgium and France

Country	Area (sq km)	Population (July 2010 est.)	Population Growth (2010) %	GDP – real growth rate (2009) %	Inflation rate (2009 est.) %	Workforce (2009 est.) Million	Unemployment rate (2009) %
Belgium	30,528	10,414,336	0.094	−2.7	0	5.08	7.9
France	643,427	64,420,073	0.55	−2.5	0.1	28.1	9.1

Source: CIA *World Factbook*, 2010.

Contexts: economics, politics and culture

Economics

Belgium and France are among the most industrialized and advanced economies of the Western world. Until the 1980s, the French economy had been dependent on small and medium size enterprises. 'Such small firms are usually family businesses and often have a strong Catholic tradition of paternalism' (Goetschy and Jobert, 1998: 176). Although most of the large industrial companies and the financial sector have been privatized, the state still controls most of the economically important and strategic companies such as France Telecom, Renault and Air France. The main industries in France are steel, machinery, chemicals, automobiles, metallurgy, aircraft, electronics, mining, textiles, food processing, and tourism. Manufacturing is the backbone of French economic strength. Most of its main export and import partners are among the European Union members. Former colonies in Africa and new trade partners in the Middle East (mainly Saudi Arabia) and Asia (mainly Japan and China) are also important.

The Belgian economy is comparatively small but strong. It is still dependent on small and medium size enterprises. With limited natural resources the country has developed a reputation for transforming imported raw materials into finished goods for exportation. A famous example is Belgian chocolate. The Belgian economy is very open to international investments and is sensitive to the conditions of the world markets. Its main industries are engineering and metal products, motor vehicle assembly, processed food and beverages, and chemicals. It is also a producer of fresh vegetables, sugar beets and tobacco. Most of its main trade partners are from within the European Union (Eurostat, 2007).

Over the last decade both countries have introduced a number of reforms designed to boost the economy and make it more internationally competitive, to maintain social equity and to control the level of unemployment. These include reducing income taxes, controlling inflation, adjusting interest rates, reforming the pension system, and encouraging employers to introduce flexible working practices, as well as other employee relations reforms explained below.

Politics

France is a republic state with a constitutional parliamentary democracy where the head of state is an elected president. Belgium, in contrast, is a kingdom with a federal parliamentary democracy under a constitutional monarchy. In practice the countries have many common economic, political and social interests. Both are members of the European Union, and have replaced their own currencies with the euro (from January 2002). In Belgium, the federal parliament is made of two houses: the Chamber of Representatives and the Senate. As a federal state, the country comprises three autonomous regions (Flanders, Wallonia and Brussels) and three major communities (Flemish, French and German). Each region has its own legislative powers. The regions are divided into a total of 10 provinces and about 590 communes.

In France, the parliament, which holds the legislative power, is divided into the upper house and the national assembly. The Council of Ministers is appointed by the president on the recommendations of the prime minister, who is nominated by the National Assembly majority and appointed by the president. Administratively, France comprises 22 regions divided into 96 departments. French politics has been dominated by two parties on the right (*Le Rassemblement pour la République*, a De Gaullist party, and *Le Union pour la démocratie Francaise*, a combination of Independent Republicans and Christian Democrats) and two parties on the left (the Communist Party and the Socialist Party).

Culture

Belgium has been described as 'a melting pot of cultures' (Buyens et al., 2004: 129), where the French, Dutch and German cultures come together. The southern part of the country is very similar to France. According to Hofstede's (1980) classification (as explained in Chapter 2), France and Belgium are high on individualism, high on uncertainty avoidance, relatively low on masculinity and high on power distance. They have a high concern for aspects like employment security and employee freedom. The people of both countries tend to put strong emphasis on logic and rationality, with stress on individual opinions. Both countries are culturally diverse societies with a significant presence of different ethnic groups (including North Africans, Indo-Chinese, Africans, and East Europeans).

As a manager of a Japanese multinational company in France, write a report to your head office in Tokyo explaining the opportunities and threats the company faces in the French socio-economic and political context.

Labour market trends

In France, out of a population of around 64 million people about 28 million are economically active (Eurostat, 2007). The minimum working age for full-time employment is 18, but those between 16 and 18 may be allowed to work with some restrictions. The standard working week is 35 hours and the minimum annual holiday entitlement for full-time workers is 25 days plus public holidays. Belgium has a workforce of about 5 million out of a population of just above 10 million. The minimum working age is 18 for full-time employment, but those between the ages of 15 and 18 may be allowed to do part-time work. The standard working week is 38 hours and the minimum annual holiday entitlement for people in full-time employment is 20 days plus public holidays (Eurostat, 2007). (See Table 10.2.)

Table 10.2 Employment by sector in 2009 (%), Belgium and France

Sector	Belgium	France
Agriculture	2	3.8
Industry	25	24.3
Services	73	71.8

Source: CIA *World Factbook*, 2010.

In both Belgium and France overtime work is allowed in addition to the standard working-week hours. The overall limit stated in the EU working time directives is 48 hours. The state intervenes heavily in the regulation of the labour market and in employee relations. Legislation bans all kind of direct or indirect discrimination on the grounds of sex, race, colour, national origin, national or ethnic background, marital status, sexual orientation, birth, wealth, religion or belief, age, state of health, disability or physical characteristics.

The main features that have characterized the labour markets of both countries are the high levels of unemployment, the utilization of flexible working practices, the growth in female employment, the employment of immigrant workers, and the employment of older workers.

Unemployment

The rate of unemployment in Belgium has tended to be lower than that of France. The lowest rate of unemployment has been in the region of Flanders and the highest in the Wallonia region. France saw a continuous rise in unemployment over the 1980s and 1990s, more than any other OECD countries. By the middle of the 1990s about 12 per cent of the working population were unemployed. In 2005 it was still high at around 10 per cent (Eurostat, 2007). The highest rates of unemployment have been among the less educated and among unskilled young people under the age of 25. (See Table 10.3.)

Table 10.3 Unemployment rates 1990–2009 (%), Belgium and France

Country	2006	2007	2008	2009
Belgium	8.3	7.5	7.0	7.0
France	9.3	8.3	7.9	7.4

Source: OECD, 2009.

Both French and Belgian governments have introduced a number of initiatives aimed at helping young people (under the age of 25), older people (over the age of 55) and the long-term unemployed of all ages to find work. One incentive has been granting exemptions from social security contributions to employers who create new jobs through the introduction of flexible working practices.

MINI CASE STUDY 22

France: The First Employment Contract 2006

The year 2006 in France started with the introduction of a new labour law (*Contrat Première Embauche* – First Employment Contract) that made it much easier to dismiss young employees and harder for graduates and young people to be employed. The new law made it easy for employers to dismiss employees under the age of 26 at any time during their first two years in employment without

(Continued)

(Continued)

having to provide any reasons or any rewards for doing so. The government claimed that the new law would encourage employers to recruit more young people and therefore reduce youth unemployment. The unions and most students (as potential employees) disagreed, and saw the law as just a way of giving more power to employers to exploit young people. They argued that employers would have access to a pool of insecure young people by regularly firing those who reach the age of 26 and replacing them with younger people. Therefore, from February to April there were mass demonstrations spreading over most of the major French cities involving millions of people from all backgrounds, resulting in public buildings and cars being burnt, train stations blockaded, universities and high schools closed, public life disrupted and many businesses badly affected. The French government attempted to crack down on the demonstrations by arresting thousands of people, but the protests continued despite a compromise solution proposed by President Chirac on 31 March. Eventually the law had to be abandoned on 10 April 2006.

Questions

1 Do you agree with the French government's argument for introducing the new law? Why?
2 If the law had been implemented what would its implications have been for the recruitment and employment of young people?

Flexible working practices

Flexible working arrangements have been developed to enable organizations to meet labour requirements, and to meet the needs of their human resources strategies – often as part of a 'family-friendly' initiative or as part of an equal opportunities policy. The most popular forms of flexible working practice in both Belgium and France are part-time work, annual hours and temporary work (Dany et al., 2006). The use of home-based working, job sharing and teleworking is still very limited.

Part-time work is the most popular practice. In France, for instance, various types of part-time work have been introduced under the scheme called *l'orientation et retour à l'emploi* (orientation and return to employment). The level of part-time work increased slowly but quite significantly from 11.8 per cent of the workforce in 1987 to 16 per cent in 1996 (Dederichs and Köhler, 1991, 1993; Schwartzbard, 1996) and then stabilized over the last six year by moving from just under 17 per cent in 2000 to just above 17 per cent in 2006 (Eurostat, 2007). The number of women part-time workers increased from 21.8 to 28.9 per cent between 1985 and 1995 and that of men from 3.2 to 5.1 per cent over the same time (EC, 1996). In recent years the percentage of women in part-time work declined slightly from 31 per cent in 2000 to 30.7 per cent in 2006, while that of men increased slightly from 5.3 per cent to 5.7 per cent (Eurostat, 2007).

In Belgium, the number of women and men employed part-time increased steadily from 15.7 per cent in 1998 to 23.2 per cent in 2006. The rise in part-time employment has been significant for both women and men. The level of women in part-time employment increased from 39.9 per cent in 2000 to 42.6 per cent in 2006, while that of men increased from 5.5 per cent to 7.6 per cent over the same period (Eurostat, 2007). In comparison with other European countries Belgium has the lowest proportion of part-time workers. Part-time work is still primarily female. Women in Belgium work more part-time than the European average.

Female participation

In France, the female participation rate in employment has been above the EU average (Buyens et al., 2004). The participation rate of women in the labour market increased from about 46 per cent in 1963 to 57.6 per cent in 2005 (Eurostat, 2007). A number of family-friendly policies have been introduced over the last two decades and they have encouraged many women who were unable to work full-time to stay in employment and work flexibly. Unlike in the UK, where the majority of part-time employees are women who have family commitments (mainly looking after their children), most married women in France work full-time because of the excellent provision of child care facilities there (Branine, 1999).

In Belgium, the participation of women in the labour market increased significantly from 45 per cent of the working population in 1995 to 53.8 per cent in 2005 (Eurostat, 2007). It should be noted that women in Belgium tend to be more highly educated than men, but most of them work part time. Moreover, less educated women have more difficulty finding a job than less educated men, while more highly educated men have more difficulty finding jobs than more highly educated women. However, the latter earn only 89 per cent of what a male would earn in the same position with the same education (compared to an EU average of 84 per cent) (Eurostat, 2008).

ACTIVITY 2

In France from July 2006 parents with at least three children can stop work following the birth of a child and be paid €750 per month for a year to stay at home and look after their children. In relation to this legislation, a number of measures were introduced such as increased tax cuts for child care outside the home (crèches, nannies) from 25 to 50 per cent of costs (up to an annual ceiling of €2,300 per child) for all children under the age of 7, the increase in parental allowance for parents who may stop working temporarily in order to take care of a child under 20 who is seriously ill, has a disability or is recovering from an accident, and providing families with at least three children with a discount card that gives them access to a wider range of goods and services at concessionary rates. (Adapted from Antoine Math, IRES, in www.eiro. eurofound.eu.int/2005/11/features/fr0511103f.html (accessed on 18 Nov. 2006).

Questions

1 What are the reasons for introducing the recent family-friendly policies in France?
2 What would be the implications of such policies on the level of unemployment, flexible working practices and the career prospects of women in France?

Migrant labour

Both Belgium and France have large populations of migrant workers, mainly from their former colonies in Africa and recently from Central and Eastern Europe. Following European integration in 1992, many people from within the EU have come to live and work in Belgium and France as well as immigrants from outside the EU. Contrary to the widely held belief, most foreigners living legally in Belgium are from either a member state of the EU or from another industrialized nation.

Belgium and France have made transitional arrangements to control the movement of people from the new member states onto their soil and tightened their immigration policies on admitting people from outside the EU. However, such arrangements have not stopped a steady flow of legal and illegal migrant workers to work in sectors such as agriculture and construction. As well as the direct immigration of job opportunity seekers, there have also been a number of other ways by which the numbers of migrant workers have increased. One way has been the authorization of people of foreign nationalities to settle with their spouse or their parents who have already been living in the country for several years. Another important source of immigrant labour has been the employment of foreign students who completed their education in the host country.

MINI CASE STUDY 23

Your are Unwanted Unless you are Highly Skilled

Each year the Belgian government gives young foreigners the opportunity to study at public universities and technical schools and then offers them residence and work permits allowing them to seek employment after graduation. The

French parliament adopted on 17 May 2006 a proposal for a new bill on immigration and integration (*Projet de loi sur le code de l'entrée et du séjour des étrangers et du droit d'asile, CESEDA*), which provides for the promotion of 'selective immigration' through the introduction of a new type of residence permit for 'skills and talents' to be granted to immigrants whose 'personalities, abilities and projects' may contribute to the country's economy. This new bill is aimed at attracting talented and skilled immigrants whose knowledge and skills are needed. At the same time the new law proposes tougher controls on the immigration and settlement of unskilled and 'unwanted' people.

Questions

1 Argue for and against the Belgian and the French approach to attracting and keeping skilled and talented migrant labour.
2 Are the new policies of discriminating between skilled and unskilled immigrants ethically and morally acceptable?
3 What would be the consequences of the new law in France on the labour market?

Older working population

Unlike other European countries, Belgium and France do not suffer from a declining birth rate and do not yet have a serious ageing population problem. France has a growing rather than a declining generation of younger people. At the turn of the century, more than a quarter of the French population was under of the age of 20 and more than 70 per cent of the working population were between the ages of 25 and 49 (Cerdin and Peretti, 2001). Although there is not yet an acute employment problem of older people, both countries have realized the importance of keeping older, healthier and experienced employees in employment for as long as possible. In Belgium, the employment rate of those aged 55 to 64 increased by nearly 10 per cent from 21.9 per cent in 1996 to 31.8 per cent in 2005, while in France it increased from 29.4 per cent to 37.9 per cent (Eurostat, 2007). (See Table 10.4.)

Table 10.4 Age structure (%) (2009), Belgium and France

Country	0–14 years %	15–64 years %	Over 65 years %	Median age (years)	Life expectancy at birth (men and women)
Belgium	16.1	66.3	17.6	42	79.22
France	18.6	65	16.4	39.7	81

Source: CIA *World Factbook*, 2010.

The French government has realized that mobilizing older people in the labour market would help not only to strengthen French economic performance, but also reduce pressure on pensions and public finances (OECD, 2005a). Access to the Special National Employment Fund programme (*Allocation spéciale du fonds national pour l'emploi*) was restricted and steps were taken to encourage workers to remain active. In 2003, the contribution threshold for entitlement to a full pension was raised and a bonus scheme for those ready to stay at work beyond the standard retirement age was introduced. The Job Substitution Allowance Scheme (ARPE, *Allocation de remplacement pour l'emploi*) was discontinued (Jolivet, 2002; Mandin, 2003). Also, through the Social Cohesion Plan and the Health at Work Plan, the French government has managed to encourage older people to stay at work longer (OECD, 2005a). Some large companies such as Renault and Thales have already introduced innovative practices that focus on keeping people in employment by adapting their occupations or encouraging mobility and flexibility, whether in work time or at the workplace (OECD, 2005a).

Management and organization

The practice of management in both Belgium and France is heavily influenced by national laws and regulations, EU directives and overall socio-economic and political changes and global competitive pressures (see Brewster and Hegewisch, 1994; Brewster, 1995; Brewster and Harris, 1999; Brewster et al., 2004). Cerdin and Peretti (2001: 216) described the practices of management in France as 'the result of several constraints such as strong and specific regulations, a demography unique in Europe, the acceleration of internationalisation of large organizations, and sociological upheaval'. French and Belgian HR managers play a significant role in the process of decision-making. One survey (Buyens et al., 2004) found that the participation of French HR managers in the boards of directors was the highest among the EU countries. In general the practice of management in both countries is characterized by formalization and bureaucracy, elitism and respect for intellect, strategic awareness, internal partnership and empowerment of line managers.

Formality and bureaucracy

The Francophone approach to management is very formalized and highly bureaucratized. Respect for hierarchy and status is very important and that is reflected in the use of language and in the forms of addressing those in certain positions of power and status. For example, it is unusual to address one's superior by the first name or in the informal *tu* (you) rather than the formal *vous* (you). The use of *monsieur* (Sir), *Madame* (Mrs) or *Mademoiselle* (Miss) is often the normal form of address between manager and subordinate, and between the provider and the receiver of a service. In most organizations, especially in the civil service, intermediaries such as secretaries and administrators are powerful people in the provision of services because it is they who are in charge of ensuring that the bureaucratic procedures are observed.

Despite the increase in the use of information technologies and the easy access to information, communication in French and Belgium organizations is still very much dependent on the written word on paper. According to a survey by Buyens et al. (2004: 135) communication in the French-speaking regions (Wallonia and France) is often top-down. This is attributed to the large power distance culture (Hofstede, 2001) that exists in France. In large power distance countries organization structures are hierarchical and subordinates rely heavily on their leaders. Such formalities and bureaucratic procedures are apparent not only in the communication process but also in all HRM functions and especially in recruitment and selection procedures.

Elitism and intellect

The Francophone approach to management is very elitist and intellectually driven. According to Roussillon and Bournois (1997) the methods by which business leaders are produced in France reflect the importance given to authority and elitism in organizations. The concept of *cadre*, which is used to describe a manager, means literally 'a frame', as in a picture frame, or door frame, which implies a form of implicit rigidity in delegating power and making decisions from the top and passing them down the hierarchy (Boltanski, 1982). In reality it is not easy to find the exact meaning of the concept of *cadre* because in the Francophone context it is generally synonymous with successful, intellectual, young graduate (*diplomé*) managers. It carries with it a sense of prestige and pride within society, especially if the graduate is from one of the prestigious business or engineering schools (*grandes écoles*). They are simply described as the elite, (another contentious concept), referring to those few people with power and authority in society. In describing the French managers, Barsoux and Lawrence (1990) state that in a society that always respects the intellectual, the philosopher, and the serious writer, French managers typically show their intellectual talents and exercise their powers of analysis and synthesis when formulating arguments and making decisions.

In both Belgium and France, terms such as *'responsible'*, *'gérant'*, *'directeur'*, *'chef'*, and *'patron'* all define the act of managing and imply a level of authority and prestige. These concepts reflect the importance given to the elite in a social system where people operate according to an 'honour system' rather than a 'contract system' as in the USA or a 'consensus system' as in the Netherlands, for example (Roussillon and Bournois, 1997). It seems that in all aspects of life, the French tend to emphasize the importance of intellectualism and 'cleverness'. According to Schramm-Nielsen (2001: 416), intellectualism in France 'is linked to the abstract, to concepts, and to mastering mathematics, the most abstract of disciplines, the mastery of which is considered the ultimate proof of intelligence'.

Strategic awareness

In both countries there has been a growing emphasis on strategic management and the strategic role of managers in organizations. For example, according to a study by Buyens et al. (2004), more than half of HR managers in Belgium claimed to be involved in corporate strategy development from the outset, while in France more than 60 per cent of the respondents said they had been involved in corporate strategy development. Moreover, because of the increasing use of technology and the creation of many specialist management consultancies and agencies throughout the world (Muratbekova-Touron, 2008), it has become possible to pass some management functions to experts outside the firm, especially when the cost of outsourcing is lower than doing it in-house.

Internal partnership and empowerment of line managers

Management functions in many French and Belgian organizations are a shared responsibility between all departments. For example, line managers in France have 'become more and more expert in human resource management, thanks to specific training that enables them to make adequate decisions in HR matters' (Cerdin and Peretti, 2001: 223). It is believed that management is human resource management and that it is the responsibility of line managers to train employees (Buyens et al., 2004). Moreover, as Roussillon and Bournois (1997) state, French managers tend to be generalist and they rarely specialize in one particular management function or one specific sector of the economy.

Managing human resources

The practice of HRM in France and Belgium mirrors the characteristics of the Francophone approach to management. National laws and regulations, EU directives and overall socio-economic and political changes and global competitive pressures heavily influence employee relations and the functions of HRM (see Brewster and Hegewisch, 1994; Sparrow and Hiltrop, 1994; Trouvé, 1994; Brewster, 1995; Brewster and Harris, 1999; Brewster et al., 2004).

Recruitment and selection

In both Belgium and France employers use the traditional methods of recruitment and selection used in any other EU member states (Sparrow and Hiltrop, 1994), though they differ slightly in their approach and in their use of newer techniques. The organization of recruitment and selection is often decentralized to the organizational and plant levels and the use of international recruitment agencies is limited. The responsibilities for recruitment and selection are very often shared between the line and the HR managers, but in most large French companies it is still the main role of HR managers who are normally in charge of HR planning.

Recruitment

In a highly regulated labour market, French employers are required to follow certain procedures when recruiting new employees according to a code of practice for each sector of the economy. For example, in the distribution and retailing sector, all vacancies have to be advertised internally in order to give existing employees the opportunity to apply for better and/or higher jobs in their companies. However, for senior management positions it is estimated that more than 60 per cent are recruited externally. There are a number of job centres for managers such as APEC (*Agence pour l'emploi des cadres*) which recruits managers for large companies. Also, as a result of advanced information and communication technologies, more and more employers use the internet to promote themselves and advertise their job vacancies, while many job seekers look for jobs through the internet. Many websites are dedicated to the recruitment of employees for general and specialized jobs. To attract a wider pool of applicants, many French companies use US and other European websites translated when possible into English.

Graduate recruitment

Graduate recruitment is another HRM activity where the French and Belgian employers differ. While the Belgians recruit graduates from different colleges and universities and promote internal recruitment of junior managers, the French recruit graduates for junior managerial jobs directly from prestigious institutions of higher education like the *grandes écoles* (mainly *écoles supérieures de commerce* and the *Ecole nationale d'administration*). Roussillon and Bournois (1997: 243) stated that 'managerial élite in France is selected at the age of 15 by the education system which, by means of successive selection, enables certain students to go to prestigious schools which give access to the most brilliant careers'. They explained that 'a young graduate from the famous engineering school *Ponts et chaussées* may be appointed directly to the post of Area Construction Engineer'.

It is customary for young graduates to start their career in the public sector and then move to important positions in the private sector (Roussillon and Bournois, 1997). This practice is called *pantouflage*, which allows managers to move from the public to the private sector and back to the public sector in order to gain further managerial and professional expertise and to enhance their career opportunities. In Belgium the most junior managerial jobs are often filled through internal recruitment and promotions.

Selection

Although both countries use similar selection methods such as the use of application forms, interviews, psychometric tests, graphology, assessment centres and references, they differ in their level of application of these. For example, the French use interview panels less often than the Belgians, but application forms are used more often in France than in Belgium. However, the use of psychometric tests is very limited in both countries (Dany and Torchy, 1994; Buyens et al., 2004). The use of assessment centres is also still very limited in both countries. In this respect, Roussillon and Bournois (1997: 341) state that 'whereas many countries use the traditional assessment centres, French firms seem rather reticent about using them and doubtful of their value'. Graphology is traditionally used in French-speaking countries but is more practised in France than in any other country in the world.

The use of references is also popular in French-speaking countries but more so in France than in Belgium. In some cases, however, employers do not request further personal references or additional information because of the comprehensive 'dossier' that applicants are requested to submit with their job applications. Therefore it can be concluded that in both France and Belgium the traditional methods of recruitment and selection (application forms, interviews and references) are still widely used for their presumed validity and reliability. Although the internet is widely used for recruitment it is less used for the purposes of selection.

Training and development

In both countries the legislator has intervened heavily over the last 30 years in regulating the process, level and type of training that organizations have had to offer. The state has intervened directly and through legislation, and invested heavily in education which is among the best in the world, as well as in continuous training and development for all employees in public and private sector organizations.

Education

Education in France is free and obligatory from the ages of 6 to 16, when general and vocational education is provided. In France, there are three education pathways: general, vocational and technological. The general education is the same as any basic education in other EU countries. Its successful completion leads to further and higher education; whereas vocational and technological education can be obtained through educational institutions, as part of an apprenticeship scheme or through specific training programmes of short duration. Successful completion results in diplomas ranging from the CAP (*certificat d'aptitude professionnelle*, level 5) to the degree of engineer (level 1).

Higher education in France can be obtained through going to a university or to a *grande école* in business or engineering. The *grandes écoles* of France are higher education establishments outside the mainstream framework of the public universities. They are generally based on a single subject area such as administration and engineering and they are very selective in their admission of students. They are seen as prestigious, hard to get into, and the main producers of France's top scientists, politicians, and managers.

Students are admitted to higher education after successful completion of secondary school education and passing the national examination *baccalaureat*. At the university, the students study particular subjects (most universities have all disciplines) and graduate with degrees starting from a bachelor's degree (*licence*) after 4 years of higher education to a national doctorate (*doctorat d'etat*) after at least 8 years of higher education and research. It is normally harder to get accepted into a *grande école*. Applicants should have a *baccalaureat* with merit (good or very good) and should pass an entrance examination. If accepted they study a two-year preparatory course and then they have to pass a nation-wide examination before continuing their studies for a business administration or engineering degree.

Education in Belgium is also free and compulsory from the ages of 6 to 18. Education is normally regulated at the level of each of the three regions of the country but they follow similar stages: primary education from the ages of 6 to 12; secondary education from the ages of 12–18; and higher education in universities, polytechnics and vocational schools. The quality of education in science and mathematics has been one of the best in Europe (OECD, 2003). Secondary school education is divided into general, technical, vocational and art. Any pupil who qualifies with a diploma of secondary education can enrol in an institution of higher education of their choice except for medicine/dentistry, arts and engineering where entrance examinations are required. All university students pay a fixed registration fee which varies depending on the financial conditions of the student's parents. In terms of qualifications, Belgium adopts the Bologna system of a three-year Bachelor's degree and a one- to two-year masters' degree, and then the research-based doctoral degree.

Vocational and employer-provided training

Vocational training is more highly regarded in Belgium than in France, where education is mainly academic and general. In Belgium vocational education is provided in parallel with a general secondary education and is aimed at developing expertise in particular skills such as car mechanics, art design and so on. In France, over the last twenty years, in an attempt to reduce youth unemployment, vocational training has been incorporated as part of secondary school education as many pupils today attend work placements as part of their vocational secondary education. There have also been a number of avenues for young people to gain transferable skills through vocational training in an increasing number of colleges and institutes of higher education. Vocational training can be divided into training for young people and long-term unemployed, and employer-provided training.

Vocational training for young people

As explained earlier, youth unemployment is one of the major challenges for the French government. Therefore in order to reduce youth unemployment a number of vocational training schemes have been introduced. Apprenticeship employment for the 16–25 age group has been provided in the workplace and in apprentice training centres (*centres de formation d'apprentis* – CFA). In addition to the apprenticeship contract, there are three types of contract combining work and training specifically targeted at the 16–25 age group: the *contrat de qualification* (qualification contract); the *contrat d'orientation* (guidance contract); and the *contrat d'adaptation* (adaptation contract). Employers receive financial support during the period of youth training while the young person receives pay calculated as a percentage of the national minimum wage.

In Belgium, most young people receive their vocational training through technical and vocational lessons in full-time secondary education. However, there are many opportunities for young people to combine part-time work with vocational education in companies or separate institutions outside work. Vocational education schools provide technical, vocational and art training. Normally, after six years of secondary education, it is possible to undertake a year of preparation for university or to specialize in preparation for working life. It is also possible to undertake part-time study after the first two years of secondary education and work as an apprentice in an established organization to get vocational training (Buyens and Wouters, 2005).

The provision of vocational training tends to differ slightly from one community to another among the three Belgian communities (Flemish, French and German speaking). They all provide vocational training at full-time secondary schools as well as the opportunity to take part-time study in secondary schools after the first four years. While the German-speaking community does not provide vocational training outside secondary school education, the Flemish community provides apprenticeship training in industry in conjunction with part-time study and apprenticeship training in medium size enterprises in conjunction with part-time study, and the French community provides vocational training in schools and in medium size organizations and with self-employed professionals (Buyens and Wouters, 2005).

Employer-provided training

In France the law since 1971 requires all organizations employing 10 workers or more to spend a set percentage of their pay bill on training. The law has been implemented in a way that 'training takes the form of courses aimed to develop, adapt or improve workers' knowledge, and is structured as off-the-job training, either within or outside the firm' (Hocquet, 1999: 233). Employers are required by law to have a yearly company training plan which has to be designed in a way that shows how the company will acquire competencies currently needed, and how it will prepare employees for the future changes in their work due to technological developments and changes in work methods. The process of producing the annual training plan involves the management and employee representatives' committee responsible for training in the company.

The French government also introduced a law on continuous training that was aimed at reducing inequalities in skills and knowledge that had been created by the education system among the French workforce. All employees were expected to gain the skills needed through training while working (Berton and Podevin, 1991; Verdier, 1994). Individual employees have the right to take up to 20 hours of work per annum for training outside the workplace. However, many studies have shown that the greatest beneficiaries of the initiative have been the highly skilled rather than the non-skilled employees. Therefore, 'contrary to the objectives of the legislation, low-skilled categories have remained largely outside training developments, while technicians and supervisors have even greater access than managers and engineers' (Verdier, 1994: 43).

The legislation has also encouraged mid-career training and provided assistance for the improvement of managerial skills of SME managers in particular. The 2004 law on life-long learning sets priorities for workers over the age of 45 and employed for over 20 years to take advantage of a skills audit and have the right to continuous training through taking time off work to attend courses to enhance their employability potential. However, the laws on employer-provided and employee continuous training have not just improved the level of employee skills and knowledge but above all raised French employers' awareness of the importance of training for the enhancement of the performance of their organizations and for their sustainable development.

Similarly, the federal government in Belgium has been committed to the training and development of its workforce. Full-time employees are entitled to paid educational leave if they or their employers identify the need for training. Employers are required by law to provide paid leave as well as paying the tuition fees for their employees' training, but they get a reimbursement from a government training fund. Paid educational leave was expected to increase the level of development of the working population in general. Individual regions have also introduced their own initiatives aimed at employee training and development.

ACTIVITY 3

In response to the violent youth protests in poor suburbs of large cities that took place in the autumn of 2005, the French government issued new legislation in March 2006 that gives tax credits to companies that employ junior apprentices (from the age of 14) in order to promote the employment of young people. The new legislation also provides for the creation of a voluntary civil service programme aimed at the young people between the ages of 16 and 24 to prepare them for employment by providing them with training and advice for career opportunities.

Question

1 What are the advantages and disadvantages of tax credits? How effective would you expect them to be?

Rewards and remuneration

In France, since the 1980s jobs have tended to be evaluated and graded relative to others in relation to specific criteria agreed by the partners. Such criteria include the level of knowledge required for the job, the freedom of action needed to do the job, the level of responsibility required, and the level of complexity of the tasks being carried out (Donnadieu and Denimal, 1993; Jenkins and Klarsfeld, 2002). This system of pay agreement was reinforced by passing the 1982 Auroux Law which provided for wages and salaries to be negotiated annually between employers and trade unions at the sector and firm levels. Gradually, employers used their negotiating powers at the firm level to shift attention from the collective to the individual performance, making way for more individually centred payment systems. Therefore since the early 1990s, many employers have introduced a number of individually centred reward approaches that are aimed at motivating the individual employee's better performance and achievement (Marbach, 1999; Jenkins and Klarsfeld, 2002). Despite the move towards more individualized payment systems collective wage agreements are still favoured by the trade unions and by organizations that have historically had strong employee relations and a tradition of collective bargaining such as those in the steel and car manufacturing industries.

Currently most organizations in France and Belgium use performance appraisal in order to provide feedback to their employees and to reward them for individual performance, but is used more for managerial and professional jobs than for those in lower positions. Performance appraisal has been used for performance-related pay and for rewarding individual employees for their commitment and other contributions to the organization such as innovation and creativity. Also, in both countries employees are entitled to many allowances such as annual, maternity, paternity, bereavement, sick and sabbatical leave, and leave to care for dependants.

Minimum wage

Both Belgium and France have a statutory minimum wage, SMIC (*Salaire minimum interprofessionel de croissance*). It is regularly adjusted in relation to the price index of consumer goods and is sometimes raised by the government when it deems necessary. In France, it went up to 1,321 Euros per month in 2008. In Belgium the minimum wage went from 1,234 Euros per month in 2006 to 1,336 Euros in 2008 (Eurostat, 2008). In both countries, the rise in the minimum wage takes into consideration the rate of inflation, namely the retail price index, and half of the increase in the purchasing power of the average basic hourly pay of manual workers.

Performance-related pay

As in all the OECD countries, performance-related pay has always existed in the private sector and was extended to the public sector in the 1980s. Currently in all sectors of the Belgian and French economies performance-related pay schemes are related to organizational objectives. The performance of individual employees is appraised regularly through a range of different schemes. Such schemes involve a combination of individual, team-based and skill-based criteria for making such rewards (OECD, 2005b). In France, even in the civil service a form of performance-related pay, referred to as 'diligence allowance', to reward civil servants for exceptional performance has existed since the early 1950s. Performance-related pay has been introduced at all levels and in all sectors. For example, in 2004 a system of performance-related pay was tried out on the top civil servants (director's level) in six ministries (finance, defence, interior, equipment, agriculture and civil service), whereby the base salary can be increased by bonuses of up to 20 per cent for improved performance.

Employee relations

Since the early twentieth century employee relations in France have been characterized by labour organizations known for their anarchist and revolutionary beliefs, by paternalistic and reactionary employers, and by an interventionist state (Dufour and Hege, 1997; Goetschy and Jobert, 1998). This tripartite employee relations system, which exists in both Belgium and France, involving the state, federations of employers and federations of employees, has been very antagonistic and controversial.

Trade unions

Trade unions in France were not recognized until 1884, although there were many informal unions before then mainly at the local level. The first trade unions were the craft unions that later developed into industrial unions in response to the country's industrializing pace. Workers had a constitutional right to form and join trade unions but it was not until the 1980s that the Socialist government introduced major industrial relations reforms, consolidating the rights of workers to representation, participation and industrial action.

Currently, trade unions are organized at the national level into confederations. The major confederations of trade unions in France are:

1 The General Confederation of Labour (*Confédération générale du travail*, CGT), which is the largest and most influential, has historically been related to the French Communist party and claims to have just less than one million members despite the recent decline in its membership.
2 The French Democratic Confederation of Labour (*Confédération Francaise démocratique du travail*, CFDT) is the second largest trade union confederation. Originally, it was the French Confederation of Christian Workers (*Confédération Francaise des travailleurs Chrétiens*, CFTC).
3 The General Confederation of Labour (*Force ouvrière* FO) also claims to be the second largest trade union in France.
4 The fourth largest trade union confederation is the independent white-collar union, the General Confederation of Professionals and Managers (*Confédération générale des cadres*, CGC).

The organization of trade unions in Belgium is historically different from that of the French in their structure and operation as they tend to be less militant and more restricted in their activities by legally binding collective agreements and by employment laws. Trade unions are organized into confederations and federations and operate at the national, regional and local (enterprise) levels. There are three main union organizations:

1 The Confederation of Christian Trade Unions (*Confédération des syndicats Chrétiens*, CSC), which covers about 187 trade unions involving more than 1.6 million members (about 50 per cent of the unionized workforce), from mainly white-collar employees. Politically, it is a conservative organization of trade unions.
2 The Belgium General Federation of Labour (*Fédération générale du travail de Belgique*, FGTB), which covers only about 14 trade unions but has a total membership of more than 1.2 million workers from mainly blue-collar jobs, covering about 40 per cent of the unionized workforce. Politically it is a socialist organization of trade unions.
3 The Federation of Liberal Trade Unions of Belgium (*Centrale générale des syndicaux libéraux de Belgique*, CGSLB), which represents about 10 per cent of the unionized workforce.

Trade union membership and density

Trade union density, possibly for social and cultural reasons, has never been high in France. Currently only about 8 per cent of the workforce are members of trade unions (see Table 10.5). Trade unions membership has been declining since the middle of the 1980s but the number of trade unions has increased slightly because of the splitting of some large unions and the regrouping of small ones as well as the creation of others. Most new members have been in the public sector and in large private sector companies.

In Belgium, trade union membership is traditionally high but it differs from one industry to another. For example, in the steel industry and in the public sector organizations union membership is higher than in other industries. In 2007 trade union density was still around 53 per cent (see Table 10.5). This shows that while trade union membership was in decline in many EU countries it has been relatively stable in Belgium over the last 15 years.

Table 10.5 Trade union density (1999–2007), Belgium and France

Country	1999	2000	2001	2002	2003	2004	2005	2006	2007	2008
Belgium	51.6	49.3	49.9	51.2	52.2	52.9	52.9	54.1	52.9	51.9
France	8.4	8.3	8.2	8.4	8.2	8.0	8.0	7.9	7.8	7.7

Source: OECD Statistics, 2009.

Collective bargaining

In both countries, collective agreements are legally binding but they have had different approaches to collective bargaining. The French approach is very often confrontational and uncompromising. Most bargaining takes place at the national level and is centralized. The law has always played a significant role in the process and outcomes of collective bargaining. In 1968 workplace union branches (*Sections syndicales*) were set up at the level of each enterprise in order to participate in collective bargaining at the local level. It was not until the 1980s that enterprise bargaining became possible. The Auroux Report 1982 pointed out a number of serious drawbacks of collective bargaining, especially in small enterprises and for those in low income, as many employees were not covered by collective agreements and were left to the exploitation of their employers. Therefore, the Collective Bargaining Act 1982 was introduced in order to improve the prevailing collective bargaining system. Following the act, the amount of workplace-level bargaining increased significantly, although industry-level bargaining was the most favoured practice. By the mid-1990s, more than 7,500 workplace agreements were signed each year covering mainly work-time issues and wage agreements, but there were still more than 70 per cent of all agreements reached at the industry level (Goetschy and Jobert, 1998). Industrial-level agreements are still popular and French employers generally prefer them because they seem to be less problematic and do not involve most of the detailed demands that employees present at the plant level. However, multi-industry bargaining increased significantly over the 1990s. The CNPF and the CFDT supported the multi-industry agreements, which they referred to as the 'consensus approach'. Multi-industry bargaining covered a wide range of issues from those related to technological change to flexible working practices and employee training arrangements.

In Belgium, nation-wide collective bargaining agreements are negotiated every year and held in a two-year cycle between the employer federations and the union confederations covering all employees. Collective agreements at the industrial/national level set the framework for collective bargaining at the plant and branch levels. Collective agreements occur in a two-year cycle. The sector- and company-level collective agreements are normally registered with the Federal Public Service of Employment, Labour and Social Dialogue (*SPF emploi, travail et concertation sociale*).

Worker participation

There is in both countries a mechanism by which employees at the workplace participate directly or indirectly in deciding on issues that affect them and their organizations, and they have the right to access information and to consultation. Workers' participation at the enterprise level in France started in the late 1930s when the Popular Front introduced employee delegates (*délégués du personnel*) in all enterprises employing 10 workers or more.

In 1945 works committees (*comités d'entreprise*) were established in all companies that employed 50 employees or more. The works committees are made up of workers' representatives elected by all the workers of the enterprise in the same manner as the employee delegates and members of management. The role of the works committees is consultative and advisory and they have very limited decision-making powers. Every enterprise with more than 50 employees has to set up health, safety and improvement of working conditions committees. Where the enterprise has more than 300 employees an employee-training committee has to be set up as well. The committees have the right to be informed about the operations and status of the enterprise in terms of its finances, production, employment, and health and safety. The employer is required by law to meet and consult the members of the committees regularly on the progress of the business's activities and to provide a written annual report to the works committees on the status and performance of the enterprise.

The French Employee Participation Act of August 1982 gave employees the right to have their say on the organization, content and conditions of their work. Employees were expected to be involved directly or through collective bargaining. The process of worker participation normally involves about 15 employees who meet three to four times a year for about two hours. Most of their concerns were to do with the improvement of working conditions. Following the introduction of the act many companies (about 45 per cent) had agreements with unions on workers' participation, making collective bargaining at the local level optional. Despite the popularity of worker participation, collective bargaining by unions has been very much preferred. Similarly, in Belgium the works councils and committees for the protection of employees at the workplace are elected every four years.

Concerning employee representation at board level in France, two or four representatives of the works committees in private sector companies have the right to attend meetings of the board of directors or supervisory board, but their role is consultative and they do not make decisions. In the public sector, however, elected employee representatives compose up to one-third of the members of the board of directors and get involved in making decisions. In Belgium, there is no system for the representation of employees on the management or supervisory boards of private companies. Works councils and workplace health and safety committees provide employee involvement in management at the plant level. In some public sector organizations such as public transport, the railways and universities, employees have representatives on the board of directors.

The European Council of Ministers adopted the European Works Council (EWC) Directive on 22 September 1994 and it was passed into national legislation on 22 September 1996. It stated that any organization that employs at least 1,000 employees within the EU member states should establish a European Works Council (EWC). Those organizations that had in place a system for informing and consulting their employees on transnational matters when the directive was introduced did not have to comply with the strict conditions of the directive (art. 13 agreements). The company that has to have an EWC should first set up by a majority vote an elected special negotiating body (SNB) which is made up of a minimum of 3 and a maximum of 17 members representing all the countries in which the company operates. In Belgium, the EWC members have the same rights as the Enterprise Council (*Conseil d'entreprise*). In France, EWC members are designated from amongst the trade union representatives on the company's works council or national works council. Unlike France, and in response to the European directive on employee involvement to the effect that works councils should be established in companies with more than 50 employees, in Belgium a Royal Decree increased the limit to 100 employees.

Industrial action

In Belgium, although strikes are allowed, the law does not give any indication as to what does or does not constitute legal strike action. It is very often left to the courts to decide whether a strike action is legal or not. Whenever the workers vote for strike action their employers resort to the courts to protest against it and they very often win. There have even been cases when the courts imposed penalties on the strikers. It was not until March 2002 that the Belgian social partners agreed to prioritize social dialogue in the event of any industrial action before resorting to the intervention of the courts. The rate of industrial action since has been very limited but in some cases quite violent. There have been some significant strike actions over the last few years. At the national level, there was a general strike by the General Federation of Labour (FGTB) in autumn 2005 to put pressure on the government to increase unemployment benefits and to maintain the level of employment in the public sector.

In France, although industrial action is less restricted in the private sector than in the public sector, the rate of strikes has been higher in the latter than in the former, and they tend to be violent and lead in some cases to social unrest. However, strikes are today less violent and less effective than they were a decade ago or more. A few years ago it would have been unthinkable for the CGT or the FO to call off a strike without workers getting what they asked for, or at least some of what they asked for, but now it is possible. For example, on 3 October 2005 the Marseille transport authority workers called for strike action to persuade the local authorities not to go ahead with a plan aimed at contracting out public transport services to a private company. However, on 22 November 2005, they voted to end a 46-day strike without having even part of their demands met.

Settlement of industrial disputes

The settlement of industrial disputes in both countries is governed in detail by laws specifying procedures such as conciliation, mediation and arbitration. In

France, the first-instance labour court (industrial tribunal or *conseil de prud'hommes*) is an independent judicial body made up half of the members elected by employees and the other half elected by employers. It deals with all individual and collective cases related to employment contracts. All employee–employer disputes have to be the subject of an initial conciliation phase before a joint conciliation board. The conciliation process does not involve a lawyer or detailed written documentation as the parties represent themselves orally in person. When the case is referred to the industrial tribunal (*prud'hommes*) it becomes fully legal and is treated according to the law. Appeals against the rulings of the *prud'hommes* can be made before the courts of appeal.

In Belgium, as explained above, whenever the workers decide to take industrial action their employers have recourse to the courts to influence the outcome of the action. In response to employers' unilateral applications, the courts very often called off strike action and imposed penalties on the strikers. It was not until 2001 that the Belgian federal government intervened to put an end to the use of unilateral applications by employers, and since 2002 the social partners have agreed on a system of 'concertation' that is based on dialogue rather than referring their case to the courts. Recently, new legislation, the Judicial Code (Amendment) (Mediation) Act of 21 February 2005, was introduced whereby the parties in conflict can go to court, but they can also consider other dispute settlement procedures such as mediation or conciliation.

Summary

1   The Francophone approach to management is heavily influenced by national laws and regulations, EU directives, and global competitive pressures.
2   Management in both Belgium and France is characterized by formalization and bureaucracy, elitism and respect for intellect, strategic awareness, a concern for internal partnership, and empowerment of line managers.
3   The labour markets of both countries exhibit high levels of unemployment, flexible working practices, growth in female employment, and significant levels of employment of immigrant and of older workers.
4   Though the countries use similar selection methods like the use of application forms, interviews, psychometric tests, graphology, assessment centres and references, they differ in their approach and level of application.
5   In both countries there is strong regulation of the process, level and type of training that organizations have to offer.
6   Despite the move towards more individualized payment systems, collective wage agreements are still favoured by trade unions and by organizations that have historically had strong employee relations and a tradition of collective bargaining (notably in the steel and car manufacturing industries).

7   The organization of trade unions in Belgium is historically different from that in France: they tend to be less militant and are more controlled by legally binding collective agreements and employment laws.

Revision questions

Chapter 1 provides a review task designed to consolidate your learning from this chapter. Please see Box 1.2.

In addition, the following questions are designed to help you revise this chapter:

1   As an HR manager of a Chinese company in France, write a report to the company's board of directors in Beijing describing the similarities and the differences in HRM functions (recruitment and selection, training and development, rewards systems, and employee relations) between China and France.
2   Discuss the importance given to the *grandes écoles* in France and then analyse their influence on the processes of recruitment, selection and training, and development of managers.

References

Barsoux, J.L. and Lawrence, P. (1990) *Management in France*, London: Cassell.
Berton, F. and Podevin, G. (1991) 'Vingt ans de formation professionnelle continue: de la promotion sociale à la gestion de l'emploi', *Formation Emploi*, no. 34, Paris: La Documentation Francaise.
Boltanski, L. (1982) *Les Cadres*, Paris: Edition de minuit.
Branine, M. (1999) 'Part-time work in the public health service of Denmark, France and the UK', *The International Journal of Human Resource Management*, 10(3): 411–28.
Brewster, C. and Harris, H. (1999) *International HRM: Contemporary Issues in Europe*, Routledge: London.
Brewster, C. and Hegewisch, A. (eds) (1994) *Policy and Practice in European Human Resource Management*, London and New York: Routledge.
Brewster, C., Mayrhofer, W. and Morley, M. (eds) (2004) *Human Resource Management in Europe: Evidence of Convergence*, London: Elsevier–Butterworth/Heinemann, 123–58.
Buyens, D., Dany, F., Dewettinck, K. and Quinodon, B. (2004) 'France and Belgium: language, culture and differences in human resource practices', in Brewster, C., Mayrhofer, W. and Morley, M. (eds), *Human Resource Management in Europe: Evidence of Convergence?*, London: Elsevier–Butterworth/Heinemann.

Buyens, D. and Wouters, K. (2005) 'Continuing vocational training in Belgian companies: an upward tendency', *Journal of European Industrial Training*, 29(4): 312–35.

Cerdin, Jean-Luc and Peretti, Jean-Marie (2001) 'Trends and emerging values in human resource management in France', *International Journal of Manpower*, 22(3): 216–25.

Dany, F. and Torchy, V. (1994) 'Recruitment and Selection in Europe: Policies, Practices and Methods', in Brewster, C. and Hegewisch, A. (eds), *Policy and Practice in European Human Resource Management: The Price Waterhouse Cranfield Survey*, pp. 68–88, London: Routledge.

Dany, F., Bewettinck, K., Auger, C., Buyens, D. and Wilthagen, T. (2006) 'Deregulation: HRM and the Flexibility-Security nexus. Dilemma's and Trends in the French, Dutch and Belgian labour Markets', in Holt, L.H. and Mayrhofer, W. (eds), *Managing Human Resources in Europe*, London: Routledge.

Dederichs, E. and Köhler, E. (1991) *Part-time Work in the European Community: Laws and Regulations*, European Foundation for the Improvement of Living and Working Conditions, Luxembourg, Office for Official Publications of the European Communities.

Dederichs, E. and Köhler, E. (1993) *Part-time Work in the European Community: The Economic and Social Dimension*, European Foundation for the Improvement of Living and Working Conditions, Luxembourg, Office for Official Publications of the European Communities.

Donnadieu, G. and Denimal, P. (1993) *Classification-Qualification*, Paris: Editions Liaisons.

Dufour, C. and Hege, A. (1997) 'The transformation of French industrial relations: glorification of the enterprise and disaffection on the streets', *European Journal of Industrial Relations*, 3(3): 333–56.

EC (European Commission) (1996) *Equal opportunities for women and men in Europe? Eurobarometer 44.3 – Results of an opinion survey*, Directorate-General for Employment, Industrial Relations and Social Affairs, Unit V/D.5, Luxembourg: Office for Official Publications of the European Communities.

Eurostat, Statistical Office of the European Communities (2007) *Europe in Figures – Eurostat Yearbook 2006–7*, Brussels: the EC.

Eurostat, Statistical Office of the European Communities (2008) *Eurostat Yearbook 2008*, available online at: http://epp.eurostat.ec.europa.eu/portal/page/portal/product_details/publication?p_product_code = KS-CD-07-001, accessed on 6 April 2009.

Goetschy, J. and Jobert, A. (1998) 'Employment relations in France', in Bamber, J.G. and Lansbury, D.R. (eds), *International and Comparative Employment Relations*, 3rd edn, London: Sage, 169–99.

Hocquet, L. (1999) 'Vocational training as a force for equality?: training opportunities and outcomes in France and Britain', *International Journal of Manpower*, 20(3/4): 231–53.

Hofstede, G. (1980) *Culture's Consequences: International Differences in Work Related Values*, London: Sage.

Hofstede, G. (2001) *Culture's Consequences: International differences in work related values*, 2nd edn, London: Sage.

Jenkins, A. and Klarsfeld, A. (2002) 'Understanding "individualization" in human resource management: the case of "skill-based pay" in France', *International Journal of Human Resource Management*, 13(1): 198–211.

Jolivet, A. (2002) 'Active strategies for older workers in France', in Jepsen, M., Foden, D. and Hutsebaut, M. (eds), *Active Strategies for Older Workers,* Brussels: ETUI, 245–75.

Mandin, C. (2003) 'From early retirement to active ageing: the evolution of social policies for older workers in France and Germany', Fourth International Research Conference on Social Security in a Long Life Society, Antwerp, 5–7 May.

Marbach, V. (1999) *Evaluer et rémunérer les compétences,* Paris: Editions d'Organisation.

Muratbekova-Touron, M. (2008) 'From an ethnocentric to a geocentric approach to IHRM: The case of a French multinational company', *Cross Cultural Management: An International Journal,* 15(4): 335–52.

OECD (Organization for Economic Cooperation and Development) (2005a) *Ageing and Employment Policies: France,* OECD Observer, no. 251, Sept. Paris: OECD.

OECD (Organization for Economic Cooperation and Development) (2005b) *Performance-Related Pay Policies for Government Employees,* Paris: OECD.

OECD (Organization for Economic Cooperation and Development) (2009) *OECD Stats Extracts-Trade union density,* available on line at: http://stats.oecd.org/Index.aspx?DataSetCode = UN_DEN, accessed on 13 Sept. 2010.

Roussillon, S. and Bournois, F. (1997) 'Identification and development of potential for management and executive positions in France', *Career Development International,* 2(7): 341–6.

Schramm-Nielsen, J. (2001) 'Cultural dimensions of decision making: Denmark and France compared', *Journal of Managerial Psychology,* 16(6): 404–23.

Schwartzbard, O. (1996) 'La flexibilité par le temps partiel', *Le Monde Initiatives,* supplement no. 15931, 16 April.

Sparrow, P. and Hiltrop, J.M. (1994) *European Human Resource Management in Transition,* London: Prentice-Hall.

Trouvé, P. (1994) 'Managing people in France', in Garrison, T. and Rees, D. (eds), *Managing People Across Europe,* Oxford: Butterworth-Heinemann, 63–91.

Verdier, E. (1994) 'Training and enterprise in France', *International Journal of Manpower,* 15(5): 38–54.

11

Germany and the Netherlands

LEARNING OUTCOMES

The chapter is designed to help you understand, for Germany and the Netherlands:

1   The (a) economic, (b) political and (c) cultural contexts in which managers work;

2   The main trends in the labour market;

3   The typical features of (a) management policies and practices and (b) organizational structure and behaviour;

4   The main policies and practices of human resource management with regard to: (a) recruitment and selection; (b) training and development; (c) rewards and remuneration; and (d) employee relations.

Introduction

The Germanic approach to management is relevant to employment policies and management practices in Germany and the countries around it, including – for reasons of history, economics and labour relations – the Netherlands, parts of Belgium and Switzerland, and even Turkey. This chapter focuses on Germany and the Netherlands, which, despite some socio-economic and political differences, have similar management policies and practices. Germany and the Netherlands were among the six countries that established the European Economic Community (EEC) in 1957 in Rome. They are influential members of the European Union (the institution that has evolved out of the EEC). Both adopted the Euro as their national currency in 2002. (See Table 11.1 for basic statistics.)

Table 11.1 Basic statistical indicators, Germany and the Netherlands

Country	Area (sq km)	Population (July 2010 est.)	Population Growth (2010) %	GDP – real growth rate (2009) %	Inflation rate (2009 est.) %	Workforce (2009 est.) Million	Unemployment rate (2009) %
Germany	357,022	82,329,758	−0.053	−4.9	0.3	43.5	7.5
Netherlands	41,543	16,715,999	0.412	−3.9	1.2	7.754	4.9

Source: CIA World Factbook, 2010.

Contexts: economics, politics and culture

Economics

Germany and the Netherlands are industrialized countries with advanced economies. Both, however, have limited natural resources and therefore need to import raw materials – often from non-European countries. Consequently their economies are highly sensitive to international trade, to changes in world markets, and to international competitive forces. Both countries have a strong international presence, not least through the considerable foreign investment made by their multinational companies. Some of the best-known world-class brands are those belonging to German and Dutch multinational companies.

Though the German economy is dominated by large industrial organizations, the majority of the workforce is employed by small and medium size enterprises (SMEs). Germany is among the world's largest industrial producers of machinery, vehicles, machine tools, cement, steel, chemicals, electronics, food and beverages, and textiles. Its main exports are vehicles, chemicals, metals and manufactures, food products and other finished goods; and its main export partners are France, the US, the UK and other neighbouring countries. The costs of unification of old West and East Germany, the euro problems, and the 'credit crunch' recession have all constrained German economic growth in recent years.

The Netherlands is a major producer of agricultural products. It is third in the world in the export of agricultural products, after only the USA and France. The country's main industries are iron processing, machinery, food processing, electronics, petroleum refining and chemicals. The Netherlands was hard hit by the international financial crisis of 2008 because of its banks' high exposure to US mortgage-backed securities.

Politics

In Germany, the federal president is democratically elected. All political decisions and laws are made in the two chambers of representatives, the *Bundestag* and *Bundesrat*. The *Bundestag*, which is elected democratically, approves legislation, elects the federal chancellor (the head of government) and pursues the activities of the government. The *Bundesrat* represents the federal legislative and administrative system. The current federal republic of Germany comprises 16 federal states. The main political parties in Germany are the Christian Democratic Union (CDU) with Bavaria's Christian Social Union (CSU), the Social Democratic party (SPD), the Free Democratic party (FDP) and the Green party (*Die Grünen*).

The Netherlands is a democratic constitutional monarchy. The monarch does have significant political powers granted by the constitution. The Netherlands comprises 12 self-governing provinces. The monarch appoints the leader of the majority party or leader of a majority coalition as prime minister (i.e. head of the government). The government seeks advice from the national Social Economic Council on economic and social policy matters and consults with the social partners (the trade unions organizations and employers' organizations) on economic, financial, labour market, and employment policies. In the Netherlands no party has held an overall majority in parliament since the start of a parliamentary democracy in 1848. There has always been a coalition government where the Christian Democratic Appeal party (CDA) is always the main partner. The coalition has been either centre-left between the Christian Democrats and the Social Democrats or a centre-right between the Christian Democrats and the Liberals.

Culture

The two countries share many distinctive norms, values and national codes of behaviour. For example, Dutch and the Germans are known for being well organized and for having a strong desire for ordering their time through agendas and on calendars. They have a reputation for punctuality. They are known for their religious and social tolerance, and for their emphasis on self-realization, high moral values and freedom of expression.

The Netherlands is a secular country where it is estimated that more than 42 per cent of the population have no religion. The remaining 58 per cent are divided between Roman Catholic (30 per cent), Dutch Reformed (11 per cent), Calvinist (6.0 per cent), Muslim (5.8 per cent), general Protestant (3.0 per cent) and other faiths (2.2 per cent). The Dutch are known for their liberal and open policies on issues such as the use of drugs, same-sex marriage and euthanasia. In Germany, in contrast, more than two-thirds of the population are religious. It is estimated that more than 68 per cent of the population belong to the Christian faith (Protestants and Roman Catholics). There are also about three million (four per cent of the population) Muslims, mainly from Turkey, Albania and Bosnia. There is also a growing population of Jews as more than 200,000 have moved from the former Soviet Republics to live in Germany since 1991 (OECD, 2010).

ACTIVITY 1

Imagine you are a management consultant advising a Canadian manufacturing company on whether to invest in Germany. Write a report on the German economic, political and cultural context, identifying what factors might attract the Canadian company to invest in Germany.

Labour market trends

Germany is the most populated country in Western Europe, with more than 83 million inhabitants. The minimum working age for full-time employment is 15 and the average number of working hours per week for full-time employment is 36 hours, though this varies according to collective agreements from one organization to another. Most of the increase in the working population since 2001 has been due to the immigration of labour from different countries (Federal Statistical Office, Yearbook, 2004).

The unification of Germany had significant effects on the composition of the labour market. There were major changes in the structure and functioning of organizations in the former East Germany, resulting in mass redundancies, privatization of public sector companies, and a reduction in public spending. Such measures led to a rise in the level of unemployment in the east and urgent needs for vocational/occupational training, redeployment policies and the creation of new job opportunities. As one of the most industrialized countries in the world, Germany has more people employed in industry (29.7 per cent in 2008) than any other OECD state. (See Table 11.2.)

The Netherlands is a small country with a population of just below 17 million people, with a significant workforce of 7.71 million in 2009. The minimum

Table 11.2 Workforce distribution by occupation in 2009 (%), Germany and the Netherlands

Country	Agriculture %	Industry %	Services %
Germany	2.4	29.7	67.8
Netherlands	2.0	23.4	75.6

Source: CIA *World Factbook*, 2010.

working age is 16 years for full-time employment, but those in education at college or university are not allowed to work more than 8 hours per week. A 38-hour working week is the norm but, as in Germany, this varies from one sector to another depending on collective agreements. Overall, the labour markets of both countries have been characterized by a significant level of employment in the industrial sector (see Table 11.2), a relatively low level of unemployment, equal opportunities in employment, an ageing population of employees, increased youth unemployment, and an increasing population of immigrant workers.

Unemployment

Both countries have had relatively low rates of unemployment. After the unification of Germany unemployment increased significantly because of the closing down and privatization of many state-owned companies in East Germany. The number of people out of work in East Germany rose from about 5 per cent in 1990 to 12 per cent in 1991, and then to about 16 per cent by the mid-1990s, whereas in West Germany the unemployment rate increased from about 4 per cent in 1979 to about 8.2 per cent in 1993 (OECD, 1994). Although the rate of unemployment has stabilized over the last 10 years before the 'credit crunch' recession, it remains a real challenge for the German government, which continues to provide subsidies to employers to hire unemployed people through the Federal Employment Office.

Those most affected by rises in unemployment in the Netherlands have been young people under the age of 23. According to the national Central Statistical Office (CBS, 2006) about 14 per cent of all young Dutch people were unemployed in 2005. Young people, especially those with little education and members of ethnic backgrounds, have found it difficult to gain access to the labour market because of their lack of skills and the lack of opportunities for vocational training and apprenticeship. The situation of young people has been worsened by the 'last in, first out' redundancy principle. Under this principle, those employed last (who are very often young people) are the first to be made redundant when redundancies occur.

MINI CASE STUDY 24

Changing the 'Last in, First out' Principle (the Netherlands)

In April 2006, the Dutch government proposed to change the principle of 'last in, first out' by introducing the 'proportion' or 'age balance' principle, which

(Continued)

(Continued)

distributes redundancies over five defined age groups: 15 to 25 years; 25 to 35 years; 35 to 45 years; 45 to 55 years; and 55 years and older. To maintain the age profile of employees in an organization, the number of job losses should be spread across the five age groups. However, employee representatives have objected to the proposal, claiming that the change from the 'last in, first out' would make older employees prone to dismissal and that the new 'age balance' principle would be difficult to explain to the workers. Employers called for more flexibility in the law on redundancies by paying more attention to quality criteria and lowering compensation for dismissals. The unions argued that the Flexibility and Security Act already provided employers with enough leeway to hire employees to work flexibly. In response to older employees' concerns, the government has made early retirement and pre-pension options financially unattractive to older employees in order to make them stay in employment longer than previously.

Questions

1 What are the main reasons for changing the 'last in, first out' principle?
2 Analyse the different points of view here. Which one would you support most and why?

Equal opportunities and diversity

In both Germany and the Netherlands discrimination in employment on the basis of gender, race, colour, nationality, age, disability, and ethnic background is forbidden by law. However, a number of reports have shown that in both countries there are still some differences between men and women in terms of pay and promotion opportunities. According to the German Federal Statistical Office (Destatis), the average monthly income of women in Germany in 2003 was 30 per cent below that of men (Destatis, 2004). The main reason for such differences in pay between men and women is that women are less employed in the upper job categories. Only 15 per cent of female white-collar workers are in top jobs. Also about 60 per cent of men are in blue-collar skilled jobs compared with only 13 per cent of female blue-collar workers (Destatis, 2004).

More recently, the German government has attempted to address the problem by introducing a number of incentives to employers for promoting a positive work–life balance and family-friendly employment policies. The participation of women in the workplace increased from 55.3 per cent in 1995 to 59.6 per cent in 2005, but most of the increase has been in part-time employment, as the rate of female part-time employment increased from 37.2 to 45.8 per cent over the same time (Eurostat, 2007).

In the Netherlands, the Equal Opportunities Law 1994 provided for the implementation of a plan to promote the participation of women in the labour market and to reduce the imbalance between men and women in employment, training and promotions. For example, it stipulated that there should be a women's officer in all organizations that have 200 employees or more, and prohibited any kind of sex discrimination in the workplace and any type of job advertisement that is gender specific. It also stipulated equal pay for work of equal value. The Dutch government has also attempted to eliminate pay inequalities between men and women, between Dutch nationals and employees from minority groups, and between full-time and part-time employees, by introducing in December 2004 an equal pay checklist at the organizational level.

The participation of women in the Dutch labour market is one of the highest in the European Union. It rose from 39 per cent in 1990 to 63.5 per cent in 2000 and to 66.4 per cent in 2005 (Eurostat, 2007). The proportion of women holding part-time jobs is also one of the highest in Europe. The number of women working part-time increased from 68.6 per cent in 1995 to 74.7 per cent in 2005 (Eurostat, 2007). The number of men in part-time work is about 15 per cent, but is also the highest in Europe, and consists mainly of students and older people.

Older versus younger workers

Both Germany and the Netherlands have a growing population of older people, but at the same time have experienced increased youth unemployment. The median age in Germany in 2009 was 43.8 years and the number of older people (65 or over) is on the rise, representing about 20.3 per cent of the overall population (see Table 11.3). In the Netherlands, the number of older people is also significant. The median age is about 40 years and population growth is 0.46 per cent. It is estimated that about 15 per cent of the population are above the age of 65 (CIA World Factbook, 2010). The governments of both countries have introduced legislation in order to address the problem. For example, the

Table 11.3 Age structure (%) (2009), Germany and the Netherlands

Country	0–14 years %	15–64 years %	Over 65 %	Median age (years)	Life expectancy at birth (for men and women)
Germany	13.7	66.1	20.3	44.3	79.26
Netherlands	17.4	67.7	14.9	40.8	79.4

Source: CIA *World Factbook*, 2010.

Social and Economic Council of the Netherlands presented in September 2006 a recommendation entitled *Welfare Growth By and For Everyone* giving priority to a rise in employment as the best response to problems of a growing number of older people in society. It estimated that in the education sector alone more than 60,000 jobs would become available over the next 10 years because of teachers retiring. Older people, it posited, also create new jobs in the health-care and public services sectors.

Similarly, in 2006 the German government called upon employers and trade union organizations to engage in collective agreements in order to improve the working conditions and prospects of older workers, especially after announcing that the age of retirement is to be increased from 65 to 67 from 2010. It is estimated that the German population will fall by 12.5 per cent from 80 million in 1991 to 70 million by 2030 (Ulrich, 1997). The number of people over 65 will make up about 26 per cent of the population. By contrast, the number of young people under the age of 15 will fall from 15.5 per cent in 1991 to 12.8 per cent by 2030, and those between the ages of 15 to 65 will decline from 69.1 per cent to 60.5 per cent (see Ulrich, 1997). Therefore, in order to encourage those aged 55 and over to stay in employment or to return to employment, the German government launched the '50-plus Initiative' in 2006. The initiative restricted the duration of unemployment benefits for those under the retirement age to 18 months and granted companies that hire employees aged 50 or over with a subsidy of between 20 to 40 per cent of the wage for a duration of two years if the employment lasts for at least one year (Stettes, 2006). Overall, the proportion of employed people made up of older people (over 65 years old) increased steadily from 1995 to 2005: in Germany it went up from 37.7 per cent in 1995 to 45.4 per cent in 2005, while in the Netherlands it rose faster from 28.9 per cent to 46.1 per cent over the same period (Eurostat, 2007). However, according to the recent OECD Employment Outlook document (2007), the employment ratio of older persons in both Germany and the Netherlands is still lower than the European average.

ACTIVITY 2

Answer the following questions in the light of what you have read in this chapter so far:

1 List the advantages and the disadvantages of employing older people.
2 What are the main reasons for the rise in youth unemployment?
3 What would you suggest the governments of the two countries do to create job opportunities for both young and old people?

Immigrant workers

According to the United Nations Population Fund UNFPA, Germany has the third highest number of migrants in the world, as it hosts about 10 million of all 191 million migrants world wide (UNFPA, 2006). The largest community of foreign workers in Germany is of Turkish origin with about 2.3 million workers (Bernstein, 2006). The German government decided to restrict entry of immigrants from the new member states of Central and Eastern Europe (the Czech Republic, Estonia, Latvia, Lithuania, Hungary, Poland, Slovenia and Slovakia) until 2011. In the Netherlands , although the government initially (in 2004) restricted entry to workers from the new member states, there were by 2005 only about 30,000 workers from these countries, mainly employed in the agriculture, construction and manufacturing sectors. When the economy started to show comfortable growth the Dutch government decided to open its borders to Eastern European workers from 1 May 2006 in order to meet the demands for labour in agriculture, metal-working, health care, retailing, hotels and restaurants.

Management and organization

The Germanic approach to management is described by Eichenberg and Wiskemann (1997: 125) as an integrated model where 'each manager has responsibility for the personnel function and obtains advice specifically related to a particular situation, should the need arise'. They refer to companies such as Audi AG and BMW as having since the 1980s developed integrated management approaches that recognize the importance of personnel policy to technical operations. Many studies describe the Germanic approach to management as integrated, strategic and participative, as explained next.

Integrated management

The integration of management functions with corporate strategy is manifested in many German and Dutch companies. For example, the HR department typically plays a significant role in the general administration of the organization and in the strategy formulation process. It is estimated that about 80 per cent of HR departments involve line managers in their activities (Dietz et al., 2004). The responsibility for training in most organizations is solely that of line managers. In most German organizations it is the middle managers, or those in the lower management board (*Vorstand*), who run the day-to-day operations and implement strategic decisions. The role of the upper management or supervisory board (*Aufsichtsrat*) is to oversee the performance of the organization and does not interfere at the operational level (Garrison and Rees, 1994: 59).

Strategic management

Under the Germanic approach to management, managers at all levels are strategically aware of the needs of their employees and their organizations. Their integrated approach to managing enables them to get access to other units or departments and to become more aware of the different activities and of those who carry them out. The significant elements of that strategic awareness in relation to human resource management are company-led continuous training and the promotion of flexible working practices to attract and retain needed employees who would have left the organization if such flexibility had not been an option. Flexible working practices such as part-time, temporary and casual work have been pursued positively by many companies in both Germany and the Netherlands.

Over the 1980s and the 1990s part-time employment increased in both countries. The Dutch economy has been labelled the 'first part-time economy' in the world (Visser and Hemmerijck, 1997, in Horgan, 2003). As a result of the high level of flexible working in the Netherlands, the Dutch government introduced in July 1998 a new employment act governing temporary employment agencies, and in January 1999 the Flexibility and Security Act, both designed to clarify the rights of temporary workers and to protect them from exploitation by their employers. They also offer workers on temporary contracts the prospects for gaining full-time employment if they have worked temporarily for a long period. Also the Part-Time Employment Act 2000 gives part-time workers the right to increase or decrease the number of their working hours, and their employers cannot object unless on grounds of specific conflicting business interests. Part-time work in the Netherlands is by no means confined to married women who have to combine work and family commitments: it is taken by men and women at all levels. Thus flexible working practices have been used strategically to attract women and men who needed to work flexibly, not just during the period of economic hardship to reduce costs.

Participative management (co-determination)

The Germanic approach to management is participative and empowering. The law provides for a system of works councils with broad powers on a wide range of enterprise-level policy and practice, with employee representation from the work unit to the supervisory board. Co-determination (or 'self-determination' in the Netherlands) is implemented through works councils elected by all employees in an organization, creating two representative bodies, works councils and trade unions, at the workplace level. The works council members are elected directly by secret ballot by the employees of an organization, possibly in consultation with the unions. The council may form committees for fulfilling certain functions. In some cases the works councils are also the trade unions, but in most cases they are two separate and complementary bodies. The council has:

1   The right of consent for any decision on labour-related matters except in cases where the matter concerned is already agreed by a collective bargaining agreement. Such matters include working hours and holidays, payment systems and job evaluation schemes, bonus rates and performance-related pay, health and safety at work, and other work related policies.
2   The right to prior consultation on operational and business matters such as the expansion or change of activities, new investments, and the integration or transfer of control of operations as in mergers and takeovers.
3   The right to access to information such as financial statements, levels of income and output, employment levels, etc., and to have regular meetings with management to give feedback on activities and to get more information when needed. They can also demand company-wide information on job opportunities and have to be informed in writing about applicants who are being considered for a job.

Managing human resources

In the Germanic approach to management, the director of personnel or the HR manager does not have a prominent role on the board of directors. However, this does not imply that the function of HRM is not considered to be strategic. On the contrary, the personnel/HR function is very strategic to the extent that it is the responsibility of every manager in the organization. HRM strategy is considered to be part of corporate strategy and is in many organizations formalized in writing. Human resource management issues are very often brought into high-level discussions through the works councils and employee directors (Muller, 1999a,b).

Recruitment and selection

The process of recruitment and selection in Germany and the Netherlands is more regulated than in those of the Anglo-Saxon countries. Equal opportunities legislation has to be considered at all stages of a recruitment and selection process. In Germany, the Federal Labour Department (*Bundessanstalt für Arbeit*) exercises a monopoly on the allocation of labour and is responsible for the labour market policies at the federal level, while the local labour offices of the individual states (*Länder*) are responsible for employment at the local level. In other words, the process of recruitment and selection is centralized in theory, but decentralized in practice. Individual employers have a lot of freedom in recruiting and employing the workers they need, but they operate according to the national policies on labour allocation and adhere to all policies on equal opportunities. Human resource planning is carried out by most of the large organizations, as is job analysis. The use of HR consultants is very limited and only confined to specific professional activities such as advising on job specifications or giving feedback on specific employment contracts and employment conditions (Blum, 1994). Although the two countries have similar approaches to recruitment and selection, they differ in the level and types of methods used, as explained below.

Recruitment

In Germany, the process of recruitment is carried out according to guidelines set by the Federal Labour Department which require employers to state where and why a particular employee has to be recruited, how the employee should be recruited (Eichenberg and Wiskemann, 1997) and whether they will be recruited internally. The works councils play a significant role in the recruitment process as mentioned earlier. They normally insist on the internal advertising of all vacancies and on giving priority to recruiting internal candidates (Faulkner et al., 2002). When the management refuses to recruit internally and does not give genuine reasons for doing so, the works councils may refuse to approve the new appointments. When this happens, the management may consider a compromise solution to transfer employees from other plants or departments of the plant. Transfers are very often used, especially when jobs are threatened in other plants and departments. Recruiting from external sources is considered only when internal recruitment or transfer are neither viable nor available. Over the last 10 years many German companies have had to resort to external recruitment in the pursuit of certain skilled and talented employees. They advertise in targeted newspapers and recruit directly from universities. Since 1994, private employment agencies have been allowed to help companies to recruit employees externally and this has reduced the monopoly of the federal labour agencies in the labour market.

In the Netherlands, as well as the works councils playing a similar role to their German counterparts, all employers are obliged to comply with the Privacy Code of Conduct for Recruitment and Selection which was introduced in 2004 and published in the Dutch Government Gazette (30 July 2004). The code lists the purposes for which employers may gather and process data on potential applicants and specifies the rights of the applicants vis-à-vis the protection of their personal data. It also lists the types of data that can be collected on the potential applicant. It states that in addition to the usual contact details, data can be collected and processed on the applicant's nationality, place of birth, civil status, training courses attended, training acquired, current employment specifications as well as possible future qualifications, employment history, work experience and income, references and recommendations.

Selection

In both countries, a number of tests, such as aptitude, intelligence and personality tests, as well as interviews and assessment centres are often used. The works councils have the right to decide on the content of the tests. Psychometric tests and assessment centres are used more often in the Netherlands than in Germany. Application forms are used more in the Netherlands than in Germany, while references are used more in Germany than in the Netherlands (Dietz et al., 2004). The most commonly used method of selection is the interview. Most of the German companies restrict themselves to a two-step selection procedure that starts with the evaluation of application documents and then interviewing the applicant, but the process is subject to a number of legal considerations, as explained earlier. For example, an employer is not allowed to ask an applicant if she is pregnant, as this is against the principle of equal opportunities (except when the nature of the work may harm the health of a pregnant woman). For managerial and professional positions, both German and Dutch employers select their employees on the basis of specialist credentials such as the subjects studied, the nature of training and the nature of previous job experience. Often managers are required to have engineering qualifications and extensive vocational education.

Training and development

In both Germany and the Netherlands, employers are expected to have training plans and to give employees the opportunity to be trained in order to enhance their career opportunities. Employees are expected to use the opportunity given to them to improve their knowledge and skills. The law allows the workers to seek short- and long-term official leaves of absence for training. In an increasing older society, training is made available to older as well as younger employees in order to provide equal opportunities for all to meet the changing demands in the labour market. Germany spends more than €70 billion per annum on education alone. Some organizations spend up to 5 per cent of their wage bill on training. Similarly the Dutch employers spend between 3 and

5 per cent of their annual wage bills on training and development. On average, both German and Dutch employees spend about 5 days per annum on training (Dietz et al. 2004).

Education

The Germans and the Dutch are well educated and literate. In Germany, for example, more than 80 per cent of the population had completed at least upper secondary education by 2000 (Eurostat, 2002). The Germans value both general and vocational education and pay serious attention to the development of transferable skills from in education system. The standards of public education are very high and all public education is free and compulsory for the first 9 or 10 years. The German federal states are normally responsible for education at all levels. After four years of primary education, pupils enter one of the four types of secondary school:

1   the *Gymnasium* prepares the most gifted pupils for university studies;
2   the *Realschule* provides intermediary education in a variety of subjects to pupils for entry into polytechnics and institutes;
3   the *Hauptschule* provides the pupils with a wide range of vocational education opportunities; and
4   the *Gesamtschule* is a comprehensive school, similar to any British public high school, combines all of the above.

Normally the pupils go through an orientation phase during their fifth and sixth forms in order to guide them to choose the type of secondary school they attend according to their abilities, needs and achievements. Higher education was also free in the public sector until recently and is normally delivered in academic universities and special institutes and centres (*Fachhochschulen*). Normally universities provide traditional scientific education while the *Fachhochschulen* provide applied scientific education (Blum, 1994). Recent education reform legislation introduced a fee of around €500 per semester per student in all sectors of higher education from October 2006. To get access to university education, students have to have either a diploma from a vocational school or pass the *Abitur* (like the French *baccalaureat* or UK A-levels equivalent) examination. To get access to *Fachhochschulen* the student should have completed 12 years of full-time school education as well as some vocational training. Before the 1980s nearly everyone who passed the *Abitur* had access to an institution of higher education, but over the last 20 years or so entry into higher education has become more competitive.

In the Netherlands there are public and private schools (the latter are mainly Christian although there are some Muslim, Jewish, and non-religious schools). Primary and secondary school education is compulsory and is free. Children attend school from the age of 5 to 18, but in the last two years they are only asked to attend part-time while undertaking vocational training. The education system is divided into Catholic, Protestant and denominational primary and secondary school. Primary school education (*basisschool*) lasts 7 years (5–12) and secondary school education lasts 6 years (12–18). University and higher vocational education takes 4 years and students are introduced to a range of transferable skills and academic knowledge leading to a particular occupation. Most of the higher education institutions (universities and colleges) are state-owned and the education is virtually free. Many Dutch pupils pursue their education after high school to go on to vocational training or attend a university course.

Vocational training

In both Germany and the Netherlands, vocational training is part of the general education system. Workforce at all levels are encouraged to acquire transferable skills to increase their employability with a view to being accepted or retained as full-time core workforce. Vocational training is a joint venture between the employer and the state, and comprises a combination of on-the-job training and theoretical back-up in the classroom, leading to the award of nationally recognized certificates. In Germany, pupils follow a 2- to 3-year vocational training programme after the junior secondary school (*Berufsschulen*) to be prepared for a profession or a skilled occupation. There are also intermediate technical schools (ITS), the *Berufsfachschulen*, higher technical schools (HTS), the *Fachoberschule*, and advanced vocational schools (*Berufsaufbauschule*) which provide full-time and part-time vocation-specific programmes of between 12 to 36 months. Young people undertake their practical training on the job whilst attending intensive vocational training courses that provide them with the theoretical underpinnings of what they do at the workplace. This way they are well prepared for working life.

Vocational education is characterized by dualism as it combines classroom study with a work-related apprenticeship. The *Duale Ausbildung* is a special apprenticeship initiative that permits students in vocational education to study in a public school while working and learning in a company. In this respect Dickmann (2003) remarks that the skilled German worker (*Facharbeiter*) is seen as a national competitive advantage.

Many apprentice-trained employees get the chance to be trained for higher-level positions as supervisors or technicians (Finegold et al., 2000). When employees are recruited, they sign a training contract as apprentices. These contracts are registered and supervised by the Chamber of Trade and Commerce, which is normally responsible for both the content and implementation of vocational training. Data on further training and education issued by the German Federal Statistical Office on 27 April 2004 showed that between April 2002 and May 2003, about 5.1 million employees (14 per cent) participated in formal, primarily job-related, training courses. It was found that employees with a degree from a university or a university of applied sciences (*Fachhochschulen*) were most likely to take job-related further training (Federal Statistical Office, 2004). This confirms other studies' findings (Bellmann and Leber, 2003) that the more qualified German employees are, the more formal job-related further training they undertake. It was also found that, besides formal job-related training, many employees used informal means by engaging in 'self-study' to improve their job-related knowledge and skills. They used the internet widely and visited institutions such as libraries, exhibitions and museums as well as using radio, television, audio and video media and self-learning computer programmes. Moreover, most of the major German companies have their own training facilities, with smaller companies collaborating to establish joint training centres. According to a survey of 785 firms conducted by the Cologne Institute for Business Research (IW), in 2004, it was found that many companies thought that the skills of many young people were not good enough to meet their growing needs for skilled workers (IW, 2004). Therefore, the German government and employers' organizations agreed in June 2004 to a pact that commits employers to creating new opportunities for training the less-qualified young people who are currently unemployable.

As in Germany, vocational training in the Netherlands is widespread. Research conducted by the Institute for Labour Studies in the Netherlands (OSA, 2006) found that between 2002 and 2004, about 50 per cent of highly educated employees attended training courses. The Dutch government provides financial assistance for vocational training and retraining of both skilled and unskilled employees. Employers obtain grants from the government for approved training courses by covering the wage costs of workers during training, their tuition fees, and all expenses.

Management development in Germany and the Netherlands tends not to focus on functional and company-specific programmes to help in the retention of managers. Often managers have an engineering background and, unlike in the USA, most of them do not have an MBA. Although a significant number of German and Dutch students study for the European MBAs, the availability of such management development programmes at home is very limited. However, Randlesome (1994) reported that 53 per cent of top German managers expressed their desire for the MBA because of its international reputation.

MINI CASE STUDY 25

The German Training Levy

The Cologne Institute for Business Research (*Institut der deutschen Wirtschaft Köln*, IW) published in April 2004 the findings of a survey of companies' views on a new training levy proposed by the government. The government wanted all employers with at least 10 workers, excluding the casuals, whose number of in-house vocational trainees is less than 7 per cent of the total workforce, to pay a levy, if the overall number of training places available in the country is according to the federal government not enough to meet business demands. The findings show that 68 per cent of the 1,018 employers surveyed did not support the proposal. They said that it would not have the effects that the government expected and it would increase labour costs and bureaucracy. Even the companies in industries that already trained more apprentices than they needed, such as metal-working, electrical, construction and craft, rejected it. Despite its being rejected by employers, the German parliament voted in favour of it in May 2004 in order to reduce shortages of apprenticeships for young people entering the labour market. The levy was to be imposed unless German companies as a whole provided 15 per cent more apprenticeships than there were applicants. Consequently the proposed legislation was put on hold following a deal in June 2004 to commit employers to create new training opportunities. (Adapted from www.eiro.eurofound.europa.eu/2004/06/feature/de0406107f.html, accessed on 11 Jan. 2007.)

Questions

1 Discuss the main reasons for the introduction of the training levy.
2 To what extent is the employers' opposition to the imposition of the new levy justified?
3 How effectively would you expect the levy to solve the problem of shortages of trained young people? How and why?

Rewards and remuneration

In both Germany and the Netherlands, rewards and remuneration are normally based on national/federal collective and plant agreements. In most cases the forms and levels of remuneration are influenced by federal collective agreements because a large number of German and Dutch employees are affected by collective bargaining agreements concluded at the national level. Both countries have a compressed wage distribution where the ratio between the top and the lowest levels of pay is around 2.5 per cent, which is low in comparison with other industrialized countries such as the UK, with 3.4, the US, with 4.5, and France, with 3.08 (OECD, 2001). The distinction in pay between blue-collar workers, white-collar workers, and managerial staff still exists, but many large companies such as the German company Audi have moved, mainly through collective agreements, to a unified remuneration system that treats the blue- and white-collar workers equally. Wage and salary rates that are collectively agreed are set as minimum rates of pay, for the different pay scales that exist in each sector and plant. Individual employees are paid on a scale according to qualifications, skills, experience and performance. Skills are highly rated and employees with the highest skills are the highest paid. The value placed on human resources in the Germanic approach to management is reflected in comparatively high rates of pay and suggests that employees are viewed as a valuable asset and not a costly production factor (Hollinshead and Leat, 1995: 185). Works councils have the right to be involved in collective agreements and decisions related to the remuneration of employees at the plant level.

ACTIVITY 3

On 21 September 2004, the Dutch government introduced a number of measures that were aimed at improving the state of a declining economy. Such measures included a wage freeze for civil servants in 2005, tightening the eligibility requirements for disability benefits by distinguishing between completely and partially disabled, tightening the eligibility requirements for unemployment benefits by asking those who claim unemployment benefits to have worked 39 weeks of the preceding 52 weeks to be eligible, making early retirement schemes accessible only for workers who were 57 or older from 1 January 2006, and making 'golden handshake' payments to dismissed employees deductible from their subsequent unemployment benefits.

The announcement of such measures sparked trade union outrage. After a series of wage negotiations accompanied by a wave of strikes in 2005, the social partners agreed in July 2006 to increase wages by an average of 3 per cent.

Questions

1 If the new measures were good for the economy why were the trade unions (as social partners) outraged?
2 What would be the arguments for and against introducing such measures in times of economic downturn?

The minimum wage

Unlike many other industrialized countries there is no statutory general minimum wage in Germany, although the debates on introducing one have been ongoing for a number of years. There is a collectively agreed *de facto* minimum wage that differs from one sector to another and from one industry to another and is usually applied to low-paid jobs and in specific sectors of the economy such as construction, roofing, painting and the demolition industry. The main reason for not introducing a general statutory minimum wage is the negative effects that it may have on the economy. For example, a study by the German Institute for Work and Technology (*Institut Arbeit und Technik*, IAT, 2006) found that if a minimum wage of €7.50 per hour had to be introduced about 4.6 million employees (14.6 per cent of the workforce) would be entitled to a pay rise, resulting in an overall increase in labour costs of between 10 to 12 billion euros.

In the Netherlands there is a statutory minimum wage set through collective agreements each year in line with a percentage based on indexation, as stated in article 14 of the Minimum Wage and Minimum Holiday Allowance Act. There is a lower rate for younger workers under the age of 23 and a higher rate for those above the age of 23. Those at the age of 15 (minimum working age) receive about 30 per cent of an adult's wage while those at the age of 22 receive about 85 per cent of an adult's wage. In most cases the collectively agreed wages have been on average higher than the statutory minimum wages for both young and adult workers. In 2008 the government came under pressure to increase the minimum wage to 1,357 Euros per month (Eurostat, 2009).

Allowances and benefits

In both Germany and the Netherlands, employees enjoy a variety of benefits and allowances. All companies are required by law to provide their staff with sick pay, holiday pay, travelling allowances, child-care allowances, career break schemes, company doctors, etc. Such allowances have become more individualized as collective bonuses and benefits are disappearing and being replaced by performance-related pay.

Performance-related pay

Performance-related pay is being used increasingly by employers in both Germany and the Netherlands, but slightly more in the latter than in the former. In Germany it is used very often for clerical staff, while in the Netherlands it is traditionally used for those in managerial and professional positions. It is estimated that more than 80 per cent of organizations in the Netherlands, but only about 50 per cent in Germany, use performance appraisal at all levels (Dietz et al., 2004: 86). The low level of performance appraisal in Germany reflects the low level in the use of performance-related pay because pay is still widely determined through collective agreements. Even in the Netherlands, where the level of use of performance appraisal is high, it is often used for non-payment purposes. In addition, performance appraisal is very often used for developmental purposes such as the identification of training needs. For example, in November 1997, the Dutch employers' and employees' representatives agreed that pay could be adjusted to reflect employees' performance only in sectors and organizations where this is considered to be important. They could not agree on the use of performance-related pay for all types of jobs because they interpreted the issue of pay for performance differently. The employers argued that performance-related pay would replace structural annual wage increases, while trade unions saw the issue of pay for performance or merit pay as a supplement to the regular annual pay rises that were agreed through collective bargaining. Thus in both Germany and the Netherlands, pay is still determined mainly through collective agreements. Performance appraisal is very often used for developmental rather than pay purposes. The use of performance-related pay has increased but is still limited to certain clerical, managerial and professional jobs.

Employee relations

As explained earlier in the chapter, employee relations in both countries are characterized by social partnership. At the national level, employee relations issues are dealt with in line with the EU regulations and are agreed collectively between the social partners. The laws on employee relations in both countries are very much in line with the European directives. For example, the 2002 EU Information and Consultation Directive has had very little effect on the German or Dutch system of employee relations as their Works Councils Acts already covered most of the issues contained in the directive. At the industrial and organizational level employee relations have traditionally been based on a dualistic system of employee representation, where employers' associations and trade unions determine the basic minimum standards and benefits, while at the plant (local) level management and the works councils regulate the application of the agreements. In theory, it seems that trade unions and the works councils perform similar roles, but in practice they have remained fundamentally distinct. There has also been some kind of unwritten law, as custom and practice have differentiated between the role of trade unions and that of the works council. Historically trade unions have dealt with collective agreements over wages and salaries, working time, working conditions, and all aspects of employee–employer relationships that are not clearly determined by law. The role of the works councils, on the other hand, is to look after the welfare of a company's employees and to promote the interests of the company as a whole.

Trade unions

The history of trade unionism in Germany goes back to the 1848 Revolution. However, it was not until after the First World War, during the Weimar Republic, that the unions became widely accepted (Fürstenberg, 1998). However, unions were abolished between 1933 and 1945 during Hitler's National Socialism. After the Second World War, trade unions became legally recognized again and played a significant role in the development and industrialization of Germany. Trade union membership reached its peak in the 1970s at about 35 per cent. The economic recession of the 1980s contributed to the decline in trade union membership. After reunification in 1990, the German unions began to organize themselves in the new federal states, but this has had no considerable effects on the overall membership figures. About 27 per cent of the German workers were trade union members in 2006 (Eurostat, 2007).

Trade unions in Germany take a more cooperative approach with management and tend to focus on employee welfare and working conditions issues. Their objectives go beyond the workplace to include activities such as economic planning (Hollinshead and Leat, 1995), work organization, technological change and adult education activities. According to Fürstenberg (1998: 214), 'the resulting concentration on social and economic issues and the independence from political parties marks a decisive difference when compared with employment relations in France or Italy, for example'.

The role of the Dutch trade unions is similar to that of the German unions but their membership has changed in contrasting ways. For example, trade union membership increased by 7.2 per cent between 1993 and 2003, while in Germany it declined by 23.9 per cent over the same time (Eurostat, 2005). It can be seen from Table 11.4 that trade union density has been in decline since 1999 in both countries. It should be noted that most members of trade unions are older workers in full-time employment (OECD, 2009).

Table 11.4 Trade union density 1999–2007 (%), Germany and the Netherlands

Country	1999	2000	2001	2002	2003	2004	2005	2006	2007	2008
Germany	25.3	24.6	23.7	23.5	23	22.2	21.6	20.7	19.9	19.1
Netherlands	24.6	22.6	21.9	21.7	21.2	21.3	21	20.4	19.8	18.9

Source: OECD, 2009.

Works councils

As explained earlier, the practices of co-determination in Germany and self-determination in the Netherlands through works councils and supervisory boards are a strategic feature of the Germanic approach to management. According to Fürstenberg (1998), the main characteristics of works councils are:

1　They represent all employees, unionized and non-unionized, and both the blue-collar and the white-collar employees;
2　They have the right to information, consultation and co-determination;
3　They cannot take industrial action or call a strike; and
4　They get involved in deciding on a wide range of issues such as daily working hours and breaks, the fixing of piece rates, pay systems, works discipline, temporary short-term or overtime work, holiday schedules, personnel selection, occupational training, technological change, welfare services, safety regulations, and housing for employees.

Employee direct involvement in Germany goes back to the time of First World War when in 1916 works councils were set up in industries that were seen to be important for the economy. According to the Co-determination Act 1976, all public limited companies with more than 2,000 employees must have supervisory boards consisting of 50 per cent shareholder representatives and 50 per cent employee representatives. The chair of the supervisory board is usually a representative of the shareholders and has the deciding vote in the event of a tie. In smaller public limited companies with between 501 and 2,000 employees, the latter have a right to one-third of the supervisory board members. In Germany, the works councils have 'rights of consent' (article 27 of the 1971 Works Councils Act) over any decision made by management on labour-related matters unless agreed by collective bargaining with the trade unions (para. 3, art. 27). Employment problems such as protection against dismissal, allocation of workers to jobs, or entitlement to fringe benefits, are processed through the legal framework provided by the works council constitution act (*Betriebsverfassungsgesetz*) and general labour laws.

According to a report by a special commission on Germany's system of co-determination issued in November 2004, the co-determination system had to change because of increased international competitive pressures on German companies, and the increased influence of EU legislation. The German co-determination system was found to represent an obstacle to foreign investment, especially to companies that do not have experience in dealing with employee direct involvement in decision-making. Most American companies are sceptical of works councils. Moreover, it was found that the co-determination system had to be adapted to the legal framework conditions at the European level, especially the European Company Statute and its accompanying employee involvement directive. The commission suggested some changes to the scope and nature of co-determination rights at both company and workplace levels, but the proposals were rejected by the Confederation of German Trade Unions (DGB), and as a result the changes were never implemented.

In June 2004, the German government passed a bill on the establishment of European Companies in line with the EU Council Regulations on the Statute for a European Company. The law gives the German companies the choice between either the two-tier system of corporate governance that is already established in Germany (with separation between a management board and a supervisory board), or a system whereby there is a single board of directors. Those companies that choose the first option for establishing a European Company have fewer requirements for co-determination than those of German public limited companies. The law also established that foreign company subsidiaries in Germany will not have to conform to German company law in the future, and that in cases of cross-border mergers and takeovers the most comprehensive form of co-determination should apply to the newly formed company.

In the Netherlands the first Works Councils Act 1950 made the employer a member and the chair of the works council in the organization. The act, which was amended in 1971, 1979 and 1998, makes it compulsory for a works council to be set up in all public and private sector and in the profit- and non-profit-making organizations that employ 100 or more employees, or at least 35 employees for more than one-third of normal working hours. A supervisory board is also set up in large companies. The government announced in June 2004 that the Works Council Act had to be replaced by a new Employee Involvement Act in line with the EU directives on information and consultation and on employee involvement in the European Company Statute. It argued that the new legislation would make employee involvement more flexible and more effective in continuing the ongoing process of decentralized collective agreements. It was expected to increase the level of employee self-determination at the workplace.

Consequently, in October 2004 the new legislation was introduced. It changed the role of works councils in nominating members of supervisory boards in large companies with shareholder equity of at least €16 million and a workforce of at least 100 employees. The Dutch government attempted to increase the level of self-determination by giving employers and employees an opportunity to determine the structure of employee involvement in their own organizations. The Social and Economic Council (SER) became responsible for the introduction of a national body to monitor and promote the quality of employee involvement and for the organization of arbitration in disputes between employers and works councils, replacing the existing joint sectoral committees.

ACTIVITY 4

In October 2005 a new independent trade union (the Alternative Trade Union, AVV) aimed at representing young workers and freelancers was established in Holland. The AVV claimed that the conventional trade unions and employers had been concerned with the interests of older workers and ignored those of young workers. They explained that collective agreements had been concerned with issues such as early retirement, pensions and dismissal protection and ignored issues of succession planning, career development, freelancers' rights, and many others. They also argued that young employees (below the age of 55) had been paying for older ones (above the age of 55) who wish to retire early. They claim that the longer the older workers continue to work the better it is for younger workers.

Question

1 Discuss the main reasons for the introduction of the young workers' trade union. How justified was the decision?

Collective bargaining

The legal framework for collective bargaining in Germany is provided by the German Collective Agreements Act 1949. The act states that only trade unions have the right to conclude collective agreements with either employers' associations or individual employers. Collective bargaining is conducted at regional and industry levels and is generally regarded as a rather centralized procedure that is carried out through association-level agreements at sectoral level. The process, which is highly formalized, ends in most cases in satisfactory collective agreements that become legally binding and apply to all employees, regardless of whether they are union or non-union members, in the particular sector. Most collective agreements are for a short term of a one year duration and cover issues such as working hours, pay, absences, and working conditions, and they usually affect both white- and blue-collar workers (Fürstenberg, 1998). It was not until the 1990s that collective agreements started to move from the centre to become more decentralized at the plant level. Recently some companies, mainly from Eastern Germany, have refused to negotiate through the employer associations and have bargained with the unions directly.

A significant development in the system of collective bargaining in Germany has been the widespread conclusion of opening clauses within industry (sector) agreements. Most of these sectoral agreements include a number of opening clauses that enable the employers to move away from collectively agreed issues such as pay, working time or other working conditions which were initially allowed only in conditions of serious economic difficulties that could result in the company closing down. They are being extended not to prevent the company from possible closure but to save employees jobs and sustain the company's competitive advantage. As well as the move towards collectively agreed opening clauses there has also been a growth in the number of so-called company pacts for competitiveness and employment, leading to the emergence of a new form of company-level employee relations. According to a survey by the German Institute of Economic and Social Research (WSI, 2005), about 75 per cent of companies covered by collective agreements made use of one or more opening clauses. However, the survey found also that the majority of works councils (88 per cent of those surveyed) were not in favour of decentralized collective bargaining. A study of the use, distribution and impact of opening clauses in collective agreements (Kohaut and Schnabel, 2006) found that opening clauses had largely been used to avoid collectively agreed working time standards but they had been applied less frequently to reduce wages.

In the Netherlands, most collective bargaining agreements are primarily at the sector level, as only a small number of employers conclude agreements at the company level. Collective agreements are generally legally binding and cover all workers of a particular sector. They may be concluded only between an association of employees that meets the legal requirements of an association on the one hand, and an employer or association of employers on the other hand. The Collective Agreement Act (WCAO) was issued in 1927 and hardly changed until 2002. The recent developments are:

1   The extension of collective agreements to include employees who are non-trade unions members, so that they also benefit from the terms and conditions of employment agreed with the unions.
2   The decentralization of collective bargaining from the sector-wide to the company level. The decentralization of collective bargaining has led to the emergence of three layers of collective bargaining: a) those on issues that are agreed at the central or sector-wide levels; b) those that apply only to specific sub-sectors for specific provisions; and c) those that are company-specific agreements. Moreover, individual workers' agreements have also been allowed in what is called 'cafeteria' agreements on issues such as part-time work, early retirement, leave entitlement, and so on. As in Germany, some companies in the Netherlands have also opted for direct agreements with the works councils.

In both countries, the decentralization of collective bargaining has not only shifted collective agreements from the sector to the company level, but has also led to an increased role for works councils as a negotiating partner with employers over the terms and conditions of employment. However, despite the move towards the decentralization of collective bargaining most collective agreements are still decided centrally because most employers in both countries still prefer to negotiate with trade unions instead of works councils. The established and unwritten rules of accepting the credibility of centralized collective agreements cannot be changed easily in countries where trade unions are much respected for upholding agreements with employers.

Industrial action

In both Germany and the Netherlands industrial action is permitted by law but restricted to issues of employee relations only. In Germany, all strikes and lockouts must be reported to the Federal Employment Agency (BA). Article 9 para. 3 of the Basic Law or *Grundgesetz* (1949, amended 2002) guarantees employees the right to strike when the majority (usually 75 per cent) of trade union members vote in a secret ballot in favour of strike action. Overall, the number of strikes has been insignificant when taking into consideration the scale of the German economy. For example, in 2003, only 118 organizations were affected by industrial action, involving a total number of 39,692 workers, resulting in the loss of 163,281 working days; only 3,247 employees were on strike for more than a week and no strike lasted more than 24 days (Eurostat, 2007).

Similarly the level of industrial action in the Netherlands has been very low. For example, there were 31 strikes in 2006 and that was the highest number since 1989. Most of the strikes lasted less than a day and most of the disputes were over the closure of departments and branches of companies as a result of privatizations and takeovers, and negotiations about collective agreements.

MINI CASE STUDY 26

Strikes at the Netherlands Potato Starch Group

On 20 September 2005, workers at Avebe, the Netherlands potato starch group, went on strikes to protest against the decision by the company to dismiss 400 of their colleagues. The management of the company explained that the reduction of labour was necessary for the company to survive as a result of declining revenues and fierce international competition. They insisted that 400 out of a total workforce of 1,300 had to go by the end of the year. The company went to the sub-district court in an attempt to stop the strike, but the court ruled that the strike was legal and was allowed to continue.

The Dutch Union Federation (FNV) backed the strike while the Christian Trade Union Federation (CNV) did not. The former was not convinced by the company's claim while the later believed that staff reduction was important for the survival of the company. During negotiations, the FNV, which represented about 75 per cent of the workers at Avebe, suggested a redundancy plan that proposed the reduction of 100 employees through early retirement and internal redeployment.

The company was determined to go ahead with the first batch of 148 compulsory redundancies because, it claimed, that was the only way for the company to avoid an imminent closure. The FNV called for the continuation of the strike which was costing the company €2 million a day. Finally, on 6 October, the management agreed that the 148 workers who were to be made redundant would stay for 15 more months while the company tried to find alternative employment, and the unions called the strike off.

Question

1 From this case what would you consider to be the costs and benefits of a strike to the workers and to the company?

Settlement of industrial disputes

The settlement of industrial disputes in Germany and the Netherlands depends on whether the dispute is one of interest or one of right. Disputes of interest are referred to a voluntary mediation procedure. This procedure is common in the private sector. In most cases conciliation clauses in collective agreements provide for a mediation panel (in the Netherlands) or conciliation board (in

Germany), which is made of an equal number of employee and employer representatives and is normally chaired by a well-known civil servant or a politician who has to be jointly nominated. Usually the board considers a disputed case within three working days and makes a proposal within five working days. The parties in dispute have to decide on whether to accept or reject the proposal within the following six working days. If the dispute is not resolved an arbitration process has to be invoked. Where the arbitration fails to help the parties reach an agreement, the way becomes free for legal industrial action to be carried out after an obligatory period of keeping the peace has expired.

Disputes of right are those that result from the interpretation of a collective agreement. In some cases a collective agreement is reached in general, but when it comes to the details of its implementation the parties may have different interpretations of the agreement. When the dispute of right is not resolved through negotiation and arbitration, as explained above, the case is then referred to the labour courts. The labour courts are independent legal bodies made of an equal number of honorary judges from the employer and employee sides as well as a professional labour law judge. Disputes can be at the industry or sector levels between the trade unions and employers, or at the plant or company levels between the works councils and the management of the company.

Summary

1 Germany and the Netherlands are industrialized countries with advanced economies. Both depend heavily on the importation of raw materials from non-European countries.
2 The labour markets of both countries are characterized by: a significant level of employment in the industrial sector, a relatively low level of unemployment, equal opportunities in employment, an ageing workforce, higher youth unemployment, and an increasing population of immigrant workers.
3 The Germanic approach to management may be described as integrated, strategic and participative.
4 Works councils play a significant role in the recruitment process and they often insist on internal advertising of vacancies and priority for internal candidates.
5 In both countries, employers are expected to have training plans, to allocate a percentage of their wage bill to training, and to give employees the opportunity to be trained in order to enhance their career opportunities.
6 In both countries, the forms and levels of remuneration are influenced by federal collective agreements, though most companies use performance-related pay.
7 In both countries, employee relations at the national level are characterized by 'social partnership' where trade unions deal with collective agreements over wages and salaries, working time, working conditions, and all aspects of employee–employer relationships that are not clearly determined by law.

Revision questions

Chapter 1 provides a review task designed to consolidate your learning from this chapter. Please see Box 1.2.

In addition, the following questions are designed to help you revise this chapter:

1 Analyse critically the main management policies and practices that characterize the Germanic approach to management.
2 Compare and contrast the Germanic approach to management to the Chinese approach.
3 Analyse the role of works councils in Germany and the Netherlands. Compare and contrast German and Chinese works councils.

References

Bellmann, L. and Leber, U. (2003) *Economic effects of continuous training*, Berlin u.a. (gedruckt; Sammelwerksbeitrag).

Bernstein, R. (2006) 'A quiz for would be citizens tests Germans' attitudes', *New York Times*, March 29.

Blum, K. (1994) 'Managing people in Germany' in Garrison, T. and Rees, D. (eds), *Managing People Across Europe*, Oxford: Butterworth-Heinemann.

Brewster, C. (1995b) 'HRM: the European dimension', in Storey, J. (ed.), *Human Resource Management: A Critical Text*, London: Thomson International Business Press.

CBS (Centraal voor de Statistiek) (2006) *Statistics Bulletin no. 51*, available on line at: www.cbs.nl/nl-NL/menu/publicaties/periodieken/statistisch-bulletin/archief/2006/default.htm, accessed on 5 March 2009.

Destatis (German Federal Statistical Office) (2004) at www.destatis.de/presse/deutsch/pm2004/p0940042.htm, accessed 13 Feb. 2007.

Dickmann, M. (2003) 'Implementing German HRM abroad: desired, feasible, successful?' *The International Journal of Human Resource Management*, 14(2): 265–83.

Dietz, B., Hoogendoorn, J., Kabst, R. and Schmelter, A. (2004) 'The Netherlands and Germany: flexibility or rigidity?', in Brewster, C., Mayrhofer, W. and Morley, M. (eds), *Human Resource Management in Europe: Evidence of Convergence?*, London: Elsevier–Butterworth/Heinemann.

Eichenberg, S. and Wiskemann, G. (1997) 'Personnel management' in Neeves, N. and Kelly-Holmes, H. (eds), *The European Business Environment – Germany'*, London: Thomson Business Press.

Eurostat, Statistical Office of the European Communities (2002) *Eurostat Yearbook 2002: The Statistical Guide to Europe, Data 1990–2000*, Brussels: European Communities.

Eurostat, Statistical Office of the European Communities (2005) *Eurostat Yearbook 2005: The statistical guide to Europe-Data 2001–2005*, Brussels: European Communities.

Eurostat, Statistical Office of the European Communities (2007) *Europe in Figures – Eurostat Yearbook 2006–7*, Brussels: The EC.

Eurostat, Statistical Office of the European Communities (2009) *Eurostat Yearbook 2009*, available online at: http://epp.eurostat.ec.europa.eu/portal/page/portal/product_details/publication?p_product_code = KS-CD-09-001, accessed on 22 January 2010.

Faulkner, D., Pitkethly, R. and Child, J. (2002) 'International mergers and acquisitions in the UK 1985–94: a comparison of national HRM practices', *International Journal of Human Resource Management*, 13(1): 106–22.

Federal Statistical Office, Germany (2004) at http://www.eiro.eurofound.europa.eu/2004/06/feature/de0406107f.html, accessed on 26/10/2006).

Finegold, D., Wagner, K. and Mason, G. (2000) 'National skill-creation systems and career paths for service workers: hotels in the United States, Germany and the United Kingdom', *International Journal of Human Resource Management*, 11(3): 497–516.

Fürstenberg, F. (1998) 'Employment relations in Germany', in Bamber, G.J. and Lansbury, R.D. (eds), *International and Comparative Employment Relations*, 3rd edn, London: Sage, 201–23.

Garrison, T. and Rees, D. (1994) *Managing People Across Europe*, Oxford: Butterworth-Heinemann.

Hollinshead, G. and Leat, M. (1995) *Human Resource Management: An International and Comparative Perspective*, London: Pitman Publishing.

Horgan, J.M. (2003) 'High performance human resource management in Ireland and the Netherlands: adoption and effectiveness', dissertation, University of Groningen, http://irs.ub.rug.nl/ppn/252086694, accessed 27 June 2006.

IAT (Institute for Work and Technology) (2006) at www.eirofound.eu.int/2006/08/articles/de0608059i.html, accessed 30 Nov. 2006.

IW (Cologne Institute for Business Research) (2004) Survey in German at www.iwkoeln.de/data/pdf/pub/direkt44–04iwd.pdf.

Kohaut, S. and Schnabel, C. (2006) *Tarifliche Öffnungsklauseln: Verbreitung, Inanspruchnahme und Bedeutung* (in German) ISSN 1615-5831; summary in English by Sandra Vogel in www.eurofound.europa.eu/eiro/2006/06/articles/de0606019i.html, accessed 30 Nov. 2006.

Muller, M. (1999a) 'Enthusiastic embrace or critical reception? The German HRM debate', *Journal of Management Studies*, 36(4): 465–82.

Muller, M. (1999b) 'Human resource management under institutional constraints: the case of Germany', *British Journal of* Management, 10(3): 31–44.

OECD (Organization for Economic Cooperation and Development) (1994) *The OECD Jobs Study: Facts, Analysis, Strategies 1994*, available online at: www.oecd.org/dataoecd/42/51/1941679.pdf, accessed on 16 Jan. 2009.

OECD (Organization for Economic Cooperation and Development) (2001) *Trends in public sector pay in OECD countries*, Paris: OECD.

OECD (Organization for Economic Cooperation and Development) (2007) *OECD Employment Outlook 2007*, Paris: OECD, Available online at: http://website1.wider.unu.edu/lib/pdfs/OECD-Employment-2007.pdf accessed on 10 July 2009.

OECD (Organization for Economic Cooperation and Development) (2009) *OECD Stats Extracts-Trade union density*, available on line at: http://stats.oecd.org/Index.aspx?DataSetCode = UN_DEN, accessed on 13 Sept. 2010.

OECD (Organization for Economic Cooperation and Development) (2010) *International Migration Outlook 2010*, available online at: http://www.oecd.org/dataoecd, accessed 26 April 2010.

OSA (Institute for Labour Studies in the Netherlands) (2006) at EIRO, 2006/06/articles/n10606019i.html, accessed 16 Dec. 2006.

Randlesome, C. (1994) *The Business Culture in Germany*, Oxford: Butterworth-Heinemann.

Stettes, O. (2006) 'Wage incentives aim to boost employment of older workers' in www.eiro.eurofound.europa.eu/2006/08/artocles/de0608039i.html, accessed 30 Nov. 2006.

Ulrich, V. (1997) 'The macro-economy: background and issues', in Neeves, N. and Kelly-Holmes, H. (eds), *The European Business Environment – Germany'*, London: Thomson Business Press.

UNFPA (United Nations Population Fund) (2006) *State of the World Population 2006*, available at www.unfpa.org.

WSI (Germany's Institute for Economic and Social Research) (2005) *Survey findings on works councils and decentralisation of bargaining*, available online at: http://www.eurofound.europa.eu/eiro/2005/10/feature/de0510202f.htm, accessed on 10 January 2009.

12

Denmark, Norway and Sweden

LEARNING OUTCOMES

This chapter is designed to help you understand, for Denmark, Norway and Sweden:

1   The (a) economic, (b) political and (c) cultural contexts in which managers work;

2   The main trends in the labour market;

3   The typical features of (a) management policies and practices and (b) organizational structure and behaviour;

4   The main policies and practices of human resource management with regard to: (a) recruitment and selection; (b) training and development; (c) rewards and remuneration; (d) and employee relations.

Introduction

Denmark, Norway and Sweden have much in common historically, economically, politically and geographically. Norway is richer in raw materials such as oil, gas, wood and fish than Denmark and Sweden. Denmark and Sweden are members of the EU, but Norway is not. It will be seen that despite their differences they have much in common when it comes to their employment policies and management systems. (See Table 12.1 for basic statistics.)

Table 12.1 Basic statistical indicators, Denmark, Norway and Sweden

Country	Area (sq km)	Population (July 2010 est.)	Population Growth (2010) %	GDP – real growth rate (2009) %	Inflation rate (2009 est.) %	Workforce (2009 est.)	Unemployment rate (2009) %
Denmark	43,094	5,500,510	0.28	−4.7	1.3	2.84	4.3
Norway	323,802	4,660,539	0.34	−1.5	2.1	2.59	3.2
Sweden	450,295	9,059,651	0.158	−5.1	−0.3	4.91	8.3

Source: CIA *World Factbook*, 2010.

Contexts: economics, politics and culture

Economics

Scandinavian countries have industrialized later but faster than most of the other European nations. They have been transformed from a poor agrarian economy to a modern service and knowledge-based economy. For Norway and Denmark, the transformation has been due mainly to the production and exportation of oil and gas since the early 1970s.

Denmark has become a major producer and exporter of petroleum, natural gas, tinned meat, fish, machinery and instruments, chemicals, furniture, ships, meat and meat products, and dairy products. The Danish economy is based on high-tech agriculture, and modern small-scale and corporate industry. The country has enjoyed an extensive government welfare system, high income, a stable currency, a positive balance-of-payments, and high dependence on international trade.

Norway is rich in natural resources such as petroleum, fish, forests, minerals and hydropower. It is one of the largest exporters of oil in Europe, and oil revenues have made the basis for a strong economy. However, the Norwegian economy has become highly dependent on the international market because it is a major exporter (third in the world, after Saudi Arabia and Russia) of oil and gas. The Norwegian government still controls key economic sectors such oil, gas, and electricity but provides high standards of public services and a good welfare system.

The Swedish economy is also modern and highly industrialized and the country is rich in natural resources. Most of the economy is in private ownership (90 per cent) and is mainly in the industrial sector, of which engineering accounts for about 50 per cent of output. However, the public sector controls strategic and important services such as the communications and energy supply sectors, education and health care. Sweden's main industries are petroleum and gas, food processing, shipbuilding, chemicals, timber, textiles and fishing. Swedish export commodities are machinery, motor vehicles, iron and steel products, chemicals, paper products, pulp and wood. However, the engineering sector is still a significant part of the economy and creates a significant number of jobs in the manufacturing sector. Sweden is well known for the production of Volvo and Saab automobiles. It is also a leading country in IT and telecommunications, pharmaceuticals, and wood and paper, as well as being popular for IKEA furniture, and Hennes & Mauritz (H&M) fashion, and pop music.

All three countries have been hard hit by the recent world financial crisis. Their economies are dependent on a growing number of small and medium size enterprises, which rely on loans from local and international banks, and on international trade, which has been seriously affected by the credit crunch. However, since the 1980s they have provided a high standard of welfare services to their citizens. However, the cost of living is also quite high, especially in the big cities where the prices of property and food are well above the EU average.

Politics

All Scandinavian countries are constitutional monarchies with democratically elected parliamentary governments. The monarchs have little real power. Scandinavian parliaments are organized on the basis of proportional representation and general elections are held every four years. Denmark comprises 99 municipalities and 5 regions. The local governments of the municipalities are elected democratically every four years and are responsible for local services such as schools, libraries, electricity, water, child and elderly care, and other facilities. The regional governments are in charge of services such as education, health and transport.

Norway comprises 434 municipalities and 19 counties. The capital, Oslo, is a combined municipality and county. The local governments are elected for four years and have similar responsibilities to their Danish counterparts. The dominant party has tended to be the Labour party.

Sweden comprises 21 counties, 20 county councils and 290 municipalities. The county councils are responsible for issues like health care and transport, while the municipalities are in charge of social welfare services, education, and child and elderly care. They have wider powers and autonomy at the local level, including the imposition of local taxes. The Social Democrats have tended to be the dominant party.

Culture

Scandinavian countries have a common cultural heritage. Norway was part of Denmark between 1450 and 1814 and then subject to the Swedish king with self-rule between 1814 and 1905. The three countries have their own languages but they are similar and easily understood by each other. They also share a common Lutheran heritage, and moral values of equality, democracy and peaceful relations. Although few people attend church regularly or claim to be religious, they have high moral values such as respecting others, being modest, helping the needy, tolerating foreigners and minding their own business. Scandinavians tend to pay little attention to rank and status, prefer informal and direct forms of communication, dress casually and tend to be 'natural' (Schramm-Nielson, 1991). The quest for equity is profoundly rooted in the Scandinavian countries' value system. It is not surprising to find that people tend to downplay their own abilities, competence and intelligence.

Scandinavian society is still very homogeneous and possesses neither large ethnic minorities nor a social structure of sharply divided classes. The social structure is comparatively even (Parkum and Agersnap, 1994). Scandinavians tend to exhibit a positive attitude towards innovation and new ideas and an appreciation of good relationships. According to Hofstede's (2001) study they are described as having low uncertainty avoidance and small power distance, and are relatively individualistic and significantly feminine. It means that their management style reflects a culture of small power distance, which means that there is a preference for delegation of authority, limited direct management control and a high level of employee participation in decision-making. However, they have also been described as pragmatists and as having the 'ability to change easily from pleasantry to seriousness' (Parkum and Agersnap, 1994: 118).

ACTIVITY 1

Imagine you are an operations manager of a Scottish multinational company specializing in the design, development, production and marketing of video games. You have been sent on a fact-finding mission to Scandinavia.

Write a short report to your head office in Edinburgh summarizing the Scandinavian economic, political and cultural context. Which of the three countries would you recommend for the opening of a new subsidiary to produce children's video games? Why?

Labour market trends

The minimum working age for full-time employment in Denmark and Sweden is 16 years, though normally those under 18 are permitted to work only during the day and under close supervision. The standard working week for full-time employment is 40 hours. In Norway, the minimum working age for full-time work is 18 years, but those aged between 13 and 18 may work part-time with some restrictions enforced at the local level. The statutory working week for full-time employment is 37.5 hours.

Scandinavian countries have a low population growth rate and a relatively high level of economically active people. Most of the population is within the ages of 25 and 64 and there has been a decline in the number of young people and a rise in the number of older people. In general a comparatively low level of unemployment, a high level of equal opportunities, a high level of female employment, a high level of older workers and an increasing population of immigrant workers characterize the labour markets of the three countries. (See Table 12.2)

Table 12.2 Workforce distribution by occupation in 2009 (%), Denmark, Norway and Sweden

Country	Agriculture	Industry	Services
Denmark	2.9	23.8	72.7
Norway	2.9	21.1	76
Sweden	1.1	28.2	70.7

Source: CIA *World Factbook*, 2010.

Unemployment

In comparison with other European countries, unemployment in Scandinavian countries has been quite low. Historically, government policies aimed at achieving full employment. Nevertheless, unemployment is one of the main challenges for the governments of the three countries. Most sectors of the economy have been affected by the slow growth in the world economy and by international competition, despite the increased prices of oil and gas over the recent years. The manufacturing, information and communications technology, telecommunications and consultancy industries have been the most affected. Also, the strength of their currencies has led to fewer exports and contributed further to lower demand for employment.

Unemployment among the young people and the educated is a problem in the three countries. Most of those affected are between the ages of 16 and 24 years. For this age group, unemployment may be for shorter periods, but it has serious and long-lasting effects on their future income and career prospects. (See Table 12.3.) The main reasons for the high level of youth unemployment are:

Table 12.3 Age structure (%) (2009), Denmark, Norway and Sweden

Country	0–14 years %	15–64 years %	Over 65 years %	Median age (years)	Life expectancy at birth (for men & women)
Denmark	18.1	65.8	16.1	40.7	78.3
Norway	18.5	66.2	15.2	39.7	79.95
Sweden	15.7	65.5	18.8	41.7	80.86

Source: CIA World Factbook, 2009.

1 The inability of the high schools and universities to produce the skilled workforce required in the labour market;
2 The desire of some young people to delay full-time employment and take up part-time jobs on a temporary basis, in which case they are unemployed most of the time;
3 The last in, first out rule in employment, which means that young people are first to loose their jobs when redundancies occur;
4 The lack of work experience that an increasing number of employers look for; and
5 The lack of attachment to the labour market as the young unemployed who spend their time with the other unemployed lose interest in looking for employment.

Female participation

Scandinavian employers are exemplary in providing equal opportunities in employment. The rate of female employment in Denmark (71.9 per cent), in Norway (71.7 per cent) and Sweden (70.4 per cent) was the highest in Europe in 2005 (Eurostat, 2007). The main reasons for the high level of female participation in the labour market are:

1 Government intervention through legislation and policies that promote equal opportunities. Scandinavian governments provide impressive welfare support for working parents and high levels of welfare benefits, which make it possible for mothers, for example, to engage in full-time employment (Siim, 1993). For example, in Norway a new law was introduced in June 2006 on minimum gender representation on company boards of all privately owned companies.
2 The introduction of education policies aimed at the education of women in disciplines that produce needed workforce skills. For example, in the mid-1980s the interest among girls in secondary schools was raised in pursuing natural sciences and technological education. According to a report published in April 2004 (Den könsuppdelade arbetsmarknaden, SOU, 2004) by Åsa Löfström, the percentage of girls studying natural science programmes in Swedish secondary schools increased from 35 per cent in 1994 to 45 per cent in 2002. Therefore, there have been as many women as men entering the labour market with the high education qualifications needed by the economy;
3 Cultural values of equality and equity in the Scandinavian society; and
4 The popularity and spread of flexible working practices.

===== MINI CASE STUDY 27 =====

Too Short for a Volvo (Sweden)

On the 21 September 2005 the automobile company Volvo cars was ordered by the Swedish Labour Court to pay damages to a female job applicant who was rejected because she was 3 cm shorter than the minimum required height of 163 cm to do the job. The court ruled that the company was indirectly discriminating against women according to the Swedish Equal Opportunities Act 1991. The evidence provided to the court showed that about 25 to 28 per cent of the female working population would fall below the Volvo required height, but only about 1 to 2 per cent of the male working population would be affected. The company representatives claimed that a certain height was necessary to decrease the risk of injuries to shorter employees because production had increased and the assembly work meant more tasks at shoulder height than before. However, the company was unable to show any statistical evidence that the risk for damage was higher for shorter people. The court ruled that the company did not show convincingly that the demand for a certain height was appropriate or necessary in order to avoid work injuries. Therefore it had discriminated indirectly and unintentionally against the female applicant and had to pay a fine for damages caused to her. (Case adapted from: www.eiro. eurofound.eu.int/2005/11/inbrief/se05111o2n.html, accessed on 1 Dec 2006.)

Questions

1 Does the requirement of a certain height and weight constitute discrimination?
2 What are the arguments for and against the employers' claim?
3 What would be the implications of this case for the employment of women in other organizations?

Flexible working

The use of flexible working practices such as part-time work, flexitime and job sharing is well established in Scandinavian organizations, though some practices such as home-based working and teleworking are not popular because of obstacles such as the 'lack of technical equipment in the homes of the employees, insufficient follow-up at work, jobs that require a presence at the workplace and people's desire to see and meet other people ... and the insurance issues concerning, for instance, workplace safety' (Lindeberg et al., 2004: 300). Part-time work is the most popular method of flexible working, especially in service industries such as health, education, banking, retailing, catering and hospitality where the majority of employees are women. In Norway and Sweden part-time employment has been a feature of the labour market since the 1970s. However, part-time employment might also be considered as part-time *un*employment because many of the people who work part time are those who cannot find full-time work. That means, unlike in many other EU countries, part-time work is often not voluntary. Most of those who work part-time involuntarily are women in low-paid jobs within the wholesale, retail, catering and hotels sectors. Nyberg (2005) argues that while men and women seem to be similarly unemployed (women accounting for 5.1 per cent and men for 5.9 per cent in 2004), the reality is that many more women than men are unemployed because many women are employed part time and are part-time unemployed.

Scandinavian employment policies and laws encourage employers to introduce flexible working practices. For example, in June 2005 the Norwegian government approved the Worker Protection and the Working Environment Act (the AML), effective from January 2006, in order to make it easier for employers to recruit and employ temporary and fixed-term employees. It states that the employer may use temporary employment in cases where the worker is only required to perform a specific task, but it gives the right to a temporary worker to claim full-time employment after a year in employment. The law also gives the right to part-time employees to increase their working hours if such time is available in the organization.

Migrant labour

Ethnically, the population of Scandinavian countries is relatively homogeneous compared to that of most other Western European countries. This is partly because of the geographical location of these countries and partly because they were not major colonial powers like the UK or France. Immigration to Scandinavian countries started to increase from the late 1960s when some overseas students started to settle after completion of their studies. The rise in the number of foreigners over recent years can be attributed mainly to Scandinavian governments' liberal attitude towards foreign migration in general and asylum seekers in particular. Nevertheless, in comparison with other EU countries they still have the lowest population of migrant labour. Norway and Sweden have had the highest increases in population due to high levels of immigration.

Since the enlargement of the European Union into Central and Eastern Europe, the majority of emigrants to Scandinavian countries have chosen Norway as their first destination. Statistics show that some 36,276 work permits were issued to workers from the new member states entering Norway from 1 May 2004 to 31 December 2005, while Denmark and Sweden issued 6,691 and 8,768 work permits respectively during the same period (Norwegian Directorate of Immigration, UDI, 2006). In Norway, the granting of work permits to foreign workers is subject to securing an offer of full-time employment. This condition has not been a problem to many job seekers wanting to work in Norway, especially in sectors with labour shortages such as construction and agriculture. In Sweden, both the Confederation of Swedish Enterprises (SAF) and the Swedish Confederation of Trade Unions (LO) support labour immigration that is regulated and ensures that immigrant employees receive the same pay and enjoy the same working conditions as Scandinavian workers. The Confederation of Swedish Enterprise also argued for more immigrant labour because of foreseeable shortages in labour in the short and long terms. It has also argued that it would be better if employers could decide themselves which workers they want to employ without having to go through the AMS (National Labour Market Board) and other authorities and agencies. In Denmark, the social partners agreed on 13 December 2006 on the integration of immigrants and their families into the labour market. The aim of the agreement was to create a broader basis for bringing more immigrants into employment.

Management and organization

There have been a number of attempts to describe and analyse the nature and practice of management in Scandinavian countries (see Brewster and Söderström, 1994; Brewster et al., 2000; Rogaczewska et al., 2004; Schramm-Nielsen et al., 2004; Sinani et al., 2008). Generally speaking, the Scandinavian approach to management is based on social partnership, egalitarianism and consensus, the empowerment of line managers, and industrial democracy.

Social partnership

Scandinavian countries are known for having good relationships between the social partners (employers or employers' organizations, employees or employees' organizations, and the government). Managers have no objection to having a dialogue with employees' representatives and see them as partners rather than as adversaries – the opposite of the US, for example. A survey of 555 Swedish companies by the National Institute for Working Life (Levinson, 2004) found that there was a strong cooperative climate between employers and trade unions. The survey identified four phases in decision-making processes: 1) Initiation in which problems and possibilities are introduced; 2) Preparation in which practical issues are investigated; 3) Decision in which decisions are made; and 4) Implementation in which decisions are implemented. The survey found employee involvement in 15 per cent of the companies studied at the initiation stage, 74 per cent at the preparation stage, 94 per cent at the decision stage and 100 per cent at the implementation stage. In all Scandinavian countries, the social partners collaborate on incomes policy and issues related to economic and social development. Most HRM and employee relations issues are decided through collective agreement between the social partners, and mainly between the workers and management at the national and organizational levels. The process of social partnership is strengthened by the Scandinavian value system of equality, shared responsibility and management by consensus, as explained below.

Egalitarianism and consensus

In Scandinavian countries most managers tend not to use superiority of status and tend to treat their subordinates as equals. They emphasize results and getting the work done rather than authority, status and power. For example, the Danes use the phrase 'delegation of responsibility' rather than 'delegation of power' or 'delegation of authority' (Schramm-Nielsen, 1991; Parkum and Agersnap, 1994; Parkum and Agersnap, 1994; Brewster et al., 2000; Schramin-Nelsen et al. 2004). The use of autonomous work groups, for which many companies in Norway and Sweden such as Volvo are known, is evidence for the level of equal opportunities given to employees in the workplace. Autonomous work groups are self-regulating teams set up at the production line where a production team leader, who is not expected to control but to support the team, replaces the traditional supervisor. Egalitarianism is also evident in the introduction of policies aimed at promoting equality between workers in the workplace and at giving them opportunities to work flexibly.

Empowerment of line managers

A number of surveys have shown that Scandinavian countries rank highly when it comes to allocating managerial, especially HR, responsibilities to line managers (Brewster and Hegewisch, 1994; Sparrow and Hiltrop, 1994; Lindeberg et al., 2004; Rogaczewska et al., 2004). Line managers have become increasingly involved in issues related to recruitment and selection, training and development, rewards and employee relations. The involvement of line managers in HRM issues is long established and has very little to do with the rise of 'Macho' management or the 'decline' of the role of HR/personnel managers. Although line managers are involved in HR decisions, it does not mean that the role of HR managers has diminished or that it is obsolete. On the contrary, HR managers have become more influential as advisors to line managers and mediators between employees and management in countries where employee relations are characterized by a high level of cooperation between the unions and employers in what is referred to as 'industrial democracy'.

Industrial democracy

Scandinavian countries have traditionally been known for having established an enviable model of industrial democracy where employees have a legal right to representation from the workplace to the board levels. The Scandinavian approach is based on having a minimum level of employee representation at board level. Also, unlike the Germanic approach, there is no statutory works councils system in Sweden. Workplace employee participation and representation are based on the role of trade unions and their co-determination rights as set out by law. The law provides for employees' rights to information, consultation, negotiation, board-level representation and participation in decision-making. The social partners have accepted the law as a practical and useful way to work together. Usually in organizations with 50 workers or more, one-third of the company board is made of elected employee representatives. In Sweden the members of the local branches of trade unions that are bound by collective agreements with the employer appoint two (three when the organization employs more than 1,000 people) employee representatives as board members who have the right to take part in decision-making (except when it comes to collective bargaining matters, because of conflict of interest). In the public sector, the rights of employee board members are restricted to the expression of opinions and they cannot take part in making decisions, according to the 1987 Staff Representatives Order. The Swedish Co-determination at Work Act (MBL) of 1976 (amended in 1991) provided the legal framework for industrial democracy, where the managers and employee representatives have equal rights to information and decision-making. Management has to consult the workers on all major decisions affecting the organization (Hammarström and Nilsson, 1998; Nilsson, 1998; Schramm-Nielsen et al., 2004; Sinani et al., 2008). The first part of the MBL provides for the system of collective bargaining while the second part concerns employee representation, information and consultation. Section 11 of the MBL states that before an employer makes any decisions regarding important changes in its operations or in working and employment conditions for its employees, it must, on its own initiative, enter into negotiations with employee representatives in order to reach a collective agreement. Also section 19 of the MBL states that employers must regularly inform employee representatives on business performance in respect of production, finance and personnel. Employee representatives have the right to examine the organization's reports, accounts and all documents that concern its operations. Employers who do not fulfil their obligations under the MBL can be fined for damages caused to employees.

Managing human resources

The results of the Cranet Survey (see Brewster et al., 2000, 2004; Rogaczewska et al., 2004; Lindeberg et al., 2004) show that 50 per cent of organizations in Denmark, 75 per cent of organizations in Norway and 80 per cent of organizations in Sweden had a director of HRM in the top management team. They also found that most organizations had written HR policies. In organizations where the head of HRM did not have a seat on the board of directors, they still had the credibility to exercise and incorporate their ideas at different levels of the organization. This high level of HR presence at the board level is translated into policies and practices that characterize the way the main functions of HRM are carried out in Scandinavian countries.

Recruitment and selection

The process of recruitment and selection in Scandinavian countries is centralized and regulated through the use of National Employment Offices (known as National Labour Market Boards – AMSs). Most organizations recruit their employees through the AMSs but the methods used at the organizational level tend to vary from one organization to another and from one country to another. The process is influenced by: 1) the employment laws and the labour market regulations that exist in each country and those of the European Union; and 2) the conditions of the labour market in general and the participation of women in particular.

Recruitment

Most organizations in Scandinavian countries tend to use internal recruitment for managerial and professional positions, especially at the middle and junior management levels. This practice is aimed at providing a career path for managers within the organization and is used as a motivational device to retain talented and committed employees. When it is not possible to recruit a senior manager from within the organization, a recruitment agency (the AMS) is usually used to search for suitable candidates. The use of advertisements is very limited. A study by Tixier (1996) found only about 38 per cent of employers in Norway used advertisements. This is mainly because most employees are recruited through agencies. Many graduates seeking managerial and professional jobs tend to use the AMSs as well as newspaper advertisements. Some of them contact employers directly by sending unsolicited applications. However, the use of application forms is very limited and it is common to apply through a covering letter and a CV. Scandinavian employers seldom visit universities and other institutions of higher and further education to recruit graduates. However, many organizations have their own websites and they also use internet recruitment by placing their job vacancies on the internet.

Selection

As in other Western European countries, the most popular method of selection is the interview. One-to-one interviews are more frequently used in Denmark and Sweden than in Norway, while panel interviews are more common in Norway than in Denmark or Sweden. Interviews in these countries are clearly structured, well planned and last for about an hour. During the interview, the interviewer typically focuses on professional interests, aptitude, particular areas of expertise and accomplishments (Tixier, 1996). Psychometric tests are more frequently used in Denmark than in Norway or Sweden but not to the extent that they are used in the Anglo-Saxon countries. Reference checks are widely used by most companies in all three countries, while the use of assessment centres is still very limited: only the very large and the international companies normally use them (Rogaczewska et al., 2004; Lindeberg et al., 2004).

Training and development

Scandinavian governments have given a lot of attention to education, training and life-long learning. There is a strong emphasis on continuous vocational training. Their citizens are well educated and their workers are highly skilled, as explained next.

Education

In Scandinavian countries, children begin school at the age of 7 and spend 6 years in primary school and 3 years at the first stage of secondary school, which are compulsory. That means education is obligatory until the age of 16. The education sector is predominantly public and free, financed by the state and the municipalities. Scandinavian people are highly literate and well educated. For example, the rate of those who have completed at least upper secondary education in Sweden is higher than the EU average. A noticeable characteristic of the Scandinavian education systems is the emphasis on communication and language skills at all levels. Most of the population speaks two languages or more, and the English language is the most spoken second language.

The upper or second-stage secondary education from the age of 16 to 19, consists of both academic and vocational studies, including apprenticeship training. Admission to universities and specialized university-level institutions requires the successful completion of upper secondary school study in specified subjects. Universities provide higher education in different disciplines and there are also specialized institutes and colleges such as the Norwegian School of Economics and Business Administration and the Stockholm School of Economics which provide world class business and management courses.

Vocational training

Throughout the Scandinavian countries there is a strong emphasis on vocational training. It is estimated that more than half of the population has taken some form of vocational training and about a fifth of the population has attended an institute of higher education. Scandinavian countries are known for their highly skilled technicians and engineers (Rogaczewska et al., 2004: 236). Vocational training is generally considered to be an ongoing process that provides opportunities for life-long learning and advancement in a person's working career. Vocational training programmes are offered to persons who are already employed and to those who are unemployed. Successful completion of such programmes results in the award of nationally recognized qualifications for specific occupations. Vocational training comes under the overall responsibility of the labour department (ministry) and is administered by the National Labour Market Authority by cooperating with the social partners who are normally involved in identifying training needs and deciding on the content of training programmes. The government plays a great role in promoting, monitoring and evaluating programmes of vocational training.

Organizational training

As well as the vocational training provided in schools, many employees get continuous training in their workplaces. About 36 per cent of organizations in Sweden spent over 5 per cent of their payroll on training in 1999 (Lindeberg et al., 2004). Many organizations carry out regular training needs analysis in order to select their employees for on- and off-the-job training opportunities. According to Nyen et al. (2004) about 58 per cent of employees in Norway pursued work-based training activities. The share of employees in this type of training (company-led) is higher in the oil/energy-producing and quarrying sectors than in the others.

Life-long learning

In response to rising levels of unemployment and high welfare costs Scandinavian governments' strategy over the 1990s was to enhance skills levels and to promote people's employability. They introduced various initiatives that were aimed at young people and women. For example, in Denmark the 'leave from work' initiative was aimed at giving employees state-subsidized time off work for up to one year for every five years' employment, to study, to raise children or simply take a break from work. The Swedish government also introduced a bill in 2003 on individual learning and a skills development system, which involves special accounts for all employees, providing tax incentives for learning and study activities. Employers are encouraged to contribute to their employees' learning accounts. In Norway, according to a survey by Nyen et al. (2004), 11 per cent of employees in the 22–66 age group had been through some form of formal education in the course of the previous 12 months (i.e., 2003). Of these, 7 per cent had participated in what is defined as further education.

=========== MINI CASE STUDY 28 ===========

Norway in the Right Way

A study published in May 2004 reported that in 2003 about 61 per cent of employees in Norway participated in some sort of training or education, but there were significant differences in training between sectors and between employees. It was also found that women employees participated more often than men in formal education. The main reason for this is that women more often than men work in sectors where training opportunities are more available. The survey also found that 57 per cent of employees surveyed stated that they had participated in courses, seminars or others types of training that did not lead to formal qualifications. Employees spent on average 26 hours per annum on work-related training. Most employees wanted to learn through practical methods of training and preferred to study short- rather than long-term courses. It was also noticed that most of the employees who preferred to learn through practical training had low levels of formal education.

Questions

1 What are the main reasons for having such a high level of employees taking part in training and development programmes in Norway?
2 Why do you think women had more training than men? What type of jobs can women do that provide more opportunities for education and training?
3 Why might learning through practical training be more preferred than through other means?

Rewards and remuneration

Rewards and remuneration in Scandinavian countries have traditionally been decided through collective agreements between the social partners at the national level. Salaries, benefits and working conditions are agreed through collective bargaining between the various employers' associations and trade union confederations. In Norway, for example, the National Wages Board (NWB) tends not to change the agreed provisions of collective agreements and acts as an arbitrator in cases of collective agreements failure. In Sweden pay negotiations are normally carried out through the Swedish Agency for Government Employers (SAV) which is an independent association of govern-ment agencies. Since 1998, a three-year pay agreement has been adopted in both private and public sectors. However, the private sector has traditionally set the pace in pay settlements for the rest of the economy. Interestingly, the gap between white- and blue-collar wages has widened over the last decade. According to a report published by the Swedish Confederation of Trade Unions (LO) in September 2005, the average wages increased by 44 per cent for blue-collar employees and by 52 per cent for white-collar employees. Moreover, although Sweden is an egalitarian society the report shows that in 2004 the women's average wages were 93 per cent of men's.

There is no statutory minimum wage in Sweden, Norway, Denmark or Finland, as wages are determined through collective agreements for all sectors of the economy and tend to vary from one sector to another. Despite the successful tradition of collective agreements in the determination of rewards and benefits, many employers have called for more individual pay agreements and performance-related pay.

Performance-related pay

Although most organizations in Denmark, Norway and Sweden use performance appraisal, not many of them have used performance-related pay. The use of performance-related pay is more widespread in Denmark than the others because it has more manual employees than in the other countries. However, due to trade union influence, performance-related pay has not been a substitute for collectively agreed wages but rather complementary to them. In Norway more and more companies are using performance appraisal and some form of performance-related pay, but the practice is not yet widespread. Performance-related pay was established for the first time in 1997 in Denmark and Sweden (OECD, 2005). In Sweden, two surveys (1995 and 1999) showed that the use of performance appraisal was the highest in the EU, but the use of merit/performance-related pay was the lowest for all occupational levels except for manual jobs. This shows that performance appraisal is not used for reward purposes but as a developmental tool aimed at assessing the future development needs of employees.

ACTIVITY 2

In the light of what you have read so far in this chapter consider the recent employers desire to move from collective to individual rewards and performance-related pay and answer the following questions:

1 To what extent does the idea of individual rewards and performance-related pay contradict the value of equality that exists in Scandinavian countries?
2 In a workplace that is dominated by industrial democracy and collective agreements, how could performance-related pay be implemented effectively?

Employee relations

Scandinavian countries are known for having a strong tradition of trade unionism, collective bargaining agreements with limited state intervention in employee relations, and a strong sense of industrial democracy at the enterprise level. Collective agreements are legally binding and there is a comprehensive mediation system to settle industrial disputes. Trade union membership is quite high, but industrial action in the form of strikes is relatively low. While very little has changed in the Norwegian employee relations system over the last 40 years, both Danish and Swedish systems have had to be revised to bring them in line with the various European Union Directives. For example, the Swedish Working Time Act 1982 was amended in February 2005 to conform to EU Working Time Directive 93 104/EC, to include new regulations for average weekly working time, day and night requirements of rest, working time for night workers and rules for compensatory leave on occasional deviations from the current rule of day and night rest.

Trade unions

Scandinavian countries have had a well-established tradition of trade unionism since the nineteenth century. Initially the trade unions of the three countries (Denmark, Norway and Sweden) cooperated together and had similar structures and principles, and engaged in similar activities, although their cooperation was informal. In 1972 the Council of Nordic Trade Unions (NFS) was established as an umbrella organization for the trade unions in the Nordic countries, covering more than 9 million workers represented by different national trade unions. The main aim of the NFS was to coordinate trade union activities and to represent them in different international organizations (http://www.nfs.net/english/, accessed 12 March 2007).

Employees in Scandinavian countries are free to form trade unions whenever they like without having to register or seek the acceptance of the government or the courts. Trade unions have legal rights of access to company information and to initiate bargaining with employers on any issues that may affect employees. Every union has its own structure, procedures and rules about how to enter into collective bargaining with its employer. The unions are generally strong, well organized and play a significant role as members of the social partnership. Trade unions are organized into confederations covering employees in all sectors of the economy. The role of the confederation is to coordinate the bargaining process of its affiliates, represent them at international events, provide trade union education, and influence government and party policies. It is also responsible for research and signing labour market insurance schemes.

In recent years a number of trade unions have merged in order to consolidate their efforts in response to changes in employer–employee relationships for a number of socio-economic and political reasons. The main reasons for the recent mergers are: 1) to develop a stronger representation at the workplace and more influence in collective bargaining, and 2) to rationalize their structures and make greater cost savings and effectiveness. In Norway, several LO member unions have merged over the last five years. The mergers have been driven mainly by the challenges of change in employee relations and in the attitudes of the working classes. Trade unions are struggling to recruit new members and the limited membership means less income for the unions, forcing them to seek new partners for their membership and financial survival.

MINI CASE STUDY 29

Danish Union Governance

The Danish Financial Services' Union (*Finansforbundet*) introduced a new code of good trade union practice, called 'union governance', similar in principle to the concept of 'corporate governance'. The 'union governance' is based on specific rules and activities that ensure good and ethically acceptable management of trade unions. They introduced, for example, a board of complaints where the members can raise their concerns and express their dissatisfaction with the conduct of their union. The complaints are reviewed by an independent trade unions officer chosen from outside the union. The independent officer can be an arbitrator, a labour law lawyer or a professor of industrial relations. The officer monitors the views and level of satisfaction among the members, checks the accounts of the union for accuracy about finances and membership, publishes the profiles of the elected union leaders and ensures transparency in the activities and management of the unions.

Allan Bang, the President of the Financial Services Union, said in an interview with the Danish Confederation of trade Unions (LO) newsletter on 12 February 2007, that 'Union governance is a set of rules of conduct about how we would like to behave towards our members and those employers we associate with on a day-to-day basis. It is not a "pop smart" attempt to brand ourselves, but recognition of the fact that we in the trade union movement from time to time are seen as being very reactionary and obdurate. We have to recognize that everything is not perfect as it is and that mistakes happen.'

He also said that the members of the union had to be consulted before a new collective bargaining round and that their views had to be considered. He added that the composition of the governing body was very important for the success of 'union governance', but he pointed out that only 3 out of 17 members are women although more than 50 per cent of the union members are women. (Adapted from Carsten Jørgensen, FAOS, www.eurofound.europa.eu/eiro/2007/02/articles/dk0702039i.html, accessed 1May 2007.)

Questions

1 Evaluate the idea of 'union governance' in the Danish socio-economic and political context. How necessary would you say it was?
2 What type of complaints can members make against their union's management?
3 Why is the composition of the union's governing body important for the success of 'union governance'?

Trade union membership

In all Scandinavian countries there has been a slight drop in union member-ship since the mid-1990s because of economic downturn and political changes, but overall it is still quite high in comparison with other EU countries (see Table 12.4). About 80 per cent of the working population in Sweden are mem-bers of trade unions while in Denmark and Norway the membership is about 60 per cent (OECD, 2005; Eurostat, 2007). Trade union membership is consid-erably higher in the public sector, especially in the old, large and state-owned organizations, than in the private sector. This comparatively high level of trade union membership is attributed to the existing tradition of joining trade unions for protection from possible redundancies, and to the level of influence and power that trade unions had over the long period of social democratic governments (Hammarström and Nilsson, 1998; Nergaard, 2006).

Nevertheless, there have been some significant changes in the type of mem-bership over the last 10 years. There has been a shift from male- to female-dominated unions and from the younger to older trade union members. Statistical analysis of trade union membership composition in 2003 shows that in most of the Scandinavian countries women make up the majority of the white-collar unions' members (see Eurostat, 2007). Overall female trade union membership is in the majority in Sweden (51.6 per cent) and Norway (51.1 per cent) (OECD, 2006; Eurostat, 2007).

Table 12.4 Trade union density 1999–2007 (%), Denmark, Norway and Sweden

	1999	2000	2001	2002	2003	2004	2005	2006	2007
Denmark	74.9	74.2	73.8	73.2	72.9	73.3	72.4	71.7	70.3
Norway	54.8	54.4	53.9	54.5	55.1	55	54.9	54.9	53.7
Sweden	80.6	79.1	78	78	78	77.3	76.5	75.1	70.8

Source: Eurostat, 2009.

Moreover, there has been a decline in the number of young workers who are members of trade unions. Union density among workers aged 16–24 years old decreased from 62 per cent in 1993 to 45 per cent in 2000. More and more young people prefer to join unemployment insurance funds but not the trade unions with which the funds have traditionally been related. There has also been a change in attitude to trade unions, as many workers are not convinced that trade unions succeed in representing their interests. An increasing number of young workers employed on fixed-term contracts see less need for joining trade unions.

Collective bargaining

In Scandinavian countries, collective bargaining activity is on the whole stable and predictable, as collective agreements tend to be limited to customary issues such as pay and working conditions that repeat themselves on a regular basis every two to four years. Until the mid-1980s most collective agreements were conducted centrally but such agreements were not legally binding until the affiliated unions had approved them. Central agreements included a peace obligation, which means that the employer accepts to meet the unions' demand for a guaranteed period of non-industrial action. During this period local bargaining may be carried out within the terms of the agreed central arrangements. Local or workplace-level bargaining differs from one organization to another and from one industry to another. Normally the local union members are organized in small syndicates or clubs according to their type of work or level. For example in Sweden the manual workers would belong to the LO-affiliated union, the professionals would belong to the SAF-affiliated union, and so on. As explained earlier, under industrial democracy, the local unions are normally represented on the company board and in company committees such as the work environment committee and the economic committee in which the union representatives meet with management on a regular basis to discuss work-related issues, production levels, investment plans, and labour–management contract matters (Hammarström and Nilsson, 1998).

Although centralized collective agreements are the norm, since the 1980s there has been an increase in decentralized bargaining. Some private sector employers have moved away from collective to individual and from centralized to decentralized agreements. In Sweden, for example, the most important issue, wage determination, which had been traditionally agreed through central collective bargaining, became in 1991 decentralized as a result of an SAF decision to withdraw from central bargaining with the LO. At the industrial and organizational levels, the Metal Workers Union and the Engineering Employers Confederation have since the 1980s been concluding agreements without the involvement of the LO or the SAF. The unions in Sweden have gradually accepted locally agreed wage structures concluded between the management and the unions at the local level. In Norway the employers' Confederation of Enterprises and Industry (NHO) has argued for the decentralization of collective bargaining because, they argued, centralized agreements are often obstacles to competition between the organizations that are and those that are not bound by them. They called for pay and working conditions to be determined at the company rather than at the national level. They also wanted their affiliated member companies to have more freedom in the choice of collective bargaining arrangements. In their report to the government in 2000 they asked for the reform of the labour law in order to make the process of collective agreements more flexible and straightforward, including the introduction of vertical agreements and company-based agreements, but, as explained earlier, they have made very little progress and most collective agreements are still conducted through centralized collective bargaining.

Industrial action

In all Scandinavian countries, employees have the right to industrial action in all private sector organizations and in most public sector organizations, but it is only permitted 'when contracts have either expired or been properly terminated' (Hammarström and Nilsson, 1998: 235). The courts decide whether a strike action is illegal or not. A union that calls for an illegal industrial action and the individual union members who take part in the action may be sued by the employer for damages and loss of income.

The Scandinavian approach to employee relations is also known for what is called 'sympathy action' or 'secondary action', which means that unions have the right to take such actions to support or express sympathy with another union involved in a lawful industrial conflict in any of the Scandinavian countries or even in other countries. For example, when the Finnish paper industry workers went on strike on 15 May 2005, both the Swedish Paper Workers Union and the Swedish Building Workers Union started a blockade of overtime work in a sympathy action from 2 June 2005.

ACTIVITY 3

On 23 June 2002, 203 football players in the Norwegian football league's two highest divisions went on strike after failed mediation between the Norwegian Athletes Organization (NISO), a member of LO, representing the players, and the Confederation of Norwegian Business and Industry (NHO), representing the football clubs. The dispute started because of a disagreement over new employment contracts and the introduction of occupational injury insurance. The NISO wanted to see changes to the present system of transferring professional footballers so that it was regulated by collective agreements, but NHO did not want any changes to the current system of standard player contracts. Also, the NISO wanted its members to benefit from fund-based occupational injury insurance schemes and to have the right of control over their own pictures, names and autographs. Except for a commitment to a new insurance scheme, the employers (football clubs) rejected all NISO's demands. Many people, including former and respected club managers, called for an end to the strike that they thought was unacceptable and unethical. In relation to the issue of transfer of players, it was argued that the social partners had to make sure that their agreements are in line with the EU principle of freedom of movement of workers.

Questions

1 How far, and for what reasons, would you agree that the strike was unacceptable and unethical?
2 'Footballers are just workers and their transfer should be considered within the EU principle of freedom of movement.' Discuss.

Settlement of industrial disputes

In Scandinavian countries there is a difference between 'interest' disputes and 'rights' disputes. An interest dispute arises when mediation is provided after the unions have started an industrial action following one-week's notice. The mediator, who is appointed by the National Conciliation Board, has only an advisory role, and the parties do not have to accept the mediator's proposal. The number of mediation cases in relation to interest disputes is very limited because such disputes do not occur very often. A rights dispute is when there is no industrial action and the parties enter into a dispute over the interpretation of laws or agreements. They normally refer to the National Labour Court or in very small cases to the regional lower civil courts or magistrates. The verdict of the National Labour Court is final in all labour disputes. Most of the disputes involve rights and are referred to the courts.

Summary

1   Scandinavian countries industrialized later but faster than most of the other European nations. They transformed from poor agrarian economies to modern, welfare-oriented, service and knowledge-based economies.
2   Scandinavian labour markets are characterized by low levels of unemployment, a high level of equal opportunities and female employment, a high proportion of older workers, and an increasing population of immigrant workers.
3   The Scandinavian approach to management is characterized by social partnership, egalitarianism and consensus, empowerment of line managers, and industrial democracy.
4   The process of recruitment and selection in Scandinavian countries is regulated by National Labour Market Boards (AMSs). Most organizations recruit their employees through the AMS.
5   Scandinavian governments have given a lot of attention to education, vocational training and life-long learning. As well as vocational training provided in schools and universities, many employees receive continuous training in their workplaces.
6   Rewards and remuneration in Scandinavian countries have traditionally been decided through collective agreements between the social partners at the national level. Salaries, benefits and working conditions are normally agreed through collective bargaining between the various employers' associations and trade union confederations.
7   Scandinavian countries have a strong tradition of trade unionism, collective bargaining agreements with limited state intervention in employees' relations, and a strong sense on industrial democracy at the enterprise level.

Revision questions

Chapter 1 provides a review task designed to consolidate your learning from this chapter. Please see Box 1.2.

In addition, the following questions are designed to help you revise this chapter.

1   As an HR manager of a Japanese company in Sweden, write a report to the company's board of directors in Tokyo describing the main similarities and the differences in HRM functions (recruitment and selection, training and development, rewards system, and employee relations) between Denmark and Sweden.
2   Assess the effects of industrial democracy on Scandinavian industrial performance.
3   Discuss the main factors that characterize the Scandinavian labour markets.
4   Compare and contrast the Scandinavian approach to management with that of the North American approach.

References

Brewster, C. and Hegewisch, A. (eds) (1994) *Policy and Practice in European Human Resource Management: The Price Waterhouse Cranfield Survey*, London and New York: Routledge.

Brewster, C. and Larsen, H.H. (eds) (2000) *Human Resource Management in Northern Europe: Trends, Dilemmas and Strategy*, Oxford: Blackwell.

Brewster, C. and Söderström, M. (1994) 'Human resources and line management', in Brewster, C. and Hegewisch, A. (eds), *A Policy and Practice in European Human Resource Management: The Price Waterhouse Cranfield Survey*, London: Routledge.

Brewster, C. Larsen, H.H. and Mayrhofer, W. (2000) 'Human resource management: a strategic approach?' in Brewster. C. and Larsen, H.H. (eds), *Human Resource Management in Northern Europe: Trends, Dilemmas and Strategy*, London: Blackwell.

Brewster, C., Mayrhofer, W. and Morley, M. (eds) (2004) *Human Resource Management in Europe: Evidence of Convergence*, London: Elsevier-Butterworth/Heinemann.

Eurostat, Statistical Office of the European Communities (2007) *Europe in Figures – Eurostat Yearbook 2006–7*, Brussels: the EC.

Hammarström, O. and Nilsson, T. (1998) 'Employment relations in Sweden', in Bamber, J.G. and Lansbury, D.R. (eds), *International and Comparative Employment Relations*, London: Sage, 224–48.

Hofstede, G. (2001) *Culture's Consequences: International differences in work related values*, 2nd edition, London: Sage.

Levinson, K. (2004) *Joint consultation at local level-a survey of Swedish co-determination (Lokal Partssamverkan-en undersökning av svenskt medbestämmande)*, Report published by the National Institute for Working Life, Sweden.

Lindeberg, T., Månson, B. and Vanhala, S. (2004) 'Sweden and Finland: Small Countries with Large Companies', in Brewster, C., Mayrhofer, W. and Morley, M. (eds), *Human Resource Management in Europe: Evidence of Convergence*, Elsevier-Butterworth/Heinemann: London, 279–311.

Mabon, H. (1995) 'Human resource management in Sweden', *Employee Relations*, 17(7): 57–83.

Nergaard, K. (2006) 'Trade union density at stable level', in www.eiro.eurofound. eu.int/2006/05/articles/no0605029i.html, visited on 1 Dec. 2006.

Nyberg, A. (2005) 'Labour force statistics-facts or fiction? *Arbtsmarknadsstatistiken – ideologi eller verklighet?* National Institute for Working Life (*Arbetslivsinstitutet*).

Nyen, T., Hagen, A. and Skule, S. (2004) *Lifelong Learning in Norwegian Working Life: Results from the Learning Conditions Monitor 2003*, Fafo report 434, Oslo: Fafo.

OECD (Organization for Economic Cooperation and Development) (2005) 'Annex A: performance-related pay policies across 12 OECD countries: brief overview', in *Performance-related Pay Policies For Government Employees*, Paris: OECD.

OECD (Organization for Economic Cooperation and Development) (2006) *OECD Factbook 2006: Economic, Environmental and Social Statistics*, Paris: OECD.

Parkum, H.K. and Agersnap, F. (1994) 'Managing people in Scandinavia', in Garrison, T. and Rees, D. (eds), *Managing People across Europe*, Oxford: Butterworth/Heinemann, 111–21.

Rogaczewska, P.A., Larsen, H.H., Nordhaug, O., Døving, E. and Gjelsvik, M. (2004) 'Denmark and Norway: Siblings or Cousins' in Brewster, C., Mayrhofer, W. and Morley, M. (eds), *Human Resource Management in Europe: Evidence of Convergence*, Elsevier-Butterworth/Heinemann: London, 231–77.

Schramm-Nielsen, J. (1991) *Management in Scandinavia: Differences and Similarities*, Cheltenham: Edward Elgar.

Schramm-Nielsen, J., Lawrence, P. and Sivesind, K.H. (2004) *Management in Scandinavia: Culture, context and change*, London: Routledge.

Siim, B. (1993) 'The gendered Scandinavian welfare state: the interplay between women's roles as mothers, workers and citizens in Denmark', in Lewis, J. (ed.), *Women and State Policies in Europe*, Aldershot: Edward Elgar.

Sinani, E., Stafsudd, A., Thomsen, S., Edling, C. and Randoy, T. (2008) 'Corporate governance in Scandinavia: comparing networks and formal institutions', *European Management Review*, 5(1): 27–40.

Sparrow, P. and Hiltrop, J.M. (1994) *European Human Resource Management in transition*, London: Prentice Hall International.

Tixier, M. (1996) 'Cross-cultural study of managerial recruitment tools in Nordic countries', *The International Journal of Human Resource Management*, 7(3): 753–75.

UDI (Norwegian Directorate of Immigration) (2006) at www.eurofound.europa.eu/ eiro/2006/06/articles/no0606039i.html, accessed 1 Dec. 2006.

13

Greece, Italy and Spain

━━━━━━━━━ **LEARNING OUTCOMES** ━━━━━━━━━

The chapter is designed to help you understand, for Greece, Italy and Spain:

1 The (a) economic, (b) political and (c) cultural contexts in which managers work;

2 The main trends in the labour market;

3 The typical features of (a) management policies and practices and (b) organizational structure and behaviour;

4 The main policies and practices of human resource management with regard to: (a) recruitment and selection; (b) training and development; (c) rewards and remuneration; and (d) employee relations.

Introduction

Greece, Italy and Spain are member states of the European Union (EU). Italy was a founding member of the EEC (from which the EU evolved) in 1956, Greece joined in 1981, and Spain in 1986. Although geographically dispersed and historically distinct, the three countries have many political, cultural and economic features in common. Over the last couple of decades they have become increasingly similar in terms of economic trends, labour market composition, social structures and industrial challenges. Their management policies and practices may be conceived as forming a common approach, which we might refer to as the 'South European' or 'olive' approach. (See Table 13.1 for basic statistics.)

Table 13.1 Basic statistical indicators, Greece, Italy and Spain

Country	Area (sq km)	Population (July 2010 est.)	Population Growth (2010) %	GDP – real growth rate (2009) %	Inflation rate (2009 est.) %	Work-force (2009 est.) Million	Unemployment rate (2009) %
Greece	141,957	10,737,428	0.127	−2	1.2	4.98	9.5
Italy	301,340	58,126,212	−0.047	−5.1	0.8	24.97	7.7
Spain	504,782	40,525,002	0.072	−3.6	−0.8	23.04	18

Source: CIA *World Factbook,* 2010.

Contexts: economics, politics and culture

Economics

Greece's economy is dependent on trade partners within the European Union and with the nearby countries of the Balkans and the Middle East. The main exports are agricultural products and manufactured goods. Tourism is also a very significant sector, which generates about 15 per cent of GDP.

Italy has very limited natural resources: most of its needs for raw materials are imported. The strength of its economy lies with the export of industrial products, high-quality textiles, clothing and footwear, motor vehicles, chemicals, canned food and beverages, fruit and vegetables. Economic reforms have included the implementation of a gradual privatization programme, which resulted in the privatization of all major banks and large companies such as Enel, Telecom, Eni and Autostrade. The economy is dominated by privately-owned small and medium size enterprises.

In Spain, the establishment of a democratic political system from the second half of the 1970s brought economic reforms in its wake. The country has been transformed as foreign direct investment into the country increased, international trade grew, nationally strategic sectors of the economy (mainly tourism and car manufacturing) were modernized, and an increasing number of Spanish companies became international. Spain is a major producer and exporter of agricultural products such as vegetables, olives, wine and citrus fruits, as well as an exporter of poultry and fish. Its industrial products include food and beverages, chemicals, automobiles, machine tools, pharmaceuticals, textiles and footwear. Spain's main trade partners are its neighbouring countries in Europe and North Africa, as well as its former colonies in South America.

Politics

All three countries are parliamentary democracies. Greece and Italy are presidential republics, while Spain is a constitutional monarchy. In Greece, the members of parliament are elected democratically for four years. The president, who is the head of state, is elected by the parliament for five years. The president, on the recommendation of the prime minister, appoints the government. However, executive power normally resides with the prime minister, who is a democratically elected leader of the majority party following general elections. The two dominant political parties have been the Social-Democratic party (the Panhellenic Socialist Movement, PASOK), and the Conservative party (New Democracy or *Nea Dimokratia*). Greece is divided administratively into 52 districts (prefectures) and 13 geographical departments.

In Italy the president is the head of state, but very much has a symbolic role. The cabinet or the council of ministers is nominated by the prime minister and approved by the president. The parliament (*parlamento*) consists of the Senate (*Senato della Repubblica*), which is elected by proportional vote with the winning coalition in each region receiving 55 per cent of seats from that region, and the chamber of deputies (*Camera dei Deputati*), which is elected by popular vote for a five-year term. Currently, the main political parties on the right are the National Alliance party (*Alleanza Nazionale*) and Go On Italy (*Forza Italia*) of the media tycoon Berlusconi, while those on the left are the Democratic party of the left (*Partito Democratico della Sinistra*) and the Communist Refoundation on the far left (*Rifondazione Comunista*). Administratively, Italy is divided into 20 regions with considerable autonomy over the provision of health care and education services, and the collection of local taxes.

In Spain, the king is the head of state and has a symbolic role. The leader of the majority party or coalition is elected by the national assembly and appointed by the monarch as the president of the government and prime minister. The national assembly or the General Courts (*Las Cortes Generales*) is made of the senate (*Senado*), which is partly (currently 208 members) directly elected by popular vote and partly (currently 51 members) appointed by the regional legislatures, and of the congress of deputies (*Congreso de los Diputados*), whose members are elected by popular vote on block lists by proportional representation to serve for a term of four years. There are two dominant political parties in Spain: The Spanish Socialist Workers' party (*Partido Socialista Obrero Español*) which includes the Socialists' Party of Catalonia (*Partit dels Socialistes de Catalunya*) and the Socialist Party of the Basque Country (*Partido Socialista de Euskadi*); and the People's Party, which used to be the People's Coalition (*Coalición Popular*) and includes the People's Alliance party (*Alianza Popular*), The Democratic People's Party (*Partido Demócrata Popular*) and The Liberal Party (*Partido Liberal*). Administratively, Spain is made up of 17 autonomous regions and two autonomous cities. Some regions like Catalonia and the Basque Country have greater autonomy than others, especially in education, health and local government.

Culture

Greece, Italy and Spain are officially secular states, though most of their people are Christians (Roman Catholics in Italy and Spain and Greek Orthodox in Greece). Some studies of culture have classified these three countries together under the Latin European or the Mediterranean cluster, while others have treated them as separate entities. For example, Hofstede (2001) placed Spain in a Hispanic cluster, Italy in a Latin cluster and Greece in a near eastern cluster. However, his analysis leads to a conclusion that all three countries have a large power distance where the relationship between managers and subordinates is formalized and the delegation of power is very limited. He found the countries differed in other cultural values, such as uncertainty avoidance (which was stronger in Greece than in Spain or Italy). Greece was found to be more collectivist and masculine than Italy or Spain. Other studies found that Spanish managers expressed less desire for group decision-making, displayed less actual group decision-making, preferred cooperation to competition with peers, and gave higher priority to social esteem and security needs than to self-actualization and autonomy (O'Connell and Prieto, 1996).

ACTIVITY 1

Imagine you are an expatriate of an Irish multinational softdrinks company. Write an assessment of the relative merits of Greek, Italian, and Spanish contexts for investment by your company.

Labour market trends

The labour markets of the three countries are characterized by self-employment, casual and seasonal employment, high unemployment among young and unskilled people, a rising population of older workers, and a rising number of immigrant workers. The minimum working age in Greece for full-time employment is 15 years. The standard working week for full-time employees is 40 hours in the private sector and 37.5 in the public sector. Italy is one of the most highly populated countries in Western Europe with a population of more than 58 million people on an area of about 301,000 square km. The minimum working age for full-time employment is 15 years and the standard working week is 40 hours for full-time employees, but can be as low as 36 hours when agreed by collective bargaining. In Spain, the minimum working age for full-time employment is 16 years and 18 years for overtime, night-time work and work that involves hazard. The standard working week for full-time employment is 40 hours with a maximum of 80 hours of overtime per annum.

In all three countries the majority of the workforce is in the services sector. The level of employment in industry and agriculture has declined over the last two decades. In Spain the active population in the industrial sector has been relatively stable, moving from 22.3 per cent of the workforce in 1960 to 26.4 per cent in 2008. The number of those working in agriculture has declined from 30.7 per cent in 1960 to 4 per cent in 2008. The sector that has increased significantly is that of the services which employed about 27 per cent of the workforce in 1960 to 69.5 per cent in 2008 (OECD, 2007, 2009). A similar trend can be found in Greece and Italy (see Table 13.2).

Table 13.2 Workforce distribution by occupation in (2006) (%), Greece, Italy and Spain

Country	Agriculture	Industry	Services
Greece	12.4	20.4	67.1
Italy	4.7	25.2	70.1
Spain	4.2	24.1	71.7

Source: CIA *World Factbook*, 2010.

Notably, self-employment is a dominant feature of the labour market in the three countries. In the European Union, Greece has the highest proportion of self-employed people. This is apparent from the growing number of small and medium size enterprises, but the public sector is still the main job provider and much-favoured employer. In Greece, for example, most graduates prefer the security and tenure of the jobs that the public sector provides.

In all three countries, the labour market is highly regulated. Strict laws govern areas such as recruitment and selection, employee relations, redundancy and the nature of employment contracts. Though the law provides for equal opportunities in employment, the participation of women in the labour market is still low in all three countries. Moreover, labour mobility within each of the three countries is limited, as many employees tend to stay in one location because of the cost of living and the high cost of housing or the culture of not moving from one region to another.

Unemployment

Unemployment is one of the main problems in the three countries. According to Patiniotis and Stavroulakis (1997: 195), unemployment in Greece 'constantly reaches new record highs, sparked by the dwindling agricultural

Table 13.3 Age structure (%) (2009), Greece, Italy and Spain

Country	0–14 years %	15–64 years %	Over 65 years %	Median age (years)	Life expectancy at birth (for men & women)
Greece	14.3	66.6	19.2	42.2	79.66
Italy	13.5	66.3	20.2	43.7	80.2
Spain	14.5	67.4	18.1	40.1	80.05

Source: CIA *World Factbook*, 2010.

income, declining industrial production, as well as by the drastic limitation of recruitment in the public sector'. After the completion of preparations for the 2004 Olympic games, which created thousands of new jobs, many employees have been made redundant. In Spain the level of unemployment has declined from about 11 per cent in 2003 to just below 10 per cent (9.2 per cent) in 2006, but it went up to 11.32 per cent in 2008 and to 18.5 per cent in 2009 (OECD, 2005; Eurostat, 2007, 2009). In Italy unemployment is relatively lower than that in Spain and Greece but is one of the main challenges for the current government. (See Table 13.3 for age structures.)

Unemployment amongst young people in the region is among the highest in Europe. Those with limited educational and vocational qualifications are the most affected. There are also a significant number of unemployed women. For example, in 2004 in Greece, the unemployment of men and women differed substantially: the rate of female unemployment (16.8 per cent) was twice as much that of men (7.3 per cent). This is similar to Spain, where the unemployment rate of women was 14.3 per cent, compared to that of men (7.5 per cent). It should be noted, however, that since many business are small and family owned it is not easy to determine the exact level of women and young people in employment: in most cases their work is not accounted for, as the main earner is the male owner of the business. Also, many women and young people may work seasonally or temporarily, while still officially considered as full-time job seekers.

Temporary employment

The availability of employment in Southern European and Mediterranean countries tends to fluctuate according to seasons, levels of business activity and even changes in the weather. Many temporary jobs are created during the summer because of tourism and in the autumn because of the harvest of grapes, olives and other crops. It is estimated that about 49 per cent of Greek employees are in temporary and casual employment, while there are about

43 per cent in Italy and 42 per cent in Spain (Eurostat, 2007). In this respect, e Cunha et al. (2004: 163) comment that 'Spanish employers commonly flout the law by issuing temporary contracts, laying off employees and then re-contracting the same workers under yet another temporary contract'. One of the reasons for the use of temporary contracts by most organizations in Spain is the cost of full-time employees' dismissal, which is 45 days for each year of employment. Redundancy compensation in Spain has traditionally been the highest in Europe (Ferner et al., 2001). Temporary employment is also used by some organizations in order to screen the best workers for full-time employment. According to e Cunha et al. (2004: 182), in Spain 'this is quite common, for instance, in the recruitment of university graduates for organizations such as banks and insurance companies'.

Flexible working practices

Unlike temporary work which is very common in Greece, Italy and Spain, flexible working practices such as part-time work, job sharing and home-based working are not very popular. However, by 2006 the use of part-time work in Italy (13.4 per cent) was higher than in Spain (12.2 per cent) or Greece (5.9 per cent) (Eurostat, 2007). The level of part-time work in Greece is the lowest in Europe, with the exception of some new EU member states such as Slovakia (2.8 per cent), Bulgaria (2.1 per cent) and Hungary (4.1 per cent). Most of those who work part time are women. In Italy, for example, 26.7 per cent of women in employment work part time while only 4.7 per cent of men are in part-time employment. In Greece the share of part-time work is higher among women (10.4 per cent) than men (3 per cent) and is also high among those aged 15–19 (13.5 per cent) and those over 65 (15.4 per cent) (Eurostat, 2007). The reasons for the low level of flexible working employment in these countries are as follows:

1 The overriding tradition of seasonal and temporary employment has provided employers with a greater degree of numerical and functional flexibility than part-time work.
2 The relatively low participation of women in the labour market.
3 The high level of small and medium size enterprises that tend to recruit a small number of employees on a full-time basis, and when they need more workers to meet temporary changes in production, they employ temporary workers.
4 The resistance of trade unions to part-time work and other forms of flexible working that are seen to undermine full-time work and exploit employees, especially in large companies and the public sector.
5 The restrictions imposed by law on the employment of part-time workers, as can be seen from Mini Case Study 30.

MINI CASE STUDY 30

Regulating Part-time Employment in Greece

In Greece, a new law was introduced in June 2004 concerning recruitment of employees in public services and local government on fixed-term and part-time contracts. The law requires public sector employers to prepare special operational plans specifying their needs for part-time employees whenever they decide to recruit. The plan has to be approved by the relevant ministerial committee and by the Supreme Personnel Selection Council (ASEP) before the part-time employees are recruited. The part-time employment contracts that can be concluded under the new law should provide for a maximum of 20 hours per week and for no more than 18 months of part-time employment at a time. After the expiry of the contract, the employee will not have the right to be rehired until at least four months have passed. The law, aimed at reducing the level of unemployment and at providing equal opportunities in employment, stated that the part-time workers to be recruited must proportionally represent various categories of employees who have difficulties in finding full-time jobs.

Questions

1 What are the strengths and the weaknesses of the new law?
2 Compare this law with other laws on part-time work from one country or more of your choice.

Immigrant labour

In all three countries, immigrants have contributed significantly to the recent economic growth by providing manual labour that has been needed in sectors such as construction and the service sectors. For example, according to a report by the Greek National Employment Observatory/Research Informatics SA (PAEP SA, 2004) more than 43 per cent of all immigrants to Greece were employed in building and other construction work and about 26 per cent were employed as providers of personal services and cleaners. Moreover, the report showed that most of the immigrant workers were substantially qualified (22 per cent had university- and college-level degrees and 45 per cent had attended a technical or occupational school), but they were employed in manual jobs that did not require high-level educational qualifications. In other words, many immigrants were over-qualified for the jobs they had to do. The report also showed that most of the immigrants (64 per cent) worked longer than the usual 40 hours a week. Interestingly, the report also stated that most immigrants (61 per cent) found their first jobs through a relative or a friend already living in Greece. As far as the employment of immigrant labour in Italy and Spain is concerned, the situation is not dissimilar from that in Greece except for the fact that there are in the former more illegal immigrants who use these countries as a transit before moving to other European countries.

Management and organization

The southern European approach to management is characterized by the management (a) of small and medium size family-owned companies, where often the general manager is the owner of the company and close relatives control the management of the organization, and (b) a small number of large multinational companies whose management is similar to that found in industrially developed countries (Papalexandris and Panayotopoulou, 2004). Thus management policies and practices in the three countries are determined by a strong link between ownership and management, and the influence of examples of international management practice.

Ownership and management practice

Most companies in Greece, Italy and Spain are family owned. Thus in the majority of firms, the general manager is usually the owner or a member of the family of the owner. In such circumstances the style of management that is exercised tends to be paternalistic and sometimes authoritarian. Some of the small and medium size organizations have no HR departments as line managers or the owner–manager of the enterprise normally assume the position. Even in some larger companies, decision-making is still centred on the founder/owner of the firm, with very limited delegation of power. One person or a few trusted people who refuse to delegate their authority because they are afraid of losing control over the organization and its employees make decisions. This is clearly described, in the Greek context, by Papalexandris (1991: 157) who says that 'the strong individualism found among Greeks stands as a major barrier when it comes to delegating authority and accounts for the readiness of Greeks to engage in entrepreneurial activities'.

Internationalized management

Greece, Italy and Spain have attracted increasing investment by multinational companies. In the process many companies have brought with them their own production techniques and management approaches. The car industry, the retailing sector and the banking sector have required international standards of production to compete internationally. Therefore international and regional market forces as well as legal and political changes have influenced the culture of doing business in these three countries. More and more family or individually controlled companies have had to adopt professional business and management approaches (Papalexandris and Stavrou-Costea, 2004), because of:

1   Increased competition of firms from within and outside the European Union;
2   The diffusion of examples of good practice from a growing number of multinational companies operating throughout the European Union;
3   The growing number of well-educated and trained managers, not just among the members of the owner/founder family, but also among the middle and line managers entering the labour market. For example, many of the business families in Greece tend to send their children to study abroad in order to gain international and up-to-date business and management knowledge and transfer it to their family businesses;
4   EU harmonization of employment legislation that the managers of companies in these countries have to adopt; and
5   The availability of resources and technical support for the development and sustainability of small and medium size businesses in these countries. Many sectors have benefited from EU subsidies and grants.

The above factors have put the three countries in the position to compete internationally and to apply management policies and practices similar to those in other Western European countries.

ACTIVITY 2

Refer to the passage entitled 'Management and Organizations' in Chapter 10 (Belgium and France). What seem to you the main similarities and differences between the Southern European (olive) and Francophone approaches to management?

Managing human resources

Studies of HRM in European countries (Brewster and Hegewisch, 1994; Brewster et al., 2004; Myloni, 2004) have shown that the role of HR managers in the southern part of Europe is less strategic than in other EU countries in Western Europe. Only about a third of organizations in Greece and less then two-thirds in Italy and Spain had an HR/personnel manager or director on the board of directors. It is not common to find HR managers participating in the making of corporate business strategies because the HR or personnel department is still considered to have an administrative role and an executive function. Papalexandris and Stravrou-Costea (2004) found that in most Greek organizations the HR department had limited involvement in the formulation of corporate strategy and that more Italian and fewer Greek organizations involved their HR managers in corporate strategy from the outset than their EU counterparts. Also, a study by Papalexandris and Panayotopoulou (2004) found that only a third of Greek companies had the personnel director as a member of the main board of directors. However, where such personnel departments exist HRM issues are either left to line managers or shared. In larger companies the HR function is typically shared, as in Spain where, according to e Cunha et al. (2004: 173), 'there is a certain partnership between line management and the HR department in respect of major HR issues, such as pay, recruitment, training, industrial relations and workforce expansion/ reduction, which is present in both countries'.

Recruitment and selection

All three countries use similar recruitment and selection processes. They all use the traditional methods, such as application forms, newspaper advertisements, interviews, references and tests. They also tend to recruit internally for managerial positions by transferring and promoting employees who already work in the company from one location to another (Papalexandris and Stavrou-Costea, 2004). This practice can be related to the importance given in these countries to seniority, work experience, commitment and loyalty. However there are also some specific differences in relation to the type and level of methods used in each country.

Recruitment

In Greece and Italy, due to the high level of family involvement in the management of their own businesses, preference is usually given to the recruitment of new employees through word of mouth and personal recommendations. The use of recommendations and personal acquaintance with the candidate is the highest in Greece among the European countries. In Spain, however, different methods of recruitment are used. For example, headhunting has become common in private sector companies. They also use employment agencies for temporary employees to meet fluctuations in demand for labour. Moreover, all vacancies, recruitment activities, signed contracts and dismissal cases have to be registered with the National Institute of Employment (*Instituto Nacional de Empleo*, INEM). Also, newspapers in the main cities are often used for graduate recruitment and for professional/managerial positions (Diaz and Miller, 1994).

The larger the company, the more diversified the recruitment methods used in order to get the best employees possible to compete internationally. Many companies (in Spain and Italy, in particular) produce job descriptions for the posts they advertise and then try to recruit the persons who best meet the descriptions. More and more of the larger companies in the three countries use the internet to advertise their job vacancies and to attract the largest pool of applicants possible. The use of the internet has tended to cut out 'the middle man' (i.e. agencies) and has made it possible to shorten the process of recruitment, as the applicant contacts the employer directly by submitting applications online.

Graduate recruitment

Most employers for professional and managerial positions in the three countries require possession of a first degree in the relevant subject area. Depending on the size of the organization, the recruitment of managers is made through various means, ranging from the use of word of mouth to the use of newspaper advertisements and graduate recruitment agencies (Mihail, 2008). Most universities and colleges provide career services for their graduates to help them find jobs. Unlike Spanish and Italian employers, who rarely visit universities (milk round) to recruit their potential managers, many Greek employers, especially large companies, target specific institutions of higher education for their graduate recruitment. Some colleges and universities such as the American Deere College, the Business Faculty of Piraeus University and the Laboratory of Business Administration (ALBA) hold annual graduate recruitment fairs. In Italy managerial positions are filled through internal and external recruitment, but internal recruitment is often preferred in promotions. Many employers in Greece and Spain, and to a lesser extent in Italy, prefer to recruit their potential managers from among graduates of universities outside the country. Graduates from British universities are most preferred and this is evident from the number of, for instance, MBA students from Greece and Spain in the UK.

Selection

Individual interviews are the most common form of selection in all three countries. However, different ways of interviewing have been used in each country. Sifting application forms and requesting references are also widely used in the three countries, though in Greece a reference does not have to be in written form. In Spain, the short-listed candidates are normally asked to complete a standard questionnaire before the interview. Interviews are often conducted by general and/or line managers rather than by HRM specialists. In Greece, the interview may be just a formality when the candidate is recommended or introduced through word of mouth by a relative or a friend (Mihail, 2008). In Italy interviews are sometimes replaced by tests and examinations. Assessment centres are not very common in small and medium enterprises, but are frequently used by a growing number of multinational companies – more often in Italy than in Greece or Spain. Personality tests are frequently used in Spain and Italy but rarely in Greece.

MINI CASE STUDY 31

Recruiting to Order in Spain

Al Dicido is a make-to-order company located in the south of Spain. The level of orders for its products determines the number and type of employees required at any one time. It employs no more than 10 core workers on a full-time basis while the rest of its employees, whose number can be as high as 200 at any one time, are hired on a temporary basis which can be as short as a couple of hours.

Normally the company has a bank of CVs of potential applicants. It has a website and also uses the internet for attracting potential applicants. When the level of orders requires more employees, the company's HR department refers to the bank of CVs, does a pre-selection, and then invites the pre-selected applicants for interview, focusing on the specific skills demanded for the production of the required products. When the managing director was asked about the recruitment procedure, he said that the majority of new recruits were made through personal contacts. He added that because of the short-term horizon of the projects it has become increasingly difficult to have a human resource plan.

Questions

1 Who would apply to work at this company? Provide a typical profile of a temporary employee in terms of gender, age, education/qualifications, experience, etc.
2 Since most of the new recruits were made through personal contacts, why do you think the company maintained a bank of CVs?

Training and development

In all three countries, responsibility for training at the organizational level is normally shared between the HR and line managers, though this differs according to the type and size of organization. Most organizations in the three countries are aware of the importance of training and development and spend at least 1 per cent of their annual labour cost on training (Papalexandris and Stavrou-Costea, 2004). However, the level of training is still very limited in comparison with that of other industrialized countries and is in need of urgent improvement because of the high demand for an educated and skilled work-force in all three countries. However, many organizations have gone through major changes aimed at improving the quality of their employees and their products/services. Such changes have necessitated advanced programmes of employee training and development at different occupational levels. However, the three countries have had to pursue different approaches in their education, vocational training and training and development.

Education

The three countries have different, but equally effective, education systems. The Greek education system has been described as highly centralized and bureaucratic that has failed to meet the needs of the economy and the interests of different stakeholders in society (Saiti and Eliophotou-Menon, 2009). The 9-year compulsory education system in Greece involves 6 years of primary and 3 years of lower-cycle secondary education. Successful completion of the compulsory education leads to the award of a diploma called *Apolyterio* with which the pupils can either join the labour market or continue their secondary and higher education. Higher education is provided by universities and by technical education institutions. It takes 4 to 6 years to complete a degree in the university and 3 to 4 years in a technical institute. A large number of young people study for a higher degree outside Greece in countries such as the UK, Germany and the USA. The high demand and preference for qualifications from universities outside Greece by many employers has led many Greek colleges (mainly private) to offer higher degree programmes that are accredited by Western universities.

In Italy, school education starts at the age of 6 and is compulsory for 8 years. The first 5 years are for primary school education and the following 3 years are for the first stage (lower) of secondary school. The upper-secondary school education, which is not compulsory, is for 5 years before gaining access to higher education. Higher education is very selective: only a limited number of those who complete the upper-secondary school education are able to get access to publicly funded universities. The whole system of education was reformed recently, and now the upper-secondary education is reduced by one year and higher education institutions are expected to become more accessible than before.

In Spain, primary and secondary school education is free and compulsory in public schools until the age of 16. After 6 years of primary education, pupils follow 4 years of secondary education, leading to the *graduado en educacion secundaria*. In secondary education pupils can either choose to follow the BUP (*Bachillerato unificado y polivalente*) pathway of secondary general education or the FP (*Formacion profesional*) route which provides for vocational training in specific industries. To enter university, pupils must sit an entrance examination (*selectividad*). At the university a student can graduate with a diploma after 3 years or with a degree (which is equivalent to the UK masters degree) after 2 more years.

Recent economic reforms in the three countries have produced a demand for new managerial skills and thus a need for more management education. There has been a high demand for holders of management degrees such as the MBA. The number of business schools has increased, although most of them are not officially recognized by the national governments. For example, in Spain, to control the increase of business schools, an association (AEEDE) was established in the 1990s in order to set standards and to advise applicants on the best courses on offer (Diaz and Miller, 1994). Over the years 'the growing supply of first-degree courses on business, and of MBA programmes, has played a very significant role in providing organizations with a more dynamic and self-confident workforce, who feel motivated by bonuses and stock options' (e Cunha et al., 2004: 178).

Vocational training

Vocational training in the three countries is still limited, as many young people prefer to pursue general education from secondary to higher education. It is estimated that the number of those taking occupational training in Spain is the lowest in the EU (e Cunha et al., 2004: 163). Spain has a proactive approach to training. There are three types of training introduced at different levels: Regulated training at schools, which is under the control of the Ministry of Education and is administered by the regional governments; Occupational training for the unemployed, which is administered by the National Institute for Employment (INEM) and regional governments; and Continuing training for employees. The *formación professional* (vocational training), which is carried out in secondary schools rather than through work placements, has a low status and is low quality in the eyes of employers. Businesses complain that students from schools and universities are not adequately prepared for work (Filella and Soler, 1992), and they have had to provide more training for their employees.

In Greece, vocational training in the form of apprenticeship has always existed in small family-owned businesses where mainly school leavers learn skills for specific jobs by working with the 'master'. There have also been a number of state initiatives aimed at helping young people learn new skills to enable them to become employable (Patiniotis and Stavroulakis, 1997). Recently the Greek government attempted to integrate the three main training systems (initial, technical and continuing) in order to improve the occupational skills of the country's workforce and to create a 'unified vocational qualifications certification system' to grant certificates for vocational training regardless of where the training takes place (Kretsos, 2004). Vocational training in Italy is similar to that in Spain but is more organized, resourced and effective.

Organizational training

Employee training and development in all three countries is still limited. The main reason for the lack of training opportunities is very often linked to the lack of resources and finances, and the general perception of training by many employers as a cost rather than an investment. Since most companies in the three countries are small and privately owned family businesses they may not be willing to invest in training because of they lack a strategic view of training and have limited resources. In most cases the owner is the manager and has received little management education and training, 'but a lot of training from their own life experience, which they are convinced is better' (Diaz and Miller, 1994: 158). There is also the dilemma that employees tend to change their employers as soon as they get the training. Italy, which is more industrialized, spends more on training than Spain and Greece. Greek organizations, for example, spend around 2 per cent of their wage bill on training, while in Germany, for example, organizations spend at least 5 per cent of their wage bill on training (Papalexandris and Panayotopaoulou, 2004).

Nevertheless, many large employers have realized the importance of continuous training and development for their sustainability and competitive advantage in an increasingly competitive business environment. The state has also intervened by subsidizing companies that provide continuous training for their employees. The European Union has also provided subsidies to companies for vocational training, both as tax relief and as partial payment of certain training courses. Therefore, such internal and external factors have led many organizations to give more attention to the training and development of their employees. For example, according to Papalexandris and Chalikias (2002), Greek companies started to place emphasis on the use of training needs analysis, on setting training evaluation criteria, and on using on-the-job training methods, and to see the need for employees' line managers to work closely with the human resources department. A study by e Cunha et al. (2004) reported that 81 per cent of Spanish companies used systematic training needs analysis, 54 per cent used business plans, and 75 per cent evaluated the effectiveness of training. They found that 89 per cent of Spanish organizations had carried out formal evaluations immediately after training, either always or often.

Rewards and remuneration

In all three countries, different organizations apply different systems of variable pay. It has been argued that 'the increase in the use of variable pay reflects a general tendency to relate pay to performance' (e Cunha et al., 2004: 178), but the level of pay in general is normally agreed through collective bargaining. The level of pay seems to vary from one country to another, and even from one organization to another within the same country depending on the type of organization, the type of employment and the profile and performance of the employee. Traditionally countries like Italy and Spain have applied rigid salary levels with limited transparency, but over the last few years they have introduced a variety of flexible pay systems. Greece and Spain have a statutory minimum wage, whereas in Italy, as in Germany and the Scandinavian countries, minimum wages are set through sectoral collective agreements.

The minimum wage

Greece and Spain have a statutory minimum wage, while Italy, like Germany, has no minimum wage. In Greece there is a minimum wage for non-manual workers aged 19 or over and for manual workers aged 18 or over, but both minimum wages are determined annually through collective agreements with the social partners and in relation to inflation forecasts. In Spain the government sets the national minimum wage for all employees of working age and adjusts it annually after taking into consideration the rate of inflation, productivity and general economic trends. In response to changes in living standards and growth in the economy the governments of both countries have increased the rate of the minimum wages over recent years. In Greece it increased from €542.69 per month in 2000 to €862.82 per month in 2010, and in Spain from €495.60 to €738.85 over the same period (Eurostat, 2010).

Performance appraisal and performance-related pay

The use of performance appraisal is relatively new in the three countries and is more established for managerial and professional jobs than manual ones. Performance-related pay is used for professional, technical and managerial staff by most Italian and Spanish companies to a level that is higher than the EU average, while Greek companies use it slightly less (Papalexandris and Stavrou-Costea, 2004). The use of performance-related pay for clerical and manual jobs in the three countries is still lower than the EU average. There is also a difference in the pay systems between the larger and smaller organizations, as the latter tend to have an egalitarian pay system that avoids embarrassing underperforming employees who may be, very often, relatives or friends. In Greece, for example, more importance is given to the results rather than formal appraisal of performance. It is believed that achieving the expected results provides enough evidence of good performance, and therefore there is no need for a formalized appraisal system especially for manual and technical jobs. Moreover, many managers and professionals in small and medium size companies enjoy a high level of status, power and prestige, which renders their actions and behaviour unquestionable, and therefore the use of formal performance appraisal becomes inappropriate (Papalexandris and Stavrou-Costea, 2004). Moreover, in Italy, performance appraisal is also not readily accepted because of the influence of the Catholic belief that everyone tries to do their best and therefore everyone's performance is acceptable (Papalexandris and Stavrou-Costea, 2004). According to e Cunha et al. (2004: 179), 'the relative importance of variable pay for clerical and manual workers in [Spain] is very much related to the difficulties of using performance appraisals fairly'. They found that in some organizations performance appraisal was seen as a burden on management and an added task that they can do without.

Employee relations

Greece, Italy and Spain differ in their employee relations approaches because of their different histories of industrialization, labour organization and levels of state intervention. However, the common feature in all three countries is that collective bargaining is becoming less centralized and the level of industrial action has been reduced. Also, their employment laws are the result of tripartite collective agreements involving the government, unions and employers' confederations, and have to be approved by parliament. There are differences as well as similarities in the composition and role of their trade unions, in the process of collective bargaining and employee participation, in the process and level of industrial action, and in the way industrial or employee disputes are settled.

Trade unions

In Greece, the majority of trade unions are organized on the basis of occupation or occupational category. They are divided into primary-level, secondary-level and tertiary-level organizations. Primary-level organizations are autonomous trade unions that are formed with the minimal of legal formalities in small private sector enterprises. In many cases they are not well organized. Secondary-level trade union organizations are federations and labour centres. They are well organized, officially recognized and the main representatives of employees at the organizational and sectoral level. Tertiary-level trade union organizations are confederations of federations and of labour centres, representing the Greek workforce at the national and international levels. There are two major trade union confederations: 1) the Greek General Confederation of Labour (GSEE) and 2) the Greek Confederation of Public Servants (ADEDY). One of the peculiarities of trade unions in Greece is that they have often supported affiliated political parties. Most of them have party- political links in the form of factions that are made of party members who promote party policies among the workers and transfer their parties' ideology into the organization of labour.

In Italy, different types of trade unions have emerged at different times since the establishment of craft unions in the late nineteenth century. As the country industrialized the unions were organized vertically at the industrial level as industrial trade unions similar to the ones developed throughout the industrialized nations as a result of increasing mass production, and the spread of mechanization and 'Fordism' from the 1920s onwards. Industrial trade unions are still common in Italy, as in Western Europe, but they have had to adapt to the development of new forms of work and modes of production, translating them into occupational and general trade unions. There are also some enterprise unions, like those found in Japan. In terms of organization, Italian trade unions are organized into a number of confederations representing national federations and regional trade unions at sectoral and organizational levels. The main trade union confederations in Italy are: 1) the General Confederation of Italian Workers (CGILl); 2) the Italian Confederation of Workers Unions (CISL); and 3) the Union of Italian Workers (UIL).

In the mid-1970s the three trade unions confederations (CGIL, CISL and UIL) joined forces to form a united federation (*Federazione*) and agreed that their leaders would not be active politicians, but rather representatives of the working classes regardless of their political affiliations. However, the coalition split in 1984 following a disagreement over the determination of a new wage indexation system (Pellegrini, 1998). Since then the unions have remained politically independent and also independent from each other. However, they very often unite on major employee relations issues and get involved in politics by forming allegiances with political parties, especially in times of political crisis and during general elections.

In Spain, trade unions were formed over the first quarter of the twentieth century as resistance groups to fight against the exploitation of labour. Gradually they became more organized as craft unions, and then as the country developed and industrialized they grew in number and in size, and took the form of occupational associations or occupational 'corporations', depending on the legal context of their recognition by the government. Following the restoration of democracy in the mid-1970s, the unions became better structured, more organized and more powerful. They became organized mainly on industrial, occupational or geographical lines. There are single unions and umbrella-type unions grouped together on the basis of geographical area (territorial federations), industry (industrial federations) or both (trade union confederation or central trade union bodies). The top three major trade union confederations are: 1) the General Confederation of Workers (CGT); 2) the Trade Union Confederation of Workers Commissions (CCOO); and 3) the General Workers Confederation (UGT).

The two Spanish trade union confederations that have played a significant role since the passing of the Trade Union Association Bill in 1977 are the CCOO and the UGT. They have been well organized nationally and effective in negotiating annual national collective agreements and in organizing general strikes. However, in recent years their relationship with employers has generally been cooperative and based on mutual understanding of the needs of the economy, especially in times of economic crisis.

Trade union membership and density

Trade union membership in Greece varies between the private and the public sectors. It can be as high as 98 per cent of the working population in the public sector or as low as 5 per cent of workers in the private sector. Since the late 1990s trade union membership has declined in all three countries (see Table 13.4). Spain has the lowest trade union membership in comparison with Greece and Italy. Although their membership is low, trade unions in Spain are influential because they enjoy the same position as the workers' committees at the plant level and are the main negotiator, supported by legislation, in collective bargaining agreements at the regional and national levels.

Table 13.4 Trade union density 1999–2007 (%), Greece, Italy and Spain

	1999	2000	2001	2002	2003	2004	2005	2006	2007
Greece	27.9	27	26.1	25.3	24.4	23.7	23	–	–
Italy	35.4	34.7	34.2	33.6	33.5	33.9	33.8	33.4	33.3
Spain	16	16.7	15.9	16	15.8	15.5	15	14.6	–

Source: Eurostat, 2009.

Collective bargaining

Collective bargaining in Greece is still dominated by pay-related issues such as setting the increase in the minimum wage or the periods of service used for calculating benefits. In Greece, the Consultative National Employment Council is the opinion-forming body that gathers the social partners (the Federation of Greek Industries, SEV, the Greek General Confederation of Labour, GSEE, and the government) to discuss employment relations issues. The Corps of Labour Inspectors (SEPS) was set up in the late 1990s in order to enforce the implementation of labour legislation, to ensure industrial peace and to help workers and employers to understand their rights and obligations.

Collective bargaining in Italy takes place at the national, regional, industry and organizational levels. The bargaining process may coincide with a strike lasting for a few hours or a day in order to put pressure on the employer to bargain sensibly. Significant features are as follows.

1 At the national level, collective agreements through centralized and politicized collective bargaining between the union confederation and the main employers' associations play a significant role in setting the terms and conditions of employment and the levels of pay settlement.

2 At the industrial level collective agreements have involved the metals, textiles, chemicals and construction industries. Industry-level agreements tend to focus on hours of work and overtime, work profiles and job descriptions, holiday entitlement, the disclosure of information to unions, rewards and benefits, discipline, union rights and other issues affecting workers at the industry or sector levels. They also seem to be 'used to influence employers' strategies in terms of investments, subcontracting and technological change' (Pellegrini, 1998: 162).

3 Enterprise-level collective agreements have existed since the late 1960s but became widespread only after the 1970 Workers Charter, which provided for workplace union representatives. The Workers Charter of 1970 gave the right to workers to set up works councils (*Rappresentanza Sindacale Aziendale*, RSA) in the workplace. The RSA was similar in its role and structure to the German works councils (see Chapter 11). However, the RSA were not so successful because many Italian works councils were never elected in many workplaces.

In Spain, the 1980 Workers Statute recognizes the right of workers to organize and to bargain collectively. Collective bargaining over salary increases, employment conditions, benefits and entitlements, and other collectively agreed issues, is normally carried out between the employer and the unions at the national or regional levels and usually covers a period of one or two years. Moreover, there is a statutory model of worker representation within companies. In companies of 50 or more staff, employees have the right to elect a workers' committee (*comité de empresa*), which has significant powers to consult and negotiate with management. This has meant that, in spite of low levels of union membership, Spanish trade unions have been able to exert considerable influence within the firms through the support they receive in workers' committee elections.

The Spanish legislator requires all firms with 50 or more employees to form workers' committees. Committee members are elected for four years from among the company's employees, regardless of their membership in the trade unions. Each committee elects a president and an administrative assistant. The workers' committee meets regularly and has the right to access company information, namely the shareholders' report, the sales and production reports, and all policies related to employment, as well as the statistical reports on absenteeism, accidents, stoppages, etc. Workers' committees have the right to collective bargaining and to represent workers individually, as in individual disciplinary cases, and collectively, as in other matters of terms and conditions of work. Such committees cover all aspects of employee–employer relationships. Even strikes are managed through a strike committee which deals with strike negotiations and coordinates the legality and security of strike action with the unions.

It should be remembered at this point that the three countries have had to adopt the EU Directive on Information and Consultation and to introduce works councils at the workplace, but in practice each country claims to have such works councils or workers' committees in place. In Greece, for example, despite the existence of legislation on works councils since 1988, not many have been set up. Employee representation at board level exists only in public utilities and transport. There are two levels of employee representation: the highest level is the 'representative assembly of social control', which sets the company's policies. Employee representatives in the assembly constitute up to one-third, with another third from consumer groups and local authorities and one-third from government. The second level is the board of directors, to which employees elect one-third of the members. Similarly, in Italy, although the constitution gives workers the right to participate in management, employee representation at board level is limited to cases where company-level agreements provide for the involvement of employee representatives in management or supervisory boards. Also, in Spain, except in some large public sector organizations, where the parties agree to employee representation in management, there is no legal right for employees to have any representation at board level.

Industrial action

Industrial action in the form of strikes and stoppages is less frequent now in any of the three countries than it was in the 1970s and 1980s. However, despite the overall decline in strike action across the European Union, Spain and Greece are still experiencing a level of industrial action that is higher than the European average. For example, in 2004 there were 35.6 working days lost through industrial action per 1,000 employees in Spain, compared to 1.6 working days lost in Germany over the same period (Kretsos, 2004). Most strikes in Greece have been in the public sector. The main reasons for such strikes have been pay indexation to offset inflation, the creation of new pay scale regulations for public servants, the inclusion of various pay supplements in basic pay, and the repeal of the new legislation extending part-time employment to the public sector (Kretsos, 2004). Also, in Greece the courts have the power to declare a strike illegal or abusive. Employers are not allowed to replace workers on strike with others, except in certain cases in the public sector when public services have to be delivered on time by temporary workers.

MINI CASE STUDY 32

Greek Union Power

On the 17 March 2005, in Greece, all workers in the public and private sectors staged a four-hour nation-wide work stoppage and demonstrations throughout the country. It was called for by the Greek General Confederation of Labour (GSEE) and supported by the Confederation of Public Servants (ADEDY). The action was taken in response to the government's proposals to make changes in employment and insurance matters in an attempt to introduce a number of economic austerity measures in response to economic decline after 2004. The GSEE demanded real wage and salary increases to meet the rising level of inflation, an immediate increase in unemployment benefits, a reduction in flexible forms of employment, more government action to deal with re-industrialization and the move of companies to low-cost countries, and a rise in wages in Greece to bring them into line with those in other EU member states.

Questions

Consider the content of the above paragraph in the light of what you have read so far about employee relations in Greece:

1 Why do you think the unions staged a four-hour nationwide work stoppage rather than an indefinite strike?
2 How effective do you think a stoppage would be, compared to a long strike?
3 Analyse each one of the unions' demands and discuss their effects on employees.

In Italy, the right to strike in essential public services has been restricted by law since 1988. Usually there are no peace clauses in agreements and consequently strikes can be held at any stage. As a result, the level of industrial action declined significantly. There are also the so-called political strikes which are used as a form of expressing solidarity with other workers elsewhere, or to put pressure on the government to change its mind over certain employee relations issues.

The levels of strike activity and industrial action in Spain are similar to those of Greece, but the process is better organized and the action is often effective. For example, when the workers decide to go on strike they elect a strike committee to carry out negotiations. Normally five days before the strike the employer is provided with the reasons for the strike, the details of the strike activities and the possible measures that could be taken to avoid strike action. Workers are not paid during the strike but they benefit from social security and state health insurance.

Settlement of industrial disputes

The process of settling industrial disputes depends on the legal and political system of each country. For example, compulsory arbitration was the main procedure for settling employee–employer disputes in Greece until 1990 when Law 1876/1990 made compulsory arbitration the last resort and the least desirable option. The law established a voluntary settlement procedure where the first step is conciliation, the second step is mediation and the last step is arbitration. Conciliation and mediation are expected to help the parties in dispute to reach an agreement without having to refer the case to arbitration where the decision of the arbitrator is legally binding. Although the process may take longer than compulsory arbitration it helps the parties to reach more realistic agreements and therefore avoids industrial action by employees.

In Italy, arbitration is the least favoured method and is used only when collective agreements have already specified it – and with the condition that there is no prejudice to the parties' option to have recourse to the law. Arbitration can be formal or informal. In formal arbitration the arbitrator, who is a *pretore* (a single judge presiding over an ordinary civil court) makes an award that is legally binding. In cases of informal arbitration the arbitrator's award is not legally binding but is considered a 'private' agreement between the collective parties in relation to specific matters.

In Spain, the settlement of industrial disputes differs between disputes of rights and disputes of interest. Disputes of rights are related to the application of a particular issue that was agreed collectively or set by law. Disputes of interest are related to cases of industrial action such as pay and working conditions. The settlement of each type of dispute is through third-party intervention, where the first step is to refer the case to a joint collective agreement committee to decide on the use of conciliation, mediation or arbitration, depending on the severity of the dispute and whether it is of rights or of interest. Most of the disputes of rights are settled through the use of conciliation, whereas most of the disputes of interest are settled through mediation and arbitration.

Summary

1. Though geographically dispersed and historically distinct, Greece, Italy, and Spain have many political, cultural and economic features in common. They are similar in economic trends, labour market composition, social structures, and industrial challenges. Hence, the Southern European approach to management, which these countries share, is known as the olive approach.
2. The labour markets of the three countries are characterized by self-employment, casual and seasonal employment, high unemployment among young and unskilled people, and a rising numbers of older and immigrant workers.
3. The Southern European management approach is characterized by a strong link between ownership and management policies and practices, and the influence of international management.
4. The process of recruitment and selection in these three countries involves the use of traditional methods of recruitment such as application forms, newspaper advertisements, interviews, references and tests.
5. Most organizations in the three countries are aware of the importance of training and development, and spend at least 1 per cent of their annual labour cost on training, though training is still very limited in comparison with other industrialized countries.
6. Traditionally countries like Italy and Spain have applied rigid salary levels with limited transparency, but over the last few years they have introduced significant changes to their pay structures and a variety of flexible pay systems.
7. Although Greece, Italy and Spain are members of the EU and are subject to its employment laws and regulations, they differ in their employee relations approaches because of their different histories of industrialization, labour organizations and levels of state intervention.

Revision questions

Chapter 1 provides a review task designed to consolidate your learning from this chapter. Please see Box 1.2.

In addition, the following questions are designed to help you revise this chapter:

1 As an HR manager of a Chinese company considering investment in Spain, Italy, or Greece, write a report to the company's board of directors in Beijing: (a) summarizing the labour markets of Greece, Italy and Spain, and (b) outlining the implications for the decision on whether to invest in any of these countries.

2 Refer to Chapter 12 (Denmark, Norway and Sweden). What seem to you the main similarities and differences in HRM functions (recruitment and selection, training and development, rewards system, and employee relations) between the Southern and Northern European countries?

3 Discuss the main reasons for the low level of part-time employment and for the high level of temporary employment in Greece and Spain.

References

Brewster, C. and Hegewisch, A. (1994) (eds) *Policy and Practice in European Human Resource Management: The Price Waterhouse Cranfield Survey*, London and New York: Routledge.

Brewster, C., Mayrhofer, W. and Morley, M. (eds) (2004) *Human Resource Management in Europe: Evidence of Convergence*, London: Elsevier-Butterworth/Heinemann.

Diaz, A. and Miller, P. (1994) 'Managing people in Spain', in Garrison, T. and Rees, D. (eds), *Managing People Across Europe*, Oxford: Butterworth-Heinemann, 140–62.

e Cunha, C.R., Obeso, C. and e Cunha, M.P. (2004) 'Spain and Portugal: different paths to the same destiny', in Brewster, C., Mayrhofer, W. and Morley, M. (eds), *Human Resource Management in Europe: Evidence of Convergence*, London: Elsevier-Butterworth/Heinemann, 161–88.

Eurostat, Statistical Office of the European Communities (2007) *Europe in Figures – Eurostat Yearbook 2006–7*, Brussels: the EC.

Eurostat, Statistical Office of the European Communities (2009) *Eurostat Yearbook 2009*, available online at: http:\\epp.eurostat.ec.europa.eu/portal/page/portal/product_details/publication?p_product_code = KS-CD-09-001, accessed on 22 January 2010.

Eurostat, Statistical Office of the European Communities (2010) *Minimum wages: Tables, Graphs and Maps Interface*, available on line at: http:\\epp.eurostat.ec.europa.eu/tgm/table.do?tab = table&init = 1&plugin = 1&language = en&pcode = tps00155, accessed on 17 September 2010.

Ferner, A., Quintanilla, J., Varul, M. (2001) 'Country-of-Origin Effects, Host-Country Effects, and the Management of HR in Multinationals: German Companies in Britain and Spain', *Journal of World Business*, 36(2): 107–27.

Filella, J. and Soler, C. (1992), 'Spain', in Brewster, C., Hegewisch, A., Lockhart, T. and Holden, L. (eds), *The European Human Resource Management Guide*, London: Academic Press, pp. 439–82.

Hofstede, G. (2001), *Culture's Consequences: International differences in work related values*, 2nd edn, London: Sage.

Kretsos, L. (2004) *2003 Annual Review for Greece*, at www.eiro.eurofound.europa.eu/2004/01/feature/gr0401102f.html, visited 21 Dec. 2006.

Mihail, M.D. (2008) 'Graduates' career orientations and strategies in corporate Greece', *Personnel Review*, 37(4): 393–411.

Myloni, B., Harzing, A.W. and Mirza, H. (2004) 'Human resource management in Greece: have the colours of culture faded away?', *International Journal of Cross Cultural Management*, 4(1): 59–76.

O'Connell, J.J. and Prieto, J.M. (1996) *A Vertical Reading of the Cross-cultural Management Research: The Case Study of Spain*, at www.ucm.es/info/Psyap/libros/conne10.htm, accessed 22 may 2007.

OECD (Organization for Economic Cooperation and Development) (2005) *OECD Employment Outlook 2005*, Paris: OECD, Available online at: http:\\website1.wider.unu.edu/lib/pdfs/OECD-Employment-2005.pdf accessed on 21 May 2007.

OECD (Organization for Economic Cooperation and Development) (2007) *Annual Report 2007*, Paris: OECD, available online at: http://www.oecd.org/dataoecd/34/33/38528123.pdf, accessed on 16 February 2009.

OECD (Organization for Economic Cooperation and Development) (2009) *OECD Factbook 2009: Economic, Environmental and Social Statistics*, Paris: OECD, available online at: http://www.oecd-ilibrary.org/economics/oecd-factbook_18147364, accessed on 12 May 2010.

PAEP SA (the Greek National Employment Observatory/Research Informatics SA) (2004) at www.eiro.eurofound.europa.eu/ 004/10/feature/gr0410105f.html, accessed 21 Dec. 2006).

Papalexandris, N. (1991) 'A comparative study of human resource management in selected Greek and foreign-owned subsidiaries in Greece', in Brewster, C. and Tyson, S. (eds), *International Comparisons in Human Resource Management*, Chapter 9, pp. 145–58, London: Pitman Publishing.

Papalexandris, N. and Chalikias, J. (2002) 'Changes in training, performance management and communication issues among Greek firms in the 1990s: Intercountry and intracountry comparisons', *European Industrial Training*, 26(7): 342–52.

Papalexandris, N. and Panayotopoulou, L. (2004) 'Exploring the mutual interaction of societal culture and human resource management practices: Evidence from 19 countries', *Employee Relations*, 26(5): 495–509.

Papalexandris, N. and Stavrou-Costea, E. (2004) 'Italy, Greece and Cyprus', in Brewster, C., Mayrhofer, W. and Morley, M. (eds), *Human Resource Management in Europe: Evidence of Convergence*, London: Elsevier-Butterworth/Heinemann, 189–230.

Patiniotis, N. and Stravroulakis, D. (1997) 'The development of vocational education policy in Greece: a critical approach', *Journal of European Industrial Training*, 21(6): 192–202.

Pellegrini, C. (1998) 'Employment relations in Italy', in Bamber, J.G. and Lansbury, D.R. (eds), *International and Comparative Employment Relations*, 3rd edn, London: Sage, 144–68.

Saiti, A. and Eliophotou-Menon, M. (2009) 'Educational decision making in a centralised system: the case of Greece', *International Journal of Educational Management*, 23(6): 446–55.

Part IV

Case Study: EU Enlargement and its Implications for Work and Employment

Introduction

When the leaders of the European Union met in Lisbon in 2000, they envisaged that EU enlargement would result in long-term positive economic and social changes, despite the possibility of short-term negative effects. They projected a European continent that would have the most competitive knowledge-based economy in the world and be able to maintain vibrant economic growth with improved employment prospects and greater social cohesion.

Eventually the biggest enlargement of the EU occurred in 2004 when 10 new member states (NMS) from Central and Eastern Europe joined the already established member states (EU-15) in the west. The EU-15 countries agreed to the enlargement, not because they were weak and needed to strengthen their economies, but because they were already in a strong position and they wanted to develop further. In fact, between 1994 and 2003 the overall labour productivity of the EU-15 countries was much greater than those of either the USA or Japan.

However, the thought of bringing 25 (economically, socially, culturally and politically) different countries together generated many worries among the citizens of the EU-15, especially in countries where the rate of unemployment and the level of immigration had already been high. The central issue in the enlargement process has been the free movement of workers from the new and less economically developed to the old and industrialized EU member states. One of the main pillars of EU integration is the free movement of resources (including human resources) from one country to another, but some EU-15 member states have benefited from the use of a special transitional clause in the enlargement agreement that allows them to restrict entry of the new member states' (NMS') workers to their territories.

The transitional clause

According to the Accession Treaty signed in 16 April 2003 in Athens, the old EU-15 member states agreed that individual members would be able to regulate or restrict access to their labour markets following the EU enlargement, instead of adhering to the EU integration rules on the free movement of people. The agreement gave the member states the right to control the free movement of labour from the new member states for up to seven years from the accession date. This right is referred to as 'transitional clause'.

Initially, all the EU-15 member states, except the UK, Sweden and Ireland, opted to apply the transitional clause by restricting access to workers from the Central and Eastern European countries. The countries that initially decided to apply the transitional clause were concerned about the effects that the increased labour migration would have on the state welfare system and on the local labour market. However, the EU-15 member states came under pressure from employers' organizations and from trade unions.

On the one hand, employers' organizations such as the Confederation of British Industry (CBI), the Confederation of Danish Employers (*Dansk Arbejdsgiverforening*, DA) and the Swedish Employers Federation (*Svenska arbetsgivareföreningen*, SAF) were in favour of free movement of labour and of lifting all restrictions that might impede the supply of labour. They did not see any real threat to the local labour markets and argued that the trade unions and politicians had exaggerated the fear of an influx of foreign labour. They insisted that their national economies needed skilled labour from the new member states (NMS). A number of companies threatened to close their operations in the west and to move to the NMS where labour is plentiful, cheap, reliable and committed. For example, the managing director of a large UK company said: 'if the needed employees do not come to us we will go to them'. With increasing international competition and the high demand for special knowledge-based, professional and technical skills, many large employers intend to recruit from overseas in the search for talented and skilled labour.

On the other hand, most of trade union organizations, such as the Trades Union Congress (TUC) in the UK, the German Trade Union Federation

(*Deutscher Gewerkschaftsbund, DGB*), and the Spanish General Workers' Confederation (*Unión General de Trabajadores*, UGT), asked for the introduction of proper immigration laws that would protect emigrant workers from exploitation and national workers from unemployment. Some trade unions called for the creation of minimum standards of terms and conditions of employment throughout the EU countries so that low-paid employees would see no need to move from one country to another.

Most of the EU-15 member states' governments have responded to their employers' organizations' demands and have opened their borders to the flow of labour from the NMS in the hope of attracting enough skilled and qualified workers. Most of them relaxed the application of the clause within the first two years of the accession, mainly because of pressure from employers. Currently the only two countries that have decided to extend the application of the transitional clause are Germany and Austria. Germany, which already has more than 10 million foreigners (UNFPA, 2006, *State of the World Population 2006*), decided to restrict entry of people from the new member states of Central and Eastern Europe (the Czech Republic, Estonia, Latvia, Lithuania, Hungary, Poland, Slovenia and Slovakia) until 2011.

Drivers of immigration

The factors that have driven people from the new to the old EU member states include the state of the home economy, social structure, political system, labour market composition, the availability of education and training opportunities, and standards of living. Income differentials and better working conditions are often the main drivers for labour migration, but there are many other reasons why people leave their families, relatives and friends, and even prosperous and well-paid jobs, behind them and seek employment in the EU-15 countries. In reality economic incentives are not the only 'push factors' for people to leave their native countries. Despite the move of some large multinational companies (MNCs) from the west to invest in the NMS, labour migration to the EU-15 countries has continued to increase.

Evidently work is not the only motive for people to move from one country to another. Some of the emigrants from Central and Eastern Europe had professional and prestigious jobs before moving to the west to undertake lower-level jobs for which they are overqualified and over-experienced. They do such jobs because they get paid more for doing them than doing better jobs in their home countries. The jobs that multinational companies provide for them at home may not be attractive unless they are paid the same or higher than they get paid in the west – but MNCs, which pursue cheap labour in such countries, are unlikely to do so.

There are other equally important factors that push people to look for a better quality of life elsewhere. Such incentives include meeting new people and making new friends, learning a new language, facing new challenges, wanting a different climate, exploring a new country, and joining family members.

Not everyone who wants to emigrate could emigrate and benefit from the right of free movement that is granted to all the citizens of the European Union. There are many factors, economic (property, land and business ownership or/ and employment contracts), familial (disruption to family life, resentment of spouse and children, care for parents, etc.), and cultural (language barriers, fear of the unknown, prejudices, etc.), that may deter people from moving from the new to the old EU member states. These are factors that 'pull' on many potential emigrants and cause them to stay at home and decide not to work in other countries. Therefore the feared influx of workers from the Central and Eastern European countries to the west may be restricted by the 'pull factors' and only certain people of certain age (normally 18 to 25 years) may be able to move freely from one country to another and to settle in the EU-15.

Implications and responses

The drivers for emigration vary but the fact is that thousands of people decided to benefit from their right of free movement in the enlarged free market economy and to seek employment where jobs are available. Countries such as Ireland, Sweden and the UK, that have had no restrictions on the movement of labour from the NMS, attracted no more emigrants than the countries that put restrictions in place, such as Germany, Finland and France.

In most of the EU-15 countries, the feared negative effects of migrant labour on the local labour markets seem to be minimal because the transitional rules have ensured that migrant workers are treated equally and paid fairly and in accordance with the employment laws of the country. Immigrants have contributed to recent economic growth by providing manual labour. For example, according to a report by the Greek National Employment Observatory/ Research Informatics SA (PAEP SA, 2004) more than 43 per cent of all immigrants to Greece were employed in building and other construction work and about 26 per cent were employed as providers of personal services and cleaners. The report shows that most of the immigrant workers were highly qualified (22 per cent had university and college-level degrees and 45 per cent had attended a technical or occupational school), but they were employed in manual jobs that did not require high-level educational qualifications. It also shows that most of the immigrants (64 per cent) worked longer than the usual 40 hours a week.

In Italy and Spain the situation is not dissimilar from that in Greece, except that more illegal immigrants in Italy and Spain use these countries as transit points before moving to other countries such as Germany, France, the UK, Canada and the USA. Sweden has had the highest increases in population due to immigration. It is estimated that immigration contributed to more than 40 per cent of Sweden's population growth (Lindeberg et al., 2004).

Recently the European Citizen Action Service (ECAS) produced a report on the movement of labour since the enlargement of the EU in 2004. The report, entitled *Who's Still Afraid of the EU Enlargement?* (Traser, 2006), which should be read in conjunction with this case study, shows that the number of legally registered citizens from the 10 new EU countries accounted for only 0.3 per cent of the total EU-15 population, and that the correlation between the imposition of laws restricting access to labour markets in the EU-15 and the actual flow of emigrants from the NMS is not strong. More NMS nationals prefer to go to Germany or Finland, where transitional arrangements have been imposed, than to Sweden or Ireland, where there were no restrictions to labour migration from the NMS. Also, contrary to expectations, Sweden has not become a place for 'welfare tourism' (i.e. NMS nationals taking advantage of the country's excellent welfare provisions). The report concluded that the free movement of labour from the NMS to the old ones has not been a real threat to Western labour markets and has not created substantial rises in unemployment or declining levels in social welfare standards. Therefore, the report recommended, among other things, the lifting of transitional arrangements, the end of exploitation of migrant workers, and the promotion of 'circular migration' by creating job opportunities in the NMS and helping migrant workers to return to their home countries with their newly acquired knowledge, skills and experience.

It has been also argued that 'intra-EU migration is vital for the efficient use of EU labour' (*Financial Times*, 23 Aug. 2006) and that labour migration is good for economic development because of the benefits it brings to the sending and to the recipient countries. The sending countries benefit from the remittances their citizens send back, as well as from reduced unemployment and the return of a better-educated and skilled workforce in the medium to long terms. However, not all emigrants from the NMS send money back to their countries because often, as young people, they do not have family responsibilities and they intend to save for their education, buying properties and setting up businesses in their new countries. There is also a possibility that some of them may never return to work in their home countries.

One of the major problems in the NMS is the rapid ageing of their populations and their low birth rate. It has been argued that the move of skilled and specialized labour from the less affluent countries of the East to the more industrialized nations of the west will encourage what is referred to as 'brain drain' that will make the poor countries poorer and the rich richer. The situation may be worse for small countries like Latvia and Lithuania where the working conditions, public services, job opportunities and salaries are much lower than the others. It has been observed that most of the top doctors, scientists and experts who move to work in the west have found it difficult to return to their home countries because of the lack of appropriate technology and resources in addition to the much lower rewards in comparison to what they receive in the EU-15 countries. For example, a doctor in Latvia was paid about €322 per month in 2004, while their counterparts in the UK or in Ireland could earn more than €350 in an hour. Moreover, the brain drain is accompanied by 'young people desertion': most of the emigrants are young, single and educated. Therefore, the poorer EU countries may suffer economically and socially because of declining numbers of skilled, educated and young people on which their future economic development depends.

Questions

1   What were the main reactions of employer organizations and trade union organizations to the free movement of labour from the new EU member states to the old ones?
2   Discuss the common drivers of labour migration within the European Union. Explain the push and pull factors, and why work may not be the main motivator for moving from one country to another.
3   Discuss the implications of labour migration for the policy and practice of human resource management and employee relations in both the new and old member states.
4   Examine the advantages and disadvantages of labour migration for the individual emigrant, the sending (home) country and the recipient (host) country.

References

Financial Times (2006) 'Europe's eroding wealth of knowledge' August 23, 2006.
Lindeberg, T., Månson, B. and Vanhala, S. (2004) 'Sweden and Finland: small countries with large companies', in Brewster, C., Mayrhofer, W. and Morley, M. (eds), *Human Resource Management in Europe: Evidence of Convergence?*, London: Elsevier, 279–312.
PAEP SA (the Greek National Employment Observatory/Research Informatics SA) (2004) at www.eiro.eurofound.europa.eu/ 004/10/feature/ gr0410105f.html, accessed 21 Dec. 2006.

Traser, J. (2006) *Who's Still Afraid of EU Enlargement?*, European Citizen Action Service (ECAS), Brussels, www.ecas.org.

UNFPA (2006) *State of World Population 2006-A Passage of Hope: Women and International Migration*, UNFPA, available online at: http://www.unfpa.org/swp/2006/pdf/en_sowp06.pdf accessed on 20 May 2009.

Part V

Managing in Developing Countries

Activity: Circle the following areas: Africa, India, Central Europe, Eastern Europe and South America.

14

African Countries

███████████████ **LEARNING OUTCOMES** ███████████████

The chapter is designed to help you understand, for selected African countries:

1 The (a) economic, (b) political and (c) cultural contexts in which managers work;

2 The main trends in the labour market;

3 The typical features of (a) management policies and practices and (b) organizational structure and behaviour;

4 The main policies and practices of human resource management with regard to: (a) recruitment and selection; (b) training and development; (c) rewards and remuneration; and (d) employee relations.

Introduction

The aim of this chapter is to provide a general account of the policies and practices of management and organization in Africa as a whole, with the use of examples from selected countries. It examines the challenges that managers face in a continent that is usually associated with a raft of economic, social and political problems. The literature in English on management and organization in Africa is very limited and tends to focus on a small sample of countries (see Blunt and Popoola, 1985; Arthur et al., 1995; Kamoche, 2002; Kamoche et al., 2004; Jackson, 2002; Khan and Ackers, 2004; Okpara and Wynn, 2008). Hence this chapter is based on a review of the literature and also on the author's own research and experience of management in Africa. It aims to portray aspects of an African approach to management that is most representative of African countries, though for practical reasons the examples and evidence it uses come from a sample of selected countries. The evidence is drawn mainly from

Ghana and Nigeria (West Africa); Kenya and Tanzania (East Africa); and Zambia (South-east Africa). North African countries (Algeria, Egypt, Libya, Mauritania, Morocco, Sudan and Tunisia) are discussed in the next chapter, as part of the Arabic-Islamic approach to management. South Africa is not included in this chapter because of its distinctive approach to management, which is a mixture of Anglo-Saxon, African and Germanic management policies and practices. (See Table 14.1 for basic statistics.)

Contexts: economics, politics, and culture

Economics

Though Africa is a rich in natural and mineral resources, most African countries are poor and underdeveloped. The economies of most African countries have been based mainly on agriculture and on the export of raw materials (see Table 14.2). Some are major exporters of international agricultural commodities such as cocoa, coffee, tea, sugar, bananas and gum; others export minerals such as iron, gold, silver and copper. Ghana and Kenya, for example, between them produce and export international commodities such as cocoa, coffee, tea, and timber as well as gold, diamonds, oil and gas, yet they are still poor and dependent on international financial support. This paradox is found in most of Africa and is often referred to as 'the resource curse' because 'the resource-rich African countries have *not* fully exploited the true (potential) benefits of their significant natural resource wealth' (Africa Development Bank, 2007: xxi). Most African countries have been unable to industrialize and or to escape from the vicious circle of poverty, dependency and underdevelopment.

Most African countries have experienced a slow rate of economic growth, high rates of inflation, a high level of external debts, and problems with food imports, hunger, or even starvation. The economic performance of all the resource-rich countries in Africa 'has been disappointing' (Africa Development Bank Report, 2007: xxii). By the mid-1980s all African countries, one after the other, experienced economic decline, and most of them depended on foreign aid. The World Bank and the International Monetary Fund (IMF) had to intervene and to impose Economic Recovery Programmes (ERPs) on a number of countries. Consequently, most African countries had to restructure their institutions and to reform their economic and political systems in order to meet the objectives of the 'structural adjustment programmes' (SAPs) imposed by the International Monetary Fund (IMF) and the World Bank. The recovery programmes included:

Table 14.1 Basic statistical indicators of a sample of African countries

Country	Area (sq.km)	Population (2009 est.)	Population growth (2009 est.)	GDP – real growth rate (2008) %	Inflation rate (2008) %	Workforce (2008 est.)	Unemployment rate (2007) %
Angola	1,246,700	12,531,357	2.2	16.7	12.2	7,148,000	> 40
Benin	112,620	8,532,545	3.1	4.5	2.9	5,380,000	> 50
Botswana	600,370	1,842,323	1.5	5.0	7.4	288,400	7.5
Burkina faso	274,200	15,264,735	3.0	6.0	0.5	5,000,000	77 (2004)
Cameroon	475,440	18,879,301	2.19	3.3	5.3	6,759,000	> 30
C.Afr.Rep.	622,984	4,444,330	1.9	4.0	3.1	1,857,000	10
Chad	1,284,000	10,111,337	2.2	1.5	4.0	3,747,000	> 30
Congo	342,000	4,012,809	2.75	6.4	7.3	–	–
D.R. Congo	2,344,858	68,692,542	3.2	5.9	16.6	23,530,000	–
Côte d'Ivoire	322,463	20,617,068	2.13	2.3	6.3	7,346,000	> 40
Eritrea	121,320	5,502,026	2.6	1.3	25.6	–	–
Ethiopia	1,127,127	82,544,840	3.2	11.1	17.2	27,270,000	–
Gabon	267,667	1,485,832	1.9	6.2	4.5	582,000	21 (2006)
Gambia	11,300	1,735,464	2.7	7.0	5.1	400,000	–
Ghana	238,533	23,832,495	1.88	7.3	16.5	10,120,000	11–20
Guinea	245,857	9,806,509	2.4	1.5	23.4	3,700,000	–
Kenya	580,367	39,002,772	2.7	1.7	26.2	17,370,000	40–45
Liberia	111,370	3,334,587	3.6	9.4	11.2	–	> 50
Madagascar	587,040	20,042,552	2.9	6.5	10.3	–	–
Malawi	118,480	13,931,831	2.3	8.0	7.9	4,500,000	–
Mali	1,240,000	12,324,029	2.9	2.8	2.5	5,400,000	> 30
Mozambique	801,590	21,284,700	1.8	7.3	8.2	9,600,000	> 20
Namibia	825,418	2,088,669	1.0	3.6	6.6	660,000	5.2
Niger	1,267,000	13,272,679	2.9	3.2	0.9	–	–
Nigeria	923,768	149,229,090	2.0	3.8	11.5	47,330,000	4.9
Senegal	196,190	12,853,259	2.6	4.5	5.9	4,850,000	> 40
Sierra Leone	71,740	6,294,774	2.3	7.4	11.7	1,369,000	–
Tanzania	947,300	41,048,532	2.04	4.5	11.6	21,230,000	> 40
Uganda	241,038	32,369,558	2.69	8.3	12.1	14,540,000	> 30
Zambia	752,618	11,862,740	1.631	4.5	13.5	5,398,000	> 20
Zimbabwe	390,580	11,392,629	1.53	3.7	5.1	3,840,000	> 80

Source: African Development Bank, *Human Development Indicators, 2008,* vol. XXVII, pp. 27–59; *World Economic Outlook* (International Monetary Fund), Statistics, 2009, and the CIA *World Factbook,* 2010.

Table 14.2 GDP: per capita and composition by sector (%) in 2008, selected African Countries

Country	GDP – per capita (PPP) US$	Agriculture	Industry	Services
Ghana	1 500	37.3	25.3	37.5
Kenya	1 600	23.8	16.7	59.5
Nigeria	2 400	33.4	34.1	32.5
Tanzania	1 400	26.6	22.6	50.8
Zambia	1 500	19.2	31.3	49.5

Source: CIA *World Factbook*, 2010.

1   The liberalization of trade by reducing state intervention and regulation of prices, and removal of state subsidiaries of consumer goods and controls on trade activities to create fair competition in a free market economy;

2   Re-valuation of local currencies and the reform of banking and financial systems to stimulate the financial market and increase exports;

3   The privatization of state-owned companies and the encouragement of private foreign and indigenous investments across the economy;

4   The reform of public sector spending and the reduction of spending on non-essential projects, and the crackdown on institutional corruption;

5   The export of non-traditional export commodities produced through industrializing the economy and improving the economic infrastructure, thereby creating jobs and reducing poverty levels in both rural and urban areas.

Most African countries experienced difficulties with or failed to implement the IMF-imposed recovery programmes. For example, Kenya started economic liberalization in 1993 by eliminating price controls, freeing import licences and abandoning foreign exchange controls. As a result, the economy grew to about 5 per cent in 1995 and then it started to drop annually to about 1.4 per cent in 1999 and to –0.3 in 2000 (IMF, 2002 in Kamoche et al., 2004: 87–8). The expected economic recovery never materialized and, as a result, the IMF suspended its support for Kenya's economic reforms in 1997 and in 2001. Some African countries such as Nigeria and Kenya made some economic progress between 2004 and 2007, mainly because of the rise in the demand for certain export commodities such as tea, coffee, sugar, copper, oil and gas. However, the challenges of eliminating accumulated foreign debts and eradicating poverty are still considerable in most African countries, especially since the recent 'credit crunch' recession.

Politics

Most African countries have yet to establish stable political institutions and have been subject to military rulers and warlords who have thrived on corruption, injustice and economic mismanagement. Most African leaders tend to stay in power until they are removed by force (e.g.. through a *coup d'état*, assassination or violent public protest). Even after the introduction of multi-party politics in the 1990s, in most countries the elected president is still the head of state and of the government, who typically stays in power for at least two consecutive terms. Despite the introduction of democratic elections at the local (municipal), regional (provincial) and national (parliamentary) levels in most African countries there has been little change in government policies or in leadership styles.

Most African countries gained their independence in the 1960s and 1970s, but they have since experienced political turmoil, civil wars and conflicts with their neighbours. Most of them adopted socialism as a model for their socio-economic development in their post-independence era. With a few exceptions, African countries have experienced political conflicts of one type or another. Most conflicts have been influenced by tribal and ethnic allegiances. For example, Ghana was the first Subsaharan country to gain independence from Britain in 1957, but successive military governments, especially after 1966, dominated the country for decades under the name of socialism, nationalism and independence (Nowak et al., 1996; Aryee, 2004). Free and democratic elections (the African way, of course) have been introduced since 1991, but the elected president, who is both the chief of state and head of government, appoints members of government (cabinet) and has substantial political powers.

Culture

Africans have generally been described as being collectivist and masculine, and having high power distance, high uncertainty avoidance, and a short-term orientation (Hofstede, 2001). These cultural values and norms are influenced by extended families, tribal allegiances, religious beliefs, and reciprocity in social relations. Individuals have a strong sense of family, group and ethnic identity (Mendonca and Kanungo, 1996; Kamoche, 2000, 2002; Jackson, 2002; Aryee, 2004). Often ethnic rivalries have posed serious problems to national unity and political stability. At the organizational level, managers have a moral obligation to support members of their family or tribe by giving priority to family and tribe members in employment, training, pay rises, and promotion.

Moreover, religious beliefs have strong effects on African people's behaviour, relationships and work ethics. The dominant religions in Africa are Christianity and Islam. Western cultures are influential not only because of decades of colonialism, but also because of the transfer of Western education and culture to many African countries after their independence. Western languages, especially English and French, are still widely used throughout Africa and have been adopted by many countries as national languages, though all African countries are multi-lingual. For example, there are more than 70 languages in Nigeria, although English is the official language and the means of instruction in formal educational institutions.

Labour market trends

There is an imbalance in many African labour markets between a high supply of unwanted labour (unskilled and uneducated workers) and a high demand for unavailable labour (skilled and educated workers) to meet economic development needs. In general, African labour markets are characterized by high levels of unemployment, declining public sector employment, increasing informal sector employment, low participation of women in formal employment, increasing child labour and illegal employment practices, the effects of HIV and AIDS on employment, emigration of skilled and professional labour (a brain drain), and shortages of skilled and educated workers.

High unemployment

High levels of population growth, limited industrial investments, declining employment in the service and agricultural sectors, poor manpower planning and inadequate employment policies have all contributed to the current levels of high unemployment in Africa (see Table 14.1 above). Following economic and social reforms introduced in most African countries under the supervision of the IMF–World Bank, the civil service sector and the state-owned enterprises, which had absorbed most of the surplus labour, have had to downsize their operations and to reduce the cost of labour by making mass redundancies (*World Economic Outlook*, IMF, 2007). In Zambia, according to official statistics, the level of unemployment increased from about 13 per cent of the workforce in 1986 to 22 per cent in 1991 (Zambian Central Statistics Office, 1993) and then dropped to around 16 per cent in 2005 (African Development Bank, 2008).

Despite a rise in private sector employment it has not been possible to create enough jobs to reduce the increasing levels of unemployment, especially among the unskilled and uneducated young people between the ages of 15 and 25. As shown in Table 14.3, the median age is less than 20 years. A large number of school leavers with little or no skills have joined the labour market. Even those who progress onto higher and further education may find themselves unemployable

Table 14.3 Age structure (%) (2009), selected African countries

Country	0–14 years (%)	15–64 years (%)	65 years and over (%)	Median age (years)	Life expectancy at birth (total population) (years)
Ghana	37.3	59.1	3.6	20.7	60
Kenya	42.3	55.1	2.6	18.7	57
Nigeria	41.5	55.5	3.1	19	47
Tanzania	43.0	54.1	2.9	18	52
Zambia	45.1	52.6	2.3	17	39

Source: Produced from CIA *World FactBook*, 2010.

after graduation because of limited job opportunities. In response to increasing youth unemployment, some African countries introduced initiatives to help young people find employment. For example, the Nigerian government set up a national committee for dealing with youth unemployment. The Committee established the National Directorate of Employment (NDE), which was in charge of implementing the National Youth Employment and Vocational Skill Development Programme. The programme's primary aim is to provide young people, mainly school leavers, with skills in special trades that are in demand in Nigeria, such as motor vehicle mechanics, brick-laying, welding, painting, plumbing, pottery-making, etc. The NDE recommended that such skills should be gained through apprenticeship in industries, vocational centres and laboratories. Also, those who were interested in self-employment benefited from loans arranged by the NDE with financial institutions in addition to a support through the Job Creation Guarantee Loan Fund. Unfortunately, to date, the NDE has had very little effect on the rising level of youth unemployment. Similar initiatives and programmes were introduced in other African countries but they failed to achieve their objectives because of corruption, lack of planning, inadequate information and poor provision of resources.

Declining public sector employment

The public sector, including the public services (government) and the state-owned enterprises, was until recently (and still is in some countries) the main job provider and the biggest employer. However the African public sector has been characterized by disguised unemployment and under-employment because it created more jobs than needed for its operations (Kamoche et al., 2004; African Development Bank Report, 2008). One finds in many public sector organizations that three or more people do the job of one person. There is a saying: 'one milks the goat and the other holds the milking pot'. The decline in public sector employment has not been matched by any significant rise in employment in the industrial sector.

Growth of informal sector employment

The informal sector is known as the underground, unreported, undeclared and hidden economy because the activity is not declared as a tax-paying business and is not formally registered. It takes the form of street sales, backstreet stores, road-side stalls, door-to-door sales, under-the-table transactions, car boot sales, and so on, for the provision and sale of basically everything from cigarettes and peanuts to designer clothes, real and fake jewellery, precious stones and electronic goods. The sale of food and drugs (with very little control over or consideration of hygiene) is also a common occurrence everywhere in small as well as large cities.

In most African countries, the informal sector has become the only way for many citizens to earn a living. It used to be the primary source of income for the orphaned, people with special needs, and the very poor people, mainly children and women. Today even the employed, the professional and the graduate benefit from the informal sector. For example, in Zambia, Muuka and Mwenda (2004: 47–8) state that the informal sector 'tends to absorb women, youths, and, increasingly, college and university graduates, who cannot find jobs in the formal sector'. It seems, as Wood (2008: 330) comments, that the working life for many Africans 'is about insecure, marginal, and often episodic livings on the informal sector'.

Low participation of women in formal employment

In African societies, men are normally the breadwinners while women tend to look after the home and the children. This does not mean, however, that women do not work. In fact, in many African countries women do much unpaid work in and around the house and in the community. As stated above, most of those who work in the informal sector are women, but their work is neither formally recognized nor properly rewarded. Even in countries such as Ghana, Kenya and Nigeria, where equal opportunities for women have been promoted officially, many female employees tend to occupy only what are known as feminized jobs (Aryee, 2004), such as teaching, nursing, caring, health and beauty, secretarial and hospitality jobs. The reality is that there are many highly educated and very talented women in Africa whose knowledge and skills are not fully utilized because of cultural, social and economic barriers.

Child labour and illegal employment practices

Child labour is legally forbidden in all African countries (Moyi, 2002; ILO, 2002), but in reality many children as young as 10 years of age are employed in a number of African countries. According to the ILO report (2002), child labour in Africa can be found in almost all sectors, and is most common in agriculture, domestic work, mining and the informal sector. Many children are abused and exploited by their employers or their family members, who put them in jobs that are unsafe, unhealthy and potentially life threatening. Many children work for their parents or relatives and do not get paid. Their employment is not considered in some countries' laws as exploitation or child labour. For example, according to the Kenyan Child Labour Report 1998/99 (CBS, 2001), 78.7 per cent of the children who worked in Kenya had not been classified as child labour because Section 10(5) of the Children Act 2001 defines the term 'child labour' as any situation where a child provides labour in exchange for payment. Since children who work for their parents or family members are not paid, they are not considered child labour. It seems, however, that in many African countries child labour is unavoidable, especially where:

1 Parents are unemployed or employed but unable to provide for their extended families;
2 Parents are dead or unwell and there is no adult person to provide for the family, thus the elder child is forced to work and to look after younger sisters and brothers. In countries where the number of HIV and AIDS sufferers is high, many orphan children have had to work following the death of one or both parents;
3 The children live in rural areas where every member of the family is expected to work in agriculture and on farms;
4 Girls are denied their right to proper education or discouraged from going to school and they either get married very young or fall prey to exploitation as servants, domestic helpers, street vendors, etc.;
5 Poor education systems and the lack of vocational training lead many children to leave school before the age of 15 and look for employment;
6 Poverty in rural areas forces many families to send their children to the cities to stay with relatives and friends, but in most cases these children end up working as servants, cleaners, and so on;
7 Law enforcement against the exploitation of children is relaxed because of limited numbers of inspectors and/or corruption. Many African employers, especially small and medium size enterprises, are able to get away with child labour by evading the law and bribing inspectors and local authority officials.

It seems therefore that child labour is an endemic problem that will take many years to eradicate in Africa because it emanates from a complexity of social, economic and political factors.

Effects of HIV and AIDS on employment

One of the most serious phenomena of labour markets in Africa is the rise in the number of working-age people with HIV or AIDS. It has been estimated that most of those affected are among the working-age group of 20–50 years (Kamoche et al., 2004). For example, in Zambia about 83 per cent of the AIDS-related deaths occurred among the people under the age of 45 (Muuka and Mwenda, 2004: 43–4).

It is also estimated that about 70 per cent of those affected by the HIV or AIDS virus are from Subsaharan Africa (UNAIDS/WHO, 2002).

The effects of the epidemic on businesses and on the economy as a whole cannot be overlooked. Many of the HIV or AIDS sufferers are core workers in organizations and their loss can have significant implications on organizational performance and human resource management. Organizations spend a lot of money on the recruitment and training of replacement employees, and on the time lost in medical care and illness. Also, the loss of experienced employees and the psychological effects of losing a friend, a work colleague or a member of the family can have serious consequences on organizational performance. Most of the countries affected have depended on the joint United Nations Programme on HIV/AIDS (UNAIDS) to help them deal with the crisis at the national level, but still not enough is being done at the organizational level to help employers and trade unions deal with those affected and their families, and to prevent the epidemic from spreading among the workers.

Migration of skilled and professional labour

The exodus of highly educated and skilled workforce from Africa in search of employment in other countries is referred to as 'brain drain' and is one of the most serious problems facing Africa's socio-economic development (Balogun and Mutahaba, 1990). The brain drain has been the result of factors such as:

1 The lack of opportunities for growth and career development, especially for the educated and professionals;
2 The lack of freedom of expression and inability to do what one is good at because of many state restrictions, bureaucracy, interventions and direct control;
3 The lack of appreciation of one's contribution because of injustice, nepotism, discrimination and corruption;
4 The lack of opportunities to learn new skills and knowledge that are not available, not accessible or not affordable in one's country;
5 The lack of safety and security in one's home because of civil wars and political conflicts;
6 Low income because of low wages and salaries for the same job done at home. In some African countries the monthly salary of a doctor in a hospital is less than a week's wage in a supermarket in a Western European country;
7 Joining family members, relatives or friends living abroad;
8 Studying abroad and staying there after the completion of one's studies because of being offered employment opportunities or benefiting from the host country's employment schemes and immigration policies; and
9 Just being lured by and attracted to the style and standards of living in economically developed countries.

The brain drain results from many African countries' lack of 'a clear and forward-looking employment policy and managerial practices that are conducive to the attraction and retention of skilled and specialized human resources' (Kamoche et al., 2004: 97). Many skilled and professional employees have no wish to emigrate to Western countries if given the opportunity to work and earn a decent income in their own countries. In recent years many African professionals, experts and skilled workers have preferred to move to other more prosperous African countries such as South Africa, Botswana and Namibia, to North African countries such as Libya and Tunisia, and to Middle Eastern countries such as Saudi Arabia and the United Arab Emirates, rather than going to Western Europe or America. This change of direction arises mainly because of limited employment opportunities, the fear of discrimination, the difficulties in getting work permits, and low financial rewards in Western Europe in comparison with, for example, working in other African countries or in the Arab Gulf States.

MINI CASE STUDY 33

Africa: Give Me One Reason Why I Should Stay

When an African doctor was leaving his country for employment in a British hospital, he was asked by the immigration officer at the airport of his home country, 'Why are you leaving your country to work abroad?' He replied, 'Give me one reason why I should stay'.

Questions

1 Based on the material in this chapter, what reasons can you think of for why the doctor might emigrate?
2 And what reasons could you suggest to him for staying?
3 What policies would you suggest for restricting the flow of emigration of skilled professional workers?

Shortages of skilled and educated labour

African labour markets are characterized by severe shortages of skilled and educated workforce because of the brain drain, on the one hand, and the lack of education and vocational training opportunities on the other. There is an urgent need throughout Africa for skilled workers who meet the demands of a free market economy that requires the use of modern technology and new managerial and organizational knowledge and skills. There is significant shortage of managers who are able to face the challenges of organizational development. Many managers lack not just formal management education but also the opportunity to learn how to do things properly. Although there is a surplus of university graduates in many African countries, there are not enough experts and skilled workers.

Management and organization

A number of studies have concluded that the practice of management and organization in African countries is nothing more than an administrative process that is politically induced and culturally influenced. This administrative process has often been described as centralized, bureaucratic, politicized and tribal (see Blunt and Popoola, 1985; Kiggundu, 1989, 1991; Blunt and Jones, 1992; Budhwar and Debrah, 2001; Kamoche, 2002; Harvey, 2002; Khan and Ackers, 2004; Kamoche et al., 2004; Okpara and Wynn, 2008). The centralization of management decision-making reflects the strong culture of power distance maintained by African managers. The overwhelming use of bureaucracy reflects the overriding public sector management style inherited from the colonial era. The politicization of management practices reflects governments' control of all aspects of organizational structure and operations. Tribally and family inspired management, or what is called '*ubuntu* management' in some African countries, reflects the strong cultural influence on management policies and practices.

Centralization of decision-making

Management in most African countries has been described as centralized and authoritarian (Kiggundu, 1989; Blunt and Jones, 1992). The power and authority bestowed to African managers have consolidated an authoritarian leadership style where the managers are respectfully obeyed and their decisions are carried out unquestioned. The attitudes of managers towards their subordinates and employees' views of their leaders enforce the existence of a strong power distance culture. For example, subordinates may act out of fear of punishment and they are too dependent on their managers. The prevalent attitude among all employees is 'check with the boss' because employees lack the authority to do anything without approval (Arthur et al., 1995; Aryee, 2004). There is a sense of powerlessness and helplessness that leads to passive behaviour among employees (Blunt, 1983; Kiggundu, 1989, 1991). Aryee (2004: 126) states that in Ghana, for example, 'the centralization of decision-making authority has made employees aware of the need to have a good relationship with their superior if they are to have a successful career'. This type of relationship tends to create passiveness in employees, who may be afraid to voice any contradictory opinions even when they know the leader is wrong. As stated above, it is not acceptable in almost all African cultures to contradict one's superior, and therefore there is a tendency to accept that the superior knows best. Employees follow detailed instructions given to them by their managers even when they have done the job many times before. This act of authoritarian leadership reflects the existence of a social structure that is dominated by a belief in seniority, social class and social divisions in wealth and status. The delegation of authority is only made to relatives and trusted close friends (Kiggundu, 1989). This right to manage gives many managers the opportunity to indulge in corrupt activities and to build around them an entourage of friends and relatives to protect them and cover for their actions. It can be concluded, therefore, that many African managers use authoritarian management to cover for their managerial incompetence.

Public sector management and bureaucracy

Management in Africa is often described as public sector-style management (referred to as 'parastatal'). The term 'public sector management', in this context, is synonymous with government bureaucracy. It is a term that, according to Blunt and Jones (1992), denotes lethargy, inertia, complacency, ineptitude and red tape. The bureaucracy of the public sector is very much inherited from the colonial administration. According to Blunt (1983: 139), 'Western forms of organization which were used to reinforce and maintain colonial administrative systems have in many cases simply served the same purpose for different masters.' Everything in the public sector is done according to prescribed rules and regulations, oblivious of the realities of the time or the needs of citizens. Managers of public sector organizations are merely civil servants and administrators who have developed a dependence on bureaucratic status, symbols and rules. Although bureaucracy may be good when used effectively, it can be very bad for the organization and its employees when used excessively unnecessarily. Bureaucracy in African organizations tends to stifle creativity, stop innovation and deter the introduction of new initiatives. Even when managers and employees are creative and able to make effective and strategic decisions, they may not be able to do so because of bureaucratic structures and control systems imposed on their organizations by government agencies. Crippled by unproductive and ineffective bureaucratic procedures, many civil servants and managers of state-owned organizations seem to take pride in filling in forms, pilling up files on their desks and making clients wait outside their offices. The length of queues of people waiting to have their documentation signed or stamped, or to be seen by an officer, tends to be used as a performance indicator of how busy the civil servant can be. Often, matters that require urgent attention are delayed for weeks on a pretext of non-availability of resources and/or insufficient information to accomplish a given task. This type of bureaucratic management is practised in many public and private sector organizations throughout Africa.

Politicization of management practices

The business environment of developing countries is highly politicized (Blunt, 1983; Blunt and Jones, 1992; Srinivas, 1995) because the state is simultane-ously the largest employer, the legislator, and the main decision-maker. Political patronage tends to overshadow economic considerations in organiza-tional decision-making. The managers of state-owned organizations and top-level civil servants are usually appointed by the state because of their loyalty to the political system or their links with people in government. It is not sur-prising to find that the managers of state-owned organizations are retired politicians, former civil servants and former army officers. For example, the 1979 constitution of Nigeria states that the president appoints and deploys top-level public service officers, institutes administrative reforms when nec-essary, and creates or merges ministries and departments when desirable. State-appointed managers are likely to do what the government wants them to do, regardless of what they think about the organizations they manage. Therefore management decisions may be made without due consideration or formulation of realistic plans or strategic thinking. Managers find themselves squeezed between the organizations they are responsible for and the extra-organizational bodies they are accountable to. Hence they are very often obliged 'to satisfy individual or collective interests outside the organization' (Kiggundu, 1989: 57), even at the expense of not meeting their organizational objectives and the needs of their employees. Many managers can find it dif-ficult to maintain principles of objectivity and meritocracy regarding disci-pline, promotion and performance management because of external pressures and direct intervention by politically or ethnically motivated individuals and government institutions.

Ubuntu management

It has been argued that the above description of management in Africa as cen-tralized, bureaucratic and politicized is a misinterpretation, because these features 'are not African *per se*' (Khan and Ackers, 2004: 1338) and are 'mostly representative of a post-colonial heritage' (Jackson, 2002: 1002). African man-agement, on the contrary, some would argue, is more people-centred and less rationally determined than Western models. It is captured by the African con-cept of *ubuntu* (Mbigi and Maree, 1995; Kamoche et al., 2004): '*Ubuntu* is said to signify an indigenous African philosophy of management which captures the complex social relations between people and the idea of caring for others as though they were members of one's own family' (Kamoche et al., 2004: xvii). In other words, as Mbigi and Maree (1995) have explained, *ubuntu* is basically a 'humanist' and 'communal' orientation of management. It is based on the ethic of 'I exist because of others': as a parent you exist because of your family, as a teacher you exist because of your pupils, as a leader you exist because of those you lead, and so on.

Thus the concept of *ubuntu* management is generally characterized by a strong emphasis on the importance of family and tribe, kinship relations and nepotism, and respect for age and seniority, where relationships are based on trust and are valued over achievements and organizational performance. It is very unlikely in African society that a younger person will oppose the opinion of an older person. This does not mean, however, that talented and skilled young employees are denied respect and promotion (Jackson, 2002; Kamoche, et al., 2004; Khan and Ackers, 2004). There is a difference between merit and respect in the workplace. Older persons are respected because they are considered to be wiser, more experienced citizens, and parents. Organizations are often managed like extended families, where managers are expected to take care of their employees' material and personal needs, and like for their subordinates what they like for themselves. This 'organizational familism' (Aryee, 2004: 125) brings the family to the organization and the organization becomes part of the extended family. For example, in the case of bereavement in one employee's family the whole factory or department closes for the day and all employees go to the funeral. The employer is also expected to offer help to cover the cost of the funeral. The same support from the employer and work colleagues is expected at weddings and when a new baby is born. The relationship between the leader and the subordinates is 'more personalized than contractual' (Aryee, 2004: 126). The dependence of people on each other within the African community requires a high level of teamwork and collaboration that can only operate through consensus in making decisions and paternalistic relationships. As a result, managers of formal organizations may exercise some form of centralized and authoritarian leadership but are bound by the African values of 'groupism, familyism and communalism' (Kamoche, 2000: 60) to look after their employees as members of their families and tribes even when they are not.

The combination of authoritarian management with *ubuntu* management has often contributed to excessive use of nepotism and favouritism. It produces managers with a tendency to ignore organizational norms of merit and qualifications by giving preference to members of their own family, ethnic group or geographical group. Nepotism is generally seen as an unethical or unfair practice in many societies, but when taking into consideration the African social structure, ways of life and cultural values, the practice of nepotism is not always a bad thing. In the African context, nepotism can be good for organizational stability, easy transfer of power and smooth continuity of operations (Khan and Ackers, 2004). It can be the only way to strengthen positive family ties that boost morale, maintain loyalty and improve job satisfaction of employees in the workplace.

MINI CASE STUDY 34

'Ubuntu existe partout'

When a researcher asked Mr Omar Bango, the chief executive of the National Telecommunications Company in Mali, 'Could you describe the type of management in your state-owned company?', Mr Bango replied, '*Système de géstion Française*' (the French management system).

It is true that Mali inherited the French system of administration and the French language is used in all of its institutions. However, when the manager was asked to describe the type of management in his enterprise, his account sounded nothing like the French system: rather it sounded just like *ubuntu* management. The researcher responded, 'Mr Bango, what you have said is *ubuntu* management, isn't it?' Mr Bango replied, '*Ubuntu existe partout en Afrique*' (*ubuntu* exists everywhere in Africa).

Questions

1 Describe the main features of *ubuntu* management in Africa.
2 Describe the main features of management and organization in France (see Chapter 10).
3 Compare and contrast the two systems.

Managing human resources

Management of human resources in Africa mirrors the type of management and organization that exists in African organizations (see Blunt and Jones, 1992; Budhwar and Debrah, 2001; Kamoche et al., 2004; Okpara and Wynn, 2008; Wood, 2008). The functions of HRM are influenced by the practice of authoritarian, bureaucratic, politicized and *ubuntu* management.

Recruitment and selection

The process of recruitment and selection in Africa depends on the type of employer, job and sector. There is a difference in the process, nature and methods of recruitment between public, private and foreign-owned organizations. In foreign-owned organizations the use of human resource planning and the production of job descriptions are very common. In private sector organizations there is a very limited use of human resource planning or job analysis, and most jobs do not have clearly defined job descriptions. Most of the privately owned small and medium size enterprises (SMEs) rely on friends and relatives (of the owners and the employees) and unsolicited applications to fill in vacancies. The common method of recruitment is word of mouth. Some of the larger private sector companies have gradually adopted recruitment and selection practices similar to the ones found in foreign-owned enterprises. The use of media advertising and the internet are common methods of recruitment among the large firms.

In public sector organizations, human resource planning is widely used as part of the country's national economic planning, though sometimes in reality the process is nothing more than an administrative activity which involves the collation of 'estimates' and unreliable information for bureaucratic purposes. In many cases the plans do not make much sense, although they are given serious consideration by the government (Blunt, 1983). Most of the public sector job vacancies are advertised in the local and national media, namely newspapers, magazines, radio and television (Muuka and Mwenda, 2004: 40), but a number of studies have found that the most popular forms of recruitment in African public sector organizations are newspapers advertisements, followed by notice boards and visits to universities and colleges (Arthur et al., 1995; Anakwe, 2002; Khan and Ackers, 2004; Okpara and Wynn, 2008). For example, a study by Anakwe (2002) found that the process of recruitment used by companies in Nigeria included advertising in the local and national newspapers and on radio and television, visits to schools and colleges, and internal referrals of relatives and friends. He also observed that the sense of 'belonging' within Nigerian society is very strong, and recruitment can often be carried out by hiring employees' family members and friends.

African managers, in general, tend to recruit applicants from their family, village and ethnic group. In Kenya, for example, 'while jobs may be advertised in the papers, particularistic approaches are fairly common, and involve nepotism and various other forms of favouritism' (Kamoche et al., 2004: 90). However, Aryee (2004) reported that in Ghana, visits to universities and colleges have declined while the number of unsolicited applications has increased significantly: many unemployed people are contacting as many employers as they can. The high level of unemployment has led to an increase in unsolicited job applications resulting in a constant pool of applicants to choose from. Companies have no shortage of applicants for their vacancies, but in most cases current employees bring in most of the application forms from friends and relatives looking for jobs. Also, many public and foreign-owned companies are finding it difficult to recruit people with the knowledge base and aptitude they look for. Therefore, some of them resort to the use of headhunting and poaching to attract skilled, professional employees. According to Kamoche et al. (2004: 91), 'the use of recruitment agencies and poaching has become common given the high number of entry-level employees, and high unemployment levels'.

Training and development

Throughout Africa, the number of primary and secondary school enrolments rose from thousands to millions in most countries, and universities and higher education centres and institutes have proliferated as the number of students increase annually and double every five years (African Development Bank Report, 2008). However, despite all the efforts and the money spent on education and training very little improvement has been achieved. African countries are still underdeveloped and in serious need of educated and skilled workers at all levels for many reasons, including the adoption of inadequate education systems, the implementation of inappropriate education and training programmes, inefficient management of education and training bodies and institutions, insufficient or non-existent organizational training, and culturally influenced training methods.

Inadequate education systems

African countries inherited a colonial educational system that had been designed to serve the needs of colonial administrations. It produced enough clerks for the civil services and some semi-literate foremen and line managers to work in farms and firms producing export commodities. Most African countries did not change their educational systems to meet their socio-economic needs until the late 1980s, when the education systems were 'partially' reformed. Unfortunately the new education systems, which have been politically imposed with little consideration for the needs of the current labour markets, have resulted in graduates with lower educational standards than the previous ones. Moreover, the current methods of management education and training provide very little scope for learning how to solve problems, deal with people, and think strategically in a free market economy.

Inappropriate education and training programmes

As explained above, in many African countries the supply of labour does not meet the demand. There are many university and college graduates who cannot be employed because they are not qualified for the jobs that are being created. For example, while the economy needs scientists, engineers, financial analysts, computer experts and other skilled and professional employees, the national education systems have produced a surplus of lawyers, historians, teachers, linguists, translators and the like from the arts and social science disciplines. Moreover, many African students are not taught how to translate the principles of free market economy management into the practicalities of African economies, social structures and political systems. Even those who were trained in Western countries find themselves unable to apply their knowledge and skills successfully in their own countries, and have to rely on conventional methods, politically oriented approaches, and poorly resourced programmes.

Inefficient management of education and training bodies and institutions

In countries where those responsible for the provision and delivery of public education – such as headmasters and principals of primary and secondary schools, directors of institutes and centres of higher and further education, deans of faculties, university rectors/presidents/vice-chancellors, and inspectors of education – and the like are appointed by the state for political, ethnic, family or friendship reasons, many of them are neither qualified to manage nor committed to the success of the education and training bodies and institutions they find themselves responsible for. It is not uncommon to find that those in charge of universities are idle politicians who have very limited managerial skills or academic experience. It is not surprising to find state-appointed inspectors of schools taking bribes in return for producing positive reports. In many African countries there are no real performance indicators, no league tables and no real control over the management of education institutions. Most vocational training centres and institutes are poor and under-funded (Kamoche et al., 2004). According to Debrah (2004: 79), such institutes and centres 'share common problems of inadequate staff – both in quantity and quality, lack of modern training equipment, facilities, and lack of teaching material'.

Insufficient organizational training

The level and nature of training at the organizational level is a reflection of the conditions at the national level. With the exception of foreign-owned and some large and newly privatized (formerly state-owned) companies, many organizations provide their employees with very little or no training at all (Blunt and Popoola, 1985; Kamoche et al., 2004; Okpara and Wynn, 2008). For example, in Ghana, 'large private sector organizations like Ghana Airways, Barclays Bank, Ghana Commercial Bank, and Standard Bank have training schools where low to middle-ranking employees are periodically sent for refresher courses' (Aryee, 2004: 1270), but in small and medium size enterprises (SMEs) where the owner is the founder and manager, training is limited to the apprenticeship of members of the family or tribe. Therefore only basic and traditional skills are transferred from one generation to another. This process does not allow for innovation and creativity or for the learning of new and advanced techniques of production and skills of service provision.

Moreover, most SMEs in Africa see training as a cost rather than an investment in their employees, and so training is used only when necessary or when the government and international agencies provide it for free. For example in Kenya, Kamoche et al. (2004: 94) stated that 'training is largely treated as a cost, and the economic situation has made it even more difficult for managers to view training as an investment'. Realizing the importance of cost as a problem for many organizations striving to train their employees, most African governments have introduced financial incentives and initiatives, such as the Nigerian Industrial Training Fund, to help employers provide on-the-job training for their employees. But such initiatives have had little success.

The influence of culture on training

In Africa, the provision of education, training and development opportunities at all levels is influenced by the culture of nepotism and ethnic favouritism (Blunt and Popoola, 1985; Blunt and Jones, 1992; Arthur et al., 1995; Kamoche et al., 2004). The process of training and the methods used in teaching are also influenced by cultural norms and values. For example, the trainees usually prefer lectures rather than group discussions since they wish to learn from the instructor's experience (Srinivas, 1995). The way the teaching is conducted makes the learner very passive and uncritical: the teacher is perceived as being in a position of authority that should be respected and followed. The learner is very dependent on the teacher, who is an information transferer rather than a knowledge provider. In most cases, the role of the teacher/trainer is to transfer as much information as possible to the learner with very little consideration of the relevance or validity of such information to the recipient. The learner memorizes the information provided and writes it in examinations. This is how many Africans learn and obtain qualifications that have very little use in the workplace.

ACTIVITY 2

Refer to the passage on Training and Development in Chapter 7 (Japan and South Korea). What seem to you to be the main similarities and differences between Japanese and African approaches to training?

Rewards and remuneration

In most African countries the government sets the income and rewards policy. Normally the government determines the minimum wage and pay rises for employees in the public sector that in turn influences the determination of rewards and pay structures in the private sector. Whereas, the level of rewards in foreign-owned and private sector organizations depends on whether the workers are unionized or not. In organizations that do not recognize trade unions, the rewards are determined by management and are agreed with individual employees. In organizations that recognize trade unions, the rewards and working conditions are determined through collective agreements. However, in most countries the agreed terms and conditions of employment and pay structures have to be registered with the ministry of finance or ministry of labour, depending on the country's government policy. Any collective agreement that does not comply with the government's guidelines relating to wage and salary levels is not registered and therefore is not legally binding. For example, in Nigeria, collective agreements on wages have to be registered with the Ministry of Labour which then decides on whether they become legally binding in line with Wages Board and Industrial Councils Act. It is illegal for an employer to agree with employees a collective or an individual increase in wages without the approval of the Minister of Labour. It means that in any case, with or without collective agreements, it is still the government that determines the wage and salary levels for all sectors of the economy.

As they move into a free market economy many African countries have also attempted to move from seniority to merit-based pay, but performance appraisal is rarely implemented effectively. Some public sector employees, including the police and customs officers, tend to supplement their income by asking for and taking bribes for their services. Also, in most African countries there is an informal welfare system at the national and organizational levels.

Minimum wage

Most African countries have a national statutory minimum wage that is determined by the government through a presidential, royal or ministerial decree or by a state-appointed tripartite committee. At the organizational level, most organizations have a base pay that normally consists of the minimum statutory wage and other benefits and allowances (Fashoyin, 2008). For example, Ghana has a minimum wage that is determined by a Tripartite Committee on Salary and Wages which takes into consideration the state of the economy and the price index in determining the national minimum wage. However, in most African countries the minimum wage is not adhered to (Kamoche et al., 2004). On the one hand there are employers, especially in the private sector and in rural areas, who pay less than the minimum wage because of the availability of cheap labour in need of employment for any wage. On the other hand, many employers in large cities, especially in banking and the large companies, provide higher wages than the minimum wage. Also, most public sector organizations and large privately owned companies offer a number of generous benefits and allowances for transport, accommodation and medical care, as well as the statutory paid annual leave and maternity leave.

From seniority to merit-based pay

Until the 1990s when most African countries were required to reform their economies in line with the IMF targets, many employers related pay to seniority. The longer an employee stayed with the company the higher the pay. There was a very limited use of job evaluation or performance appraisal. Pay rises and promotions were based on seniority, length of service and managerial judgement. Following the liberalization of African economies and the growing willingness to adopt individualistic and free market economic approaches to employee relations, more and more employers have had to reward their employees on the basis of merit and individual performance. Therefore, concepts such as performance appraisal, performance-related pay, value for money, corporate governance and accountability have all become part of the government's political discourse and employers' management policies. However, despite the use of performance appraisal in many organizations, most rewards are still seniority-based (Kamoche et al., 2004). Annual increments are still offered to public sector and government employees on the basis of seniority despite the introduction of performance-related pay initiatives.

Performance appraisal

Performance appraisal in African countries, when implemented, is sometimes considered an annual ritual to be disposed with as quickly as possible. It is an administrative process of completing forms and files to meet the head office's deadlines. What happens thereafter ceases to be of concern to most appraisers until the following year when the next 'exercise' becomes due. The process does not really form the basis for a continuous performance monitoring and improvement procedure by which individual employee performance can be evaluated effectively. The reasons for this are mainly to do with the lack of awareness of the importance of performance appraisal and with the type of culture in Africa. In many African cultures it is not acceptable to evaluate employees' performance or to criticize them for not achieving their objectives. It is not easy for African employees to accept the Western concept of performance management with its emphasis on setting specific goals and objectives or giving face-to-face criticisms, and practices such as peer and subordinate evaluation (Aryee, 2004). It is believed that since workers always think that they have done their best, even when things go wrong there is no need for performance appraisal. This belief seems to stand in the way of introducing an open and interactive performance appraisal system. Performance appraisal is very often interpreted negatively as a lack of trust in employees and is seen as a threat to employees' livelihood. It is, therefore, resisted by whatever means possible.

Supplementary pay

In most African countries, many public sector employees, including the police and the customs officers, tend to supplement their pay by taking bribes in return for their services. Even when salaries have improved, some employees are accustomed to corrupt practices to supplement their incomes. In some countries it is impossible to get things done without paying bribes. Giving a bribe to a public or civil service employee is regarded as just like giving a tip to a waiter in a restaurant. Bribes are given in return for most public services. In some countries there is 'an informal tariff' for everything, from getting a permit to having a wedding party to applying for a passport or for an export licence certificate. Also, it is often very easy to avoid paying high fines for committing offences by giving the police or customs officers a small bribe.

Promotion by decree

The promotion of employees in many African countries' organizations, especially in the public sector, is very subjective and has very little to do with an individual's achievements or performance. Promotions are very often decided on the basis of how well employees fit in with the group or how much their managers value them. Company directors and managers of government services are promoted by ministerial or presidential (depending on the level of the position) decree on the basis of seniority, loyalty and connections. In some countries, such as Nigeria, the Public Service Commission, a government body, makes and confirms all senior appointments and promotions in the civil service. The procedure is usually inflexible and there is no provision for accelerated promotion. For example, if a scheme of service requires the completion of three years' service before promotion, that employee is made to wait until this requirement is met, and then the employee is promoted irrespective of how well he or she has performed.

Informal welfare system

African societies have an informal welfare system that makes it possible for citizens to support each other. This informal welfare system keeps the members of families and tribes tied together. In many villages, families support each other financially, physically and morally. At the organizational level, work colleagues support each other in good and bad times. Employers also tend to take care of their employees' needs by, for example, providing company loans to build a house, buy a car, and so on. Expenses that occur as a result of bereavement (funeral costs), weddings, legal battles (court fees), moving house, etc., are fully or partly funded by the employer, friends, work colleagues and family members.

MINI CASE STUDY 35

Performance Appraisal in the Nigerian Civil Service

According to a group of Nigerian civil servants who attended a course in public sector management reform in the UK, the civil service performance appraisal system in their organizations tended to rely heavily on personality traits. This means that factors taken into consideration in performance reviews are viewed subjectively – for example, cooperativeness, judgement, intelligence or initiative. These traits were difficult to assess because every appraiser was able to define them differently from the others. Many appraisers were often unsure of what they were rating. In such circumstances there is always the possibility of bias and prejudice.

It was also noticed that the approach diverted attention from the job performed to the person performing it. Appraisers were restricted to ticking off against predetermined trait ratings, with very little space to make any comprehensive comments. The process seemed to offer an easy way out for those appraisers who did not monitor their appraisees' performance or were not sure what they had been required to assess. Some appraisers had little to say about their appraisees' performance for the simple reason that they did not know much about them, because the appraisers were not always the line managers. The whole process seemed an administrative ritual for the sake of it.

Questions

1 Identify the main problems with such an appraisal system.
2 How would you suggest it could be improved or reformed?

Employee relations

Most African countries have well-documented employment policies and employment laws that cover all aspects of employer–employee relations. However, they tend not to be fully implemented. Some policies and regulations were produced by colonial administrations and later amended by local employment lawyers and international experts with little consideration of the needs of the working classes of the countries concerned. For example, in Ghana, the Industrial Relations Act of 1958 (amended in 1965) provides for employees' right to organize trade unions, to bargain collectively and to organize collective industrial action. The act covers all employee–employer relations, from the issues that should be covered by collective bargaining agreements to discipline, termination and the settlement of industrial disputes (Debrah, 2001, 2004). In practice, such policies and regulations may be no more than ink on paper. There is a big difference between what is written or said in legal and political circles and what is implemented or practised in the workplace. Even when trade unions are recognized and employees are free to form and to join trade unions, genuine collective bargaining is very rare and industrial action is very often prohibited. In general, employee relations in Africa are characterized by weak and poorly organized trade unions, controlled collective bargaining and restricted or even banned industrial action.

Trade unions

African trade union movements originated in the colonial era and many unions participated in the struggle for independence. For example, the first trade union organization in Nigeria was established in 1912 as the Nigerian Civil Service Union. In Ghana, the Ghanaian Trades Union Congress was formed in 1945. By the time the colonials left there was already a well-established trade union tradition in most African countries. In some sectors of the economy, such as mining, transport, agribusiness, the railways and construction, trade unions retained strong political and industrial influence in the post-independence period, but the one-party state that dominated African political systems at that time either outlawed trade unions or made them part of the state apparatus and put them under its control. For example, in Kenya, all workers have the right to form a union with seven or more members, but the union has to be registered with the Trade Unions Registrar. The registrar has the power to reject a trade union application if it is thought that there already exists a sufficient representation 'of the whole or of a substantial proportion of the interest in respect of which the applicants seek registration' (Trade Unions Act, sec. 16). It is not easy to get a union registered because the registrar always finds a reason to refuse the application. There were cases when the union was not registered because the secretary or the treasurer of the proposed trade union was not fluent enough in the English and Swahili languages. Thus the government, through the power given to the registrar, controls and restricts the freedom of association of employees.

In summary, even when trade unions have formally been allowed to organize freely and to bargain collectively, they have often proved practically ineffective because of:

1 Declining employment in public sector organizations that recognize trade unions and used to absorb most of the surplus labour;
2 The increasing number of private sector organizations that do not recognize trade unions;
3 Governments' economic liberalization policies aimed at attracting foreign direct investment. Most African governments have introduced legislation aimed at restricting trade union activities by giving 'employers a loophole to undermine the rights of workers' (Debrah, 2004: 82), and to attract foreign investors who are very often reluctant to invest in countries where trade unions are highly active.
4 The change in trade unions' attention to activities that many employees do not see as serving their direct interests. For example, many unions have been concerned with problems related to privatization, child labour and the effects of HIV/AIDS on employment (Debrah, 2004), instead of being concerned about better rewards and working conditions for their members.

Collective bargaining

In theory, collective bargaining is provided for by law in most African countries. It is a process that was inherited from the colonial industrial relations systems. Even in the post-independence period, when the majority of African countries opted for a one-party political system and a socialist approach to management, which did not require the institution of trade unionism and collective bargaining in Western terms, many workers' organizations retained their constitutional right to employee involvement and collective bargaining. Very often a nominal tripartite collective bargaining process takes place between the government, the unions and employers' representatives at the national level in order to determine the overall wage increases and employment policies. In most African countries the tripartite dialogue is seen as a national forum for cooperation between the trade unions, the employers and the state on issues of economic and social development. In practice, however, genuine collective bargaining never happens and most of the tripartite collective agreements at the national level are dominated by the state. At the organizational level, collective bargaining is very limited or non-existent (Fashoyin, 2008). In some countries, the negotiating parties are required by law to register their collective agreements with a government body such as the Prices and Incomes Board (PIB) in Ghana or the Ministry of Labour in Kenya, where the Trade Dispute Act (part 3) states that all collective agreements have to be lodged with the ministry within 14 days of their execution before they can be registered with the industrial court. Once the agreement is registered with the industrial court it becomes legally binding on both parties and it replaces any individual contracts signed with the employer. This process maintains the state's control of collective bargaining at the organizational level because the registration of the agreement can be refused whenever it is deemed not to be in the government's and the employers' interests.

Industrial action

In Africa, industrial conflict in the form of strikes is very often influenced by political and cultural factors. In some countries strikes are only permitted in selected private sector enterprises, while in others although strikes are allowed in most sectors, they have to be approved by the minister of labour or the industrial court. When a strike is approved, the police and the local authorities have to be informed in advance of the strike action. In Kenya all disputes have to be registered first with the ministry of labour that normally acts as arbitrator, appoints a mediator, or refers the case to the industrial court. Trade unions are not allowed to take industrial action during the mandatory cooling-off period of at least 21 days. It is the ministry of labour that decides whether strike action is legal or not. Therefore it is practically impossible to get approval for a legal strike because the ministry always tries to make the parties reach an agreement by imposing a mediator. When the negotiations break down, the ministry refers the case to the industrial court, which very often finds a reason to make the strike illegal. Strikes are not allowed in what the law defines as 'essential services'. These are: electricity; water; health; sanitary; air traffic control; civil aviation; fire; air transport; supply and distribution of fuel, petrol, power and oil; telecommunications, post and telegraphs; public transport; ports and docks; teaching; local government; and railways services. In other words, most of the sectors employing a large number of the working population are barred from taking industrial action.

Settlement of industrial disputes

African governments use various methods of settling industrial disputes, including the use of force. For example, in Ghana, the Industrial Relations Act 1965 provides that all disputes should be negotiated at the organizational and/or national/industrial level between the unions and management. It is stipulated that when the negotiating parties fail to reach an agreement the case will be referred to the Minister of Labour through the Chief Labour Officer for conciliation or arbitration. Similarly, in Kenya a report has to be made in writing to the Minister of Labour within a specified time during the dispute, and it is the minister who decides whether the matters on which the dispute has arisen are appropriate to proceed under the Trade Dispute Act or not. When the dispute is deemed to be in accordance with the act, the Minister has the power to recommend the start of conciliation, investigation or inquiry. Most of the disputes are settled through conciliation, which involves a public officer or any industrial relations expert or a conciliation panel, appointed by the Permanent Secretary and the Chief Industrial Relations Officer, meeting the two parties in dispute separately to help them to reach an agreement.

MINI CASE STUDY 36

Kenya: Flowers with Tears

In January 2006, the flower workers at a farm near Naivasha in Kenya went on strike over workplace injuries and unfair allocation of places in an education programme. Their employer responded by making more than 1,000 of its 4,500 employees redundant because they failed to give the 21 days obligatory notice before going on strike. In response to their employer's action and in support of the dismissed employees the remaining workers organized a peaceful demonstration, but the government sent the police to stop what they claimed was an illegal industrial action. The police used tear gas to disperse the demonstrators and that resulted in injuring several workers. A peaceful demonstration ended in tears and injuries.

Questions

In analysing this case consider two scenarios:

1 What might have happened if the workers had been unionized and the company had recognized trade unions?
2 To what extent do you think the company and the police actions were justified? Why?

Summary

---

1 The most common approach to management in Africa involves the implementation of a set of employment policies and management practices that are culturally bound and politically influenced.
2 The economies of African countries have been based mainly on agriculture and on the export of raw materials. Most of them have been unable to industrialize or to move away from the vicious circle of poverty, dependency and underdevelopment.

3   The majority of African countries have yet to establish stable and democratic political institutions and have been at the mercy of military rulers and warlords who have thrived through corruption, injustice and economic mismanagement.

4   Africans have been described as collectivist and masculine, and having high power distance, high uncertainty avoidance, and short-term orientation. These cultural values and norms are influenced by extended families, tribal allegiances, religious beliefs, and reciprocity in social relations.

5   African labour markets are characterized by high unemployment, declining public sector employment, increasing informal sector employment, low participation of women in formal employment, increasing child labour and illegal employment practices, the effects of HIV and AIDS on employment, migration of skilled and professional labour, and shortages of skilled and professional labour.

6   The process of management and organization in Africa is generally characterized by the centralization of management decision-making, widespread bureaucracy that reflects overriding public sector management, politicization of management practices, and the tribal and family inspired '*ubuntu* management'.

7   The process of recruitment and selection in Africa depends on the type of employer, the job and the sector. There is a difference in the process, nature and methods of recruitment between the public, private and foreign-owned organization. The common method of recruitment is word of mouth, but some larger private sector companies have gradually adopted recruitment and selection practices similar to those found in foreign-owned enterprises.

8   African countries have a shortage of educated and skilled workers as a result of the adoption of inadequate education systems, the implementation of inappropriate education and training programmes, inefficient management of education and training bodies and institutions, insufficient or non-existent organizational training, and culturally influenced training methods.

9   In most African countries, the government determines the minimum wage and pay rises for employees in the public sector. This in turn influences the determination of rewards and pay structures in the private sector. As they have moved towards free market economics many African countries have attempted to move from seniority- to merit-based pay, though performance appraisal is rarely implemented effectively.

10 Most African countries have employment policies and employment laws covering all aspects of employer–employee relations, though they are never fully implemented. There is a big difference between what is written and what is implemented or practised in the workplace. Even when trade unions are recognized and employees are free to form and to join trade unions, genuine collective bargaining is rare and industrial action is often prohibited.

11 It seems that neither African socialist systems nor the development of African capitalism have been successful in creating investments that could yield economic growth, reduce the increasing levels of unemployment and eradicate poverty.

Revision questions

Chapter 1 provides a review task designed to consolidate your learning from this chapter. Please see Box 1.2.

In addition, the following questions are designed to help you revise this chapter:

1 Discuss the view that African countries are victims of their own making because most of them have been unable to manage their natural resources effectively.
2 Refer to Chapter 11 (Germany and the Netherlands). What do you think are the main similarities and differences between the African and Germanic management approaches and labour market trends?
3 What are the main reasons for the weakness of trade unions in Africa? How do trade unions compare, in terms of role and status, with those in the United Kingdom?

References

African Development Bank (2007) *African Development Report 2007*, available online at: http://www.afdb.org/en/knowledge/publications/african-development-report/african-development-report-2007/, accessed on 16 March 2009.

African Development Bank (2008) *African Economic Outlook 2007/2008*, available online at: http://books.google.co.uk/books?id = mnyUL7Fql0MC&pg = PT442&lpg = PT442&dq = African + Development + Bank + 2008 + unemployment + statistics&source = bl&ots = 75V2Kwj898&sig = X8Ak5RnT_s_dguu8L-b10j8d4F8&hl = en&ei = 7OuUTL, accessed on 18 March 2009.

Anakwe, U.A. (2002) 'Human resource management practices in Nigeria: challenges and insights', *International Journal of Human Resource Management*, 13(7): 1042–59.

Arthur, W., Woehr, D.J., Akande, A. and Strong, M.H. (1995) 'Human resource management in West Africa: Practices and perceptions', *International Journal of Human Resource Management*, 6(2): 347–67.

Aryee, S. (2004) 'HRM in Ghana', in Kamoche, K.N., Debrah, Y., Horwitz, F. and Muuka, G.N. (eds), *Managing Human Resources in Africa*, London: Routledge, 121–34.

Balogun, M.J. and Mutahaba, G. (1990) 'The dilemma of the brain drain', in C. Grey-Johnson (ed.), *The Employment Crisis in Africa: Issues in Human Resource Development Policy*, Mount Pleasant, Harare: African Association for Public Administration and Management.

Blunt, P. (1983) *Organizational Theory and Behaviour: An African Perspective*, London: Longman.

Blunt, P. and Jones, M.L. (1992) *Managing Organizations in Africa*, New York: Walter de Gruyter.

Blunt, P. and Popoola, O. (1985) *Personnel Management in Africa*, London: Longman.

Budhwar, S.P. and Debrah, Y.A. (eds) (2001) *Human Resource Management in Developing Countries*, London: Routledge.

CBS (Central Bureau of Statistics) (2001) *The 1998/99 Child Labour Report*, CBS: Ministry of Finance and Planning, Republic of Kenya.

Debrah, Y.A. (2001) 'Human resource management in Ghana', in Budhwar, P. and Debrah, Y. (eds), *Human Resource Management in Developing Countries*, London: Routledge, 190–208.

Debrah, Y.A. (2004) 'HRM in Tanzania', in Kamoche, K.N., Debrah, Y., Horwitz, F. and Muuka, G.N. (eds), *Managing Human Resources in Africa*, London: Routledge, 69–86.

Fashoyin, T. (2008) 'Employment relations in Zambia', *Employee Relations*, 30(4): 391–403.

Harvey, M. (2002) 'Human resource management in Africa: Alice's adventures in wonderland', *The International Journal of Human Resource Management*, 13(7): 1119–45.

Hofstede, G. (2001) *Culture's Consequences: International differences in work related values*, 2nd edition, London: Sage.

ILO (International Labour Organization) (2002) *ILO's International Program on the Elimination of Child Labour (IPEC): Country profile: United Republic of Tanzania*, Geneva: ILO.

IMF (International Monetary Fund) (2002) 'Kenya: selected issues and statistical appendix', *IMF Country Report no.02/84*, Washington: IMF.

IMF (International Monetary Fund) (2007) *World Economic Outlook 2007: Globalization and Inequality*, available online at: http://www.imf.org/external/pubs/ft/weo/2007/02/pdf/text.pdf, accessed on 16 March 2009.

Jackson, T. (2002) 'Reframing human resource management in Africa: a cross-cultural perspective', *International Journal of Human Resource Management*, 13(7): 998–1018.

Kamoche, K.N. (2000) *Sociological Paradigms and Human Resources: An African Context*, Aldershot: Ashgate.

Kamoche, K.N. (2002) 'Introduction: human resource management in Africa', *International Journal of Human Resource Management*, 13(7): 993–7.

Kamoche, K.N., Nyambegra, S.M. and Mulinge, M.M. (2004) 'HRM in Kenya', in Kamoche, K.N., Debrah, Y., Horwitz, F. and Muuka, G.N. (eds), *Managing Human Resources in Africa*, London: Routledge, 87–101.

Khan, A.S. and Ackers, P. (2004) 'Neo-pluralism as a theoretical framework for understanding HRM in sub-Saharan Africa', *International Journal of Human Resource Management*, 15(7): 1330–53.

Kiggundu, M.N. (1989) *Managing Organizations in Developing Countries: An Operational and Strategic Approach*, Hartford, CT: Kumarian Press.

Kiggundu, M.N. (1991) 'The challenges of management development in sub-Saharan Africa', *Journal of Management Development*, 10(6): 32–47.

Mbigi, L. and Maree, J. (1995) *Ubuntu: The Spirit of African Transformational Management*, Rannburg, South Africa: Knowledge Resources.

Mendonca, M. and Kanungo, R. (1996) 'Impact of culture on performance management in developing countries', *International Journal of Manpower*, 17(4/5): 66–75.

Moyi, P. (2002) *Child Labour, Povery and Schooling in Ghana and Kenya: A Comparative Analysis*, available online at: http://paa2007.princeton.edu/download.aspx?submissionId=71929, accessed on 16 Sept. 2010.

Muuka, G.N. and Mwenda, K.K. (2004) 'HRM in Zambia', in Kamoche, K.N., Debrah, Y., Horwitz, F. and Muuka, G.N. (eds), *Managing Human Resources in Africa*, London: Routledge, 35–51.

Nowak, M., Basanti, R., Horvath, B., Kochhar, K. and Prem, R. (1996) 'Ghana, 1983–1991', in IMF (ed.), *Adjustment for Growth: The African Experience*, Occasional Paper 143, Washington, DC: IMF, 22–47.

Okpara, J.O. and Wynn, P. (2008) 'Human resource management practices in a transition economy: challenges and prospects', *Management Research News*, 31(1): 57–76.

Srinivas, K.M. (1995) 'Globalization of business and the third world: challenges of expanding the mindsets', *Journal of Management Development*, 14(3): 26–49.

UNAIDS/WHO (2002) *AIDS Epidemic Update 2002, Joint United Nations Program on HIV/AIDS*, Geneva: World Health Organization.

Wood, G. (2008) 'Introduction: employment relations in Africa', *Employee Relations*, 30(4): 329–32.

Zambian Central Statistics Office (1993) *Zambia Demographic and Health Survey 1992*, Lusaka: CSO, Zambia.

15

Arab Countries

███████████████████ **LEARNING OUTCOMES** ███████████████████

The chapter is designed to help you understand, for Arab countries:

1   The (a) economic, (b) political and (c) cultural contexts in which managers
    work;
2   The main trends in the labour market;
3   The typical features of (a) management policies and practices and (b) organ-
    izational structure and behaviour;
4   The main policies and practices of human resource management with regard
    to: (a) recruitment and selection; (b) training and development; (c) rewards
    and remuneration; and (d) employee relations.

Introduction

There are 22 Arab countries as members of the League of Arab States. They
have a number of common interests, though they differ significantly in land
area, political orientation and availability of natural resources. They may be
divided regionally into:

1   The Cooperation Council for the Arab States of the Gulf (CCASG), which are
    known as the Gulf Cooperation Council (GCC) states or, for short, the Arab Gulf
    States (Bahrain, Kuwait, Oman, Qatar, Saudi Arabia and the United Arab Emirates);
2   The Magrebian countries or the Arab countries of western North Africa (Algeria,
    Libya, Mauritania, Morocco and Tunisia);
3   The western Arabian countries or the Nile River countries (Egypt and Sudan);
4   The northern Arabian countries or the Arab Mashreq countries (Jordan, Iraq,
    Lebanon, Palestinian authorities [West Bank and Gaza Strip], and Syria); and
5   The Southern Arabian countries (Comoros, Djibouti, Somalia and Yemen).

On the surface, the above countries seem to differ to a great extent, but in reality they have much in common in terms of historical background, religion, culture, language and developmental challenges. They also have in common a number of management practices and policies that are influenced by Arabic and Islamic cultural norms and values. This 'Arabic-Islamic' management approach is the outcome of a combination of inherited and adopted (but conditioned) employment and management policies and practices. (See Table 15.1 for basic statistics.)

Contexts: economics, politics and culture

Economics

The Arab countries are at different stages of their development, ranging from the industrializing to the underdeveloped. Most of them are members of the Organization of the Petroleum Exporting Countries (OPEC) and they control more than 60 per cent of the world's oil reserves (see Table 15.2). The Arab Gulf states have been transformed from relying on subsistence agriculture, fishing and pearl diving before the 1970s to vibrant manufacturing and major oil producing and exporting economies. For example, Saudi Arabia, Kuwait, Qatar and the UAE have developed significant international markets and fast-growing economies that are based on the production and exportation of oil and oil derivatives, trade activity, and a large industrial and manufacturing sector. However, the majority of Arab countries have experienced depressed economic conditions, especially between the mid-1980s to about 2004, due to fluctuations in oil and gas prices and political instability in the region. Some of them, such as the UAE, Jordan and Bahrain, have also been severely affected by the 'credit crunch' recession.

Tourism is another important economic sector in the Arab world. There is not a single Arab country that does not have fabulous tourist attractions. Countries such as Egypt, Jordan, Tunisia, Dubai, Yemen and Morocco are already world-famous tourist destinations, but the others possess many historical sites, beautiful sea resorts, spectacular deserted lands, and a rich culture. Even petroleum producing countries such as Algeria, Libya and the Gulf States have started to focus their investment on tourism in order to reduce their reliance on revenues from the export of oil and gas. The contribution of tourism to Dubai's GDP is higher than that of the oil sector (Suliman, 2006). Moreover, some of the non-oil producing countries, such as Jordan and Tunisia, have concentrated on promoting sectors such as tourism and manufacturing for foreign currency generation.

Table 15.1 Basic statistical indicators for most Arab countries

Country	Area (sq km)	Population (July 2009)	Population growth rate (2009 est.) %	GDP – real growth rate (2008 est.) %	Inflation rate (2008) %	Work force (2008) (millions)	Unemployment rate (2008) %
Algeria	2,381,740	34,178,188	1.196	3.5	4.4	9.464	12.8
Bahrain	741	727,785	1.285	6.3	7.0	0.557	13.5
Egypt	1,00,1450	83,082,869	1.642	7.2	18.3	24.6	8.7
Iraq	438,317	28,945,657	2.507	7.8	2.8	7.74	18.2
Jordan	89,342	6,342,948	2.264	5.6	14.9	1.615	12.6
Kuwait	17,820	2,691,158	3.547	8.5	10.6	2.088	3.3
Lebanon	10,400	4,017,095	1.107	6.3	10.0	1.481	9.2
Libya	1,759,540	6,310,434	2.170	5.9	10.4	1.640	18.6
Mauritania	1,030,700	3,364,940	2.399	3.5	7.3	1.318	25–30
Morocco	446,550	34,859,364	1.479	6.2	3.8	11.290	9.5
Oman	309,500	3,418,085	3.138	6.4	12.5	1.200	10.6
Qatar	11,586	833,285	0.957	13.4	15.2	1.119	0.4
Saudi Arabia	2,149,690	28,686,633	1.848	4.4	9.9	6.740	11.8
Sudan	2,505,813	41,087,825	2.143	6.6	14.3	11.920	18.7
Syria	185,180	20,178,485	2.129	5.1	15.7	5.593	8.6
Tunisia	163,610	10,486,339	0.989	4.4	5.0	3.660	14.1
United Arab Emirates	83,600	4,798,491	3.689	7.5	15.8	3.266	2.4
Yemen	527,970	22,858,238	2.786	3.8	3.6	6.641	20–25

Source: CIA *World Factbook*, 2010 and World Bank, 2009.

Table 15.2 Share of the petroleum sector in the economies of the Arab members of OPEC (2008)

	Algeria	Iraq	Kuwait	Libya	Qatar	Saudi Arabia	United Arab Emirates
Oil/gas export earnings (%)	95	90	95	95	85	90	85
Oil/gas budget revenues (%)	60	–	80	60	70	80	65
Oil/gas GDP (%)	30	–	50	25	60	45	25
Oil proved reserves (billion bbl)	12.2	115	104	43.66	15.21	266.7	97.8
Oil production (million bbl/day)	2.18	2.385	2.741	1.875	1.208	10.78	3.046
Oil exports (million bbl/day)	1.891	1.83	2.349	1.542	1.043	8.728	2.703
Natural gas reserves (trillion cu m)	4.502	3.17	1.794	1.54	25.26	7.319	6.071
Natural gas production (billion cu m)	85.7	1.88	12.7	15.9	76.98	80.44	50.24
Natural gas exports (billion cu m)	59.67	0	0	10.4	56.78	0	7.567

Source: Compiled from different sources including the OPEC website and the CIA *World Factbook,* 2009.

Table 15.3 Workforce distribution by occupation in 2008 (%), selected agricultural Arab countries

Country	Agriculture	Industry	Services
Algeria	14	23.4	62.6
Egypt	27	22	51
Libya	17	23	59
Morocco	44.6	19.8	35.5
Sudan	70.8	9.2	20
Syria	19.2	14.5	66.3
Tunisia	35	23	42

Source: Compiled from country data, World Bank, 2008, and the CIA *World Factbook*, 2010.

Agriculture is still an important sector in Arab countries such as Algeria, Egypt, Lebanon, Morocco, Oman, Sudan, Syria and Tunisia. For example, in Sudan agriculture employs more than 70 per cent of the workforce and contributes more than 30 per cent of the country's GDP and over 60 per cent of its export revenues (see Table 15.3).

The telecommunications industry is one of the fastest-growing sectors in most Arab countries. For example, Jordan has become the information and communications technology (ICT) centre of the Middle East because of its success in establishing a number of ICT networking services such as the development of e-government (Branine and Analoui, 2006). Similarly Egypt, Tunisia and the UAE have established ICT network centres with high international standards. The recent spread of internet cafés throughout many Arab countries is an indication of an increasing demand for the use of the internet by the public, and hence the growth the ICT industry.

All Arab countries have introduced economic reforms in order to improve their national economies. They started by reducing state controls over the economy, encouraging foreign investment, eliminating state monopolies over the import of consumer goods, and privatizing state-owned enterprises. However, such economic reforms have had very little success. Most of them have been unable to attract significant foreign investment outside the hydrocarbons sector. Revenues from high oil prices, increasing tourism activity and the export of agricultural products pushed the economic growth of the region to an average of more than 6 per cent between 2002 and 2007, before some countries became seriously affected by the recent international financial crisis. However, the majority of Arab countries have not been affected by the credit crunch because of a low debt culture where people do not take bank loans and of the use of Islamic banking that does not operate with interest. Taking into consideration the natural and human resources in Arab countries, the current levels of economic growth are still unsatisfactory. The low levels of economic growth in most Arab countries can be attributed to factors such as corruption, bureaucracy, inappropriate financial institutions, lack of entrepreneurial spirit, lack of research and development, an uneducated and unskilled workforce, unemployment, injustice, political conflicts, and international investors' lack of confidence in domestic markets.

Politics

Arab countries differ significantly in their political institutions. They range from absolute monarchies (such as Saudi Arabia and most of the GCC states), through constitutional monarchies (such as Jordan and Morocco), popular democracies (such as Algeria, Tunisia, Egypt, Mauritania and Yemen), and special democracies (such as Libya, Syria, Lebanon and the Sudan), to special constitutional monarchies (such as Bahrain and Kuwait). In countries such as Algeria, Tunisia and Egypt, the political system is divided into executive, judiciary and legislative authorities. The executive authority is vested in the council of ministers led by the head of government (prime minister) and the president as the head of state with substantial political power. The legislative authority comes under the publicly elected people's assembly (parliament). There is also an upper house called the *Shura* council in Egypt and the *Uma* council in Algeria. The role of the upper house is to offer advice and to approve the people's assembly laws. In absolute monarchies such as the kingdom of Saudi Arabia and other Gulf states, the monarch (king, sultan or emir) is the head of government and head of state. For example, in Saudi Arabia, although there is a consultative council (*Majlis al-Shura*) which consists of 90 members representing the different tribes and communities throughout the country, the members are appointed by the king and any policies they make have to be approved by him and his council of ministers. Some Arab countries have recognized multi-party politics, while others cling to the one-party regime or absolute monarchy and introduce no more than some closely monitored and limited local or municipal elections. Despite some political reforms and multi-party elections, most Arab governments are still far from being democratic.

Culture

Over 90 per cent of Arabs are Muslims. There are about 2 billion Muslims in the world, making up almost 25 per cent of the world's population, and only just over 300 million are Arabs. In all Arab countries, Arabic is the national official language, while other languages such as French and English are widely used in business, commerce and administration. In terms of Hofstede's cultural dimensions, Arab countries are described as highly collectivist, masculine, authoritarian (strong power distance), risk evading (high uncertainty avoidance) and short-term orientated. A study of the GCC countries by Mellahi and Wood (2003) found two types of relationships; the in-group and the out-group. The in-group (tribe or extended family) is highly collectivist while the out-group (those outside the family ties such as expatriate workers) is highly individualistic. It is very important for managers of international companies to understand these types of relationships and to utilize them appropriately if they want to operate successfully in Arab countries.

ACTIVITY 1

Imagine you are a senior manager of a multinational company considering the opening of a subsidiary in Algeria, Egypt, Saudi Arabia or the UAE. Consider the economic, political and cultural context. What do you think are the most and least attractive aspects of investing in each one of these countries?

Labour market trends

Arab countries have the most regulated labour markets in the world: the government controls all employment aspects in both public and private sectors. The Gulf states have more regulated and restricted labour markets than the others because they employ a high number of foreign workers. In general, Arab labour markets are characterized by an uneven composition and distribution of labour, a high level of youth unemployment, a declining level of public sector employment, a move from the employment of foreign to national (indigenous) labour, a surplus of unskilled and uneducated workforce, the increasing entry of women into the labour market, increasing foreign investments, a significant level of child labour and illegal employment practices, and the emigration of skilled and professional labour (a 'brain drain').

Uneven composition and distribution of labour

In countries such Algeria, Egypt, Mauritania, Morocco and Sudan there is a surplus of manual and skilled labour, while in others, especially the Gulf states, there are shortages of all kinds of labour. The most significant imbalance in the labour market is the uneven composition of labour between the nationals and non-nationals in the Gulf states (Kuwait, Qatar,

Table 15.4 GCC countries' population and workforce distribution between nationals and non-nationals (2009)

Country	Population	Nationals %	Non-nationals %	Total workforce (millions)	Nationals %	Non-nationals %
Bahrain	727,785	66.82	33.18	0.557	56	44
Kuwait	2,691,158	52.02	47.98	2.088	33	67
Oman	3,418,085	83.12	16.88	1.220	38	62
Qatar	833,285	25.45	74.55	1.119	18	82
Saudi Arabia	28,686,633	80.57	19.43	6.740	20	80
United Arab Emirates	4,798,491	26.10	73.90	3.266	15	85

Source: Compiled from government statistics and from the CIA *World Factbook*, 2010.

Saudi Arabia and the UAE). Most of their workforce (more than 80 per cent) is made of non-nationals (see Table 15.4). They are highly dependent 'on imported, ready-made human capital of all types and skills to run and manage most of the technological and sophisticated operations' (Ali and Al-Kazemi, 2006: 84). It is estimated that more than 97 per cent of employees in private sector organizations are foreigners who do jobs that nationals do not or cannot do. Most nationals do not like to do manual jobs and they prefer to work in government institutions doing managerial and professional jobs.

In turn, many private sector employers do not prefer to hire the nationals because they are seen as more expensive and less productive than the non-nationals. The nationals 'prefer the lucrative employment packages of the public sector', while private sector employers 'prefer the often more productive, lower paid expatriates' (Abdalla, 2006: 135). Foreign workers, mainly from Asian countries, are 'imported' in to work for as long as they are needed and then sent home. Normally foreign workers are given work permits to work in specific jobs with designated employers and under the sponsorship of a local person or employing organization. The sponsor is called the *kafeel*. Foreign workers cannot change employment without the consent of the *kafeel* and the approval of the current employer. This practice is designed to control the flow and movement of foreign labour and to restrict the level of employee turnover, but in reality the flow of foreign workers continued while unemployment among the nationals started to rise.

Unemployment and youth unemployment

Unemployment in all Arab countries is one of the major challenges facing their governments. It can be seen from Table 15.1 above that, according to

Table 15.5 Age structure of selected Arab countries (%) (2009)

Country	0–14 years %	15–64 years %	65 years and over %	Median age (years)	Life expectancy at birth (years for total population)	GDP per Capita (ppp), US$ (2008)
Algeria	25.4	69.5	5.1	26.6	74.02	6,900
Egypt	31.4	63.8	4.8	24.8	72.12	5,800
Jordan	31.3	64.5	4.2	24.3	78.87	5,200
Kuwait	26.4	70.7	2.9	26.2	77.71	57,500
Libya	33.0	62.7	4.3	23.9	77.26	14,200
Morocco	30.0	64.7	5.2	25.0	71.8	4,500
Oman	42.7	54.5	2.8	18.8	74.16	20,200
Qatar	21.8	76.8	1.4	30.8	75.35	111,000
Saudi Arabia	38.0	59.5	2.5	21.6	76.30	20,500
Sudan	40.7	56.8	2.5	19.1	51.42	2,200
Syria	35.9	60.8	3.4	21.7	71.19	4,600
United Arab Emirates	20.4	78.7	0.9	30.1	76.11	44,600

Source: Compiled from government statistics and from the CIA *World Factbook*, 2010.

official statistics, most Arab countries have more than 10 per cent of their workforce unemployed (the real figures may be far higher).

Table 15.5 shows that the population of Arab countries is very young, and as a result more young people are joining the labour market each year. The problem is that the economies of Arab countries are unable to create new jobs for the growing number of job seekers not just from the unskilled and the uneducated but also from a growing number of skilled and university graduates. In all Arab countries more university graduates are joining the labour market, but there are few jobs for them. Some countries have done nothing to deal with this escalating problem. Others have introduced employment policies aimed at creating employment for young people, but none of the policies introduced so far have been successful. For example, the *Sanad* and the *Intilaaqah* programmes in Oman, and the *Tanmia* programme in the UAE, were aimed at providing training and support to young people to help them to find jobs or to set up their own businesses, but they did not do enough to create new job opportunities and to absorb the excess labour among young people.

From foreign to national labour employment: localization

After their independence, the majority of Arab countries had to depend on expatriates (i.e. a non-national workforce) to meet their shortages of professional and skilled labour. While most of them depended on expertise from their former colonial powers, some also needed Arab-speaking workforce that was imported from other Arab countries – especially Egypt, Iraq and Syria, because these countries had a surplus of such employees. However, by the mid-1980s, as the indigenous workforce increased, most Arab countries started to replace foreign by national employees in what came to be known as 'nationalization'. Hence, new concepts such as Algerianization, Emiratization, Qatarization, Omanization, Saudization and so on, were introduced into the vocabulary of employment policies in Arab countries (Yousef, 2004, 2005). For example, to reduce their countries' dependency on foreign workers the governments of Qatar, Oman, Saudi Arabia and the UAE have:

- restricted the issue of work permits and do not renew the expired ones;
- imposed a quota system of nationals and non-nationals governing private sector recruitment (at least 10 per cent of the workforce should be national);
- paid nationals higher wages than expatriates doing the same or similar jobs;
- restricted the issue of visas in large blocks to make it harder for employers to bring in large numbers of foreign workers at any one time;
- made the process of recruiting expatriates more expensive for recruitment agencies and private sector employers by increasing administration fees, visa fees and transfer costs; etc. (See Abdalla, 2006: 131; Mellahi, 2006: 99–100.)

Most of the Gulf States have not achieved their intended labour nationalization targets. It has proved impossible in countries such as Qatar and the UAE to dispose of foreign workers because foreigners are needed to do many jobs that the nationals do not or cannot do. These countries' economies have grown faster than their populations and there is still a shortage of labour in a number of sectors.

MINI CASE STUDY 37

I Did Not Meet the Locals (the Gulf States)

A visitor to Abu Dhabi once said, 'I did not meet the locals and all the people I met and spoke to were foreigners. Perhaps the locals were on holiday outside the country.' Taking into consideration the labour market trends in the Gulf states, discuss the advantages and disadvantages of adopting a national approach to employment (i.e. replacing non-nationals with nationals).

Public versus private sector employment

Until the mid-1990s, over 70 per cent of enterprises in the Arab countries were owned and controlled by the state (World Bank, 1997). Most of the state-owned enterprises were large and had monopolies over the production of goods or provision of services in their sectors. However, except for the hydrocarbons industry, many of these state-owned companies were unable to operate efficiently because of bad management, inadequate utilization of resources, limited skilled workforce, over-employment, and cumbersome state bureaucracy. Describing public sector management in Qatar, Abdalla (2006: 127) writes: 'Despite the huge financial support given to it, the public sector is blamed for stifling initiative, suppressing innovation, inviting mismanagement, operating at a low level of efficiency and impairing economic growth (when the oil revenues are excluded)'. By the 1990s most public sectors had become ineffective, unproductive and in serious need of restructuring and rationalization. Among the economic reforms were the privatization of state-owned companies and the encouragement of private sector investments. The private sector was expected to create new jobs and to stimulate economic growth, but in practice the closing down of some, and the privatization of other, state-owned companies resulted in job losses.

The public sector remains the main job provider and the most preferred employer in Arab countries. The problem of public versus private sector employment is twofold. On the one hand, in all Arab countries a job in government and in public sector institutions in general is seen as a citizen's right and is the most preferred because of, as for example in Kuwait, 'prestige, higher salary and lucrative compensation packages, and for job security' (Ali and Al-Kazemi, 2006: 83). On the other hand, a job in the private sector is not desirable because of poor wages, the delay in paying employees and the bad treatment of employees. In most private sector enterprises, the owner is the manager who hires and fires employees at will and has very little respect for employment laws and regulations. Moreover, in the Gulf states, foreign workers are recruited to work in the private sector not just because they are paid lower wages, but they also have more relevant skills, they are easier to control, they are seen to work harder, and they are generally more disciplined and obedient than the nationals (Atiyyah, 1994, 1996; Ali and Al-Kazemi, 2006).

Foreign investment

There has been a flow of foreign investment into some Arab countries, especially the Gulf states where there has been strong consumer spending and over-dependence on goods and services produced and distributed by multinational companies (MNCs). Almost all major MNCs of the world can be found in the Gulf states, from the big oil producing companies to small producers of household goods and fastfood restaurants. MNCs have brought

Table 15.6 Male and female employment by sector (%) (2005)*, selected Arab countries

Country/sector	Agriculture		Industry		Services	
	%Male	%Female	%Male	%Female	%Male	%Female
Algeria	20	23	26	28	54	49
Egypt	28	39	23	6	49	55
Jordan	4	2	23	15	73	83
Morocco	41	53	23	15	36	32
Oman	7	5	11	14	82	81
Saudi Arabia	5	1	24	1	71	98
Syria	24	58	31	7	45	35
UAE	9	0	36	14	55	86

*Data unavailable on Arab countries not included.

Source: World Development Indicators, 2007, pp. 48–51 from the ILO database, Key Indicators of the Labour Market, 4th edn.

their own international workforce of managers and experts, as expatriates from the home or third country nationals, and benefited from the employment of the already available, skilled and hard-working foreign labour because there are not enough employees among the host country nationals. The presence of MNCs in the Gulf states has contributed to the growth of foreign labour. The governments of other Arab countries such as Tunisia, Egypt, Sudan, Algeria and Morocco have encouraged foreign direct investment with the aim that MNCs would create new jobs and transfer knowledge and technology. With the exception of Tunisia and, to some extent, Egypt, most of the Arab countries outside the Gulf region have been unable to attract significant foreign investment in industrial and manufacturing projects.

Female employment

There has been a significant rise in female employment throughout the Arab world (World Bank, 2007; ILO Report, 2007). Even in the most conservative countries, such as Saudi Arabia, Oman and Yemen, more than 60 per cent of female graduates are employed (Moghadam, 2005). There has also been a significant rise in the number of women entrepreneurs, some of whom have been very successful (see CAWTAR and IFCGEM, report 2007). However, despite the increase in female employment, many women are still segregated into certain jobs in services sectors such as education, health, hospitality and public administration (see Table 15.6). Most of the women who work in Arab countries are among the well-educated and highly qualified members of society, while the majority who do not have access to formal education and training are unemployed.

Child labour and illegal employment practices

Although the minimum age for employment in Arab countries is 16 years and the laws prohibit the use of child labour or any form of forced employment, many young people between the ages of 12 and 16 are employed, especially (a) in rural areas where children help their families by working in agriculture and (b) in big cities where poor children are forced to work in homes, factories and in the informal sector. Child labour is increasing for reasons similar to the ones mentioned in Chapter 14. Another problem in some Arab countries is the illegal employment of foreign workers in dangerous working conditions in the construction, manufacturing and hospitality sectors.

Immigration of skilled and professional labour

Many doctors, professors and skilled workers from all Arab countries, especially Egypt, Iraq, Jordan and Algeria, have emigrated to Europe and the US in search of employment, for reasons similar to the ones stated earlier in Chapter 14.

Management and organization

Studies of management and organization in Arab countries have demonstrated the significance of cultural and political influences on managerial behaviour and have recognized the importance of Islam, tribalism, state control and Western influence in shaping the contemporary management practice and organizational behaviour in Arab countries (Muna, 1980; Ali, 1990, 1995, 1998, 2004; Weir, 1998, 2001; Kuran, 2004). These studies reveal the existence of a hybrid of inherited and adopted but conditioned management systems throughout the Arab world. The inherited management policies and practices are derived from traditional tribal ways of living and from the colonial administration. The adopted management policies and practices, which were politically imposed over the 1960s to 1980s, were either socialist ones copied from the Soviet Union or capitalist ones copied mainly from the UK and the US. However, both the inherited and the adopted management systems have been conditioned by Arabic traditions and norms, and by Islamic values and principles of management and work behaviour (see Branine and Pollard, 2010).

Inherited management policies and practices

Arab countries inherited a mixture of traditional tribal leadership and Western colonial administration. This mixture has produced a type of management and leadership that is authoritarian, centralized, politically oriented, paternalistic and bureaucratic.

Authoritarianism

Authoritarianism in Arab countries is mostly inherited from the practices of the former colonial powers. It is also influenced by the customs and traditions that existed within the tribal leadership system. It has been observed that Arab managers tend to be either extremely authoritarian (Kaynak, 1986) or very consultative (Muna, 1980; Ali, 1990). Authoritarianism has established a tradition of management by conformity and obedience, where the role of managers is to tell their subordinates what to do and how to do it. Arab managers do not like to be criticized by their superiors and they tend to be aggressive and offensive to their subordinates, and very defensive when challenged by their colleagues. They rely on fear, rather than respect, and they act like army officers, though without the discipline of an army life. They give orders and do not like to be ordered, and they tell rather than ask their subordinates. For example, in Morocco, according to Benson and Al Arkoubi (2006: 277), 'those who are of high status are seen as having legitimate power over those at a lower status'. Managers from the Arab Gulf states tend to be more authoritarian than their counterparts in other Arab countries, and they tend to be more authoritarian with foreign workers than with the nationals. They are accustomed to obedient and respectful foreign workers (mainly Asians) who either do what they are told or risk of being punished or deported. However, when subordinates are nationals, especially when they are among the members of the family or tribe of the manager, they are usually consulted and listened to. Nationals may disagree with their managers because they are protected by the state and by the status of their family and tribe. In this type of national–national relationship, the managers tend to be paternalistic and act like elder members of a family.

Paternalism

Arab managers value loyalty over efficiency and they rely upon family and friends for getting things done. They run their organizations as family units, especially in privately owned enterprises. For example, describing management in Qatar, Abdalla (2006: 128) states that managers have 'a strong loyalty to in-group and a preference for paternalistic managerial styles'. Paternalism is apparent in the implementation of HRM functions, as explained below.

Centralization of decision-making

In Arab countries the process of decision-making is usually highly formalized and centralized. The delegation of power and authority is very limited because of low trust between the leaders and the subordinates, and the prevalence of political gamesmanship at the national and organizational levels (Al-Faleh, 1987; Abdalla and Al-Homoud, 2001). For example, in Tunisia, according to a study by Yahiaoui and Zoubir (2006: 240), the 'subordinates must always request permission from management even for minor decisions'. However, in the absence of proper management training, many such managers use the privilege of the post they hold to abuse their position of power and get involved in corruption and nepotism.

Politically oriented management

Being a manager in Arab countries is a political privilege that carries with it many economic and social benefits. Senior managers of state-owned companies and public sector institutions are usually appointed by a ministerial or presidential decree on the basis of their loyalty to the government in power or their links to the ruling family and personalities in high places. In other words, senior managers' appointment is often political and hence their role is to transfer the government's policies from the national to the organizational levels. In this way, organizational structure and culture becomes a carbon copy of the political system in power. According to Ali (1992), such a structure reinforces the concept of absolute right and wrong and the 'do not rock the boat' attitudes that exist at the national and tribal levels. Mellahi (2006: 105) points out that 'any approach that does not conform to acceptable norms is considered a threat to established authority and organizational stability and therefore is not welcomed'. Senior managers and officials are expected to do what the government wishes or they will lose the power and status they hold. Therefore, in order to stay in power, senior managers tend to have good relationships with the government and may attempt to build their own niches of passive technocrats, stubborn bureaucrats and bewildered administrators loyal to the regime in power.

Bureaucracy

Managers in Arab countries often use bureaucratic procedures to impose their authoritarian management styles. They are trained to have a strong capacity for dealing with top-down bureaucracy. In the pursuit of making sure that the paperwork is in reasonably good order, many managers and administrators give less importance to interpersonal communication or to the urgent needs of employees, customers and suppliers.

Adopted management policies and practices

Adopted management policies and practices were introduced after independence as part of nation-building and economic development strategy. In the 1960s and 1970s most of the Arab countries adopted a socialist ideology and introduced models of production and management copied from the Soviet Union. By the early 1990s they abandoned socialism and introduced free market economic reforms that necessitated the adoption of Western capitalist management systems.

Adopted socialist management systems

Examples of adopted socialist management systems are to be found in the history of Egypt, Algeria, Syria, Libya, Iraq and Yemen. In Algeria, for example, the Self-Management system (1962–9) and the Socialist Management of Enterprises system (1971–90) were imposed on all state-owned enterprises through codes of practice and charters under the banner of socialism, often with very little consideration of the needs of employees or the condition of the economy (see Clegg, 1971; Lazreg, 1976; Zeffane, 1981; Branine, 1994). Similar attempts to introduce 'Soviet-oriented' management systems were made in Egypt, Syria and Libya (see Brynen et al., 1995), but they were all abandoned because they were ineffective.

Adopted capitalist management systems

Most of the Arab Gulf states have adopted capitalist modes of production and employment. They often aspire to adopt Western management practices for their socio-economic development. In recent years, however, all Arab countries have introduced free market economic reforms and have attempted to transfer management policies and practices from Western countries, mainly from the UK and the US. Today, the forward diffusion of capitalist management theories and practices to Arab countries is apparent in all aspects of life, from the increasing presence of multinational companies (MNCs) to the daily exposure of indigenous managers to Western management thinking. Ali and Al-Kazemi (2006: 91) argue that 'MNCs in the areas of high technology, insurance, marketing, hospitality, and processing have flourished. These companies interact with a wide range of local businesses and government agencies, making knowledge transfer in management and HRM a reality'. In the UAE, for example, expatriates have 'played a very important role in creating a strong awareness about the importance of the human factor in all types of organizations' (Suliman, 2006: 67). Moreover, a study by Yahiaoui and Zoubir (2006: 241–2) found that 'Tunisian firms have adopted Western practices. The State, too, appropriated such practices as part of a national project to bring the development of Tunisian firms to the level of Western companies.'

There has been a high level of forward diffusion of management theories and practices from the West to the Arab countries through MNCs' investments and the teaching of Western management education. Some theories and practices have been transferred with success, but it has not been easy to implement them because the practice of management in general and HRM in particular in Arab countries are severely conditioned by traditional norms and cultural values, and by the religion of Islam.

Factors conditioning management and organization in Arab countries

The factors that have conditioned the practice of management in Arab countries are not necessarily all Islamic: some of them emanated from the traditions and norms that had existed in those countries even before the arrival of Islam.

Traditional norms and values

Traditionally, Arabs are status conscious, prefer the use of direct, face-to-face communication, have high respect for age and seniority, and tend to get things done through intermediaries in the form of connections and kinship relations. These traditional cultural values have great impact on the process of management in Arab countries.

Status consciousness

According to Wilkins (2001: 263), 'Arab culture emphasizes status in all areas of society, family and work'. The status of being a manager carries with it a lot of privileges as well as high financial rewards. In the Gulf states, people are treated differently depending on their gender, position, family, age, qualifications, titles, and the type of jobs they do (Abdalla, 2006). In short, the main sources of power and status are:

- Family and tribe. The family's name has more importance and holds more power in some Gulf states than knowledge and expertise.
- Relationship to the state apparatus. In countries where the state controls everything, the closer the person is to the government, the higher their status.
- Position in the organization. The higher the person is in the organizational hierarchy the more powerful they get and the higher their status.
- Relationship to the management of the organization. The closer employees are to the management the more protected they feel and the higher their status.
- Degrees and qualifications. The higher the qualification (doctor, engineer, etc.) the higher the prestige and status in society, family and work. In countries such as Egypt, Jordan, Kuwait, Saudi Arabia and the UAE people prefer to be addressed by their qualifications' titles.

This status-conscious culture has conditioned the way organizations are structured and decisions are made. Organization structures in Arab countries are hierarchical, relationships are formalized and decisions are centralized.

Nepotism (wasta)

The practice of nepotism and favouritism in Arab countries is known as *wasta* or *ma'rifa* (in Arabic). It is also known in Algeria, Tunisia and Morocco as *le piston* (in French). The concept of *wasta* means literally to go in between, and *le piston* is the bolt that holds parts of an engine together, but in practice both concepts imply a type of favouritism and nepotism. It is inherited from the tribal system and the traditions of kinship identity relations that existed in Arab countries before the arrival of Islam, which were later strengthened through the bureaucratic procedures inherited from the colonial administration. The act of nepotism is forbidden in Islam, but it seems that the customs and attitudes of Arabs may override their belief system in many cases. El-Said and McDonald (2001) argued that the first source of high transaction costs in Jordan is reflected in a tribal mentality that is based on the concept of *wasta*. They explain that 'through *wasta*, businessmen can obtain import, export and production licenses, evade taxation, and even ignore rules and regulations, therefore increasing their profits through unproductive and inefficient means' (p. 77). They add that 'everything, no matter how simple it is, requires a *wasta* in Jordan' (El-Said and McDonald, 2001: 77). The practice of *wasta* can develop from special kinds of relationship (*ailakat*) between members of one community and reciprocal exchange of favours in dealing with people (*mouamalat*). Powerful and influential people have strong relationships (*ailakat*) and good dealings (*mouamalat*) with the right people, and it is only through them that problems of their friends and relatives can be solved and their needs can be met.

Face-to-face interaction

Arab culture is based on face-to-face interaction. Talking directly is often a more preferred way of communication than sending letters, memos or e-mails. In the workplace, managers and their employees prefer direct contact with each other because it is believed that the face-to-face interaction produces trust, sincerity, support and commitment. In business meetings, Arabs tend to dislike, and become sceptical of, people who are silent most of the time. They prefer talkative people because they perceive them as friendly, open-minded and courteous. It is not surprising to find that many Arab managers deal with work-related problems outside the workplace. Business deals are often conducted outside the workplace (Mellahi, 2006) in places like the mosque, the café, the market, the club or social gathering (*majliss* or *diwaniyah*). The act of dealing with work-related issues face-to-face outside the workplace is also used as a tactic of saving face in an informal rather than a formal working environment.

Saving face

In Arab countries any action that may result in shame or a loss of face to anyone is 'avoided at all costs' (Abdalla, 2006: 137). In the workplace, managers tend to avoid direct conflict and confrontation with their employees, clients and customers, and with other managers and government officials because that can result in a loss of face and embarrassment to one party or another (Weir, 2000; Ali, 2004; Mellahi, 2006; Hatem, 2006). Direct and public criticisms are avoided because they are seen as insults rather than criticisms. Discussing the importance of face-saving in Saudi Arabia, Mellahi (2006: 106) states that

> Saudi individuals tend to avoid getting directly to the topic or the business at hand (this is considered as rude behaviour and a sign of impatience) and prefer instead to loop around by starting with introductory greetings and social talk before getting to the business at hand. Relaxed and long informal settings lend themselves to such decision-making processes.

It is also reported that Arab managers prefer to use a third party to convey a message, especially when the message is negative, to avoid the loss of face

(Hatem, 2006). Avoiding conflict and direct criticism to avoid the loss of face has significant implications on managing human resources. For example, managers may find it difficult to administer performance appraisals and to implement performance-related pay or to make their employees redundant, while workers may find it difficult to take industrial action or to enter into adversarial face-to-face collective bargaining with their employers.

Respect for age and seniority

Being old in Arab countries is generally seen as a positive attribute: old age implies wisdom, sacrifice, and enduring commitment to society. Old people are respected and put in the position of one's parents. The young are expected to respect the old, and the junior to obey the senior. It is difficult for many young and talented managers to give orders or to criticize those who are older or have more experience than them. This type of working relationships has many implications for the management of human resources.

Islamic values and principles

The practice of management in Arab countries is strongly conditioned by Islam. In Islam, all human activities are understood in the context of 'vicegerency' (istikhlaf): humans are the vicegerents or the trustees of God on earth. The purpose of life is to worship God and to be a good trustee of God in all earthly activities. This act of trusteeship is based on two foundations. The first is Aqeeda, which is the belief (eman) in the oneness of God (Tawhid), his angels, his books, his messengers, the Hereafter and Day of Judgement, and in the divine destiny, both the good and the evil thereof. The second foundation is Shari'a or Islamic law, which explains the rights and wrongs of implementing the five pillars of Islam, and regulates all kinds of relationships between people and between people and other creations on earth. The source of reference for both Aqeeda and Shari'a are the holy Koran (revealed book) and the Hadith (what the Prophet Mohammed said or did, and this is referred to as Sunnah).

Many verses of the Koran and many Hadiths are about justice and honesty in trade, courtesy and fairness in employee–employer relations, acceptable financial transactions and appropriate means of production. They also encourage humans to learn new skills and to strive to do good work that benefits the individual and the community. Management is crucial in Islam and having a leader is obligatory in most circumstances of life. The Prophet Mohammed said, 'when three are on a journey, they should appoint one of them as their leader'. Moreover, Islam emphasizes the importance of work in society to the extent that 'life without work has no meaning and engagement in economic activities is an obligation' (Yousef, 2001: 153). In Islam working is obligatory for those who are able to work, and self-reliance is a virtue as well as a source of self-fulfilment and success. Since humans are trustees of God on earth and their activities are acts of worship, work is an act of worship. Work is not just a necessity for earning a livelihood, it is to strive to utilize and enjoy the bounties of God for the benefit of oneself and the community. Therefore, work ethics in Islam include having the desire for perfection, seeking rewards in life and in the Hereafter, and exerting effort without excess or waste of resources (Al-Buraey, 1988). Whatever the task a Muslim performs it is carried out with the intention to worship God, to earn a right (*halal*) income and to live a good (*tayeb*) and respectable life.

Therefore, when guided by Islamic values and principles, Arab managers see their role as a moral, spiritual and physical activity that is not only driven by material (earthly) objectives but by rewards in the afterlife. Employment relationships go beyond the written and psychological contract between an individual and an employer by having a religious dimension because both parties are responsible before God for their actions and are God's covenants or trustees on earth. In this context, many reviews of literature on management in Islam (see for example Al-Buraey, 1988; Tayeb, 1997; Mubarak, 1998; Rosen, 2002; Ali, 2004) have identified some of the main Islamic management principles that should have conditioned the practice of management in Arab countries, as follows:

Intention (nya)

In Islam every act should be accompanied by intentions. The Prophet Mohammed is reported as saying that actions are recorded according to intention, and a person will be rewarded or punished accordingly. When he emigrated from Mecca to Medina many people followed him to Medina. He said to them, 'Actions are but by intention and every person shall have but that which he intended. Thus he whose migration was for Allah (God) and His Messenger, his migration was for Allah and His Messenger, and he whose migration was to achieve some worldly benefit or to take a woman in marriage, his migration was for that for which he migrated' (narrated by Boukhari and Muslim as a correct *Hadith* and reported in *An-Nawawi's Forty Hadiths*, trans. Ibrahim and Johnson-Davies, 1977: 26).

The implications of this principle for management are that employees should not, for example, be punished for making unintentional mistakes and should be rewarded or punished for their intended actions, ideas, plans and strategies, rather than merely for the outcomes of their activities which may be affected by external factors beyond their control. This also accentuates the importance of human resource planning and strategic decision-making.

Forever mindful of the Almighty God (taqwa)

Taqwa implies that a person refrains from behaving unjustly and commands his/her soul to move from the state of *ammara* (the prone-to-evil level), which is the primitive stage that man shares with animals, to the state of *lawama* (self-reproaching level), in which man is conscious of evil and struggles through repentance, to the highest level of *mutmainna* (the righteous level), when the mind is perfectly in tune with good deeds, piety and justice. At this highest level of *taqwa*, managers are happy to be criticized for their actions, treat their subordinates equally and fairly, and consult those concerned before making decisions.

Truthfulness (sidq)

The concept of *sidq* implies doing and saying what is right to the best of one's knowledge. It is forbidden in Islam to lie or to cheat in all circumstances. There are many verses in the *Koran* that emphasize the virtues and values of truthfulness. Managers as well as subordinates are reminded by the belief in God not to be guided by personal feelings that may divert them from the right path of justice, care and trustworthiness. They are asked to be patient, to fulfil their contractual duties, to be honest and to work hard, while seeking God's love and mercy. Honesty and trustworthiness are central to effective management. They safeguard humans from temptation to misuse the resources entrusted to them. The love of truth reflects the notion of personal responsibility for every uttered word and reinforces organizational attempts to evaluate and assess practice or investigate roots of problems.

Kindness and care while feeling the presence of God (ehsan)

The word *ehsan* has several meanings. It means being generous, seeking perfection and amelioration in one's doings, completeness of faith, and most important of all doing good deeds. It also implies basic human relations such as solidarity, cooperation, sympathy, compassion, forgiveness and brotherhood, and to care for and to help each other to do what is good and to avoid what is bad, as stated in the *Koran*: 'Help one another in benevolence and piety. But help not one another in sin and transgression' (ch. 5, verse 2). The value of *ehsan* is related to the concept of *eman*, which is explained above. Every activity in one's life should be carried out for God's sake and in the interests of other people as well as oneself. Managers with a high level of *ehsan* promote the training and development of their employees and encourage employee involvement and participation in decision-making.

Justice (adl)

Justice (adl) in Islam as in many other communities is a virtue and a human right. The ultimate justice is that of God. All people are equal despite their differences in wealth, health, prestige, profession, status, gender, colour, race and knowledge. What truly count are their actions and deeds. The Prophet Mohammed made it clear that people are equal when he said: 'An Arab has no superiority over a non-Arab, nor a non-Arab over an Arab, nor is a white one to be preferred to a black one, nor a black one to a white one, except in piety (righteousness)' (narrated as a correct *Hadith* by Boukhari and Muslim). In organizations where justice prevails, employees are treated and rewarded equally and fairly. Managers should treat their subordinates with respect and courtesy, and never look down on them or ignore their views and suggestions.

Trust (amana)

The concept of *amana* or trust is a core value that governs social relationships, as every person is held accountable for his/her actions. The *Koran* states: 'O you that believe! Betray not the trust of God and the apostle nor misappropriate knowingly things entrusted to you' (ch. 8, verse 27). A manager or leader is an *ameen* or a trustee who should respect the trust bestowed on him/her by superiors or employers and subordinates or employees. Any act of misuse of resources or mismanagement is seen as a violation of trust. An organization is an *amana* or a trust of those who own it and those who work in it.

Perfection (etqan)

The word *etqan* or perfection in Islam means the continuous striving to do better in what one does all the time. In other words, *etqan* is work behaviour that is related to a state of passion for excellence (*alfalah*). In an organizational context, striving to do better all the time requires managers and employees to work harder and improve the quality of their products and services through the promotion of learning, training, innovation and creativity.

Sincerity and keeping promises (ekhlas)

In Islam, keeping promises is a religious obligation. It is a sin to intentionally break one's promises. Breaking one's word is not Islamic and characterizes a person as a hypocrite. Sincerity infuses trust and confidence in an organization or a community and creates a culture of trustfulness, cooperation, loyalty and commitment.

Consultation (shura)

It is stated in the *Koran*, referring to the believers, that 'their matters are *shura* among them' (ch. 42, verse 38), which means they make collectively agreed decisions on worldly matters, so long as their actions do not contradict or deviate from the prescribed text (*Koran* and *Sunnah*). In organizations, managers are expected to seek advice and to consult with their subordinates before making decisions.

Patience (sabar)

Patience is the highest virtue of believing in God. Those who are patient in this life are the most rewarded in the Hereafter. Many verses of the *Koran* and many *Hadiths* emphasize the importance of patience. At the organizational level, being patient in making decisions reduces the possibility of making mistakes and increases the chances of success in negotiations.

MINI CASE STUDY 38

The World Goes Around: Islamic Management

From his studies of management in Arab countries Weir (1998; 2000) concluded that in many key issues the fundamentals of Islamic belief and management in Arab countries are similar to the current trends in Western management. Weir (2000) reported a study of Western motivation theories by Mubarak (1998), who concluded that the idea of motivation was widely theorized by Muslim scholars such El-Ghazzali (1058–1111), Ibn Taymiyya (1263–1328), and Ibn Khaldun (1332–1406) before the European Renaissance period and centuries before Western industrialization. Weir (2000) also suggests that the practice of 'management by walking about' which is related to best practice in Western management was practised by the Caliph Omar Ibn Al Khattab (the second companion of Prophet Mohammed), 'who visited his people to see and hear at first hand their problems and grievances' (Weir, 2000: 506). Also, from a study of total quality management (TQM) in an electronic manufacturing firm in Casablanca (Morocco), D'Iribarne (2002) reported that many of the respondents found it easy to learn the principles of TQM because they reinforced the teachings of Islam.

Question

1 What similarities can you find between the Western and Islamic approaches to management described in this book?

Managing human resources

The management of human resources in Arab countries is heavily influenced by traditional norms and values, and the principles and values of Islam discussed above.

Recruitment and selection

The process of recruitment and selection in Arab countries is in theory similar to that in most Western countries. Vacancies are normally advertised and applicants are short-listed and then interviewed and/or tested before the offer of employment is made. In practice, however, the process is influenced by socio-economic, political and cultural factors that may make it merely a bureaucratic and administrative formality. In some Arab countries the government specifies the procedure for recruitment and selection, according to a code of practice or a decree, making it a government affair and a real bureaucratic process. As explained below, the process is neither systematic nor objective.

Recruitment

In most Arab countries, job analysis is hardly known of and proper recruitment procedures are never used. Vacancies are normally filled through connections, and jobs are normally offered to family members, relatives and friends with very little consideration of competency and achievement. In most cases vacancies are filled before they are advertised, and new employees are hired without necessarily having vacancies. Because of the high level of unemployment in some countries, many job seekers attempt to improve their chances by sending applications to as many organizations as possible, asking for jobs or requesting to have their names put on a waiting list.

The most common method of recruitment is word of mouth and connections (*wasta*). Some jobs are never advertised formally because word of mouth spreads quicker than written text. When a job vacancy becomes available the first person to hear about it contacts a friend or a relative who is looking for a job, asks them to apply for it and then helps them to get it. Describing the recruitment process in the UAE, Suliman (2006: 66) said that it 'was, mainly, based on family members, relatives, friends and favourable word of mouth. Advertising a job would, usually, take place in prayer meetings, parties or any other social gathering.' Also, according to Ali and Al-Kazemi (2006: 89), 'most of the hiring and promotion in Kuwait, especially in the government sector, is influenced highly by social connectivity, tribal identity, and political and sectarian allegiances.'

It is also a common practice to hire new employees without necessarily having vacancies, especially when friends and relatives apply for jobs. Friendship and kinship relations seem often to take precedence over qualifications, as managers feel obliged to support their relatives and friends in getting employment. It is not surprising to find that in some cases a job description is produced and a job application form is completed only after the job has been offered. This is common when a member of the family or relative/friend is already employed in that organization. Through family connections, managers already know their job applicants before they employ them. According to Mellahi and Wood (2003: 375), about 80 per cent of employees recruited by SMEs in Algeria were known by their employers before they applied to work for them. They argued that this practice reinforces the importance of trust in employment relationships, especially in countries that are torn by political instability and tribal allegiances. In some cases, especially in the private sector, managerial jobs have to be obtained through recommendations regardless of knowledge and qualifications because of the trust factor. Application forms and documents that are not followed up through the use of *wasta* are often lost or ignored. Abdalla (2006: 135) argues that in the Gulf states 'the strong in-group orientation' encourages the use of *wasta* because 'some decision-makers prefer to appoint "people of trust and loyalty" rather than "people of competence"'. Also, applying for jobs in public sector enterprises, which are still a significant source of employment and job creation in most Arab countries (Gardner, 2003; Abdalla, 2006; Hatem, 2006; Branine, 2006), can be a traumatizing experience because of the amount of documentation one has to produce.

Selection

In most Arab countries, the selection of employees is based on recommendations, qualifications and loyalty. Those who are recommended by friends, relatives and people in high positions may be given no tests and no formal interviews. Also, it seems that the more academic certificates, degrees and diplomas the person holds, the better his/her chances of getting employed. It is generally believed that the knowledge acquired through education is enough to start a career. Exemption from national military service is also a prerequisite for getting a job in some Arab countries. The selection of employees for managerial and professional jobs is based on qualifications, especially Western-acquired qualifications, language ability (fluency in at least one foreign language), and perceived loyalty to the government in power (in public sector) or the owner of the business (private sector) rather than ability, experience and knowledge.

In the Gulf states there is a difference in recruitment and selection between nationals and foreign workers. Nationals are recruited and selected as explained above, but foreign workers, who make up the majority of the workforce, are recruited through the outsourcing of specialized agencies abroad. Agencies apply different methods of recruitment depending on the countries they recruit from and the jobs they look for. Normally, once selected the foreign worker holds a work permit for a specific occupation with a specific employer or sponsor (*kafeel*). The sponsorship process has become big business for the nationals who deal with recruitment agencies because they receive a payment for each foreign worker they sponsor. For example, Abdalla (2006: 135) explains that in Qatar the recruitment of foreign employees 'has become a thriving business for foreign and Qatari employment offices and for intermediaries, who benefit from the employers and the job seekers in the form of commissions, transportation fees, and cash guarantees'. Foreign individuals work or do business under the mercy of national sponsors (*kafeel*), and they are not allowed to stay in the country, change employment, or move from one employer to another without the endorsement of the *kafeel*. Commenting on such practices in Kuwait, Ali and Al-Kazemi (2006: 85) note that they provide the Kuwaitis with 'a means to generate wealth easily and to control expatriates, they lead to less optimal utilization of talent and prevent expatriates from freely exercising their natural rights for lawful business opportunities that are suitable for their skills and qualifications'. It should be stressed that this process of recruiting and employing foreign workers seems unique to the Gulf states.

Training and development

Except for a limited number of countries such as Jordan, Kuwait and Qatar, that spend between 5 to 9 per cent of their GDP on human resource development and have developed the best education systems in the region (Ali, 1996; World Bank, 2007), Arab countries do not spend enough – or cannot afford to spend more – on education and training. At the national level, all Arab countries have invested heavily in education and vocational training, but as Mellahi (2006: 112) argues, for example in Saudi Arabia, 'there is considerable concern over the employability of graduates from universities and vocational training colleges, raising questions about the effectiveness of some academic courses and the vocational training policy'. There is an urgent need in all Arab countries for better education systems, stronger vocational training and more training programmes in general, and management development (in particular at the organizational level) in order to meet the increasing demands for efficient and competent workers in all sectors of the economy.

Vocational training

Vocational training is very limited and will tend to be offered to those who become excluded from formal education. For example, in Algeria, over 92 per cent of those who attended vocational training courses in 1998 were young people who had been excluded from general education (CNES, 1999). In a report on vocational education and training in Algeria, the European Training Foundation (2003) stated that technical and vocational education and training (TVET) was used as an option for pupils who had dropped out of general education schools. It served as a social outlet, rather than a gateway to the labour market. In the Gulf states, there are many colleges of further education and vocational training, but their programmes are too theoretical and the teaching is lecture-based. There is no room for practical work or innovation, as students grasp theoretical information for use only in examinations.

Organizational training

At the organizational level, selection of employees for training is rarely made on the basis of training needs analysis. The decision on who should or should not be on a training programme is made by managers who normally see training as a cost to the organization and a favour to their employees rather than as an investment for the future. Big companies in Saudi Arabia, Kuwait and the United Arab Emirates have their own training centres, but they are often under-utilized. In other countries, spending on training is very limited and does not exceed 1 per cent of the total expenditure in most enterprises. There is a general lack of awareness of the importance of continuous training. Many small and medium size enterprises have no training facilities and provide no training opportunities to their employees. In the Gulf states, the private sector, which is dependent on foreign labour, does not care about training because when new skills are required it is cheaper to hire new workers than to invest in the current ones.

Management development

It was not until recently that Arab countries paid much attention to management development. In the Gulf states this has become a big business for national and international consultancy training agencies (Wilkins, 2001; Budhwar et al., 2002). Also, the growing affluence of that part of the world has allowed faster growth in education opportunities and more exposure of managers to European and North American management education. More and more managers have benefited from state scholarships to study abroad for further and higher degrees or to attend workshops, conferences and seminars. According to Weir (2000: 505), 'more Gulf managers hold university degrees than their counterparts in the US, UK, France, Germany and Japan. Gulf managers receive more management training per year than American and British managers.' There is still, however, a shortage of managers in marketing, finance, HRM and operations management, as well as of skilled and professional workforce throughout the Arab world.

ACTIVITY 3

Refer to the passage entitled 'Training and Development' in Chapter 11 (Germany and the Netherlands). What seem to you to be the main similarities and differences between the Germanic and the Arabic-Islamic approaches to training?

Rewards and remuneration

Arab countries differ significantly in their levels of income and reward systems. The oil rich states of the Gulf pay high salaries and provide good benefits and allowances, whereas other Arab countries differ according to their level of wealth and population size (see Tables 15.1 and 15.5 above). In all Arab countries the government determines the grades and levels of payment and pay rises in all state-controlled organizations and institutions. Most employees receive a basic salary and bonuses depending on their jobs, age, experience and position within the organization. The state's welfare system provides for sickness and disability allowances, old age pensions, family allowances and unemployment benefits, but such allowances differ from one country to another. They are quite high in the Gulf states and low in other countries. There is a statutory minimum wage in few Arab countries, and until recently all rewards were seniority-based. Pay in the Gulf states is also nationality-related and there is a big difference in pay between the indigenous and foreign workforce. The use of performance appraisal and performance-related pay is still very limited but is increasing in both public and private sectors.

Seniority-based pay

Until recently, seniority-based pay was the norm in all Arab countries. Workers were, and still are to a great extent, paid according to their age, work experience and qualifications. Pay is normally related to work experience rather than to performance and competency. When it comes to deciding pay rises, how hard or how much better one works may well matter less than how long one has been employed. It is only recently that some Arab countries such as Tunisia, Jordan, Algeria and Egypt have introduced a comprehensive reward system that takes into consideration the qualifications, experience, performance and competency of the employee in deciding the level of pay and pay rises (Yagoubi, 2004; Hatem, 2006; Yahiaovi and Zoubir, 2006).

Nationality-based pay

Nationality-based pay is a peculiar system that is only practised in the Gulf states (mainly Kuwait, Qatar, Saudi Arabia and the UAE), where employees are paid according to their nationalities or, to be more specific, according to the passports by which they enter the country. In general, nationals are paid higher than foreigners for doing similar jobs. In the private sector, where the majority of workers are foreign, wages are relatively low and are set individually depending on the individual's nationality, race, qualifications, looks, and so on. In some organizations, Western passport holders are paid more highly even than nationals for certain jobs, such as those in the banking and insurance sectors. Employees from other Arab countries such as Egypt and Lebanon earn higher than employees from South-east Asia, and so on. The locals (nationals), especially those who work in public sector organizations, are usually paid generously for the posts they hold rather than the work they do. Public sector wages and salaries are much higher than those of the private sector by as much as ten times. For example, according to statistics from the Saudi Ministry of Planning, the average salary of Saudi nationals was about 7,034 Saudi riyals in 2000, while that of non-Saudis doing the same job was about 2,354 Saudi riyals (cited in Mellahi, 2006: 115). When nationals work in the private sector they often demand about six times the salary of a skilled foreign worker. This is one of the main reasons for hiring non-nationals rather than nationals to work in private sector organizations.

Pay for goodwill

Payment for goodwill is another particularly Arab payment system that is practised more often in the Gulf states. Employees receive an occasional pay rise or bonus because the ruler (king, emir or president) or the owner of the organization wants to be grateful. For example, the ruler may decide to increase public sector employees' wages following the marriage or the birth of a member of his family, or to increase all the wages of the health service workers following a successful operation or treatment to him or to any member of his family. Similarly, in the private sector, the business owners may increase wages or give bonuses on good occasions and in festive seasons such as the month of Ramadan and the Eid celebrations. In some cases, these goodwill pay rises and bonuses are given to nationals only rather than to all employees, so discrimination is possible and very often expected and accepted.

Performance appraisal

The use of job evaluation and performance appraisal is very limited and is mainly practised in large private and foreign-owned organizations and joint ventures that have been influenced by Western HRM practices. And yet these approaches are not effective even in the latter because of cultural influences. Most Arab governments have attempted to introduce performance measurements and performance indicators to improve the quality of public sector products and services and to reduce public spending, but such measurements and indicators are very often used for administrative rather than developmental purposes. Abdalla (2006: 136) argues that performance appraisal systems in the public sector are 'mostly traditional (as they are carried out by the supervisor), authoritative, and centralized (the employee has no say), subjective (based on the impressions of the superiors and selected others, and not actual results), and confidential'. The practice of performance appraisal in the private sector depends on the size and type of organization. In small family businesses the owner–manager appraises employees' performance through managerial judgement, usually without the use of any formal performance appraisal methods. Large private sector organizations have introduced performance appraisal but with little success because both managers and employees have resisted it. Performance appraisal seems to go against the cultural values of avoiding direct criticism, face-saving, and respect of other people's contribution.

Performance-related pay

All Arab countries have had to reform their economies and to review their income policies. As a result, most of them have decentralized their payment systems by giving power to private sector employers to decide their own pay structures. Also the national wage negotiation process has been decentralized by allowing public enterprises to negotiate their wages and working conditions independently with their employees within the limits of the civil service wage scale, which is set by the government. However, there is little evidence that performance-related pay has been fully implemented or successful in any of the Arab countries studied so far.

Employee relations

Employee relations systems in Arab countries are centralized and strictly controlled by the state authorities through different administrative bodies. In the Gulf states, there are no trade unions and there is no collective bargaining. Strikes are not allowed and no industrial conflict is tolerated in countries such as Saudi Arabia, Qatar and the United Arab Emirates. Recently these countries came under pressure from the ILO and other international organizations to give the workers more freedom of association and the right to collective bargaining. Some of them, such as Bahrain, Qatar and Oman, have permitted the setting up of labour committees and associations for certain professional jobs, but they are at their very early stages and are short of trade unions in their operations.

In the Gulf states, the relationship between management and workers depends on ownership (public or private) and type of employees (nationals or foreigners). In the absence of Western-type systems of employee relations there are unwritten rules of employee relations tacitly based on the country's social relations. It is believed, for example, that managers have a duty to protect their subordinates, who in turn have to show loyalty and obedience to their leaders. Managers attempt to achieve and maintain a conflict-free work environment by seeking to resolve any employment problems directly by using the laws in force or the laws of custom and practice. As far as foreign workers are concerned, they often have no rights of any kind except for the wages they receive. The employer determines all kinds of rewards and allowances depending on the nationality of the foreign employee, as explained earlier.

In other Arab countries, employees have the right to form and join trade unions, and to bargain collectively, but the activities of trade unions are very often restricted to social and welfare issues and they are controlled by the state, as explained below.

Trade unions

In general, trade unions in Arab countries are either non-existent or are weak and ineffective because they are controlled by the state or made part of the state apparatus. They usually support the decisions made by the government and avoid any kind of confrontation with the government. Most employment laws such as the Labour Law (*Code du travail*) introduced in Morocco in 2004 and the Unified Labour Law no. 12 of 2003 in Egypt have given workers the right of association, collective bargaining and industrial action, but at the same time strengthened the power of employers by giving them the right to de-recognize trade unions and to dismiss employees on economic grounds. Trade unions are prohibited from associating with political parties and/or receiving funds from foreign donors. Most of the national trade unions federations are state-sponsored and controlled. They exist as long as their role is no more than being an intermediary body between the government and the trade unions they represent.

Collective bargaining

In the Gulf states where trade unions are not allowed, there are no formal mechanisms for collective bargaining. Informal and formal discussions or negotiations may take place between the management and individual workers (nationals), but agreements in the form of promises by management are not legally binding, although in most cases the management sees a moral obligation to honour them. In other Arab countries where trade union are allowed, collective bargaining is normally centralized and takes place between the employers' organization and the national trade union federation under the 'supervision' of the state. In most cases the process is an administrative formality in order to rubber stamp the state's employment policies (for example, for more details on trade unions and collective bargaining in Algeria, see Branine et al., 2008).

Industrial action

In the Gulf states, any form of industrial action is strictly forbidden. Industrial action by national or foreign workers is interpreted as an act of betrayal and social unrest that may result in instant dismissal and deportation in the case of foreign workers. In other countries where industrial action is legally allowed, strike activity is still very limited because of the many legal restrictions that make it almost impossible to organize legal strikes. In Algeria, for example, workers may organize a secret ballot to go on strike only after 14 days of mandatory conciliation or mediation. Also, the Industrial Relations Law 1990 stipulates that any action taken with the aim of either disturbing the operation of establishments that provide public services or obstructing traffic or freedom of movement in public places may be considered a terrorist act, liable to a punishment of up to 20 years in prison. Any strike action can be seen as obstructing traffic or freedom of movement in public places and can therefore be refused. This is the case in all other Arab countries where strikes are permitted in theory but they are not allowed to happen in practice.

Settlement of industrial disputes

In countries, such as the Gulf states where there are no formal industrial disputes and no procedures for the settlement of disputes, individual cases of grievances and complaints are dealt with informally or formally, depending on the severity of each case, by the senior management. In other countries, such as Algeria, Egypt and Tunisia most collective industrial disputes are dealt with at the national level through formal conciliation and arbitration.

Summary

1   Despite rich natural and human resources, the Arab countries' economic performance has been weak. This may be attributed to corruption, bureaucracy, inappropriate financial institutions, lack of entrepreneurial spirit, lack of research and development, high unemployment, injustice, political conflicts, and the lack of international investor confidence in domestic markets.
2   Arab labour markets are characterized by an uneven composition and distribution of labour, a high level of youth unemployment, a declining level of public sector employment, a move from the employment of foreign to national (indigenous) labour, a surplus of unskilled and uneducated workforce, increasing entry of women into the labour market, increasing foreign investment, a significant level of child labour and illegal employment practices, and the immigration of skilled and professional labour.
3   Most of the Arab countries inherited organizational approaches that are a mixture of traditional tribal leadership and Western colonial administration.
4   The process of recruitment and selection in Arab countries is often an administrative formality because in most cases vacancies are filled before they are advertised and new employees are hired without there necessarily being vacancies. The most common method of recruitment is word of mouth and connections (*wasta*).
5   There is an urgent need for better education systems, stronger vocational training, more training programmes in general, and management development.
6   Arab countries differ significantly in their levels of income and reward systems. The oil rich states of the Gulf pay high salaries and provide good benefits and allowances, whereas other Arab countries differ according to their level of wealth and population size. The use of performance appraisal and performance-related pay is still very limited, though on the rise.
7   Employee relations systems in Arab countries are centralized and strictly controlled by the state authorities. In the Gulf states, there are no trade unions and no collective bargaining. In other Arab countries, employees have the right to form and to join trade unions, and to bargain collectively, but the activities of trade unions are very often restricted to social and welfare issues and are controlled by the state.

Revision questions

Chapter 1 provides a review task designed to consolidate your learning from this chapter. Please see Box 1.2.

In addition, the following questions are designed to help you revise this chapter:

1 Discuss the main ways in which traditional norms and values have influenced management practices in Arab countries.
2 What other main factors, beyond traditional norms and values, have conditioned the practice of management in Arab countries?
3 Refer to Chapter 18 (South America). In a table, list the main similarities and the main differences between the Arab and South American countries in terms of (a) labour market trends and (b) recruitment and selection.

References

Abdalla, I. (2006) 'Human resource management in Qatar', in Budhwar, P. and Mellahi, K. (eds), *Managing Human Resources in the Middle East*, London: Routledge, 121–44.

Abdalla, I. and Al-Homoud, M. (2001) 'Exploring the implicit leadership theory in the Arabian Gulf states', *Applied Psychology: An International Review*, Special Issue, 50(4): 506–31.

Al-Buraey, M.A. (1988) *Administrative Development: An Islamic Perspective*, London: Kegan Paul.

Al-Faleh, M. (1987) 'Culture influence on Arab management development: a case study of Jordan', *The Journal of Management Development*, 6(3): 19–34.

Ali, A.J. (1990) 'Management theory in a transitional society: the Arabs' experience', *International Studies of Management and Organization*, 19(2): 22–37.

Ali, A.J. (1992) 'Islamic work ethics in Arabia', *Journal of Psychology*, 126(5): 507–20.

Ali, A.J. (1995) 'Cultural discontinuity and Arab management thought', *International Studies of Management and Organization*, 25(3): 3–6.

Ali, A.J. (1998) 'The typology of the Arab individual: implications for management and business organizations', *International Journal of Sociology and Social Policy*, 18(11/12): 1–19.

Ali, A.J. (2004) *Islamic Perspectives on Management and Organization*, Cheltenham and Northampton, MA: Edward Elgar.

Ali, A.J. and Al-Kazemi, A. (2006) 'Human resource management in Kuwait', in Budhwar, P. and Mellahi, K. (eds), *Managing Human Resources in the Middle East*, London: Routledge, 79–96.

Atiyyah, H.S. (1994) 'Effectiveness of Management Training in Arab Countries', *The Journal of Management Development*, 10(7): 22–30.

Atiyyah, H.S. (1996) 'Expatriate acculturation in Arab Gulf countries', *The Journal of Management Development*, 15(5): 37–47.

Benson, P.G. and Al Arkoubi, K. (2006) 'Human resource management in Morocco', in Budhwar, P. and Mellahi, K. (eds), *Managing Human Resources in the Middle East*, London: Routledge, 273–90.

Branine, M. (1994) 'The rise and demise of participative management in Algeria', *Economic and Industrial Democracy: An International Journal*, 15(4): 595–630.

Branine, M. (2006) 'Human resource management in Algeria', in Budhwar, P. and Mellahi, K. (eds), *Managing Human Resources in the Middle East*, London: Routledge.

Branine, M. and Analoui, F. (2006) 'Human resource management in Jordan', in Budhwar, P. and Mellahi, K. (eds), *Managing Human Resources in the Middle East*, London: Routledge, 145–59.

Branine, M. and Pollard, D. (2010) 'Human resource management with Islamic management principles – A dialectic for a reverse diffusion in management', *Personnel Review*, 39(6): 712–27.

Branine, M., Fekkar, A.F., Fekkar, O. and Mellahi, K. (2008) 'Employee relations in Algeria: a historical appraisal', *Employee Relations*, 30(4): 404–21.

Brynen, R., Rorany, B. and Noble, P. (eds) (1995) *Political Liberalization and Democratization in the Arab World*, vols 1&2, Boulder: Lynne Rienner.

Budhwar, P., Al-Yahmadi, S. and Debrah, Y. (2002) 'Human resource development in the Sultanate of Oman', *International Journal of Training and Development*, 6(3): 198–215.

CAWTAR (Centre of Arab Women for Training and Research) and IFCGEM (International Finance Corporation Gender Entrepreneurship Markets) (2007) *Women Entrepreneurs in the Middle East and North Africa: Characteristics, Contributions and Challenges*, Report at www.cawtar.org/Assets/Documents/pdf/Women_Entrepreneurs_in_the_ME_Jun07.pdf, accessed 21 May 2008.

Clegg, I. (1971) *Workers' Self-management in Algeria*, London: Penguin.

CNES (*Conseil National Economique et Social*) (1999) *La Relation Formation-Emploi*, Commission Relations de Travail, XIVeme session pleniere, November, 59pp, Algiers: CNES [in French].

D'Iribarne, P. (2002) 'Motivating workers in emerging countries: universal tools and local adaptations', *Journal of Organizational Behaviour*, 23: 243–56.

El-Said, H. and McDonald, F. (2001) 'Institutions and joint ventures in the Middle East and north Africa', in El-Said, H. and Becker, K. (eds), *Management and International Business Issues in Jordan*, Binghamton, NY: International Business Press, 65–83.

European Training Foundation (2003) *General survey of vocational education and training in Algeria*, Country Report, EU: Turin.

Gardner, E. (2003) 'Creating Employment in the Middle East and North Africa', at www.imf.org/external/pubs/ft/med/2003/eng/gardner, accessed 12 Nov. 2004.

Hatem, T. (2006) 'Human resource management in Egypt', in Budhwar, P. and Mellahi, K. (eds), *Managing Human Resources in the Middle East*, London: Routledge.

Ibrahim, E. and Johnson-Davies, D. (1977) (Trans.) *An-Nawawis' Forty Hadith*, 2nd edn, Damascus: The Holy Koran Publishing House.

ILO (International Labour Organization) (2007) *Global Wage Report 2008/09*, ILO: Geneva.

Kaynak, E. (ed.) (1986) *International Business in the Middle East*, Berlin: Walter de Gruyter.

Kuran, T. (2004) 'Why is the Middle East is economically underdeveloped? Historical mechanisms of institutional stagnation', *Journal of Economic*

Perspectives, 18(3), available online at: www.aeaweb.org/jep/contents/Summer 2004.html.

Lazreg, M. (1976) *The Emergence of Classes in Algeria: A Study of Colonialism and Socio-political change*, Boulder, CO: Westview Press.

Mellahi, K. (2006) 'Human resource management in Saudi Arabia', in Budhwar, P. and Mellahi, K. (eds), *Managing Human Resources in the Middle East*, London: Routledge, 97–120.

Mellahi, K. and Wood, G.T. (2003) 'From kinship to trust: changing recruitment practices in unstable political contexts', *International Journal of Cross Cultural Management*, 3(3): 369–81.

Moghadam, V.M. (2005) 'Women's economic participation in the Middle East: what difference has the neoliberal policy turn made?', *Journal of Middle East Women's Studies*, 1(1): 110–46.

Mubarak, A. (1998) *Motivation in Islamic and Western Management Philosophy*, PhD Thesis, University of Bradford, UK.

Muna, F.A. (1980) *The Arab Executive*, London: Macmillan.

Rosen, L. (2002) *The Culture of Islam: Changing Aspects of Contemporary Muslim Life*, Chicago: University of Chicago Press.

Suliman, A.M.T. (2006) 'Human resource management in the United Arab Emirates', in Budhwar, P. and Mellahi, K. (eds), *Managing Human Resources in the Middle East*, London: Routledge, 59–78.

Tayeb, M. (1997) 'Islamic revival in Asia and human resource management', *Employee Relations*, 19(4): 352–64.

Weir, D. (1998) 'The fourth paradigm', in Shamali, A.A. and Denton, J. (eds), *Management in the Middle East*, Kuwait: Gulf Management Centre.

Weir, D. (2000) 'Management in the Arab Middle East', in Tayeb, M. (ed.), *International Business: Theories, Policies and Practices*, London: Prentice-Hall.

Weir, D. (2001) 'Management in the Arab World: a fourth paradigm?', Paper submitted to EURAM Conference, Sophia Antipolis, France, 2 Dec.

Wilkins, S. (2001) 'Management development in the Arab Gulf states – the influence of language and culture', *Industrial and Commercial Training*, 33(7): 260–5.

World Bank (1997) *World Development Indicators*, Feb., Washington, DC: World Bank.

World Bank (2007) *Youth–An Undervalued Asset: Towards a New Agenda in the Middle East and North Africa*, Policy Note, No.43372, Human Development Department, MENA Region (MNHD), Washington, DC. World Bank.

Yagoubi, M. (2004) 'HRM in Tunisia', in Kamouche, K., Debrah, Y., Horwitz, F. and Muuka, G.N. (eds), *Managing Human Resources in Africa*, London: Routledge, 151–67.

Yahiaoui, D. and Zoubir, Y.H. (2006) 'Human resource management in Tunisia', in Budhwar, P. and Mellahi, K. (eds), *Managing Human Resources in the Middle East*, London: Routledge, 233–49.

Yousef, A.D. (2001) 'Islamic work ethics: a moderator between organizational commitment and job satisfaction in a cross-cultural context', *Personnel Review*, 30(2): 152–69.

Yousef, T.M. (2004) 'Development, growth and policy reform in the Middle East and north Africa since 1950', *The Journal of Economic Perspectives*, 18(3): 91–114.

Yousef, T.M. (2005) 'The changing role of labour migration in Arab economic integration', Paper prepared for a policy seminar on 'Arab Economic Integration: Challenges and Prospects', held in Abu Dhabi on Feb. 23-4.

Zeffane, R. (1981) 'Participative management in Algeria', in Mansfield, R. and Poole, M. (eds), *International Perspectives on Management and Organizations*, London: Gower, 67-75.

16

India

The chapter is designed to help you understand, for India:

1 The (a) economic, (b) political and (c) cultural contexts in which managers work;

2 The main trends in the labour market;

3 The typical features of (a) management policies and practices and (b) organizational structure and behaviour;

4 The main policies and practices of human resource management with regard to: (a) recruitment and selection; (b) training and development; (c) rewards and remuneration; and (d) employee relations.

Introduction

Although India's economic experience has much in common with that of other emerging economies, in many ways it stands alone as 'a cultural island' (see Sparrow and Budhwar, 1997; Budhwar et al., 2008). This chapter focuses on India. However, for comparative purposes Tables 16.1 and 16.2 provide statistics on some other emerging economies.

Table 16.1 Basic statistical indicators, selected emerging economics

Country	Area (sq. km)	Population (July 2009 est.)	Population growth (2009) %	GDP – Real growth rate (2008) %	Inflation rate (2008 est.) %	Work force (2008 est.) millions	Unemployment rate (2008) %
India	3,287,263	1,166,079,217	1.548	7.4	8.3	525.5	9.1
Iran	1,648,195	66,429,284	0.883	6.5	25.6	24.35	12.5
Mexico	1,964,375	111,211,789	1.13	1.3	5.1	42.32	4
South Africa	1,219,090	49,052,489	0.281	3.1	11.3	17.79	22.9

Source: CIA, *World Factbook*, (2010), and World Development Indicators, 2009.

Contexts: economics, politics and culture

Economics

India's economy is potentially one of the strongest in the world because of its 'large industrial output, technological knowledge and extensive reserve of skilled manpower' (Basu, 2007: 665). After more than 40 years of centralized economic planning, with moderate growth, in 1991 the Indian government embarked on the implementation of substantial liberalization economic policies that have transformed the country from a state-regulated to a free market economy. A number of important austerity measures were introduced over the 1990s in order to 'correct the fiscal imbalance, to bring about structural adjustments and to attract foreign direct investments' (Saini and Budhwar, 2004: 115). Such reforms included review of trade and exchange policy, the public sector, the banking sector and foreign investment (Budhwar, 2003; see also *The Columbia Journal of World Business*, 1994). In 1995 India adopted the charter of the WTO as a major trade partner in the world economy. The economic liberalization process has attracted significant foreign direct investment (FDI). The inflow of FDI has created a growth in employment and led to the transfer of technology, knowledge and skills from industrialized nations. Also, since most of the FDI was for export products, the export sector grew significantly from about 6 per cent in the 1980s, to an average of 10 per cent in the1990s, and to an average of 20 per cent by the mid-2000s (Government of India, 2005).

India's economy is still predominantly agricultural. The agricultural sector employs about 60 per cent of the working population, though it contributes by about 17.6 per cent to the GDP. India is self-sufficient in the production of food grain and many agricultural products. The industrial sector is still relatively small: it employs about 12 per cent of the working population, though it contributes about 29 per cent of the GDP.

The major contributor to India's economic growth is the service sector (53.4 per cent in 2008), especially IT software services. According to Bhattacherjee and Ackers (2008: 18), 'the most impressive growth has been in information technology, the export of software and IT-enabled business services: between 1991/92 and 2004/05, IT services exports grew at a phenomenal 47.6% per year'. In this respect, India is described as the electronic housekeeper of the world (Budhwar et al., 2006). The IT services sector has provided new employment opportunities and set the foundation for sustainable economic growth. Although the recent international financial crisis slowed down the level of economic growth from about 9 per cent in 2007 to 7.4 per cent in 2008, and increased the rate of inflation from around 6.4 percent to 8.3 per cent, India still has one of the highest rates of economic growth in the world.

Politics

India is a republic and one of the largest constitutional democracies in the world. It has been politically stable since its independence from Great Britain in 1947. The political system is designed along the 'Westminster model' where the parliament is the highest political institution that consists of the two houses of *Rajya Sabha* (the upper house) and *Lok Sabha* (the lower house). The political party or the coalition of parties that gets the majority of seats in the *Lok Sabha* following general elections forms the government (Budhwar, 2003). The head of the state is an elected president who has limited political powers while the head of government is a publicly and democratically elected prime minister who is chosen by parliamentary members of the majority party. The president on the recommendation of the prime minister appoints the members of India's federal government.

As in most emerging economies, the sustainability of India's future economic growth depends on the stability of its political system and the stability of international economic and financial institutions. Commenting on the Indian political system, Basu (2007: 674) observes that 'the strong democratic set-up in India involving public opinion in every strategic issue can be of enormous value for a sustainable development process. An open and multiparty democratic system has its own problems, particularly in countries like India where the number of political parties are innumerable and the level of political corruption is arguably extremely high. '

Culture

India consists of a mixture of religious, ethnic, caste and linguistic groups that are historically, regionally and socially differentiated (Sinha and Sinha, 1990; Budhwar, 2003; Budhwar et al., 2008). As one of the most ancient nations in the world, India has a long history that is rich with traditional values, norms and religious beliefs. Among the major religions, according to 2001 census, are Hinduism (80.5 per cent), Islam (13.4 per cent), Christianity (2.3 per cent), Sikhism (1.9 per cent), and others (1.8 per cent). There are about 3,000 castes and ethnic groups. There are about 200 languages and 500 dialects, but the two official and most spoken languages are Hindi and English. About 75 per cent of the population communicates through different languages belonging to the Indo-Aryan group (Hindi, Assamese, Bengali, Gujarati, Kashmiri, Marathi, Oriya, Punjabi, Sindhi, Urdu, etc.) and the rest (about 25 per cent) of the population speak languages belonging to the Dravidian family. More than 40 per cent of the population speak Hindi (Office of the Registrar General, 2001).

The British cultural influence is very strong. The British strengthened the system of elitism, feudalism and class values during their imperial rule of

India. They established institutions that were based in their operations on bureaucracy, hierarchy, discipline and subjugation. The legacy of such values still pervades the different institutions and classes of the current Indian society. Obviously the inherited culture of elitism and the class system have widened the gap between the rich and the poor, and have deepened the inequality of the caste system. For a comprehensive review of India's history and national culture, please refer to Husain (1992).

Indian society is based on strong family bonds where people rely on each other for moral and financial support. Indian people 'search for security and prestige within the confines of the near and dear' (Banerjee, 2008: 370); because Indian society is 'more harmonious and less competitive in nature, people believe in in-group performance', and they 'strive for individual achievement but they are also ready to share it with others' (Banerjee, 2008: 374). Also, symbols and signs, and rituals and customs, play a vital role in Indian culture, as well as respect for the elderly, the senior, the superior, the educated, the wealthy, and leaders. This translates into work behaviour (Singh, 1990; Sinha and Sinha, 1990).

In terms of Hofstede's (1991) cultural dimensions, India is rated as relatively low on individualism and masculinity, high on power distance and uncertainty avoidance, and is a long-term orientation nation (Singh, 1990; Kanungo and Mendonca, 1994; Sinha and Kanungo, 1997). According to Budhwar (2001: 80), the high power distance 'reflects the hierarchical nature of Hinduism (evidenced by the caste system), the early socialisation process that highlights the importance of family structure and remnants of British colonial influence'. The low masculinity culture 'is reflected in a paternalistic management style and preference for personalised relationships rather than a more divorced performance orientation' (p. 81).

MINI CASE STUDY 39

Global Products for Local Tastes (India)

Many multinational companies in India have had to adapt their products and services to the national languages and cultures. For example, McDonald's served vegetarian instead of beef burgers and LG used the Hindi language to rename its range of washing machines, refrigerators and colour TVs. However, the same companies did not have to change anything when they invested in the UK.

Questions

1 Discuss the importance of understanding the Indian culture to foreign companies investing in India.
2 Write a short report describing the threats and opportunities to foreign investors wishing to set up joint ventures in India.

Labour Market Trends

India has the second largest population in the world after China. The major problem facing the Indian government is the creation of sufficient jobs to meet the increasing surplus of labour. Reducing unemployment levels is no doubt the biggest challenge.

The recent decline in employment is related to the sharp decline in manufacturing and in public sector enterprises that were labour intensive and employed most of the organized and unionized labour. However, economic reforms have led to an increase in urban employment, especially in IT services and in foreign-owned companies. There have been significant shifts in the structure of employment as the 'share of both casual employment and regular wage employment has fallen whereas the share of self-employment for all categories of workers has significantly risen' (Bhattacherjee and Ackers, 2008: 20). Overall, the labour market is characterized by increased youth unemployment, a high level of agricultural employment, a rise in IT services employment, an increase in jobs created by foreign direct investment, the domination of informal sector employment, low female participation in the labour market, the existence of child labour and illegal employment practices, and a significant level of skills shortages.

Unemployment

Economic reforms led to the introduction of drastic austerity measures to improve the performance of public and private sector organizations. Among such measures was the downsizing of many organizations to eliminate their surplus labour. Voluntary retirement schemes as well as early retirement packages had to be introduced at a time when the labour market demand for labour was already much lower than the supply. Many young and highly qualified people are unable to find employment. Unemployment rates have risen across all sectors of the economy, 'but this has occurred largely due to an increase in the number of active job seekers rather than an increase in the size of the unemployed' (Bhattacherjee and Ackers, 2008: 20).

Agricultural employment

It is estimated that about 60 per cent of employment is created in the agricultural sector. However, although the majority of the workforce is in agriculture only about 15 per cent of the workforce 'is estimated to fall in the category of wage/salary employment' (Saini and Budhwar, 2004: 113). Most of the working population are in the informal sector. Rural employment in general declined by about 15 per cent between 1984 and 2004. In a large country that is trying to be self-sufficient in the production of its food (grains, rice, poultry, fish, vegetables, spices) agriculture is a very important sector that will always be used to absorb the surplus labour, but the problem is that more and more young and educated job seekers are not willing to work in agriculture.

Increasing employment in IT

India is known for its IT software services sector which accounts for more than 25 per cent of export earnings and employed about 2 million people in 2008. Software services are provided in either project-oriented, IT outsourcing, or support and training services (Kuruvilla and Ranganathan, 2008). IT outsourcing is the new engine of India's economic growth in this sector (Bhattacherjee and Ackers, 2008). However, support services and call centres for a large number of different industries account for about 40 per cent of the IT sectors' employment and about 43 per cent of its revenues (Kuruvilla and Ranganathan, 2008: 48). According to Gurtoo (2009) a number of studies of IT services as well as case studies of big companies such as the National Thermal Power Corporation, Indian Oil Corporation and Veerat National Bank Limited, have shown that 'information technology (IT) related changes aligned with reforms have increased productivity and overcome competition' (p. 525).

However, the increase in the service sector has not created a similar increase in employment because the share of employment in services has been less than half the increase in the services output. In reality the drivers in the diversification of job creation outside the agricultural sector have been manufacturing and construction, followed by trade, hotels and restaurants (Mohanty, 2009).

Employment and foreign direct investment

The liberalization process and the stable political system attracted much foreign direct investment (FDI). For example, by the year 2000 there were more than 15,000 multinational companies in India (Budhwar, 2001) and the number has increased significantly since then. MNCs have been attracted to India by the availability of an English-speaking, competent, highly educated and skilled workforce that provides effective and efficient work for very low wages. They have also benefited from the existence of a well-established infrastructure, which supports efficient international communication services, and sophisticated international technology networks as well as the existence of a large and strong software industry and an increasing number of blue-chip companies throughout India (Raman et al., 2007: 698). For example, in 2006 about 25.6 per cent of all FDI in research and development projects was directed to India, and the major investors were US MNCs such as Intel, IBM, Motorola and Microsoft (Huggins et al., 2007). This increasing FDI created substantial job opportunities in the manufacturing and industrial sectors. In this respect, Basu (2007: 674) notes that 'world-class businesses that have emerged in knowledge-based industries are transforming India into a key global player'. However, FDI has created jobs for the select few; few people can get jobs to work for foreign companies.

Informal sector employment

The National Commission for Enterprises in the Unorganized Sector (NCEUS) in India defined the informal sector as a sector where employees do not generally 'enjoy employment security (no protection against arbitrary dismissal), work security (no protection against accidents and illness at the work place) and social security (maternity and health care benefits, pension, etc.)' (NCEUS, 2007: 3). In general, the informal sector can be described as a form of self-employment at a small scale, as already explained in Chapter 14 of this volume. In 2001, there were only 28.14 million (about 7 per cent) in organized (formal) employment out of a workforce of 402 million (Office of the Registrar General, 2001). Thus almost 93 per cent of the working population were employed in the informal or unorganized sector.

The rate of regular employment decreased by about 19 per cent between 2000 and 2005, while self-employment increased significantly. It is estimated that nearly 97 per cent of all the new jobs created between 1999/2000 and 2004/5 were in the informal sector. The formal economy produced about 1.4 million new jobs while the informal economy produced more than 41.9 million net new jobs over the same period (Mohanty, 2009). There has been a process of informalization of the formal sector because more and more regular jobs have been created in the informal economy.

Female participation in the labour market

Women are respected in Indian culture but, as Budhwar (2003: 71) states, 'respect does not always translate into equality in the workplace, in earnings or in society in general'. This is endorsed by Bhattacherjee and Ackers (2008: 28), who confirm, that 'there has been no large scale or spectacular induction of women into the workforce'. Many women are denied access to formal employment and are confined to doing jobs from home or to work in the informal sector. A significant proportion (about 12 per cent) of the self-employed workers in non-agricultural employment between 2000 and 2005 worked from home and most of them were female (NCEUS, 2007: 57). Also, according to the NCEUS (2007), about 30 per cent of the female non-agricultural self-employed work from home, as opposed to only 6.5 per cent of males. About 49 per cent of the female self-employed in manufacturing worked from home as opposed to 20 per cent of males. Most of the females who worked from home were in the manufacture of textile products and wearing apparel.

Although the recent reforms have resulted in better education, foreign investment and the development of new sectors such as the software industry, call centres, and hospitality, which can and have to some extent provided opportunities to an increasing number of women to get access to the labour market, women are still under-represented in many sectors of the economy. Research by Budhwar and Sparrow (2002b) concludes that 'Indian male managers appear to exercise their superiority and assertiveness over their female employees by expressing their reluctance to recruit them irrespective of their performance during the recruitment process' (cited in Budhwar et al., 2008: 83). They also state that this phenomenon is cultural because such behaviours are influenced by the traditional roles of men and women in Indian society, where men are the breadwinners and women are housewives. The low level of female participation in the labour market is also the result of a high level of illiteracy and low education levels among the women of India.

Child labour and illegal employment practices

India is a large country with a large population, making it an attractive location and transit place for the exploitation of men, women and children. As can be seen from Table 16.2, more than 30 per cent of the population of India is under the age of 14. Many school-age children are forced to work as domestic servants, factory workers, beggars and street vendors. Illegal employment practices such as not considering the health and safety of employees, not paying

Table 16.2 Age structure (%) (2009), selected emerging economies

Country	0–14 years %	15–64 years %	Over 65 %	Median age (years)	Life expectancy at birth
India	31.1	63.6	5.3	25.3	69
Iran	21.7	72.9	5.4	27	71
Mexico	29.1	64.6	5.4	26.3	76
South Africa	28.9	65.8	5.4	24.4	50

Source: CIA *World Factbook*, (2010).

employees their full wage entitlements, and nepotism and corruption, are very common especially in the small enterprises whose owners have no respect for and do not implement employment laws. Also, many vulnerable people are held in debt bondage and forced to work in brick kilns, rice mills, restaurants and factories.

Skill shortages

It can be argued that in a country with a large population like India, which is very often described as having the world's largest pool of scientifically trained, English-speaking graduates, there should be no shortage of skilled workforce. In reality many industries suffer from acute shortages of skilled and professional employees (Kuruvilla and Ranganathan, 2008; Bhattacherjee and Ackers, 2008). For example, in the software industry, for which India is known, a study by Kuruvilla and Ranganathan (2008) found that there had been shortages of programmers in common software skills such as proficiency in Java, C++, ERP, SAP and J2EE and in specialized skills such as data warehousing, Citrix-certified enterprise administrators, Cisco-certified network professionals, and the like. They also reported shortages of employees with managerial skills such as systems administrators and project managers. There was also a need for IT consultants, researchers, architects, and managers with international vision. They observed that the shortage 'appears to be more critical at the middle and upper management levels and in high-skill categories' (Kuruvilla and Ranganathan, 2008: 52). It has been estimated that the annual demand for software employees will surpass the supply by about 235,000 jobs by 2010 (2008: 51).

ACTIVITY 1

Imagine you are a labour market consultant: write a report of no more than 1,000 words to the ILO (International Labour Organization) describing the strengths and weaknesses of the Indian labour market, highlighting any potential problems that may affect the Indian economy in the future.

Management and organization

India inherited much of the British system of administration and management, especially in the administration of the civil service and the railways network. However, a new breed of managers has developed over the years. As Budhwar (2001: 83) pointed out, currently Indian managers internalize two separate sets of values, the Indian and the Western. On the one hand they tend to assimilate

Western and Japanese managers as a result of their education and training in the West or Western-accredited Indian management institutions. On the other hand, their management behaviour is influenced by strong family traditions, social relationships and religious beliefs. In practice 'these two sets of values co-exist and are drawn on as frames of reference depending on the nature of problems that people face' (Budhwar et al., 2008: 84). Also, from a study of leadership in selected Indian organizations, Kakar et al. (2002: 241) identified four types of business organizations with their particular management systems and leadership styles, as follows:

1   Medium to large organizations that are family owned and have established links with foreign companies through joint ventures and business collaborations. Their management is a hybrid of Western and traditional Indian practices. Most of their top management have been exposed to Western practices through management education such as studying for an MBA in Western or Indian universities.
2   Indigenous small to medium size organizations that are family owned and follow traditional Indian management practices where managers are authoritarian and paternalistic.
3   Subsidiaries of multinational companies. They are managed according to their parent organizations' management policies and practices.
4   Entrepreneurial ventures that are small enterprises owned by young professionals. They are small but they have a large market exposure, especially those in IT services. Their management is yet to be defined but it tends to vary depending on the type of business and the experience of its owners.

According to Suar et al. (2006: 96) management in India differs between the private and the public sectors. They argue that private sector companies operate in a fairly competitive environment and they 'emphasise high task, close relationships, participation, and caring for employees', while the public sector companies operate in a protected environment that is 'isolated from market pressures, low task, impersonal work environment, and bureaucratic set-up with too many rules and regulations for employees without actual practice'. Therefore it can be concluded from the above studies that the practice of management in India varies from one type of organization to another and from one sector to another, but it is generally described as authoritative and paternalistic, and integrated and international.

Authoritative and paternalistic management

Sinha (1979, 1995) describes Indian management and leadership styles as 'bureaucratic and authoritarian' on the one hand, and 'nurturant–task' on the other. The 'nurturant–task' (NT) style overlaps with authoritarianism on one side and participative leadership on the other. The authoritarian leader is power-oriented while the NT leader is task-oriented. The former neither cares for subordinates nor understands their problems, while the latter 'expresses nurturance in terms of care, consideration, warmth, support and affection for his/her subordinates, and a deep interest in their growth and well-being' (Suar et al., 2006: 98). In this context, Indian managers are said to have preference for *authoritative* rather than *authoritarian* management because they are strict and demanding but caring and supportive just like the paternalistic head of an Indian family (Sinha, 1979; Kakar et al., 2002). This type of leadership derives, according to Budhwar (2001: 81), from the 'use of familial and cultural values (such as affection, dependence and need for personalised relationships) to temper the form and structured task direction expected in situations of high power distance'.

It seems that complicated family relations and strong power holders have been responsible for the continuation of a paternalistic managerial style in India (Budhwar, 1999, 2003). The family-owned business houses, which have dominated the Indian economy since the time of British rule of India, inherited a management system that was based on bureaucratic procedures, hierarchy, status consciousness, and mechanisms of control. Saini and Budhwar (2004: 120) stated that these inherited values 'have helped to strengthen hierarchical superior–subordinate relationships which act as a kind of mechanism of social control on the managed'. It also makes the decision-making process less decentralized. According to Kakar et al. (2002: 240), there is always 'a tendency to centralize power and control' which makes collaborative team effort and criticism of management very limited or non-existent. However, a study by Raman et al. (2007) found that Indian managers emphasize the importance of teamwork and both informal and formal communication channels with their employees throughout the organization. They argued that there was 'a strong belief in the organization that changes, even small ones, need to be well communicated to all employees. Informal meetings are often convened to discuss issues and also to elicit suggestions for corrective action' (p. 707). Therefore a combination of inherited and acquired managerial behaviour has produced managers who tend to be authoritative and paternalistic at the same time, depending on the issues they deal with, the subordinates they lead, and the economic environment in which they operate.

Integrated and international management

More and more Indian managers have been educated in Western countries or in Indian institutions of education that are established along the lines of Western education systems (Sparrow and Budhwar, 1997; Budhwar et al., 2008). This type of 'hybrid' management style has grown over the years to control the Indian economy. The Indian economy has benefited significantly from foreign direct investment, which brought in technology and know-how. In India the spread of multinational companies has no doubt led to the development of a cluster of different management systems adopted from Western countries as well as Japan. Gradually most organizations that are influenced by MNCs adopt some kind of standardized international management practices. It is argued that many Japanese and American companies have transferred their management practices to India with only small modifications (Budhwar and Björkman, 2003; Saini and Budhwar, 2004). Also, as Kakar et al. (2002: 241) argue, 'Indian management culture ..., among all of India's various cultures, is arguably the most exposed to forces of modernization and globalisation'.

An increasing number of family business groups have grown large and multinational in their operations. Some of them have entered into joint ventures with Western companies and become in need of Western management practices. Kakar et al. (2002: 242) explain that the managers among the family members 'have almost always been professionally trained in well-known institutions of higher learning in India or in universities in Europe, the UK and the US'. Also, their employees, especially the middle and upper managers, who are not members of the family, have been educated in institutions that 'have exposed them to Western management values' which are different from the traditional cultural values of the established Indian families.

Managing human resources

Research by Budhwar (2000), Ramaswamy and Schiphorst (2000), Ramaswamy (2000), Budhwar and Khatri (2001) and Budhwar and Sparrow (2002a, b) found that there had been low representation of HR managers at the board level and that there has been a significant devolution of HRM responsibilities to line managers. They also found that Indian companies have started to give more attention to training and development than any other HRM functions. The liberalization of the economy, and the socio-economic reforms that accompanied it, have required the development of an effective and efficient workforce that is 'capable of taking on the challenge thrown up by the new economic environment' (Saini and Budhwar, 2004: 115). Also, in another study of HRM policies and practices in 76 subsidiaries of MNCs in India, Björkman and Budhwar (2007) found that the majority of the firms studied, which had different subsidiary units in India, had appointed an HR manager who was in charge of implementing HRM policies throughout the country. They also found that one of the main tasks of these HR managers 'was to manage the tension between expectations from corporate headquarters for a global approach to HRM and the need to adapt practices to the (micro) local conditions facing a specific unit while bearing in mind the advantages associated with national integration and standardization of HRM practices' (Björkman and Budhwar, 2007: 605).

All the above studies have agreed that the practice of HRM in India is influenced by the socio-economic and political context in which organizations operate. There have been some changes in employment policy but the practice, especially in employee relations and recruitment and selection, is still heavily influenced by cultural norms and values.

Recruitment and selection

Recruitment

In India, there is a difference between the recruitment of the more qualified (white-collar) and the less qualified (blue-collar) employees. Companies tend to recruit their white-collar employees by advertising externally through agencies, whereas they recruit blue-collar employees through both external and internal advertising, especially internally through introductions and recommendations. From a study of a US-based outsourcing services provider in India, Raman et al. (2007: 704) found that while the company did not advertise in newspapers for employee recruitment, it depended 'on a variety of sources like head hunters, job portals, fairs, and internal employee referrals'. There was also a preference for internal over external recruitment. However, regardless of the approach used, new employees are normally recruited according to commercial, family and political considerations (Budhwar et al., 2008). For example, family businesses prefer to hire family members, friends and relatives through recommendations and word of mouth. Large companies tend to use headhunting and poaching, as they compete with each other for better skilled and talented employees, to the extent that poaching employees from competitors has led some companies to form 'non-poaching pacts' with each other. Normally the competitors agree that none of them poaches employees from others' current pool of employees, or hires others' employees within three months of their leaving employment. However, there has been very little success in keeping such agreements (Kuruvilla and Ranganathan, 2008).

Selection

In a country where there is a surplus of labour there is high demand for jobs. The selection process is quite tough and rigorous because employers have many applicants to choose from. A study by Raman et al. (2007: 704) found that the selection process in the IT outsourcing services involved 'a test followed by a minimum of two rounds of interviews'. However, since there are strong family ties and many managers tend to recruit friends and relatives, the process of selection is very often tainted by nepotism and favouritism at all levels (Budhwar, 2000, 2003; Ramaswamy, 2000).

Graduate recruitment

India has one of the largest numbers of graduates in the world (Asher and Nandy, 2006; Fairell et al., 2005). Each year millions of college and university graduates join the labour market but, as explained earlier, it has become more and more difficult for the new graduates to find employment. Indian employers have a wider pool of graduates to choose from and the process of graduate recruitment and selection has become more complex and sophisticated. As far as the recruitment of professionals and those for managerial jobs is concerned, each organization applies its own staffing policies depending on their size, ownership and type of operations. Some owners of family businesses tend to 'recruit managers from their own families, castes and communities, reinforcing old customs, values and beliefs' (Budhwar, 2001: 81), while others tend to recruit graduates with 'MBAs at the entry level from lower-tier business schools rather than the "elite" ones, if at all' (Raman et al., 2007: 704) because of the fear that graduates with MBAs from good business schools may leave quite early to work for their competitors.

MINI CASE STUDY 40

I Need a Good Reference (India)

Latit Kumar is a graduate from Mumbai University with a first class degree in biotechnology. He completed an MBA (biotechnology) from a British university and returned home to look for employment. He had three job interviews during the first six months of his return, but after each interview he was told that his references were not good enough. He sent an email to his MBA programme tutor in the UK asking for a good reference.

Questions

1 Why are references so important for employment in India?
2 To what extent will a reference from the MBA programme tutor help Latit Kumar to be employed? Why?

Training and development

Studies of HRM in India have confirmed that Indian employers see human resource development (HRD) as the main function of HRM and the only activity for improving organizational performance (Rao, 1999; Saini and Budhwar, 2004; Raman et al., 2007). The term HRM has been replaced by HRD as the main people management function that can advance the Indian economy and society to the level reached by industrialized countries (Rao, 1999). When HRM is taught in colleges and universities it is described by Indian academics as HRD. This started in the 1980s, when the central government Ministry of Education was renamed the Ministry of HRD. Currently, the training of employees is provided by a number of national institutes that are centrally funded and expected to provide a variety of training courses to job seekers throughout the country to make them more employable. The emphasis given to training and development for organizational success in a competitive and free market economy does also reflect the importance given to education and learning in Indian society.

Education and learning

Education is highly valued by the Indian people and is seen as a means of gaining recognition and status in society. The Indian education system is funded and run mainly by the central and state governments, and is made available to all classes of society regardless of their income or location. Higher education institutions are known for their world-class standards and the international reputation of their scholars. For example, India's first-tier and second-tier engineering institutions, such as the IITs [Indian Institutes of Technology] and the Regional Engineering Colleges, produce top-quality graduates that are recognized all over the world (Chatterjea and Moulik, 2007). However, according to a recent study by Kuruvilla and Ranganathan (2008), despite the high quality of the first-tier and second-tier institutions, it is actually the third-tier colleges that produce the most engineers at undergraduate and postgraduate levels, and it is this type of college that is under-funded and suffering from acute shortages of resources. Therefore Kuruvilla and Ranganathan (2008: 59) state that 'government spending on research and development is considerably lower in India (0.0843% of the country's GDP in 2007) than in some competing countries (2.8% of South Korea's GDP, for example)'. They add that declining government spending on higher education as a proportion of GDP from about 1 per cent in 1971 to 0.4 per cent in 2006 have made India's postgraduate education and research system unable to 'generate high-level skills of the kind that are required for growth in the high end of the industry, particularly the software and R&D segments' (Kuruvilla and Ranganathan, 2008: 59).

Vocational education and training

In India, vocational education is centralized and comes under the control of the federal Ministry of HRD, and is normally offered by schools at the senior secondary stage. There are also a number of specialized vocational training institutions, privately and publicly owned, throughout the country. Apprenticeship is also offered by some employers, but this is very limited and much below expectations. In general, the performance of state-regulated vocational training is far from satisfactory (Vladimir et al., 2003; Saini and Budhwar, 2004). There is a need for more publicly and privately funded programmes to improve the knowledge and skills of an increasing number of job seekers, especially among the young and the unemployed.

Organizational training

The recent economic reforms have put great pressure on Indian employers to train more employees to face the challenges of international competition in a free market economy and to meet the demands of current and future economic growth. Gurtoo (2009: 524) comments that 'the systems need to be overhauled and the workforce needs to be retrained to perform new roles, meeting new and more stringent requirements of performance'. Therefore many large companies have invested in preparing their employees to take up professional and managerial positions through the introduction of 'tailor made management development programmes' (Raman et al., 2007: 704). Also, some large firms in the IT industry have established a number of academic–industry collaborations. For example, Honeywell, Sun, Microsoft and Intel have all established links with IIT Mumbai. However, in comparison with other emerging economies, such as South Korea, Mexico and Brazil, organizational training in India is still too rare and is very limited to a small number of companies and sectors of the economy.

ACTIVITY 2

Refer to the section on Training and Development in China and Hong Kong, Chapter 8, and compare and contrast the practices of training in China and India.

Rewards and remuneration

Until the reforms of the 1990s, the state was the largest employer and it was the politicians who determined the rewards structure for centralized policies' sake. Rewards were primarily determined by the central government through its incomes policy and basic pay regulations. As a result of economic reforms, all ceilings on pay were removed in January 1994, but as far as top management pay is concerned the board of directors is still required to take Section 198 of the Indian Companies Act 1956 into consideration. The results of a survey by Jaiswall and Firth (2007: 23) show that 'higher salaries are determined by performance and have not simply resulted from removal of restrictions on managerial pay limits or taxation leverages'. Companies are now allowed to set up their own reward and compensation packages, but they have to state the rationale behind each award paid to a top manager and explain the relationship of pay to corporate performance. The removal of restriction here does not exclude the government from control and imposition of rewards systems that it sees as appropriate to the country's economic conditions.

Basic pay, benefits and allowances

Indian employees receive a basic salary and a number of benefits, allowances and bonuses depending on the type and nature of employment, as well as the seniority and experience of the employee. It is estimated that about 50 per cent of the total pay of a manager is made of rewards above the basic salary (Jaiswall and Firth, 2007). Benefits and bonuses 'play a significant role in attracting and retaining top management talent' (Jaiswall and Firth, 2007: 4). Also, it is common for employees to receive payment in kind to avoid paying taxes, although income tax rates have been reduced in recent years.

Performance appraisal and performance-related pay

Recent studies have confirmed that many Indian organizations use performance appraisal metrics to determine rewards above basic pay (see Björkman and Budhwar, 2007; Raman et al., 2007; Jaiswall and Firth, 2007). Although a system of performance appraisal is hard to implement fully because of cultural and political influences, most of the large Indian companies, joint ventures and foreign companies have in place systems of assessing the performance of their employees and have introduced performance-related pay. For instance, a study of MNCs in India by Björkman and Budhwar (2007) found that the majority of multinational firms studied had used performance appraisal and performance-related pay, but they also found that 'several firms reported considerable resistance among their employees towards providing negative performance feedback, and low levels of subordinate involvement in goal setting' (p. 605).

ACTIVITY 3

As an HR manager of a joint venture in Mumbai, you have been asked to review the current reward policy and to suggest a new policy that is more appropriate to India's social and economic structure. What type of reward policy would you suggest and how would you implement it?

Employee relations

India inherited the British industrial relations system, but since independence many state-imposed employment laws have been introduced to regulate employee–employer relations. The government has always argued that it has to intervene in order to promote industrial peace and uphold social justice (Bhattercherjee, 2001; Venkata Ratnam, 1995, 1996; Venkata Ratnam and Verma, 1998; Sodhi, 1999; Saini and Budhwar, 2004; Badigannavar, 2006). Hence, the government has been able to implement its employment policies through a consultative tripartite organization called the Indian Labor Conference, which involves representatives from employers, trade unions and the state. The conference is held annually to discuss and decide policies on employee relations.

In an attempt to reform the system of employee relations in response to the general economic reforms, the government set up the second National Labour Commission (NLC) in 1999. The Commission was tasked to rationalize the existing labour laws for organized labour and to introduce legislation that ensured minimum labour standards for unorganized labour. In its first report in 2002 it made the following recommendations:

1   Organizations were to set up effective labour–management partnerships that would improve the commitment of employees to both quality and productivity in their organizations;
2   Employers were expected to invest in multiple-skills training in order to develop a flexible and mobile workforce with many employment opportunities;
3   Employers were expected to recognize trade unions and to promote the use of decentralized collective bargaining;
4   The introduction of severe penalties against unions that resort to 'illegal' strike action; and
5   Employers were not requested to get state permission for introducing labour reductions, but they should give their employees two months' notice.

However, most of the above recommendations are yet to be fully implemented because of trade union resistance to them (Bhattacherjee and Ackers, 2008).

Trade unions

The formal recognition of trade unionism was made in the Trade Unions Act of 1926 in parallel with the development of industrial relations and personnel management in the United Kingdom. Employees have a constitutional right to form and to join trade unions. However, trade union density has been very low and has rarely exceeded 10 per cent of the total workforce.

Before the economic reforms of the 1990s, the state was the largest employer and public sector employment led to the development of stronger public sector unionism, resulting in the growth of trade unions from 4,624 in 1951/2 to

11,614 in 1961/2 (Bhattacherjee and Ackers, 2008: 7). Most of the public sector employees were members of the Congress party-controlled Indian National Trade Union Congress (INTUC), and therefore it was obvious that the unions in the public sector had a welfare and a non-adversarial role. However, the role of trade unions has changed gradually to become more cooperative and less militant (Venkata Ratnam, 1995; Budhwar, 2001, 2003). According to Budhwar (2003: 76) the main reasons for the change of trade union role are:

1   The failure of a number of strikes such as those in Bombay (textile mills; Hindustan Lever), West Bengal (Dunlop Rubber and Bata India) and Pune (Telco);
2   The loss of faith and confidence in militant trade unionism as a result of the failed strikes.

However, Indian trade unions are still influential in large organizations and they often intervene in HRM functions by getting involved in the recruitment of new employees, distribution of bonuses and re-allocation of employees. Also, as the number of independent and regional trade unions has increased since the 1980s, the power and influence of the state-controlled and politically affiliated trade unions has started to decline. As a result, the density of trade unions has changed from one sector to another and from one type of employee to another. For example, it does not exceed 3 per cent in the non-agricultural sector, but it represents more than 35 per cent in the organized labour (Frenkel and Kuruvilla, 2002). Also, the majority of employees in public sector enterprises are unionized while most of the workers in urban private sector enterprises are not unionized (Bhattacherjee and Ackers, 2008).

Collective bargaining

Until the late 1990s collective bargaining had been centralized and conducted by the state at the national level and in line with the Industrial Disputes Act of 1947, which did not require employers to recognize representative trade unions as the main bargaining partner and did not request the employees and trade unions to bargain in good faith. Moreover, the act did not make collective bargaining agreements legally binding. Now collective bargaining is becoming less centralized and is moving from the national to the industry and the unit levels. There are different levels of collective bargaining ranging from the plant (organization) to the national level, depending on the type of sector and organization. For example, in private sector enterprises collective bargaining takes place at the plant level between the management and the local trade unions, which may or may not be linked to the national unions that are normally affiliated to parliamentary political parties. In most public sector enterprises, collective bargaining takes place at the industry and/or national level between the centralized trade union federations that are affiliated to political parties and the state as the employer. In other words, until the recent reforms, 'the structure of bargaining was thus very centralized, usually at the national level, but in some regions at the industry level, and in a few cases in the private sector bargaining was at the enterprise level' (Bhattacherjee and Ackers, 2008: 8).

Industrial action

In the 1990s, India ranked the highest in the world in the number of days lost annually through lockouts and strikes (ILO's *World Labour Report*, 1997–8), but in reality most of the days lost were employer-imposed lockouts rather than the result of trade union-led industrial action (Perry, 2006). For example, almost 60 per cent of the 230 million days that were lost between 1991 and 2000 were the result of employer-imposed lockouts (Bhattacherjee and Ackers, 2008: 22). Employee- and trade-union-initiated industrial action, in the form of strikes, is very limited in public sector enterprises. The main reason for the low level of strikes in India is that the Industrial Disputes Act of 1947 made it almost impossible for employees to take legal industrial action. Nevertheless when strikes do take place they tend to last for a long time. In recent years most industrial disputes have been in the private sector and mainly in manufacturing, but in comparison to other emerging economies and taking into consideration the size of the country, the level of industrial action is very low.

Settlement of industrial disputes

The process for the settlement of industrial disputes in India is set out in the Industrial Disputes Act (IDA) of 1947 as a four-stage procedure of negotiation, conciliation, arbitration and adjudication.

1 Negotiation between the management and workers in any organization that employs more than 100 workers should be through works committees that are made of an equal number of representatives of management and workers (sec. 3 of the IDA 1947), and joint management councils related to employee welfare, health and safety, discipline, productivity, changes in work practices, vocational training and holidays (IDA amendment of 1958).
2 Conciliation between management and employees is normally led by a government-appointed conciliation officer for a specific area or a defined industry to help settle the dispute. The conciliation officer is expected to meet and interview the representatives of the two parties in dispute and to complete the case within a period of two months. The officer plays a significant administrative role rather than a judicial one. If the conciliation fails to help settle the dispute, the case is referred to arbitration.
3 Arbitration, according to section 73A of the IDA 1947, is led by an arbitrator who is a court judge or a senior person who has been in a high position in public office (Budhwar, 2003), and who listens to the claims of the two parties and then makes

a decision which is final and legally binding. References to arbitration are not popular in India because of the adversarial relationship it implies between management and labour (Venkata Ratnam, 1995; Ramaswamy and Schiphorst, 2000; Budhwar, 2000, 2003).

4 Adjudication is the final stage of conflict settlement and is the most common method of settling labour disputes in India (Budhwar, 2000, 2003). Cases of adjudication are normally referred to the labour courts, or to the national or industrial tribunals, depending on the type, level and size of industrial conflict.

Summary

1 India and other countries with emerging economies share experiences of successful economic reforms that have necessitated the adoption of similar management and organizational approaches, despite their historical, cultural and geographical differences.

2 India's economy, like that of many emerging economies, is still predominantly agricultural. The industrial sector is still small and employs about 12 per cent of the working population, though it contributes about 29 per cent of the GDP. The major contributor to India's economic growth is the service sector (53.4 per cent in 2008), especially in IT and software services.

3 India is a multicultural state that consists of a mixture of religious, ethnic, caste and linguistic groups that are historically, regionally and socially differentiated.

4 The Indian labour market is characterized by increasing unemployment levels, especially among the young people, a high level of agricultural employment, a rise in IT service employment, an increase in jobs created by foreign direct investment, the domination of informal sector employment, a low rate of female participation in the labour market, the existence of child labour and illegal employment practices, and significant skills shortages.

5 The practice of management and organization in India may be described generally as authoritarian, paternalistic, centralized, international and integrated.

6 New employees in India are recruited according to commercial, family and political considerations thanks to a word-of-mouth approach. The term HRM has been replaced by HRD as the main people management function that can advance the Indian economy and society to the level reached by industrialized countries.

Revision questions

Chapter 1 provides a review task designed to consolidate your learning from this chapter. Please see Box 1.2.

In addition, the following questions are designed to help you revise this chapter:

1 Critically discuss the main management issues that characterize the Indian approach to management. Analyse each issue in comparison to similar issues in the Chinese management approach.
2 As an expatriate in India, write a letter to the head office of your company describing the socio-economic context and the conditions of the labour market in the host country. What advice would you give to potential expatriates?
3 As an HR manager of a Japanese company in India, write a report to the company's board of directors in Tokyo describing the similarities and differences in HRM functions (recruitment and selection, training and development, rewards system, and employee relations) between India and Japan.

References

Asher, M.G. and Nandy, A. (2006) 'Demographic complementarities and outsourcing: implications and challenges for India', *RIS Discussion Paper no. 111*, New Delhi: Research and Information System for Developing Countries.

Badigannavar, V. (2006) 'Industrial relations in India', in Morley, M.J., Gunnigle, P. and Collings, D.G. (eds), *Global Industrial Relations*, London: Routledge, 198–217.

Banerjee, S. (2008) 'Dimensions of Indian culture, core cultural values and marketing implications: an analysis', *Cross Cultural Management: An International Journal*, 15(4): 367–78.

Basu, P.K. (2007) 'Critical evaluation of growth strategies: India and China', *International Journal of Social Economics*, 34(9): 664–78.

Bhattacherjee, D. (2001) 'The evolution of Indian industrial relations: a comparative perspective', *Industrial Relations Journal*, 32(3): 244–63.

Bhattacherjee, D. and Ackers, P. (2008) 'Managing employment relations in India: old narratives and new challenges', *Working Paper Series*, WPS no. 618, Jan, Calcutta: Indian Institute of Management.

Björkman, I. and Budhwar, P. (2007) 'When in Rome...? Human resource management and the performance of foreign firms operating in India', *Employee Relations*, 29(6): 595–610.

Budhwar, P. (1999) 'Indian management style and HRM', in Tayeb, M. (ed.), *International Business*, London: Pitman, 534–40.

Budhwar, P. (2000) 'Human resource management in India', in Budhwar, P.S. and Debrah, Y.A. (eds), *Human Resource Management in Developing Countries*, London: Routledge, 75–90.

Budhwar, P. (2001) 'Doing business in India', *Thunderbird international business review*, 43(4): 549–68.

Budhwar, P. (2003) 'Culture and management in India', in Warner, M. (ed.), *Culture and Management in Asia*, London: Routledge Curzon, 66–81.

Budhwar, P. and Björkman, I. (2003) 'A corporate perspective on the management of human resources in foreign firms operating in India', *International HRM Conference*, 4–6 June, Limerick, Ireland.

Budhwar, P. and Khatri, N. (2001) 'Comparative human resource management in Britain and India: an empirical study', *International Journal of Human Resource Management*, 13(5): 800–26.

Budhwar, P. and Sparrow, P. (2002a) 'An integrative framework for determining cross-national human resource management practices', *Human Resource Management Review*, 12(3): 377–403.

Budhwar, P. and Sparrow, P. (2002b) 'Strategic HRM through the cultural looking glass: mapping cognitions of British and Indian HRM managers', *Organization Studies*, 23(4): 599–638.

Budhwar, P., Varma, A., Singh, V. and Dhar, R. (2006) 'HRM systems of Indian call centres: an exploratory study', *International Journal of Human Resource Management*, 17(5): 881–97.

Budhwar, P.S., Woldu, H. and Ogbonna, E. (2008) 'A comparative analysis of cultural value orientations of Indians and migrant Indians in the USA', *International Journal of Cross Cultural Management*, 8(1): 79–105.

Chatterjea, A. and Moulik, S.P. (2007) 'Academic research in India', in Basu, K. (ed.), *The Oxford Companion to Economics in India*, New Delhi: Oxford University Press, 461–7.

The Columbia Journal of World Business (1994) Special Issue, Spring.

Fairell, D., Kaka, N. and Stürze, S. (2005) 'Ensuring India's offshoring future', *McKinsey Quarterly*, Special Edition, 74–84.

Frenkel, S. and Kuruvilla, S. (2002) *Logics of action, globalization, and employment relations change in China, India, Malaysia, and the Philippines*, Retrieved on 12 April 2010 from Cornell University, School of Industrial and Labor Relations site: digitalcommons.ilr.cornell.edu/cbpubs/4/.

Government of India (2005) *Economy & employment stats, facts and figures*, Federal Ministry of Commerce, Government of India, available on line at: www.indianindustry.com/trade-information/trade-statistics.html, accessed on 23 March 2010.

Gurtoo, A. (2009) 'Adaptation of Indian public sector to market-based economic reforms: a resource-based perspective', *International Journal of Public Sector Management*, 22(6): 516–31.

Hofstede, G. (1991) *Cultures' Consequences: Software of the Mind*, London: McGraw-Hill.

Huggins, R., Demirbag, M. and Ratcheva, V.I. (2007) 'Global knowledge and R&D foreign direct investment flows: recent patterns in Asia Pacific, Europe and North America', *International Review of Applied Economics*, 21(3): 437–51.

Husain, A. C. (1992) *The National Culture of India*, New Delhi: National Book Trust.

ILO (International Labour Organization) (1998) *World Labour Report 1997/8*, Geneva: ILO.

Jaiswall, M. and Firth, M. (2007) 'Top management compensation and firm performance in the emerging markets: evidence from India', *Working Paper Series*, WPS no. 602, May, Calcutta: Indian Institute of Management.

Kakar, S., Kets de Vries, M.F.R., Kakar, S. and Vrignaud, P. (2002) 'Leadership in Indian organizations from a comparative perspective', *International Journal of Cross Cultural Management*, 2(2): 239–50.

Kanungo, R.N. and Mendonca, M. (1994) 'Culture and performance improvement', *Productivity*, 35(3): 447–53.

Kuruvilla, S. and Ranganathan, A. (2008) 'Economic development strategies and macro- and micro-level human resource policies: the case of India's "outsourcing" industry', *Industrial and Labour Relations Review*, 62(1): 39–72.

Mohanty, M. (2009) 'The dynamics of employment generation in post-reform India', *Working Paper Series*, no. 640, June, Calcutta: Indian Institute of Management.

NCEUS (National Commission for Enterprises in the Unorganised Sector) (2007) *Report on the Conditions of Work and Promotion of Livelihoods in the Unorganised Sector*, New Delhi: NCEUS, Government of India.

Office of the Registrar General (2001) *Census of India 2001*, available on line at: www.censusindia.net/, accessed on 23 March 2010.

Perry, L.J. (2006) 'Lockouts and strikes: some comments on the experience of India and Australia', *Australian Bulletin of Labour*, Wednesday, March 1st, 2006, available online at: www.allbusiness.com/human-resources/1184525-1.html, accessed 17 September 2010.

Raman, S.R., Budhwar, P. and Balasubramanian, G. (2007) 'People management issues in Indian KPOs', *Employee Relations*, 29(6): 696–710.

Ramaswamy, E.A. (2000) *Managing Human Resources*, Delhi: Oxford University Press.

Ramaswamy, E.A. and Schiphorst, F.B. (2000) 'Human resource management, trade unions and empowerment: Two cases from India', *International Journal of Human Resource Management*, 11(4): 664–80.

Rao, T.V. (1999) *HRD Audit: Evaluating the Human Resource Function for Business Improvement*, New Delhi: Response Books/Sage.

Saini, D.S. and Budhwar, P.S. (2004) 'HRM in India', in Budhwar, P.S. (ed.), *Managing Human Resources in Asia-Pacific*, London: Routledge.

Singh, J.P. (1990) 'Managerial culture and work-related values in India', *Organization Studies*, 11(1): 75–101.

Sinha, J.A. and Sinha, D. (1990) 'Role of social values in Indian organizations', *International Journal of Psychology*, 25: 705–25.

Sinha, J.B.P. (1979) *The Nurturant Task Leader*, New Delhi: Concept.

Sinha, J.B.P. (1995) *The Cultural Context of Leadership and Power*, New Delhi: Sage.

Sinha, J.B.P. and Kanungo, R. (1997) 'Context sensitivity and balancing in Indian organization behaviour', *International Journal of Psychology*, 32: 93–105.

Sodhi, J.S. (1999) *Industrial Relations and Human Resource Management*, New Delhi: Shri Ram Centre for Industrial Relations and Human Resources.

Sparrow, P.R. and Budhwar, P. (1997) 'Competition and change: mapping the Indian HRM recipe against world wide patterns', *Journal of World Business*, 32(3): 224–42.

Suar, D., Tewari, H.R. and Chaturbedi, K.R. (2006) 'Subordinates' perception of leadership styles and their work behaviour', *Psychology and Developing Societies*, 18(1): 95–114.

Thomas, A.S. and Philip, A. (1994) 'India: management in an ancient and modern civilisation', *International Studies of Management and Organisation*, 24(1/2): 91–115.

Venkata Ratnam, C.S. (1995) 'Economic liberalisation and the transformation of industrial relations policies in india', in Verma, A., Kochan, T.A. and Lansbury, R.D. (eds), *Employment Relations in the Growing Asian Economies*, London: Routledge.

Venkata Ratnam, C.S. (1996) *Industrial Relations in Indian States*, New Delhi: Global Business Press.

Venkata Ratnam, C.S. and Ghandra, V. (1996) 'Sources of diversity and the challenge before human resource management in india', *International Journal of Manpower*, 17(4/5): 76–108.

Venkata Ratnam, C.S. and Verma, A. (eds) (1998) *Challenge for Change: Industrial Relations in Indian Industry*, New Delhi: Allied Publishers.

Vladimir, G., Aggarwal, A., Grover, A., Kumar, A. and Juneia, Q.L. (2003) *Industrial Training Institutes of India: the efficiency study report*, Geneva: ILO.

17

Central and Eastern Europe

=========== **LEARNING OUTCOMES** ===========

The chapter is designed to help you understand, for Central and Eastern Europe:

1   The (a) economic, (b) political and (c) cultural contexts in which managers work;

2   The main trends in the labour market;

3   The typical features of (a) management policies and practices and (b) organizational structure and behaviour;

4   The main policies and practices of human resource management with regard to: (a) recruitment and selection; (b) training and development; (c) rewards and remuneration; and (d) employee relations.

Introduction

While all Central and Eastern European (CEE) countries share a historical legacy of communist rule and centrally planned economic policies, each has its own social and cultural characteristics that has made it able to reclaim its unique national identity in the post-communist era. Though they have exhibited similar economic infrastructures and development policies, occupational and employment regulations, and management experiences, they differ in their wealth creation capabilities, availability of resources, and the size of their current economies.

These former 'communist bloc' countries can be divided into three groups (*Business Monitor International*, 2009) as follows:

1 Central Europe and the Baltic states (Czech Republic, Estonia, Hungary, Latvia, Lithuania, Poland and Slovakia);
2 Russia and the Commonwealth of Independent States (CIS) (Armenia, Azerbaijan, Belarus, Georgia, Kazakhstan, Kyrgystan, Moldova, Russia, Tajikistan, Turkmenistan, Ukraine, Uzbekistan);
3 South-east Europe (Albania, Bosnia-Herzegovina, Bulgaria, Croatia, Macedonia, Montenegro, Romania, Serbia and Slovenia).

These countries are all at different levels in the process of completing a radical transformation since the collapse of communism in the late 1980s and early 1990s, from a planned to a free market economy. This transition has necessitated the adoption of particular management policies and practices that are capitalist in orientation but still influenced by communist legacies, as well as national cultural values and local economic conditions.

It is not practically possible to cover all CEE countries within a single chapter, and so the focus here is on selected countries. (See Table 17.1 for basic statistics.)

Contexts: economics, politics and culture

Economics

Most of the CEE countries are in long-term transition from command to free market economies. The majority of them have significant material resources for export, a respectable level of industrialization and technological development, and a significant agricultural sector. So far, in dealing with the challenges of the transition, some of them have made significant socio-economic changes by reforming their political systems, liberalizing their economies and gaining full access to the European Union (EU). Others are still a long way from establishing credible free market economic institutions. Important economic reforms have included the privatization of state-owned enterprises, the encouragement of foreign direct investment, the restructuring of the banking and fiscal system, and the reduction of state control of the economy. The privatization process has resulted in a significant decline in employment: most privatized enterprises rationalized their operations by introducing mass redundancies.

Foreign direct investment (FDI) has been seen as crucial for economic liberalization, the transfer of needed technology and management know-how, the enhancement of economic growth, and the creation of new jobs. Thus maintaining a flow of FDI has been a key element of the transition from centrally planned to free market economies. For instance, foreign investment in the

Table 17.1 Basic statistical indicators of selected CEE countries

Country	Area (sq.km)	Population (2009 est.)	Population growth (2009 est.)%	GDP – real growth rate in 2009 (2008) %	Inflation rate (2009) %	Workforce (2009 est) Millions	Unemployment rate (2009) %
Bulgaria	110,879	7,204,687	–0.79	–4.9 (6.1)	1.6	3.2	9.1
Croatia	56,594	4,489,409	–0.052	–5.2 (2.4)	2.4	1.196	16.1
Czech Republic	78,867	10,211 904	–0.094	–4.1 (2.5)	1.1	5.38	9.3
Estonia	45,228	1,299,371	–0.632	–14.1 (–3.6)	–0.4	0.7	14.3
Hungary	93,028	9,905,596	–0.257	–6.7 (0.6)	2.1	3.8	10.8
Latvia	64,589	2,231,503	–0.614	–17.8 (–4.6)	3.3	1.205	16.6
Lithuania	65,300	3,555,179	–0.279	–15 (2.8)	4.2	1.656	13.7
Poland	312,685	38,482,919	–0.047	1.7 (5.1)	3.4	16.99	8.9
Romania	238,391	22,215,421	–0.147	–7.1 (7.3)	5	9.33	7.6
Russia	17,098,242	140,041,247	–0.467	–7.9 (5.6)	11.9	75.81	8.9
Slovakia	49,035	5,463,046	0.137	–4.7 (6.2)	1.6	2.365	12.1
Slovenia	20,273	2,005,692	–0.113	–7.8 (3.5)	0.8	0.914	9.4
Ukraine	603,550	45,700,395	–0.632	–14.1 (2.1)	12.3	20.4	4.8

Source: Compiled from Eurostat (2010) and CIA *World Factbook* (2010).

Table 17.2 Real GDP growth rate between 2000 and 2009 (%), selected CEE countries

Country	2000	2001	2002	2003	2004	2005	2006	2007	2008	2009
Bulgaria	5.4	4.1	4.5	5.0	6.6	6.2	6.3	6.2	6.1	−4.9
Czech Republic	3.6	2.5	1.9	3.6	4.5	6.3	6.8	6.1	2.5	−4.1
Estonia	10.0	7.5	7.9	7.6	7.2	9.4	10.0	7.2	−3.6	−14.1
Hungary	4.9	4.1	4.4	4.3	4.9	3.5	4.0	1.0	0.6	−6.7
Lithuania	3.3	6.7	6.9	10.2	7.4	7.8	7.8	9.8	2.8	−14.8
Poland	4.3	1.2	1.4	3.9	5.3	3.6	6.2	6.8	5.1	1.7
Romania	2.4	5.7	5.1	5.2	8.5	4.2	7.9	6.3	7.3	−7.1
Slovakia	1.4	3.5	4.6	4.8	5.0	6.7	8.5	10.6	6.2	−4.7
Slovenia	4.4	2.8	4.0	2.8	4.3	4.5	5.8	6.8	3.5	−7.8

Source: Eurostat 2010, http://epp.eurostat.ec.europa.eu/tgm/, accessed 3 May 2010.

automobile and electronics industry has flourished over the years and has benefited immensely from the availability of a skilled workforce and the favourable investment and taxation policies of many of the CEE governments.

Moreover, most of the CEE countries introduced radical fiscal and financial reforms to stimulate economic growth and, for some, to meet the conditions for their accession to the European Union. They have had to reduce their budget deficits and to control the level of inflation. As a result, their economies grew by an average of 5 per cent between 2000 and 2007 (see Table 17.2). However, the 'credit crunch' recession has made it difficult to maintain growth. With the exception of Poland, which has sustained positive (1.7 per cent) economic growth in 2009, all CEE economies (see Table 17.1) contracted significantly as a result of the recent international financial crisis.

Dependence on foreign income through the export of raw materials, and finished commodities, and in the form of tourism, has made these countries vulnerable to changes in world economic conditions. Although most of the CEE countries made considerable progress in reforming their economies, many are still far from establishing sustainable free market economies and face significant long-term challenges, including unemployment, inflation, institutional corruption, poor infrastructure, and the exodus of their skilled workforce.

Politics

Most CEE countries have gone through spells of political instability and change at the national, regional and local levels. While most of them have been relatively politically stable, some are still in the process of building the institutions necessary for democratic governments. All of the CEE countries are republics with parliaments and governments elected by popular vote. The head of state is normally a democratically elected president who has substantial political powers, while the head of government is a prime minister who is normally the leader of the largest party.

The Russian Federation is made of 46 oblasts, 21 republics, 4 autonomous okrugs, 9 krays, 2 federal cities, and 1 autonomous oblast. The federal assembly consists of an upper house, the Federation Council, which is made of members appointed by the top executive and legislative officials in each of the 84 federal administrative units, and a lower house, the State Duma, which is made of members elected by popular vote on a proportional representation system.

All the CEE countries that became members of the EU (Bulgaria, Czech Republic, Estonia, Hungary, Latvia, Lithuania, Poland, Romania, Slovakia and Slovenia) have had to harmonize their laws and regulations with those of the other countries in the EU, and to adjust their employment policies in line with those of Western Europe.

Culture

Each country has reclaimed its traditional values, historical heritage and language after years of Soviet cultural influence. Until the late 1990s, many people in Western Europe and North America had very little knowledge of the CEE countries. Perhaps the main images that came to mind of 'the Soviet bloc' were those of Soviet military parades in the Red Square. Such images frequently tarnished the cultural reality in individual countries, with their diverse traditions, norms and values. In reality, different people with various linguistic and ethnic backgrounds 'encompass the vast geographical mass that makes up the lands east of the former Iron Curtain' (Channon and Dakin, 1995: 25).

The CEE countries are religiously and ethnically mixed. However, the influence of the Soviet era cannot be underestimated. For example, Russians make up about 18 per cent of the Ukraine's population and 25 per cent of Estonia's population, Hungarians make about 10 per cent of Slovakia's population, and Poles make about 8.5 per cent of the Lithuanian population (Eurostat, 2009). After years of religious oppression under communism, most of the CEE countries have returned to their pre-communist beliefs, namely Roman Catholicism, Christian Orthodoxy (various denominations) and Islam (in the Russian Federation and former Soviet states), though many people are still either non-believers or non-practising believers.

Generally speaking, the cultures of most of the CEE countries have been scored in relation to Hofstede's cultural dimensions as: moderate to high for power distance; moderate to high for uncertainty avoidance; moderate to low for masculinity; moderate to low for individualism; and low in long-term orientation (Hofstede, 1993; Todeva, 1999; Kolman et al., 2003; Huettinger, 2008). None the less, there are marked cultural differences both (a) between the CEE countries and (b) between them and Western European countries (see Jankowicz, 1994; Kolman et al., 2003). It is predicted that in the coming years these countries will see significant shifts in value orientations following political and economic changes (Kolman et al., 2003; Mailand and Due, 2004), especially following their accession to the European Union.

Labour market trends

With the introduction of free market economic reforms and the liberalization of the economy, employment declined substantially in manufacturing because of the closure of large state-owned manufacturing companies, while it increased slightly in the services sector (Stockhammer and Onaran, 2009). As shown in Table 17.3, all CEE countries have a modest agricultural sector, which creates a significant number of jobs for people in rural areas. The fertile soil of countries such as Romania and Ukraine, which supplied more than a quarter of the Soviet market for agricultural products, meat and poultry, means that they remain significant producers of food products for home consumption and export. The services sector has also improved, resulting in the creation of employment in banking, transport and hospitality.

Table 17.3 Workforce distribution by occupation in 2009 (%), selected CEE countries

Country	Agriculture	Industry	Services
Bulgaria	7.5	36.4	56.1
Czech Republic	3.6	40.2	56.2
Estonia	2.8	22.7	74.5
Hungary	4.5	32.1	63.4
Lithuania	12.2	30.2	57.6
Poland	17.4	29.2	53.4
Romania	26.7	26.2	47.1
Russia	10	31.9	58.1
Ukraine	15.8	18.5	65.7

Source: Compiled from Eurostat (2010) and CIA *World Factbook* (2010).

Current 'transitional' labour market trends include a shift from employment in state-owned large companies to privately owned medium and small size enterprises, and from a job-creating heavy industries and manufacturing sector to a downsized light industries and service sector. These shifts and other socio-economic and political changes have resulted in CEE labour markets characterized by company closures, downsizing and mass redundancies, a surplus of well-educated and highly skilled workers, declining levels of female employment, and limited use of flexible working practices.

From state-owned large companies to privately owned small and medium size enterprises

In most CEE countries, private ownership was not spoken about: under communism, it was seen as a taboo subject and an unethical business practice. The whole economy was dominated by state-owned large companies, which were the main job creator and the major employer in all sectors. However, most of these companies were heavily subsidized by the state, loss-making, and unsuitable for a competitive capitalist business environment. With the introduction of economic reforms, most of the state-owned companies found themselves unable to compete in either international or national markets because of their low-quality products and high costs (Nelson and Taylor, 1995). Therefore, one of the main objectives of the transition from planned to free market economies was the privatization of state-owned companies. Hence in a very short time after the collapse of communism, private businesses flourished and attitudes to private ownership changed. Private ownership has become 'a sign of a largely irreversible commitment to market-economic transformation' (Wagner, 1996: 75).

However, the sale of public assets through privatization was poorly conducted because of lack of financial expertise and of appropriate regulations for the transfer of ownership from public to private. Most of the CEE countries had underdeveloped capital markets and unrealistic privatization programmes. The paperwork involved in setting up small businesses and having to meet the requirements of a number of regulatory and funding authorities has often hindered entrepreneurs from buying state-owned companies or setting up their own businesses.

The crucial factors for small business survival and growth are: clarity of business objectives; identification of training needs; effective use of resources; and effective and transparent links between productivity, rewards and product or service quality. These factors are often non-existent in many organizations in the transitional economies. Small businesses have the potential to contribute to the transition process in a number of ways, but most of the newly created businesses in CEE countries are not yet familiar with a market driven by customers' tastes and choices. They have had to operate in unstable and uncertain business environments in which many risks are often involved, including the ones associated with high interest rates, inflation and unstable foreign exchange. Increased taxation and the withdrawal of state subsidies have put even further pressure on the development of small businesses. The risks created by the liberalization of the economy can be too high to contemplate, especially when the human resources available are neither trained nor confident at doing business successfully.

Company closures, downsizing and mass redundancies

The Soviet economy was based on the policy of 'industrializing industries' that promoted the establishment of heavy industrial companies that would subsequently lead to the growth of light industries. The Soviets invested heavily in heavy industry such as machine building and metallurgy, and neglected light industry and the service sector (Kumssa and Jones, 1999). The process of 'industrializing industries' required a constant supply of skilled labour, especially engineers, who were mass-produced in institutes of science and technology. Also, many manual jobs were created in large manufacturing plants where the emphasis was on quantity rather the quality of products. Large complexes of heavy industrial plants were able to absorb the surplus of labour and to eliminate unemployment. In a planned labour market, there was no accounting for unemployment, and every person who could work, male or female, was employed.

It was very soon realized in the post-communist era that the heavy industrial sector had been suffering from overcapacity and widespread overstaffing and was in need of urgent downsizing (Kenny and Trick, 1994). Privatization of state-owned companies and the closure of many loss-making manufacturing companies resulted in mass redundancies and a surplus of well-educated and highly skilled workers in search of employment at home and abroad.

A well-qualified and skilled workforce

One of the positive outcomes of communism has been the availability of a well-educated and highly skilled workforce throughout the CEE countries. The policy of industrializing industries required the education and training of as many people as possible in science and technology. The closure of large manufacturing plants and the continuing work of institutions of higher, further and vocational education, producing many new graduates, resulted in the availability of a surplus of well-educated and highly skilled labour. Many foreign investors benefited from the availability of skilled labour when they moved their businesses to the CEE countries, and many companies in Western European countries were able to meet their skills shortages by recruiting emigrants from the CEE countries. It can be seen from Table 17.4 that the majority of the population in the CEE countries is at the working age of 15–64 years. This is conducive to economic growth and prosperity.

Table 17.4 Age structure (%) (2009), selected CEE countries

Country	0–14 years %	15–64 years %	Over 65 %	Median age (years)	Life expectancy at birth (men and women)
Bulgaria	13.8	68.5	17.7	41.4	74
Czech Republic	13.6	71	15.5	40	77
Estonia	14.9	67.5	17.6	40	73
Hungary	15	69.3	15.8	40	74
Lithuania	14.2	69.6	16.2	39	75
Poland	15	71.6	13.4	38	76
Romania	15.5	69.7	14.7	38	73
Russia	14.8	71.5	13.7	38	66
Ukraine	13.8	70.3	15.9	40	68

Source: CIA World Factbook, 2010.

Female employment

In the communist era, women were expected to assume a number of roles in society as mothers, workers and 'household managers' as part of an attempt to impose a social structure of gender equality. In a planned labour market, the governments issued policies such as 'generous maternity leave and day care benefits [that] encouraged women to work, and female labour market participation rates were high compared with those of other countries' (Brainerd, 2000: 138). By the 1980s, the participation of women in the labour market was well over 60 per cent (Blau and Ferber, 1992). However, according to Lange (2008: 329), the communist rhetoric of bolstering equality in the labour market 'did not translate into giving women access to the same career opportunities as men'. This supports the point made by Pollert (2005: 220), that 'women's strong representation among professionals and associated occupations . . . reflects their educational gains during communism, but they failed to advance further up the occupational hierarchy'.

The post-communist era saw a reverse in women's participation in the labour market as many CEE governments introduced employment policies and adopted family values that emphasized the role of women in society as mothers first and workers second. Such conservative policies (Pascall and Manning, 2000; Pollert, 2003; Lange, 2008) led to a steady decline in the participation of women in the labour markets of most of the CEE countries over the 1990s. Although the proportion of female/male employment has been relatively stable over the 10 years from 1999 to 2009 (see Table 17.5), it is still very low in comparison with that of Western European countries. Women in the CEE countries are highly educated and skilled, but they have benefited 'less from their qualifications than their male counterparts' (Lange, 2008: 331).

Table 17.5 Employment by gender between 1999 and 2009 (%), selected CEE countries

Country	1999 M/F	2001 M/F	2003 M/F	2005 M/F	2007 M/F	2009 M/F
Bulgaria	–	53/47	56/49	60/52	66/58	67/58
Czech Republic	74/57	73/57	73/56	73/56	75/57	74/57
Estonia	66/58	65/57	67/59	67/62	73/66	64/63
Hungary	63/49	63/50	64/51	63/51	64/51	61/50
Lithuania	64/59	59/56	64/58	66/60	68/62	60/61
Poland	64/51	59/46	57/46	59/47	64/51	66/53
Romania	69/58	68/57	64/52	64/52	65/53	65/52
Slovakia	64/52	62/52	63/52	65/51	68/52	68/53
Slovenia	67/58	69/59	67/58	70/61	73/63	71/64

Source: Eurostat (2010), http://epp.eurostat.ec.europa.eu/tgm/, accessed 03/05/2010.

Flexible working

Full-time work, 8 hours a day, 5 to 6 days a week, was the norm in the communist era when the supply and demand for labour were centrally planned and every citizen who was able to work was offered secure lifetime employment. Flexible working practices such as part-time work, job sharing and home-based working were generally unheard off. There was very little flexibility in the workplace or in the labour market as a whole.

It seems that not much has changed in the post-communist era, despite the economic reforms: full-time employment is still the favoured employment policy and practice. It can be seen from Table 17.6 that part-time employment in the CEE countries is very low in comparison to Western European countries, and it even declined between 2000 and 2008 in most CEE countries.

Table 17.6 Part-time employment in selected CEE countries in comparison with some Western European countries (% of total employment)

Country	2000	2002	2004	2006	2008
Bulgaria	–	2.5	2.4	2.0	2.3
Czech Republic	5.3	4.9	4.9	5.0	4.9
Estonia	8.1	7.7	8.0	7.8	7.2
Hungary	3.5	3.6	4.7	4.0	4.6
Lithuania	10.2	10.8	8.4	9.9	6.7
Poland	10.5	10.8	10.8	9.8	8.5
Romania	16.5	11.8	10.6	9.7	9.9
Slovakia	2.1	1.9	2.7	2.8	2.7
Slovenia	6.5	6.1	9.3	9.2	9.0
Denmark	21.3	20.0	22.2	23.6	24.6
The Netherlands	41.5	43.9	45.5	46.2	47.3
Sweden	19.5	21.5	23.6	25.1	26.6
United Kingdom	25.1	25.3	25.7	25.3	25.3

Source: Eurostat (2010), http://epp.eurostat.ec.europa.eu/tgm/, accessed 02/02/2010.

As a labour market consultant, write a report of no more than 1,500 words for a multi-national company wanting to invest in the CEE countries, describing the strengths and weaknesses of the CEE labour markets, and highlighting any potential employment problems and opportunities in investing in such countries.

Management and organization

The CEE countries inherited a legacy of highly centralized, very bureaucratic and authoritarian management policies and practices created according to ideologically planned economic arrangements. This type of Soviet management system is described by Ardichvili and Gasparishvili (2001: 229) as managerial behaviour that 'was marked by meticulous rule-following, a lack of initiative, and contentment with inferior product quality'. Managers of this sort are described by Puffer (1996: 18–19) as 'micro managers and macro puppets'. The transition from a command economy to a market-based one needs clear understanding of the mechanisms by which market economies work, which is usually in uncertain and competitive environments. The question here is: do CEE countries have managers who understand such mechanisms?

The transition to a market economy is not without its problems. Restructuring, adjustment, repositioning, redeployment, and competition are only examples of the realities of a free market economy. The transition, however, means the introduction of piecemeal as well as radical structural changes including deregulation, privatization of public sector organizations, and reform of the banking and taxation systems. Downsizing, subcontracting, outsourcing, relocating and redeploying are examples of what many companies are accustomed to in a capitalist economic system. In the CEE countries, the downsizing of the labour force has been one of the strategic choices for small business creation and organizational change, but there has been very limited management expertise available for implementing such strategies (Redman and Keithley, 1998).

It can be concluded that the current transitional approach to management involves a mixture of inherited communist practices and adopted post-communist capitalist policies. Meyer-Sahling (2009: 513) argues that communist legacies 'can be expected to be only one among many determinants of administrative reforms in East Central Europe', because one should not underestimate the effects of the accession to the EU, the influence of foreign direct investment, and the influence of financial and economic crises of recent times on shaping the current management systems in the CEE countries, which are described as authoritarian, experimental and taking initiatives.

Authoritarian management

Mrozowicki and Van Hootegem (2008: 199) describe management in the CEE countries, especially in the SMEs and larger foreign-owned companies, as 'hier-archical, authoritarian and anti-union'. They also state that the preferred approach is to have 'individualized paternalist relations with the best skilled, full-time, core employees, while simultaneously using low wages, overtime and violations of work contracts to minimize employment costs in the segment of lower-skilled, often female, young and contractual workers' (p. 199). This sup-ports an earlier study by Ardichvili et al. (1998), which found that Russian managers tended to employ autocratic leadership styles, liked to make crucial management decisions individually, and did not consult with their subordinates or peers. Another study by Ardichvili and Gasparishvili (2001) found that Russian managers were 'much more competitive and individualistic' and they were 'less likely to provide their employees with support and opportunities for growth'. This finding endorses an earlier study by Puffer (1996), who found that Russian managers had 'strong achievement motivation ("the sky is the limit"), but being cynical, not trusting anyone, and tending to rely on themselves alone (or on a very limited in-group) in all business dealings' (cited in Ardichvili and Gasparishvili, 2001: 238). Ardichvili and Gasparishvili (2001: 238) concluded that the collapse of communism 'created conditions for the emergence of more independent, ruthless and isolated business leaders in Russia'.

Similarly, in a study of management and governance in Bulgaria and the Slovak Republic, Takei and Ito (2007) found that Slovak managers tend to be moody, unfair and arrogant, make unclear decisions, and have negative atti-tudes towards their employees. The study also listed a number of problems of managing in both countries, such as: poor communication about corporate policies and strategic directions, one-way (top-down) communication flow, poor feedback from superiors, unclear and unfair performance appraisal and feedback, poor coaching and supporting for problem-solving, unclear career paths, poor information disclosure and sharing, unfair rewards and treatment, poor initiative and passive attitudes of employees, weak employee participa-tion, no incentives for improvement and suggestions of improvements, reac-tive and passive attitudes, and unclear rules and structure.

Experimental management

The ongoing socio-economic and political reforms in the CEE countries have given managers of enterprises new roles that they were not familiar with. In the communist era, managers of state-owned enterprises were not expected to have any particular managerial skills to do their jobs. The criteria for becoming managers were academic qualifications and loyalty to the party. By Western standards, performance expectations were often very low. The newly created economic conditions required new kinds of managerial skill for coping with the demands of change. New skills to manage projects, build teams and maintain organizational commitment in employees became necessary.

Many of the new activities, such as downsizing, human resource accounting and performance management, were unheard of or seen as unethical capitalist practices. In command economies there was a very limited concern about individual performance, but managers have since had to devise ways of assessing individual employee performance, to reward, control and (at times) dismiss staff. Managers have been required to think more about survival, and more strategically. It seems that 'the culture, training and experience have not prepared managers for the task of becoming efficient' (Nelson and Taylor, 1995: 13). Opportunities for restructuring, streamlining and downsizing are great, but they require managers with the determination, knowledge and skills needed for their successful introduction. The new managerial roles are challenging to many managers, who have had to experiment with different types of management and leadership styles.

Moreover, a number of studies (see Clement et al., 1994; Redman and Keithley, 1998; Peiperl and Estrin, 1998) have found that managers in CEE countries are generally well educated and quite business-minded, but in need of commercial expertise of the kinds used in free market economies. They also need leadership skills and experience of human resource management practices that are normally associated with free labour markets. There are relatively few shortages in engineering expertise and operational skills, but acute need for financial and change management skills.

It has been argued that one of the problems of management in transitional countries is the inability to see, set and manage priorities. Faced with a number of new problems, most of them have come to terms with situations that they have never experienced before. Hence, they are eager to experiment with new approaches and management techniques whenever possible. For example, one of the new challenges for managers is maintaining a high level of employee motivation in a free market economy where work performance is individually appraised and employees are individually rewarded. Because of their lack of experience in motivating employees, many managers have experimented with a variety of rewards, and even threats, to achieve their objectives.

Initiative management

The transition to a free market economy has required the relocation of decision-making powers from the state to individual managers of mainly privately owned enterprises. In the past, the implementation of national plans needed operational and financial support from a number of intermediaries, ranging from ministries and state councils to national banks, but the shift to a free market economy has created a vacuum between the state apparatus and managers who are expected to implement the reform policies, because there were no established mechanisms for the decentralization process and for the delegation of authority. Since the direct control of the state is taken away, managers of enterprises are left alone to come up with solutions to economic, commercial and managerial problems not experienced before. They have had to use their initiative to manage their enterprises in different business circumstances. However, in some cases the inherited organizational structures and the heavy intervention by some governments have restricted managers from using their managerial initiatives (Channon and Dakin, 1995). The problem is that some of the current organizations and business institutions in the CEE countries do not allow for proactive and market-oriented managers to take the initiative. They are still 'managers who continue to rely more on networks of connections than on superior business performance; and managers who encourage initiative and creativity in their workers co-existing with those who continue to follow the "don't rock the boat" philosophy of organizational behaviour and management' (Ardichvili and Gasparishvili, 2001: 230).

MINI CASE STUDY 41

It Works in the West (Poland)

Olga Pawlowska was appointed managing director of Polska Electronica in 2005 and she was determined to turn the company around from being loss-making and heavily subsidized to being a profit-making and independent organization. When she was asked, how will you do it, she replied: 'it works in the West'. She also said: 'I would like all my managers to be proactive, not reactive, and to be experimental in their roles.'

Questions

1 What do you think Olga Pawlowska meant by replying: 'it works in the West'?
2 Explain what you think she meant by 'proactive not reactive and experimental in their roles'.

Managing human resources

A number of studies (see Jankowicz, 1998; Morley et al., 2008) confirm that managing human resources in Central and Eastern Europe is not clearly defined, not well documented, and is still emerging as the transition unfolds. In the communist era, general managers were personnel managers and mere administrators whose main task was to implement the government-imposed manpower plans. The crucial role of management was to make sure that the technical and operational aspects of the production system were met. There was little need for human resource management because the government controlled all aspects of employment and employee relations.

The transition to the adoption of a free market economy has required managers to manage their human resources effectively and rationally. The function of managing human resources became one of the main challenges for all managers because it presented them with a new set of tasks that had been previously unknown to them. For example, many erstwhile managers of large public sector enterprises have had to come to terms, perhaps for the first time, with concepts such as downsizing, rationalization and cost reductions. Staff audit, performance appraisal, interviewing, collective bargaining, retraining, redeployment, recruitment and selection, job evaluation, rewards management, and employee motivation were all different, if not new, HR functions that required HR professionals to implement them effectively in a competitive and free market economy.

Recruitment and selection

Under the command economy, the supply of and the demand for labour were forecasted and planned by the state according to a national five-year plan. Every person who was able to work was assigned to a particular job depending on his/her qualifications and skills. All jobs were allocated according to a national employment plan executed by local recruitment bureaus in different locations throughout the country, and every employee was guaranteed a job for life. However, the move from a command to a free market economy in the CEE countries has shifted the responsibility for recruitment and selection from the state-allocated recruitment bureaus to the managers of individual organizations. Managers were used to employees coming to them as ordered, and now they have to look for and select only the employees they need. Now managers have to advertise their job vacancies, receive applications, short-list candidates, and select their potential employees.

Current recruitment and selection procedures in any of the CEE countries tend not to be any different from what is practised in Western European countries. Jobs are advertised through the use of different methods ranging from newspaper advertising to the use of the internet. Application forms are very often used and the selection process involves the use of interviews and tests. However, although the procedure is the same, the approach differs from one country to another. Current approaches to recruitment and selection in the CEE countries are influenced by labour market trends, as outlined below.

Too many applicants to choose from

As explained earlier, the CEE countries have a surplus of well-educated and skilled workforce and the majority of the population is at the working age of 15–64 years. Employers receive a high number of applications for every job vacancy they advertise. The process of recruitment and selection is difficult and time consuming not just because of the high volume of applications but also because many managers are not well trained in how to sift through applications, short-list applicants, and interview and test candidates.

Applicants in high demand

Since many companies, especially the growing number of SMEs, cannot afford either to invest heavily in the training of their current employees or to spend on advertising their job vacancies widely and conducting lengthy recruitment and selection processes, they tend to use the direct approach of poaching and head-hunting the employees they need from other companies. There is a high demand for professionals and managers with special knowledge and skills in certain professions such as accountancy, finance, people management, marketing, employment law, and quality control. Poaching and headhunting have become the most convenient approach to staffing new and fast-growing organizations.

Applicants by recommendation

Although the workforce is educated and skilled, companies are frequently looking for, as a regional manager of a multinational company put it, 'a 25-year-old who speaks English, is self-motivated, attracted to the West, with a well-connected father' (cited in Channon and Dakin, 1995: 27). What is interesting in this description is the phrase 'with a well-connected father'. Perhaps this is from the legacy of the Soviet era or part of the 'Eastern' culture. The use of recommendations from family members, friends and relatives is very common when applying for jobs. To get the job one wants, one needs to be fixed up by someone who knows those in the right places. The process of recruitment and selection becomes very often redundant when applicants are 'parachuted' in through recommendations from those in the senior management of the organization.

ACTIVITY 2

Discuss the following statement:

As an HR manager for Central and Eastern Europe and the CIS, I found that one of the greatest challenges – and a key to success – was the selection of suitably qualified and reliable people. The local people are well qualified technically and well educated. But they lack good business skills by Western standards, particularly in the key areas of marketing, sales, finance and office administration. Also, local managers lack the 'softer' skills required to manage a customer-focused business. Whatever approach is taken to recruit local staff, my advice is to define the key skill requirements of the job, because job titles are meaningless. (Louise Smith, consultant and former HR manager, in *People Management*, 15 June 1995, p. 27)

Training and development

As already stated above, one of the positive outcomes of communism in the CEE countries is a well-educated and skilled workforce. The CEE countries inherited good education systems and a strong culture of learning. However, the content of education of the Soviet era was different from what is needed today in a free market economy. People were educated and trained to serve a different economic system and to meet the objectives of a different ideology than that of the current political and business environment. In order to integrate the local employees into a free market economy and culture, substantial training and development is required. In the mid-1990s, concepts such as profitability, quality, competition and motivation were still alien to many managers, and they have since had to become familiar with them and use them on a daily basis.

Most studies of management in transitional economies agree that the main problem for a successful transition is the lack of trained professionals, bankers, entrepreneurs and other types of managers (Nelson and Taylor, 1995; Marcic, 1995; Wagner, 1996). There is a need for more management training and development in order to enhance the abilities and knowledge of expert staff and managers to help them to meet the present and future demands of their countries' economies. There should be greater investment in education, training and development at the national and organizational levels. It is not enough to rely on governments as the main providers of education and vocational training: local and foreign employers also need to invest in the training and development of their employees.

Organizational training

Currently, most of the large state-owned companies, multinational companies and joint ventures provide some basic training, mainly in the form of induction, to their newly recruited employees. Some of them take a reactive approach by providing training only in response to their employees' requests. Training needs analysis is not very often conducted and most employers spend only a small fraction of their budgets on training and development.

Many employees are eager to learn new knowledge and skills, and they take such training seriously whenever they are given the opportunity. For example, a study by Cyr (1996) of the success factors for the creation of effective organizational learning in international joint ventures in the Czech Republic, Hungary and Poland, found that local employees had a strong desire for learning new knowledge and skills to enable them to reach Western standards of performance. They were highly motivated to learn in order to demonstrate their real abilities to their managers and to earn enough compensation.

MINI CASE STUDY 42

Training for Changing Times (the CEE Countries)

The multinational computer company ICL was one of the first companies to invest in the CEE countries in the 1960s. As one of the early settlers, ICL experienced the change from a command to a free market economy and has had to adapt and adjust to the socio-economic and political challenges those countries have had to face. During the communist era, the company produced and sold computer hardware and software in Poland, Czechoslovakia and Russia, and had only to get on well with the government agencies they sold to and to make sure that they supply the quantity of products required each year. Most of ICL's employees were local and they were well trained to do the tasks at hand. Today the company is competing in an open market where the government has very little influence on the quality and quantity of computers produced and the services provided. The management of ICL is no longer looking for hardware salespersons but for people who understand the business they sell to. They have had to re-educate and train their employees to do things differently and to try to retain them, otherwise they move on to work for their competitors. Mike Campbell, international director of personnel for ICL, was reported as saying: 'Initially, money was the big retention factor, but now other factors are coming into play, such as training and development and long-term job opportunities. Potential employees want to know how secure your company is and what future opportunities they might have, including career moves to other countries' (*People Management*, 15 June 1995, p. 26).

Questions

1 What type of training had the company provided to its employees under the command economy of CEE countries?
2 Why has the company had to change its training policies?
3 What type of training should the company now provide to its employees and how it should be implemented?

Rewards and remuneration

Under communism, all employees in the CEE countries were rewarded according to qualification, position and seniority or time spent at the organization. Pay scales were determined by the state according to a national system of job classification that gathers jobs into functional categories. Employees were paid for the jobs they hold not for the work they do. The wages were not very different between posts and levels. Also, to keep inflation rates at their lowest, and in the absence of any kind of price competition, the wages were kept very low and prices of household and consumer goods were highly subsidized by the government. There were no incentives to encourage employees in similar employment to do better than each other because the difference in performance was not normally recognized and formally rewarded. Collective rewards in the form of pay, benefits and bonuses were allocated to all employees regardless of the level of their performance.

CEE countries have adopted wage determination policies based on collective agreements at the organizational level, but in most organizations the status quo still prevails. Most of the local companies, public sector organizations and privately owned SMEs still pay their workers according to qualifications and seniority. Despite the liberalization of the economy and the rewards system, studies have confirmed that there is very limited use of performance-related pay, most rewards are based on managerial judgements, the minimum wage has become irrelevant, and there are rising wage inequalities.

Limited use of performance-related pay

A study by Trif (2007) found that in Romania the wage structure had changed to some extent to being linked to collective or individual performance only, when possible, but qualifications and seniority were still the most important criteria in determining employees' wages (as under communism). However, it was also found that since the pay is still based on qualifications and seniority some companies are replacing bonuses with performance-related pay. Many employers do not pay high wages but provide good social benefits to their employees. Benefits and allowances such as food vouchers, medical care and accommodation are provided by many employers, especially large companies and public sector organizations. Studies by Aro and Repo (1997) and Trif (2007) found that the majority of organizations studied in Slovakia, Czech Republic, Bulgaria and Romania provided health services to their employees.

Rewards based on managerial judgements

In many developing countries it is the managers, especially those of SMEs, who decide who gets paid what and who gets promoted to where. Most rewards are based on managerial judgements regardless of the minimum wage and the regulations in place. Managers in the CEE countries are no exception. According to Trif (2007: 250) managers in Romania, for example, had a high influence on wages and social benefits in their organizations.

Rising wage inequalities

A study by Newell and Socha (2007) of the rise in wage inequalities in Poland concluded that the growing employment in the private sector had been the cause. Private sector employers tend to differentiate between their employees less on the basis of performance than on the basis of age, gender, ethnicity, family relations, location and so on (Puffer and Sheksnia, 1996).

The gap in pay between the levels of an organization is widening. Senior managers are paid 6 to 8 times higher than the average pay in their organizations. Low-paid employees are often pleased to be employed because of the threat of unemployment: indeed, many job seekers would accept a pay level below the minimum wage (Puffer and Sheksnia, 1996). However, with the exodus of many skilled workers to work in Western European countries, some employers are finding it difficult to attract and retain skilled workers. Therefore they have had to offer wages well above the minimum wage. So the minimum wage has tended to become irrelevant. Also, because of the fear of losing key employees through poaching and headhunting, many 'companies are increasingly finding they have to offer incentives to retain key staff, including higher wages, long-term career development and training, and long-service bonus schemes' (Channon and Dakin, 1995: 27, 29).

ACTIVITY 3

As an HR manager of a Russian–French joint venture with branches throughout Russia, you have been asked to review the current reward policy, which is still traditional, and to suggest a new policy that is more appropriate to the staff of a multinational company. What reward policy would you suggest and how would you implement it?

Employee relations

Since the breakdown of communism, the system of employee relations in the new CEE countries has been determined by the economic policies of the new market economy. Most of the CEE countries have had to review their employment and employee relations laws in response to the requirements for EU accession, the influx of foreign direct investment and the growing number of privately owned companies (Aguilera and Dabu, 2005; Stockhammer and

Onaran, 2009; Ost, 2009). However, despite the changes that have been introduced over the last two decades, 'many trade unions in CEE remained locked in the past and unable to develop offensive strategies under new, more difficult and unfriendly conditions' (Mrozowicki and Van Hootegem, 2008: 199).

Trade unions

Following the fall of communism (and especially between 1992 and 1995), trade union influence and power increased significantly (Aro and Repo, 1997). They emerged as strong, organized and free unions that promised to protect the interests of the working classes in the face of increasing capitalist exploitation. According to Trif (2007: 248), 'a Romanian union representative indicated that immediately after 1989 the unions were very strong and some had extreme demands, but as they got more experience, they became more realistic and constructive'. In this respect, Mrozowicki and Van Hootegem (2008: 200) also commented that 'the unions that emerged from the anti-communist movement had difficulties in reconciling their engagement to promoting market reforms with their mission of protecting workers against the negative effects of the same economic transformation'.

By the late 1990s the power of trade unions had declined at the organizational level, especially in CEE countries where private sector enterprises had increased significantly (see Pollert, 1999, 2000). While many large and highly unionized companies were closed down or privatized, most of the privately owned enterprises became non-unionized (Aguilera and Dabu, 2005; Kohl and Platzer, 2007). According to Stockhammer and Onaran (2009: 322), the 'early transition period also witnessed the foundation of independent unions and conflict between old and new unions'. It can be seen from Table 17.7 that trade unions membership continued to decline even after the late 1990s. As their membership declined, the unions became less organized, underfunded, weaker and in need of government support.

So far, all indications show that trade unions in the CEE countries are now weak and lack the support of the working class (Crowley and Ost, 2001; Meardi, 2002; Ost, 2005). There is a deep sense of powerlessness among the workers (Mrozowicki and Van Hootegem, 2008) because they have lost faith

Table 17.7 Union membership 2000 and 2007 (%), selected CEE countries

Country	2000	2001	2002	2003	2004	2005	2006	2007
Czech Republic	29.5	–	21.66	–	22.25	–	20.96	–
Hungary	–	22.46	–	18.47	–	17.82	–	16.86
Poland	–	17.60	–	19.18	–	–	14.36	–
Slovakia	36.25	32.83	31.12	29.92	27.78	25.82	23.61	–

Source: OECD Statistics, 2009, http://stats.oecd.org/Index.aspx, accessed on 6 Nov. 2009.

in trade unionism and solidarity movements. It seems that solidarity is a thing of the past and it cannot be reinvented in the face of the current economic and political climate (Hyman, 1999; Ost, 2005; Mrozowicki and Van Hootegem, 2008).

It should be noted that there are many differences in the nature, type and coverage of collective bargaining between the CEE countries. For example, collective bargaining agreements cover only about 20 per cent of employees in Latvia and Lithuania, where many private sector employers do not recognize trade unions. By contrast it is 100 per cent in Slovenia, where large public sector organizations dominate the economy.

Collective bargaining

In centrally planned economies the mechanism of collective bargaining is not considered to be important for setting the terms and conditions of employee relations. Since trade unions were part of that state apparatus and subordinated to the communist party, there was no genuine bargaining procedure: it was the state that decided the wages of all employees and all aspects of employee–employer relations. In countries such as Bulgaria, Hungary and Poland, there were some very limited and party-controlled negotiations taking place at the enterprise level regarding operational issues, but most of the crucial employment and rewards decisions were determined by the state.

It was not until the 1990s that mechanisms for free collective bargaining were legally established, but they remained heavily regulated and still directly or indirectly influenced by the state at the national level where important employee relations decisions are made (Meardi, 2000, 2002). For example, in countries such as Poland, each year a tripartite commission sets the framework for collective bargaining at the national level in order to control the power of trade unions, although most collective bargaining agreements are conducted at the organizational level between the unions and management. Also, in Romania, only a single collective agreement is to be negotiated at any one level and it should cover all employees in the bargaining unit. The law prescribes all the requirements that the negotiating parties should meet before they are legally permitted to enter into collective bargaining agreements. When these collective agreements are 'concluded at national and sectoral levels' they 'only provide minimal frameworks for negotiations at company level' (Trif, 2007: 244). Moreover, in Russia, the labour code provides for employees to request collective bargaining through their trade unions but only one agreement is permitted per enterprise. Also, in most of the CEE countries, collective agreements are written and then registered with a specified office at the ministry of labour.

Currently, all CEE countries have established mechanisms for collective bargaining, though there are significant differences between them. Some trade unions still prefer the cooperative, national and state-endorsed bargaining structure, while others are adopting Western European approaches which range from the more cooperative, as in Scandinavian countries, to the more adversarial, as in France and the UK. For example, from a comparative study of trade union strategies in the printing industry in the Czech Republic, Hungary and Slovakia, Gennard (2007) concluded that the unions in the three countries were not in favour of an adversarial bargaining strategy and preferred the cooperative approach in negotiations. Also, Mrozowicki and Van Hootegem (2008: 199) maintain that trade unions in Poland and other CEE countries retained their bargaining power in the public sector organizations and in large, privately owned companies where collective agreements had been traditionally negotiated through collective bargaining. They also assert that collective bargaining was uncommon in the newly founded national and foreign privately owned companies, which are not union-friendly.

MINI CASE STUDY 43

To Negotiate or Not to Negotiate (Romania)

Vladimir Dzurinda, the new leader of a well-established industrial trade union that represents more than 3,500 employees in a large manufacturing plant in Bucharest, Romania, once said: 'it is hard to concentrate on one issue and get it settled because there are changes beyond everyone's control. For example, we find it very difficult to discuss the terms and conditions of employment because shortages of raw materials cause disruption to production and you cannot put the blame fully on management.'

Questions

1 What do you think are the main issues on which the trade unions normally negotiate with their employers' representatives?
2 Are there issues that cannot be negotiated because they are beyond the control of the employer? Justify your answer with the use of examples.

Industrial action

Under communism, industrial action in the form of strikes, walkouts and stoppages were not permitted. Under the mechanisms of a free market economy, all CEE countries have legislation that protects the rights of employees to take industrial action and to go on strike. However, in practice, industrial conflicts seldom end in industrial (strike) action. This can be attributed to two reasons. First, the new regulations on strikes have made the process of organizing a legal strike very cumbersome for the unions. It involves a lengthy and bureaucratic procedure before a legal strike action can be taken. Second, because of the legacy of the Soviet era, many employees still believe that strikes are bad for the economy. For example, Trif (2007) found that in Romania, even trade unions believe that a strike action should be taken only when necessary and in exceptional cases.

The settlement of industrial disputes

All CEE countries have procedures for the settlement of industrial disputes, but since such disputes are limited, the extent to which such procedures are effective is not yet known. Collective agreements are very often reached through collective bargaining between the unions and management at the organizational level. The negotiations are usually influenced by external pressures such as the conditions of the economy and state intervention rather than by industrial action. When the negotiating partners find it difficult or fail to reach an agreement, they seek a third party intervention through mediation or arbitration which is provided by an independent employee relations body.

Summary

1 The transition that the CEE countries have had to make has necessitated the adoption of particular management policies and practices that are capitalist in orientation, though still influenced by communist legacies and national cultural values and economic conditions.

2 In dealing with the challenges of the transition, some countries have reformed their political systems, liberalized their economies and gained full accession to the European Union (EU). Others are still a long way from establishing credible free market economic institutions.

3 Important economic reforms have included the privatization of state-owned enterprises, the encouragement of foreign direct investment, the restructuring of the banking and fiscal system, and the reduction of state control of the economy.

4 The current 'transitional' labour market trends are characterized by a shift from employment in state-owned large companies to privately owned small and medium size enterprises, and from a job-creating heavy industry and manufacturing sector to a downsized light industry and services sector.

5 The shifts in labour market trends have resulted in company closures, downsizing and mass redundancies, a surplus in well-educated and highly skilled workers, declining levels of female employment and limited use of flexible working practices.

6 A number of studies have found that a mixture of authoritarian management, experimental management, and initiative management characterizes the current transitional approach to management in the CEE countries.

7 The nature of managing human resources in Central and Eastern Europe is not clearly defined, not well documented, and is still emerging. The function of managing

human resources has become one of the main challenges for all managers because it presents them with a new set of tasks that had been unknown to them.

8   The move from the command to free market economies in CEE countries has shifted the responsibility for recruitment and selection from the state-allocated recruitment bureaus to the managers of individual organizations.

9   There is a need for more management training and development in order to enhance the abilities and knowledge of expert staff and managers to help them to meet present and future demands of their countries' economies. More investment in education, training and development is required at the national and organizational levels.

10 Despite the liberalization of the economy and the rewards system, studies have confirmed that there is very limited use of performance-related pay, most rewards are based on managerial judgements, the minimum wage has become irrelevant, and there are rising wage inequalities.

11 As their membership has declined, trade unions in the CEE countries have become less organized, underfunded, weaker and in need of government support.

Revision questions

Chapter 1 provides a review task designed to consolidate your learning from this chapter. Please see Box 1.2.

In addition, the following questions are designed to help you revise this chapter:

1   Analyse critically the main management and organization issues that characterize the transitional approach to management of CEE countries. Discuss each one of them in comparison with the North American approach (Canada and the US).

2   Imagine you are an HR manager of a British multinational company in Poland. Write a report to the company's board of directors in London describing the main similarities and the main differences in HRM functions (recruitment and selection, training and development, rewards system, and employee relations) between the CEE countries and the UK.

3   Discuss the effects of national culture and the legacy of communism on the current labour markets and management policies and practices in selected CEE countries.

References

Aguilera, R. and Dabu, A. (2005) 'Transformation employment relations systems in central and eastern Europe', *Journal of Industrial Relations*, 47(1): 16–42.

Ardichvili, A., Cardozo, R.N. and Gasparishvili, A. (1998) 'Leadership styles and management practices of Russian entrepreneurs: implications for transferability of western HRD interventions', *Human Resource Development Quarterly*, 9(2): 145–55.

Ardichvili, A. and Gasparishvili, A. (2001) 'Socio-cultural values, internal work culture and leadership styles in four post-communist countries', *International Journal of Cross Cultural Management*, 1(2): 227–42.

Aro, P.O. and Repo, P. (1997) *Trade Union Experiences in Collective Bargaining in Central Europe*, Budapest: ILO-CEET.

Blau, F.D. and Ferber, M.A. (1992) 'Women's work, women's lives: a comparative economic perspective', in Kahne, H. and Giele, J.Z. (eds), *Women's Work and Women's Lives: The Continuing Struggle Worldwide*, Boulder, CO: Westview Press, 324–46.

Brainerd, E. (2000) 'Women in transition: changes in gender wage differentials in eastern Europe and the former Soviet Union', *Industrial and Labor Relations Review*, 54(1): 138–62.

Channon, J. and Dakin, A. (1995) 'Coming to terms with local people', *People Management*, 15 June: 24–9.

Clement, R.W., Payne, F.W. and Brockway, G.R. (1994) 'Training central and eastern European managers: the Hungarian experience', *Journal of Management Development*, 13(4): 53–61.

Crowley, S. and Ost, D. (2001) 'Conclusion: making sense of labor weakness in postcommunism', in Crowley, S. and Ost, D. (eds), *Workers After Workers' States: Labor and Politics in Postcommunist Eastern Europe*, Lanham, MD: Rowman and Littlefield, 219–33.

Cyr, D.J. (1996) 'Implications for learning: human resources management in EastWest joint ventures – special issues on managerial learning in the transformation of eastern Europe', *Organizational Studies*, Spring.

Eurostat, Statistical Office of the European Communities (2009) *Eurostat Yearbook 2009*, available online at: http://epp.eurostat.ec.europa.eu/portal/page/portal/product_details/publication?p_product_code = KS-CD-09-001, accessed on 22 January 2010.

Gennard, J. (2007) 'Managing membership decline in a hostile environment: the case of the print unions in the Czech Republic, Slovakia and Hungary', *European Journal of Industrial Relations*, 13(1): 89–108.

Hofstede, G. (1993) 'Cultural constraints in management theories', *The Academy of Management Executive*, 7(1): 81–94.

Huettinger, M. (2008) 'Cultural dimensions in business life: Hofstede's indices for Latvia and Lithuania', *Baltic Journal of Management*, 3(3): 359–76.

Hyman, R. (1999) 'Imagined solidarities: can trade unions resist globalization?', in P. Leisink (ed.), *Globalization and Labour Relations*, Cheltenham: Edward Elgar, 94–115.

Jankowicz, A.D. (1994) 'The new journey to Jerusalem: mission and meaning in the managerial crusade to Eastern Europe', *Organisation Studies*, 15(3): 479–507.

Jankowicz, A.D. (1998) 'Issues in human resource management in central Europe', *Personnel Review*, 27(3): 169–76.

Kenny, B. and Trick, B. (1994) 'Developing management education in the former communist countries of Europe', *European Business Review*, 94(1): 30–8.

Kohl, H. and Platzer, H. (2007) 'The role of the state in central and eastern European industrial relations: the case of minimum wages', *Industrial Relations Journal*, 38(6): 614–35.

Kolman, L., Noorderhaven, N.G., Hofstede, G. and Dienes, E. (2003) 'Cross-cultural differences in central Europe', *Journal of Management Psychology*, 18(1): 76–88.

Kumssa, A. and Jones, J.F. (1999) 'The social consequences of reform in transitional economies', *International Journal of Social Economics*, 26(1/2/3): 194–210.

Lange, T. (2008) 'Communist legacies, gender and the impact on job satisfaction in central and eastern Europe', *European Journal of Industrial Relations*, 14(3): 327–46.

Mailand, M. and Due, J. (2004) 'Social dialogue in central and eastern Europe: present state and future development', *European Journal of Industrial Relations*, 10(2): 179–97.

Marcic, D. (1995) 'Challenges and opportunities of teaching management in a post-socialist society', *Executive Development*, 8(5): 26–31.

Meardi, G. (2000) *Trade Union Activists, East and West: Comparison in Multinational Companies*, Aldershot: Gower.

Meardi, G. (2002) 'The Trojan Horse for Americanization of Europe? Polish industrial relations towards the EU', *European Journal of Industrial Relations*, 8(1): 77–99.

Meyer-Sahling, J.H. (2009) 'Varieties of legacies: a critical review of legacy explanations of public administration reform in east central Europe', *International Review of Administrative Sciences*, 75(3): 509–28.

Morley, M.J., Heraty, N. and Michailova, S. (eds) (2008) *Managing Human Resources in Central and Eastern Europe*, London: Routledge.

Mrozowicki, A. and Van Hootegem, G. (2008) 'Unionism and workers' strategies in capitalist transformation: the Polish case reconsidered', *European Journal of Industrial Relations*, 14(2): 197–216.

Nelson, E.G. and Taylor, J. (1995) 'New ventures and entrepreneurship in an Eastern European context: a training and development programme for managers in state-owned firms', *Journal of European Industrial Training*, 19(9): 12–22.

Newell, A. and Socha, M. (2007) 'The Polish wage inequality explosion', *Economics of Transition*, 15(4): 733–58.

Ost, D. (2005) *The Defeat of Solidarity: Anger and Politics in Postcommunist Europe*, Ithaca, NY: Cornell University Press.

Ost, D. (2009) 'The End of Postcommunism: Trade Unions in Eastern Europe's Future', *Eastern European Politics and Societies*, 23(1): 13–33.

Pascall, G. and Manning, N. (2000) 'Gender and social policy: comparing welfare states in central and eastern Europe and the former Soviet Union', *Journal of European Social Policy*, 10(2): 240–66.

Peiperl, M. and Estrin, S. (1998) 'Managerial markets in transition in central and eastern Europe: a field study and implications', *The International Journal of Human Resource Management*, 9(1): 58–78.

Pollert, A. (1999) *Transformation at Work in the New Market Economies of Central Eastern Europe*, London: Sage.

Pollert, A. (2000) 'Ten years of post-Communist central and eastern Europe: labour's tenuous foothold in the regulation of the employment relationship', *Economic and Industrial Democracy*, 21(2): 182–209.

Pollert, A. (2003) 'Women, work and equal opportunities in post-communist transition', *Work, Employment and Society*, 17(2): 331–57.

Pollert, A. (2005) 'Gender, transformation and employment in central eastern Europe', *European Journal of Industrial Relations*, 11(2): 213–30.

Puffer, S. (1996) 'Leadership in a Russian context', in S. Puffer (ed.), *Business and Management in Russia*, Cheltenham: Edward Elgar, 38–56.

Puffer, S.M. and Shekshnia, S.V. (1996) 'Compensating local employees in post-communist Russia: In search of talent or just looking for a bargain?', *Compensation & Benefits Review*, 26(1): 35–9.

Redman, T. and Keithley, D. (1998) 'Downsizing goes east? Employment restructuring in post-socialist Poland', *The International Journal of Human Resource Management*, 9(2): 274–95.

Stockhammer, E. and Onaran, Ö. (2009) 'National and sectoral influences on wage determination in central and eastern Europe', *European Journal of Industrial Relations*, 15(3): 317–38.

Takei, H. and Ito, Y. (2007) 'Human resource management and governance in central and eastern Europe – case studies in Bulgaria and Slovak Republic', *Policy and Governance Working Paper Series*, no. 119, Graduate School of Media and Governance, Keio University, Japan.

Todeva, E. (1999) 'Models for comparative analysis of culture: the case of Poland', Posted at Surrey Scholarship Online, http://epubs.surrey.ac.uk/entrepstrategy/8, accessed 6 March 2010.

Trif, A. (2007) 'Collective bargaining in eastern Europe: case study evidence from Romania', *European Journal of Industrial Relations*, 13(2): 237–56.

Wagner, H. (1996) 'Transformation process and J-curve problem', *International Journal of Social Economics*, 23(10/11): 73–87.

18

South America

LEARNING OUTCOMES

The chapter is designed to help you understand, for South America:

1   The (a) economic, (b) political and (c) cultural contexts in which managers work;

2   The main trends in the labour market;

3   The typical features of (a) management policies and practices and (b) organizational structure and behaviour;

4   The main policies and practices of human resource management with regard to: (a) recruitment and selection; (b) training and development; (c) rewards and remuneration; and (d) employee relations.

Introduction

The Latin American approach to management is the outcome of the common past experiences and current challenges of most of the countries in the region. As Elvira and Davila (2005b: 2166) state, 'Latin American organizations are embedded in their historical tradition even though globalization forces have deeply changed the region. These combined historical and global processes have determined unique characteristics for business management and created a hybrid management model'. This chapter attempts to explain the main characteristics and functioning of this hybrid Latin American approach to management and organization.

Table 18.1 Basic statistical indicators of selected South American countries

Country	Area (sq. km)	Population (2009 est.)	Population growth (2009 est.)	GDP – real growth rate (2009) %	Inflation rate (2009) %	Workforce (2009 est.) millions	Unemployment rate (2009) %
Argentina	2,780,400	40,913,584	1.053	−2.5	6.2	16.380	9.6
Bolivia	1,098,581	9,775,246	1.772	2.8	4.3	4.536	8.5
Brazil	8,514,877	198,739,269	1.199	0.1	4.2	95.210	7.4
Chile	756,102	16,601,707	0.881	−1.5	1.7	7.420	10.1
Colombia	1,138,914	45,644,023	1.377	−0.1	3.0	20.030	12.0
Ecuador	283,561	14,573,101	1.497	−2.0	5.4	4.770	9.8
Paraguay	406,752	6,995,655	2.364	−3.5	2.5	2.983	7.9
Peru	1,285,216	29,546,963	1.229	1.0	1.2	10.26	9.2
Uruguay	176,215	3,494,382	0.466	0.6	7.3	1.636	7.9
Venezuela	912,050	26,814,843	1.508	−1.5	27.3	12.670	10.9

Source: Compiled from World Economic Outlook (IMF), Statistics, 2009; and the CIA *World Factbook* (2010).

Contexts: economics, politics and culture

Economics

South American economies depend on agriculture and the export of raw materials. They are also heavily dependent on international trade. The continent has much fertile land and plentiful natural resources, notably zinc, copper, petroleum and uranium. Most South American countries experienced economic recession in 1999–2001. From 2003, there was a slow but strong recovery because the region enjoyed an export boom of considerable proportions, thanks to an increase in demand for, and in the international prices of, the main export products (such as soya, crude oil, copper, gold). This recovery coincided also with an increase in foreign direct investments by multinational companies. However, the region's economies suffered as a result of the recent 'credit crunch' recession.

The establishment of the South American countries' free trade association (Mercosur) has contributed to the development of economic stability and confidence, which has attracted multinational companies (MNCs) to invest in the region. The economic liberalization programmes introduced across South America included market deregulation and the privatization of state-owned companies. Privatization programmes included the sale of 'key sectors such as telecommunications, mining, energy, petroleum, finance, airlines, transportation and infrastructure industries' (Casanova, 2005: 2175). As in many developing countries, the privatization of public utilities was resented by the general public, national organizations, trade unions and left-wing political parties. In countries such as Venezuela some of the privatized companies have been nationalized. In terms of their impact on labour markets, some of the economic reforms carried out in the 1990s were disappointing: production per employee grew by only 0.21 per cent annually between 1990 and 2005, while unemployment and informal employment increased over the same period (ILO, 2006). Latin American countries lagged behind in terms of productivity in comparison with the rest of the world (World Economic Forum, 2005). The gradual, partial, success of economic reforms only came after 2005, when most of the South American countries entered a period of recovery and economic growth as a result of increased exports and a move from agriculture-based to more industrialized and service-oriented economics.

Argentina is a world leader in the export of beef and a number of agricultural products such as wheat, corn and soyabeans. About a quarter of Argentina's export revenues come from soya, wheat, corn and meat. Brazil is South America's most improved economy and has become a leading economic power. Both Argentina and Brazil experienced economic crisis between 2001 and 2003, but recovered quite fast before the recession towards the end of the decade. Brazil's economy has much improved to a record trade surplus as productivity gains doubled, with high commodity prices contributing to the surge in exports. Brazil is a major producer and exporter of agricultural products such as coffee, soyabeans, corn, cocoa, sugarcane and beef. Brazil has become a leading member of 'the G-20 alliance of developing countries, strengthening the voice of poor agricultural exporters at the World Trade Organization' (*Financial Times*, 15 Sept. 2004: 19).

Chile has had one of the highest rates of economic growth in South America over the last 10 years, combined with low inflation and high prices for export commodities such as copper. As a result, Chile attracted many foreign investments, especially after signing a free trade agreement with the US and the EU member states.

Bolivia, Colombia and Ecuador have the lowest GDP per capita in the region. Their large natural gas and petroleum reserves have yet to be fully exploited. Colombia is a major producer and exporter of coffee, bananas, coal and cut flowers. It is also the world's largest producer of narcotics such as cocaine, opium poppy and cannabis. Ecuador is very dependent on the export of hydrocarbons, which accounts for more than 50 per cent of its export revenues. Venezuela is a founding member of OPEC and has benefited from the high oil prices since 2003. Venezuela's economy is highly dependent on the export of oil, which accounts for more than 90 per cent of export earnings and 50 per cent of the federal budget.

Politics

All South American countries are republics or federal republics and have democratically elected governments. Most of them have presidents who are both chief of state and head of government. The legislative body in most South American countries is made of a bicameral national congress (*Congresso Nacional*), though electoral systems vary. The Republics of Ecuador, Peru and Venezuela have a unicameral national congress (*Congresso Nacional*) or national assembly (*Asamblea Nacional*). The continent's current democratization process and political stability are somewhat fragile. Politics in South America can be volatile, and so there is a risk of reversion to military rule and dictatorship in the face of poor economic performance, institutional corruption, or apparent injustice. However, South American countries are currently more politically united and supportive of each other than at any time before.

Culture

Most South Americans (over 75 per cent) are at least nominally Roman Catholics. With the exception of Brazil, where Portuguese is the national language, South American countries have Spanish as their national language, together with local traditional languages. When applying Hofstede's (2001) cultural dimensions, South American countries may be classified as collectivists and relatively masculine, high in power distance and high in uncertainty avoidance (see also Garibaldi de Hilal et al., 2009). Religious symbols and rituals are very important in people's lives. For example, wearing the cross or having images of the Virgin of Guadalupe in the workplace are commonplace. Family ties are highly respected and people value personal relationships at work and in all aspects of society (Olivas-Luján et al., 2009).

ACTIVITY 1

Imagine that you are a manager of a multinational company that is planning to open new subsidiaries in Argentina, Bolivia and Chile. Write a report to explain the main (a) opportunities and (b) threats involved in investing in these countries. Be sure to take into consideration in your report the economic, political and cultural contexts.

Labour market trends

The South American labour markets are rather fragmented and heterogeneous: nearly 33 per cent of the workforce is located in rural areas and more than 50 per cent of those in employment are 'self-employed, domestic workers, unpaid family workers or wage-earning workers in micro-enterprises with up to five employees' (ILO, 2006: 7). The workforce is generally young, educated, works long hours, is poorly paid, and is insecure (ILO, 2006: 5). As shown in Table 18.2, more than a quarter of the population of most South American countries is under the age 14 and the majority of the population is at a working

Table 18.2 Age structure (%) (2009), selected South American countries

Country	0–14 years %	15–64 years %	65 years and over %	Median age (years)	Life expectancy at birth (for men and women)
Argentina	25.6	63.5	10.8	30	76.56
Bolivia	35.5	60.0	4.5	21.9	66.89
Brazil	26.7	66.8	6.4	28.6	72.00
Chile	23.2	67.8	9.1	31.4	77.34
Colombia	28.9	65.4	5.6	27.1	72.81
Ecuador	31.1	62.7	6.2	25	75.30
Paraguay	36.7	58.1	5.2	21.9	75.77
Peru	29.1	65.2	5.7	26.1	70.74
Uruguay	22.4	64.3	13.3	33.4	76.35
Venezuela	30.5	64.3	5.2	25.5	73.61

Source: Compiled from government statistics and from the CIA *World Factbook*, 2010.

age of 15–64. In general, South American labour markets are characterized by: high levels of unemployment, especially among the young people; agricultural employment; declining public sector employment; informal sector employment; self-employment; and short-term employment.

Unemployment

Unemployment, especially among the young people, has been one of the major challenges to governments in South America in recent years. Rural–urban migration increased the supply of unskilled and uneducated manual labour in large cities, adding to unemployment. Limited housing in the cities has led to the spread of shantytowns. It can be seen from Table 18.3 below that the average rate of unemployment is officially over 8.5 per cent in South America. In 2005, there were about 57 million young people of working age, of whom around 9.5 million (or about 42 per cent of total unemployment in the region) were jobless. More than 20 per cent of young people (15–25 age group) neither study nor work, and two-thirds of this group were women, 'many of whom became mothers at an early age' (ILO, 2006: 50–1). Youth unemployment 'is significantly higher than that of adults, and young women face high levels of exclusion' from the labour market (ILO, 2006: 19). It has been argued, however, that the main reason for the high level of youth unemployment is that many young people lack the skills and the know-how needed by current economic development. The recent economic reforms have necessitated a skilled and professional workforce that the current labour market is unable to supply. There is an urgent need for youth training programmes and vocational education.

Many initiatives have been introduced in order to help provide employment for young people. Most such initiatives involve the provision of opportunities for learning new skills. Some South American governments introduced legislation that allowed enterprises to cut the benefits and allowances of young employees in return for investment in training them in new skills but, according to the ILO report (2006), in countries such as Peru only about 7 per cent of young people had benefited from such schemes and 'many enterprises used them to cut costs rather than provide training' (ILO, 2006: 51). In Brazil, where 44 per cent of those aged of 16–24 are unemployed, the First Employment Programme (PPE) was introduced in 2003 in order to create new jobs for young people who had no work experience, did not complete secondary education and came from low-income families (Marshall, 2004: 31). The programme offers employers different financial incentives to retain current young employees and to attract more, depending on the company size and type of activity, but many employers did not benefit from such incentives because it was not necessary for them to invest in training new employees while they can attract many experienced and already trained employees seeking employment.

ACTIVITY 2

If you were responsible for finding ways to promote employment opportunities for young people in South American countries, what policies would you suggest?

Agricultural employment

Economic liberalization has led to the opening of new international markets for the export of agricultural products other than bananas, sugar, coffee and cocoa. Though, as shown in Table 18.3, agriculture is an important sector in South America, with the exception of Bolivia, Colombia and Paraguay, it does not create employment for a significant number of people. Despite the increase in agricultural and food products from countries such Argentina and Peru, the sector has not been able to create enough jobs for the increasing number of job seekers, partly because agriculture has become highly mechanized and less labour intensive than it used to be. Also, as the workforce is becoming more educated, many of those who look for jobs feel too qualified to seek employment in agriculture. In the countries where agriculture and animal husbandry is still the major employer, the means of production are still 'traditional, with low productivity, few links to agro-industry, and dependent on low-capital technology and an unqualified workforce, all of which partly explains the low

Table 18.3 Workforce distribution by occupation in 2009 (%), selected South American countries

Country	Workforce millions	Agriculture %	Industry %	Services %	Unemployment rate %
Argentina	16.38	1.0	23	76	9.6
Bolivia	4.536	33	19	48	8.5
Brazil	95.21	10	22	68	7.4
Chile	7.42	11.2	23	65.8	10
Colombia	20.03	21.4	18.1	60.5	12
Ecuador	4.77	6	20	74	9.8
Paraguay	2.983	21	20	60	7.9
Peru	10.26	1	22	77	9.0
Uruguay	1.636	8	16	76	7.9
Venezuela	12.67	7.2	25.3	67.5	7.4

Source: Compiled from government statistics and from the CIA *World Factbook*, 2010.

wages and the limited income among producers dependent primarily on this type of farming' (ILO, 2006: 59). Many jobs created in rural areas are in 'very small-scale family agricultural units' (ILO, 2006: 60).

Declining public sector employment

As a result of economic reforms, the role of most South American governments 'changed from actively protecting a large part of the domestic productive sector to a State creating the environment for private activities' (Ernst, 2005b: 23). The privatization of state-owned companies and the reductions in public spending since the 1990s have resulted in mass redundancies and a significant decline in public sector employment (ILO, 1999). This change has led to 'a shift of skilled workers into informal or small-scale activities' (Casanova, 2005: 2181). The decline in public sector employment has also led to a growth in informal sector employment.

MINI CASE STUDY 44

Marcopolo Brazil

Marcopolo is a medium size bus manufacturer from Brazil. After gaining more than 50 per cent of the local market, it turned to the international market. It introduced new, varied, and competitive designs to meet the demands of international customers. For example, it designed a 22-seat minibus that is suitable for the crowded Mexico City and a bus with a retractable roof for Saudi Arabia to use during the season of Haj (pilgrimage).

According to Carlos Zignani, Marcopolo's head of investor relations, the low-cost base and flexible working methods of his company would ensure competitiveness. He said: 'our larger competitors are good at producing big amounts of the same product. We are better at smaller, customized orders'. (Case developed from the *Financial Times*, 15 Sept. 2004, p. 19.)

Questions

1 Which labour market trends might have contributed to making Marcopolo an international company?
2 What are the likely implications of Marcopolo's international success for the Brazilian labour market?

Informal sector employment

The informal sector tends to thrive in countries where there is economic crisis, poverty and lawlessness. The informal sector is becoming the largest employer in South America. In Brazil nearly a third of jobs are created by the informal sector (cited in Elvira and Davila, 2005c). Many people prefer the informal sector, rather than being formally registered as self-employed individuals or as business employers, because of high taxation, lack of incentives for small businesses, and excessive bureaucratic procedures. Some informal sector enterprises 'prefer to operate on the fringe of the law and thus enjoy higher profits than their legally operating competitors, despite the risk of discovery and sanctions' (ILO, 2006: 57–8).

Also, according to the ILO (2006: 17), 'poverty is the reason why most people create or accept a job in the informal economy'. Many of those who work in the informal economy have very low income and lack social protection. They enter into 'a vicious circle of poverty which is very difficult to break' (ILO, 2006: 17). Most of these are young people, who become vulnerable to social unrest and fall prey to organized criminal gangs and anti-establishment groups. A UNDP report on *Democracy in Latin America* (2004) showed that in countries where there had been a high proportion of people in informal sector employment, there was low support for democracy. It was found that 54.7 per cent of Latin Americans would prefer an 'authoritarian regime' to a democratic one because the former provided a better social welfare system than the latter.

Self-employment

An increasing number of skilled and professional individuals and groups are setting up their own businesses that are formally registered as micro, small, or medium size enterprises. Self-employed people enjoy more independence and flexibility in their employment than those in the informal sector because their employment is recognized and supported by the state. They also avoid the bad image that the informal sector has in the community. However, many such businesses fail because of high taxes, competition, bureaucracy and red tape, lack of resources, limited experience and expertise, and poor organization and management.

Temporary, seasonal and short-term employment

Temporary, seasonal and short-term employment contracts are very common in most countries of South America, especially in the privately owned enterprises. For example, the number of workers employed temporarily in Colombia increased from 20 to 40 per cent of the working population between 1992 and 2001 (Ogliastri et al., 2005). To cut labour costs, increase profits and respond easily to fluctuations in demand for their goods and services, many private sector enterprises 'have learned to apply new organizational principles of flexible manufacturing and just-in-time and zero-defect methods, adapting them to their own needs and circumstances' (Ernst, 2005a: 23). They have also introduced temporary and short-term employment that suits their business needs. In agriculture, which is the largest sector, most jobs are seasonal, as workers are employed en mass during the harvest time (summer and autumn) and then released to join the dole queue in other times.

Multinationals and employment

A significant aspect of South American labour markets has been the growth of foreign direct investment by multinational companies. Such investment has created an appreciable level of employment for the indigenous workforce (Elvira and Davila, 2005b). However, most recent investment has been based on the production of export commodities for international markets and has created employment for only a small number of skilled workers. Hence the growth in foreign investment 'has not been sufficient to alter significantly the main structures of the labour market and to create job opportunities for all' (ILO, 2006: 6). This was confirmed by a comparative study of foreign direct investment in Argentina, Brazil and Mexico by Ernst (2005b: 6–7), who stated that MNCs 'are not as important for employment in Argentina, Brazil and Mexico as they are in China.'

MINI CASE STUDY 45

Say South America, You Get Football

'South American countries are known for their outstanding football teams and star players. International victories have ... cemented the popularity of football within Brazilian culture and have paved the way for growing commercialisation' (*Financial Times*, 26 April 2000, p. 6). Football has become a big business that has attracted huge international investment around the world. Multinational companies have exploited the popularity of certain South American teams and players to promote their products, but they have created very few employment opportunities for the local people. The manager of a Brazilian football club once said, 'Foreign companies exploit the popularity of football in South America to make money for other parts of the world.'

Questions

1 Discuss the effects football can have on the labour markets in South America.
2 What opportunities are there for multinational companies to use football to create new investments and create new job opportunities in South America? By what means?

Increasing employment of women

Better education of women has meant greater opportunities to become employable in all sectors of the economy. For example, according to Casanova (2005: 2182), in Argentina, Brazil, Colombia, Ecuador, Guatemala and Panama 'progress with women's education was reflected in a greater number of years of schooling, with more girls reaching the middle and higher stages of education'. However many women are employed in low-paid jobs and 'concentrated in areas such as politics, public administration, education, medicine, art, NGOs/services and absent from managerial positions in business organizations' (Elvira and Davila, 2005c: 2270). Also, many women have been employed by multinational companies in agribusiness and in manufacturing of goods for exports or in the provision of services in low-paid jobs. Although more and more women are entering the labour market, gender inequality is still widespread (Olivas-Luján et al., 2009). Elvira and Davila (2005c: 2270) argue that there had been some improvement in employment opportunities for women, but that discrimination still exists in pay and promotion opportunities. 'While more men hold higher positions in organizations women tend to concentrate in support roles.' In theory, all countries have equal opportunities legislation; in practice many women are paid less than their male counterparts and are discriminated against in training and promotion opportunities.

Though there has been a rise in female employment because of agribusiness for exports, 'much of this employment is seasonal, insecure and low paid, with poor labour standards or health and safety provision' (Barrientos, 1999: 2). For example, women do more than 51 per cent of non-agricultural jobs in the informal sector and the rate of unemployment among the female workforce is 40 per cent higher than that of male unemployment (ILO, 2006). In Latin America generally there have been many obstacles that prevent women from entering the labour market and achieving their potential through career progression. There is discrimination in the workplace and pressure from the family and society.

Child labour

It was estimated in 2005 that a total of 5.7 million children aged between 5 and 14 years worked in Latin America (ILO-IPEC, 2005). This represents more than 5 per cent of the total number of children in the region in 2005 (ILO, 2006: 11). Most countries have implemented policies aimed at controlling and preventing the employment of children. However, there are still many employers in all South American countries that exploit children in low-paid and potentially dangerous jobs. Unless joint national and international action is taken, the problem of child labour will persist and may become even worse in the poorest countries. The ILO report on employment in South America proposed a number of policies to help to eradicate child labour and exploitation (see ILO, 2006: 33).

Labour migration

Labour migration is endemic in South America. It was estimated that in 2005 there were more than 20 million migrant workers in Latin America and the Caribbean (ILO, 2006). Most of the intra-regional migration is to Argentina, Costa Rica and Venezuela, where mainly multinational companies have created jobs for emigrant workers in the production of export goods. Emigration outside the region is mainly to the United States, Spain and Canada. Many of the people who emigrate beyond the region are non-professional and unskilled employees who decide to leave their countries not just for economic reasons but also because of political conflicts, injustice, racial discrimination, or civil war.

Management and organization

Managers in South American use a combination of national and international management policies and practices depending on the size and type of organization, and on whether the organization is public or private. The large and privately owned organizations, mainly in the industrial and services sectors, tend to adopt more internationally inspired management practices, while the small and medium size enterprises and organizations of the public sector tend to use more local management practices (Parnell, 2008; Gomes and Gomes, 2009).

However, management is socially constructed and culturally influenced. The Latin American approach to management and organization in general and the management of human resources in particular have been described as 'humanistic' or 'person-centred' (Elvira and Davila, 2005c: 2267) because of managers' concern for the welfare of their subordinates and their willingness to maintain a harmonious working environment in which every employee is a member of a community that respects the legitimate authority.

Person-centred approach

The Latin American approach to management is person-centred because of the importance that managers give to social relations at work and their concern for the welfare of employees and their families. Elvira and Davila (2005c) argue that this approach to management might appear to be irrational from a business point of view, but it can be clearly understood when considered in the context of Latin American culture, which gives 'precedence to people's needs over system consistency'. They explain this point further: 'labour laws can be bent to suit a firm's survival needs and therefore protect workers from unemployment' (Elvira and Davila, 2005c: 2274). Individual employees are made to feel members of the organization's community. Organizations are seen as social entities where people get to work together rather than economic entities where people are hired to do jobs to earn a living.

Authoritarian management

Most South American countries have been dominated at one point or another by the authoritarian governments of military dictators who appointed the managers of state-owned companies and of all public sector institutions on the basis of their loyalty to the government (Parnell, 2008; Garibaldi de Hilal et al., 2009). In such contexts, employees who express opinions contrary to those of management are easily dismissed, and in some cases they are accused of destabilizing the system and then severely punished. Moreover, HRM practices such as recruitment, training and promotion are often influenced by vertically organized social networks and state-controlled economic institutions: those in power are obeyed because of their authority status and their control mechanisms (Garibaldi de Hilal et al., 2009; Rodriguez and Gomez, 2009). Elvira and Davila (2005c: 2278) point out that the cultural value of respect for authority in Latin America makes people 'appreciate closeness to the person in authority' and that 'Latin Americans value status within a hierarchy because it indicates social distance between the higher-up and his subordinates'.

Centralized approach

At the organizational level, there are very few horizontal relationships and managerial authority is seldom delegated. The process of decision-making is centralized. Organization structures are hierarchical. Consequently, it is not surprising to find very passive and dependent subordinates who expect their leaders to tell them what to do all the time. In such organizations, 'information generally flows from top to bottom' (Elvira and Davila, 2005b: 2169). The centralization of decision-making is exercised through the use of excessive bureaucracy and many rules and regulations. Organizations may have policies that they never implement and procedures that are followed only when necessary.

Red tape is widespread and there are many people, called *enchufados* (in Argentina) and *despachantes* (in Brazil), whose role is to go-between government officials and those who need a service to be done.

Procedural formality and formal behaviour

Procedural formality is the prerequisite of bureaucracy and involves respect for authority and the need to follow procedures to the letter. However, the existence of procedural formality does not imply respect for rules and regulations or the achievement of better organizational performance (Parnell, 2008; Garibaldi de Hilal et al., 2009; Gomes and Gomes, 2009). On the contrary, it is often no more than a rubber-stamping activity based on the need to be *seen* to be doing the right thing rather than doing things right. Procedural formality in the Latin American approach to management is strengthened by a code of formal behaviour whereby employees are expected to respect the chain of authority in the organization. Thus job titles and qualifications have a great significance in employee relationships. Also, in many companies appearance is highly rated and employees are requested to adhere to a strict dress code.

Paternalism

The South American economy is increasingly dominated by family-owned small and medium size enterprises. Most of the managers are the owners of enterprises or members of their families, who run businesses as family units (Rodríguez and Ríos, 2009). According to Elvira and Davila (2005a,b), among the manifestations of respect for authority are benevolent paternalism and avoidance of public conflict and confrontation with supervisors. They explain the dominant benevolent paternalism as a 'leadership style where a supervisor has the personal obligation to protect his/her subordinates and in some cases to safeguard the personal needs of workers and their families' (Elvira and Davila, 2005b: 2167). In many indigenous companies, and in the small and medium ones in particular, there is a sense of commitment and loyalty to the organization in which one works. Paternalism is also manifested in collective celebration, where employees celebrate national and religious festivities at their workplace rather than with their families at home (Gomes and Gomes, 2009; Rodríguez and Ríos, 2009). Also, the loyalty and seniority of employees is celebrated in what is referred to as ceremonial recognition, where all employees celebrate their colleagues' recognition and reward for their achievements and loyalty to the organization.

Face-to-face communication

In South America, managers prefer personal contacts and to communicate face-to-face with each other and with their subordinates and seniors (Elvira and Davila, 2005b; Garibaldi de Hilal et al., 2009). Conflict is avoided not just between leaders and subordinates, but also among leaders and subordinates. Elvira and Davila (2005b) argue that benevolent paternalism and the climate of harmony and good employee relations that companies seek to maintain, make it important to have face-to-face communications, personal contacts and social interactions in the workplace. However, communication is very often vertical, and in many South American organizations, because of centralized decision-making, information flows from the top to down the organizational hierarchy.

ACTIVITY 3

Read the passage entitled 'Management and Organization' in Chapter 14 (Africa). What three main similarities and three main differences can you find between Latin American and African management?

Managing human resources

A number of recent studies (Elvira and Davila, 2005a,b,c; Durán-Palma et al., 2005; Durán-Palma and López, 2009; Garibaldi de Hilal et al., 2009; Rao, 2009; Renwick, 2009; Rodriguez and Gomez, 2009; Rodríguez and Ríos, 2009) have concluded that although the practice of HRM in South American countries is changing towards the adoption of more rational, objective and performance-driven methods, it is still heavily and directly influenced by national culture. This influence is clearly apparent in the process of recruitment and selection.

Recruitment and selection

Most of the small and medium size companies which dominate the South American economies recruit their employees through informal contacts made by friends and relatives. Personality traits and social relations are important factors in the recruitment and selection process (Abarca et al., 1998; Elvira and Davila, 2005b; Rodriguez and Gomez, 2009). In some companies, priority in recruitment is given to family members or close relatives because 'family traditions in the workplace are so strong' and it is believed that 'trust, loyalty and responsibility will be guaranteed by having family members at work' (Elvira and Davila, 2005b: 2167). However, the ILO (2006: 65) report on employment in Latin America states that the use of personal contacts may be efficient in such labour markets, but it may not be fair because it provides job opportunities, 'particularly with regard to good jobs, for a select few (those people who have such personal relationships), while a large section of the working population will be excluded'.

Recruitment

While word of mouth and personal contacts are the norm and exist in all organizations regardless of their size or type of ownership, many large state-owned and multinational companies tend to hire their employees through traditional recruitment and selection methods. They also use headhunting and national as well as international recruitment agencies to fill their vacancies. However, 'the problem is that in some countries, many placement agencies function without any sort of regulation or control. Private agencies often charge excessive fees to jobseekers, who may even have to agree to hand over their first wage packet if they are placed in employment' (ILO, 2006: 65).

Selection

South American employers tend not to use sophisticated selection methods such as psychometric and personality tests or assessment centres. In most cases a recommendation followed by a meeting (interview) are enough to offer someone a job. When a relative or a friend recommends a job applicant, the interview may become just a formality. The selection for managerial and professional jobs often takes into consideration physical appearance, gender, age, the birthplace, ethnic origins as well as the qualifications and experience of the applicants.

MINI CASE STUDY 46

Young and Handsome from Lebanese Immigrants (Argentina)

In 1994 a jewellery shop in Buenos Aires placed an advertisement in a local newspaper for a shop assistant. The job advertisement stated: 'we seek to employ a young and handsome man who is a descendant of Lebanese immigrants with knowledge and experience in the sale of jewellery and precious stones'.

Questions

1 How is the advertisement discriminatory?
2 Discuss the reasons that might make this advertisement apparently acceptable in a South American country.

Training and development

Economic liberalization and foreign direct investment have required more trained and better-skilled employees to meet the demands of growing free market economies. For example, many high-tech industries are finding it difficult to employ highly skilled employees from among the national population. Therefore, education and training are very important for the economic development of South American countries. However, it seems that this is the area where most of them have not done enough. The current wide gap in skills and education levels in South American countries cannot be reduced by just relying on government to invest in education and vocational training: it requires the involvement of the stakeholders concerned.

Organizational training

At the organizational level, many companies provide some basic education and training to their employees in order to close the educational gap that exists in society. 'There is a general conviction in Latin America that it is advisable to leave to the enterprises the responsibility for training their own workers whenever possible' (Ducci, 1997: 170). However, even large companies often provide very little pre-employment training or skills development to their employees, and depend on the use of on-the-job training. According to Elvira and Davila (2005c: 2270), when it comes to organizational training 'there are notable differences between what firms do in practice and what managers say they are doing'. Moreover, most small and medium size enterprises (SMEs) devote only a small fraction of their budgets to the training and development of their employees, and since companies of this size are the most affected by economic and financial crises, they have been unable to invest in the training and development of their employees without the support of the state.

Most South American governments have introduced a number of financial incentives to encourage employers to provide more training opportunities to their employees. For example, the governments of Argentina, Brazil and Chile introduced tax incentives for enterprise training (Ducci, 1997), but many companies did not take them up because of 'the complexity of the mechanisms for receiving tax reductions' (Ducci, 1997: 171). Many employers thought there were too many formalities involved in the process of getting a training programme approved and then being reimbursed for it via tax rebate. In Chile, the government introduced in 2003 a system where employers 'undergo training in lieu of paying a fine for a labour violation, once the cause for the violation has been rectified' (ILO, 2006: 80). However, the problem is that many South American employers do not seem to be aware of the importance of employee training for the improvement of their organizational performance. Most of them do not use training needs analysis in order to know the training needs of their employees, and many lack expertise in implementing training programmes (Ducci, 1997). Employers in South America need to invest more in the training of their employees, and especially MNCs, to bring new knowledge and skills to the host country rather than just exploiting the available raw materials and already trained human resources.

Apprenticeships

Until recently the main way to learn a new skill at work was through apprenticeship. Since most businesses in South America are small and family-owned, many young and new employees have had to learn how to do their jobs properly from the old and the experienced employees. In countries where public education is inadequate and not widely accessible, many young people join the labour market at an early age and learn new skills through on-the-job training and apprenticeship. As businesses grow and more MNCs invest in South America, new training methods are introduced, though on-the-job training or learning by doing has been the norm in most organizations for the reasons explained above.

Vocational training

The high number of school leavers and the increasing rate of youth unemployment in most South American countries are symptomatic of prevailing poor education systems and poor or non-existent vocational training opportunities. Some of these countries seem to have realized the severity of the current problems and have attempted to invest in vocational training in order to help young people learn the skills that make them employable. For example, in Argentina, the Ministry of Labour, Employment and Social Security had introduced initiatives 'aimed at integrating technical education and training in the provinces with training under programmes for unemployed young people' (ILO, 2006: 52). Similar initiatives have been introduced in Brazil, Chile and Colombia. In Chile a computer literacy programme has been introduced in order to improve the employability skills of young people. The programme is financed by the Ministry of Labour National Training and Employment Service (SENCE) in order to reduce youth unemployment. In Colombia, the *Emprender* (start-up) fund, administered by the National Service for Training (SENA), has been set up in order to support young people to receive vocational training and start up their own businesses (ILO, 2006).

Moreover, there has also been an increase in the number of Higher Technology Institutes (*Institutos Superiores Tecnológico*, ISTS) over recent years. Such institutes give the opportunity to secondary-school leavers to learn transferable skills by attending short-term courses. A number of students are fully or partially sponsored by their current or potential employers. Moreover, students can also benefit from an educational loan (*créditos educativos*), which they have to pay back during a set period of employment time after graduation. This post-secondary education training is often described as being far from adequate because of the lack of facilities, the use of outdated teaching methods and the poor relationship between them and the industrial sector. These institutes rely on business enterprises and other non-governmental bodies for funding. For example, Peru's TECUP generated more than US$18 million from 175 enterprises in sponsorship, and US$13.6 million in external funding from bodies such as the Inter-American Development Bank, the European Union, the Canadian government, the German state of Baden Württemberg, and the Open University in Cataluña in Spain. Also, in Brazil, PLANFOR was introduced in 1996 in order to improve the skills and knowledge of the unemployed, the unsecure workforce, small entrepreneurs, and the self-employed. According to a study by Marshall (2004: 33), more than 11 million workers were trained under the PLANFOR programme between 1996 and 2001, but the amount was 'short of the envisaged 15 million or 20% of the labour force each year'.

Management education and training

In countries where there are few highly qualified and well-trained managers, many employees try to make it to the top through promotions. However, many promotions are made on the basis of loyalty, hard work, managerial judgement and achievements rather than management qualifications and managerial experience. Recent economic reforms have required managers to have up-to-date free market economic skills and to think strategically in turbulent times. Except for a limited number of large national and multinational companies, most employers are unable to provide the training they need to meet the demands of the new South American economies. National governments have resorted to international organizations such as the UNDP (United Nations Development Programmes) for technical and financial support to deliver management training programmes to managers, mainly from public sector institutions and state-owned organizations. As a result, a number of management training centres supported financially by international organizations have been set up in various countries (Ducci, 1997). However, as Ducci (1997: 174) points out, 'although large and medium-sized enterprises could solve the problem within the enterprises themselves, or with the help of private training agencies and specialized advisory services, small enterprises could not'. There is more to be done in order to train current and potential managers to learn the skills and the knowledge needed to manage organizations in the newly reformed economies of South America.

Read the passage entitled 'Training and Development' in Chapter 7 (Japan and South Korea). What (a) similarities and (b) differences can you find between the Japanese and South American approaches to training?

Rewards and remuneration

Before the economic reforms introduced by most of South American countries in the 1990s, workers were rewarded according to state-imposed pay policies that were used 'essentially as a means of compensating for loss of purchasing power, by means of diverse and sometimes complex indexation mechanisms' (ILO, 2006: 67). Since the 1990s South American employers have been allowed to use a wide variety of monetary and non-monetary rewards, especially when they need to attract and retain skilled and competent employees. In order to control inflation, neither the governments nor employers have been in favour of rewarding high wages. Although there is a minimum wage in most countries it has become increasingly irrelevant as basic pay is coming to be individually agreed between employers – especially in the SMEs, who may have very little respect for employment laws and have employees who are thankful just to be employed.

Large national and international companies have introduced performance-related pay but performance appraisal has not been properly implemented. The wage gap between the educated (professionals and managers) and the non-educated and unskilled workers is quite high and is widening (Elvira and Davila, 2005c). The more educated and skilled the employee, the better the reward. Casanova (2005: 2182) confirms that 'as the skill differential between those with university education and those without increased, the pay gap between higher-skilled workers and lower-skilled ones has also been widening'. South American countries are still characterized by unjust distribution of wealth (the gap between the rich and the poor has been widening), unacceptable levels of poverty as the majority of the population is under the poverty line, job insecurity because of the high level of unemployment, an increasing number of self-employed, and a large number of people living on work in the informal sector.

Minimum wage

The minimum wage in South America is traditionally set for political and social reasons rather than just economic ones. Governments have often used it as a means of redistribution of national wealth and of reducing income inequality in societies where the majority of the population is poor. The basic pay in the majority of countries is the minimum wage that is normally decided by

Table 18.4 South American countries with a national minimum wage (2007)

Country	Level of minimum wage (MW) income (PPP in US$)	Level of MW/GDP per capita %	Changes in minimum wages (MW) over the GDP per capita (2001–7) %
Argentina	553	49.92	16.73
Bolivia	199	59.60	−17.36
Brazil	267	33.07	5.39
Chile	377	32.43	−11.39
Colombia	389	69.41	−8.99
Costa Rica	446	51.95	−8.35
Ecuador	443	73.83	−9.24
Guatemala	335	85.58	11.43
Paraguay	569	152.23	94.62
Peru	326	50.14	−16.42
Uruguay	219	22.62	4.91
Venezuela	382	37.70	−12.05

Source: ILO, *Global Wage Report* 2008/9, IL0: Geneva, pp. 90–1.

the government after taking into consideration changes in the price index of necessary commodities and the conditions of the national economy. For example, in Chile wages are adjusted every two years in relation to 'increases in GDP, thereby ensuring that the poorest segment of the population also feels that it is benefiting from growth' (ILO, 2006: 68). In Brazil, minimum wage increases are negotiated annually between the state, employers' associations and employee (trade union) organizations. This is becoming the norm in the majority of South American countries. The minimum wages of most countries have not increased, and have even decreased, in relation to the increases in GPD since 2001 (see Table 18.4).

Rewards and the family

When it comes to pay and employment benefits and allowances, the family plays a significant role, especially in pay rises and promotion decisions (Abarca et al., 1998; Elvira and Davila, 2005b). If it were not for their families, many employees would not have been employed. As explained earlier, many people are employed through recommendations by relatives and friends. Also, many people work in small and medium size enterprises that are owned by family members who determine the type and level of rewards they receive for the jobs they do.

Pay inequalities

The wage gap between the educated and the non-educated is to some extent justified, but inequalities in pay also exist in relation to gender and ethnic background. Despite the introduction of laws that forbid discrimination in rewards on the basis of race, gender, nationality and ethnic background, many female employees are paid much less than their male counterparts, and those from indigenous races are paid much less than those from mixed or white races. For example, 'in Peru mixed race workers earn 70 per cent less than white workers, and indigenous workers 40 per cent less than mixed race workers, which is clear evidence of discrimination within the labour market' (ILO, 2006: 18). Female employees earn about 66 per cent of the monthly wage of their male counterparts (ILO, 2006: 12).

Limited employment benefits

In South America, many workers have no contract of employment and they are easily hired on a temporary basis in the informal sector and in SMEs: most of them do not receive the benefits and the allowances to which they are legally entitled (Barrientos, 1999; Ferrer and Riddell, 2009). Most of those who work get no more than basic pay, while those who do not work get either no or very little unemployment benefits.

Performance appraisal

The liberalization of South American economies has necessitated the reform of the rewards system. This has meant that employers have had to introduce performance-related pay and to implement forms of performance appraisal. However, it has not been easy to implement performance appraisal because of social and cultural influences. According to Elvira and Davila (2005b: 2168), reward systems in Latin American countries 'could become contentious when based on performance appraisal' because 'the impact of performance appraisals is tinted by a work culture that avoids conflicts between superior and subordinates'. Performance appraisal is often avoided by employees and is rarely used by managers, especially in family-owned SMEs. In large companies where performance management and performance-related pay have been introduced, the process has often not been effective: performance appraisal may not be objective or may just be an administrative process. The main reasons for this is lack of awareness by all employees of the importance of performance appraisal for organizational success, and the culture of avoiding conflict between managers and their subordinates over reward issues.

Employee relations

Each South American country has its own industrial relations system, but they have much in common when it comes to trade union organization and structure. Employment laws differ slightly, depending on the type of government and the level of industrialization of each country. Many of them are in effect little more than just ink on paper and have been introduced in response to pressure from international organizations, mainly the International Labour Organization (ILO), the International Confederation of Free Trade Unions (ICFTU), the World Federation of Trade Unions (WFTU), and the World Confederation of Labour (WCL). Employers can easily avoid, if not ignore, the implementation of employment laws and regulations. A number of reports have shown 'evidence of frequent violations of fundamental rights at work' (ILO, 2006: 11). The number of complaints submitted to the Committee on Freedom of Association in relation to employees denied freedom of association increased from 164 to 194 between 1995 and 2005, and there has been a significant decline in the cases covered by collective agreements (ILO, 2006).

Moreover, in countries such as Argentina, Colombia and Peru, the economic reforms introduced in the 1990s have given more power to employers than employees. For example, employers are allowed not to recognize trade unions and to recruit and dismiss employees easily. Also, 'in many cases, social protection mechanisms providing pensions, health care and occupational accident and illness cover were abandoned' (ILO, 2006: 3). Overall, the recent economic reforms have weakened trade unions' power and undermined the process of collective agreements.

Trade unions

Until the mid-1990s, most trade unions in South America were either banned or tightly controlled by the state. In most cases, trade unions had no alternative but to align themselves with the ruling party and become part of the government's organizational and administrative institutions. Such state-controlled trade unions weakened the ability of the working classes to express freely their legitimate grievances. Many of the ordinary members of the trade union movement became isolated and intimidated by trade union leaders who became preoccupied with issues of state interest, rather than representing the interests of the workers. With the introduction of economic and political reforms, and the relaxation of state control of trade union activities, many trade unions have had to change their role in response to national and international pressure.

However, the new role of trade unions is more cooperative and proactive than adversarial. 'Instead of pressuring employers to improve working conditions under these difficult competitive circumstances, some unions have proactively offered alternatives that would benefit both the company and employment by reducing manufacturing related costs, not labour costs' (Elvira and Davila, 2005c: 2268). In the majority of South American countries, workers are now entitled to form and join trade unions, though most unions are still under the control of the state and many of them have very little impact on employee relations.

In Argentina, all workers except military personnel have a constitutional right to join and form trade unions at industry, company or branch level, but for a trade union to be recognized it has to be officially registered. It is not easy, however, for a trade union to be registered because of bureaucratic procedures and political prejudices. A number of trade union applications have been refused registration. For example, the CTA (*Central de los Trabajadores Argentinos*) has repeatedly been denied official recognition (ILO, 2007). Similarly, in Brazil, all workers, with the exception of the military, the fire fighters, the uniformed police and those in government services, are allowed by the constitution and the labour code to form and join trade unions, but according to the *unicidade* system, or the geographically based single union system, each territorial area (region) can only have one trade union per occupational or economic activity. This has made it difficult to organize national trade union federations and centres. Although there are various federal laws that recognize many of the confederations that were established after the 1980s, the federal high court recognizes only those unions that come under the *unicidade* system.

Collective bargaining

In the majority of South American countries collective bargaining is a procedural activity that takes place between the management of the organization and employee representatives (trade unions) at the national, regional, provincial or organizational level. The process has changed from negotiation over the terms and conditions of employment to cooperation over issues such as cost reduction, productivity improvement, and eradication of child labour (Elvira and Davila, 2005c). However, in some countries only selected trade unions are allowed to engage in collective bargaining with their employers. For example, in Argentina only the trade union that is certified by the Ministry of Labour as 'union personality' is allowed to engage in collective bargaining activities. To become a certified 'union personality', the union has to be officially registered, have a membership of more than 20 per cent of the workers in the organization, and be a major trade union representing workers in the relevant industry within a given geographical area. Also, only collective agreements that are approved by the Ministry of Labour become legally binding.

Industrial action

In most South American countries, the right to take industrial action in the form of strikes and lockouts is allowed in private sector enterprises and selected non-strategic state-owned organizations. For example in Argentina the right to strike is guaranteed by article 14b of the national constitution. In Brazil, the right to strike is provided by the 1988 constitution to all workers except those in the services, where trade unions are not allowed. However, the constitution contains a number of restrictions on how, where and when strikes are permitted. Since such restrictions are open to different interpretations, it has often not been possible for workers in both public and private sector organizations to exercise their right to industrial action. However, in countries where trade unions are well organized they do take industrial action and organize effective strikes. In May 2007 Volkswagen Brazil was forced, following a six-day strike, to cancel its plans to dismiss 1,800 employees, and agreed to start negotiations with the unions to reach a satisfactory agreement.

Settlement of industrial disputes

Settlement of industrial disputes depends on the type of legislative system and employment laws of each country. Currently the majority of South American countries use a combination of conciliation and arbitration processes. However, in most cases the government, rather than a member of an independent body, appoints the conciliator or the arbitrator. Collective agreements become legally binding only when approved by a government institution such as the Ministry of Labour.

Summary

1 The Latin American approach to management is the outcome of common past experiences and current challenges of most of the countries in the region. The approach is described as a unique hybrid management system that characterizes business management in South America.
2 The gradual and partial success of economic reforms became apparent only after 2005, when most of the South American countries entered a period of recovery and economic growth as a result of increased exports and a move from agriculture-based to more industrialized and service-oriented economies.
3 The current democratization process and political stability in most Latin American countries is fragile. There is a risk of reverting to military rule and dictatorship.
4 Religious symbols and rituals are very important in people's lives in South America. People value family ties and personal relationships at work and in all aspects of society.
5 High levels of unemployment, especially among young people; agricultural employment; declining public sector employment; informal sector employment; self-employment; and short-term employment characterize the current labour markets in South America.
6 The Latin American approach to management and organization may be described as humanistic or person-centred, but also centralized, authoritarian, paternalistic and interactive.

7 The recruitment and selection of employees occurs mainly through word of mouth and personal contacts, though many large state-owned companies and multinational companies operating in South America tend to hire their employees through the use of traditional recruitment and selection methods.

8 Levels of education and training are not yet sufficient to meet the requirements of a modern workforce.

9 Since the 1990s, South American employers have been allowed to use a wide variety of monetary and non-monetary rewards, Although there is a minimum wage in most countries, it has become increasingly irrelevant as basic pay is often individually agreed.

10 Recent economic reforms have weakened trade union power and undermined the process of collective agreements.

Revision questions

Chapter 1 provides a review task designed to consolidate your learning from this chapter. Please see Box 1.2.

In addition, the following questions are designed to help you revise this chapter.

1 What seem to you the three main characteristics of the South American approach to management? What do you consider to be the main strengths and weaknesses of this approach?

2 Imagine you are a Spanish expatriate working in Argentina. Write a memo to the head office of your company summarizing the labour market in the host country and the main implications for potential investments.

3 Imagine you are an HR manager of a French company in Brazil. Write a brief report to the company's board of directors in Paris summarizing the similarities and differences in HRM functions you have found between France and Brazil.

References

Abarca, N., Majluf, N. and Rodriguez, D. (1998) 'Identifying management in Chile: a behavioural approach', *International Studies of Management & Organizations*, 28(2): 18–37.

Barrientos, S. (1999) 'Women's employment, agribusiness in Latin America – Free trade or fair?' *Employment Studies Paper no. 26*, Working Paper Series, University of Hertfordshire Business School, UK.

Casanova, L. (2005) 'Latin America: economic and business context', *International Journal of Human Resource Management*, 16(12): 2173–88.

Ducci, M.A. (1997) 'New challenges to vocational training authorities: lessons from the Latin American experience', *International Journal of Manpower*, 18(1/2): 160–84.

Elvira, M.M. and Davila, A. (2005a) 'Culture and human resource management in Latin America', in Elvira, M.M. and Davila, A. (eds), *Managing Human Resources in Latin America: An Agenda for International Leaders*, Oxford: Routledge, 3–24.

Elvira, M.M. and Davila, A. (2005b) 'Special research issue on human resource management in Latin America', *International Journal of Human Resource Management*, 16(12): 2164–72.

Elvira, M.M. and Davila, A. (2005c) 'Emergent directions for human resource management research in Latin America', *International Journal of Human Resource Management*, 16(12): 2265–82.

Ernst, C. (2005a) 'Trade liberalization, export orientation and employment in Argentina, Brazil and Mexico', *ILO Employment Strategy Papers*, paper 2005/15, Employment Analysis Unit, Employment Strategy Department, ILO: Geneva.

Ernst, C. (2005b) 'The FDI–employment link in a globalizing world: the case of Argentina, Brazil and Mexico', *ILO Employment Strategy Papers*, paper 2005/17, Employment Analysis Unit, Employment Strategy Department, ILO: Geneva.

Ferrer, A.M. and Riddell, C.W. (2009) *Unemployment Insurance Savings Accounts in Latin America: Overview and Assessment*, Social Protection Discussion Paper Series No. 0910, The World Bank. Available online at: http://siteresources.worldbank.org/SOCIALPROTECTION/Resources/SP-Discussion-papers/Labor-Market-DP/0910.pdf, accessed on 20 Sep. 2010.

Garibaldi de Hilal, V.A., Wetzel, U. and Ferreira, V. (2009) 'Organizational culture and performance: a Brazilian case', *Management Research News*, 32(2): 99–119.

Gomes, R.C. and Gomes, L.O.M. (2009) 'Depicting the arena in which Brazilian local government authorities make decisions: what is the role of stakeholders?', *International Journal of Public Sector Management*, 22(2): 76–90.

Hofstede, G. (2001) *Culture's Consequences: International differences in work related values*, 2nd edn, London: Sage.

ILO (International Labour Organization) (2006) *Decent Work in the Americas: An Agenda for the Hemisphere, 2006–15*, Report of the Director-General, 16th American Regional Meeting, Brasilia, May 2006, ILO: Geneva.

ILO (International Labour Organization) (2007) *Global Wage Report 2008/9*, ILO: Geneva.

ILO-IPEC (2005) *Building the Future, Investing in Children: An Economic Study of the Costs and Benefits of Eradicating Child Labour in Latin America*, San José: Costa Rica.

Marshall, A. (2004) 'Labour market policies and regulations in Argentina, Brazil and Mexico: programmes and impacts', *ILO Employment Strategy Papers*, paper no. 2004/13, Employment Analysis Unit, Employment Strategy Department, ILO: Geneva.

Ogliastri, E., Ruiz, J. and Martinez, I. (2005) 'HRM in Colombia', in Elvira, M.M. and Davila, A. (eds), *Managing Human Resources in Latin America: an agenda for international leaders*, Oxford: Routledge, Chapter 9.

Olivas-Luján, R.M., Monserrat, I.S., Ruiz-Gutierrez, A.J., Greenwood, A.R., Gómez, M.S., Murphy Jr, F.E. and Bastos F. Santos, M.N. (2009) *Employee Relations*, 31(3): 227–44.

Parnell, A.J. (2008) 'Strategy execution in emerging economies: assessing strategic diffusion in Mexico and Peru', *Management Decision*, 46(9): 1277–98.

Renwick, D. (2009) 'The origins of employee wellbeing in Brazil: an exploratory analysis', *Employee Relations*, 31(3): 312–21.

Rodríguez, D.M. and René Ríos, F. (2009) 'Paternalism at a crossroads: labour relations in Chile in Transition', *Employee Relations*, 31(3): 322–33.

Rodriguez, K.J. and Gomez, F.C. (2009) 'HRM in Chile: the impact of organisational culture', *Employee Relations*, 31(3): 276–94.

UNDP (United Nations Development Programme) (2004) *Democracy in Latin America: Towards a Citizen's Democracy*, Buenos Aires.

World Economic Forum (2005) *Global Competitiveness Report 2004–5*, WEF: Geneva.

Part V

Case Study: Making Poverty History

In September 2000 world leaders gathered at a United Nations meeting to pledge to eradicate world poverty. They agreed on a set of eight targets, called the Millennium Development Goals (MDGs), to be met by 2015. They were to:

1   Reduce the proportion of people living in poverty (on less than $1 a day) and malnutrition by 50 per cent;
2   Ensure that all children are able to complete primary education;
3   Eliminate gender disparity in primary and secondary education;
4   Cut the under-five death rate by two-thirds;
5   Reduce the maternal mortality rate by three-quarters;
6   Halt the spread of and begin to reduce HIV/AIDS and other diseases;
7   Cut the proportion of people without sustainable access to safe drinking water and sanitation by 50 percent;
8   Reform aid and trade with special treatment for the poorest countries.

However, five years later the Human Development Report (UNDP, 2005), entitled *International Cooperation at a Crossroads: Aid, Trade and Security in an Unequal World*, found that very little progress had been made: there were still more than 1,200 children dying of poverty every hour, about 2.5 billion people (40 per cent of the world's population) living on less than $2 a day, and more than 10.7 million children dying before their fifth birthday each year.

The report sought to establish the scale of the challenge that would be facing the world over the coming years to 2015. It focused on three major areas – aid, trade and security – where cooperation and action were needed to meet the MDGs. It stated that international aid or development assistance suffers from underfinancing and poor quality, international trade is conducted in unequal and unfair conditions, and the poorest countries are the most affected by a failure to prevent conflict or to seize opportunities for peace in an increasingly unsafe world. The report emphasized that the cause of world poverty is very human and includes factors such as inappropriate economic policies, ineffective and insufficient aid, local and regional conflicts, and continuous debt. Nelson Mandela was reported as saying: 'Massive poverty and obscene inequality are such terrible scourges of our times – times in which the world boasts breathtaking advances in science, technology, industry and wealth accumulation – that they have to rank alongside slavery and apartheid as social evils' (cited in the UNDP, 2005).

The timing of the Human Development Report (HDR) coincided with a global campaign to make poverty something of the past. The campaign was led by international charities, religious groups, trade unions, artists and musicians, and human rights activists to put pressure on and to lobby world leaders in general and the heads of the major industrial economies (G8) in particular before their summit meeting in Gleneagles, Scotland, in July 2005. The G8 Summit meeting provided an opportunity to put pressure on the leaders of the richest countries in the world to take immediate action to eradicate poverty from the world. They vowed to end export subsidies, to give more aid for development projects in countries in need, and to waive the repayment of unpaid debts by some of the poorest countries in the world. Their pledges were widely welcomed and were seen as a positive step by governments towards the eradication of poverty. In this respect, the Band Aid founder Bob Geldof said: 'The reality is that only politics created this dilemma and only politics can resolve it'.

This case study is designed to indicate the extent to which progress has been made in relation to aid, trade and security since the G8 Summit meeting in 2005, to explore the means by which poverty can really become history, and to discuss the managerial and organizational problems and challenges for the achievement of such an objective.

Aid, trade and security

The three main elements required for the achievement of the Millennium Development Goals (MDGs) and to eradicate poverty from this world are the effective use of international aid, fair international trade, and peace within and between countries. These have yet to be met. Poverty is generally defined as a situation in which a major part of the population lives at or below income sufficient to meet their basic needs for food and shelter. Currently, many poor countries suffer from depressed economic conditions, unstable political regimes, social and political conflict and unrest, population growth, rural–urban migration, the exodus of intellectuals, increased unemployment, and an unskilled workforce.

The need for sustainable and developmental aid programmes

More than 40 percent of the world's population live in poverty and more than two-thirds of the world's poorest depend on foreign aid. The HDR asserted that aid could only be effective if invested in building human capital by improving the economic infrastructure and establishing institutions for effective education and health care. In other words, as the Chinese proverb says: 'don't give me a fish today and I will starve tomorrow, teach me how to fish and I will never starve.'

The HDR (2005) states that when the MDGs were agreed the development assistance glass was three-quarters empty and leaking because the international aid budgets had been subject to deep cuts. Now the glass is almost empty: most of the aid sources, public and private, have dried up. Aid programmes have only been able to respond to emergencies and short-term crises rather than investing in sustainable long-term development projects.

The need for fair international trade and more foreign direct investment

Unfair trade regulations and structural inequalities within and between countries have combined to reduce the potential for human development. The trade policies of rich countries continue to deny the poor countries and poor people their fair share of global wealth and prosperity (HDR, 2005). Most of the developing countries (LDCs) in the world are endowed with rich natural resources (such as oil, gas, diamonds, uranium, copper, iron, tea, coffee, sugar, fish and forestry), yet they lack the capital and advanced technology, as well as entrepreneurial and technical skills, required for sustainable economic development. They have been unable to attract foreign investments that are badly needed for the creation of jobs and enhance their economies.

According to Musila and Sigué (2006: 577), to reduce the level of poverty in African countries by half they should achieve and maintain an economic growth at an average GDP rate of at least 7 per cent. To achieve this level of growth, they 'need huge investment injection in various sectors of Africa's economies such as agriculture, industry, education, and health' (577). The share of FDI to Africa represents less than 10 per cent of the world FDI. Still only few African countries benefit from such investment because most of them go to the most prosperous and developed countries rather than to the poor ones. 'About 63 per cent of the FDI directed to Africa during 1995–9 was concentrated in only five countries – Angola, Egypt, Morocco, Nigeria and South Africa' (578). Most of the other countries are not attractive to foreign investors for many reasons, including political instability, lack of economic infrastructure, poor incentives for investment, corruption and conflicts.

Many poor countries depend on a single product such as tea, coffee, bananas and coco for exports. The prices of these products are subject to fluctuations in the world financial market. The economies of such countries are vulnerable to changes in world markets. In the absence of fair international trade policies, the poor countries are disadvantaged and are unable to compete with the rich and industrialized nations. Also, their need for economic development has required the use of modern technology and foreign investment but created problems of technology transfer, negative balance of payments as they import more than they export, organizational restructuring, high levels of inflation, increasing the need for foreign currency, more foreign debts, a lack of consumer goods, bad living conditions, and social and political unrest. In addition, there are serious regional disparities in wealth.

The need for peace, equality and justice

One of the main causes of poverty is war. Most of the poor countries suffer from civil wars, conflicts with their neighbours, or foreign occupation. Wars disrupt the livelihoods of people, create economic chaos, reduce foreign and local investments and increase unemployment. The Human Development Report (UNDP, 2005) puts the blame on conflicts for poor nutrition and public health, devastation of livelihoods, poor standards of education, and setbacks in prospects for economic growth. The uncertainty and risk created by wars is a major deterrent to the flow of foreign investment to many poor countries.

Social and economic symptoms such as poverty, unemployment and crime are also exacerbated by a lack of equality, justice, and fair and effective state welfare systems. As the gap between the poor and the rich widens, social unrest and the incidence of crime increase. Being poor often means malnutrition, bad housing conditions, poor health and poor or no education. This is compounded by poor or non-existent means of public transport and limited health services. As a result, corruption or personal gain from one's status or position is seen in some poor countries as a social right and privilege.

How can the three elements identified above – effective aid, trade, and peace – be achieved? It follows from the discussion provided in the preceding five chapters of this book that the root problem to achieving economic growth and prosperity in LDCs is managerial and organizational.

Management and organization

From a study of globalization, growth and poverty, Akoum (2008: 228) concluded that 'it is not simply scarcity of resources that is plaguing the poor, but it is rather the misuse of resources and their improper distribution'. The actual situation of management and organizations in LDCs is a complex phenomenon, especially where opportunities for development, in terms of labour and raw materials, are available but not properly used. The main weakness in such organizations is the inadequate use of resources and the lack of competent managers and efficient management practices. Unnecessary bureaucratic procedures and bad managerial policies and practices have hindered the prospects for successful organizational changes.

Moreover, the social and political prestige of corrupt leaders, the belief in master and servant relationships, and the cultural values of paternalism have contributed to the establishment of organizations that are often state-controlled and centrally planned, culturally bound and politically determined, poorly designed and badly managed, and in need of expertise, experience, technology, finance, good management, and a trained workforce. These organizations have become characterized by: 1) low organizational performance and poor productivity; 2) inability to provide continuous supervision of business operations; 3) failure to maintain equipment regularly; 3) limited prosperity to undertake innovation and creative initiatives; 4) strategic decisions being made by individuals to achieve personal goals; 5) low general standards of accounting, record keeping and management control; 6) unawareness of the need for managerial training and development; 7) centralization of authority and limited delegation of responsibility; 8) ineffective and unwise employment policies; and 9) rampant acts of nepotism and corruption.

There is a need for modern and up-to-date management knowledge and skills to deal with the existing managerial and organizational problems by adopting and then adapting new managerial thinking to meet the requirements of change, encouraging the exchange of managerial experiences through all means including job rotation and study abroad, developing executive and line managers through regular training schemes at home and abroad; and encouraging freedom of expression, speech and innovation. To eradicate poverty, new jobs have to be created through local and foreign investments in order to reduce unemployment, because unemployment in many countries means no income and hence living in poverty.

Conclusion

Poverty is man-made and its eradication is an ethical, economic, social and political obligation of humankind. It is one of the main challenges for governments throughout the world. However, although it has been five years since the G8 Summit meeting in Gleneagles, and there are only five years to the target date (2015) for meeting the MDGs, very little progress has been made towards making poverty history. In fact poverty is now a reality in more countries than before. The whole world has become under threat of a serious economic recession that has been created by an international financial crisis. Despite some fair-trade initiatives and the writing off of some poor countries' unpaid debts, most of the poor countries have become poorer than before.

Questions

1 Explain the importance of meeting each of the eight MDGs.
2 Discuss critically each of the three elements (effective aid, trade, and security) for the eradication of poverty. What or whom do you blame for the lack of progress in achieving each of the three elements?
3 Analyse the main characteristics of management and organization in developing countries. Try to go beyond the case study by using examples from what you have read or experienced.
4 Discuss the extent to which the current management policies and practices in poor countries are the main cause of their poverty.
5 To what extent would you agree or disagree with the statement that 'rich countries become richer as long as the poor countries become poorer'.

References

Akoum, F.I. (2008) 'Globalization, growth, and poverty: the missing link', *International Journal of Social Economics*, 35(4): 226–38.

Casanova, L. (2005) 'Latin America: economic and business context', *International Journal of Human Resource Management*, 16(12): 2173–88.

Musila, J.W. and Sigué, S.P. (2006) 'Accelerating foreign direct investment flow to Africa: from policy statements to successful strategies', *Managerial Finance*, 32(7): 577–93.

UNDP (2005) *Human Development Report 2005*, New York: Hoechstetter Printing.

Part VI

Conclusion

19

Emerging Issues and Future Challenges in Managing Across Cultures

▰▰▰▰▰▰▰ **LEARNING OUTCOMES** ▰▰▰▰▰▰▰

This chapter is designed to help you to analyse and discuss critically, from the point of view of managing across cultures, the following issues:

1   Management of diversity implementation and of equal opportunities policies;
2   Adoption of flexible working practices and family friendly policies and ethical issues arising therefrom;
3   The application of information technology;
4   Environmental challenges.

Introduction

We have seen from the preceding chapters that a number of management and organizational issues, policies and practices are common to most countries in the world. They include such issues as diversity, quality, flexibility, equality, ethics and information technology. There are also common labour market trends, problems and challenges such as unemployment, the employment of women, immigrant labour, the older workforce, and skills shortages. Such issues and challenges have become increasingly important to national and international managers operating in different countries. This chapter outlines how crucial the management of diversity and equality are to organizational effectiveness and how important the use of flexible working practices and the adoption of family friendly policies have become to gaining organizational competitive advantage. It will also discuss the need for international managers to understand ethical and non-ethical behaviours and practices when managing resources in different countries. Other topics include the use of the internet and the need to develop in employees a sense of environmental awareness. The increasing use of information and communications technologies has transformed the ways by which managers operate across cultures and borders. Also, one of the challenges facing managers in different countries is not just how to save the 'Earth', the environment, but how to make employees aware of environmental issues in their workplaces. Thus this chapter outlines an agenda for future research in cross-cultural management.

Managing diversity

It is very unusual these days to find organizations that are made of a uniform workforce where all employees are members of the same race, ethnic background, nationality, age, gender and physical abilities. Therefore, since no organization's workforce is the same it means there is a diverse workforce that has to be managed effectively (Carell et al., 2000). However, the strategic approach to managing diversity may differ from one country to another and from one organization to another depending on the composition of the workforce, the labour market trends, the size of organizations, the level of state intervention, the type of employment policies in place, the level of trade union power and influence, and the employment legislation in force.

There are various interpretations of what constitutes the management of diversity in different societies. In some societies it may be no more than 'a proportional representation of various demographic and social groups in the workplace. To others, it may involve overcoming cultural prejudice and instilling new values about difference in the organization' (Prasad and Mills, 1997: 13), while to others it may be more strategic and involve all the policies and practices that attract and retain a diverse workforce in organizations. Some studies have described it in the context of 'a melting pot' (Davis and Newstrom, 1985), while others call it 'a tossed salad' (Moorhead and Griffin, 1995), but it can be described as no more than a process of looking after 'a garden of many flowering plants'.

Describing the importance of managing diversity in the USA, Davis and Newstrom (1985: 406) wrote: 'The United States historically has been called a "melting pot" of people from all parts of the world, so it is important to give these people equal access to jobs regardless of their backgrounds. In this way they have a fair chance to earn their way into the mainstream of society and become self-sufficient.'

The above metaphor is both too general and too specific. It is general because it refers to all the people from around the world who seek employ- ment and possibly citizenship in the United States. It is no more than a political statement that does not explain how a diverse workforce can be man- aged at the organizational level. At the same time it is too specific because it refers to a specific socio-economic context, which is the United States, and it does not explain how multinational companies manage diversity in different countries.

Commenting on Davis and Newstrom's (1985) interpretation of managing diversity, Moorhead and Griffin (1995: 523) argue that 'rather than a melting pot, the workplace now resembles a tossed salad of different flavours, colors, and textures. Rather than assimilate those who are different into a single organizational culture, the current view is that organizations need to celebrate the differences and use the variety of talents, perspectives, and backgrounds of all employees.' They also state that 'valuing diversity is not just the right thing to do for workers, it is the right thing to do for the organization, finan- cially and economically' (Moorhead and Griffin, 1995: 526).

Moorhead and Griffin's (1995) interpretation of managing diversity pro- vides a good description of the type of diverse workforce that exists in con- temporary organizations. However, although it emphasizes the importance of managing diversity to the organization and to the individual employee, it does not really help with how different employers in different countries can man- age diversity effectively. In other words, using the salad analogy, how are the different flavours, colours, and textures mixed together to make the salad taste better!

Alternatively, managing diversity in any organization in any country may be described as a process of looking after a garden of different types of flowering plants. The issue is not so much the existence of many different type of plants, or many different types of employees in the organization, but rather looking after them properly and effectively. Different types of plant require different types and amounts of fertilizer and water, sunlight, warmth, etc. Similarly, different employees have different needs. Managing diversity involves looking after every individual employee just like looking after every plant in the gar- den. This process requires managing change effectively and adapting to changes in the workforce to meet organizational objectives.

If managing diversity is to succeed in an organization it is vital for employers to recognize the fact that they have to change to adapt to employee differences rather than just expecting employees to fit in with existing practices. It is not only advisable that an organization adapt to diversities in the labour market, it is essential for their long-term survival, because 'failure to adjust to the growing diversity of the workforce can result in conflict, low productivity, absenteeism and turnover' (Rosenfeld and Wilson, 1999: 406).

Thus it should be recognized that managing diversity in any organization in any country or in any society requires:

1 The treatment of all employees on an individual level. Managers should recognize that differences in people can bring value to the organization when employees are given individual consideration with individual solutions to their particular needs. As Kandola and Fullerton (1994: 8) state, 'harnessing these differences will create a productive environment in which everybody feels valuable and their talents are fully utilised in such a way that organizational goals are met'.

2 An appreciation of the distinction between managing diversity and equal opportunities in organizations. It will be seen in the next section that managing equality is fundamentally different from managing diversity.

ACTIVITY 1

One of the problems that multinational companies face is whether or not to implement a standardized diversity programme across subsidiaries in different countries. In your opinion how should multinational companies manage their diverse workforce? Discuss how and why they should use standardized or different diversity programmes in different countries.

Managing equality

As we have seen in the preceding chapters, most countries in the world have equal opportunities policies in place, yet discrimination still exists at different levels. Employers are pressed by national and international employment laws to treat their job applicants and employees equally and fairly. Many employers in different countries claim to be equal opportunities employers but they still discriminate against women, people from ethnic minorities, older people and people with special needs. It seems that stereotyping is the underlying cause of discrimination and arises from a need to impose personal or group desires on others. We have seen from the preceding chapters that there has been a significant growth in female employment and in the employment of immigrant labour globally, but it is still the case that those most discriminated against by national and multinational employers in many countries are women and people from ethnic minorities, especially in promotion and pay rewards. According to Adler (2002: 743), 'most global managers know their companies can no longer afford to ignore potential talent "simply because it's wearing a skirt" or because it holds a passport different from that of the founding executives'. The growth of gender equality and increasing participation of women in international management and business is increasingly apparent in many multinational companies, but still very limited (Adler, 1997, 2002; Selmer and Leung, 2002; Linehan, 2002; Linehan et al., 2001; Van der Boon, 2003; Taylor et al., 2002).

Employment of women

Although there has been a significant increase in the employment of women in many countries, most women have been discriminated against in employment, promotion and pay. Women not only tend to be employed in low-paid jobs, they are also facing different kinds of unfair discrimination, and the trend is far from establishing real equality between women and their male counterparts in the workplace.

As far as the employment of women in multinational companies is concerned, until the 1990s very little attention was paid to women expatriates as international managers, advisors, consultants or trainers (Caligiuri and Cascio, 1998; Stroh et al., 2000). Most of the literature on expatriation refered to women as partners or spouses of expatriates rather as expatriates themselves.

Frequently cited reasons, which are no more than myths (Adler, 1987), for the low level of women expatriates in international business are:

1 Unwillingness of host country nationals to have Western women as their managers. This may be true in some countries but there is no evidence for a widespread rejection of women expatriates by host country employees. A combination of organizational and socio-cultural factors contribute to the minimal representation of women in expatriate management positions, and most of them have very little to do with the conditions of the host country or its people (Linehan and Scullion, 2001; Linehan et al., 2001). This was supported by studies of female expatriates in Hong Kong (Westwood and Leung, 1994) and in Japan (Taylor and Napier, 1996; Volkmar and Westbrook, 2005: 474). In fact, most of the 'masculine' countries, such as Japan, South Korea, the Middle East and Africa, that promote few of their women into important managerial positions, treat foreign women with the respect they normally bestow to male expatriate managers. Employees tend to open up more to their female managers, resulting in better collaboration, higher employee morale and more productivity (Adler, 1984; 2002; Linehan and Scullion, 2001; Linehan et al., 2001).

2 Unwillingness of women in general to seek international career progression through international assignments. Adler (1984) found that women were as interested in

international assignments as their male colleagues, and that once sent abroad, were as successful, if not more so.

3 Unwillingness of women to work abroad because it was too great a risk for them to work abroad. For example, 'single women were considered to be vulnerable to harassment and the isolation in a foreign land too much for them to bear' (Altman and Shortland, 2001: 141). At the same time married women could not travel without their husbands and their children.

The reality is that many companies have been unwilling to send their female employees abroad (Caligiuri and Cascio, 1998; Altman and Shortland, 2001). Studies found that many female managers believe that companies offer them more limited opportunities to work abroad than they offer to their male counterparts. Multinational companies offer fewer opportunities for women overseas than at home (Adler, 1993, 1997). Research conducted by Linehan (2000) found that although organizations may give women the opportunity for promotion and career development in their home country managerial hierarchy, few women were given the same opportunities through international management assignments. A study by Linehan and Scullion (2001) of 50 senior female managers in Europe found that it was 'much more difficult for female managers to be selected for an international assignment than their male counterparts' (Linehan and Scullion, 2001: 218). For example, home country senior managers did not select married women for international assignments unless they asked for such assignments. They also found that the lack of mentoring and networking relationships had been the most significant informal barriers to women's international career development. They also found a lack of pre-departure training for female expatriates, as only 5 out of the 50 female executives interviewed said they had some pre-departure training for international assignments. Interestingly they found that no partner or family member of the five female executives, who said they had training, had been involved in the pre-departure training (Linehan and Scullion, 2001: 224). Moreover, a study by Selmer and Leung (2002: 353) found that 'although both men and women are hired because they possess required management abilities, a general tendency to neglect executive development, combined with sex role expectations, may create an environment in which women are less likely than men to receive support and developmental opportunities.'

A number of studies (Adler, 1984; Vance et al., 2006; Forster, 1999; Stroh et al., 2000; Altman and Shortland, 2001; Mayrhofer and Scullion, 2002; Selmer and Leung, 2002; Dowling et al., 2008) have documented experiences of female expatriates in different countries and have concluded that assignment location, previous cross-cultural experience, spouse/partner satisfaction, and level of employer support are the factors that determine the success of female expatriate assignments. According to Dowling et al. (2008: 129–30), recent surveys (ORC, 2002; GMAC GRs, 2005) have shown that the level of female employment as expatriates increased significantly but, as Selmer and Leung (2002: 348) state, 'although many companies have re-examined their reluctance to send women abroad, the number of female expatriates is till relatively low, although with an increasing trend'.

Employment of ethnic minorities

We have seen from the preceding chapters that most countries in the world have experienced a rise in migrant labour and the presence of a significant number of people from different nationalities. In theory it seems that both national and multinational companies could benefit from the surplus labour created by immigration and have a pool of labour from different countries to choose from, but in practice they do not or cannot employ people from ethnic minorities because of many national restrictions such as the use of work permits, licences, etc. Hence in many countries, not just in Western countries, ethnic minorities are often the most affected by inequalities and discrimination in work and employment.

Employment of older people

One of the common labour market trends in most of the industrialized countries that are included in this volume is the increasing number of older and healthy people who still have much to offer, as active employees, although they are very often discriminated against in work and employment. The rapid increase in global ageing is 'one of the most important demographic changes in human history' (Powell and Cook, 2009: 388), and it has significant socioeconomic and political implications (Bengtson and Lowenstein, 2003). Therefore lay and academic concern with the potentially increasing net costs of having an older population has burgeoned since the 1970s and has resulted in a raft of theories that have linked age to wider social and economic issues including aspects of age discrimination in work and employment (see Branine and Glover, 1997; Glover and Branine, 2001).

The need for international equal opportunities policies

There is a need for clear and well-understood equal opportunities policies that should be designed to eliminate discrimination on unlawful or unfair grounds and to promote positive action where necessary, to redress the effects of past discrimination and to promote equality in employment. In theory there are many national and international policies that aim to ensure that all existing and potential employees receive equal consideration and that every employee from the top down in the organization is committed to the elimination of unlawful and unfair prejudice. Yet such policies have not resulted in an international working environment where all forms of discrimination or oppressive behaviour are unacceptable. Often such policies have not been translated into practice in recruiting, selecting, training, transferring, treating and rewarding employees.

MINI CASE STUDY 47

Can't Go or Won't Go: Female Expatriates

Although the employment of women managers is on the increase, there are still fewer female than male expatriates. Some employers argue that female employees cannot work effectively abroad because of cultural and environmental differences, while some researchers argue that many female managers are not allowed to work in different countries by their management, family, government, etc.

Question

1 If you were an HR manager of a multinational company, what would you do to promote the employment of women international managers?

Managing flexibility

The concept of flexibility in employment refers, in general, to the process by which the time and patterns of work are arranged in a way that meets employees' and employers' needs. It can be also concluded from the countries covered in this volume that the labour markets of most countries in the world are characterized by the use of flexible working practices and flexible management and organization practices. The rise in the use of flexible working practices is closely related to a number of economic, political and social changes (Nord et al., 2002; Felstead et al., 2002; de Ruyter and Burgess, 2003; De Cieri et al., 2005). Today, the main aim of much organizational change is flexibility, allowing organizations to survive and to be competitive in a complex and uncertain business environment. Organizations of different sectors, sizes and types have been forced by economic, social and political pressures to look for alternative ways of improving their employment relations and their responsiveness to fluctuations in their activities (Pettinger, 1998). The standard pattern of working from 9 a.m. to 5 p.m., five days a week, under a permanent contract, is no more the norm in many industrialized countries. Non-standard ways of employment have been adopted extensively (Lewis and Lewis, 1996).

Organizations operate in a world of increasing globalization and as a result are faced with greater competition, changes in demographic trends, and growing concerns over shortages in skilled labour. The demand for more highly skilled workers and new technologies leads to a reorganization of work and the increasing need for flexible working hours (Pettinger, 1998). Therefore, most countries have experienced a significant increase in part-time work, job sharing, temporary work, flexitime, home-based working, teleworking, freelancing, etc. Such forms of employment have been associated with increased levels of outsourcing, subcontracting, networking, franchising, and niche marketing. Global trends in flexible labour can be seen as a manifestation of the dynamics of international labour markets. There is no doubt that 'labour markets around the world are becoming more segmented, fragmented and fractured' (Felstead and Jewson, 1999: 17). Moreover, the introduction of policies that offer employees the opportunity to balance home and work commitments has become an important part of many companies' strategic commitment to their employees in different countries. For example, Ford's Worklife Initiative provides for transitional work arrangements, flexitime, telecommuting, child care, parenting, care of the elderly, wellness and fitness. Many companies in the US and the EU offer attractive packages aimed at retaining and enticing back employees who cannot work full-time (Nord et al., 2002; Felstead et al., 2002; De Cieri et al., 2005).

Flexible working practices

Flexible working practices such as part-time work, job sharing, temporary work, flexitime, home-based working, etc., are used by employers in order to retain their valued employees and to basically respond to their needs, because they might otherwise have to leave their jobs. However, countries differ in their use of flexible working practices according to their social structures, cultures, employment laws and regulations, and their levels of economic growth (Felstead and Jewson, 1999).

Social processes within labour markets and workplaces are shaped and influenced by relationships between economic institutions and the wider social system. According to Felstead and Jewson (1999), an understanding of the growth in flexible working practices cannot be complete without an analysis of broader societal contexts (welfare systems, family structures and gender relations). In many countries opportunities for working flexibly are still very limited, and when practised they were introduced by private sector and multinational companies because most of their workforce work full-time in public sector organizations. Among the countries of the EU, the Netherlands, which is characterized by a highly regulated market, has the highest proportion of part-time workers (Allan and Daniels, 1999). Similarly, the Scandinavian countries have high levels of part-time and temporary employment. The UK has a high proportion of part-time employees, but most of them are women who have chosen to be so voluntarily for family and domestic reasons, while in other European countries such as France, Germany and Italy it seems that unemployment and government policies have contributed to an increase in part-time employment among women and men of all ages.

Although there is no conclusive evidence of a direct relationship between deregulation of the labour market and flexible employment (Brewster and Scullion, 1997; Standing, 1997), there is some evidence of flexible working practices being introduced as a result of employment legislation aimed at reducing unemployment or creating equal opportunities in employment. 'The governments of European countries such as Germany, France and Spain have been actively involved in the process of regulating and re-regulating their labour markets in order to reduce unemployment' (Branine, 1999: 424). In many Western countries employment legislation concerning the minimum wage, the number of hours worked in a week, redundancy rights and benefits, maternity and paternity provisions, has contributed to the use of flexible working. Such regulations are not new in many developing countries, but their implementation seems to be geared towards full-time employment. We have seen from the preceding chapters of this volume that full-timeness, or working full time, is still the norm in many countries, although part-time work is on the increase.

Family-friendly policies

The main factors that have sparked a growing interest in implementing family-friendly policies include demographic changes, changes in family values and expectations, changes in business needs and objectives, the overlapping roles of work and family, and government legislation. Increasing competition is forcing organizations to consider all methods of improving quality and reducing operating costs. Considerable savings on recruitment and training can be made if employees are encouraged to stay by providing family-friendly policies and flexible working practices. Many national and international organizations have realized that it would be more cost-effective to employ people flexibly by offering them the opportunity to balance work and family commitments, than to lose them and have to recruit and train new ones. What is important for good business is the retention of skilful and experienced employees regardless of their age, gender, ethnic origin or disability. Therefore the implementation of family friendly policies has become a commonplace activity in many industrialized countries over the world.

The term 'family-friendly policies' is used to describe employment policies that may help employees to combine their work and family commitments. These include a wide range of provisions that can be classified into five schemes:

1   Leave for family reasons such as maternity and paternity leave, school holiday leave, wedding and funeral attendance, and breaks as a result of a problem or illness in the family. Maternity leave for a certain time after the birth is a principal right for all women in the world. Some organizations, especially in Western, industrialized countries offer their female employees enhanced conditions in the form of extended leave or additional maternity pay to improve the retention of skilled and experienced employees.
2   Flexible working practices such as job sharing, part-time work, annual hours, home-based working, flexitime, and flexiplace.
3   Career break schemes allow employees to take a break for a specific period and then return to work (Wooding, 1995). They are normally considered for those who have child-care responsibilities, those caring for dependants, those who would like to study, and those who may be involved in voluntary work. This policy may appeal to women who want take a break in order to have a family or those people who may want to update their skills and qualifications.
4   Childcare facilities such as: crèche facilities, vouchers, allowances and holiday provisions; elderly care facilities such as home care visits, club services and medical attendance; and disabled care facilities such as the provision of transport, accessibility, medical help, etc.
5   Special leave arrangements that are granted when employees need to be absent from work in circumstances not covered by sick leave, annual leave, maternity leave, family leave or flexible working arrangements. Instances where such arrangements may be used include bereavement, adoption or domestic problems.

There are many examples of successful implementation of family friendly policies by private and public sector organizations in different countries (Stredwick and Ellis, 1998; Felstead and Jewson, 1999; Dastmalchian and Blyton, 1998; Felstead et al., 2002; De Cieri et al., 2005), but the credibility of the flexibility thesis is widely discussed and heavily criticized (Pollert, 1988a,b; Blossfeld and Hakim, 1997; Nord et al., 2002). There is no doubt that the number of flexible working practices has increased, but, as Payne and Payne (1993) argue, such an increase may be partly in response to the growth in service sector jobs which tend to be non-standard and the growth in demand for flexible working from employees who prefer to work flexibly for various reasons. Flexible working meets the demands of many sections of the population, such as young people studying, older people before and after retirement, people suffering from a partial incapacity to work full time, and those employees with caring responsibilities.

Ethics in managing across cultures

When operating in different countries, international managers have to consider many ethical issues that are influenced by different societies' norms and cultural values. What can be acceptable in one country may be unethical and immoral in another. We have seen in Part V of this book that nepotism, for example, is widely used in many African, Asian and Middle Eastern countries in recruitment and selection, but, although it exists in some Western countries, it is seen as an unprofessional and unacceptable activity. One of the dilemmas that international managers face in different countries is the extent to which they allow the use of culturally determined practices such as *guanxi* in China or *wasta* in Arab countries. Although such practices may be seen as unethical in the home country it is very likely that they will be accepted and practised in the host countries in the best interest of the company's business operations and competitive advantage. For example, a study by Becker and Fritzsche (1987) of different ethical perceptions among American, French and German managers found that 39 per cent of American managers thought that paying money (bribes) for business favours was unethical, whereas only 12 per cent of the French and none of the Germans thought the same.

Moreover, many multinational companies invest in developing countries where labour is cheap and they sometimes employ children and illegal immigrants. The same companies in some countries but not in others see such practices as unethical. In this respect, McVeigh (2007) comments that it is obscene that in the UK people can earn more through loyalty card schemes than the people who produce the goods they buy. Also, Foot and Hook (2008: 354) point out that 'while people in the UK continue to expect clothes and food at cheap prices this is often also achieved at the expense of overseas workers who may be working long hours in poor conditions for less than a living wage'

In addition, many common concepts such as friendship, loyalty, commitment, reliability, delegation, agreement, involvement, participation, etc., are open to different interpretations by people of different cultures. In some countries the line between friendship and work relationships is tacitly drawn, resulting in respect for authority and fair rewards for achievements, but in others, establishing friendship relations overrides work relationships, resulting in nepotism and abuse of status power.

Managing information technologies

Information technologies involving storing, transmitting, exchanging and retrieving information have changed the way people are managed throughout the world. The internet (world-wide) or the intranet (organization based) is simply an electronic device that makes the processing and transfer of information fast and easy. Through the use of this device, information flows between offices and across national borders through a network of computers. It is normally used to support a lot of applications such as the discovery of information (browsing and information retrieval), fast and inexpensive communication (email, instant messaging, blogs, skyping, information transfer) and collaboration (two or more people can work together or share common resources or servers). Computers provide the basic unit for storing, retrieving, processing, sending, receiving, generating and managing information (Turban et al., 1999). The information itself can be in the form of words, numbers, pictures, moving images, graphics and sound. Information is shared via satellite, television, mobile phones and computers.

The use of information technologies has made it possible for organizations to be more flexible and more efficient in times of economic hardship and increasing competition. For example, we have seen from the case study at the end of Part II of this volume how US multinational companies resorted to the use of video-conferencing to reduce the need for travelling. Also, a great example of the international use of the internet occurred when Philips celebrated its 100th anniversary in 1991: the president of the company used a televised world-wide conference to explain the company's prospects to the entire workforce (*The Economist*, 1995). Other uses of the internet and intranet are for entertainment, education and electronic commerce. With the use of the internet every firm becomes international without having to open subsidiaries in other countries. A small company can easily sell its products or provide services throughout the world via the internet.

In short, the use of the internet has changed the way organizations operate and the way employers interact with their customers, suppliers and employees. The spread of information between the headquarters of a multinational company and their employees in different countries is more effective than ever before (Turban et al. 1999; Sparrow et al., 2004). Information flows instantly from one part of the world to another, and a communication network can be created within minutes if not seconds. Managers can have instant access to their employees' personal and contract details, educational and training records, and information on appraisal, discipline, absences, etc.

The applications of information technologies in the management of human resources are significant, wide-ranging and increasingly important. For example:

1 The use of the internet has made it easy for employers to advertise their job vacancies and for applicants to access them. Most organizations have online job applications and they even conduct interviews online or via video-conferencing. Since many people world-wide have access to the internet the reponses from applicants reflect a diversity of people with various backgrounds, expertises, experience and qualifications. According to Brewster et al. (2007: 101–2), the use of the internet allows international organizations to widen their pool of recruitment at relatively low cost, attract specific job applicants with a desired skills match, target sources of graduate recruitment such as MBA career centres, and 'improve on traditional advertising approaches by targeting particular lifestyle or culture-fit groups (such as expatriates or people who consume services similar to those provided by the host firm)'.

2 The application of information technologies has also become a useful tool for national and international organizations to train their employees. Companies use intranets and the internet extensively to educate and train their employees because in this way training costs are reduced and training programmes can reach as many people as possible, even if they are employed in different subsidiaries around the world. There are also a number of software packages that are designed for individual and group learning and for personal self-development in different disciplines.

3 Moreover, the administration of the payroll for employees world-wide has been widely facilitated through the use of computer software and networking technologies. The transfer of cash by means of electronic transfers and other global networks has facilitated not just the way employees are paid, but also the way customers pay for the goods and the services they buy and the way employers pay their suppliers and their clients.

4 Team-working can be enhanced by the use of advanced information and communication technologies. Information can be shared through the internet, issues can be discussed online, and decisions can be made or solutions to problems can be given through video-conferencing, blogging, etc. This IT-based process can result in greater creativity, mutual learning, more rapid response times, effective problem-solving, and so on. Virtual teams can be easily set up, giving instant access to information and immediate exchange of ideas and solutions to work-related performance and quality problems.

5 The use of information and communication technologies can lead to significant reductions in the cost of travelling and associated expenditure on accommodation and subsistence, as well as saving time and effort. A further aspect of flexibility resulting from the use of IT is that multinational companies can relocate work and gain from lower labour and mobility costs (Taylor and McIntosh, 1998).

However, there are a number of political, social, economic and technological factors that affect the international applications of the internet across cultures. For example, not all governments support the use of the internet in all aspects of life. Many countries impose restrictions on internet access. There are also taxation, security and intellectual property issues that differ from one country to another with respect to the use of the internet for domestic and business purposes.

Managing environmental awareness and employee well-being

There has been much debate in recent years about global warming and the need to reduce the level of carbon monoxide gas into the atmosphere. Every government in the world has been asked to take whatever action possible to contribute to saving the planet. The environment has become a concern of everyone on the globe. A number of studies (see, for example, Ramus, 2002; Fernández et al., 2003; Hong et al., 2009) have argued that organizations of all sizes should take innovative environmental action to become sustainable and to contribute effectively to environmental initiatives. Therefore one of the main challenges of managing across cultures is managing environmental awareness and employee well-being. In other words, one of the main tasks of international managers is to make their organizations environmentally friendly and their employees aware of environmental issues. While making employees environmentally aware, international managers have to take care of the well-being of their employees by providing a safe and healthy working environment. This is more easily said than done, because there is very little evidence of multinational companies actively training their employees to be aware of environmental issues in the workplace or doing enough with regard to health and safety of their employees.

Most organizations have in place policies and procedures on health and safety in order to ensure that all the legal requirements are fulfilled for the safety of their employees, customers and visitors, but the risks when operating across cultures are much higher than they may prepare for. The risks are high in developing countries because of poor health services, poor hygiene, and the spread of certain life-threatening diseases. We have seen in Chapter 14 that one of the main problems of management in some African countries is the high level of employees with HIV and AIDS. Also, an increasing risk of managing across cultures is international terrorism. The events that followed the 9/11 attacks, as explained in the Part II case study in this volume, have had profound effects on management across cultures, not just for US companies but for all companies world-wide.

Summary

Issues such as diversity, quality, flexibility, equality, ethics, and information technology have featured throughout this book, though each chapter has revealed a different approach to management. There are also similar labour market trends, problems and challenges, such as unemployment, the employment of women, immirgrant labour, the older workforce, and skills shortages, that all countries have had to deal with in recent years. Such issues and challenges have become increasingly important to national and international managers operating in different countries. The main themes and issues that have emerged in importance in recent years are:

1 The management of diversity and equality has been crucial to organizational effectiveness.
2 The use of flexible working practices and the adoption of family-friendly policies have become important to gaining organizational competitive advantage.
3 International managers need to understand ethical and non-ethical behaviours and practices when managing resources in different countries.
4 The increasing use of information and communications technologies has transformed the ways managers operate across cultures and borders.
5 Managers of contemporary organizations need to develop in employees a sense of environmental awareness to contribute to protecting the environment from potential disasters.

Revision questions

1 Discuss critically the different approaches to managing diversity in different countries.
2 Evaluate the recent developments and challenges in implementing equal opportunities policies across cultures.
3 Analyse the factors that have led to organizations adopting flexible working practices and family-friendly policies, and the different ways in which they have done so.

References

Adler, N.J. (1984) 'Women in international management: where are they?', *California Management Review*, 26(4): 78–89.

Adler, N.J. (1987) 'Pacific basin managers: a *gaijin*, not a woman', *Human Resource Management*, 26(1): 169–92.

Adler, N.J. (1993) 'An international perspective on the barriers to the advancement of women managers', *Applied Psychology: An International Review*, 42(4): 289–300.

Adler, N.J. (1997) *International dimensions of organizational behaviour*, 3rd edn, Cincinnati, OH: South-Western College Publishing.

Adler, N.J. (2002) 'Global managers: no longer men alone', *International Journal of Human Resource Management*, 13(5): 743–60.

Allan, A. and Daniels, L. (1999) *Part-time Workers*, Exeter: Short Run Press.

Altman, Y. and Shortland, S. (2001) 'Women, aliens and international assignments', *Women in Management Review*, 16(3): 141–5.

Becker, H. and Fritzsche, D.J. (1987) 'A comparison of the ethical behaviour of American, French and German managers', *Columbia Journal of World Business*, Winter, 87–95.

Bengtson, V.L. and Lowenstein, A. (eds) (2003) *Global Ageing and Challenges to Families*, New York: De Gruyter.

Blossfeld, H.P. and Hakim, C. (eds) (1997) *Between Equalization and Marginalization*, Oxford: Oxford University Press.

Branine, M. (1999) 'Part-time work in the public health service of Denmark, France and the UK', *The International Journal of Human Resource Management*, 10(3): 411–28.

Branine, M. and Glover, I. (1997) 'Ageism in work and employment: thinking about connections', *Personnel Review*, 26(4): 233–44.

Brewster, C. and Scullion, H. (1997) 'A review and agenda for expatriate HRM', *Human Resource Management Journal*, 7(3): 32–41.

Brewster, C., Sparrow, P. and Vernon, G. (2007) *International Human Resource Management*, 2nd edn, London: CIPD.

Caligiuri, P.M. and Cascio, W.F. (1998) 'Can we send her there? Maximizing the success of western women on global assignments', *Journal of World Business*, 33(4): 394–416.

Carrell, M.R., Elbert, N.F. and Hatfield, R.D. (2000) *Human Resource Management: Strategies for Managing a Diverse and Global Workforce*, 6th edn, Orlando: Dryden Press.

Dastmalchian, A. and Blyton, P. (1998) 'Organizational flexibility in cross-national perspective', *The International Journal of Human Resource Management*, 9(3): 437–44.

Davis, K. and Newstrom, J.W. (1985) *Human behaviour at work: Organizational behaviour*, 7th edn, New York: McGraw-Hill.

De Cieri, H., Holmes, B., Abbot, J. and Pettit, T. (2005) 'Achievements and challenges for work/life balance strategies in Australian organizations', *International Journal of Human Resource Management*, 16(1): 90–103.

de Ruyter, A. and Burgess, J. (2003) 'Growing labour insecurity in Australia and the UK in the midst of job growth: beware the Anglo-Saxon model', *European Journal of Industrial Relations*, 9(2): 223–43.

Dowling, P.J., Festing, M. and Engle, A.D., Sr (2008) *International Human Resource Management*, 5th edn, London: Thomson Learning.

The Economist (1995) 'Only communicate: thoroughly modern corporations know no borders', June 24.

Felstead, A. and Jewson, N. (1999) *Global Trends in Flexible Labour*, London: Macmillan Business.

Felstead, A., Jewson, N., Phizacklea, A. and Walters, S. (2002) 'Opportunities to work at home in the context of work–life balance', *Human Resource Management Journal*, 12(1): 54–77.

Fernández, E., Junquera, B. and Ordiz, M. (2003) 'Organizational culture and human resources in the environmental issue: a review of the literature', *International Journal of Human Resource Management*, 14(4): 634–56.

Foot, M. and Hook, C. (2008) *Introducing Human Resource Management*, 5th edn, London: Prentice-Hall.

Forster, N. (1999) 'Another glass ceiling? The experiences of women expatriates on international assignments', *Gender, Work and Organization*, 6(2): 79–91.

Glover, I. and Branine, M. (eds) (2001) *Ageism in Work and Employment*, Aldershot: Ashgate.

GMAC (Global Relocation Services) (2005) *Global Relocation Trends 2005 Survey Report*, Warren, NJ: GMAC, available online at: http://www.businessfordiplomaticaction.org/learn/articles/2005_global_relocation_trends_survey_gmac_grs.pdf, accessed on 22 April 2010.

Hong, P., Kwon, H. and Roh, J.J. (2009) 'Implementation of strategic green orientation in supply chain: An empirical study of manufacturing firms', *European Journal of Innovation Management*, 12(4): 512–32.

Kandola, R. and Fullerton, J. (1994) *Diversity in Action: Managing the Mosaic*, London: Chartered Institute of Personnel and Development.

Lewis, S. and Lewis, J. (eds) (1996) *The Work-Family Challenge: rethinking employment*, London: Sage.

Linehan, M. (2000) *Senior Female International Managers: Why So Few?*, Aldershot: Ashgate.

Linehan, M. (2002) 'Senior female international managers: empirical evidence from western Europe', *International Journal of Human Resource Management*, 13(5): 802–14.

Linehan, M. and Scullion, H. (2001) 'Challenges for female international managers: evidence from Europe', *Journal of Managerial Psychology*, 16(3): 215–28.

Linehan, M., Scullion, H. and Walsh, J.S. (2001) 'Barriers to women's participation in international management', *European Business Review*, 13(1): 10–18.

Mayrhofer, W. and Scullion, H. (2002) 'Female expatriates in international business: empirical evidence from the German clothing industry', *International Journal of Human Resource Management*, 13(5): 815–36.

McVeigh, K. (2007) 'Asda, Primark and Tesco are accused over clothing factories', *The Guardian*, 16 July, p. 1.

Moorhead, G. and Griffin, R.W. (1995) *Organizational behaviour: Managing people and organizations*, 4th edn, Boston: Houghton Mifflin.

Nord, W.R., Fox, S., Phoenix, A. and Viano, K. (2002) 'Real-world reactions to work–life balance programs: lessons for effective implementation', *Organisational Dynamics*, 30(3): 223–38.

ORC (Organizational Resources Counselors) (2002) *Worldwide Survey of International Assignments Policies and Practices*, New York: ORC.

Payne, J. and Payne, C. (1993) 'Unemployment and Peripheral Work', *Work, Employment and Society*, 7(4): 513–34.

Pettinger, R. (1998) *Managing the Flexible Workforce*, London: Routledge.

Pollert, A. (1988a) 'The "flexible firm": fixation or fact?', *Work, Employment and Society*, 2(3): 281–316.

Pollert, A. (1988b) 'Dismantling flexibility', *Capital and Class*, 34(1): 42–75.

Powell, L.J. and Cook, G.I. (2009) 'Global ageing in comparative perspective: a critical discussion', *International Journal of Sociology and Social Policy*, 29(7/8): 388–400.

Prasad, P. and Mills, A.J. (1997) 'Managing the organizational melting pot: dilemmas of diversity at the workplace', in P. Prasad, A.J. Mills, M. Elmes and A. Prasad (eds.), *Managing the Organizational Melting Pot: Dilemmas of Workplace Diversity*, Newbury Park, CA: Sage, pp.3–27.

Ramus, A.C. (2002) 'Encouraging innovative environmental actions: what companies and managers must do', *Journal of World Business*, 37: 151–64.

Rosenfeld, R. and Wilson, D. (1999) *Managing Organizations*, 2nd edn, London: McGraw-Hill.

Selmer, J. and Leung, A.S.M. (2002) 'Career management issues of female business expatriates', *Career Development International*, 7(6): 348–58.

Sparrow, P., Brewster, C. and Harris, H. (2004) *Globalizing Human Resource Management*, London: Routledge.

Standing, G. (1997) 'Globalization, labour flexibility and insecurity: The era of market regulation', *European Journal of Industrial Relations*, 3(1): 7–37.

Stredwick, J. and Ellis, S. (1998) *Flexible Working Practices*, London: IPD.

Stroh, L.K., Varma, A. and Valy-Durbin, S.J. (2000) 'Women and expatriation: revisiting Adler's findings', in Davidson, M.J. and Burke, R.J. (eds), *Women in Management*, London: Sage.

Taylor, J. and McIntosh, E. (1998) 'Managing human resources in the information age', in Towers, B. (ed.), *The Handbook of Human Resource Management*, 2nd edn, Oxford: Blackwell.

Taylor, S. and Napier, N. (1996) 'Working in Japan: lessons from western expatriates', *Sloan Management Review*, 37(1): 76–84.

Taylor, S., Napier, N.K and Mayrhofer, W. (2002) 'Women in global business: introduction', *International Journal of Human Resource Management*, 13(5): 739–42.

Turban, E., McLean E. and Wetherbe, J. (1999) *Information Technology for Management,* 2nd edn, London: Prentice-Hall.

Van der Boon, M. (2003) 'Women in international management: an international perspective on women's ways of leadership', *Women in Management Review*, 18(3): 132–46.

Vance, C.M., Paik, Y. and White, J.A. (2006) 'Tracking bias against the selection of female expatriates: Implications and opportunities for business education', *Thunderbird International Business Review*, 48(6): 823–42.

Volkmar, J.A. and Westbrook, K.L. (2005) 'Does a decade make a difference? A second look at western women working in Japan', *Women in Management Review*, 20(7): 464–77.

Westwood, R.I. and Leung, S.M. (1994) 'The female expatriate experience: coping with gender and culture', *International Studies of Management and Organization*, 24(1): 64–85.

Wooding, N. (1995) *Understanding Flexibility – A Guide to Flexible Opportunities Inside the Workplace*, Llanelli, UK: Campaign for Opportunity 2000.

Glossary

Acculturation: A situation where individuals and groups of people respond to cross-cultural contacts and, while retaining their own cultural values and norms, they adopt new cultural values and norms to meet their social and economic needs. See also *Adaptation*.

Adaptation: A process of accepting and dealing positively with the terms and conditions of a new and different socio-cultural environment, and becoming able to accommodate the perspectives of another culture and respond successfully to its demands, rules and regulations. It is a change of behaviour from the norms of a home to those of a host culture in what is referred to as *cognitive adaptation*.

Affirmative action: Taking positive action to increase the representation of certain groups in society (for example ethnic groups, women and old people) in areas of education, employment and business.

Anthropology: The study of human communities and their origins by focusing on the ways of life and people's behaviours in past and the present contexts.

Arbitration: A process by which a third party is required to help two or more groups to reach an agreement. The third party (arbitrator) has the power to ask the disputing parties to accept the proposed solution.

Association of South East Asian Nations (ASEAN): An economic organization that was established in 1967 between Asian countries to promote exports of their goods to other nations.

Autocratic leadership: Leaders who attempt to control all aspects of managing an organization by determining the policies and procedures, instructing members what to do or make, and having a subjective and impersonal approach to dealing with subordinates. It is also referred to as 'authoritarianism'.

Belief system: A way of thinking about and perceiving relationships and dealing with others within a society. Religions, ideologies and philosophies are examples of belief systems.

Brain drain: The migration of highly educated and skilled workforce from one country to another in search of employment and better standards of living and working.

Bureaucracy: An organizational process that is based on hierarchy of status, division of labour and formalization of rules and procedures.

Capitalism: A socio-economic system that is based on policies to promote the production and distribution of goods and services that accumulate capital and create profit. It is also related to the promotion of a free market economy.

Caste system: A hereditary system of segregation that is found on the Indian subcontinent where social status and class are determined at birth and conditioned by religious or other social beliefs.

Centralization: The concentration of power and control among very few people who make the decisions in an organization.

Centrally determined economy: An economy in which a central committee or institution of government decides on the allocation of resources and services according to a periodic plan.

***Chaebol*:** Korean; *chaebol* translates as 'financial clique'. In practice they are family-controlled and -owned conglomerates, structured into a number of companies in various businesses. They are similar to the Japanese *kobal*, *zaibatsu* and *keiretsu*

Chiefdom: A form of kin leadership that is found in countries where the political system is based on a relationship between the tribe and the state. The chief of the tribe or the village has substantial local powers.

Co-determination: A system of employee representation that requires workers and their managers to make collective management decisions. It is historically practised in Germany.

Collective agreement: An agreement between employers and trade unions over the terms and conditions of employment, normally the outcome of collective bargaining. In some countries such as the US and Canada collective agreements are legally binding, while in others such as the UK they are not.

Collective bargaining: A process by which one or more employers negotiate the terms and conditions of employment with one or more employee representatives or trade unions.

Collectivism: Individualism versus collectivism is one of the sociologist Geert Hofstede's cultural dimensions. Among other things, he suggested that in collectivist societies, people from birth onwards are integrated into strong, cohesive in-groups, which they continue to protect in exchange for unquestioning loyalty throughout their lifetime.

Colonialism: The economic, political and social domination of a territory and its people by a foreign power for a period of time.

Communism: The opposite of capitalism. It is an ideology/political theory that promotes the common ownership of the means of production in an economic system. Its most famous example is the command economy of the Soviet Union between 1917 and 1991.

Comparative advantage: Based on the theory of international trade, that a country should specialize in the production and export of goods that it can produce more cheaply and efficiently than others.

Comparative management: A field of study that covers the differences and similarities in management approaches within and between different countries and their impact on the trends and developments in international trade and business activity in different cultural settings.

Competencies: The levels and types of knowledge, skills and experience needed by an individual or a group of individuals to carry out the tasks or the functions assigned to them in an organization.

Competency-based pay: A reward system that recognizes employees' competence in applying their knowledge and skills in doing their jobs.

Competitive advantage: Based on the theory that a country's international competitive position depends on having the conditions that give it an advantage in producing a particular good or service.

Competitor: A person or an organization that competes with another person or organization for the use of the same resources (as inputs), the production of the same products or the provision of the same services (as outputs).

Confucianism: A moral philosophy and a system of ethical conduct that promotes harmony, peace and good morals in family life and society in general. Confucianism comes from the teachings of Confucius (551–479 BC), whose thinking still guides Chinese society with respect to learning, hierarchical relationships, standards of morality and social virtues.

Corruption: The misuse of public positions of power and authority for personal gains. It involves practices taken outside the formal legal framework of an organization to achieve individual or group benefits.

Cross-cultural: A situation where individuals from different cultures interact and attempt to understand each other's culture. The term is very often used in comparative studies of societies, international management and international business.

Cross-cultural awareness: This happens when a person gains cross-cultural knowledge and skills that enable her/him to understand and to appreciate the norms and values of a culture.

Cross-cultural communication: A process of dealing and communicating with people from different cultures. It has been developed into a subject of study that focuses on how people from different cultures communicate with each other in business, social and political activities.

Cross-cultural competence: Describes the individual's ability to recognize cultural differences and similarities, and to deal effectively with people across cultures.

Cross-cultural management: Knowledge, skills, awareness and competencies of managing across-cultures. According to the organizational theorist Nancy Adler, 'cross-cultural management explains the behaviour of people in organizations around the world and shows people how to work in organizations with employees and client populations from many different cultures' (*International Dimensions of Organizational Behavior*, 4th edn, 2003, p. 11).

Cross-cultural sensitivity: Describes the individual's ability to understand and react swiftly and appropriately to the situations, conditions, behaviours and contexts of cultural differences. It requires a high level of cross-cultural awareness and competency.

Cultural convergence: Based on the idea that societies become culturally similar because of globalization, industrialization, information and communications technologies, and international education.

Cultural divergence: This is is the opposite of cultural convergence, and is based on the idea that societies become more culturally different because of increasing differences in belief systems, norms and values, educational opportunities, and political and economic systems.

Cultural diversity: A situation where there are differences in behaviours among a social group because of differences in ethnicity, race, nationality or belief systems.

Cultural identity: Refers to the common cultural norms and values by which members of a group or society can be identified. People identify themselves as belonging to a group or society when they share a common set of norms and values.

Cultural norms: A set of behaviours that are typical of specific cultures and by which members of groups develop their cultural identities. They can be learnt early in life from parents, teachers and the environment in which one grows up and interacts with others. Norms can be written or unwritten rules and ways of behaving in a particular social context.

Cultural values: The virtues by which a culture of a group can be identified. They can be forms of a belief system, behaviours, customs and relationships that people of a group value in their cultures.

Culture: There are many definitions of culture, but it is generally referred to as the shared norms, values, customs, traditions, rituals, arts, folklore, history, heritage and institutions of a group of people. For example, the sociologist Geert Hofstede defines culture as the 'collective programming of the mind which distinguishes members of one group or category of people from another' (*Cultures and Organizations: Software of the Mind*, 1991, p. 260).

Culture clash: When two or more cultures meet and their differences result in misunderstandings and a problematic working or social environment.

Culture shock: A state of anxiety, frustration and tension that is expressed physiologically and/or psychologically by a person when coming to terms for the first time with an unfamiliar cultural context and not knowing how to behave. People often experience it when they move from one country or culture to another.

Decentralization: A process whereby decision-making authority is transferred from the higher to the lower levels of an organization. It is the opposite of centralization and often associated with empowerment.

Democracy: A system where on the basis of majority votes, the people, either directly or through their representatives, decide what is to be done. In politics, governments are elected through public vote in fair, free and transparent elections.

Developing countries: This term is usually used interchangeably with terms like underdeveloped, less developed, third world, or poor countries, and they are also referred to as the 'South' or the 'East'. Countries on the opposite end of the spectrum are termed industrialized, developed, or rich countries, and are simply summarized as 'the West'.

Diffusion: A process of moving behaviours, policies and practices from one culture to another, either directly or indirectly, formally or informally. It can be forward or reverse diffusion. Forward diffusion involves developing a global employment strategy that enables local employees to learn the knowledge and skills that make them globally employable. Reverse diffusion is part of the national identification process as international managers are informed of the national characteristics of organization and management in different countries.

Discrimination: Actions and behaviours that can be seen as a denial of equal treatment, rights and opportunities in an organization or society. It is illegal in the laws of many countries to discriminate by making unjust distinctions that are based on race, age, gender, religion, political affiliation, marital status, colour, nationality, sexual orientation, and physical or mental disability.

Diversity: It is a recognition and understanding of individual differences in an organization and realization that individuals have their unique needs, abilities and potentials. It is often related to *managing diversity*.

Downsizing: A process of restructuring an organization by reducing the number of employees to increase organizational efficiency.

Economic growth: A country's increase in national income over a specific period because of growth in production and services as a result of increasing investments, and technological development.

Economic integration: When two or more countries agree to enhance their economic cooperation by increasing the level of trade and reducing or abolishing tariff barriers among them.

Employee relations: Used in broad terms to refer to the process of developing, maintaining and improving employee relationships within an organization by having direct and indirect methods of contact with employees.

Empowerment: A process of giving the workers the power to make decisions over their work.

Ethnic group: A group whose members share similar cultural norms and values, history, race, nationality and/or belief systems that make them different, to some extent, from other ethnic groups.

Ethnocentric: A belief in the superiority of one's own ethnic group over others. In managing across cultures, multinational companies prefer to have their managers from the home rather than the host country and to apply the home country organizational culture and management practices in their foreign subsidiaries.

Expatriate: A person who has left his or her own country to live and work in another country. In managing across cultures, expatriates are usually employees of multinational companies who move from the home country to live and work in the company's host country.

Family-friendly policies: Employment policies that may help employees to combine their work and family commitments. These include a wide range of provisions such as: 1) leave for family reasons like maternity and paternity leave, school holiday leave, wedding and funeral attendance, career breaks and sabbaticals, and breaks as a result of a problems or illness in the family; 2) Flexible working practices such as job sharing, part-time work, annual hours, home-based working, flexitime, and flexiplace; 3) Career break schemes to allow employees to take a break for a specific period and then return to work; 4) Care facilities such as child care, elderly care and disabled care; and 5) Special leave arrangements that are granted when employees need to be absent from work in circumstances not covered by sick leave, annual leave, maternity leave, family leave or flexible working arrangements.

Feminity: Masculinity/feminity is one of the sociologist Geert Hofstede's cultural dimensions. According to Hofstede, 'Feminity pertains to societies in which social agenda roles overlap (i.e. men and women are supposed to be modest, tender, and concerned with the quality of life)' (*Cultures and Organizations: Software of the Mind*, 1991, p. 83).

Flexibility: The concept of flexibility in employment refers, in general, to the process by which the time and patterns of work are arranged in a way that meets employees and employers' needs.

Flexible working practices: Work practices such as part-time work, job sharing, temporary work, flexitime, home-based working, etc. that are used by employers in order to retain their valued employees and to basically respond to their needs because they might otherwise have to leave their jobs. However, countries differ in their use of flexible working practices according to their social structures, cultures, employment laws and regulations, and their levels of economic growth.

Foreign direct investment (FDI): The investment of equity funds of an organization in other countries.

Freedom of association: Giving the right to workers to form and join trade unions and to bargain collectively. In most countries this right is protected by law.

Geocentric: When no culture is seen as superior than the other. Geocentric organizations are those that depend on international teams of managers regardless of their country of origin or nationality. Neither the host nor the home country culture dominates the process of making decisions in a geocentric multinational company.

Global market: International business environment, including international labour market.

Globalization: A disputed concept that is used to describe the causes of international transformations in society, economy and geography. Current perceptions and interpretations of globalization vary, not least because of the multi-disciplinary nature of the phenomenon: from the globalization of trade to the globalization of arts, language and types of food, there are almost as many conceptualizations of globalization as there are disciplines. In society, the sociologist Anthony Giddens sees globalization as 'the intensification of world-wide social relations which links distant localities in such a way that local happenings are shaped by events occurring many miles away and vice versa' (*The Consequences of Modernity*, 1990, p. 4).

Graduate recruitment: A process of searching for and obtaining potential job applicants from graduates in sufficient quantity and quality so that employers can select the most suitable candidates to fill in their job vacancies.

Grande école: in the French system of higher education, a *grande école* is a highly selective and prestigious school or institution from which the country's top managers and political leaders graduate. A *grande école* can be an *école nationale* or an *école superieure*.

Guanxi: A Chinese term which literally means 'relationships' or 'connections'. In practice, it is a reciprocal act of doing favours in the sense of a favour being repaid at some time after the original one is given, and because the original recipient may not have anything immediately useful to give to the donor in return. It is related to the confucius saying, 'do not expect returns when you provide a service to others but do not forget when others provide a service to you'. *Guanxi* is very important in doing business with the Chinese.

Home country nationals or parent country nationals (PCN): The citizens of the country where the multinational company originates. They are also called expatriates.

Host country nationals (HCN): The citizens of the country where the multinational company has subsidiaries. They are also called the nationals or the local employees.

Illegal employment practices: Such as not considering the health and safety of employees, not paying employees their full wage entitlements, the employment of children, nepotism and corruption. They are very common in developing countries, especially in the small enterprises whose owners have no respect for and do not implement employment laws.

Immigrant workers: Are those who move to another country in search of employment and/or better standards of living.

Indigenous people: The native people of a land or territory that was later occupied or populated by people of foreign nationalities. For example, the aborigines are the indigenous people of Australia. The concept of 'indigenous' is also used to refer to the locals or the nationals of a country.

Individualism: Individualism/collectivism is one of the sociologist Geert Hofstede's cultural dimensions. According to Hofstede, 'individualism pertains to societies in which the ties between individuals are loose: everyone is expected to look after himself or herself and his or her immediate family' (*Cultures and Organizations: Software of the Mind*, 1991, p. 51).

Informal sector: Is known as the underground, unreported, undeclared, and hidden economy because the activity is not declared as a tax-paying business and is not formally registered. It takes the form of street sales, backstreet stores, roadside stalls, door-to-door sales, under-the-table transactions, car boot sales, and so on.

International human resource management: Human resource management policies and practices used to manage human resources in organizations operating in different countries.

Japanization: The adoption of Japanese management techniques such as quality circles, total quality control systems, just-in-time and so on by companies in other countries.

Kaizen: In Japanese it means 'continuous improvement' involving all employees, and is linked to low-cost high-productivity manufacturing systems.

Keiretsu: In Japanese it means a group of companies with strong long-term associations. They are characterized by cross-shareholdings and having one main bank.

Labour force participation rate: The ratio between the economically active (all those currently employed and those looking for employment) and the nation's total working-age population.

Labour market: A geographical area (local, national international) or occupational sector (public or private) where labour is in supply and demand.

Liberalization: Implementing policies and procedures that reduce government controls on the economy and allow market forces to determine the level of economic activity.

Life expectancy: The length of time that a person can, on average, expect to live in a given society.

Localization: A process of replacing foreign employees with local ones. It was introduced in some Middle Eastern countries under the concept of, for example, Emiratization, Omanization, Saudization and so on.

Managing across cultures: Is a two-way process that involves national and international employees and employers of different organizations in different countries and cultural settings. It can be defined simply as the process of *managing local employees globally and global employees locally.* Every employee is expected to act locally and think globally. Understanding this process leads not only to gaining knowledge of different national contexts and to comparing them, but also to learning the knowledge and skills of managing resources internationally in different national contexts.

Managing diversity: The treatment of all employees on an individual level. Managers recognize that differences in people can bring value to the organization when employees are given individual consideration with individual solutions to their particular needs. As Kandola and Fullerton (*Managing the Mosaic,*

1994: 8) state, 'harnessing these differences will create a productive environment in which everybody feels valuable and their talents are fully utilised in such a way that organizational goals are met'.

Market economy: An economy determined by the law of supply and demand in the allocation of resources and where businesses are mainly in private ownership. It is often referred to as free market economy and is the opposite of the command or planned economy.

Masculinity: Masculinity/feminity is one of the sociologist Geert Hofstede's cultural dimensions. Hofstede (*Cultures and Organizations*, 1991: 83) defines masculinity as it 'pertains to societies in which social roles are clearly distinct (i.e. men are supposed to be assertive, tough and focused on material success whereas women are supposed to be more modest, tender and concerned with the quality of life)'.

Mercosur: In South America, a subregional free trade association that was formed between Argentina, Brazil, Paraguay and Uruguay to promote economic cooperation.

Minimum wage: The statutory minimum pay that is determined by government as the lowest level of earning per hour or month.

Multiculturalism: The view that is based on the principle of cultural diversity of different nations as distinctive cultural identities. Different cultures and ethnic groups are formally recognized and legally protected from discrimination.

Multinational Enterprise (MNE): A company that has its headquarters in one country and operates in different countries. They are also referred to as Multinational Companies (MNCs) or Transnational Companies (TNCs).

Nation: A social grouping of people related by a common history, heritage, language, norms and values, legal system, territorial homeland and objectives. It is also used to mean a *country* or a *nation-state* when it has its own administrative, judicial and political systems by which it can be identified.

Nepotism: The act of favouring relatives and friends in employment, promotion, treatment and pay by those in positions of authority and power.

North American Free Trade Agreement (NAFTA): A regional free trade agreement between Canada, Mexico and the United States.

Organization for Economic Cooperation and Development (OECD): An international organization of 30 industrialized and industrializing countries that provides a forum for the discussion and dissemination of information on economic, social and political issues, and monitors the economic performance and policies of its member states.

Organizational culture: The shared values of employees, rules and procedures, policies and strategies, images and symbols, and the vision of management that together make the organization. In managing across cultures, the type of organizational culture concerned is 'corporate culture' which is characteristic of multinational companies whereby the culture of the headquarters influences that of the subsidiaries and vice versa.

Outsourcing: Seeking human resources from outside the business to get some non-core activities such as building maintenance and cleaning, computer services, security, payroll, transport and training, temporary employment, printing, catering, recruitment, etc. done by other providers.

Particularism: Universalism versus particularism is one of the cultural value dimensions proposed by Trompenaars and Hampden-Turner (*Riding the Waves of Culture*, 1997). This dimension concerns the extent to which behaviours and rules are applied universally or specifically to particular situations. In particularist societies people tend to be more relaxed with the application of rules and recognize the unique circumstances around a particular rule.

Paternalistic management: A management style where managers treat employees as members of their families. Paternalism is common in African, Arab and Chinese cultures.

Performance appraisal: A periodic process of identifying, evaluating and discussing the performance of an employee with the aim of making future developmental and reward decisions.

Performance-related pay: Is a reward policy that links an individual's pay to his or her performance. Normally, the better the performance, the higher the pay.

Political instability: Occurs in countries where governments are unstable because of civil war, social and political conflict, corruption, religious tensions and wars.

Polycentric: The opposite of ethnocentric is polycentric, where the host country management is preferred over the use of expatriates. Subsidiaries are treated as distinct national entities with some decision-making autonomy.

They are managed with a minimum of intervention from the headquarters personnel.

Power distance: Large versus small power distance is one of the sociologist Geert Hofstede's cultural dimensions. Hofstede (*Cultures and Organizations*, 1980) argued that societies differ from one another in the extent to which power and authority are exercised among people. Power inequality is more tolerated in some societies than in others. The level of power differentiation (or distance) is influenced by national norms and values concerning status, wealth, gender, age, religion, race and education.

Pragmatism: Not showing emotions of anger or satisfaction to others. A common attitude is that what is good can be better and what is bad can be worse.

Repatriation: The process of an expatriate returning home after the completion of an overseas assignment. It involves the re-induction and the re-integration of the expatriate to his/her former working and social environment.

Strategic alliances: The formation of working partnerships between multinational firms operating in different countries with the aim of strengthening their international market positions.

Strategic awareness: Being aware of the importance of linking organizational policies and procedures to corporate strategies and objectives.

Stratification: A situation where there are social divisions based on unequal access to resources and unequal distribution of wealth and power in a society.

Third country nationals (TCN): Citizens of countries other than the host or the home country of a multinational company.

Trade unions: An organization of workers that is usually related to the type of work they do and its aim is to bargain collectively with the employer for better terms and conditions of employment.

Trade union density: The ratio of the workforce that is a member of trade unions.

***Ubuntu* management:** A people-centred and less rationally determined African management style that is generally characterized by a strong emphasis on the importance of family and tribe, kinship relations and nepotism, and respect for age and seniority, where relationships are based on trust and are valued over achievements and organizational performance.

Uncertainty avoidance: High versus low uncertainty avoidance is one of the sociologist Geert Hofstede's cultural dimensions. Uncertainty avoidance concerns the extent to which people in a culture feel nervous or threatened by uncertainty and ambiguity and create institutions and rules to try to avoid uncertainty.

Unemployment: The ratio of the labour force who are willing to work but cannot be employed.

Wasta: The practice of nepotism and favouritism in Arab countries is known as *wasta* or *ma 'rifa* (in Arabic). It is also known in Algeria, Tunisia and Morocco as *'le piston'* (in French). The concept of *wasta* literally means to go between, and *'le piston'* is the bolt that holds parts of an engine together, but in practice both concepts imply a type of favouritism and nepotism.

Welfare state: The provision of social benefits from public funds to citizens with low or no income. Such benefits include a free or subsidized health service, education, transport and accommodation, as well as social security payments.

Westernization: A process of adopting and adapting to Western cultures and free market economic modes.

Works council: A workers' representative body at the workplace which normally involves representatives from management, workers and trade unions to establish a two-way communication: employees–management and trade unions–management.

World Trade Organization (WTO): An international organization which regulates international and multilateral trade agreements among its member states and settles trade disputes between them.

Zaibatsu: In Japanese, are the old forms of *keiretsu*, which are similar to Korean *chaebol* (q.v.).

Index